94

(1009)

(346)

$14.95

STEVE BENNETT

300 La.

357- 4323

Accounting Principles for Management

An Introduction

SECOND EDITION

Robert E. Seiler

Charles E. Merrill Publishing Company
A Bell & Howell Company
Columbus, Ohio

Published by
Charles E. Merrill Publishing Company
A Bell & Howell Company
Columbus, Ohio 43216

This book was set in Helvetica and Times Roman.

The Production Editor was Susan Sylvester-Glick.

International Standard Book Number 0-675-08726-0

Library of Congress Catalog Card Number 74-25935

Printed in the United States of America

2 3 4 5 6 7 8 9 10—79 78 77 76 75

Preface

Accounting Principles for Management (second edition) is designed for use in a college- or university-level course of one semester or one quarter which covers those accounting principles of primary interest to managers. The material has been arranged to build logically from one topic to the next, so that financial guidance and measurement of the enterprise is covered first, followed in sequence by cost accumulation and analysis topics, planning and control systems, and applications of cost data to specific decision areas.

As in the first edition of this text, purely procedural matters have been reduced to a minimum. While some procedural work is inherent in any problem-oriented course such as accounting, the intent of the author has been to reduce this type of material to only that necessary to insure an understanding of the most important concepts. The objectives of this second edition are (1) to introduce additional topics and to expand those areas of most significance to managers, (2) to incorporate the suggestions of the many educators who used this text during its first edition, (3) to insert a greater number and variety of end-of-the-chapter materials, and (4) to rearrange the topics and present them in their most logical, pedagogically sound sequence. To accomplish these objectives, major new materials have been inserted throughout the text. The more significant expansions may be summarized as follows:

1. A new introductory chapter has been added to provide a more solid foundation for the course.
2. The chapters on analysis of financial statements and flow of funds have been greatly expanded to make them more easily understood and to emphasize the more important aspects.

3. The chapters on cost behavior and introduction to manufacturing costs have been enlarged to include additional matters and to strengthen their content.

4. Appendices illustrating the journalization of cost flows have been placed at the end of the chapters treating cost accumulation systems and standard costs. While journal entries have been omitted in the explanatory materials throughout the text, their inclusion in the form of appendices will assist those instructors who wish to use this mechanism to illustrate the accumulation of costs and their flow through the accounts.

5. The chapter on the analysis of cost and revenue data has been expanded and major additions inserted to make it more meaningful and more easily understood.

6. The topics of capital budgeting and the use of costs in the pricing decision have been expanded into separate chapters, thereby giving these important topics the additional emphasis they deserve.

7. Learning objectives have been placed at the beginning of each chapter to assist students in mastering the materials, and a glossary of all the new terms introduced has been inserted at the end of each chapter. The combination of learning objectives, a chapter summary, and a glossary of new terms provides a unique and powerful learning platform.

8. The number of problems and exercises has been increased by 11 percent. In addition, discussion questions have been included in each chapter to provide another teaching and home assignment mechanism.

9. The solutions to selected exercises have been placed in the appendix at the back of the book to aid students in learning the chapter material and solving their assigned homework problems. Those exercises for which answers are included are indicated in the text by the asterisk (*) placed beside the exercise number.

10. A solution time has been indicated for each exercise and problem to aid both instructor and student in using the end-of-chapter materials. It is extremely important that the solution times be interpreted correctly, for they represent the *average time required for an average student who has already studied and who has a reasonably good grasp of the chapter materials*. If the student must return to the text discussion to review or to restudy the pertinent materials, the time required to work the problem could be longer than that indicated. In addition, the indicated time is dependent upon whether the instructor has discussed and lectured on the pertinent topics, working out examples similar to the assignment material, or whether the student is basically "on his own." The solution times have been placed in the text to assist instructors in selecting problems and exercises for assignment and to provide students with a rough feel for their individual solution times in relationship to that required by other students.

The author wishes to acknowledge his indebtedness to all those who have contributed to the second edition of *Accounting Principles for Management*. The number who contributed is much too large to permit listing individual names, for suggestions and recommendations incorporated in this edition have come from a large number of users of the original text. Thus, while individual names are not listed, each contribution is sincerely appreciated. Responsibility for errors of omission or commission must, of course, be assumed by the author, who welcomes any suggestion or comment for further improvement of this text.

Houston, Texas   *Robert E. Seiler*

Contents

PART 1

Enterprise Analysis

chapter 1

Nature of Control and Planning Information

This is an introductory chapter designed to provide an overview of the text. You should read this chapter, rereading several times if necessary, until you have achieved the following:

1. An understanding of the nature of management control and the complexities of the management decision process.
2. An appreciation of the role of financial data in the control and decision processes.
3. A recognition of management's need for measures of efficiency and effectiveness of (a) the overall enterprise and (b) the detailed operating segments of the enterprise.
4. An understanding of the need for generally accepted accounting principles in enterprise measurement and the overriding need for relevance in segment analysis.

Nature of Planning and Control

Management control is the process by which executives are able to guide an organization so that its objectives are met. If the control process is well executed, the organization will be both efficient and effective in the use of its resources. Note that control can be exercised only after objectives have been

3

formulated, for without objectives there can be no means of knowing whether or not the organization is progressing satisfactorily.

The management control process may be summarized in the following steps:

1. Formulating plans for meeting the objectives of the organization. This step includes separation of the plans into a coordinated course of action for each employee and each segment of the business.
2. Communicating these plans to each person affected by them.
3. Gathering information on individual performance, as well as performance of the organization as a whole.
4. Identifying those areas needing attention and formulating new plans for moving the organization closer to its objectives.

The objectives of the organization may be good or bad, but the control process insures the utilization of its resources in the manner best designed to achieve those objectives. For this reason, characteristics of the control process will be the same for a church, a political organization, a profit-oriented business, or a charitable organization. Although the objectives of these groups are entirely different, the processes by which their executives exercise control should be quite similar.

Objectives for a profit-making business in a competitive economy may include maximization of profit, command of an increased share of the market, or maintenance of a constant rate of growth. Objectives of a charitable hospital, on the other hand, may include maximization of the number of people served, an increase in the scope of services, or a decrease in the time required to recover from certain illnesses. In all cases, however, plans must be made, performance information must be gathered, weak areas or inadequate performance must be identified, and new plans must be formulated.

The Decision
Process

The decision process which management follows may be described as (1) identifying the more pressing problems which require solution, (2) identifying and measuring all the significant elements which are related to the problem, (3) projecting the probable results of each feasible solution, and (4) selecting that solution which maximizes the long-range objectives of the company. There is no clear-cut starting or stopping point in this process, for the solution to one problem invariably poses new problem areas requiring further consideration. The existence of competitors, a normal condition in our free enterprise system, automatically presents problems in the form of competitive pressures. Even non-competitive companies such as public utilities encounter problems in the form of the maze of governmental regulation.

The circular management process is illustrated graphically in Exhibit 1–1. The number of elements for which financial data may be needed is almost infinite, but it is critical that financial data concerning revenue inflows and expense outflows be available for the completion of steps 1, 4, and 5.

EXHIBIT 1–1

The Continuous Decision Process

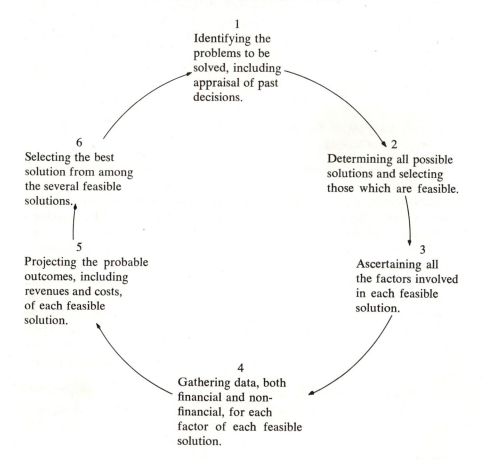

1

Identifying the problems to be solved, including appraisal of past decisions.

6

Selecting the best solution from among the several feasible solutions.

2

Determining all possible solutions and selecting those which are feasible.

5

Projecting the probable outcomes, including revenues and costs, of each feasible solution.

3

Ascertaining all the factors involved in each feasible solution.

4

Gathering data, both financial and non-financial, for each factor of each feasible solution.

To illustrate this process, assume that management identifies a major problem in the area of employee morale which is affecting the company's productivity. A possible solution would be the construction of a cafeteria to provide a comfortable facility for employees' lunch and coffee breaks. Another possible solution would be to grant pay increases, and still another solution would be the provision of expanded group insurance and pensions. Each of the three possible solutions is feasible, but selection of the best plan depends upon its cost and the ultimate effect upon employee morale and productivity. Gathering the necessary data on costs and the probable benefits of a potential solution is perhaps the most difficult part of the process, especially since the final effect cannot be known with certainty in advance. However, an intelligent decision cannot be reached without information on the relative costs of each of the feasible solutions and the expected increases in productivity from each. Furthermore, after a decision has been implemented, it is necessary to determine actual costs as they are incurred and the actual benefits realized. If the results are less than expected, or the costs excessive, the process of searching for a better solution must continue.

The need for adequate and timely information is critical to the decision process; for, without proper information, an incorrect or costly solution to a problem may be selected. Use of irrelevant information can sometimes be more costly than the use of data which lack absolute accuracy. One of the basic purposes of this text is to indicate those areas where irrelevant data may distort an analysis of expected costs and benefits.

Internal vs. External Data Needs

Financial data about the organization are important to external groups as well as to internal management personnel. External, within this context, refers to persons outside the immediate management of the company, such as stockholders, creditors, or governmental agencies. Internal, on the other hand, includes the management personnel working within the company.

Although financial data concerning an enterprise are frequently furnished to persons outside the organization, the emphasis in this text is on the uses and applications of financial data in the solution of problems faced by management. Financial data include all information which may be reduced to monetary terms and would encompass, for example, such items as the cost of operating a drill press, the merchandise sales of a particular branch store, and the salaries paid to the company's employees. Detailed data such as these are primarily for the use of internal management and are not usually of interest to persons outside the immediate management of the company.

External parties are primarily interested in the enterprise as a whole, while internal management would also be interested in the operations of each segment of the firm. An individual investor holding stock in Montgomery Ward and Company, for example, is an external party who would be interested only in the financial condition and profitability of the entire company, and this individual would normally find detailed financial information on the operations of each retail outlet of the company of little use.

On the other hand, the management of Montgomery Ward and Company must have operating data on each outlet. These data are necessary for locating inefficiencies, reducing costs, and increasing the company's overall profits. Thus the needs of management for financial data are more diversified, more detailed, and less well defined than are the needs of external persons.

Those who manage a business need periodic accounting information on all facets of the company's operations, including detailed information on the sources of incomes and the nature of all expenses incurred. Financial information for management planning and control purposes must be sufficiently detailed so that unprofitable products may be identified, excessive expenses located, inefficient operating areas spotted, and the efficiency of employees measured. Indeed, the consistent and diverse needs of management for financial information can be satisfied only by relatively frequent and detailed accounting reports.

Informational Needs of Management

The needs of management for information may be summarized into three broad areas:

1. Data which reveal how closely the company's objectives are being met. This has sometimes been called *score-keeping* information.
2. Data answering questions about the operations or individuals which need attention in order to bring the organization closer to its objectives. This has been called *attention-directing* information.
3. Data answering specific questions about the best way to perform a specific task or the best solution to a given problem. This may be called *problem-solving* information.

There is considerable overlap between these areas; and, in many cases, elements of all three will be found in the same accounting report. For illustrative purposes, however, consider the following examples:

Score-keeping: An income statement which compares actual profit with anticipated profits.

Attention-directing: A departmental expense report for the welding department of a factory, which indicates an above-normal monthly use of welding rods.

Problem-solving: A cost report prepared to help determine whether product A or product B should have the higher selling price, indicating that the cost to manufacture product A is greater than the cost to produce product B.

Control and Planning Levels

The type of information and the frequency with which it is reported differ from one level of management to another. Top management, at the level of director or president, is involved in strategic planning and in the formulation of broad company policy. The data needed at this level are more condensed than those needed at lower levels and are concerned as much with outside events as with activities within the company. A decision by the president or his executive committee to introduce a new line of products requires outside information relative to the size of the potential market, any existing competition, and the nature of customer acceptance. However, information from inside the organization would also be required for this decision, including such data as expected costs to manufacture the product and the impact such production would have on existing facilities. Note that the information required for this type of decision, whether gathered from inside or outside the organization, is forward-looking and is more concerned with *strategic planning* than with operating control.

Middle management, which is characterized by such levels of responsibility as vice-president of marketing, vice-president of production, controller, treasurer, and division manager, requires information of a more detailed nature than does top management. Management at the middle level is charged with the responsibility of guiding the operations of a part of the organization and placing its strategic plans into operation. Monthly and sometimes weekly operating reports are needed at this level, with information on individual products, departments, or sections which lie within that individual's span of control. The activities of these executives may be characterized as *management control*.

Lower-level executives, such as a department head, departmental foreman, or section chief, need data in considerable detail and with increased frequency. Daily and weekly operating reports are frequently used at this level, much of it in non-financial terms. Foremen in production departments need information on units produced, hours worked, and the efficiency of individual workmen. Where possible, such data are reported daily and weekly, so that inefficiencies may be corrected as quickly as possible.

The partial organization chart in Exhibit 1–2 illustrates the several levels of management responsibility and the points at which strategic planning, management control, and operating control fit within the organization. Although planning and control cannot always be neatly assigned to exact levels within the organization, the illustration does emphasize the differing control and planning levels. The accompanying outline summarizes the nature of the data requirements at these three levels.

Data Requirements for Levels of Management

Level	Information Characteristics
Top management	Concerned with the entire enterprise
	Summarized in nature
	Future-oriented
	Heavily external in nature
	More estimates are required
Middle management	Focused on one aspect of the business
	More detailed
	Reported frequently
	Internally oriented
	Reported with more accuracy, using fewer estimates
Lower management	Focused on lesser activities
	Great detail required
	Daily or weekly reports needed
	Source of data almost totally internal
	Greater accuracy required

Line and Staff Functions

Some of the activities in an organization are designed to provide support for the primary operating activities. The machinery repair department in a factory, for example, has as its primary function the servicing of equipment used in other departments. The payroll department, as a further example, serves the other activities of the business by calculating earnings and preparing the paychecks

EXHIBIT 1–2
Partial Organization Chart

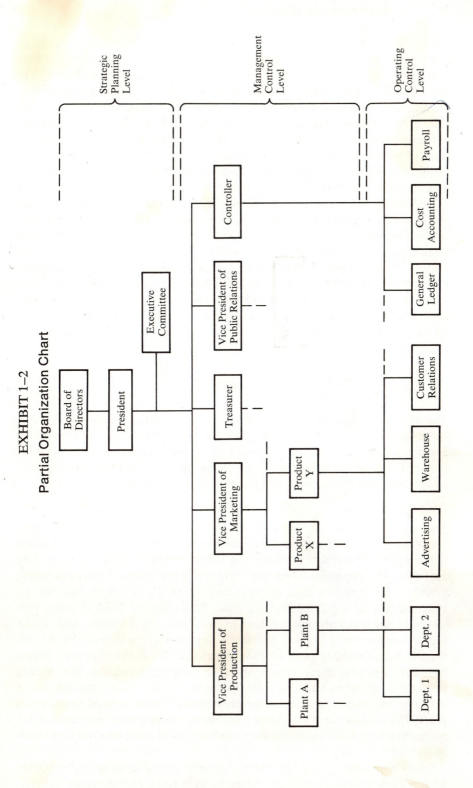

of employees. Such functions are called *staff functions,* because they exist to provide service and information to other departments.

A *line function* exists where there is a direct line of authority, such as a vice-president who supervises the work of the department head, who in turn directs the activities of the supervisor, who is in charge of a machinist. In such cases, a direct line of command exists, and orders are issued down the line. Orders do not arise from a staff function, nor should the staff become involved in the issuing of orders and directives or in corrective action. The staff function should perform its appointed duties without hindering the line executives in their process of exercising control.

Accounting and report-preparing activities are staff functions. The *controller,* who is the chief accounting officer, is charged with the responsibility of establishing the framework of financial and budgetary reports and of seeing that these reports are issued on time and without error. However, neither he nor his staff should become involved in the process of actually correcting situations that need attention. Note that in Exhibit 1–2 the controller and his staff, along with the vice-president of marketing and the vice-president of production, answer to the president. The controller assists these two vice-presidents by the preparation of reports, but only the vice-presidents have the authority to issue orders to their subordinates.

Sources of Financial Information

The various sources of financial information are too numerous to describe exhaustively in this text, especially since financial data include all data which are stated in terms of money. However, two broad categories of financial information are so frequently employed in management's control and decision-making activities that some discussion of each is warranted.

Accounting Data

Accounting is traditionally considered to be the systematic process of gathering, condensing, reporting, and analyzing the results of events which have affected the company. There is no uniform rule for determining which events or data are sufficiently important to warrant inclusion in the systematic data-gathering process. Management's need for information will dictate which data will be systematically accumulated and reported. Production of finished units, purchases of raw materials, sales of units to customers, check writing, and similar actions are invariably deemed sufficiently important to be included in the systematic record-keeping process. Past experience has shown that such events have sufficiently significant effects upon the company to warrant the expense of establishing and maintaining a data-gathering system. In fact, the data are of sufficient importance to warrant the preparation of standardized financial reports. The *balance sheet* and *income statement,* for example, are standardized accounting reports which reflect the overall results of these relatively standardized events.

Many companies include in their systematic record-keeping and reporting process such data as the mileage driven by each truck (for purposes of determining when certain maintenance should be undertaken) or the daily gross weight of products shipped to customers (to provide an immediate barometer of sales activity). These are also accounting data, even though not expressed in dollar amounts, because they are the product of the systematic data gathering and reporting processes undertaken by the company. Periodic reports are employed to convey such data, and they constitute a major part of the company's information system.

Non-Accounting Data

A large portion of the financial information needed by management is of a non-accounting nature. This means that the data will not have been accumulated and reported in the normal recurring process of data-gathering and reporting. A bakery, for example, may occasionally need such data as the per capita consumption of bread in the major cities of the U.S., or the expected population increases in certain geographical areas for the next ten years, or even trends in the yield of wheat per acre in the United States. Information such as this is not accumulated systematically by the company's accounting activities and must be gleaned from other sources outside the company. These data are as important to management as those produced by the accounting system but will not be accumulated and reported on a regular basis—either because regular reporting would be too expensive or because such data are needed only at infrequent intervals.

Measuring Enterprise Performance

One of the most significant measurements that financial data provide at the strategic planning and management control level is that of enterprise profitability and financial condition. The three financial reports which are traditionally used to reflect these economic events are the *income statement,* the *balance sheet,* and the *statement of changes in financial position.*

Income Statement

This report is designed to reflect the revenues earned by the enterprise during a specified period of time—usually monthly, quarterly, or annually—the expenses incurred during that same period of time, and the resulting profit or loss. The profitability which this statement indicates is one of the most important barometers of management's effectiveness and is carefully studied by managers, owners, creditors, and governmental agencies. A complex network of generally accepted accounting principles is necessary to insure that the income of one company is calculated in a manner that will permit comparison with other companies.

Balance Sheet

This report is a financial report designed to reflect the properties which are owned and used by the organization and the equities in those properties. This statement is not designed to reflect the current market value of the properties;

it reflects the *cost* of the assets at the time of investment and whether they were invested by owners or creditors. The balance sheet is primarily designed to report the properties under the control of management and is valuable from an owner's standpoint in the calculation of the return which is being realized on his investment. This information is also valuable from the manager's standpoint, because the return on investment reflects his ability to use the properties entrusted to him in earning profits for the owner. A complete set of generally accepted accounting principles is necessary for the preparation of this statement to insure its consistency and comparability from one accounting period to another.

Statement of Changes in Financial Position

This statement is frequently called a statement of the flow of funds and is designed to reflect the funds which have become available to the company during the period and what they were used for. It is prepared from data appearing on the income statement and the balance sheet and reflects management's use of the funds available to it during the period.

The data reflected in these three financial reports are accumulated through the accounting system and consist almost entirely of internal information. A series of business documents, journals, ledgers, and other accounting devices is required to capture and summarize the data which they contain. It is important to remember that these reports are of extreme importance to management, as well as to outside persons, because they reflect the effectiveness of management's use of the properties entrusted to it by the owners.

Measuring Managerial Effectiveness

Financial data relative to the company's profitability is the primary means by which the effectiveness of management is measured and reported to the company's owners. Net income is an especially important measure of management's ability to employ the assets invested in the company in such a manner that the owners will realize an adequate return on their investment. Management's decisions relative to such events as establishing selling prices, determining production quantities, acquiring plant and equipment, and granting salary increases to employees will directly affect the profit which the company is able to earn. Thus the income statement of a company is a reflection of management's ability to compete and to reach workable solutions to the company's problems.

Unfortunately, the reported profit for any one year is an imperfect measurement of management's actions during that particular year, because net income is the result of a stream of actions, many of which were instigated in prior years. The decision to construct a plant may have been made decades ago, and hiring an administrative staff may be the product of training efforts extending over a number of years, but they both have considerable effect upon the current year's profit. However, for all its imperfections, the amount of profit reported on the income statement remains the primary measure of management's effectiveness in utilizing the company's resources. For this reason every manager and every owner of a business should have a working knowledge of the elements that go into the determination of accounting net income.

A complex framework of principles and concepts has been developed to provide a basis for determining net income, financial position, and the flow of funds. This framework constitutes "the body of generally accepted principles of accounting." These principles are determined not by a central authority, but by general agreement of the profession. Furthermore, there is no single authoritative writing which contains a comprehensive list of these principles, and they do not constitute a set of fixed or irrefutable rules. The complete literature of the profession comprises the source from which they are drawn. These principles are in turn based upon a set of assumptions and concepts about our business environment and the objectives to be accomplished by measuring net income and financial position.

Information for Operational Control

In addition to data which provide a measure of enterprise profitability and financial position, as described in the preceding section of this text, management has a constant need for information about the internal operations of the company. The balance sheet, income statement, and statements of funds provide data for strategic planning and for the formulation of broad company policies, but this type of information cannot provide satisfactory daily operating controls.

Some of the major information gathering and reporting techniques which are employed for operational control are standard costs, budgeting systems, contribution margin reports, responsibility accounting, and return on investment calculations. These techniques are described below in order to illustrate the nature of the information needed for operating control.

Standard costs are predetermined costs, reflecting what the costs to manufacture a product or perform an operation *should* be. When actual costs are compared to these standards, the differences provide a basis for quickly determining what products or operations are below expectations and need attention. Standard costs are most frequently employed in manufacturing operations.

Budgeting systems are methods of predetermining the expenses which should be incurred in selling, administrative, and other operational areas. The budgeted amounts for the advertising department for the month of February, for example, indicate to the advertising manager how much he can spend that month. Without this budgetary guide he could not keep his advertising activity properly coordinated with the other activities of the business, and losses and inefficiencies would result. Actual expenses are compared with budgeted amounts in weekly, monthly, and annual reports to insure that budgets are not exceeded; in case a budget is exceeded, the responsible official must be ready to justify the excess spending.

Responsibility accounting is a system whereby budget reports, standard cost reports, and contribution margin reports are prepared to reflect the activities for which one particular individual is responsible. The partial organization chart shown earlier in Exhibit 1–2 indicates separate areas of responsibility for advertising, warehousing, and customer relations, all under the control of the manager of product X. Another manager is responsible for product Y. The reports prepared in a responsibility accounting system would report separately the expenses, costs, and contribution margin of each area and each subarea in the organization chart.

Contribution margin reports are financial statements prepared to report the contribution which a particular segment of the business is making toward the profit of the company. The segment may be a product line, a sales territory, or a particular department, and the control reports are constructed to reflect only those revenues, costs, and expenses which are directly associated with that segment.

Return on investment calculations are made for each segment of the business which earns revenue, or for which revenue calculations can be made. The amount of return on investment is determined by dividing the profit, or contribution margin, by the amount of the investment in assets which was necessary to earn that profit.

$$\frac{\text{Profit}}{\text{Investment in assets}} = \text{Return on investment}$$

The managers of product X and product Y, as shown in the partial organization chart in Exhibit 1–2, would each have a return on investment amount calculated periodically to ascertain the effectiveness with which they are using the assets under their control. In this way their effectiveness can be compared, even though their contribution margins are different, and the assets they use are not equal in amount.

Consistency and Relevance

Management needs an almost infinite amount of information, and the preceding discussion has indicated that these informational needs center around (1) enterprise measurements and (2) segment analysis. Enterprise measurement, through the income statement, balance sheet, and statement of funds flow, must be prepared in a consistent manner, so that the resulting data will be comparable, either between companies or from one reporting period to the next. A body of generally accepted accounting principles has been developed to insure consistency and adequacy in the preparation of statements for the enterprise as a whole.

On the other hand, there is no universally accepted body of principles surrounding an analysis of segments of the business. Management is free to construct its reports in any way deemed appropriate, to use or not to use a budgetary system, or to change its method of calculating return on investment at any time it wishes. For internal management purposes, *relevancy* is the most important attribute of the information and control system. The inclusion of irrelevant costs in a cost report, for example, could lead to incorrect decisions and ultimate reduction in the profits of the company.

Consider the following simplified example of a situation in which irrelevant costs may be used and an incorrect decision reached.

Problem   Management is attempting to decide between (1) use of a commercial trucking line to transport its finished product to a new market in another state, or (2) use of the company's own existing truck fleet. Present monthly costs of the company's own truck fleet have been determined as follows:

Salaries of drivers	$10,000
Insurance, licenses, and taxes on trucks	10,000
Gas and oil	6,000
Total	$26,000
Miles driven	100,000 mi.
Cost per mile	$.26

If the company's truck fleet is used, a new driver must be hired, although it will not be necessary to purchase new trucking equipment. On the other hand, the commercial carrier has quoted a price of $.20 per mile.

Analysis   The overall cost of $.26 for the operation of the company's truck fleet cannot be compared with the $.20 per mile quoted by the commercial trucking line. If the company's existing truck fleet is used, the only additional costs to be incurred will be salaries and gas and oil. The insurance, licenses, and taxes will not increase if the company's own trucks are used. The salaries ($10,000) and gas and oil ($6,000) average only $.16 per mile, which is lower than the price quoted by the commercial line. Had the irrelevant costs of insurance and taxes been included in the analysis, an incorrect decision might have been reached.

Sunk cost = some already been spent; irrelevant for decision making.

Summary

The management process is a constant series of setting goals and objectives, locating problem areas, and arriving at solutions to the identified problems. Some of the goals and problems relate to the enterprise as a whole, while others relate to smaller segments of the business.

The accounting system within a company is the primary method by which data are gathered and reported for managerial decision making, planning, and control. The accounting system is the primary information system and includes the gathering of data for income statements and balance sheets, as well as the gathering and reporting of data for operating and cost control and for contribution margin analysis of smaller segments of the company.

While generally accepted accounting principles must be employed in reporting enterprise data to persons outside the company, their use is not necessary for internal measurements. Consistency and relevance are the primary attributes of the internal operating control system.

New Terms

The following new terms were introduced in this chapter. They are defined at the point where they were introduced, and you should have a working knowledge of each one before completing your study of this chapter.

Accounting data Information about a company's transactions which is gathered and reported in a systematic, periodic, recurring process.

Balance sheet A financial report reflecting the properties used by the business and the sources and equities in those properties.

Budgetary system Systems of predetermining what revenues, costs, and expenses should be realized in the coming period. The system usually includes reports which match actual amounts with the predetermined amounts.

Contribution margin report A financial report which reflects the profit contribution of a segment of the company.

Income statement A financial report which reflects the revenues and expenses applicable to the period and the resulting net income or loss.

Management control Process of guiding an organization toward its objective.

Organization chart A formal listing of responsibility areas, with indication of lines of command and staff support.

Relevant data Data which apply to the problem being analyzed.

Responsibility accounting An accounting system which matches accounting reports with areas of responsibility within the company.

Return on investment A ratio, usually expressed as a percentage of profit to investment.

Standard cost A predetermined cost, usually indicating the expected cost to be incurred for manufactured products.

Strategic planning Formulating plans which will affect the entire company for several years in the future.

Questions

1. Define the following terms:
   a. Management control
   b. Strategic planning
   c. Organization chart
   d. Accounting data
   e. Income statement

   f. Balance sheet

   g. Statement of changes in financial position

   h. Standard cost

   i. Budgetary system

   j. Responsibility accounting

   k. Contribution margin

   l. Return on investment

   m. Relevant data

2. a. Describe the management control process, and explain why the formulation of objectives is a necessary part of this process.

   b. List some of the objectives of the bookstore which serves the members of your class. Indicate the way in which the management of that store would determine whether these objectives are being met.

3. a. How do you think management identifies the problems which it must resolve?

   b. After the problem has been identified, how do you think management assesses the importance of turning its attention to that problem in relationship to the other problems which are in the process of solution?

4. The amount of sales made by department six of a large department store is included in the store's daily sales report. Indicate whether this information is score-keeping, attention-directing, or problem-solving to the following:

   a. The manager of that department, who has a sales budget

   b. The store manager, who is trying to decide whether to eliminate the department

   c. The budget officer, who is trying to estimate the sales budget for the department for the coming year

   d. The owner of the store, who is concerned with the total profit made by the store

5. Indicate whether the following would be strategic planning, management control, or operating control:

   a. Establishing prices for next year's catalog

   b. Measuring the number of units Mary completed today

   c. Determining whether salesmen meet their quotas for the week

   d. Determining whether the cost to produce product X is the same as the cost analysts had estimated it would be

   e. Determining whether an advertising campaign was successful

6. For each item listed in question 5 above, indicate the type of information which management would require in order to reach a decision or to resolve the matter. Indicate whether this information would be gathered from within the company or from an outside source.

7. Define "staff function" and "line function," and distinguish between the two. In which category does the accounting function belong? Why?

8. Contrast the nature of the information needed by top management with that needed by lower-level operating management in regard to:
   a. Which contains more estimates
   b. Which should be reported more frequently
   c. Which is usually gathered from internal sources
   d. Which is narrower in scope

9. Name the three financial reports which are prepared to measure the financial affairs of the enterprise as a whole, and describe what each is designed to reflect. *7, 11+12*

10. Name and describe the major techniques through which management is able to obtain operating control over daily activities.

Exercises *(2)*

1-1   Return on Investment (*15 minutes*)   The XYZ Company has a plant in New York, which was built twenty years ago at a cost of $500,000 and which earned a profit of $60,000 this year. The company also has a plant in California, which was built three years ago at a cost of $750,000 and which also earned a $60,000 profit this year. The plants are identical in size and in operations, except that the one in California cost more to build due to inflation.

12%

Instructions
12% 8% a. Calculate a rate of return on each plant.
use replacement plan b. Comment on the problem of interpreting the rate of return as a measure of managerial effectiveness in this situation. *If you compare them you should use replacement costs, not historical costs,*

1-2   Line vs. Staff Functions (*15 minutes*)   Company A hired James Whitmore last month to head the Accounting Department. On hiring Whitmore, the president of the company told him to "prepare financial reports that tell my people how they are doing; and when you find them not performing up to standard, do something about it!"

Company B hired Lester Frost as its controller and chief accounting officer. He was assigned the responsibility for determining what reports should be prepared, for whom, and what type of information they should contain. He was told to point out where major differences existed between company expectations and actual performance, but not to become personally involved in corrective action.

Instructions
Comment on the effectiveness of these two approaches, indicate which one you favor, and detail what problems you would anticipate in the approach you dislike.

record book keeper ← score keep.

Test 03.

1–3   **Score-keeping, Attention-Directing, and Problem-Solving** (*10 minutes*)

Instructions

For each of the following activities within the accounting function, discuss whether it is primarily directed toward score-keeping, attention-directing, or problem-solving:

attention-directing a. Recording and reporting sales by territories in a report to the president of the company

problem-solving b. Analyzing the profit that a new product would make if it were introduced to the company's customers

score-keeping c. Calculating the payroll for the week

problem-solving d. Analyzing the equipment to ascertain whether a plant rearrangement would be of value

attention-directing e. Preparing a budget for the sales department for the following month

score-keeping f. Preparing an invoice for sales to a customer

attention-directing to the middle manager g. Explaining a variance in the performance report of the welding department

p - refer to the supervisor

1–4*   **Line vs. Staff Functions** (*10 minutes*)   Exhibit 1–2 contains a number of line functions and some staff functions.

Instructions

a. Describe the line of command from the board of directors to the advertising department.

b. Describe the nature of the staff function performed by the payroll department for the advertising department.

c. Suppose the advertising department of product Y exceeded its budget in March, with a larger payroll than was indicated. How and to whom would this fact be reported by the controller? How and by whom do you think corrective action should be taken?

Problems (1)

1–5   **Analysis with Irrelevant Data** (*15 minutes*)   A friend is trying to decide whether to keep his old car or buy a new one. He paid $4,000 cash for the old one six years ago and feels that he could keep it running for another two years. It has a present market value of $800. The new car he is considering has a list price of $5,000, and the dealer has offered a trade-in allowance of $1,000 on the old car.

Instructions

State which of the above information is relevant and which is irrelevant to the decision to keep or buy. Also list some other factors not included which may be relevant.

* Solutions to exercises marked with an asterisk can be found in the appendix.

1-6

*use cash out lay
to see how
much profit.*

Analysis with Irrelevant Data (*30 minutes*)   Management is attempting to decide whether to put in a cafeteria for its employees on a non-profit basis with prices just high enough to cover costs. If it does install the cafeteria, the following costs will be incurred:

New equipment (total cost, with an average expected life of ten years)	$100,000.00
Existing equipment, original cost ten years ago (not presently in use; no plans for future use; market value $2,000; remaining useful life of five years)	40,000.00
Cafeteria salaries, monthly	3,200.00
Food materials, average per meal	.83
Space costs (space, not presently being used. This amount is assigned to the cafeteria on a square-foot basis.)	7,000.00

The company has 1,000 employees who will eat in the cafeteria each day, five days per week, fifty weeks per year. If the company does not install the cafeteria, an outside caterer has offered to bring hot meals to the building for $1.00 each, using only the company's old equipment and space for serving.

*Sal - 38,400
Food + Mat. 250,000
$/400 yr - A*

-0-

5,900

250,000 meals

Instructions

a. Prepare an analysis showing the costs of installing the cafeteria compared to the costs of using the outside caterer.

yes

b. What other information would you want before reaching a decision? State the sources from which this information would come.

*250,000
.83
750,000
20000 000*

1-7

Selecting Relevant Costs (*30 minutes*)   Suppose you own an automobile and have agreed to carry three friends to a football game in a city located 200 miles away. They have agreed to split the travel cost equally with you for the 400-mile trip. Arriving back on the campus after the two-day trip to the game, you gather the following information on the costs of operating your automobile:

Gas for the 400-mile trip	$ 18.00
Oil change while at the game	5.00
Parking while at the game	3.00
Speeding ticket on the way to the game	15.00
New tire bought on the way to the game to replace a blowout	30.00
Major tune-up last week	36.00
Original cost of the car, bought new last year	3700.00
Annual license tags	25.00
Annual insurance on the car	210.00

Instructions

Compute the cost to be divided among the travelers. If any of the costs listed in the problem should not be included, state why not; include any costs not listed if you feel they should be included.

1-b installing new

ME. $10,000 N.E.
400 (Cx. eg.)
38,400 Sal.
207,500 Adm.
$256,300

Using caterer:
$250,000 meals
250,400 (Ex. eg.)
$250, *save $5,900 Sav. in marketable securities*
+ 3,000 Employee moral

chapter 2

Measurement of
Financial Position

have to have a bal. sheet.

This chapter continues the discussion of management's need for information concerning the overall operations of the enterprise. You should achieve the following from your study of this chapter:

1. A knowledge of the nature, purpose, and uses of the statement of financial position
2. The ability to construct and interpret the contents of the statement of financial position
3. An appreciation of the basic accounting assumptions which underlie the measurement of enterprise financial position and net income

Need for a Measure of
Financial Position

At periodic intervals, operating management must have information concerning the organization's financial position. Since one of the basic objectives of the organization is the maintenance of a sound financial position with adequate resources for current and future operations, management cannot guide the organization toward that objective unless there is periodic measurement to indicate the strength of the company's financial position.

This same type of information is also needed by many persons outside the immediate management of the company, and the accounting system of every company is designed to furnish, in standardized form, a statement of financial position. This statement is frequently referred to as a _balance sheet_. The balance sheet is submitted to management on a monthly basis but is usually released to external groups only quarterly or annually. The balance sheet is designed to reflect the properties which are owned by the organization and the sources of these properties. This type of information answers questions concerning the immediate availability of funds to pay debts as they become due, the amount of resources which have been permanently committed to land and buildings, and the amount of resources which are presently committed to inventory and uncollected receivables. Comparison of last year's financial position with that of the current year provides information concerning the company's growth and the extent to which management has been able to strengthen the debt-paying ability of the company.

If a company is unable to pay its debts, it may be declared bankrupt or be forced to terminate its operations. Management must guard against this eventuality by insuring that the financial position of the company is not jeopardized by excessive debt, an overinvestment in such properties as land and buildings, which cannot be used to pay debt, or an overexpansion of inventories, so that immediate cash resources are depleted. The balance sheet, or statement of financial position, was one of the earliest financial statements to be prepared, having originated centuries ago in the trading centers of the Mediterranean area. Its form and content have become highly standardized to permit comparison from one period to another and from one company to another.

Framework of the Balance Sheet

The balance sheet derives its name from the fact that it is divided into two balancing sections whose money amounts must be equal in total. It contains a listing of the properties invested in the business and the equities, or rights, which various groups have in these properties. The balance sheet is based upon the equation:

$$\text{ASSETS} = \text{EQUITIES}$$

The term "assets" is commonly used in accounting reports to indicate properties. While the term "asset" and "property" are synonymous, accounting terminology is somewhat standardized, and the term "assets" is more frequently used.

The term "equities" may be defined as a right in property or a claim against assets. The equation ASSETS = EQUITIES is a way of expressing the fact that the amount of property equals the rights to or claims against that property.

There are two principal types of equity—those of the creditor and those of the owner. A creditor's equity is called a liability and is a debt or obligation representing the creditor's rights in the assets of the company. Owners' equity is sometimes called proprietorship, or capital, and represents the owners' rights in the assets of the business. The balance sheet equation is thus expanded to include these commonly used terms as follows:

$$\text{ASSETS} = \text{LIABILITIES} + \text{OWNERS' EQUITY}$$

The assets section of the balance sheet, which appears first, lists all the properties which belong to the business. The equities section follows, listing all equities which owners and creditors have in those properties.

EXHIBIT 2–1

R. J. TALON COMPANY
Balance Sheet
December 31, 19X1

ASSETS		EQUITIES	
		LIABILITIES	
Cash	$ 5,074	Accounts payable	$ 36,420
Accounts receivable	12,963	Taxes payable	14,210
Inventory	41,720	Total	$ 50,630
Buildings	160,000	OWNERS' EQUITY	
Equipment	38,000	Capital stock	200,000
Land	10,000	Retained earnings	17,127
	$267,757		$267,757

The basic framework of the balance sheet is illustrated in Exhibit 2–1. Note that the two sides of the statement contain equal dollar totals and that the assets and equities have been segregated into several categories. These categories are called *accounts*. Account titles may differ slightly from one company to another.

Nature of Equities

In general an equity may be defined as a property right. If an individual purchases an automobile which costs $4,000, paying $1,000 in cash and signing a note payable for the remaining $3,000, both the purchaser and the holder of the note have an equity in the automobile. The purchaser has a $1,000 equity, and his creditors have a $3,000 equity in the $4,000 automobile. The concept of an equity is sometimes difficult to grasp, but it is basic to an understanding of the balance sheet.

The technical definition of "equity" as applied to accounting developed from a colloquial usage meaning "the amount or value of a property or properties above the total of the liabilities." The term "owners' equity" thus assumed meaning as the amount of properties left to the owner after the payment of all liabilities.

The owners' equity is sometimes called a "residual equity." The term "residual equity" is based upon the legal right that creditors have a prior claim against the company's assets. If a company goes out of business, its creditors must be paid in full before any assets may be distributed to the owners.

Although the liabilities have a preferential claim on assets and rank ahead of owners' equity in case the business ceases operations, there is no relationship between specific liabilities and specific properties. A creditor may have an equity in the properties of a business without having legal title to or a claim against any specific item of property. The balance sheet shown in Exhibit 2–1 indicates that the company owes accounts payable of $36,420. Should the company fail to pay its debts, any one or several of the company's assets may be taken by the company's creditors to satisfy these claims. In the case that the total assets are insufficient to satisfy all claims, the creditors share pro rata, and there will, of course, be nothing distributed to the owners.

Balance Sheet Classifications

Since the balance sheet is designed primarily as a means of reporting a company's financial status, the assets and equities are usually *classified* in a manner that assists in interpreting the statement. Classification means a grouping of assets and liabilities according to their nature. The major classifications of assets are (1) current assets, (2) fixed assets, and (3) other assets; the major classifications of liabilities are (1) current liabilities and (2) long-term debt. Owners' equity is usually placed after the liabilities. Exhibit 2–2 illustrates the arrangement of a classified balance sheet with appropriate subtotals.

EXHIBIT 2–2

LANTON AND JONES COMPANY
Balance Sheet
December 31, 19X1

ASSETS			EQUITIES		
Current assets			*Current liabilities*		
Cash	$ 15,000		Accounts		
Accounts			payable	$ 82,000	
receivable	73,000		Taxes payable	13,000	
Inventory	119,000		Salaries payable	9,500	
Supplies on hand	8,000				$104,500
		$215,000	*Long-term debt*		
			Mortgage		
Fixed assets			payable in		
Equipment	$ 63,000		19X7		180,000
Buildings	182,000		Total		
Land	20,000		liabilities		$284,500
		265,000			
			Owners' equity		
Other assets			Capital stock	$200,000	
Land held for			Retained		
possible			earnings	25,500	
expansion		30,000	Total owners'		
			equity		225,500
			Total		
Total assets		$510,000	equities		$510,000

Current Assets

For classification in the balance sheet, current assets are those which are expected to be realized in cash or sold or consumed during the next normal operating cycle of the business. A normal operating cycle, in the absence of special circumstances, is assumed to be one year. In addition to cash, the principal current assets are accounts receivable from customers and inventories. These assets are usually converted into cash within one year. In addition, any office supplies or store supplies which are on hand as of the balance sheet date fall within the definition of current assets, since they are reasonably expected to be consumed during the next operating cycle. Certain prepaid amounts—those amounts which have been paid in advance—are also considered current assets according to the definition given above. When rent or salaries are paid in advance, the payment gives rise to an asset which appears in the balance sheet as prepaid rent or prepaid salaries and should be classified as a current asset.

The various current assets are normally listed within the current assets section of the balance sheet in the order in which they are expected to be realized in cash, or as they otherwise become available for debt-paying purposes. Thus, the usual order is cash, followed by receivables, inventory, supplies on hand, and the prepaid items. Current assets would include the following:

1. *Cash* consists of funds on deposit in banks, or on-hand undeposited, which are available for immediate disbursement.
2. *Marketable securities* consist of investments which have been acquired with cash in excess of that required for immediate needs. The intent of management must be to sell these investments within the next year; if the intent is not to sell them, these assets cannot be classified as current.
3. *Accounts receivable* represent amounts owed to the company which the company expects to collect within a year. Sometimes *Trade Receivables*, which arise from sales to customers, are shown separately from *Other Receivables*—especially if the other receivables are significant in amount. If it is collectible within one year, regardless of its origin, a receivable can be listed as a current asset.
4. *Notes receivable* are receivables evidenced by a legal document called a note. The existence of the legal document makes these receivables more readily transferable should the company wish to sell or discount them to raise immediate cash. For this reason, they are separated from Accounts Receivable in the balance sheet.
5. *Inventory* represents finished goods or merchandise ready to sell to customers, work in process which can be completed and sold within the next year, and raw materials which will be consumed in the next year. These assets must appear on the balance sheet at cost, rather than at their sales value.

6. *Prepaid expenses* are assets which have been paid in advance, but which will cease to exist or have "usefulness" in the next year. These expenses include prepaid rent, prepaid taxes, prepaid salaries, and prepaid inurance.

In summary, three criteria must be satisfied before an asset may be classified as a current asset. The item must be (1) convertible into cash, (2) consumed within the next accounting period, which is normally one year, and (3) converted into cash or consumed in the normal course of the company's operations. Land which a retail grocery company owns for possible expansion of its operations could not be classified as a current asset, even though it could be sold for cash in the next year, because it does not meet the third criterion. Selling its land is not a "normal" transaction for a retail grocery store. In this case, land must be placed in another classification within the balance sheet. On the other hand, land held for resale by a real estate firm would appear as a current asset on that company's balance sheet, because selling land is a normal transaction for that company. Office supplies for either company could be properly listed as a current asset, however, for this asset will normally be consumed in the course of the next year's operations.

Fixed Assets

Fixed assets are those assets which are used in the normal operations of the business, have a life longer than the usual one-year accounting period, and will not be sold in the normal course of business. Fixed assets include buildings, equipment, machinery, land, and similar assets which are actually employed in the operations of the company. The land described earlier, which was being held for expansion purposes by a retail grocery store and which was not actually being used in current operations, could not be included among that company's fixed assets. (Note that such an item appears in Exhibit 2–2 under *Other Assets.*) However, land used as part of the company's parking lot for customer use would be included as a fixed asset.

Although there is no prescribed sequence for listing items within the fixed asset section of the balance sheet, they are frequently listed in the order of their length of life—those with the shortest life being listed first. Thus a possible sequence could be: Tools, Equipment, Trucks, Machinery, Buildings, and Land. This sequence is less than exact, however, because certain pieces of equipment may have a life longer than that of a truck, while other pieces of equipment may not last as long as some of the tools. Thus, sequencing becomes more a matter of preference than of exactness.

Fixed assets appear in the balance sheet at their original cost, rather than at their market value. This cost is reduced each accounting period through the process of *depreciation*, so that over the life of the asset its cost will be equitably and systematically included in the determination of the company's profit. The process of calculating and recording depreciation will be explained in the next chapter, but it is necessary to recognize at this point that the balance sheet reflects the original cost of fixed assets *less the accumulated depreciation to date*. The usual balance sheet presentation would be as follows:

Fixed assets

Machinery, at cost	$ 67,000	
Less accumulated depreciation	15,000	$ 52,000
Buildings, at cost	243,500	
Less accumulated depreciation	109,000	134,500
Land		25,000
Total fixed assets		$211,500

Other Assets

Occasionally a company has assets which are neither current nor fixed; these assets may be classified as "other assets," and include such items as investments which will be held for several years, and non-operating properties, such as land, which are being held for expansion purposes. This classification usually appears below the fixed asset section, and since it contains a variety of items, the listing is usually in order of importance, the largest item being listed first. The assets in this group may be sometimes divided into two separate sections, *Investments* and *Deferred Charges,* if the amounts are material. The investments category contains the company's permanent investments, including properties held for future use, and the deferred charges contains intangible items such as goodwill and the cost of extensive plant rearrangements.

Current Liabilities

Current liabilities are those which will be paid within the next accounting period or, expressed another way, those which will require the expenditure of a current asset. Current liabilities include accounts payable, notes payable, taxes payable, rent payable, and other debts which will become due within the next year. There is no prescribed sequence for listing liabilities in the current liabilities section, although they are frequently listed according to the significance of their amounts, the largest being placed first.

Accounts payable represent debts payable within the next accounting period which are owed to suppliers who have provided materials or services. Such debts are usually unsecured; if the supplier has been given a note payable signed by the company, this amount should be separately classified under *Notes Payable*. Some notes payable have due dates which will not occur until much farther in the future, and these should not be included in current liabilities.

Taxes payable are obligations owed to local, state, or federal government agencies for taxes. The amounts must sometimes be estimated, but they should be included in Current Liabilities if due within one year.

Accrued liabilities are debts which are not yet due, usually items for which the company has not received a bill or invoice. Salaries owed employees for work performed prior to the pay date would give rise to an accrued liability for salaries payable, and rent owed a landlord—even though it's not payable until the end of the year—would give rise to an accrued liability entitled Rent Payable.

Deferred income is a type of liability which exists because the company has received an advance payment for services or materials. The company owes the payer either a refund or the agreed service or material, and a current liability exists until that obligation is satisfied.

Long-Term Debt

Long-term debt includes those liabilities which are not due within the next accounting period (one year). Examples of long-term debt would be a note payable, due in five years, or a twenty-year mortgage payable on the company's fixed assets. Long-term debt usually necessitates periodic interest payments, but the accrued interest liability thus created would appear in the balance sheet as a current liability if it is to be paid within a year.

Note that the balance sheet illustrated in Exhibit 2–3 has a classification entitled *Long-Term Debt,* which consists of the traditional types of liability existing in this industry which have a due date more than one year in the future.

Ownership Equity

There are three principal forms of business ownership: proprietorships, partnerships, and corporations. A *proprietorship* is owned by a single individual and is formed or discontinued with relative ease. A *partnership* is a business owned by two or more individuals. Other than the agreement among the several partners, there are comparatively few regulations and restrictions that pertain to a partnership. The *corporate* form of business ownership is quite different from a proprietorship or partnership. A corporation is given existence by state law and exists as a separate "person," distinct and apart from its owners.

All of the larger business enterprises in our country and a major portion of the smaller companies are corporations. The corporate form of organization has certain advantages, including the ease with which ownership shares may be traded without disruption of the business and the limited liability of the shareholders in case of bankruptcy.

The owners' equity in a corporation—that is, the "stockholders' equity"—is composed of two parts: (1) the original investments of the owners and (2) the earnings retained in the business. The investment of the individual owners is evidenced by stock certificates issued to them by officers of the company in exchange for cash or other assets. The stockholders have an equity in the assets of the business equal to their original investment, and all profits (or losses) made by the corporation accrue to them.

EXHIBIT 2-3

ALLENTOWN CIRCUS, INC.
Balance Sheet
December 31, 19X1

ASSETS

Current assets		
Cash		$ 972,936
Accounts receivable		85,630
Deferred 19X2 show costs and other prepaid expenses		636,420
Total current assets		$1,694,986
Property and equipment, at cost		
Leasehold improvements		$ 826,524
Railroad equipment		955,483
Railroad equipment under construction, not being depreciated until completed		320,000
Circus equipment		362,400
Animals		496,434
Automobiles and office equipment		121,339
		$3,082,180
Less—Accumulated depreciation		232,655
Total property and equipment, net		$2,849,525
Other assets		
Circus memorabilia, not being amortized		$ 566,974
Investment in circus program book rights, being amortized through 19X3, net		223,750
Deferred debt issuance cost, being amortized through 19X8		110,540
Goodwill, not being amortized		3,894,625
Total other assets		$4,795,889
Total assets		$9,340,400

LIABILITIES AND SHAREHOLDERS' INVESTMENT

Current liabilities		
Accounts payable		$ 472,501
Accrued interest		122,500
Other accrued liabilities		164,000
Federal and state taxes payable		608,257
Current portion of long-term debt—		
Note payable to bank		600,000
Liability for purchase of circus program book rights		78,750
Total current liabilities		$2,046,008
Long-term debt, net of current portion		
Note payable to bank, payable $600,000 annually through 19X4		$1,800,000
7% subordinated notes payable, due November, 19X6		3,500,000
Liability for purchase of circus program book rights, due 19X3		266,805
Total long-term debt		$5,566,805
Shareholders' investment		
Common stock		$ 780,000
Paid-in surplus		349,500
Retained earnings		598,087
Total shareholders' investment		$1,727,587
Total liabilities and shareholders' investment		$9,340,400

The primary investment of the stockholders is reflected in the balance sheet as *capital stock*. Although shares of capital stock are transferable and are traded frequently on the stock exchanges, such transactions are personal transfers of ownership from one individual to another. The original investment remains with the company as permanent capital, even though ownership of the shares may change hands. The common stock of $780,000 in Exhibit 2–3 reflects this type of investment. The paid-in surplus of $349,500 appearing immediately after the common stock also reflects a part of the owner's investment. The par value of a share of stock is an amount assigned to each share in the articles of incorporation; and, when stockholders invest more than this amount, the difference is called "paid-in capital." The paid-in capital is shown separately because of legal differences arising from the assignment of a par value for the capital stock.

The second part of stockholders' equity is that portion of the company's earnings of the current and prior years which has been retained for expansion purposes. Many large corporations began with small investments by the original owners and grew through retention of earnings. That portion of stockholders' equity resulting from the retention of profits is called *retained earnings*. The total of the capital stock and retained earnings constitutes the total stockholders' equity in the business.

Segregation in the balance sheet of the stockholders' investment for capital stock and the company's retained earnings provides important information for stockholders and creditors. Capital stock and paid-in capital represent a permanent investment, which normally is not withdrawn until the company ceases to operate. Retained earnings, on the other hand, represents an owners' equity created by profits, which may be distributed to the owners in the form of dividends. The distinction between capital stock and retained earnings is so important that state laws require careful distinction between these two elements of ownership.

Concepts Underlying
The Balance Sheet

One of the primary purposes of a balance sheet is to provide a basis for comparing a company's financial position with that of other companies, or with that of the same company in prior years. Consistency and uniformity in the preparation of these statements is of paramount importance if comparability is to be maintained. A complex body of accounting principles has been formulated for this purpose, and many of these principles are discussed in this text. However, the principles are based upon a number of assumptions, or concepts, concerning the environment in which the financial measurement process operates, and a knowledge of these concepts and assumptions is necessary for an understanding of the meaning of a balance sheet.

The general definition of a concept is "a mental image, or an opinion." Accounting concepts, then, are the basic images or assumptions which, for purposes of determining net income and financial position, have been formulated about the economic setting in which accounting operates. Since they are assumptions rather than facts, these concepts are subject to neither proof nor disproof. However, their usefulness as a basis for financial reporting has given them general acceptance.

The five basic accounting concepts are (1) the entity concept, (2) the going concern concept, (3) the cost concept, (4) the stable-dollar concept, and (5) the periodicity concept.

The Entity Concept

Each business is assumed to be a separate entity, and its financial position and profitability must not be distorted by the inclusion of the properties or transactions of other persons or businesses. In some cases, the separate legal entity of a business is clearly evident. All corporations, for example, are separated by law from their stockholders. However, the legal distinction between a proprietorship or partnership and the owners' personal assets or transactions is an arbitrary one derived for purposes of measuring net income and financial position. Thus, when the entity is not clearly defined by law, the assumption must be made that the business is a separate entity.

The business as a whole is the accounting entity for purposes of reporting to those outside the immediate operations of the company, such as creditors, governmental agencies, or stockholders who do not participate actively in the company's management. For the purposes of internal management, however, parts of the same business may be divided into separate accounting entities. The management of a company with branches in different cities frequently treats each branch as a separate accounting entity. Separation in such cases facilitates the financial measurement of each branch. Similarly, management sometimes divides the company's operations into territories, each territory or region comprising a separate entity within the business. Thus there are no universally applicable rules for determining what is to be considered an accounting entity. Usefulness is the only criterion which can be established—that is, if information is required concerning the profitability or financial position of an organization or any part thereof, that organization should be considered an accounting entity and separate financial reports should be prepared. However, the usefulness of the data obviously must be weighed against the cost of its accumulation.

The Going Concern Concept

assume that the co. will last forever

Unless there is strong evidence to the contrary, a business is assumed to have a life expectancy longer than that of any of its assets. The going concern concept provides the foundation for periodic profit measurement and balance sheet preparation. The net amount at which a fixed asset is carried on the balance sheet (cost less accumulated depreciation) represents that cost applicable to its remaining productive life. Consequently, the going concern concept is compatible with the periodic allocation of the cost of assets over their expected useful life. Although voluntary or involuntary liquidation is a possibility in any company, the entity should be considered a going concern until liquidation is imminent. During the liquidation period, the balance sheet and income statement are not utilized, and another type of statement called a *Realization Statement* is prepared.

The Cost Concept

The accounting process of measuring net income and financial position does not attempt to measure the changes in market value of the company's productive assets. The process is designed to record the asset at cost and to retain this cost in the accounts until the asset is sold, consumed, or otherwise disposed of. Cost is defined as the cash or cash equivalent given up for the asset in an arm's length, or bargaining, transaction between two individuals.

Cost is an objective amount resulting from a market transaction. Estimates of present market value, on the other hand, usually lack objectivity because there is no transaction to measure the present market value of an asset if it is not actually sold. Thus, use of market values instead of cost could result in a lack of confidence in accounting reports.

The Stable Dollar Concept

The accounting process is designed to record and report transactions which can be measured in terms of dollars. The implication is that each dollar in an accounting report is exactly like every other dollar on the report. No distinction is made between dollars on the balance sheet resulting from the purchase of a depreciable asset thirty years ago when the dollar had two or three times its present purchasing power, and those supplies or fixed assets which were bought with current dollars of lesser purchasing power.

The balance sheet reflects assets acquired at different dates with dollars of unequal purchasing power, and the income statement reflects dollars of revenues and expenses which are of unequal purchasing power. However, accounting is not designed to reflect changes in the purchasing power of money. Accounting is designed to account for the *number* of dollars invested in a business, the dollar cost of its assets, and the *number* of dollars of profit or loss which the business earns. Whether these dollars are equal or unequal in value or purchasing power is not reflected in the financial statements.

The Periodicity Concept

The periodic preparation of a balance sheet and an income statement might be described as a sampling or testing of a company's financial affairs. The exact profit or loss accruing to the owners cannot be determined until the business finally ceases operations. Profits reported in one accounting period may be offset by unforeseen losses which are not discovered until many accounting periods into the future. The periodicity concept indicates that the profitability of a business can be reliably measured by periodic statements and that revenues and expenses can be properly matched within these accounting periods.

There are two major problems in applying the periodicity concept. The first involves the selection of a period which is sufficiently long to be representative, but short enough to provide current information; the second is the selection of the most satisfactory method of associating revenues and expenses within this period. These problems are discussed further in the next chapter.

Summary

The balance sheet is designed to furnish interested persons outside the company, as well as management, with information concerning the financial position of the company. The balance sheet, which is the traditional statement prepared for this purpose, is a listing of properties employed in the operations of the company and the existing equities in those properties. The statement is classified to facilitate its interpretation, and current assets and current liabilities are set apart from other assets and liabilities. Owners' equity is segregated from other equities and is divided in corporate balance sheets into capital stock and retained earnings. This separation is necessary in order to reflect the sources of owners' investments and because, due to the special nature of a corporation, retained earnings are legally available for dividends, while the original stockholder investment normally is not.

The balance sheet lists assets at their cost rather than at their market value. The cost concept is the basis for recording depreciation and spreading the cost of an asset over its useful life; the going concern concept also underlies the process of depreciating assets; for a business must be assumed to have a life sufficiently long to accomplish the depreciation process. The stable dollar, periodicity, and entity concepts are also an underlying part of the traditional financial measurement process, which includes the preparation of a balance sheet and an income statement.

specific item

New Terms

Account   A category of asset, liability, or equity (including revenues and expenses) which appears in the financial statements or bookkeeping records.

Asset   A property or thing which has value and usefulness.

Capital stock   The amount invested by stockholders of a corporation as owners' equity.

Current assets   Assets which will be converted into cash in the normal course of business within the next accounting cycle.

Current liabilities   Debts due to be paid within the next accounting cycle.

Depreciation   That portion of the cost of an asset which has been considered expense due to wear, tear, and obsolescence.

Equity   A right or claim in a property or in assets.

Fixed assets   Assets with a life longer than one year which are used in the operations of the business.

Long-term debt   Debt which is due after more than one accounting period in the future.

Retained earnings   Reinvested earnings of a corporation.

Questions (1)

1. Define the following terms:
   a. Balance sheet
   b. Asset – *property with owned.*
   c. Equity – *ɔ*
   d. Account
   e. Current asset – *anything use 1 yr. or business cycle (ɔ) Insurance*
   f. Fixed asset *Prepaid expense – Ins. – used in the operation of business*
   g. Depreciation – *something loose value of wear & tear bring down to salvage value.*
   h. Current liability
   i. Long-term debt *takes longer than 1 yr.*
   j. Capital stock –
   k. Retained earnings – *money retain from business*

2. What is the basic equation upon which the balance sheet is constructed?

3. What is a classified balance sheet? Name the classifications of assets. Name the classifications of equities.

4. Define "current asset" and give several examples.

5. Define "fixed asset" and give several examples.

6. Name several assets which would be included in the classification of Other Assets, and state why they would be in that grouping.

7. Distinguish between "depreciation" and "decrease in market value."

8. Define "current liability" and give several examples.

9. Define "long-term debt" and give several examples.

10. Distinguish between a partnership and a corporation.

11. Distinguish between capital stock and retained earnings.

12. Describe the entity concept.

13. Describe the going concern concept.

14. Describe the cost concept.

15. Describe the stable-dollar concept.

16. Describe the periodicity concept.

17. Do you think that the balance sheet is designed to reflect the value of the properties which a company owns? If not, state what the purpose of this financial statement is.

18. Exhibit 2–3 is the balance sheet of a circus. Do you think the "Animals" classifications of assets would be subject to depreciation in the same way as the circus equipment? How would you determine the annual depreciation of an elephant?

Exercises (2)

2-1   **Balance Sheet Equality** *(15 minutes)*   Each horizontal line in the following table has been taken from a different balance sheet. In each case one amount has been omitted, as indicated by the question marks.

	Cash	Receivable from Customers	Supplies on Hand	Payable for Supplies	Capital stock	Retained earnings or (Loss)
a.	$1,000	$3,000	190	$500	$3,200	$400
b.	2,000	1,000	$800	100	3,000	700
c.	1,400	1,100	450	150	3,000	-2(?)
d.	700	2,500	500	580	4,000	(800)
e.	1,450	400	850	200	2250	250

Instructions
Compute the amount required for each omitted item if the balance sheet is to be made to balance.

2-2   **Relationship of Owners' Equity and Profit** *(10 minutes)*   The Bryson company had assets of $10,000 and liabilities of $3,000 at the beginning of the year. At the end of the year it had assets of $9,000 and liabilities of $1,000.

Instructions
Compute the amount of the net income or loss realized during the period.

2–3   Balance Sheet Construction *(15 minutes)*   Assume that the following amounts were taken from a balance sheet dated as of the last day of the current month:

Cash	$ 4,000
Owner's investments	11,000
Supplies	200
Income for the year (retained earnings)	3,000
Machinery and equipment	12,000
Receivable from customers	750
Taxes payable to the government	2,050
Wages payable to employees	900

Instructions
Reconstruct the balance sheet.

2–4   Balance Sheet Construction *(15 minutes)*   The Holtam Company had the following assets, liabilities, and owners' equity accounts on December 31 of 19X1:

Cash	$ 2,000	Land	$ 3,000
Payable to creditors	3,200	Merchandise on hand	7,400
Trucks	8,000	Retained earnings	12,500
Capital stock	30,000	Notes payable to the	
Buildings	41,000	bank, due in	
Receivable from		three months	5,000
customers	1,600	Mortgages payable,	
Salaries payable		due in four years	10,000
to employees	2,300		

Instructions
Prepare a balance sheet using these amounts.

2–5   Classification of Assets and Liabilities *(10 minutes)*   Listed below are the items on the balance sheet of a company:

Notes payable	Cash
Accounts receivable	Accounts payable
Capital stock	Land
Mortgages payable in 1980	Retained earnings
Inventory	Buildings
Store equipment	Taxes payable
Office supplies	Prepaid insurance
Permanent investment in	Land held for future expansion
government bonds	

Instructions
Indicate in which balance sheet classification each item should be placed.

2–6*   Preparation of a Balance Sheet *(20 minutes)*   Listed on the following page are items from the records of the Jade-Wait Corporation as of December 31, 19X1:

Capital stock	$20,000	Accounts receivable	$ 7,500
Cash	3,750	Buildings	6,000
Notes payable	2,500	Land	2,250
Store equipment	3,250	Retained earnings	6,225
Merchandise inventory	14,100	Office equipment	1,900
Taxes payable	375	Accounts payable	7,825
Office supplies	100	Store supplies	175
Mortgages payable		Prepaid insurance	650
in 1980	2,500	Salaries payable	250

Instructions

Prepare a classified balance sheet.

2–7   **Preparation of a Balance Sheet** *(20 minutes)*   The data below were taken from the records of the Model Construction Company as of December 31, 19X1:

Cash	$ 4,000	Inventory	$25,000
Accounts payable	11,000	Salaries and wages	
Land	10,000	payable	700
Accounts receivable	8,000	Retained earnings	15,800
Mortgage payable in		Prepaid insurance	2,000
1980	21,000	Sales fixtures	1,500
Buildings	29,000	Property taxes payable	1,000
Capital stock	30,000		

Instructions

Prepare a classified balance sheet.

2–8*   **Violation of Accounting Concepts** *(25 minutes)*   In each of the following cases one or more generally accepted accounting concepts have been violated.

Instructions

Name the concepts violated and state how they were violated.

a. The ending merchandise inventory is placed on the balance sheet at its present sales value.

b. A letter is received from a customer inquiring whether a certain item is carried in stock and what the price is. The company had the item in stock and answered the letter to that effect. At that time an entry was made recording an accounts receivable and a sale to that customer.

c. Depreciation is not recorded in those years when profits are low and is brought "up-to-date" when profits are high.

d. A fire occurred on December 31, the last day of the accounting period, completely destroying two of the company's automobiles. The company left the automobiles on the balance sheet and deferred their write-off until the next accounting period.

e. Assets which had been bought several years ago were fully depreciated by the beginning of the current year. Since the assets were still useful, the company continued to depreciate them in excess of their cost.

2–9   **Recording Costs Under a Lease-Purchase Agreement** *(20 minutes)*
The J. Evans Construction Company specializes in large earth-moving contracts such as dams and roads. The company's operations utilize a number of costly pieces of heavy machinery, which are acquired on a lease-purchase option. Under these agreements the company leases the machinery on a monthly basis, and 80 percent of the lease payments may be applied to the purchase of the equipment at any time the company wishes to buy it. The company's accountant records each lease payment as 20 percent lease expense and sets up the other 80 percent in the asset account for equipment. The equipment account is then depreciated on a five-year basis. Approximately one-half of the time the company does not buy the equipment; and, in such cases, any balance remaining in the asset account is written off as a lease expense of the year in which the equipment is returned to the dealer.

Instructions
Describe the company's procedure in relation to any accounting concepts which may have been violated.

2–10   **Recording the Cost of Land** *(20 minutes)*   The Starlight Gas Producing Company acquired a tract of land by giving the original owner of the land shares of stock in the company. The land had previously been listed for sale at $130,000; the present market value of the stock given to the land owner is $140,000; and an experienced appraisor hired by the company indicated that the land has a value of $150,000. How should the land appear on the company's balance sheet? Discuss the use of each of the three possible amounts, indicating for each the accounting concepts, if any, which would be involved.

2–11   **Branch Losses** *(20 minutes)*   The Ideal Sales Company opened its sixth branch office on January 1 of the year just ended, and a significant operating loss was realized by the branch during the year. Operating losses for individual branches are not unusual during their first year, and in a number of previous cases losses had been recorded as an asset entitled Deferred Organizational Losses. The losses were then written off as expenses over a five-year period. The company's president defended this treatment on the grounds that the first-year loss was a necessary cost of creating the branch and that the loss was incurred in order to realize profits in future years. He argued further that profits of future years are better measured if they absorb a portion of the original "starting-up" loss. Finally, he stated that since this procedure had been followed in several prior cases, it would be necessary to continue in the interests of consistency and conservatism.

Instructions

Discuss the procedure used by the Ideal Sales Company, especially as related to the periodicity concept and the conventions of conservatism and consistency.

2–12   **Automobile Trade-ins** *(20 minutes)*   An automobile dealer has a new automobile in stock, for which he paid the manufacturer $2,000. The car has a list price of $2,900. A customer agrees to pay $1,800 cash plus his old car for the new automobile. The customer's old car has a current value of $600, but with an expenditure of $100 for repairs, it would have a sales value of $800. How should the dealer compute profit on the sale of the new automobile? The sales manager wants to record the sale using the list price of $2,900; the president feels $2,600 should be considered the sales price; and the accountant argues that $2,400 is more nearly correct. What, if any, accounting concepts would be violated by use of the $2,900 list price or the $2,600 amount suggested by the president?

2–13   **Depreciation vs. Increase in Value** *(15 minutes)*   A company acquired a machine for $40,000 on June 3. The company's machinists designed a special patented adaptor for the machine at a cost of $1,200, and the machine performed operations which no similar machine could perform. As a result of the unique adaptor, the machine had a resale value considerably in excess of the total $41,200 cost. The company's accountant wishes to record no depreciation on the machine during the current year because the market value exceeds original cost. What, if any, accounting concepts would be violated by this treatment?

Problems (2)

2–14   **Preparation of a Balance Sheet** *(25 minutes)*   Presented below are data gathered by the Donaho Company for the year ending December 31, 19X1:

Cash	$ 4,050
Payable to creditors for merchandise	7,800
Store supplies on hand	600
Wages payable to employees	1,200
Merchandise inventory	17,550
Receivable from customers	3,400
Capital stock	12,040
Buildings	5,700
Land	2,000

Mortgage payable due 1980	6,000 ✓
Retained earnings	4,305 ✓
Commissions payable to salesmen	750 ✓
Office supplies on hand	120
Taxes payable to the federal government	1,325

Instructions

Prepare a classified balance sheet for the Donaho Company.

2–15   **Balance Sheet Classifications** *(20 minutes)*   The following items were taken from the balance sheet of a company:

Land	Mortgage payable (due in
Patents *other asset.*	1986)
Accounts payable	Prepaid insurance
Retained earnings	Equipment
Cash	Accumulated depreciation on
Federal income taxes payable	equipment
Merchandise inventory	Office supplies
Investments (to be sold next month) C.A.	Six-month note payable
Investments (not to be sold)	Six-month note receivable
Accounts receivable	
Capital stock	

Instructions

Indicate the balance sheet classification in which each of the items would be placed.

2–16   **Preparation of a Balance Sheet from Transactions** *(30 minutes)* The following transactions were completed by The Forbes Corporation during the year ending December 31, 19X1:

a. Cash in the amount of $10,000 was invested, capital stock was issued, and the company began operations.

b. Cash totaling $6,000 was spent for office furniture.

c. A total of $2,000 was spent for a truck.

d. The company earned a profit of $700, all of which was received in cash.

e. Supplies which cost $60 were purchased but not paid for. None of the supplies was consumed.

f. Merchandise inventory of $1,000 was bought for cash. None of the merchandise had been sold.

g. Cash totaling $1,000 was borrowed from the bank, for which the company gave a note payable due in six months.

Instructions

Prepare a balance sheet as of December 31 with classified assets, liabilities, and owners' equity.

2–17   **Matching Costs With Revenues** *(25 minutes)*   The Griswold Company, a manufacturer of paints and various kinds of paint products, employs an accounting year ending each December 31 for accounting purposes. A competitor of the company who was in financial difficulty decided to discontinue business. On December 6, 19X5, the Griswold Company's vice-president offered the competitor $100,000 for his entire stock of raw materials and finished goods. Having little choice, the competitor accepted the offer. The materials and paints thus purchased would have cost $170,000 if purchased from the Griswold Company's regular sources of supply, and the vice president feels that they can be sold to the company's regular customers for $200,000. An entry was made on December 19 placing the inventory on the books at $170,000 and recording a profit for the $70,000 excess of the inventory value over cost.

When the materials and finished products were examined more carefully by the Griswold Company's engineers, the need was found for a special additive to bring the quality of the paints up to that of the Griswold Company's standards. This additive cost $35,000. In July of 19X6, the additive was bought, and the inventory cost was increased by $35,000, from $170,000 to $205,000.

The inventory was sold in 19X7 for the $200,000 which the vice president originally thought could be realized.

Instructions

Answer the following questions:

a. What, if any, generally accepted accounting concept was violated?
b. What effect should the purchase, added costs, and final sale have had on profits during 19X5, 19X6, and 19X7? If you disagree with the procedure followed by the Griswold Company, how do you think the transactions should have been recorded? Show what profit or loss actually relates to 19X5, 19X6, and 19X7.

2–18   **Profit Calculations From Owner's Equity** *(30 minutes)*   On December 31, 19X4 and 19X5 the ABC Company had the following assets and liabilities:

	19X4	19X5
Cash	$ 5,500	$ 5,600
Accounts receivable	10,000	11,500
Merchandise inventory	19,000	18,000
Accounts payable	11,500	11,700
Prepaid insurance	800	700
Mortgage payable	25,000	20,000
Building	38,000	38,000
Accumulated depreciation—building	3,000	4,900
Machinery and equipment	12,000	12,000
Accumulated depreciation—machinery and equipment	4,000	5,200
Taxes payable	1,300	—0—

During 19X5 the owner withdrew $5,000 of his invested capital.

Instructions

1. Compute the owner's equity at the end of each year. (Prepare balance sheets for the two years, with the owner's equity as the amount to balance them.)

2. Compute the profit the company made during 19X5. (Calculate the change in owner's equity, taking into consideration the withdrawal of capital.)

2–19 **Balance Sheet Classifications** *(20 minutes)*   A company has the following classifications on its balance sheet:

Current assets	Current liabilities
Fixed assets	Long-term debt
Other assets	Owners' equity

Instructions
Indicate which of the classifications the accounts listed below would appear in:

Cash	Prepaid rent
Furniture and fixtures	Accumulated depreciation
Wages payable	Office furniture
Unearned revenue	Buildings
Accounts payable	Delivery trucks
Cleaning supplies	Merchandise inventory
Capital stock	Retained earnings
Accounts receivable	Office equipment
Office supplies	Mortgages payable, due 1986
Prepaid insurance	Land
Notes receivable in six months	Temporary investments

2–20 **Application of Stable Dollar Concept** *(30 minutes)*   Assume that the value of the dollar has declined steadily at a rate of 2 percent annually. Using 1949 as the base year, the dollar would have had a 100 percent purchasing power that year, but only 98 percent in 1950, 96 percent in 1951, 94 percent in 1952, and so on, until 1975 when the purchasing power would be 48 percent. This decline means in essence that one dollar would buy only 48 percent as much real goods in 1975 as it would have bought in 1949.

The income statement of the Papermill Company is shown below, with data on the year of acquisition of the assets which have been depreciated or amortized during 1975:

Sales (in 1975 dollars)		$150,000
Cost of goods sold (merchandise acquired in 1974)		100,000
Gross margin		$ 50,000
Operating expenses		
Depreciation (assets acquired in 1949)	$30,000	
Insurance expense (policy paid in 1973)	5,000	
Supplies expense (bought in 1975)	3,000	
Advertising expense (bought in 1975)	1,000	
Total operating expenses		39,000
Net income		$ 11,000

Instructions

1. The above statement is correctly prepared and does not violate any generally accepted principles of accounting. However, in order to emphasize the difference between accounting for the number of dollars and the purchasing power of dollars, you are to convert the income statement so that all amounts are stated in terms of 1975 dollars. Thus the cost of goods sold, for example, would be multiplied by the fraction 50/48, or the ratio of the year of acquisition to the current year:

$$\frac{\text{Year of acquisition index (50 percent)}}{\text{1975, Current year index (48 percent)}}$$

Similarly, depreciation and insurance will require adjustment to convert these expenses to 1975 dollar values, using the ratios of their year of acquisition.

2. Write a brief description of the differences between profit calculations based upon the number of dollars and profit measurement based upon the purchasing power of the dollar.

chapter 3

Measurement of Net Income

Learning Objectives

This chapter continues the emphasis on enterprise measurement, with a focus on the net income of the enterprise. You should achieve the following from your study of this chapter:

1. An understanding of the several concepts of income and why the accounting concept facilitates intercompany and interperiod comparisons.
2. A knowledge of the nature and content of single-step and multistep income statements.
3. An understanding of the meaning of depreciation, the several acceptable methods of calculating depreciation, and their effects on the determination of net income.
4. An understanding of the several acceptable inventory cost flow methods and their effects on the determination of net income.

Concepts of Income

Income is difficult to describe with an all-inclusive, precise definition. This is due partly to the existence of several different concepts of income. Four concepts will be examined briefly in this chapter, primarily to strengthen the understanding of the concept generally used in preparing financial reports for management. These four concepts are:

1. The economic, or purchasing-power concept
2. The legal concept
3. The cash basis concept
4. The generally accepted accounting concept

Economic Concept

The economic concept of income holds that income is the amount which can be consumed during a period and leave the individual as well-off at the end of the period as at the beginning. The term "well-off" implies that the individual's assets have retained their purchasing power, or market value, and under this concept it is possible to have more dollars at the end of the period than at the beginning, but have no more purchasing power. To illustrate, assume that an individual had $9,000 in his bank account at the beginning of the period and $10,000 at the end of the period. Assume also that inflation had produced a 10 percent decline in the purchasing power of the dollar, so that one dollar at the end of the year will buy what ninety cents would have bought at the beginning. Thus, the individual's present $10,000 has no more purchasing power than his original $9,000, and under the economic concept there would be neither a profit nor a loss, since the purchasing power of the assets has not changed.

Under the economic concept, changes in the market value of a company's assets due to factors other than inflation must also be included in the computation of income. Thus, assuming a stable value of the dollar, land with a market value of $57,000 at the beginning of the period and $60,000 at the end of the period would have produced a $3,000 income, even though it has not yet been and may never be sold.

Although the arguments in favor of the economic concept are strong, this concept has a number of serious limitations when applied to a systematic measurement of net income. Two of the most significant disadvantages are the lack of objectivity and a lack of consistency. Use of market value destroys the objectivity of the amounts, for the market value of unsold properties is in many cases only a guess, subject to manipulation by the person preparing the estimate. In addition, attempting to measure "purchasing power" of money or other liquid assets is a complex task; and, to date, the economic concept of income has not become a generally accepted accounting principle.

Legal Concept

Many types of legal arrangements are concerned with the determination of income in a specific situation and thus specify in considerable detail how income is to be determined. Documents such as those dealing with estates, trusts, and bequests frequently specify the type of revenues which will be considered in the determination of net income and the time at which they will be recognized as earned. Such documents also specify the nature and timing of the expenses which are to be recognized. The income computations specified in these documents are not uniform, and their results vary widely.

Legal income may thus be defined as income computed in accordance with some method prescribed by legal means. If an individual establishes a trust fund for his children, placing an apartment building which he owns into the trust, the legal document establishing the trust may specify how income is to be calculated. Depreciation on the building, for example, may be specifically excluded from the calculation, or it may be included, depending upon the wishes of the person establishing the trust. "Taxable income," as another example, is a legal concept of the income which is subject to tax; consequently, taxable income must be determined in accordance with the methods prescribed by the tax code and the related regulations. To date, the use of a rigid legal definition of net income for purposes of measuring enterprise net income is not generally considered preferable, because it tends to be inflexible and is subject to the personal biases of the politicians who would have to establish the methodology.

Cash Basis Concept

The cash basis concept of income is based entirely upon the receipt and disbursement of cash. If a company had a beginning cash balance of $7,000 and had $8,000 at the end of the period, it would, according to the cash basis concept, have a $1,000 income. This concept has been rejected as an equitable measure of net income, because it ignores changes in all other assets and liabilities and assumes that cash alone is the measure of income or loss. Although this method is prescribed in some legal documents and is acceptable for computing taxable income in the case of many individuals, it is not acceptable for general accounting purposes. Since the timing of cash receipts and disbursements is clearly within management's control, the method is not a valid measurement of enterprise net income.

Accounting Concept

The generally accepted accounting concept, or *accrual basis* of determining income, is based upon a prescribed point at which revenue is considered earned and a careful matching of expenses with that revenue. Although a few exceptions are permitted, revenues are in general not considered realized until a completed sale to a customer has taken place. Thus, an increase in the market value of an asset is not sufficient justification for recognizing revenue, for sale of the asset is necessary before the revenue can be considered earned. Furthermore, the generally accepted accounting concept is concerned with the *number* of dollars rather than with their purchasing power.

The accounting computation of net income is based upon the process of "matching" revenues with the expenses incurred in earning those revenues. This matching process is accomplished by careful assignment of revenues to the accounting period in which they are realized and the assignment of expenses to those accounting periods in which they are incurred.

The accuracy of the net income or loss for any one accounting period is directly dependent upon the degree of precision exercised in assigning revenues and expenses to the correct period. Considerable judgment and technical knowledge are usually required if net income is to be computed and reported with an acceptable degree of accuracy.

The matching of revenues with expenses has given rise to many of the procedures and methods included in the framework of generally accepted accounting principles. The processes of accruing expenses and recording deferred revenues and expenses are examples of these procedures. Office supplies and insurance coverage, as another example, do not become expenses until they have been consumed or have expired, and the point at which they are paid is irrelevant to the process of determining accounting net income.

Concepts of Income Illustrated

To illustrate the different concepts of income, suppose that a company had the following assets and liabilities at the beginning of the year, shown at both cost and market value.

	Cost	Market Value
Cash	$ 1,000	$ 1,000
Land	20,000	17,000
Debts owed to creditors	(500)	(500)
	$20,500	$17,500

Suppose further that, during the year, commissions of $50,000 were earned and received in cash, and salaries of $40,000 were earned by employees. Of this, only $37,000 was paid to the employees and the remaining $3,000 was unpaid. Thus the assets and liabilities at the end of the year were as follows:

	Cost	Market Value
Cash	$14,000	$14,000
Land	20,000	20,000
Debts owed to creditors	(500)	(500)
Salaries owed to employees	(3,000)	(3,000)
	$30,500	$30,500

If there was no change in the purchasing power of the dollar during the year, the company's economic income would be $13,000, or the difference between the $17,500 net market value of the company's properties at the beginning of the year and the $30,500 value at the end of the year.

The cash basis income, however, would be $13,000. This income is the difference between the beginning balance of cash, $1,000, and the ending balance of $14,000. Finally, the company's net income computed in accordance with generally accepted accounting principles would be $10,000. This amount is the difference between the revenues considered earned during the period (total commissions of $50,000) and the expenses incurred in earning that revenue (the full $40,000 of salaries earned by employees).

The Income Statement

The income statement is a formal accounting statement employed to present the amount of revenues realized during the period as a result of completed transactions, the expenses incurred in earning that revenue, and the residual income or loss. It is prepared to reflect the net income of the company in accordance with generally accepted principles of accounting. Usually the statement reflects all the major categories of revenue and expense in order to provide additional information concerning the nature of the company's operations. The degree of detail which is used differs considerably from one company to another, and some latitude is permitted in the arrangement of the statement.

Exhibit 3–1 shows the income statement of the Lewis Furniture Corporation. Note that data for three years are furnished in order to provide a basis for ascertaining any trends in the company's profitability. The final amounts at the bottom of the statement are normally entitled Net Income; and, in the case of the Lewis Furniture Corporation, these amounts indicate a substantial growth in profits during the three-year period.

The form of an income statement is not rigidly prescribed, but at a minimum the arrangement should permit identification of three important amounts. These are (1) income from operations, (2) extraordinary and non-recurring items, and (3) net income. However, other subtotals may appear, especially one showing gross margin on sales.

EXHIBIT 3–1

LEWIS FURNITURE CO.
Income Statement
For the Year Ended December 31:

	19X3	19X2	19X1
Sales to customers	$3,254,000	$2,963,000	$2,437,000
Other revenues	265,000	190,000	210,000
Total revenues	$3,519,000	$3,153,000	$2,647,000
Cost of merchandise sold	2,115,000	1,874,000	1,523,000
Salaries and wages	642,000	603,000	584,000
Depreciation	210,000	206,000	193,000
Federal income tax	112,000	60,000	30,000
Transportation out	105,000	93,000	91,000
Advertising and public relations	193,000	182,000	180,000
Total operating expenses	$3,377,000	$3,018,000	$2,601,000
Net operating income	$ 142,000	$ 135,000	$ 46,000
Gain on sale of properties	130,000		15,000
Uninsured fire loss		(76,000)	
Correction of prior year's depreciation			(18,000)
Net income to retained earnings	$ 272,000	$ 59,000	$ 43,000

Single-Step and Multistep Statements

The income statement prepared by management for release to persons outside the company is usually condensed and contains a minimum of subtotals and classifications. Exhibit 3–1 reflects this type of statement, frequently called a single-step statement because revenues are grouped together, as are operating expenses and costs. The amount of detail reflected in such a statement can be reduced, because external groups are primarily interested in operating income and final net income; in such cases great detail can sometimes be more confusing than helpful.

Management may wish to reflect more detail in the income statement than Exhibit 3–1 contains, showing—for instance—intermediate totals for gross margin and a segregation of selling and administrative expenses. This type of statement is frequently called a *multistep income statement* and is more adaptable to the needs of management than to those of persons outside the company's operations. The income statement of the Lewis Furniture Company shown earlier has been rearranged in Exhibit 3–2 to reflect a multistep, classified income statement. Note that the greater detail in Exhibit 3–2 makes this type of statement more difficult to interpret, although more subtotals are included. It is for this reason that the more condensed single-step statement is used for reporting enterprise net income to persons outside the company.

Income Statement Classifications

The classifications of revenues and expenses which appear on an income statement will differ from company to company, because their sources of revenue may not be the same, and their expense and cost categories may differ. However, the financial statements of most companies will contain accounts for sales, cost of merchandise sold, gross margin, operating expenses, non-operating gains and losses, and net income. Each of these is described below.

Sales   The major source of revenues from the sale of products is shown under the heading of *sales*. However, the term sales is not used for revenues from professional services or for income from investments. For these revenues such terms as professional fees, interest income, and dividend income are more commonly used.

Cost of merchandise sold   This section reflects the cost of the merchandise which was delivered to customers in return for cash or accounts receivable. It is computed by adding the beginning inventory, purchases, and transportation-in to determine the cost of the total merchandise available during the period and subtracting from this total the unsold inventory at the end of the period. This section appears only in the income statements of those companies which sell products, and in many cases the term *cost of sales* is used.

Sometimes management wishes the company's income statement to reflect the detailed amounts which enter into the computation of the cost of merchandise sold, such as beginning inventories, purchases of merchandise, transporta-

EXHIBIT 3-2

LEWIS FURNITURE COMPANY
Income Statement
For the Year Ended December 31:

	19X3		19X2		19X1	
Sales to customers		$3,254,000		$2,963,000		$2,437,000
Cost of merchandise sold		2,115,000		1,874,000		1,523,000
Gross margin on sales		$1,139,000		$1,089,000		$ 914,000
Other revenues		265,000		190,000		210,000
Total		$1,404,000		$1,279,000		$1,124,000
Selling expenses						
Salaries and wages	$260,000		$263,000		$284,000	
Depreciation	100,000		101,000		93,000	
Transportation out	105,000		93,000		91,000	
Advertising	140,000		130,000		135,000	
Total Selling expense		$ 605,000		$ 587,000		$ 603,000
Administrative expenses						
Executive salaries	$300,000		$265,000		$230,000	
Clerical wages	82,000		75,000		70,000	
Depreciation	110,000		105,000		100,000	
Public relations	53,000		52,000		45,000	
Total administrative expenses		545,000		$ 497,000		$ 445,000
Total operating expenses		$1,150,000		$1,084,000		$1,048,000

LEWIS FURNITURE COMPANY
(Continued)

	19X3	19X2	19X1
Income from operations before taxes	$ 254,000	$ 195,000	$ 76,000
Federal income tax	112,000	60,000	30,000
Income after taxes	$ 142,000	$ 135,000	$ 46,000
Non-operating gains and losses			
Gain on sale of properties	$ 130,000		$ 15,000
Uninsured fire loss		$ (76,000)	
Correction of prior year's depreciation			(18,000)
Total	$ 130,000	$ (76,000)	$ (3,000)
Net income to retained earnings	$ 272,000	$ 59,000	$ 43,000

tion, and ending inventories. In such cases, the presentation is usually in the following format:

Sales		$634,090
Cost of merchandise sold		
Inventory, January 1, 19X1	$ 72,100	
Merchandise purchases	396,530	
Freight-in	21,900	
Total available for sale	$490,530	
Less inventory December 31, 19X1	81,420	
Total cost of merchandise sold		409,110
Gross margin		$224,980

This arrangement permits the beginning inventory and merchandise purchases, with the related transportation cost, to be added together to determine the total merchandise available for sale. The ending inventory is subtracted from this total to ascertain the cost of the merchandise sold during the year.

Gross profit on sales   The gross profit on sales is the difference between revenue inflow from sales and the cost of merchandise sold. This amount is sometimes called the *gross margin* or the *mark-up*. If the company is to be profitable, its gross profit must exceed its operating expenses; and, for this reason, the gross profit is one of the most important amounts appearing on the income statement. Upward or downward trends in gross profit are of considerable importance in judging the company's profit potential. Note that the gross profit of the Lewis Furniture Company shown earlier in Exhibit 3–2 increased in dollar amount from 19X1 to 19X2 and again in 19X3, although the margin expressed as a percentage of sales declined each year (amounts rounded to thousands).

	Sales	Cost of Merchandise Sold	Gross Margin	Margin as a Percentage of Sales
19X1	$2,437	$1,523	$ 914	37%
19X2	2,963	1,874	1,089	36%
19X3	3,254	2,115	1,139	35%

This indicates that the company has not been able to market its products so that the same percentage of gross profit is received from each dollar of sales. This is not necessarily bad, for lowered gross margins may be due to reduced unit sales prices, which in turn cause more units to be sold. It is the interaction of sales volume, sales prices, and the cost of merchandise sold that results in the gross margin figure.

Operating expenses   A company's operating expenses include all those incurred in the buying, selling, and administrative functions of the business. These activities are frequently divided into two sections, as indicated in Exhibit 3–2, so that the selling expenses and the administrative expenses appear separately. Selling expenses include all those incurred directly for the purpose of selling merchandise. The expenses incurred in connection with salaries of sales personnel, advertising, store supplies, and insurance on merchandise, for example, are directly associated with the sales effort and in a classified income statement would be included in the selling expense category. The administrative expense classification includes all administrative and operating expenses, such as office supplies, administrative salaries, office salaries, utilities, and rent.

Net income from operations   The net income from operations is the residual after total operating expenses have been subtracted from gross profit on sales. This amount represents the income realized by the normal operations of the company before unusual, non-recurring items are added or subtracted. In a multistep income statement, the operating income before federal income taxes is usually shown.

Non-operating gains and losses   A company's operating income reflects the ability to earn profits in the normal course of events. However, every company has unusual transactions from time to time, such as fire losses, gains or losses on the sale of fixed assets, and corrections of accounting errors made in prior years. These events, when material in amount, should be reported separately immediately after operating income. Exhibits 3–1 and 3–2 both reflect this arrangement. Note that the non-operating items have changed the final net income figures materially and would, if not separately shown, increase the possibility of misinterpreting the statements.

Net income   The net income is the final amount on the statement and represents the difference between all revenues and all expenses assigned to the period. A loss is frequently shown in red or in parentheses to distinguish it clearly from a profit.

The parentheses shown in the Non-Operating Gains and Losses section of Exhibit 3–2 indicate losses, while gains in that same section do not appear in parenthesis.

Fixed Assets as Deferred Costs

Fixed assets are by definition those with relatively long lives which are used in the operation of a business and not intended for resale. The cost of a fixed asset with a limited useful life must be allocated to those periods during which it has usefulness. The cost of such assets as buildings, equipment, limited franchises, and patents must be apportioned to those years during which they contributed to the company's earning ability. On the other hand, assets such as land, trade names, and perpetual franchises, which do not have a limited useful life, may not be subject to depreciation or amortization.

Accounting for fixed assets and the related periodic depreciation expense is based upon the concept of the accounting entity as a going concern with an unlimited life. Depreciation is the process of systematically spreading the cost of a fixed asset over its useful life so that the cost is properly matched with revenues. The going concern and the periodicity concepts are the basis for the depreciation process. Fixed assets are in a practical sense deferred costs, and the depreciation process is a means of apportioning this deferred cost to the appropriate accounting periods.

Primary emphasis in the depreciation process is placed on a systematic and fair apportionment of the cost of using the fixed assets. The balance sheet does not attempt to reflect the market value of fixed assets. The current market value of a fixed asset is not significant in the accounting process, since the assumption must be made that the business will continue indefinitely and that the asset will eventually be consumed in the normal operations of the business.

Nature of Depreciation

Depreciation is the systematic allocation of the cost of an asset over its useful life. It is a process of allocation, not of valuation. Depreciation for any year is the portion of the cost of the asset which is allocated to that year and should not be confused with any decline in the market value of the asset. It is possible that the market value of the asset may actually increase during the same year that depreciation expense is being recorded. This is as it should be, for changes in market value are irrelevant to the process of allocating the cost of a depreciable asset.

The portion of the cost of a fixed asset to be assigned to an accounting period is difficult to measure. The life of the asset and any salvage proceeds which may be received when it is ultimately disposed of cannot be known definitely in advance, and must be estimated. Even in those rare cases when the *physical* life of an asset may be determined accurately, estimates of the *useful* life must nevertheless be made. Assets are frequently sold or scrapped before the end of their physical lives because they are superseded and become obsolete. A typewriter, for example, may have a twenty-year physical life but may still be replaced each five years because the company officials want impressive new office equipment at all times.

The cost to be assigned to an accounting period may be determined in several ways. Acceptable methods include the (1) straight-line, (2) service hours, (3) units of output, (4) constant percentage of a declining balance, and (5) sum-of-the-years' digits methods.

Straight-Line Depreciation

The straight-line method is applicable to those assets which make an equal contribution to operations during each year of their productive lives. This method allocates to each year an equal amount of the asset's depreciable cost.

The annual straight-line depreciation expense is computed by dividing the depreciable cost of the asset by the number of years in its productive life. Depreciable cost is the cost recorded in the asset account less the estimated net proceeds which are expected to be realized when the asset is sold, traded, or otherwise disposed of. The computation is expressed in the following formula:

$$\text{Annual depreciation} = \frac{\text{Cost} - \text{Estimated salvage}}{\text{Estimated years of life}}$$

$$\frac{25,000 - 5,000}{10 \text{ yr}} = 2,000$$

If a company pays $10,200 for an asset which is expected to have a salvage value of $200 after five years of use, the annual depreciation expense is $2,000, computed as follows:

$$\frac{\$10,200 - \$200}{5} = \$2,000$$

The straight-line method has the advantage of simplicity, but it is not an appropriate depreciation method in those cases where the asset does not contribute uniformly to operations during each year of its useful life.

Service Hours Depreciation

If the use of an asset is not uniform during its life and if its life can be estimated in terms of service hours, a logical allocation of costs results from use of the service hours method. When this method is used, an hourly depreciation rate is computed by dividing the depreciable cost of the asset by the estimated number of service hours in its life. The computation is expressed in the following formula:

$$\text{Depreciation cost per service hour} = \frac{\text{Cost} - \text{Estimated salvage}}{\text{Estimated number of service hours}}$$

If the asset described above, a machine with a depreciable cost of $10,000, is expected to have 50,000 service hours of productive life, the depreciation per service hour would be $.20 ($10,000 ÷ 50,000 hours). Suppose further that during the first year of the machine's life it is used 12,000 hours. The depreciation expense for the year is $2,400 (12,000 × $.20). If the machine is operated 8,000 hours during the second year, the depreciation expense is $1,600 (8,000 × $.20). Exhibit 3–3 illustrates the computation of the annual depreciation expense for the entire life of the machine, using assumed amounts for the service hours operated each year.

EXHIBIT 3–3

Year	Hours Used	Estimated Cost Per Hour	Depreciation Expense
1	12,000	$0.20	$ 2,400
2	8,000	.20	1,600
3	11,000	.20	2,200
4	13,000	.20	2,600
5	6,000	.20	1,200
Total			$10,000

Estimation of an asset's total service hours may be subject to considerable error; consequently, this method of computing depreciation should be used only in those instances in which the asset's total service hours can be estimated with some degree of accuracy.

Units of Output Depreciation

The units of output method of computing periodic depreciation is similar to the service hours method. The total life of the asset is estimated in terms of the total number of units it will produce, and a unit depreciation rate is computed by dividing the depreciable cost by the estimated total units of output.

If the machine described previously, with a net depreciable cost of $10,000, is expected to produce 20,000 units during its productive life, the depreciation expense per unit is $0.50. Exhibit 3–4 illustrates the computation of the annual depreciation expense for the entire life of the machine, using assumed amounts for the units produced each year.

EXHIBIT 3–4

Year	Units	Unit Cost	Depreciation Expense
1	3,000	$0.50	$ 1,500
2	5,000	.50	2,500
3	6,000	.50	3,000
4	4,000	.50	2,000
5	2,000	.50	1,000
Total			$10,000

Declining Balance Depreciation

Depreciation expense may be computed by applying a constant percentage to the undepreciated cost (cost less accumulated depreciation of prior years) of the asset. This method was accepted for determining depreciation for tax purposes by the Revenue Act of 1954 and has been adopted by many companies since that time.

The formula[1] to determine the percentage is as follows:

$$\text{Declining balance depreciation rate} = 1 - \sqrt[n]{\frac{\text{Salvage value}}{\text{Cost}}}$$

where "n" is the number of years of useful life. Since salvage value must be used in the formula, an arbitrarily small salvage value is sometimes used when the asset has no salvage value. By applying this formula to the machine discussed previously with a $10,200 cost and a five-year life, a constant rate of 55 percent is determined. Exhibit 3–5 illustrates the application of the constant rate to the undepreciated balance each year. The asset is never fully depreciated when this method is used, but by the end of the asset's life the undepreciated balance approximates the estimated salvage.

For the fifth year, the depreciation expense is $218. Fifty-five percent of $418, the undepreciated balance at the beginning of that year, is $230; how-

---

1. The derivation of this formula is beyond the scope of this text. It is included here to illustrate the means by which the percentage figure is computed.

EXHIBIT 3–5

Year	Undepreciated Balance at Beginning of Year		Constant Percentage	Depreciation Expense
1	Total cost	$10,200	55	$ 5,610
2	($10,200 — $5,610)	4,590	55	2,525
3	(4,590 — 2,525)	2,065	55	1,136
4	(2,065 — 1,136)	929	55	511
5	(929 — 511)	418	55	218
Total				$10,000

ever, total depreciation of an asset can never exceed its depreciable cost, and the expense is thus the remaining $218 of the $10,000 depreciable net cost. Note that the full $10,200 cost of the asset is used when this method is applied; no salvage value is deducted when the percentage is applied to undepreciated cost, although salvage value was included in the computation of the percentage.

Accountants who advocate this method of computing depreciation argue that repairs and maintenance are greatest during the latter years of the life of the asset, and that depreciation computed by the constant percentage method tends to equalize the combined depreciation expense and maintenance expense for each year of the asset's life. These accountants argue further that in some cases the revenue-producing ability of the asset declines as the asset grows older. An apartment house, for example, commands higher rentals when it is new than in later years.

The general acceptance of this method did not occur until 1954 when it became acceptable for determining income for federal income tax purposes. The tax regulations allow the constant percentage to be *no greater than twice the straight-line rate.* In the above example, the asset with a five-year life would have a 20 percent straight-line rate, so that—for tax purposes—a percentage of no greater than 40 percent could be used. Almost all of the companies using the declining balance method employ rates in conformity with income tax limitations. For this reason the declining balance method is frequently referred to as the "200 percent method," which is twice the straight-line rate, or the "double" declining balance method.

Sum-of-the-Years' Digits Depreciation

The sum-of-the-years' digits method is similar to the declining balance method and results in larger depreciation charges in the early years of the life of the asset. The annual depreciation is determined by multiplying the depreciable cost by a fraction. The numerator is the number of years in the remaining life of the asset from the beginning of that year, and the denominator is the total of digits representing the years of the asset's life. Exhibit 3–6 illustrates the computation of the annual depreciation expense by the sum-of-the-years' digits method.

The fraction is applied to the depreciable cost, that is, cost less estimated salvage value. Since the total of the fractions is 1, the total depreciation expense of all years is equal to the amount to which the fractions are applied. Note that the fraction used in the first year is 5/15. The five is the highest digit in the year's life and the fifteen is the sum of the years' digits. The numerator of the fraction decreases by one each year, going from 5/15 to 4/15, to 3/15, etc.

The arguments in support of the sum-of-the-years' digits method are similar to those for the method based on a constant percentage of a declining balance. The sum-of-the-years' digits method has also been acceptable for income tax purposes since 1954.

EXHIBIT 3–6

Year	Fraction	Depreciable Cost	Depreciation Expense
1	5/15	$10,000	$ 3,333
2	4/15	10,000	2,667
3	3/15	10,000	2,000
4	2/15	10,000	1,333
5	1/15	10,000	667
Total of the years' digits	15		$10,000

Comparison of Depreciation Methods

Exhibit 3–7 compares the annual depreciation expense determined by each of the methods discussed in the preceding sections. Observe that the depreciation expense in any one year can vary substantially, depending on the method by which it is computed. However, the total depreciation expense for the five years is $10,000 (the depreciable cost), regardless of the method used. The choice of a depreciation method affects the amount of depreciation expense in any one year but not the total amount of depreciation charged against revenue over the entire life of the asset. Note, for example, the variance in depreciation expense of the first year as computed by the methods previously discussed.

EXHIBIT 3–7

Comparison of Various Depreciation Methods

Year	Straight-line	Service Hours	Units of Production	Constant % of Declining Balance	Sum-of-the-Years' Digits
1	$ 2,000	$2,400	$ 1,500	$ 5,610	$ 3,333
2	2,000	1,600	2,500	2,525	2,667
3	2,000	2,200	3,000	1,136	2,000
4	2,000	2,600	2,000	511	1,333
5	2,000	1,200	1,000	218	667
Total Depreciation	$10,000	$10,000	$10,000	$10,000	$10,000

At the end of the fifth year, the balance in the asset account on the balance sheet is still the $10,200 original cost, and the balance in the accumulated depreciation account on the same statement is $10,000, leaving a book value of $200. When the asset is sold or otherwise disposed of, these two amounts are removed from the accounts, and a gain or loss results when the asset is sold for more or less than the $200 net book value.

One of the major problems confronting those who must measure periodic income is the selection of a method of assigning depreciation to accounting periods. Straight-line, declining balance, sum-of-the-years' digits, units of production, and a number of variations of these methods are being used to determine net income. Although the results of applying one or the other of these methods are different, strong arguments may be advanced for any one of them.

In the interests of an adequate interpretation of the financial statements, the depreciation method should be disclosed. Financial reports submitted by management to its stockholders frequently provide these data in the form of footnotes or as other supplemental information. Changes in the *amount* of the periodic depreciation expense resulting from revised estimates of the asset's life or salvage value are sometimes necessary, but changes in the *method* should not be made without full and adequate disclosure of the effects, usually for a period covering several years after the change.

Measuring the Cost of Merchandise Sold

Matching the cost of units sold with revenues received from their sale presents another complex problem in the measurement of net income. The inventory account on a company's balance sheet reflects those costs associated with unsold units which are available for sale. The manner by which these costs are assigned to the cost of merchandise sold during the accounting year affects the determination of net income for the period. Alternative choices are available in the determination of the cost of merchandise sold; if the units available for sale during the period have been acquired at different costs, the cost assigned to the unsold units may be that of the first purchase, the last purchase, or the average of all purchases. These methods frequently produce substantially different results.

To illustrate the problems encountered in assigning a unit cost to the items in the ending inventory, suppose a company selling automobile tires had the following identical tires available for sale during January, acquired at different times and at different unit costs:

	units	Cost	= 4 L
Beginning inventory	8 tires @ $10.00 each =	$ 80.00	
Purchases			
January 2	10 tires @ 12.00 each =	120.00	
January 12	20 tires @ 13.00 each =	260.00	
January 26	15 tires @ 14.00 each =	210.00	
January 31	5 tires @ 15.00 each =	75.00	
Total available for sale	5 8	$745.00	

BI=25

On January 31 there are twenty tires in the ending inventory, determined by a physical count. Since the tires are identical, there is a question of which cost to assign to them. Four methods by which costs may be assigned to these twenty tires are (1) identifiable cost, (2) first-in-first-out, (3) last-in-first-out, and (4) average cost. The following illustrations of these four methods are based on the data above.

Identifiable Cost

The individual units of some products can be specifically identified. Automobile tires were selected for this example because they are marked with a serial number and can be traced for specific sales. Thus, continuing the example, if twelve of the tires in the ending inventory were determined to have been purchased on January 12 and the other eight on January 26, the amount of the ending inventory would be computed as follows:

		Cost of the Ending Inventory by Identifiable Cost Method	
Beginning inventory	8 @ $10.00	Sold	
Purchases:			
January 2	10 @ 12.00	Sold	
January 12	20 @ 13.00	12 @ $13.00 =	$156.00
		8 Sold	
January 26	15 @ 14.00	8 @ 14.00 =	112.00
		7 Sold	
January 31	5 @ 15.00	Sold	
Total ending inventory		20	$268.00

The cost of the merchandise sold for the period would then be $477, computed as follows:

Total available for sale	$745.00
Less ending inventory	268.00
Cost of merchandise sold	$477.00

Not all companies sell products which can be specifically identified with unit costs. Only those companies whose merchandise has identifiable markings would attempt to identify specific units with specific invoice prices, and then only when the resulting data are considered worth the clerical cost. If identifiable unit costs cannot be determined or do not justify the clerical effort of unit identification, the inventory must be determined by a *flow of costs*. The first-in-first-out, last-in-first-out, and average methods of inventory pricing are assumptions based on an assumed flow of costs, rather than on specific identification.

First-In-First-Out

One assumption concerning the flow of costs is that the first units bought are the first units which are sold. This method is called first-in-first-out (FIFO). Continuing the example used previously, under the FIFO method the ending inventory is valued at the cost of the last twenty tires purchased, since the first units available are assumed to have been sold first. The FIFO computation is illustrated as follows:

		Cost of the Ending Inventory by First-in-First-out Method
Beginning inventory	8 @ $10.00	Sold
Purchases		
January 2	10 @ 12.00	Sold
January 12	20 @ 13.00	Sold
January 26	15 @ 14.00	15 @ $14.00 = $210.00
January 31	5 @ 15.00	5 @ 15.00 = 75.00
Total ending inventory		20 $285.00

The cost of merchandise sold is $460.00, computed as follows:

Total available for sale	$745.00
Less ending inventory	285.00
Cost of merchandise sold	$460.00

The FIFO inventory is an acceptable assumption as to the flow of costs, even though it may be possible to identify specifically the units in the ending inventory and trace the actual invoice cost of each unit. The FIFO method attaches an actual cost to the units in the ending inventory, and the costs need not be the specific costs of the units in the inventory.

It is important that this method and those that follow be understood as a *flow of costs* and not an attempt to identify the actual flow of units. In a period of changing prices, as the example indicates, the FIFO method results in an inventory valuation for balance sheet purposes that is a realistic approximation of the latest costs.

Last-In-First-Out

The last-in-first-out (LIFO) inventory method is the opposite of the FIFO in that it assumes that the last units bought were the ones which were sold. Therefore, the ending inventory is assigned the costs of the oldest units in the cost pool. The cost of the inventory of the twenty units used in the preceding examples would be determined as follows using the LIFO method:

		Cost of the Ending Inventory by Last-in-First-out Method
Beginning inventory	8 @ $10.00	8 @ $10.00 = $ 80.00
Purchases:		
January 2	10 @ 12.00	10 @ 12.00 = 120.00
January 12	20 @ 13.00	{ 2 @ 13.00 = 26.00
		18 Sold
January 26	15 @ 14.00	Sold
January 31	5 @ 15.00	Sold
Total ending inventory		20 $226.00

The cost of merchandise sold is $519, computed as follows:

Total available for sale	$745.00
Less ending inventory	226.00
Cost of merchandise sold	$519.00

Average Cost

The average cost inventory method assigns to each unit the average of the cost of the units available for sale during the period. The average unit cost is determined by dividing the number of units available for sale into the total cost of the merchandise available for sale, as follows:

	Units	Total Cost
Beginning inventory	8	$ 80.00
Purchases		
January 2	10	120.00
January 12	20	260.00
January 26	15	210.00
January 31	5	75.00
Total	58	$745.00

Average cost is $745.00 ÷ 58 units, or $12.84. The ending inventory is twenty units at $12.84, or $256.80. The cost of merchandise sold is determined as follows:

Total available for sale (58 @ $12.84)	$745.00
Less ending inventory (20 @ $12.84)	256.80
Cost of merchandise sold (38 @ $12.84)	$488.20

Comparison of Inventory Methods

When prices are rising or falling, the four inventory valuation methods will produce different balance sheet inventory amounts and different costs of merchandise sold for each year within a business cycle. The ending inventories and costs of units sold computed above, each from the same set of facts but using a different inventory valuation method, are compared in Exhibit 3–8.

EXHIBIT 3–8

Comparison of Inventory Methods

	Specific Identification	FIFO	LIFO	Average
Total available for sale	$745.00	$745.00	$745.00	$745.00
Less ending inventory	268.00	285.00	226.00	256.80
Cost of merchandise sold	$477.00	$460.00	$519.00	$488.20

Comparison of the cost of merchandise sold resulting from each method reveals that the FIFO method produced a significantly lower cost of sales figure than did the LIFO method. This will be the case when costs are increasing, as reflected by the tire dealer's purchases; but the opposite is true when costs are falling. The effects of using one or the other of these methods in times of changing price levels is one of the most important points brought out in this chapter. In addition, the following aspects of the several methods must be kept in mind:

1. Inventory valuation methods other than specific identification *assume a flow of costs* that may differ from the physical flow of units. The methods differ in that the cost used may be the earliest, latest, average, or specific cost.

2. The method selected by a company to compute its ending inventory and cost of merchandise sold must be followed consistently. Although the company may apply different valuation methods in the determination of the cost of different inventory components—such as the inventory of different plants belonging to the same company—the method applied to a specific component cannot be changed without violating generally accepted accounting principles.

3. The FIFO method assigns the most recent costs to the ending inventory and earlier costs to the cost of goods sold. The LIFO method, on the other hand, assigns the earliest costs to inventory and the most recent costs to the cost of goods sold. Thus FIFO produces a higher profit than LIFO when costs are rising.

FIFO and LIFO Concepts Compared

Two entirely different concepts of business income underlie the FIFO and LIFO inventory methods. Suppose that during the current accounting period a company buys an item of merchandise for $5, sells it for $8, and pays $6 for an identical unit of merchandise to replace the item sold. Is the gross profit on the sale $3, determined by the difference between the $8 selling price and the $5 cost of the original unit? Or is the gross profit $2, determined by the difference between the $8 selling price and the $6 cost of the replacement item? Since a business is assumed to be a going concern, with maintenance of a minimum inventory a prerequisite to continuing in business, all items sold must be replaced; thus perhaps only $2 should be considered the gross profit.

These two concepts of income are reflected by the LIFO and FIFO inventory valuation methods, as illustrated in the following comparative partial income statements:

	LIFO	FIFO
Sales	$8	$8
Cost of merchandise available for sale		
(one unit at $5 and one at $6)	$11	$11
Ending inventory	5	6
Cost of merchandise sold	6	5
Gross profit	$2	$3

Use of either the FIFO or the LIFO inventory method will produce identical results when there is no change in the price of purchased units. However, when prices fluctuate either upward or downward, the inventory method selected by a company has a direct effect upon both the inventory in the balance sheet and the cost of merchandise sold in the income statement. The differences in the inventory and the net income will increase sharply when there are pronounced increases or declines in prices.

Use of FIFO more nearly approximates the physical flow of units in most but not all companies, and the primary argument of those who favor this method is that since the oldest units are sold first, the earliest costs should be matched against revenue. However, those who support the LIFO method maintain that it is not necessary to follow the physical flow of units, and that matching the latest cost with revenue is as valid as matching the early cost.

Summary

The meaning of "net income" is not always clearly understood unless the concepts employed in its calculation are known. Accountants, economists, and attorneys sometimes interpret net income differently, and the possibility of miscommunication is strong unless the methods and assumptions which have been used are understood. The accounting concept which is more generally used in measuring enterprise net income for financial reporting to managers and owners is based upon an accrual concept, or a careful matching of revenues and expenses.

The income statement is designed to reflect the revenues and expenses which are considered applicable to the period. Sometimes all revenues are grouped together, all expenses are grouped together, and a single-step income statement is prepared. This arrangement contains a minimum of detail and is used principally for reporting to owners and parties outside the company. For the purposes of internal management, a multistep statement is frequently used. This arrangement contains intermediate subtotals for gross profit, operating profit before taxes, non-operating and non-recurring items, and net income after taxes. It may also contain expense subtotals for operating functions within the business, such as selling, administrative, and warehousing expenses.

Two of the most important elements in the determination of net income are the cost of goods sold and the depreciation expense. Each of these presents special problems in the determination of net income, for there are several different methods which may be utilized.

Depreciation is subject to straight-line, declining balance, and sum-of-the-years' digits methods, and each of these may be conceptually correct. The accounting profession has not singled out one particular technique as being correct, and rightly so, for a rigidly prescribed method would in many cases produce results more undesirable than having several acceptable methods. The cost of goods sold may also be calculated by several different methods; the three most frequently used are FIFO, LIFO, and average cost. These methods produce materially different cost of goods sold and ending inventory amounts when prices rise or drop sharply during the period. However, both LIFO and FIFO are defendable as cost flow methods, and both may be conceptually justified. It is for this reason that information concerning both the inventory method and the depreciation method which a company utilizes should accompany the income statement. Such information is necessary for a correct interpretation of the net income amount.

New Terms

Accrual basis income   Income determined by matching revenues and expenses through a process of deferrals and accruals in order to assign them to the correct period.

Average inventory method   An inventory method which assigns an average cost to each unit.

Declining balance depreciation   A depreciation method which applies a constant percentage to the remaining undepreciated cost of the asset.

FIFO inventory method   An inventory method which assigns the cost of the earliest unit in inventory to the units being sold.

Gross margin   Difference between sales and cost of goods sold.

LIFO inventory method   An inventory method which assigns the latest cost of the units in inventory to the unit being sold.

Multistep income statement   A statement which shows a number of intermediate totals.

Non-operating gain or loss   Gain or loss arising from sources other than those normal and recurring for the company.

Single-step income statement   A statement which groups all revenues together and all expenses together with a minimum of subtotals.

Straight-line depreciation   A method which allocates the cost of an asset equally to the years of its life.

Sum-of-the-years digits method   A depreciation method based upon the calculation of a fraction which utilizes the sum of all the years of an asset's life.

Questions/

1. Define each of the following terms:
   a. Accrued revenue
   b. Single-step income statement
   c. Multistep income statement
   d. Gross margin
   e. Non-operating loss
   f. FIFO method
   g. Sum-of-the-years' digits method

2. Distinguish between the economic, cash basis, and generally accepted accounting concepts of net income in respect to (a) increases in the market value of fixed assets, (b) declining purchasing power of money, and (c) receipt of cash from a customer in payment of merchandise purchased last year.

3. Define depreciation and discuss whether it should cover the full physical life of an asset or its economic life to the company. Is it possible for these two lives to be different?

4. Why has the accounting profession permitted several methods of computing depreciation and calculating the cost of goods sold, instead of agreeing on one acceptable method and insisting that all companies use that one?

5. John, Jim, and Jack each bought an identical new Chevrolet this year. John will use his as a taxicab and drive 40,000 miles per year; Jim will use his as a business car and drive 25,000 miles per year; Jack will use his as a personal car and drive 10,000 miles per year. What life would you give each automobile for purposes of depreciation?

6. Maxine Tollhouse sells vacuum cleaners as a door-to-door salesperson. She paid $100 for the single unit which she maintains as inventory and keeps it with her during her sales demonstrations. Yesterday she sold the unit for $180 and paid $120 for another like unit in order to continue her work. Did she make $80 or $60 profit on the sale?

7. Describe how the cost of a fixed asset, with the exception of land, would be a form of deferred cost.

8. Describe the relationship between an income statement and a balance sheet of the same company. Do the amounts on the income statement in any way enter into the construction of the balance sheet?

9. Why are subtotals such as gross margin, operating net income, and net income after taxes shown on multistep income statements? Are these amounts of more interest to stockholders or to operating management?

10. How would you classify the following on an income statement—as operating or as non-operating gains and losses:
    a. Gain on the sale of land (manufacturing company)
    b. Loss due to fire in the building (bank)
    c. Inventory obsolescence losses (clothing manufacturing company)
    d. Fee to consultants to design an accounting system (insurance company)
    e. Loss on sale of stocks and bonds (brokerage firm)
    f. Employee embezzlement loss (bank)
    g. Contribution to a political party (retail store)

11. The ABC company was formed on January 2 and immediately purchased 100,000 units of merchandise at $5 per unit. Later during the year they purchased another 100,000 units at $6 per unit. Sales were 150,000 units,

and the owner wants to pay as little income tax as is legally possible for the year's operations. Would you advise him to use LIFO, FIFO, or average inventory to compute the cost of goods sold?

Exercises (2)

3–1*   **Concepts of Income** *(30 minutes)*   The Matson Commission Agency had assets and liabilities as follows on December 31, 19X1.

	Cost	Market Value
Cash	$ 500	$ 500
Accounts receivable	150	150
Buildings	15,000	12,000
Land	5,000	3,000

During the year, the company earned commissions of $27,000 but collected only $23,000 of this amount in cash. Salaries expenses of $24,000 were incurred, but only $23,000 was paid in cash. Advertising expenses of $6,000 were incurred but not paid. At the end of the year the company had the following assets and liabilities:

	Cost	Market Value
Cash	$ 500	$ 500
Accounts receivable	4,150	4,150
Buildings	15,000	14,000
Land	5,000	5,000
Advertising payable	(6,000)	(6,000)
Salaries payable	(1,000)	(1,000)

Instructions
Prepare (1) an income statement prepared in accordance with accepted accounting principles, (2) computations to reflect the cash-basis income, and (3) computations to reflect the economic income.

3–2   **Single-Step Income Statement** *(15 minutes)*   The Trade-Winds Company accumulated the following data during the year ending December 31, 19X1.

Rent paid	$ 2,000
Utilities paid	500
Fees received from clients	14,000
Salaries paid to employees	6,000
Taxes paid	400
Rent received from sublease of part of the building	600
Supplies paid for	200
Insurance policy for the year	100

The revenues from clients and from the tenant were all received in cash, but $200 of the rent paid was for the first month of the coming year, and the insurance policy had not been paid for by December 31.

Instructions

Prepare a single-step income statement for the year.

3–3   **Single-Step Income Statement** *(15 minutes)*   Lytle and Company is a firm of professional real estate appraisers. The transactions completed by the company during 19X1 are summarized as follows:

a. Earned $27,000 in professional fees, of which $2,700 has not yet been collected from clients.

b. Paid salaries of $18,300, and owes $200 additional salaries.

c. Purchased supplies costing $930 during the year. Of this amount, $100 is not yet paid for, and $210 is unused.

d. Paid $200 rent each month during the entire year.

e. Paid federal income taxes on the income of the business for the year, $1,150.

Instructions

Prepare a single-step income statement for the year.

3–4*   **Multistep Income Statement** *(20 minutes)*   The Strane Company uses an accounting period ending on July 31, and had accumulated the following data by the end of the accounting year 19X1:

Salaries expense	$ 7,000
Fuel	2,400
Revenues from the sale of products	56,500
Insurance	1,000
Federal income taxes	2,100
Cost of the products sold	28,000
Supplies used	700
Advertising	3,200
Utilities	2,000
Rent	4,100
Gain on sale of fixed assets	2,000

Instructions

Prepare a multistep income statement which reflects gross profit, net operating income before extraordinary gains, net income after extraordinary gains, and net income after federal income taxes.

3–5   **Selection of Data for an Income Statement** *(20 minutes)*   Lloyd Harris operates an advertising agency and prepares advertising copy, which he places in newspapers, on radio, and occasionally on TV. He receives a lump sum amount from a client and uses this amount to advertise the client's products in the most effective manner.

The agency had a cash balance at the beginning of the year of $2,130 and received $205,100 during the year. A total of $103,000 was paid for advertising on radio and TV and $40,000 for newspaper advertising. Payments were also made as follows: salaries, $28,000; supplies, $2,000; rent, $3,600; and taxes, $5,000. Included in the $205,100 received was a $10,000 payment received from a customer for services to be performed during January of the next year, and $5,000 borrowed from the bank to be repaid in one year without interest.

Instructions
Prepare an income statement for the current year.

3–6 **Preparation of an Income Statement from Transactions** *(25 minutes)* The Trell Company began operations on January 1 of the current year, completing the following transactions:
a. The owner invested $2,000 cash to begin the business.
b. Completed services of $173,000 for customers, of which $160,000 was received in cash.
c. Paid $12,000 for advertising.
d. Paid salaries of $110,500.
e. Purchased and consumed office supplies of $2,000; of this amount $350 had not been paid for by the end of the year.
f. Owed the state government $3,450 for taxes for the current year.
g. Owed employees another $1,675 in salaries, in addition to that already paid.
h. Was sued by an irate client for $5,000, but the suit was settled out of court for $3,000, which has been paid.

Instructions
Prepare a single-step income statement.

3–7 **Depreciation Calculations** *(15 minutes)* A company acquired a truck at a cost of $11,000. The expected life is four years and at the end of that time it is expected to have a value of $1,000.

Instructions
Compute the depreciation expense for the truck for each of the four years of its life using the following methods:
1. Straight-line
2. Sum-of-the-years' digits
3. Declining balance, using twice the straight-line rate

3–8 **Depreciation Calculations** *(15 minutes)* Sam Gotlieb purchased a delivery truck for his delicatessen. Because of planned expansion of his business he plans to drive it the following number of miles each year during its four-year life:

19X1	14,000 miles
19X2	26,000
19X3	40,000
19X4	50,000

The cost of the truck was $4,800 and its estimated salvage value is $900.

Instructions

Compute the depreciation expense for each year of the truck's life using (1) a mileage basis and (2) the sum-of-the-years' digits method.

3–9* **Computation of Depreciation** *(20 minutes)* The Opal Company purchased a new truck on December 31, 19X3 for $5,500. The truck had an estimated life of five years or 100,000 miles and an estimated salvage value of $500. The truck was driven 10,000 miles in 19X4, 25,000 miles in 19X5, and 15,000 miles in 19X6.

Instructions

Compute the depreciation expense for 19X4 ,19X5, and 19X6 using the following methods:
1. Straight-line
2. Sum-of-the-years' digits
3. Units of output based upon a 100,000 mile life
4. Constant percentage of a declining balance (use a 40 percent rate)

3–10 **Selection of an Amortization Method** *(10 minutes)* A copyright was acquired by a publishing house on January 1, 19X1, at a lump sum cost of $12,320 for a novel written by a popular author. The publishing company estimated at that time that the book would remain popular for five years.

Instructions

Which of the various methods described in this text would best fit the amortization of the cost of the copyright? Defend your selection.

3–11 **Assignment of Costs and Computing Depreciation** *(20 minutes)* The Listman Company purchased a truck on January 1, 19X5. The dealer's list price was $3,061.22, and he allowed a 2 percent discount for the cash purchase. The Listman Company then paid $200 to a metal shop for welding special racks to the body of the truck. They paid $40 for a 19X5 truck license and $240 for a two-year liability insurance policy. The truck has an estimated life of five years and an estimated salvage value of $250.

Instructions

1. How should the payments for the truck, the special racks, the license, and the insurance be treated, as an expense of the year 19X5, as a part of the cost of the truck, or in some other way?
2. Compute the depreciation which would be recorded on December 31 of each year of the truck's life if (a) the company uses

straight-line depreciation and (b) if the company uses a constant percentage of a declining balance method at a 40 percent rate.

3–12 **Selection of a Depreciation Method** *(15 minutes)* The Abott-Jones Corporation was formed on January 1, 19X1, for the purpose of acquiring thirty new apartment houses. The apartment houses cost a total of $1,300,000 and are expected to have a life of fifty years. Rentals during the early years are expected to be higher than in later years, when the apartments become older and less attractive. Maintenance and repairs are also expected to be higher in the later years of the apartments' useful lives.

Mr. Abott, who owns 50 percent of the stock of the company, maintains that straight-line depreciation should be used for the apartment houses. He contends that if rental revenue is higher and repairs are lower in early years, profits are greater in those years and the income statement should reflect that fact. He can see little reason for using a depreciation method that produces a greater depreciation expense and thus reduces profits in the early years of the life of the buildings. He argues that sum-of-the-years' digits and other accelerated depreciation methods defer profits to later years.

Mr. Jones, who owns the remaining 50 percent of the company's stock, argues that actual net income on the apartment house venture cannot be known exactly until the end of the life of the assets, and net income should be computed evenly over the life of the venture. He contends that lower depreciation expenses in the later years of the useful life of the asset should offset lower revenues and higher maintenance costs.

Instructions
What would you recommend as a depreciation policy for the company?

3–13 **Selection of a Depreciation Method** *(10 minutes)* The Ledmetter Manufacturing Company manufactures plastic products, and its catalogue contains some 2,000 different plastic items, ranging from electric outlet plugs to radio cabinets. A separate steel multiple-mold is used for casting each product, and these molds cost approximately $200 each. The molds normally last from five to ten years, but there is no assurance that the product for which the mold was designed will be carried in the company's catalogue for that period of time. When the product is discontinued, the mold is sold for scrap.

Instructions
The company's accountant is not sure what depreciation method or what life to use in depreciating the molds. What would you recommend? What asset records would you suggest be maintained for the molds?

3–14   **Inventory Methods** *(15 minutes)*   A company had the following purchases and sales of merchandise during the month of December:

Dec. 1 balance	100 units @ $10 each
Dec. 8 purchase	80 units @ $11 each
Dec. 12 sales	90 units
Dec. 24 purchase	150 units @ $12 each
Dec. 29 sales	120 units

Instructions
Compute the cost of goods sold and the cost of the ending inventory using (1) LIFO, (2) FIFO, and (3) average cost.

3–15   **Inventory Calculations** *(20 minutes)*   The following data apply to inventory transactions of the Boston Products Company during April:

	Units	Unit cost
Beginning inventory	1,000	$2.30
Purchases:		
April 1	3,000	2.40
April 11	5,000	2.50
April 22	4,000	2.45
April 29	2,000	2.60

There were 3,000 units in the ending inventory.

Instructions
Compute the cost of the ending inventory and the cost of merchandise sold, showing all computations, for each of the following:
1. FIFO
2. LIFO
3. Average cost

3–16   **Inventory Calculations** *(20 minutes)*   The Grace Company had an inventory of 2,000 units on June 30, with a unit cost of $1.70 each. During the month of July, the following purchases were made:

July 7	900 units at $1.75
16	1,200 units at 1.80
30	1,000 units at 1.85

Sales during the month were as follows:

July 9	1,000 units
25	1,800 units

Instructions
Compute the cost of the ending inventory, using the following:
1. LIFO
2. FIFO
3. Average

3–17   **Inventory Calculations** (*25 minutes*)   The Freeport Company had the following units available for sale during the month of July:

Beginning inventory	20 units @ $20 each	= 4 00
Purchases:		
July 3	50 units @ $21 each	1 0 5 0
July 14	100 units @ $22 each	2 2 0 0
July 26	30 units @ $23 each	6 9 0

On July 31 there were 40 units in the ending inventory.

Instructions
Compute the cost of the ending inventory and the cost of merchandise sold using the following:
1. The specific identification method if 30 units were left from the July 14 purchase and 10 from the July 3 purchase.
2. The FIFO method.
3. The LIFO method.
4. The average cost method.

Problems

3–18   **Economic and Cash Basis Income** (*20 minutes*)   The following accounting statement is available for the Barker Corporation:

Balance Sheet
For the year ended Dec. 31

	19X1	19X2
Cash	$ 15,000	$ 25,000
Accounts receivable from customers	—0—	12,000
Inventory	10,000	16,000
Building, purchased Dec. 31, 19X1	75,000	75,000
Accumulated depreciation	—0—	(3,000)
Land, purchased Dec. 31, 19X1	25,000	25,000
Total assets	$125,000	$150,000
Notes payable to suppliers	75,000	65,000
Owner's equity	50,000	85,000
Total equities	$125,000	$150,000

The market value of the building is now estimated at $78,000 and the value of the land is $30,000, other values remaining unchanged.

Instructions
Compute the economic income and the cash basis income for the year 19X2.

3–19   **Computation of Accounting, Cash Basis, and Economic Income** *(35 minutes)*   The Dresson Warehousing Company, Inc., had the following assets and liabilities on January 1:

	Cost	Market Value
Cash	$ 700	$ 700
Inventory	7,000	7,100
Buildings	12,000	13,000
Land	3,000	8,000
Accounts payable	(1,500)	(1,500)

At the end of the year the company had the following assets and liabilities:

	Cost	Market Value
Cash	$ 1,400	$ 1,400
Accounts receivable	2,000	2,000
Inventory	7,000	6,800
Buildings	12,000	12,500
Land	3,000	15,000
Accounts payable	(2,000)	(2,000)
Salaries payable	(700)	(700)

The company had collected cash of $21,000 on its total sales of $23,000, had bought and paid for merchandise costing $16,000, all of which had been sold, and had incurred salaries expenses of $5,000 but had paid only $4,300 to its employees. The $500 increase in accounts payable was for the purchase of office supplies which had not been paid for but which had been consumed.

Instructions
1. Prepare an income statement reflecting accounting income.
2. Compute the economic income, measuring only the change in the net market value of the company's assets and liabilities.
3. Compute the cash-basis income.

3–20   **Accounting, Cash Basis, and Economic Income** *(35 minutes)* The Flagstone Company had the following assets and liabilities on January 1, 19X1:

	Cost	Market Value
Cash	$ 2,100	$ 2,100
Inventory	21,000	21,300
Buildings	36,000	39,000
Accounts payable	(4,500)	(4,500)

At the end of the year the company had recorded these assets and liabilities:

	Cost	Market Value
Cash	$ 4,200	$ 4,200
Accounts receivable	6,000	6,000
Inventory	21,000	20,400
Buildings	36,000	38,000
Accounts payable	(6,000)	(6,000)
Salaries payable	(2,100)	(2,100)

The company had collected cash of $63,000 on its total sales of $69,000, had bought and paid for merchandise costing $48,000—all of which had been sold—and had incurred salaries expenses of $15,000, but had paid only $12,900 to its employees. The $1,500 increase in accounts payable was for the purchase of office supplies which had not been paid for but which had been used.

Instructions

1. Prepare an income statement reflecting the accounting income.
2. Compute the economic income, measuring only the change in the net market value of the company's assets and liabilities.
3. Compute the cash-basis income.

3–21 **Preparing Financial Statements** (*35 minutes*)   Robert Smith had $1,000 cash, which he invested in a newly formed business called Smith's Concession Company. He then paid $200 cash to the owners of a ball park for the exclusive right to sell cold drinks, popcorn, and peanuts for a three-day period beginning July 6 while a circus was in town. He purchased cold drinks, popcorn, and peanuts the day before the circus began at a cost of $700. He hired five students to sell the items in the stands and paid them $30 each for the three-day period. He also paid a sign maker $15 for several signs clearly stating the prices he was charging for the cold drinks, popcorn, and peanuts. At the close of the three-day period, he had collected $1,200 in cash from sales and had returnable cold drinks on hand that had cost $70.

Instructions

Prepare an income statement and a balance sheet for Smith at the end of the three-day circus.

3–22 **Estimated Income Statement** (*35 minutes*)   Henry Story is considering the formation of a business on January 1 of the current year to operate a small printing shop. He has estimated that an investment of $5,000, with all the owners' equity belonging to him, will be sufficient to begin the business. This $5,000 will be used to buy presses, which cost $4,000. He will need one month's supply of inks and papers, which cost $1,200, but he will not have to pay for these until the following month. He will have to hire one helper, which he estimates will cost $400 per month. In addition, he will have to rent space in a small building for $175 per month, and his utility expenses for telephone and electricity will be $50 per month. He believes that he can secure orders and complete printing work for his customers for a total of $2,500 during the first month. If the depreciation on the printing press will be $200 per month, will he make a profit during the first month?

Instructions

1. Prepare an estimated income statement for the month of January using Story's estimated data.
2. At the end of January, Story's records indicated that his actual printing revenues were $2,200 and that he had $400 of the inks and supplies on hand. All other costs and expenses were exactly as he had estimated. Prepare an income statement for the month of January reflecting the results of actual operations.

3–23   Selection of Data for an Income Statement *(20 minutes)*   The Northwest Company is a real estate agency which was formed on January 1 by three brothers. None of them recognized the need for gathering financial information until the end of the first year of operation. At that time a question arose concerning how profitable the company had been. You have been asked to help them construct financial statements for the year. They present you with the following information:

Commissions received in cash during the year	$60,000
Commissions earned but for which no cash has been received	5,000
Salaries paid to employees	14,000
Rent through November on the office building (paid)	5,500
Rent for December on the office building (unpaid)	500
Office supplies purchased for cash and consumed during the year	700
Income received by one of the brothers on rental of his personal home	3,000
Advertising paid for during the year	20,000
Advertising completed but not yet paid for	1,000
Telephone costs paid during the year	450
Telephone costs for December (unpaid)	40
Repairs on office furniture in December, not yet paid	120
Purchase of a company automobile on December 30, paid for by $1,000 cash and a note payable to the bank for the balance. Total cost, $3,000.	3,000

Instructions

Using whatever part of the data you deem appropriate, prepare an income statement for the year ending December 31, 19X1.

3–24   Preparation of a Balance Sheet and an Income Statement *(40 minutes)*   The amounts below were taken from the records of the Trajer Shipping Company as of December 31, 19X1;

Cash	$ 1,000	Sales	$210,000
Accounts receivable	3,000	Cost of merchandise sold	140,000
Inventory	14,000	Sales salaries	36,000
Investment in land		Advertising	8,000
for expansion	20,000	Store supplies	1,100
Equipment	33,800	Office salaries	10,000
Trucks	18,600	Office supplies	800
Accounts payable	6,000	Taxes on property	5,000
Notes payable, due in		Interest expense	3,200
six months	3,000		
Mortgages payable,			
due in five years	50,000		
Capital stock	20,000		
Retained earnings (at the			
beginning of the year)	5,500		

Instructions

Using the appropriate amounts, prepare a multistep income statement for the year. Then add the profit computed in this statement to retained earnings. With the new balance of retained earnings, prepare a classified balance sheet, using the remaining figures given in the problem.

3–25   **Preparation of a Balance Sheet and Income Statement** *(40 minutes)*
The following data of the Wilson Company were accumulated during the year ended December 31, 19X1:

Cash on hand	$ 1,250
Salary expenses	11,000
Revenue from the sale of products	60,000
Accounts receivable	3,000
Rent expense	1,000
Office furniture	6,000
Merchandise inventory on hand	9,700
Cost of merchandise sold	35,000
Interest expense	800
Equipment	12,000
Equipment repairs	2,900
Accounts payable	3,000
Notes payable (1979)	12,000
Capital stock	15,000
Retained earnings	(To be computed)
Rent payable	1,000
Office furniture repairs	700

Instructions

Separate the data appearing on a balance sheet from that for an income statement and prepare a single-step income statement and a classified balance sheet. The amount of the retained earnings is not given; this figure will be whatever amount is necessary to bring the balance sheet into balance.

3–26   Preparation of a Balance Sheet and Income Statement *(40 minutes)*
The Stewart Company began operations on January 1, and accumulated the following financial information during the year:

Mortgage payable on building	$15,000
Cash	2,000
Revenue from the sale of products	73,600
Merchandise on hand	11,000
Cost of merchandise sold	51,000
Trucks	5,000
Amounts payable to creditors	1,900
Amounts receivable from customers	4,000
Buildings	22,500
Owners' investment in common stock	25,000
Rent expense	11,200
Salaries expense	6,050
Salaries payable to employees	850
Advertising expense	3,600

Instructions
Separate the data needed for the balance sheet from that needed for an income statement and prepare the two financial statements. The owners' investment of $25,000 does not include the profits of the current year; these profits must appear as Retained Earnings in the balance sheet.

3–27   Effect of Depreciation Methods upon Disposition of an Asset *(40 minutes)*
1. A company purchased a truck for $3,000 cash. At that time $60 was paid for extra-heavy springs to make the truck more serviceable. The truck has a salvage value of $200 and an estimated life of four years. Should the $60 be treated as an expense or as part of the cost of the truck?
2. Compute the depreciation for the first and the second year of the truck's life, using straight-line and sum-of-the-years' digits depreciation.
3. Without consideration of the income tax aspects, write in narrative form a justification for the use of a depreciation method such as the sum-of-the-years' digits.
4. Assume the truck is sold after two years' use for $1,300. Compute the gain or loss which would have to be recorded if the company had used (1) straight-line and (2) sum-of-the-years' digits depreciation.
5. Write in narrative form a description of the effects of the depreciation methods upon the periodic determination of net income when the asset is sold early in its estimated life.

3–28   Effect of Different Inventory and Depreciation Methods *(60 minutes)*   The Jackson Company and the Grant Company were formed on January 1, 19X5. They are identical in every respect, except that the Jackson Company employs a LIFO inventory method, and, for depreciation, a constant percentage of 20 percent on the declining balance (twice the straight-line amount), while the Grant Company uses a FIFO inventory method and straight-line depreciation.

During 19X5, both companies made purchases as follows:

February	1	100 units @ $21 each
April	13	200 units @ $22 each
June	21	200 units @ $23 each
August	7	100 units @ $24 each

The ending inventory for both companies was 120 units, and the office and store equipment had a ten-year life and no salvage value. The trial balances of the two companies on December 31, 19X5, before the inventory or depreciation expense was recorded, were as follows:

	Jackson Company		Grant Company	
Cash	$ 1,000		$ 1,000	
Accounts receivable	3,000		3,000	
Office equipment	7,000		7,000	
Store equipment	12,000		12,000	
Accounts payable		$ 2,100		$ 2,100
Capital stock		20,000		20,000
Sales		21,800		21,800
Purchases of merchandise	13,500		13,500	
Salaries expense	5,000		5,000	
Supplies	1,000		1,000	
Utilities	800		800	
Property tax expense	400		400	
Insurance expense	200		200	
	$43,900	$43,900	$43,900	$43,900

Instructions
1. Prepare income statements for the two companies.
2. Which of the two companies, in your opinion, is the more profitable? Prepare a schedule explaining the difference in the net income or loss of the two companies.

3–29 **Comparative Statements with Straight-Line and Sum-of-the-Years' Digits Methods** *(60 minutes)* The Baker Company purchased electronic data processing equipment from The International Calculator Company on January 1, 19X5, for $1,230,000 plus installation costs of $140,000. The Baker Company paid $370,000 in cash and signed a two-year 6 percent note payable for the balance. A calendar year is used for depreciation purposes, and interest on the note is paid each December 31.

During 19X5, the Baker Company made sales of $2,940,630, with cost of merchandise sold of $1,660,400 and operating expenses of $664,900, exclusive of interest expense and depreciation on the data processor. The company pays 50 percent of its net income in federal income taxes and subtracts the federal tax as the final item on the income statement to arrive at net income after taxes.

Instructions

Prepare three different income statements for the year, one for each of the three separate assumptions given below for depreciation:

1. Straight-line depreciation on the data processor, and it has an estimated life of five years and $100,000 salvage value.
2. Sum-of-the-years' digits depreciation, using the five-year life and $100,000 salvage value.
3. Constant percentage of a declining balance depreciation. (Use 40 percent, since this method is limited to twice the straight-line depreciation, or 40 percent, for tax purposes.)

3–30   **Calculation of Depreciation Cost** *(25 minutes)*   The Marton Company acquired a machine on December 31, 19X2, for $55,000. It had an estimated life of five years, and the company's engineers estimated it would produce 100,000 units of the company's product and would have a salvage value of $5,000. The machine produced 13,000 units in 19X3, 22,000 in 19X4, and 28,000 in 19X5.

Instructions

Compute the depreciation expense for 19X3, 19X4, and 19X5 using the following methods:

1. Straight-line
2. Sum-of-the-years' digits
3. Units of production
4. Constant percentage of a declining balance, using a 40 percent rate

3–31   **Calculation of Depreciation Cost** *(25 minutes)*   A high-speed press was bought by the Frontier News Company on January 1, 19X1. The press cost $53,000 and had an estimated life of five years, or 20,000 hours, and a $3,000 salvage value. The press was used 3,600 hours in 19X1, 4,200 hours in 19X2, 5,000 hours in 19X3, 4,000 hours in 19X4, and 3,200 hours in 19X5.

Instructions

Compute the depreciation for each year of the asset's expected life, using the following methods:

1. Straight-line
2. Sum-of-the-years' digits
3. Declining balance, using a 40 percent rate
4. Service hours

3–32 **Comparative Statements with LIFO, FIFO and Average Costs** *(40 minutes)*   The Logston Company had a beginning inventory on January 1 containing 500 units which cost $2.50 each. During January purchases were made as follows:

Jan. 5	1,000 units @ $2.60 each
14	1,500 units @ $2.70 each
21	800 units @ $2.75 each
30	500 units @ $2.80 each

The company sold 3,500 units during the month for $5 each, and had selling and administrative expenses of $8,050.

Instructions
Prepare three income statements for January, using FIFO, LIFO, and average costs. Show the beginning inventory, purchases, and ending inventory in each of the income statements.

3–33 **Comparative LIFO and FIFO Income Statements** *(60 minutes)*
The purchases and sales data for the three products which the Tobar Company sells are given below for the month of January:

	Product A	Product B	Product C
Sales price per unit	$10.00	$20.00	$25.00
Beginning inventory	100 @ $6.00	100 @ $10.00	50 @ $12.00
Purchases:			
January 10	300 @ $6.50	200 @ $11.00	50 @ $13.00
January 19	100 @ $6.40	50 @ $12.00	100 @ $14.00
January 30	50 @ $6.80	50 @ $12.50	20 @ $13.50
Units in the ending inventory	140	70	60

Instructions
Assuming that the selling and administrative expenses were $6,300, prepare two income statements for the company for the month, one using a LIFO inventory method and the other a FIFO inventory method. Show all computations.

3–34 **Comparative Statements with FIFO, LIFO, and Average Cost** *(60 minutes)*   The Jacksonville Appliance Company was formed on January 1, and during the year the company purchased the following units:

January	1	1,000 units @ $200 each
March	14	2,000 units @ $210 each
May	23	500 units @ $220 each
September	7	1,500 units @ $230 each
November	12	1,000 units @ $240 each

The company's condensed trial balance on December 31 was as follows:

Cash	$ 16,000	
Accounts receivable	122,000	
Fixed assets	390,000	
Liabilities		$ 75,000
Capital stock		644,000
Retained earnings		–0–
Sales		1,720,000
Purchases	1,315,000	
Sales salaries	300,000	
Office salaries	200,000	
Depreciation expense	50,000	
Supplies used	40,000	
Insurance expense	6,000	
	$2,439,000	$2,439,000

On December 31, there were 1,200 units in the ending inventory. Since the company is newly formed, a decision must be made concerning the inventory method which the company will use in this and the following years.

Instructions
Prepare three separate income statements, one for each of the following inventory assumptions:
1. FIFO
2. LIFO
3. Average

3–35   **LIFO and FIFO Methods Contrasted** (*30 minutes*)   The Yeargan Company is newly formed. Its first monthly income statement was prepared by the company's accountant on January 31, 19X1, and appears in condensed form as follows:

Sales	$100,000
Cost of goods sold (700 units)	70,000
Gross profit	$ 30,000
Selling and administrative expenses	28,000
Net income before taxes	$ 2,000
Income taxes	1,000
Net income after taxes	$ 1,000

The significance of the amounts on the statement was discussed at an executive conference, which was attended by the president, controller, and vice-president in charge of sales.

The president, upon inquiry, was informed that a FIFO method had been used. He was further informed that 1,000 units had been purchased; the first 700 units cost $100 each, and the 300 units in the ending inventory cost $110 each. The president believes that a normal inventory must be maintained to stay in business and that had a LIFO inventory method been used, a loss instead of a profit would have been reported. Furthermore, an income tax of 50 percent would have to be paid on the $2,000 before-tax net income, placing an additional drain on the company's cash at the same time that inventory replacement units are costing more.

Instructions
1. Reconstruct the income statement using a LIFO method.
2. Write a short description of the different concepts of income which the LIFO and FIFO inventory methods represent.

chapter 4

Analyzing
Financial Statements

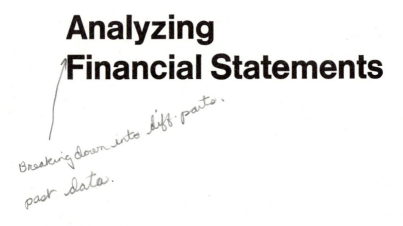

*Breaking down into diff. parts.
past data.*

Learning
Objectives

This chapter describes the methods by which the management of a company analyzes a balance sheet and income statement. The utilization of comparative statements and financial ratios is emphasized, and upon completion of this chapter you should:

1. Understand the nature and use of comparative financial statements.
2. Be able to recognize the existence and importance of trends in financial data.
3. Be able to calculate the basic financial ratios and understand their significance.
4. Recognize the limitations of financial statements and know when a particular ratio or trend is meaningful.

Nature of
Statement Analysis

Financial statement analysis consists basically of separating financial statements into parts, examining one part in relationship to another part, and drawing from the relationship some conclusions about the company as a whole. A person concerned about the ability of a company to pay its debts in the near future would want to relate assets available for the payment of debt to the amount of debt presently owed. Another person interested in the company's long-range ability to earn profits would relate the company's profits to its total assets, to the owners' equity, or to the amount of sales which the company is able to generate. Still another individual may wish to measure the relationship of interest expense on long-term debt to the company's net income, thereby gaining an insight into the ability of the company to meet its interest obligations. Each person analyzing the statements obviously has a reason for making his analysis, and his purpose will dictate which relationships are of significance.

Unfortunately, individual ratios or relationships by themselves will rarely provide complete answers to the questions which have led to the analysis of financial statements. Usually two or more ratios will bear upon the question, and trends in these relationships over several accounting periods must be considered. From a banker's point of view, for example, the safety of a loan which he has made to one of the customers of his bank will depend not only upon the company's current profitability and debt-paying ability, but whether one can expect the company's profitability to continue favorably into the future. Thus trends in the financial condition of the company are more important than a single relationship which presently exists.

Evaluation of Risk, Profitability, and Potential

The analysis of financial statements is usually undertaken in order to measure current financial condition and past profitability; and, from these measurements, conclusions are drawn about the future of the company. Because financial position and profitability are interdependent, they cannot be completely isolated and measured separately. Safety of a loan to the company, for example, depends upon both the current financial position and the future profitability of the company, since a strong financial position today may be weakened by future operating losses.

The analyst must consider several factors individually and then combine them to form an overall evaluation. For example, if a banker is considering a company's application for a large loan, he first attempts to form a judgment concerning the company's present financial position. Next he judges the profitability of the company. Finally, he will bring to bear all his knowledge of economic, legal, and technological events that may affect the company's future. This latter information usually cannot be found in the financial statements and is basically a matter of relating the impact of economic and political events to the company and its operations. However, the starting point in the banker's analysis will always be a study of the company's past financial history and its current financial position.

Comparative Statements

One of the most effective means of analyzing financial statements and appraising a company's operations is through a comparison of amounts. A comparative statement is one containing data for several periods. A company's financial statements are usually compared with the previous years' figures, but comparisons are also made with data from similar companies, or with industry-wide averages. Annual reports to stockholders almost always contain comparative financial data for the current year and for the preceding year, and they frequently contain summarized financial data reaching back for as many as ten years. The purpose of such a presentation is to provide data for comparative analysis. Industry-wide averages are available from trade associations and from national publications which present financial data classified by type and size of company and sometimes by geographical groupings, such as midwest, east, northwest, etc.

Trends

A trend may be defined as a general direction or inclination. The determination of trends through comparative analysis is a common method of analyzing financial statements. This method is illustrated in Exhibit 4–1, which provides income statement data for a five-year period. The data are taken from the income statements of the same company and reflect the changes which have occurred in the company's sales, expenses, and profit during that period. The trends evident in these statements indicate that while sales have increased steadily, from $50,000 in 19X1 to $70,000 in 19X5, both cost of merchandise sold and expenses have increased correspondingly, so that profits have remained almost constant. Consequently, the potential of the company for increased profits without serious managerial effort to reduce costs appears relatively dim. Insight into the future of the company is thus gained by an analysis of the comparative statements covering several years.

EXHIBIT 4–1
Trend Analysis

Sample

	19X1	19X2	19X3	19X4	19X5
Sales	$50,000	$54,000	$61,000	$68,000	$70,000
Cost of merchandise sold	30,000	33,000	38,000	44,000	45,000
Gross profit	$20,000	$21,000	$23,000	$24,000	$25,000
Expenses	17,000	18,500	20,000	20,800	21,900
Net profit	$ 3,000	$ 2,500	$ 3,000	$ 3,200	$ 3,100

Changes From the Prior Year

The method most frequently used to report financial data in comparative form is the presentation of current data with data of the prior year, utilizing adjacent columns. This type of statement is called a comparative statement, and Exhibits 4–2 and 4–3 illustrate a comparative income statement and a comparative balance sheet. Reporting both current and prior years' data makes possible the calculation of an amount of change as well as a percent of change. Note that both amount and percent of change appear in the illustrated comparative statements for each item and for all totals and subtotals.

The amount and percentage changes for the Maplewood Company indicate that the trend in sales is favorable, since sales increased $20,000, or 5 percent, over the prior year. The trends of the cost of merchandise sold and expenses are unfavorable, since the cost of merchandise sold increased $22,000, or 8.1

EXHIBIT 4–2

MAPLEWOOD COMPANY
Comparative Income Statements
For the Years Ended December 31, 19X4, and 19X5

Base yr.

	19X5	19X4	Increase or (Decrease) Amount	Percent
Sales	$420,000	$400,000	$20,000	5 %
Sales returns	10,000	8,000	2,000	25 %
Net sales	$410,000	$392,000	$18,000	4.6%
Cost of merchandise sold	292,000	270,000	22,000	8.1%
Gross profit	$118,000	$122,000	($ 4,000)	(3.3%)
Selling expenses	35,000	30,000	5,000	16.7%
Administrative expenses	63,000	60,000	3,000	5 %
Total expenses	$ 98,000	$ 90,000	$ 8,000	8.9%
Net income before taxes	$ 20,000	$ 32,000	($12,000)	(37.5%)

percent, and expenses increased $8,000, or 8.9 percent. As a result, the trend in profits is unfavorable, since profits decreased by $12,000, or 37.5 percent. A conclusion may be drawn that the increased sales volume is insufficient to offset the increased expenses and higher cost of merchandise sold.

On the comparative balance sheet for the Maplewood Company, which is illustrated in Exhibit 4–3, note that both the amount and the percent change between 19X4 and 19X5 are shown, as well as the change in asset and equity totals. The statement indicates that although there was little change in total assets, the company's current assets increased by $19,000, or 13.7 percent, while fixed assets decreased by $15,000, or 8.1 percent. Total equities changed only slightly, but liabilities decreased by $16,000, or 23.9 percent, while owners' equity increased by $20,000, or 7.8 percent.

While percentage change in a particular account is significant, the percentage of change must be interpreted concurrently with the dollar amount of change. In Exhibit 4–3 cash increased by $6,000, or 85.7 percent. Inventory, on the other hand, increased by a greater amount, $9,000; but the change was only 11.1 percent more than the prior year's inventory.

Computing Change Between Years

Note that the amount of change between the two years in a comparative statement is computed for each item in the statement, with parentheses used to reflect decreases. Changes in subtotals are computed, as well as totals at the bottom of the statement. These totals and subtotals are used in the computation of some of the more important ratios, and it is helpful to the analyst to have the amount and percentage of their change available.

Change expressed as a percentage is computed by dividing the dollar amount of change in an account by the dollar amount of the account in the earlier year. Note that in Exhibit 4–3 the 85.7 percent change in cash is the result of divid-

EXHIBIT 4–3

MAPLEWOOD COMPANY
Comparative Balance Sheets
December 31, 19X4, and 19X5

	19X5	19X4	Increase or (Decrease) Amount	Increase or (Decrease) Percent
Current assets				
Cash	$ 13,000	$ 7,000	$ 6,000	85.7%
Accounts receivable (net)	45,000	40,000	5,000	12.5%
Inventory	90,000	81,000	9,000	11.1%
Prepaid expenses	10,000	11,000	(1,000)	(9.1%)
Total current assets	$158,000	$139,000	$19,000	13.7%
Fixed assets				
Land	$ 19,000	$ 19,000	–0–	–0–
Buildings (net)	95,000	105,000	($10,000)	(9.5%)
Machinery and equipment (net)	56,000	61,000	(5,000)	(8.2%)
Total fixed assets	$170,000	$185,000	($15,000)	(8.1%)
Total assets	$328,000	$324,000	$ 4,000	1.2%
Liabilities				
Accounts payable	$ 37,000	$ 54,000	($17,000)	(31.5%)
Accrued payables	14,000	13,000	1,000	7.7%
Total current liabilities	$ 51,000	$ 67,000	($16,000)	(23.9%)
Owners' equity				
Common stock	$200,000	$200,000	–0–	–0–
Retained earnings	77,000	57,000	$20,000	35.1%
Total owners' equity	$277,000	$257,000	$20,000	7.8%
Total equities	$328,000	$324,000	$ 4,000	1.2%

ing the $6,000 change by the $7,000 balance in the prior year. One limitation of this type of analysis is the inability to express as a percentage any change from a positive to a negative amount in succeeding years—such as a profit in 19X4 to a loss in 19X5—or any change from a zero balance in an account.

The technique of calculating the amount and the percentage of change is illustrated in Exhibit 4–4. The first four items illustrate situations in which

EXHIBIT 4–4

Calculation of Percentage Change

	19X5	19X4 (Base)	Amount of increase or (decrease)	Percentage of increase or (decrease)
(a)	$10,000	$8,000	$2,000	25.0%
(b)	3,000	5,000	(2,000)	(40.0%)
(c)	–0–	1,000	(1,000)	(100.0%)
(d)	(2,000)	3,000	(5,000)	(166.7%)
(e)	1,000	0–	1,000	not expressible
(f)	2,000	(400)	2,400	not expressible

the amount of change and the 19X4 base year amount are compatible and a percentage may be calculated. The last two items illustrate cases where the amount of change is not compatible with the base year, and calculations of a percentage are misleading or meaningless. In case (e) the base year is zero, and calculations are not possible when the denominator is zero. In case (f) the $400 negative amount is not compatible with the $2,400 positive amount of change, and a percentage calculated from these two amounts would be misleading. If a percentage were calculated, the result would be a 600 percent increase ($2,400 ÷ $400). This 600 percent increase is misleading, because either a negative $2,400 or a positive $2,000 would produce a 600 percent change from a negative $400 base.

Common-Size Statements

The calculation of trends and the comparison of amounts are sometimes facilitated by substituting percentage figures in place of dollar amounts. This is accomplished by replacing the amounts in financial statements with percentages, utilizing the traditional financial statement format. Such statements are called common-size statements. A base amount, such as sales in the income statement or total assets in the balance sheet, is used, and all amounts are reported as percentages of this base.

Expressing each amount in the income statement as a percentage of net sales facilitates comparisons between different amounts in the same statement and also between similar expenses in successive income statements. Through a comparison of changes in the percentages, a relative change is made more apparent. A relative change is frequently more significant than a change in dollar amount. The income statement of the Maplewood Company, previously shown with dollar amounts in Exhibit 4–2, is reduced to a common-size income statement in Exhibit 4–5. Note that net sales and not gross sales is used as a

Break dollar amt down

EXHIBIT 4–5

MAPLEWOOD COMPANY
Comparative Common-Size Income Statements
For the Years Ended December 31, 19X4, and 19X5

	19X5	19X4
Sales	102.0%	101.8%
Sales returns	2.0	1.8
Net sales	100.0%	100.0%
Cost of merchandise sold	71.2	68.9
Gross profit	28.8%	31.1%
Selling expenses	8.5%	7.7%
Administrative expenses	15.4	15.3
Total expenses	23.9%	23.0%
Net income before taxes	4.9%	8.1%

study this

100 percent base in each year, permitting sales returns to be deducted from gross sales in the usual fashion.

Balance sheets are reduced to common-size by expressing each item as a percentage of total assets. The balance sheet of the Maplewood Company, previously shown with dollar amounts in Exhibit 4–3, is reduced to a common-size balance sheet in Exhibit 4–6. Note that both Total Assets and Total Equities are 100 percent, since they must be equal in dollar amount.

EXHIBIT 4–6

MAPLEWOOD COMPANY
Comparative Common-Size Balance Sheets
December 31, 19X4, and 19X5

	19X5	19X4
Current assets		
Cash	4.0%	2.2%
Accounts receivable (net)	13.7	12.3
Inventory	27.4	25.0
Prepaid expenses	3.1	3.4
Total current assets	48.2%	42.9%
Fixed assets		
Land	5.8%	5.9%
Buildings (net)	28.9	32.4
Machinery and equipment (net)	17.1	18.8
Total fixed assets	51.8%	57.1%
Total assets	100.0%	100.0%
Liabilities		
Accounts payable	11.3%	16.7%
Accrued payables	4.2	4.0
Total liabilities	15.5%	20.7%
Owners' equity		
Common stock	61.0%	61.7%
Retained earnings	23.5	17.6
Total owners' equity	84.5%	79.3%
Total owners' equity	100.0%	100.0%

Ratio Analysis

Ratio analysis of a company's financial statements is a process of calculating relationships between amounts within a single set of financial statements. This process, which is illustrated in Exhibit 4–7, utilizes subtotals to indicate the comparison of current assets to current liabilities, current assets to fixed assets, and current liabilities to owners' equity. Each of these basic comparisons is indicated by an arrow.

The data in Exhibit 4–7 indicate that the $54,000 amount invested in current assets, which represents present debt-paying ability, is approximately three times the $18,000 of current liabilities; consequently, the present debt-paying ability of the company appears sound. The $87,000 of owners' equity in the statement is almost five times the $18,000 in creditors' equity, indicating that the major part of the risk is borne by owners rather than creditors. The data also reflect an approximately equal amount of current and fixed assets, which provides an indication of the relative amounts of liquid assets and permanently committed assets.

EXHIBIT 4–7
Condensed Balance Sheet Illustrating Ratio Analysis

Current assets	$ 54,000	Current liabilities		$ 18,000
Fixed assets	51,000	Common stock	$50,000	
		Retained earnings	37,000	87,000
	$105,000			$105,000

Ratios are computed from historical data and may change from one period to the next. For this reason the change in a ratio itself is significant in the analysis of financial statements. The relationship of total debt to total owners' equity, for example, may indicate that, over a period of years, an increasing proportion of risk is being borne by creditors. Consider the following data:

Year	Total Owners' Equity	Total Liabilities	Ratio of Owners' Equity to Debt
19X2	$52,000	$21,000	2.5 to 1
19X3	60,000	25,000	2.4 to 1
19X4	63,000	30,000	2.1 to 1
19X5	70,000	35,000	2.0 to 1

These data indicate that the owners' share of the risk, in terms of funds committed to the business, has decreased each year, from $2.50 to each $1.00 of liabilities down to $2.00 for each $1.00 of creditors' equity. The increasing share of risk borne by creditors becomes evident through this analysis, and both management and creditors would find this trend of interest.

Analysis of Working Capital

Net working capital is the difference between total current assets and total current liabilities, representing the amount of current assets which would be available for operations if current liabilities were fully paid. Changes in the amount and composition of a company's working capital are important in the analysis of a company's financial position, and a number of significant ratios have been developed to measure working capital relationships. Consider, for example, the items comprising Exhibit 4–8.

The balance sheet in the exhibit shows total current assets of $50,000, which will be converted into cash or consumed in the normal course of business

Bankers - short Term. [handwritten margin note]

should the listed according to liquidity. [should they be reversed] [handwritten margin note]

EXHIBIT 4–8

Partial Balance Sheet

CURRENT ASSETS		CURRENT LIABILITIES	
Cash	$ 2,000	Accounts payable	$12,000
Accounts receivable	15,000	Notes payable	4,000
Marketable securities	8,000	Accrued wages payable	3,000
Inventory	25,000	Other accrued payables	1,000
Total current assets	$50,000	Total current liabilities	$20,000

during the next operating cycle, which is usually one year. The current liabilities of $20,000 represent amounts which much be paid during the next accounting period. Thus, the company has $30,000 of net working capital ($50,000 less $20,000).

Analysis of the amount, nature, and adequacy of working capital is a frequently applied technique of evaluating the current financial position of a company. The following comparisons and ratios are the more significant aspects of this technique:

Current ratio   *CA ÷ CL = ratio 2:1* [handwritten]

Acid-test ratio   *C + R + MS = 1.25:1* [handwritten]

Turnover of net working capital   *N. Sales / Av. work. cap.* [handwritten]

Turnover of inventory   *CGS / Av. Inv.* [handwritten]

Number of days' sales in accounts receivable   *365 × End boj. 9 A/R / Sales* [handwritten]

Current Ratio   The current ratio, which measures the relationship of current assets to current liabilities, is computed by dividing current assets by current liabilities. Using amounts from Exhibit 4–8, the current ratio would be computed as follows:

$$\frac{\text{Current assets (\$50,000)}}{\text{Current liabilities (\$20,000)}} = 2.5 \text{ to } 1$$

There is no minimum current ratio which indicates a satisfactory current position. A current ratio of less than one to one indicates a strong possibility that a company may not be able to pay its current liabilities as they become due, especially if receivables are not collected or merchandise inventory becomes obsolete. On the other hand, an extremely high current ratio, such as five to one or eight to one, may indicate that nonproductive current assets, such as accounts receivable, are excessive and that assets are not being employed in an optimum manner. A satisfactory current ratio falls in a range somewhere between the extremes and differs from one industry to another. Trade publications of many industries frequently publish data on the upper, median, and lower ranges of current ratios of companies in that industry.

The point at which a current ratio becomes inadequate or excessive depends on the nature of the business, the composition of the current assets, and the personal judgment of the analyst. A current ratio considered satisfactory for a stable business may be considered inadequate for a highly speculative business, or the existing current ratio of a company might be considered satisfactory by one credit grantor and unsatisfactory by another.

The composition of the current assets affects the significance of the current ratio. To illustrate, consider the following data relative to Marliene's and Terry's, two ladies' hat shops:

	Marliene's	Terry's
Cash	$ 400	$ 4,000
Accounts receivable	5,000	7,000
Inventory	10,600	5,000
Total current assets	$16,000	$16,000
Total current liabilities	$ 8,000	$ 8,000
Current ratio	2 to 1	2 to 1

Both companies have equal dollar amounts of current assets and current liabilities and thus have equal current ratios. However, there are two significant differences in their current financial position. Terry's has a considerably larger cash balance for meeting daily expenditures. On the other hand, Marliene's has a much larger inventory of ladies' hats, which are highly subject to obsolescence. Even though the current ratio and the dollar amount of current assets and liabilities are identical, Terry's appears to have a much stronger working capital position because of the large cash balance and the low inventory.

Acid-Test Ratio   The acid-test ratio, sometimes called the *quick ratio* or *quick current ratio,* is designed to measure the immediate ability of a company to meet its current liabilities. The acid-test ratio measures the relationship between the amount of current assets which are *immediately* available for debt-paying purposes and the total amount of current liabilities. Inventory and prepaid expenses are not considered to be immediate sources of cash, and only cash, receivables, and marketable securities are included in the asset side of this ratio. Since receivables and securities can usually be converted into cash very quickly with only a limited loss on realization, they are included in the calculation of the ratio. Using amounts from Exhibit 4–8, the computation of the acid-test ratio proceeds in the following manner: *Good figure for acid test is 1:1.*

$$\frac{\text{Cash ($2,000) + Receivables ($15,000) + Marketable securities ($8,000)}}{20,000} = \frac{\$25,000}{20,000} = 1.2 \text{ to } 1$$

Although there is no specific point at which an acid-test ratio may be considered excessive or deficient, a ratio above one to one is generally considered a satisfactory indication of a company's immediate ability to meet its current debts.

Turnover of Working Capital   A high current ratio and a high quick ratio are desirable from the standpoint of debt-paying ability. However, a balance must be maintained between financial safety and the efficient use of working capital. A company should not have more funds tied up in working capital than can be used efficiently in its profit-making ventures. Efficiency in the use of working capital is measured by the turnover of working capital. The turnover is computed by dividing net sales by the average net working capital employed during the period. Using amounts from Exhibits 4–2 and 4–3, the computation of the working capital turnover is as follows for 19X5:

	19X4	19X5
Current assets	$139,000	$158,000
Current liabilities	67,000	51,000
	$ 72,000	$107,000

Average working capital (72,000) + 107,000 ÷ 2 = 89,500

$$\text{19X5 turnover of working capital} = \frac{\text{Net sales}}{\text{Average working capital}}$$

$$= \frac{\$410,000}{89,500} = 4.6 \text{ times}$$

An average of the monthly working capital figures is preferable if the amounts are available. However, if monthly amounts are not available, the working capital at the beginning and end of the year are added and their total divided by two to arrive at a simple average.

The turnover of working capital is an indicator of the number of times cash was invested in inventory, inventory was sold, and the resulting receivables were collected. There is no specific measure of an acceptable working capital turnover, but a company's turnover may be compared with the industry-wide average or with data from prior years to indicate the efficiency of the company's use of working capital.

Turnover of Inventory   The turnover of inventory measures the number of times inventory has been sold and replaced during the year. It is computed by dividing the cost of goods sold during the period by the average inventory. Average inventory should be used whenever possible, either by averaging monthly inventory amounts or by using an average of the beginning and ending inventories. Using amounts from Exhibits 4–2 and 4–3, the inventory turnover for 19X5 is computed as follows:

$$\frac{\text{19X5 Cost of merchandise sold}}{\text{19X5 Average inventory}} = \frac{\$292,000}{(\$90,000 + 81,000) \div 2} = 3.4 \text{ times}$$

There is no established rule-of-thumb for judging what constitutes an adequate inventory turnover. A relatively low inventory turnover is normal for a furniture store, and a relatively high turnover is normal for a grocery supermarket. An inventory turnover significantly lower than the average for the industry probably indicates that a company is carrying an excessively large inventory and is subjecting itself to inefficient use of financial resources, as well as to losses from obsolescence.

Number of days' sales in accounts receivable   The number of days' sales in accounts receivable, considered in conjunction with the company's credit terms, provides an indication of the collectibility of the receivables and the efficiency with which the collection policy is being administered. The calculation is made by dividing the ending balance of accounts receivable by the sales for the year, and multiplying the resulting figure by 365 days. If a company made sales of $50,000 during the year and had $5,000 of uncollected receivables, one-tenth of the year's sales were uncollected. Multiplying the 365 days in a year by one-tenth gives 36½ days' sales which lie uncollected in accounts receivable. The number of days' sales in accounts receivable would thus be computed as follows:

$$365 \text{ (days in a year)} \times \frac{\text{Ending balance of accounts receivable (\$5,000)}}{\text{Sales (\$50,000)}}$$

$$365 \times 1/10 = 36½ \text{ days' sales in accounts receivable}$$

If the company sells on twenty-day terms and there are 36½ days' sales in accounts receivable, there is an indication that a significant portion of the receivables are past-due. On the other hand, if the company sells on forty-day terms and there are 36½ days' sales in accounts receivable, there is greater likelihood that the receivables are sound and collectible.

Analysis of Equity

The ratio of owners' equity to total debt is a means of measuring the relative risks borne by creditors and by owners. Using assumed amounts, the ratio of owners' equity to total debt is computed as follows:

$$\frac{\text{Total owners' equity (\$70,000)}}{\text{Total debt (\$20,000)}} = 3.5 \text{ to } 1$$

From a creditor's viewpoint, the ratio should be high, because the stockholders would be assuming the major portion of the risks. The stockholders' equity in the assets of the business disappears first in case of losses, and a higher owners' equity indicates a greater protection for the creditors. On the other hand, from a stockholder's viewpoint, a low ratio may be desirable. If earnings from borrowed funds are greater than the interest paid for those borrowed funds, the profit differential accrues to the owners. The ratio of owners' equity to debt varies greatly from one industry to another and comparisons with industry averages are a frequent use of this ratio.

Analysis of Profitability

Methods of measuring a company's profitability are (1) net income as a rate of return on total assets, (2) net income as a rate of return on owners' equity, (3) earnings per share of common stock, (4) net income as a percentage of net sales, and (5) the number of times bond interest is earned. While all of these measures are necessary to evaluate fully the company's profitability, generally the owners and prospective investors are interested in net income as a rate of return on assets, on owners' equity, and on a per-share basis; creditors are interested in net income in relation to the interest on long-term debt; and managers are interested in net income as a percentage of sales.

Rate of return on total assets   Earnings may be measured by relating the net income earned during a year to all the assets used to earn that income. The rate is computed by dividing net income by total assets on the balance sheet at the end of the year.

$$\frac{\text{Net income (\$12,000)}}{\text{Total assets (\$200,000)}} = 6\% \text{ return on total assets}$$

If there is a significant change in the amount of assets during the year, the average assets should be used in the computation. The return on total assets is a measure of how well management has used the assets entrusted to it, and the rate is frequently compared with the return realized by other companies within the same industry. It is also compared with the rate realized by the company in prior years, or to the rate of return which is considered normal for the risks involved. Management frequently establishes a desired rate of return and formulates its operating plans upon this target rate.

Rate of return on invested capital   Net income may also be measured as a rate of return on total owners' investment. The rate is computed by dividing the net income by the average owners' equity for the period. Using assumed amounts the calculation would be made as follows:

$$\frac{\text{Net profit (\$12,000)}}{\text{Average owners' equity (\$100,000)}} = 12\% \text{ return on owners' investment}$$

An average of the monthly owners' equity should be used if the amounts are available; otherwise, the owners' equity at the beginning and end of the year are averaged. A large investment or withdrawal of capital made near the end of the year should be excluded when the computation of average owners' investment is made to prevent distortion of the rate. The rate of return on total owners' equity is especially significant because it provides a comparison of the rate of return earned by funds invested in the business with rates of return that might be earned by alternative uses of the funds.

Earnings per share   One of the most frequently used expressions of profitability is the amount of earnings per share of capital stock. There are two basic types of capital stock, however, and the calculation of earnings per share necessitates an assignment of earnings to each class. The two types are *preferred* stock and *common* stock.

Preferred stock   Holders of preferred stock enjoy certain privileges which holders of common stock do not have. These rights must be stated in the corporate charter and generally consist of preferences in the distribution of profits and in the right to receive assets upon liquidation of the company. Obviously, limits must be set on the preference given preferred shares. The earnings preference is limited to a stated dollar amount each year, or a percentage of the par value. The preference as to liquidation is usually stated as a fixed dollar "liquidating value." In the absence of a specified liquidating value, the preference of preferred stock is limited to its par value. Thus a share of preferred stock may be described as $100 par value, 6% dividend preference, with a $120 liquidating value. This means that the preference on earnings is $6 per year (6% of the $100 par value), and each share would receive $120 when the company liquidates, before the common shareholders receive anything.

Common stock   Common stock is a residual equity, receiving what is left after the preferences of all preferred shares have been satisfied. Common stock is a risk or speculative stock. If the company is highly profitable, the common stockholders will receive the major portions of the profit, since the preferred stock receives a fixed amount; if the company's profit is small, common stockholders will receive a small return, if any.

Common stockholders are normally given the right to vote and to select the management of the company, while this vote is normally withheld from the preferred stockholders. The right to manage the company is usually reserved for the common stockholders, since they must bear the major share of the risks and since preferred stockholders have preference in the distribution of assets in liquidation.

Calculation of earnings per share   To illustrate the calculation of earnings per share, assume that a company with a net profit of $46,000 has the following classes of stock:

1. Preferred stock—1,000 shares of $100 par value, 6%, $110 liquidating value.
2. Common stock—5,000 shares, $100 par value.

The earnings per share of preferred stock is $6.00, and the 1,000 shares would have a total claim of $6,000 on the annual net profit. That would leave the remaining profit of $40,000 for the common stock. The earning per share of common stock would then be $8.00, calculated as follows:

$$\frac{\text{Net profit (\$46,000)} - \text{The claim of preferred shares (\$6,000)}}{\text{Number of common shares (5,000)}} = \$8\,\text{share}$$

The amount of earnings per share is significant to the common stockholder, because it expresses the company's profitability in terms of earnings available for common stock dividends. Trends in the earnings per share are so important that annual reports to stockholders frequently contain these data for the last five to ten years.

Book Value   Book value is the dollar equity of each share of stock in the net assets (assets less liabilities) which appear on the balance sheet. Thus, if a company has net assets of $10,500, and 100 shares of stock are outstanding, the book value is $105 per share ($10,500 ÷ 100 shares). Total owners' equity may also be used to compute the book value of a share of stock, since net assets (assets less liabilities) are exactly equal to total owners' equity.

Book value per share may be defined as the amount each share of stock would receive if the assets were all sold without gain or loss, all liabilities were paid, and the remaining cash was divided among the shares of stock outstanding. To illustrate further, suppose a corporation has the following condensed trial balance:

Assets	$65,000	
Liabilities		$10,000
Common stock (400 shares, $100 par)		40,000
Retained earnings		15,000
	$65,000	$65,000

The corporation has 400 shares of stock outstanding and a total owners' equity of $55,000; the common stock plus the retained earnings represent owners' equity. The book value of each share of common stock, determined by dividing the $55,000 owners' equity by the 400 shares, is $137.50 per share.

Book value becomes more difficult to compute when both preferred and common shares are outstanding. When two classes of stock are outstanding, the total owners' equity must first be divided between the two classes. The *liquidating value* of a share of preferred stock is used to determine the equity of preferred stock, and par value is used if the stock has no specified liquidating value. Common stock is assigned the balance of the owners' equity after preferred shares have been assigned their equity.

To illustrate, suppose a company has the following condensed trial balance:

Assets	$120,000	
Liabilities		$ 15,000
Preferred stock (300 shares, $100 par,		
6%, $110 liquidating value, no		
unpaid dividends)		30,000
Common stock (500 shares, $100 par)		50,000
Premium on preferred stock		8,000
Retained earnings		17,000
	$120,000	$120,000

The owners' equity is assigned to each class of stock as follows:

Total owners' equity ($30,000 + $50,000 + $8,000 + $17,000) = $105,000
Applicable to preferred stock (300 shares with a liquidating value
of $110 per share)   =   33,000
    Balance applicable to common $ 72,000

Book value per share of preferred: $33,000 ÷ 300 shares = $110.00
Book value per share of common: $72,000 ÷ 500 shares = $144.00

Book value is not a valid measure of the market value of a share of stock, since the owners' equity as it appears on the books does not reflect either the current market value of the assets or the ability of the company to earn profits. Book value cannot be interpreted significantly without a knowledge of the nature of a company's assets and their true market value. However, an increase or decrease in book value per share from one period to another does have significance, for it indicates the *change* in dollar equity per share.

Price-Earnings Ratio   The relationship between the earnings per share of common stock and the price at which that share is currently selling on the open market is called the *price-earnings ratio.* If a company has per share earnings of $2.00 and that stock is quoted on the stock market at a price of $26, the stock is said to have a thirteen to one price-earnings ratio. The calculation is made as follows:

$$\frac{\text{Market price per share of stock}}{\text{Earnings per share}} = \frac{\$26}{\$2} = 13 \text{ to } 1$$

Can be used to figure what price to sell stock for when first going public.

Price-earnings ratio is dependent upon data (market price per share) which are not in the financial statements and which must be gathered from external sources. The ratio may change from one day to the next, since the market price of the shares is subject to considerable fluctuation. This ratio fluctuates so quickly that it is not published in a company's financial reports to stockholders.

Net income as a percentage of sales   The relationship between profit and sales is so direct that the net income realized during an accounting period is frequently measured as a percentage of net sales. The calculation would be made as follows, using assumed amounts:

$$\frac{\text{Net income (\$12,000)}}{\text{Net sales (\$400,000)}} = 3\%$$

When net income is expressed as a percentage of sales, the rate reflects the effect of changes in sales volume on the company's profitability. For example, if net income was 2½ percent of sales in the preceding year and is 3 percent during the current year, the trend would be favorable, provided sales have not decreased significantly.

The nature of the business must be considered when judging the adequacy of net income as a percentage of sales. A dealer in exclusive art objects would command a higher rate of profit on sales than a high-volume department store, because art objects carry a much greater mark-up over cost. For this reason, the net profit as a percentage of sales can be compared to that of other companies in the same industry, but it will differ greatly from one industry to another.

Number of times bond interest is earned   Bonds payable represent a form of long-term debt requiring fixed periodic interest payments. The ability of a company to pay its fixed interest charges is determined primarily by its ability to earn a profit, and for this reason the relationship between profits and interest is significant.

Bond interest is deductible in the computation of the company's income tax liability; consequently, the amount of earnings available for bond interest is the net income before income taxes and before bond interest expense has been paid. The number of times bond interest is earned is determined by the following computation:

$$\frac{\text{Net income } (\$12,000) + \text{Income taxes } (\$3,000) + (\text{Bond interest } \$5,000)}{\text{Bond interest } (\$5,000)} =$$

$$\frac{\$20,000}{\$5,000} = \text{Bond interest earned four times}$$

This ratio is a means of expressing the margin of safety in the company's ability to meet its bond interest expense. If the company cannot meet these fixed expenses, the bondholders or mortgagor may take over the assets of the company if they are pledged as security.

Summary

The specific techniques used in the analysis of a financial statement depend upon the purpose for which the analysis is made. Most analyses consist of drawing relationships among several items in the financial statements and ascertaining what trends, if any, exist for those relationships. Financial statements cannot provide specific indices of profitability and financial position, but they do provide data for gathering general impressions. Absolute indices are not possible because the same figure means different things to different people. A figure that would be an acceptable company profit to a group of employees in the company's labor union might be considered insufficient by creditors, and even grossly insufficient by owners. The analysis of financial statements provides data for comparing profit to investment or to the amount of sales or to the total assets of the business, but the adequacy of the profit figure is dependent upon the person making the analysis.

The format of financial statements is designed to assist in their analysis. Comparative statements which show the amount and the percentage of change from one period to the next are prepared to call attention to the more significant changes, and common-size financial statements are used to emphasize relationships. The precise classification of items within a balance sheet as current assets, fixed assets, current liabilities, long-term debt, and owners' equity is also designed to assist in the analysis. These subtotals facilitate such comparisons as current assets with current liabilities, liabilities with owners' equity, or fixed assets with long-term debt.

The analysis of present financial position is undertaken by studying the current balance sheet. Such indices as the current ratio, acid-test ratio, and working capital turnover are calculated for this purpose. Financial position in the long run, however, is indicated by an ability to generate profits; and return on investment calculations and debt-to-equity ratios are useful gauges for this purpose. The profit-making ability of the company is the aspect of greatest interest to both internal and external groups, and the measurements which reflect this ability include the ratio of profit to total assets, to owners' equity, and to sales, and profit as an amount per share of capital stock. Trends in sales

Summary of Ratios

Name	Computation	Significance
Analysis of Working Capital		
Current ratio	$\dfrac{\text{Current assets}}{\text{Current liabilities}}$	Short-run debt-paying ability
Acid-test ratio	$\dfrac{\text{Quick current assets}}{\text{Current liabilities}}$	Short-term liquidity
Turnover of working capital	$\dfrac{\text{Sales}}{\text{Average working capital}}$	Efficiency of use of working capital
Turnover of inventory	$\dfrac{\text{Cost of goods sold}}{\text{Average inventory}}$	Efficiency of use of inventory
Number of days' sales in accounts receivable	$\dfrac{365 \times \text{Ending accounts receivable}}{\text{Sales}}$	Effectiveness of collections
Analysis of Equity		
Owners' equity-to-debt	$\dfrac{\text{Owners' equity}}{\text{Total liabilities}}$	Relative risks borne by owners and creditors
Analysis of profitability		
Net income as return on assets	$\dfrac{\text{Net income} + \text{Interest}}{\text{Average total assets}}$	Earning power of assets
Net income as return on capital	$\dfrac{\text{Net income}}{\text{Average owners' equity}}$	Earning power of owner investment
Earnings per share of common stock	$\dfrac{\text{Net income} - \text{Preferred dividends}}{\text{Number of shares of common stock}}$	Earnings accruing to each share of common
Net income on sales	$\dfrac{\text{Net income}}{\text{Sales}}$	Ability to earn net income as related to sales
Number of times bond interest earned	$\dfrac{\text{Net income} + \text{Interest} + \text{Taxes}}{\text{Bond interest}}$	Coverage of fixed interest obligations
Price-earnings ratio	$\dfrac{\text{Market price of common shares}}{\text{Net income per share}}$	Relationship of earnings and price of shares

and in net profits are observed as closely as any other amounts because of the importance of these figures in the measurement of financial position and profitability.

New Terms

Book value   The amount each share of stock would receive if the company sold its assets for the amount on the books and liquidated the company.

Common-size statement   A financial statement containing percentages instead of dollar amounts.

Common stock   A class of stock which receives what is left of earnings after preferred shares (if any) have received their share.

Comparative statement   A financial statement containing several years' data for comparison purposes.

Preferred stock   A class of capital stock having a preference on earnings and assets in the event of liquidation.

Trend   A general direction or inclination.

Working capital   The amount of current assets less current liabilities.

Questions

1. Define the following terms which were introduced in this chapter:
   a. Comparative statement
   b. Common-size statement
   c. Trend
   d. Working capital
   e. Book value
   f. Common stock
   g. Preferred stock

2. Describe the general purposes for which financial statements are analyzed. What would the following groups want to obtain from a company's financial statements:
   a. Managers
   b. Owners
   c. Prospective investors
   d. Governmental agencies
   e. Organized labor

3. Why is comparison of amounts the basic means of evaluating figures that appear in financial statements? With what data can amounts in a set of financial statements be meaningfully compared?

4. Describe how each of the following is computed, and give the significance or meaning of each:
   a. Current ratio
   b. Acid-test ratio
   c. Turnover of working capital
   d. Turnover of inventory
   e. Number of days' sales in accounts receivable
   f. Debt-to-equity ratio
   g. Return on total assets
   h. Return on owners' equity
   i. Earnings per share
   j. Book value
   k. Net income as a percent of sales
   l. Number of time bond interest is earned

5. Describe how a common-size balance sheet is prepared, stating what is used as the 100 percent base. What is the base for an income statement?

6. Explain why the composition of current assets must be considered in the evaluation of the adequacy of a company's working capital. Is it possible for a company to have too much cash? Too much accounts receivable? Too much inventory? Defend your answers.

Exercises

4–1   **Nature and Meaning of Ratios** *(25 minutes)*   The following analytic measures were described in this chapter:
   a. Current ratio
   b. Acid-test ratio
   c. Turnover of net working capital
   d. Turnover of inventory
   e. Number of days' sales in accounts receivable
   f. Net income as a rate of return on owners' equity
   g. Net income as a rate of return on total assets
   h. Earnings per share on common stock
   i. Net income as a percentage of net sales
   j. The number of times bond interest is earned
   k. Book value
   l. Price-earnings ratio

Instructions
Describe how each is computed and its significance. Give an example of each, using assumed amounts.

4–2*

po this

Computation of Ratios *(15 minutes)*   The trial balance of the Rommel Company follows:

Cash	$ 1,000	
Receivables	2,000	
Inventory (no change since last year)	3,000	
Fixed assets	10,000	
Accounts payable		$ 1,000
Accrued taxes payable		2,000
Common stock ($50 par)		10,000
Sales (all on credit)		27,000
Cost of goods sold	18,000	
Selling expenses	6,000	
	$40,000	$40,000

Instructions
Using data from this trial balance, compute the following:
1. Current ratio
2. Acid-test ratio
3. Number of days' sales in accounts receivable
4. Inventory turnover
5. Earnings per share of common stock
6. Price-earnings ratio if common stock is selling for $150 per share

4–3*   **Mechanics and Meaning of Ratios** *(25 minutes)*   The condensed balance sheet of the Donovan Company is as follows on December 31:

Cash	$ 30,000	Accounts payable	$ 60,000
Accounts receivable	30,000	Mortgage payable	
Merchandise inventory	80,000	(6%) in five years	100,000
Fixed assets (net)	180,000	Common stock	
		($100 par)	120,000
		Retained earnings	40,000
	$320,000		$320,000

The net income for the year was $14,000.

Instructions
Compute the following significant ratios to indicate the soundness of the financial condition of this company. For each ratio indicate how it is computed, and its significance.
1. Current ratio
2. Acid-test ratio
3. Earnings per share
4. Ratio of owners' equity to debt
5. Net income as a return on invested capital
6. Price-earnings ratio if the common stock is selling for $175 per share

4–4   **Current Liquidity Ratios** *(20 minutes)*   The following data were
extracted from the financial statements of a company:

Current assets (beginning of the year)	$ 77,000
Current assets (end of the year)	63,000
"Monetary" assets (cash, receivables and investments	
at end of year)	31,500
Average finished goods inventory	50,000
Accounts receivable (end of year)	20,000
Current liabilities (beginning of year)	21,000
Current liabilities (end of year)	19,000
Sales (all on credit terms)	500,000
Cost of merchandise sold	300,000

Instructions
Using the above data, compute the current ratio, the acid-test ratio,
the turnover of net working capital, the inventory turnover, and the
number of days sales in accounts receivable.

4–5   **Comparison of Current Position Using Ratios** *(20 minutes)*
Given below are selected data from the financial statements of two
companies:

	Company A	Company B
Cash	$ 3,000	$ 1,000
Accounts receivable	12,000	5,000
Inventory	6,500	15,000
Prepaid insurance	500	1,000
Accounts payable	2,000	5,800
Notes payable (due in 6 months)	8,000	1,800
Accrued wages payable	1,000	1,200

Instructions
From this information, compute the current ratio and the acid-test
ratio of each of the two companies. Then compare the composition
of the current assets and state which of the two companies in your
opinion has the stronger current financial position.

4–6   **Computation of Change** *(15 minutes)*   The following data were
drawn from a company's financial statements:

	Prior Year	Current Year
a. Net income	$ 5,000*	$ 7,000*
b. Accounts receivable	6,000	4,000
c. Inventory	20,000	15,000
d. Notes payable	–0–	10,000*
e. Gain or loss on sale of assets	3,000	1,000*
f. Investments	5,000	–0–
g. Net loss	2,000	1,000

Instructions

Compute the amount of change and the percentage of change. All amounts starred (*) are credits. If a percentage change cannot be computed, indicate this fact.

4–7   **Computation of Ratios** *(30 minutes)*

Presented below are four unrelated problems. Compute for each part the requested data.

1. The current ratio of a company is 2.3 to 1, and its acid-test ratio is 1 to 1. If the inventories and prepaid expenses amount to $520,000, what is the amount of current liabilities?
2. A company has total current assets of $500,000 and total current liabilities of $250,000. The board of directors declares a cash dividend of $50,000. What is the current ratio after the declaration but before payment? What is its current ratio after payment of the dividend?
3. A company has current assets of $100,000 and current liabilities of $40,000. The board of directors declares a $10,000 stock dividend. What is the current ratio immediately after the declaration? What is the current ratio after the stock dividend is issued?
4. A company has current assets of $18,000 (of which $6,000 is inventory) and current liabilities of $9,000. What is the current ratio? What is the acid-test ratio? If the company borrows $5,000 cash from a bank on ninety-day loan, what will its current ratio be? What will the acid-test ratio be?

4–8   **Computation of Ratios** *(30 minutes)*   The balance sheet of a company for 19X4 and 19X5 appears below.

	December 31:	
	19X4	19X5
Cash	$ 23,500	$ 24,800
Accounts receivable	37,900	50,000
Inventory	10,000	11,000
Investments, temporary	20,000	12,000
Equipment	60,000	65,000
Land	10,000	20,000
Accumulated depreciation	(19,000)	(25,000)
Total assets	$142,400	$157,800
Accounts payable	42,500	40,800
Long-term notes (due 1980)	18,000	10,000
Total liabilities	$ 60,500	$ 50,800
Capital stock ($100 par)	50,000	82,000
Paid-in capital in excess of par	10,000	15,000
Retained earnings	21,900	10,000
Total stockholders' equity	$ 81,900	$107,000
Total equities	$142,400	$157,800

The profit for 19X5 was $11,000.

Instructions

Compute the following:
1. Net working capital for 19X4 and 19X5
2. Current ratio for 19X4 and 19X5
3. Owners'-equity-to-debt ratio for 19X4 and 19X5
4. Return on total assets for 19X5
5. Return on owners' equity for 19X5
6. Book value per share for 19X5

4–9 **Calculation of Ratios** *(30 minutes)* The balance sheets of a company as of December 31, 19X4 and 19X5 are shown below. The profit for 19X5 was $103,000 before taxes and $70,000 after taxes.

	December 31,	
ASSETS	19X4	19X5
Current assets		
Cash	$ 35,000	$ 45,000
Accounts receivable	55,000	65,000
Inventory	90,000	110,000
	$180,000	$220,000
Fixed assets		
Equipment	117,000	143,000
Less: Accumulated depreciation	30,000	43,000
	$ 87,000	$100,000
Investments		
Land	13,000	—0—
Total assets	$280,000	$320,000
EQUITIES		
Current liabilities		
Accounts payable	35,000	45,000
Long-term liabilities		
Bonds payable (8% interest)	200,000	200,000
Shareholders' equity		
Common stock ($100 par)	40,000	40,000
Retained earnings	5,000	35,000
Total equities	$280,000	$320,000

Instructions

Compute the following ratios:
1. Current ratio for 19X4 and 19X5
2. Acid-test ratio for 19X4 and 19X5
3. Owners'-equity-to-debt for 19X4 and 19X5
4. Number of times bond interest was earned in 19X5
5. After-tax return on total assets in 19X5
6. After-tax return on owner's equity in 19X5
7. Book value of common stock shares in 19X4 and 19X5

Problems (3)

4–10   **Computation and Analysis of Ratios** *(30 minutes)*   The balance sheet and the income statement of the Fox Company are presented below:

<table>
<tr><td colspan="2" align="center">FOX COMPANY
Balance Sheet
December 31, 19X5</td><td colspan="3" align="center">FOX COMPANY
Income Statement
Year Ended December 31, 19X5</td></tr>
<tr><td colspan="2" align="center">ASSETS</td><td></td><td></td><td></td></tr>
<tr><td>Cash</td><td>$ 10,000</td><td>Sales</td><td></td><td>$400,000</td></tr>
<tr><td>Accounts receivable</td><td>70,000</td><td>Beginning inven-</td><td></td><td></td></tr>
<tr><td>Merchandise inventory</td><td>40,000</td><td>tory</td><td>$ 30,000</td><td></td></tr>
<tr><td>Prepaid expenses</td><td>1,000</td><td>Purchases</td><td>300,000</td><td></td></tr>
<tr><td>Fixed assets</td><td>100,000</td><td></td><td>$330,000</td><td></td></tr>
<tr><td></td><td>$221,000</td><td>Ending inventory</td><td>40,000</td><td></td></tr>
<tr><td colspan="2" align="center">EQUITIES</td><td>Cost of goods sold</td><td></td><td>290,000</td></tr>
<tr><td>Accounts payable</td><td>$ 10,000</td><td>Gross profit</td><td></td><td>$110,000</td></tr>
<tr><td>Wages payable</td><td>4,000</td><td>General and admin-</td><td></td><td></td></tr>
<tr><td>Payroll taxes payable</td><td>1,000</td><td>istrative expenses</td><td></td><td>80,000</td></tr>
<tr><td>Bonds payable, 6% due</td><td></td><td></td><td></td><td></td></tr>
<tr><td>1982)</td><td>50,000</td><td>Net income before</td><td></td><td></td></tr>
<tr><td>Common stock</td><td></td><td>taxes</td><td></td><td>$ 30,000</td></tr>
<tr><td>($100 par value)</td><td>120,000</td><td>Federal income taxes</td><td></td><td>12,000</td></tr>
<tr><td>Retained earnings</td><td>36,000</td><td>Net income after</td><td></td><td></td></tr>
<tr><td></td><td>$221,000</td><td>taxes</td><td></td><td>$ 18,000</td></tr>
</table>

Instructions

1. Using these statements and assuming that net working capital and inventory have not changed since January 1, 19X5, compute:
   a. The current ratio
   b. The acid-test ratio
   c. The turnover of net working capital
   d. The inventory turnover
   e. The number of days' sales in receivables
   f. The ratio of owners' equity-to-debt
   g. Net income after taxes as a rate of return on total assets
   h. Net income after taxes as a rate of return on invested capital
   i. Earnings per share
   j. Number of times bond interest is earned
   k. Price-earnings ratio if the stock is selling for $300 per share
2. Comment briefly on whether or not you think the company is in sound financial position with an acceptable profitability. Also comment on any weaknesses which the ratios indicate to you.

4–11   **Comparison of Companies Using Ratios** *(40 minutes)*   Presented below are statistics drawn from the annual reports of four companies.

	Com- pany A	Com- pany B	Com- pany C	Com- pany D
Net income for the year after taxes	$30,000	$30,000	$10,000	$150,000
Shares of preferred stock outstanding	1,000	5,000	100	10,000
Par value of preferred stock	$100	$10	$100	$50
Preferred stock dividend rate	6%	5%	6%	4%
Shares of common outstanding	2,000	10,000	1,000	3,000
Par value of common stock	$100	$10	$100	$100
6% bonds outstanding (face value)	$80,000	$100,000	$25,000	$750,000
Federal income taxes paid	$10,000	$12,000	$3,000	$60,000
Retained earnings	$73,000	$25,000	$12,000	$190,000

Instructions

1. Using these data, compute for each company the number of times bond interest is earned, the return on total owners' investment, the per share book value of common and preferred stock, and the earnings per share of common stock. Preferred dividends have not been paid for the current year but have been paid for all prior years. The retained earnings include the current year's net income.

2. Assuming that the net income after taxes of each of the four companies will continue at the present level, rank the four companies in the order in which you would prefer to invest in their common stock, if stock could be acquired at book value. (Place the most desirable first.) Describe briefly how you arrived at the ranking.

4–12   **Comparison Using Ratios and Common-Size Statements** *(40 minutes)*   Harold Phenny is considering the purchase of an investment in common stock and is attempting to relate the financial position of two corporations whose stock is under consideration. The balance sheets of the two companies are presented below:

COMPANY A

ASSETS			EQUITIES		
Cash	$ 1,800		Notes payable	$17,000	
Accounts receiv-			Accounts payable	16,800	
able (net)	26,600		Accrued taxes		
Inventory	34,400		payable	6,600	
Total current			Total current		
assets		$62,800	liabilities		$40,400
Land	$ 5,000		Common stock		
Buildings (net)	9,900		($100 par)	$15,000	
Total fixed			Retained earnings	22,300	
assets		14,900	Total owners'		
			equity		37,300
Total assets		$77,700	Total equities		$77,700

COMPANY B

ASSETS		EQUITIES		
Cash	$ 3,000	Notes payable	$ 5,000	
Accounts receiv-		Accounts payable	4,000	
able (net)	12,000	Accrued taxes		
Inventory	15,000	payable	4,000	
Total current		Total current		
assets	$30,000	liabilities		$13,000
Furniture and fix-		Common stock		
tures (net)	6,000	($100 par)	$10,000	
		Retained earnings	13,000	
		Total owners'		
		equity		23,000
Total assets	$36,000	Total equity		$36,000

Instructions

1. Prepare common-size statements for the two companies to facilitate comparison.
2. Compute the current ratio, acid-test ratio, owners' equity-to-debt ratio, return on total assets, return on total investment, and earnings per share for both companies. Net income of Company A was $4,000, and net income of Company B was $3,000.
3. Which would you consider the better investment if both stocks could be bought for their book values?

4–13   **Analysis Through Ratios and Trends** *(40 minutes)*   Shown below are comparative balance sheets of the Wayhouser Company for 19X3, 19X4, and 19X5. Also presented are operating data for each of the three years.

Comparative Balance Sheets

	19X3	19X4	19X5
ASSETS			
Current Assets:			
Cash	$ 1,200	$ 1,900	$ 400
Accounts receivable (net)	14,800	12,400	10,400
Inventory	14,800	16,200	19,800
Total current assets	$30,800	$30,500	$30,600
Fixed Assets:			
Equipment (net)	$ 9,800	$12,000	$12,800
Buildings (net)	15,700	16,300	18,000
Land	5,000	5,000	5,000
Total fixed assets	$30,500	$33,300	$35,800
Total assets	$61,300	$63,800	$66,400

Comparative Balance Sheets
(continued)

	19X3	19X4	19X5
EQUITIES			
Current Liabilities:			
Notes payable (due in six months)	$ 7,500	$ 3,000	$ 5,000
Accounts payable	6,300	11,200	13,400
Accrued salaries and taxes	1,200	1,600	2,900
Total current liabilities	$15,000	$15,800	$21,300
Long-term Debt:			
Notes payable (due 1975)	—	—	$ 5,500
Total debt	$15,000	$15,800	$26,800
Owners' Equity:			
Common stock ($100 par)	$30,000	$30,000	$30,000
Retained earnings	16,300	18,000	9,600
Total owners' equity	$46,300	$48,000	$39,600
Total equity	$61,300	$63,800	$66,400

Operating Data for the Year Ending:

	19X3	19X4	19X5
Total sales	$100,000	$105,000	$93,000
Reported net income, after taxes	5,000	5,700	(2,400)
Dividends paid	3,000	3,000	3,000
Non-operating gains (or losses) not on the income statement (directly to retained earnings)	(1,500)	(1,000)	(3,000)

Instructions

1. Compute the following for each of the three years:
   a. Current ratio
   b. Owners' equity-to-debt ratio
   c. Acid-test ratio
   d. Return on total owners' investment
   e. Earnings per share of common stock
   f. Price-earnings ratio if the stock was selling for $167 in 19X3, $285 in 19X4, and $120 in 19X5
2. Discuss the financial condition of the company on December 31, 19X5, and the trends evidenced by the comparative data and ratios.
3. Comment on the company's policy of reporting net income, especially as related to non-operating losses, and the effects such a policy has on computations of earnings per share and return on investment.

4–14 **Computation of Ratios** *(40 minutes)*   The balance sheet and income statement of The Austin Service Company for 19X5 are shown below.

AUSTIN SERVICE COMPANY
Balance Sheet
December 31, 19X5

ASSETS		EQUITIES	
Current Assets		*Current Liabilities*	
Cash	$ 3,210.20	Accounts Payable	$ 4,300.00
Accounts Receivable	8,740.00	Notes Payable	3,000.00
Inventory	13,090.95	Total Current	
Supplies on Hand	600.00	Liabilities	$ 7,300.00
Total Current			
Assets	$ 25,641.15		
		Long-Term Debt	
Fixed Assets		6% Bonds Payable	40,000.00
Buildings	$ 70,000.00	Total Liabilities	47,300.00
Land	5,000.00		
Equipment	45,000.00	*Owners' Equity*	
Total Fixed Assets	120,000.00	Common Stock $100	
		par value	80,000.00
		Retained Earnings	18,341.15
Total Assets	$145,641.15	Total Equities	$145,641.15

AUSTIN SERVICE COMPANY
Income Statement
For the Year Ended December 31, 19X5

Sales	$128,222.18	
Less Cost of Sales	89,543.03	
Gross Margin		$38,679.15
Expenses		
Wages & Salaries	$ 5,735.00	
Tax Expense	910.00	
Depreciation Expense	9,420.00	
Advertising Expense	1,600.00	
Interest Expense	2,400.00	
Miscellaneous Expense	721.00	
Total Expenses		20,786.00
Net Income Before Taxes		17,893.15
Less Income Taxes		8,000.00
Net Income After Taxes		$ 9,893.15

Instructions

From these data compute the following ratios:

1. Current ratio
2. Acid-test ratio
3. Owner's equity-to-total-debt ratio
4. Inventory turnover
5. Number of days' sales in accounts receivable
6. Return on owners' equity
7. Return on total assets
8. Number of times bond interest earned
9. Net income per share of common stock
10. Book value per share of common stock
11. Price-earnings ratio if the stock is selling for $124 per share

4–15   **Computation and Meaning of Ratios** *(45 minutes)*   The financial statements of the Davidson Garden Supply Company are given below and on the following page.

DAVIDSON GARDEN SUPPLY COMPANY
Balance Sheet
December 31, 19X5

ASSETS			EQUITIES		
Current Assets			*Current Liabilities*		
Cash	$	950	Accounts payable		$ 3,000
Accounts receivable		3,000	Rent payable		1,000
Merchandise inventory		9,820	Total current liabilities		$ 4,000
Total current assets		$13,770			
			Long-term Liabilities		
Fixed Assets			6% notes due in 19X5		12,000
Equipment		$20,000	Total liabilities		$16,000
Office furniture		6,000			
Total fixed assets		26,000	*Stockholders' Equity*		
			Common stock, $100 par		$15,000
			Retained earnings		8,770
			Total capital		23,770
Total assets		$39,770	Total equities		$39,770

Instructions

1. From these data compute the following ratios:
    a. Current ratio
    b. Acid-test ratio
    c. Number of days' sales in Accounts Receivable
    d. Inventory turnover
    e. Ratio of owners' equity to debt
    f. Return on total assets

DAVIDSON GARDEN SUPPLY COMPANY
Income Statement
For the Year Ended December 31, 19X5

Revenue from sale of products		$59,350
Less costs of goods sold		35,000
Gross margin		$24,350
Salary expenses	$11,000	
Supplies consumed	1,080	
Interest expense	720	
Equipment expense	2,900	
Office furniture expense	700	
Total costs and expenses		$16,400
Net profit for the year		$ 7,950

   g. Return on owners' equity

   h. Net income per share of common stock

2. For each of the above ratios, state the meaning, and tell how each helps to provide an insight into the financial status of the company.

4–16   **Use of Comparative Financial Statements** *(45 minutes)*   Financial data for the Tribb Processing Company for 19X4 and 19X5 appear below:

	19X4		19X5	
Cash	$ 1,000		$ 2,000	
Accounts receivable (net)	3,000		5,000	
Inventory	14,000		18,800	
Bond sinking fund investments	20,000		25,000	
Equipment (net)	33,800		29,800	
Trucks (net)	18,500		13,500	
Accounts payable		$ 6,000		$ 5,000
Notes payable (due in 6 months)		3,000		1,000
Mortgages payable (1979)		50,000		50,000
Common stock		20,000		20,000
Retained earnings		5,400		11,300
Sales		210,000		220,000
Cost of merchandise sold	140,000		148,000	
Salaries	36,000		37,000	
Advertising	8,000		8,000	
Utilities	1,100		1,100	
Supplies	800		1,000	
Rent	6,000		6,000	
Depreciation on equipment	4,000		4,000	
Depreciation on trucks	5,000		5,000	
Interest expense	3,200		3,100	
	$294,400	$294,400	$307,300	$307,300

Instructions

1. Prepare a comparative income statement and a comparative balance sheet, with both the amount of change and the percentage change indicated on both statements. *p. 88 (Ex.)*
2. Comment on any favorable or unfavorable conditions indicated by the comparative statements.

4–17 **Computation and Meaning of Ratios** *(40 minutes)* The following statements were prepared for the Willowby Company for 19X1:

WILLOWBY COMPANY
Income Statement
For the year ended December 31, 19X1

Sale of products		$100,000
Cost of products sold		70,000
Gross margin		$30,000
Operating expenses:		
Rent expense	$ 5,000	
Advertising	500	
Salaries expense	16,000	
Insurance	500	
Truck	3,000	
Supplies expense	1,000	
Office expenses	900	
Total operating expenses		26,900
Net income for the year		$ 3,100

WILLOWBY COMPANY
Balance Sheet
December 31, 19X1
ASSETS

Current Assets:		
Cash	$ 200	
Accounts receivable	10,000	
Merchandise inventory	14,000	
Total current assets		$ 24,200
Fixed Assets:		
Office furniture	15,000	
Equipment	25,000	
Total fixed assets		40,000
Total assets		$ 44,200

EQUITIES

Current Liabilities:		
Salaries payable to employees	$ 800	
Accounts payable to suppliers	8,000	

Balance Sheet
(continued)

Rent payable	1,000	
Total current liabilities		$ 9,800
Owners' Equity:		
Common stock ($100 par value)	30,000	
Retained earnings	4,400	
Total owners' equity		34,400
Total equities		$ 44,200

Instructions

1. Using the data given, compute the following:
   a. Current ratio
   b. Acid-test ratio
   c. Number of days' sales in Accounts Receivable
   d. Inventory turnover
   e. Owners' equity-to-debt
   f. Return on total assets
   g. Return on owners' equity
   h. Book value per share
   i. Net income per share of common stock
2. For each of the above ratios comment on its meaning and how it provides information on the financial status of the company.

4–18   **Comparison with Industry Averages** *(50 minutes)*   The Zello Company is a large chain laundry and dry cleaning firm. Its trial balance was as follows at the end of its first year of operations in 19X1:

THE ZELLO COMPANY
December 31, 19X1

Cash	$ 2,000	
Accounts receivable	1,300	
Prepaid insurance	800	
Office supplies on hand	500	
Equipment	18,700	
Delivery trucks	6,300	
Accounts payable		$ 1,400
Notes payable		2,200
Capital stock		20,000
Revenue from services		200,000
Salaries expenses	130,000	
Office expenses	29,000	
Other expenses	35,000	
	$223,600	$223,600

William Zello, president and principal stockholder, read an article in a monthly journal published by the Laundry and Dry Cleaning Trade Association. The article quoted the following as averages for all companies in the industry:

	Revenue and expenses, by operating areas, as a per cent of total revenue		
	Laundry	Dry Cleaning	Total
Revenue	40%	60%	100%
Plant expenses:			
Salaries—plant	20%	20%	40%
Supplies—plant	5	5	10
Heat and power	3	2	5
Total plant expenses	28%	27%	55%
Profit after plant expenses	12%	33%	45%
Office expenses:			
Salaries—office			20%
Supplies—office			5
Insurance, taxes, and licenses			3
Advertising			10
Total office expenses			38%
Net income after all expenses			7%

Zello was interested in comparing his business with the average company in his industry, but found that his framework of ledger accounts did not permit a thorough comparison. He instructed his bookkeeper to give him the necessary information for comparative purposes and, as a result, received the following data:

Revenue: $76,000 from laundry and $124,000 from cleaning.

Salaries expense included plant salaries of $90,000, of which $48,000 was laundry and $42,000 cleaning. Office salaries were $40,000.

Office expenses included plant supplies of $20,000 and office supplies of $9,000. The plant supplies were applicable in equal amounts to laundry and dry cleaning.

Other expenses included $11,000 of heat and power, $6,000 of insurance, taxes, and licenses, and $18,000 of advertising. The heat and power is applicable $6,000 to laundry and $5,000 to dry cleaning.

Instructions
1. Prepare a statement, using Zello Company amounts and percentages, and in the same form as the statement containing industry averages.

2. Analyze the Zello Company's financial data and compare them with the average in the industry. Ascertain in view of this comparison whether laundry and dry cleaning are each producing a reasonable profit after plant expenses; if not, determine which area indicates excessive expenses.

4–19   **Analysis for Acceptance or Rejection of a Loan Application** *(45 minutes)*   The Rainbow Company was formed five years ago. On January 6, 19X6, its balance sheets for 19X4 and 19X5, with a related income statement, were presented to a loan officer of the First State Bank. The president of the Rainbow Company had submitted these statements in support of a loan request. The desired loan was for $15,000, to be repaid in two annual installments of $7,500 each on 12/31/X6 and 12/31/X7, plus 6% interest on the unpaid balance. The loan is needed to finance the increased receivables and inventory of the Rainbow Company which had resulted from expanded operations.

RAINBOW COMPANY
Comparative Balance Sheets

ASSETS

	12/31/X4	12/31/X5
Cash	$ 6,275	$ 450
Accounts receivable	9,000	19,000
Inventory	14,000	17,000
Prepaid insurance	2,250	1,350
Prepaid rent	1,000	1,250
Fixed assets	50,000	50,000
Accumulated depreciation	(21,600)	(27,000)
	$60,925	$62,050

EQUITIES

Accounts payable	$ 6,000	$ 5,000
Note payable to bank (due in 6 months)	1,000	2,500
Accrued salaries payable	900	500
Accrued interest payable	25	50
Capital stock ($100 par)	45,000	45,000
Retained earnings	8,000	9,000
	$60,925	$62,050

RAINBOW COMPANY
Statement of Income and Retained Earnings
For the Year Ending December 31, 19X5

Sales	$100,000
Cost of goods sold	70,000
Gross profit	30,000

Statement of Income and Retained Earnings
(continued)

Expenses		
Salaries	$14,850	
Depreciation	5,400	
Rent	2,750	
Insurance	900	
Interest	100	24,000
Net income		$ 6,000
Retained earnings, 12/31/X4		8,000
		$ 14,000
Less: dividends paid		5,000
Retained earnings, 12/31/X5		$ 9,000

Profits in recent years have been as follows:

19X2	$ –0–
19X3	500
19X4	3,000
19X5	6,000

The only dividend was in 19X5, when $5,000 was paid.

Instructions
Analyze these statements, computing all significant ratios which you feel are appropriate. Do you think the loan to the Rainbow Company would be a good financial risk for the First State Bank (ignoring other factors not given in the case)?

4–20 **Comparison with Industry Averages** *(60 minutes)*   Presented below are condensed balance sheets of Krabbe, Inc., as of December 31, 19X4, and 19X5, and income statements for each of the two years then ended. Also presented are data taken from trade publications representing the average in the industry. Percentages have been computed for certain key figures in the income statement.

Comparative Balance Sheets

	Krabbe, Inc.		Industry Average
ASSETS	Dec. 31, 19X4	Dec. 31, 19X5	Dec. 31, 19X5
Cash	$ 700	$ 1,200	$12,000
Accounts receivable (net)	10,800	13,600	7,000
Notes receivable	1,200	1,500	200
Inventory	8,900	13,500	8,500
Equipment (net)	22,000	19,800	8,725
Real estate (net)	42,800	42,000	20,000
Total assets	$86,400	$91,600	$56,425

Comparative Balance Sheets
(continued)

EQUITIES	Krabbe, Inc. Dec. 31, 19X4	Dec. 31, 19X5	Industry Average Dec. 31, 19X5
Accounts payable	$10,000	$10,200	$ 5,000
Notes payable (6 months)	4,400	4,700	1,425
Mortgages payable (1989)	14,400	5,000 19,900	6,425
Capital stock ($100 par)	70,000	70,000	40,000
Retained earnings	2,000	1,700	10,000
Total equities	$86,400	$91,600	$56,425

Comparative Income Statements

	Krabbe, Inc. 19X4 Amount	Per Cent	19X5 Amount	Per Cent	Industry Average 19X5 Amount	Per Cent
Sales (net)	$90,000	100%	$80,000	100%	$100,000	100%
Cost of sales:						
Inventory, Jan. 1	9,100		$ 8,900		$ 7,500	
Purchases (net)	67,300		60,600		81,000	
	$76,400		$69,500		$ 88,500	
Inventory, Dec. 31	8,900		13,500		8,500	
Cost of sales	$67,500	75	$56,000	70	$ 80,000	80
Gross profit	$22,500	25	$24,000	30	$ 20,000	20
Expenses:						
Purchasing department (detail omitted)	$ 1,800	2.0	$ 2,000	2.5	$ 1,500	1.5
Selling department:						
Salaries	$ 7,200	8.0	$ 8,000	10.0	$ 6,000	6.0
Advertising	1,800	2.0	2,000	2.5	2,200	2.2
De'ivery	900	1.0	1,200	1.5	600	.6
Collections	450	.5	560	.7	300	.3
Bad debts	900	1.0	1,600	2.0	300	.3
Miscellaneous	450	.5	640	.8	100	.1
Total selling	$11,700	13.0	$14,000	17.5	$ 9,500	9.5
General and administrative (detail omitted)	5,400	6.0	6,400	8.0	3,000	3.0
Total expense	$18,900	21.0	$22,400	28.0	$ 14,000	14.0
Net operating profit	$ 3,600	4.0	$ 1,600	2.0	$ 6,000	6.0

Instructions

Has the financial position and profitability of Krabbe, Inc., been strengthened or weakened during the past two years? Compute all significant ratios to substantiate your answer.

If you were owner and manager of Krabbe, Inc., would you consider the present financial position and profitability of your company better than the industry average? What weaknesses can you spot by comparing Krabbe, Inc. with the average? What might be done to strengthen these weak areas?

chapter 5

Analysis of Changes in Financial Position: Flow of Funds

Learning Objectives

This chapter continues the analysis of financial statements and is concerned with the overall measurement of an enterprise. The focus is on an analysis of the flow of funds. Upon completion of your study of this chapter you should:

1. Understand the meaning of working capital funds and be able to distinguish them from cash funds.
2. Know the various sources of funds and how funds are applied.
3. Be able to analyze a balance sheet and income statement to determine sources and applications of funds.
4. Understand the role which depreciation expense has in the analysis of funds flow and in the recapture of an investment made in depreciable assets.

Nature of Funds

Information concerning the sources and disposition of the funds which became available during the year is of vital importance to those who manage the financial affairs of a company. The need for information concerning the flow of funds has resulted in the development and use of a separate financial statement called the *Statement of Changes in Financial Position*. This statement, the balance sheet, and the income statement constitute the basic set of financial reports for the enterprise as a whole. Although the balance sheet and income statement provide information concerning financial position and profitability, a considerable amount of additional information is contained in the statement of funds flow to answer such questions as the following:

How much expansion can we undertake without having to borrow additional monies from the bank?

Although the net income is increasing, why is our working capital decreasing?

Will enough funds be available to replace our plant when it becomes obsolete?

The statement of changes in financial position is designed to help answer such questions. The statement is sometimes called the *Statement of the Flow of Funds* or the *Statement of Changes in Working Capital Funds,* and its preparation and uses are described in this chapter.

There are several different concepts of funds used in accounting today. Cash funds and working capital funds are two of the most widely used, and both are described below.

Cash Funds

A company's cash fund is basically the cash which is available in its bank accounts for use in normal daily operations. Deposits into the bank accounts provide information concerning sources of cash, and the checks that have been written provide information concerning its disposition. However, management is usually able to control the timing of disbursements and to some extent may be able to affect the timing of cash receipts. For this reason, information concerning the flow of cash is useful only for a fairly narrow range of planning purposes.

Well-managed companies rarely let large amounts of cash accumulate in their bank accounts. If cash in excess of immediate requirements is available, it is invested in short-term securities or other readily marketable assets which earn interest and which can be sold as the need for cash arises. On the other hand, when the cash balance is less than is needed for current operations, monies are borrowed from the bank on a short-term basis. It is for this reason that flows of cash are too narrow to reflect meaningfully the funds which are of long-range significance to the company.

Working Capital Funds

The definition of funds which is most frequently encountered in the financial statements includes all the working resources of the company and encompasses all current assets and current liabilities. The total funds which a company has at its disposal are not always received or disbursed in the form of cash, and working capital is a more useful concept for planning purposes. Sales may be made, creating receivables which are yet to be collected and which have not yet had an effect upon cash. Merchandise may have been acquired but not yet paid for, so that cash itself has not been affected, although the financial position of the firm has. It is for these reasons that all current assets and current liabilities must be considered when the analysis of the flow of working capital funds is made.

Most businessmen find that including only cash in the definition of funds is too narrow and the broader definition is more meaningful. The basis of working capital funds has become the more generally accepted concept for reporting purposes and is more applicable to a company's long-range planning than cash funds. A concept of funds which encompasses all working capital is natural when one considers that short-term credit is frequently used by management as a substitute for cash and that both temporary investments and accounts receivable may be readily converted into cash at management's discretion.

$$CA - CL = WC$$

Flow of
Working Capital

Working capital, for purposes of preparing a Statement of Balance Sheet Changes or a Statement of Funds Flow is defined as the excess of current assets over current liabilities. Since current liabilities are normally paid with current assets, subtraction of total current liabilities from total current assets indicates the net funds employed in a "working" or "current" capacity. The working capital fund is thus composed of the cash, temporary investments, receivables, inventory, and other current items available for operations after all current liabilities have been covered.

Total current assets	$27,400
Less: Total current liabilities	10,300
Net working capital	$17,100

EXHIBIT 5–1

Flow of Working Capital

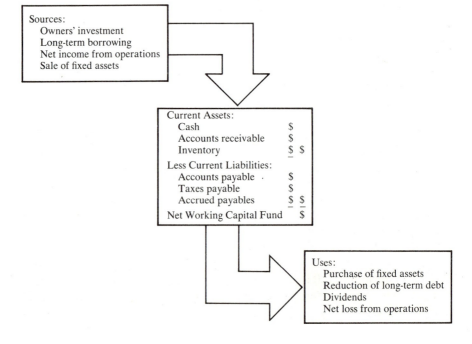

Working capital is provided by profits and consumed by losses. When a profit is earned, the inflow of cash or accounts receivable from revenues is greater than the outflow of merchandise and the liquid assets used to pay expenses. Therefore, working capital is provided by the sale of fixed assets, by long-term borrowing, or by a net profit, and is applied to the purchase of fixed assets, payment of long-term debts, a declaration of dividends, or a net loss. The flow of working capital is illustrated in Exhibit 5–1, and the major inflows and outflows from the pool of working capital are shown.

Both net income and net loss from operations are shown in Exhibit 5–1; however, a company will have either a net income or a net loss from operations during a given accounting period and it cannot have both.

Sources and
Applications of
Working Capital

The primary sources of working capital are net income, sales of assets, borrowing with long-term debt, and owners' investments. The primary uses of funds are for the purchase of non-current assets, for the payment of long-term debt, for dividends to owners, and for net losses. Each of these sources and applications is described below in terms of its effect upon the company's net working capital and is further illustrated in Exhibit 5–2. The numbers in Exhibit 5–2 correspond with the paragraph numbers which follow.

EXHIBIT 5–2
Sources and Applications of Funds

Sources of Funds		Application of Funds	
Current assets	Current liabilities ③	Current assets ⑥	Current liabilities
②		⑤	
Fixed assets ①	Long-term debt ④	Fixed assets ⑦	Long-term debt ⑧
Deferred charges	Owners' equity	Deferred charges	Owners' equity

Sources

1. *Net income*. Profits increase working capital, since revenue inflows exceed expense outflows. Net income is thus one of the primary sources of working capital funds.
2. *Sale of fixed assets*. When fixed assets are sold, the proceeds received by the company constitute a funds inflow. This transaction is rather infrequent but can be a major source when a material amount of fixed assets are sold.
3. *Long-term borrowing*. When funds are borrowed with the incurrence of long-term debt, there is an inflow of funds. Even if the long-term debt is incurred directly in the purchase of a fixed asset, such as issuing bonds pay-

able in payment of a new building, there is an inflow of funds from the long-term debt matched with an outflow of funds for the building.

4. *Owners' investment.* When the owners of a business invest assets, there is an inflow of funds, regardless of whether the investment is in cash or in property. If fixed assets are invested, there is a source of funds (owners' investment) matched by an application of funds (acquisition of fixed assets).

Applications

5. *Purchase of non-current assets.* Funds are applied when non-current assets are acquired. Even though short-term notes are issued in payment instead of a cash disbursement, there is, nevertheless, an outflow of funds.

6. *Payment of long-term debt.* Payment of long-term debt constitutes a very frequent application of funds. Since current assets are decreased when the debt is paid, there is an outflow of working capital.

7. *Payment of dividends.* When dividends are declared and paid, there is an obvious decrease in the company's working capital. The decrease constitutes an application of funds.

8. *Net losses.* Losses occur when revenues are less than expenses. The net difference is an outflow of working capital, and continued losses can seriously impair a company's working capital position.

The Statement of Changes in Financial Position

The Accounting Principles Board of the American Institute of Certified Public Accountants issued an opinion in 1971 to the effect that financial statements purporting to present both financial position (balance sheet) and the results of operations (income statement) must include a statement summarizing changes in the company's financial position. Since that date the title "Statement of changes in Financial Position" has been widely used.

The reason for emphasizing balance sheet changes in the title of the statement is that the statement reflects the changes between the company's beginning balance sheet amounts and those at the end of the year. The statement of changes in financial position is illustrated in Exhibit 5–3. Note that the statement is in two parts, both of which place emphasis upon changes in working capital. The first section of the statement is entitled Statement of Changes in Financial Position. This section reflects the various sources of working capital and their applications. The final and most significant figure at the bottom of this first section is the net change in working capital during the year. The second section of the statement reflects the changes in individual working capital accounts.

In Exhibit 5–3 the working capital has increased by $2,054 during the year, and a number of sources and uses of funds during the period are indicated. However, this $2,054 net increase in working capital must be further analyzed to determine the change in individual current asset and current liability accounts. The increase may have been the result of decreases in current liabilities, increases in current assets, or an offsetting combination of both. A schedule of

EXHIBIT 5–3

ALTON AND BALLOTTI COMPANY
Statement of Changes in Financial Position
Year Ended December 31, 19X2

Sources of working capital

Net income	$ 3,792	
Proceeds from sale of fixed assets	762	
Borrowed on five-year bank note	12,000	
Issue of common stock	20,000	
Total sources of funds		$36,554

Applications of working capital

Expended for plant and equipment	$17,000	
Retirement of bonds payable	5,000	
Dividends declared	7,500	
Set aside in asset replacement fund	5,000	
Total funds applied		34,500
Net increase in working capital		$ 2,054

Schedule of Working Capital Changes

	Balances as of December 31,		Changes in Working Capital	
	19X1	19X2	Increase	Decrease
Current assets				
Cash	$ 1,200	$ 1,900	$ 700	
Receivables	12,900	12,100		$ 800
Allowance for uncollectable accounts	(654)	(800)		146
Inventory	15,700	21,000	5,300	
Total current assets	$29,146	$34,200		
Current liabilities				
Accounts payable	$10,700	$ 9,700	1,000	
Notes payable	—	4,000		4,000
Total current liabilities	$10,700	$13,700		
Working capital	$18,446	$20,500		
Increase in working capital				2,054
			$7,000	$7,000

changes in each current asset and current liability account is therefore necessary and appears as the second section of the statement. This section is entitled *Schedule of Working Capital Changes*.

The schedule of working capital changes provides a detailed analysis of the individual working capital accounts. Both the beginning and ending balances of all current asset and current liability accounts are shown, with the resulting increase or decrease. The net change in working capital as reflected at the bottom of this schedule must equal the final figure in the first section of the statement. Note that the $2,054 increase in working capital reflected by sources and applications in the first part of Exhibit 5–3 also appears as the increase in working capital in the second section, where the detailed changes are reflected. Note further that the $2,054 increase in working capital in the schedule of working capital changes is entered in the decrease column, so that the totals of both increase and decrease columns will balance.

Separating Working Capital and Nonworking Capital Accounts

The preparation of a statement of changes in financial position begins with an analysis of balance sheet changes. The changes in balance sheet accounts, other than working capital items, indicate either sources or applications of working capital funds. This may be noted in Exhibit 5–4, wherein all balance sheet changes are computed, and the working capital and nonworking capital account changes are separated. In this illustration, the working capital has decreased by a total of $4,000, since the increase in accounts payable and the decrease in inventory more than offset the increase in cash and receivables. The net change in the working capital accounts must equal the change in the nonworking capital accounts, because the increases or decreases in working capital are either derived from or applied to nonworking capital accounts. Thus both the individual changes in working capital accounts as well as the sources and applications of working capital are determined from an analysis of balance sheet changes.

Assuming that the entire change in retained earnings in Exhibit 5–4 was the result of the net income earned during the period, the statement prepared from these data would indicate a $1,000 source from net income, a $3,000 application for the purchase of land, a $2,000 application to the retirement of bonds payable, and a resulting decrease in working capital of $4,000.

The net change in a nonworking capital account may be the result of some decreases, offset by some increases. The causes of changes in the balance of retained earnings, for example, can be ascertained only after an analysis of the transactions affecting the retained earnings account. The $1,000 net change in retained earnings in Exhibit 5–4 was assumed earlier to be entirely from net income, but it could have been a net income (a source) of $5,000, offset in part by dividends of $4,000 (an application). Further, the $3,000 increase in the land account in Exhibit 5–4 could have been the net result of the sale of one parcel of land and the purchase of another. In all cases, each source and each application should appear separately in the statement.

EXHIBIT 5-4

Analysis of Balance Sheet Changes

	Balance Sheet		Changes			
			Working Capital Accounts		Nonworking Capital Accounts	
	Dec. 31, 19X1	Dec. 31, 19X2	Increase	Decrease	Applications	Sources
Cash	$ 1,000	$ 3,200	$2,200			
Receivables	2,000	3,800	1,800			
Inventory	10,000	8,000		$2,000		
Land	20,000	23,000			$3,000 (purchase)	
Buildings	50,000	50,000				
Total assets	$83,000	$88,000				
Accounts payable	$ 8,000	$14,000		6,000		
Bonds payable, 1980	20,000	18,000			2,000 (payment)	
Common stock	50,000	50,000				
Retained earnings	5,000	6,000				$1,000 (profit)
Total liabilities and capital	$83,000	$88,000				
Net decrease in working capital			4,000			4,000
			$8,000	$8,000	$5,000	$5,000

Assuming the land account and the retained earnings account to contain the sources and applications mentioned above, the ledger accounts for 19X2 would contain the following data:

Land			Retained Earnings		
Beginning balance $20,000					Beginning balance $5,000
					Net income 5,000
	Sale, at cost $6,000		Dividends $4,000		
Purchase of land 9,000					

These data must then be reflected in the statement of changes in financial position as follows:

Sources of working capital		
Operations (net income)	$5,000	
Sale of land	6,000	
Total sources		$11,000
Applications of working capital		
Purchase of land	$9,000	
Dividends	4,000	
Retirement of bonds payable	2,000	
Total applications		15,000
Net decrease in working capital		$ 4,000

Funds Provided By Operations

The funds provided by (or applied to) operations are not fully reflected by the net income (or loss) figure appearing on the income statement. Included in the computation of net income or loss are items such as depreciation and amortization of intangible assets which do not require an outlay of working capital funds. These expenses must be added to net income to ascertain the actual amount of funds provided by operations. Exhibit 5–5 is given as an illustration of an income statement wherein the net income figure does not reflect the full inflow of funds from operations. Items requiring adjustment are indicated with arrows.

EXHIBIT 5–5

WALTON FLOORING COMPANY
Income Statement
For the Year Ending December 31, 19X2

Revenues		
Fees earned	$79,000	
Interest on investments	2,000	
Gain on sale of land	3,000	
Total incomes		$84,000

Adjustment item

Sale of Fixed assets

Income Statement
(continued)

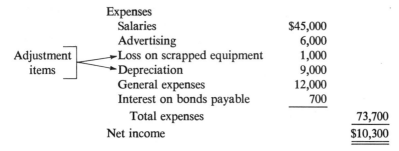

Expenses		
Salaries	$45,000	
Advertising	6,000	
Loss on scrapped equipment	1,000	
Depreciation	9,000	
General expenses	12,000	
Interest on bonds payable	700	
Total expenses		73,700
Net income		$10,300

Depreciation and losses on scrapped equipment showing in the income statement did not require an outlay of funds when the expense was recorded. Neither a reduction in current assets nor an increase in current liabilities resulted from recording the depreciation or the loss on scrapped equipment. Working capital was therefore not affected when these expenses were recorded. Consider, for example, the entries which would have been recorded at the time depreciation and loss on scrapped equipment were first entered in the books.

Dec.	31	Depreciation expense	$9,000	
		Accumulated depreciation		$9,000
		To record annual depreciation		
Dec.	31	Accumulated depreciation	5,000	
		Loss on scrapped equipment	1,000	
		Equipment		6,000
		To record scrapping of equipment		

Although depreciation and loss on scrapped equipment were recorded as expenses, thus reducing the net income, no outflow of funds is involved, and these amounts must be added back to the reported income to ascertain the actual funds inflow due to operations.

At the same time, some of the incomes or gains in the income statement do not accurately reflect the true source of the inflow of working capital funds. The gain on the sale of fixed assets, shown in the previous illustration, for example, does not reflect the total source of funds which the company realized from the sale of the asset. The total funds provided by the sale of the asset are measured by the proceeds received from the sale itself. The gain on the sale, as shown on the income statement, must be added to the net book value of the sold asset to determine the actual funds received when the asset was sold. To provide an illustration, assume that the following entry was made to record the sale of land:

July	7	Cash	$8,000		
		Gain on sale of land		$3,000	
		Land		5,000	
		To record sale of land			

The land account reflects a $5,000 decrease, while the $3,000 gain on the sale appears in the income statement. The full $8,000 of funds received from the sale of land should appear as a single source, and the $3,000 gain on the sale is subtracted from net income so that the source of the funds can be shown correctly as coming from the sale of assets. Thus, the $10,300 net income as shown in Exhibit 5–5, adjusted for non-fund items, and the $8,000 from the sale of land would appear in complete detail in the statement of changes in financial position as follows:

Sources of working capital
　From operations
　　Reported net income — $10,300
　　Add:　Depreciation — 9,000
　　　　　Loss on scrapped equipment — 1,000
　　　　　　　　　　　　　　　　　　　$20,300
　　Less:　Gain on sale of land — 3,000
　　　Total funds provided by operations — $17,300
　From sale of land — 8,000
　　Total sources of working capital — $25,300

Preparing the Statement

Preparation of the statement of changes in financial position is facilitated by use of a work sheet. The work sheet begins with the balance sheet amounts at the beginning and end of the period and does not include income statement accounts. The work sheet is primarily concerned with nonworking capital items on the balance sheet, since the sources and applications are primarily located in these accounts. Only the net working capital at the beginning and end of the year appear in the work sheet, and individual current asset and current liability accounts are not included.

The first step in the completion of the work sheet is the computation of working capital at the beginning and also at the end of the period. All current assets and current liabilities must be included in the computation. The schedule of working capital items which is the second section of the final statement may be prepared while completing this step. To illustrate the preparation and use of the work sheet, the financial statements of the Able Stationery Company will be used. They include the balance sheet accounts as of December 31, 19X1 and 19X2, and the income statement for the year 19X2, as shown in Exhibit 5–6.

There are four steps necessary to prepare the statement of changes in financial position.

1. *Separate working capital from nonworking capital accounts.* As pointed out earlier, the final statement will contain two sections, one reflecting sources and applications of working capital and the other reflecting changes in current asset and current liability accounts. The latter section should be prepared first, since changes in individual current assets and current liabilities must be known in order to determine the amount of increase or decrease in working capital.

This step completes one section of the final statement and provides the beginning and ending amounts of working capital for the other section, which

EXHIBIT 5–6

ABLE STATIONERY COMPANY
Balance Sheet Accounts
As of December 31, 19X1 and 19X2

	19X1		19X2	
Cash	$ 3,000		$ 3,500	
Accounts receivable	10,000		9,000	
Allowance for doubtful accounts		$ 1,000		$ 800
Inventory	18,000		21,000	
Prepaid insurance	700		600	
Land	4,000		7,000	
Buildings	32,000		34,000	
Accumulated depreciation—				
buildings		9,000		10,500
Patents	6,000		5,000	
Accounts payable		12,000		9,000
Notes payable		3,000		5,000
Accrued liabilities		2,000		2,400
Mortgages payable, 1980		10,000		9,000
Common stock		30,000		32,000
Retained earnings		6,700		11,400
	$73,700	$73,700	$80,100	$80,100

ABLE STATIONERY COMPANY
Income Statement
For the Year Ended December 31, 19X2

Sales		$140,000
Cost of merchandise sold		80,000
Gross profit		$ 60,000
Depreciation expense	$ 1,500	
Amortization of patents	1,000	
Salaries	30,000	
Advertising	12,400	
Supplies	6,000	
Total operating expenses		50,900
Operating income		9,100
Nonoperating gain: Gain on sale of land		1,000
Net income		$ 10,100

will reflect the sources and applications. The completion of this step and the resulting schedule of changes in current assets and current liabilities for the Able Stationery Company are shown in Exhibit 5–7.

Note that increases in current assets will increase working capital, while decreases in current assets will decrease working capital. The allowance for bad debts has just the opposite effect as its counterpart, accounts receivable. A decrease in the allowance for bad debts is an increase in working capital. Current liabilities also have an effect opposite to that of current assets. If accounts payable decrease, total working capital increases. This is readily apparent when

EXHIBIT 5–7

ABLE STATIONERY COMPANY
Schedule of Working Capital Changes
For the Year Ended December 31, 19X2

	December 31		Changes in Working capital	
	19X1	19X2	Increase	Decrease
Current assets				
Cash	$ 3,000	$ 3,500	$ 500	
Accounts receivable	10,000	9,000		$1,000
Allowance for bad debts	(1,000)	(800)	200	
Inventory	18,000	21,000	3,000	
Prepaid insurance	700	600		100
Total current assets	$30,700	$33,300		
Current liabilities				
Accounts payable	$12,000	$ 9,000	3,000	
Notes payable	3,000	5,000		2,000
Accrued liabilities	2,000	2,400		400
Total current liabilities	$17,000	$16,400		
Net working capital	$13,700	$16,900		
Increase in working capital				3,200
			$6,700	$6,700

one realizes that current liabilities are subtracted in determining working capital, and a decrease in a liability makes the amount subtracted smaller. Thus, decreases in current liabilities will produce an increase in working capital.

The net working capital at the end of both 19X1 and 19X2 are shown separately in the schedule of working capital changes, and the difference between the two is the increase or decrease in working capital during the year. In Exhibit 5–7 the net working capital at the beginning of the year was $13,700 and at the end of the year was $16,900. Thus, there was an increase in working capital during 19X2 of $3,200. This amount is also the figure needed to balance the increase and decrease columns of the statement, thus providing a check on mathematical accuracy.

2. *Prepare a work sheet to analyze nonworking capital changes.* The next step in completing the statement of changes in financial position is to prepare a worksheet which analyzes the nonworking capital accounts. The form of the worksheet is illustrated in Exhibit 5–8. Note that all nonworking capital balances at the beginning of the year are placed in the column on the left, while those at the end of the year are placed in the column on the right. There are two columns between them for analysis purposes. The net working capital amounts at the beginning and end of the year are also inserted; these amounts are available from Step 1, which was described above. Note that the $13,700

balance of working capital on December 31, 19X1, and the $16,900 balance on December 31, 19X2, are inserted in the work sheet and are used in the subsequent analysis.

EXHIBIT 5–8

ABLE STATIONERY COMPANY
Work Sheet for Preparation of a Statement of
Sources and Applications of Net Working Capital
For the Year Ended December 31, 19X2

	Balance Dec. 31, 19X1	Analysis of Changes Debit	Analysis of Changes Credit	Balance Dec. 31, 19X2
Net working capital	$13,700			$16,900
Land	4,000			7,000
Buildings	32,000			34,000
Accumulated depreciation—buildings	(9,000)			(10,500)
Patents	6,000			5,000
Total assets	$46,700			$52,400
Mortgages payable, 1980	$10,000			$ 9,000
Common stock	30,000			32,000
Retained earnings	6,700			11,400
Total equities	$46,700			$52,400

3. *Analyze all changes in nonworking capital accounts.* The most difficult part of the preparation of a statement of changes in financial position is the analysis of all changes in the accounts appearing on the work sheet. Each change in a nonworking capital account balance is an indication of either a source or an application of working capital. As each source or application is located, that account is debited or credited in the analysis columns, with the offsetting debit or credit made to either a source or application which is inserted at the bottom of the work sheet.

The basic procedure in analyzing a change in an account balance is to reconstruct the journal entry or entries which caused the change. *Working capital* is then substituted for any working capital account (current asset or current liability) which appears in the entry.

Each amount appearing in the analysis column of the completed work sheet shown in Exhibit 5–9 is explained below. The explanations are lettered to correspond with amounts on the work sheet.

(a) The balance of the buildings account increased $2,000. Analysis of the buildings account indicates that the entry made during the year to record this building expansion was:

Buildings   2,000
     Cash   2,000

EXHIBIT 5–9

ABLE STATIONERY COMPANY
Work Sheet for Statement of Working Capital
Year Ended December 31, 19X2

	Balance Dec.31, 19X1	Analysis of Account changes		Balance Dec.31, 19X2
Working capital	$13,700	(j) $ 3,200		$16,900
Land	4,000	(f) 8,000	(g) $ 5,000	7,000
Buildings	32,000	(a) 2,000		34,000
Accumulated depreciation—buildings	(9,000)		(b) 1,500	(10,500)
Patents	6,000		(c) 1,000	5,000
Total assets	$46,700			$52,400
Mortgages payable, 1980	$10,000	(d) 1,000		$ 9,000
Common stock	30,000		(e) 2,000	32,000
Retained earnings	6,700	(h) 5,400	(i) 10,100	11,400
Total equities	$46,700			$52,400
Sources of working capital				
Adjustment to net income—depreciation		(b) 1,500		
Adjustment to net income—patents		(c) 1,000		
Issuance of stock		(e) 2,000		
Gain on sale of land		(g) 6,000		
Net income for the year		(i) 10,100		
Adjustment to net income—gain on land			(g) 1,000	
Applications of working capital				
Purchase of buildings			(a) 2,000	
Payment of mortgage			(d) 1,000	
Purchase of land			(f) 8,000	
Payment of dividends			(h) 5,400	
Increase in working capital			(j) 3,200	
		$40,200	$40,200	

Cash does not appear on the work sheet, since only total working capital appears. Because the purchase of the building has consumed working capital, the necessary entry on the work sheet is a debit to building and a credit in the section for applications. The entire entry on the work sheet is:

Buildings	2,000	
Purchase of buildings (application)		2,000

Had the addition to the building been acquired with a sixty-day note payable instead of cash, the entry on the work sheet would have been the same. A decrease in working capital is effected by either a decrease in cash or an increase in current liabilities. Note that the $2,000 appears as a debit to buildings and a credit to *purchase of buildings,* which is a credit in the work sheet. The entire change in the building account has now been accounted for.

(b) The account entitled Accumulated Depreciation—Buildings was increased by $1,500 as a result of the annual entry to record depreciation expense. This entry to record depreciation was made in the company's accounting records as follows:

Depreciation expense	1,500	
Accumulated depreciation—buildings		1,500

The amount of depreciation would also be indicated by the depreciation expense on the income statement, shown previously in Exhibit 5–6. While depreciation neither provided nor consumed funds, the debit to depreciation expense affected the determination of net income, which was closed to retained earnings. The net income, which is a source of funds, must be adjusted by the amount of the depreciation to reflect the true amount of funds provided by operations. Therefore, the entry on the work sheet is a debit in the lower portion to the *sources* section for Adjustment to Net Income—Depreciation, with a credit to Accumulated Depreciation—Buildings in the upper portion of the work sheet:

Adjustment to net income—depreciation	1,500	
Accumulated depreciation—buildings		1,500

(c) The $1,000 decrease in patents was due to an entry amortizing patents as patents expense. Since this is a noncash expenditure, the entry on the work sheet is made in the same manner as the entry for depreciation expense. The debit on the work sheet is a debit to the sources section as Adjustment to Net Income—Patents, with a credit to patents in the upper section.

(d) The reduction of $1,000 in the mortgages payable account resulted from a payment of debt, and this reduces working capital. This transaction is identified as an application of funds. The entry on the work sheet would be:

Mortgages payable	1,000	
Payment of mortgage (application)		1,000

(e) The $2,000 increase in the capital stock account resulted from the issuance during the year of additional stock, at par. The transaction produced working capital and would be entered on the work sheet as a debit to Issuance of Stock in the sources section and a credit to Common Stock in the upper section.

Issuance of stock (sources)	2,000	
Common stock		2,000

(f) and (g) The $3,000 change in the land account is the result of two entries, one for the purchase of land for $8,000, and one wherein land costing $5,000 was sold for $6,000 cash. These data are usually available only through an analysis of transactions affecting the land account. The actual recorded entries and the corresponding entries on the work sheet are:

Recorded Entries on the Books			Entries on the Work Sheet		
Land	8,000		(f) Land	8,000	
Cash		8,000	Purchase of land (application)		8,000
Cash	6,000		(g) Sale of land (source)	6,000	
Gain on sale of land	1,000		Adjustment to net		
Land		5,000	income—		
			Sale of land		1,000
			Land		5,000

The work sheet entry (f) accounts for the purchase of land. The second entry (g) reflects the purchase of the other tract of land. In the second entry, the $1,000 gain on the sale entered into the determination of net income and would appear in the statement of balance sheet changes as an adjustment to net income.

(h) Dividends of $5,400 were paid during the year. The entry recorded during the year and the necessary entry on the work sheet would be:

Recorded Entry on the Books			Entry on the Work Sheet		
Retained earnings	5,400		Retained earnings	5,400	
Cash		5,400	Payment of dividends (application)		5,400

(i) The profit of $10,100 which appears on the income statement provided funds and requires an entry which credits Retained Earnings in the upper portion of the work sheet and debits Net Income as a source in the lower section.

(j) The working capital increased $3,200 during the year. This figure is available from the schedule of working capital changes prepared in step 1 and shown in Exhibit 5–7. This amount is entered as a debit on the working capital line in the upper portion of the work sheet. Since working capital, which is an asset, increased by $3,200 during the year, a debit of that amount is necessary, with the offsetting credit to Increase in Working Capital in the applications section of the work sheet.

At this point all changes in account balances have been fully explained, and their effects upon working capital have been entered in the lower part of the work sheet. The amounts in the two center analysis columns of the work sheet explain completely the events which affected the flow of working capital funds

EXHIBIT 5–10

ABLE STATIONERY COMPANY
Statement of Changes in Financial Position
Year Ended December 31, 19X2

Sources of working capital		
Operations		
Reported net profit	$10,100	
Add: Depreciation	1,500	
Amortization of patents	1,000	
Less: Gain on sale of land	(1,000)	
Total provided by operations		$11,600
Issuance of common stock		2,000
Sale of land		6,000
Total funds provided		$19,600
Applications of working capital		
Purchase of buildings	$ 2,000	
Retirement of bonds payable	1,000	
Dividends	5,400	
Purchase of land	8,000	
Total funds applied		16,400
Net increase in working capital funds		$ 3,200

during the year. The complete statement of changes in financial position can now be prepared using the amounts for sources and applications which appear in the lower section of the work sheet.

(4) *Prepare the statement of changes in financial position.* The completed work sheet contains a listing of the sources and applications of working capital funds. These sources and applications are arranged in the formal statement to reflect the sources first, followed by the applications. The final figure on the statement is the net increase or decrease in working capital.

The statement prepared from the completed work sheet is shown in Exhibit 5–10. Note that all items which affected the determination of net income, but which did not require funds, are listed as adjustments to net income. The subtotal of $11,600 presents the total funds provided by operations. Other sources are then listed to obtain the $19,600 of total sources which were available during the period. The applications are then listed and are subtracted from the total sources.

Analysis of Cash Flow

As mentioned early in this chapter, cash funds are sometimes analyzed for more short-range planning. The completion of an analysis of cash flow is similar to that of working capital flow, except that attention is focused primarily upon receipts and uses of cash. The format of the statement of cash flow is basically the same as that of a statement of working capital flow, with receipts (or sources) listed first and uses (or applications) subtracted. However, the short-range focus of the statement of cash flow makes it helpful to employ a slightly different approach in the presentation of receipts and disbursements. The statement should contain an amount for total cash receipts from customers and an amount for total cash payments for costs and expenses. The net cash inflow or outflow from operations is shown as the difference between these two totals. It takes the place of net funds from operations. All other sources and applications would be the same as those appearing in the statement of changes in financial position as previously described.

The statement of cash flow appearing in Exhibit 5–11 has been prepared from the financial data of the Able Stationery Company shown earlier in Exhibit 5–6 and used in previous examples in this chapter. Note that the applications have not changed, although the sources are reported differently. Only two items appear under the heading *Sources of Cash from Operations*. These are the cash receipts from customers and the cash payments for costs and expenses. The difference is the net cash inflow from operations. Calculation of the cash received from customers and the cash payments for costs and expenses is completed by using sales and expense data from the income statement, adjusted for changes in current asset and current liability items. This process is explained in the next section.

EXHIBIT 5–11

ABLE STATIONERY COMPANY
Statement of Cash Flow
For the Year Ended December 31, 19X2

Sources of cash		
From operations		
Received from customers	$140,800	
Paid for costs and expenses	132,900	
Net cash from operations		$ 7,900
From issuance of stock		2,000
From sale of land		6,000
Total sources		$15,900
		16,900
Applications of cash		
Purchase of buildings	$ 2,000	
Retirement of bonds payable	1,000	
Dividends	5,400	
Purchase of land	8,000	
Total applications		$16,400
Excess of applications over sources		(500)
Beginning cash balance, December 31, 19X1		3,500
Ending cash balance, December 31, 19X2		$ 3,000

Preparation of the Cash Flow Statement

The analysis of cash flow is undertaken by completing the same work sheet as that illustrated earlier in Exhibit 5–9 for the statement of changes in financial position. Only two additional steps are then necessary to convert from working capital funds to cash funds. These are the calculation of cash receipts from customers and the calculation of cash payments for costs and expenses. In illustrating the preparation of the statement of cash flow, the work sheet from Exhibit 5–9 and related data shown previously in Exhibits 5–6 and 5–7 will be used again.

Cash received from operations   The amount of sales appearing in the income statement will not reflect the total cash received from customers unless it is adjusted for any increase or decrease in uncollected accounts receivable. Any change in the allowance for bad debts must also be considered at the same time. The income statement (Exhibit 5–6) reported sales of $140,000, and the balance sheets in that same exhibit reflect a decrease of $1,000 in accounts receivable and a decrease of $200 in the allowance for bad debts. This $800 net decrease ($1,000 receivable decrease less $200 decrease in the allowance for bad debts) is added to sales to reflect the total cash received. Explained another way, the cash collections were more than all the current year's sales, because net receivables declined.

The cash received from customers, computed by adjusting sales for changes in accounts receivable and bad debts, would be:

Total sales (from the income statement)	$140,000
Add: Decrease in accounts receivable	1,000
Less: Decrease in allowance for bad debts	200
Cash received from customers	$140,800

Had accounts receivable increased, the amount of the increase would have been subtracted from sales. Similarly, an increase in the allowance for bad debts would require an addition to sales.

Cash paid for costs and expenses   The amount of change in all other working capital accounts appearing in the schedule of working capital changes, except receivables and the allowance for bad debts must be added to or subtracted from the total of the costs and expenses appearing in the income statement. The $3,000 increase in inventory, for example, must be added to costs and expenses, since the company has acquired merchandise in excess of the cost of merchandise sold. The increase in accounts payable, on the other hand, must be subtracted from costs and expenses, since accounts payable represent purchases which were not paid for during the current period. The conversion of the costs and expenses appearing on the income statement to a cash basis would be made as shown on the following page.

Note that the total costs and expenses of $129,900 appearing as the first subtotal in the statement were calculated by subtracting net income from sales. This figure represents the total expenses on the income statement. This total is then adjusted for any noncash expenses or gains. The second subtotal of $131,400 represents the total expenses adjusted for any noncash items appearing on the statement.

The final calculation adjusts the expenses for amounts paid on current liabilities, for changes in inventories, and for changes in other current assets be-

Sales (from income statement)		$140,000
Less: net income		10,100
Total expenses		$129,900
Adjustment for non-cash items		
Add: Depreciation	$1,500	
LESS Amortization of patents	1,000	
Less: Gain on sale of land	(1,000) *500*	1,500
Adjusted expenses	*500*	$131,400 *129,400*
Adjustment for other expenditures		
Add: Increase in inventory	($3,000)	
Decrease in notes payable	(2,000)	
Less: Increase in accounts payable	(3,000)	
Decrease in prepaid insurance	(100)	*2,500*
Increase in accrued liabilities	(400)	1,500
Total cash payments		$132,900 *131,900*

(handwritten margin note: "messed up" with arrow)

sides receivables and the allowance for bad debts. The final $132,900 amount appears in the completed statement of cash flow as the amount of cash payments made for operations.

The guide presented below may be followed in making adjustments to the cash payments because of changes in current asset and current liability accounts. (Do *not* use this guide for accounts receivable and allowance for bad debts, since they are adjustments to sales in computing cash inflows.)

Guide for Adjustments to Cash Payments

Total costs and expenses per income statement		$$
Add: Increase in current assets		(+)
Decreases in current liabilities		(+)
Noncash losses or expenses such as depreciation		(+)
Subtract: Decreases in current assets		(−)
Increases in current liabilities		(−)
Noncash gains		(−)
Adjusted cash payments for costs and expenses		$$

Finally, note that the $140,800 receipts from customers and the $132,900 paid for costs and expenses are matched on the statement of cash flow in Exhibit 5–11. The difference is the net cash flow from operations. All other receipts and applications are exactly as calculated in the previous section of this chapter which treated working capital flows.

In summary, the statement of cash flow is prepared by completing the following four steps:

1. Complete a work sheet similar to that described for working capital flows.
2. Adjust the sales appearing on the income statement for any change in the balance of accounts receivable and the allowance for bad debts.
3. Adjust total costs and expenses which appear on the income statement for (a) noncash items in the income statement and (b) for all changes in working capital items other than receivables and allowance for bad debts.

4. Prepare the statement so that it reflects net cash inflow or outflow from operations and includes all sources and applications identified in the work sheet completed in step 1.

The final statement of cash flow was shown earlier in Exhibit 5–11. Note that the $7,900 net cash from operations is the difference between the inflow and outflow of cash as calculated in steps 2 and 3. Note also that all other sources and applications are exactly the same as in the statement of working capital flow shown in Exhibit 5–10. These elements produce an excess of applications over sources of $500. This amount explains in full the change in the cash balance during the year; the final figure in the statement is the ending cash balance.

Summary

A company's working capital fund is an essential element in its profit-making activities. The composition of the fund, as well as the sources and applications of funds, is of primary importance to managers and owners. Sources and applications arise from the nonworking capital items which appear in the company's balance sheet, and determination of these amounts is accomplished through an analysis of all the nonworking capital accounts.

The analysis of funds flow is so important that the accounting profession has within recent years required inclusion of the statement of changes in financial position with the balance sheet and income statement. While much of the information in the statement of changes in financial position is available from the other two financial statements, a number of funds transactions may be hidden or may offset each other, so that this statement should accompany the other two for full financial reporting. Without information concerning the sources and applications of funds, data would be incomplete for such decisions as the acquisition of capital assets, undertaking additional long-term financing, or the issuance or retirement of capital stock. The data contained in the statement of changes in financial position are useful primarily for long-range planning purposes.

New Terms

Cash fund   The cash available in the bank for use in daily operations.

Fund   Any grouping of assets which has been designated for a particular purpose.

Funds from operations   The asset inflow from normal operations, usually profit adjusted for nonfund revenues and expenses.

Statement of cash flow   A financial statement showing sources and application of cash.

Statement of funds flow   A financial statement showing sources and applications of funds, usually with working capital as the fund being analyzed.

Working capital fund   The pool of working assets defined as current assets less current liabilities.

Questions

1. Define the concept of "working capital fund," and distinguish this type of fund from cash funds.

2. Indicate whether the following changes in account balances would be a working capital or a nonworking capital change. For each nonworking capital change, indicate whether it represents a source or application of funds.
   a. Increase in accumulated depreciation of buildings
   b. Decrease in buildings
   c. Increase in mortgage payable
   d. Addition to accounts payable
   e. Reported net profit for the year
   f. Patent amortization expense
   g. Increase in prepaid insurance
   h. Decrease in allowance for bad debts
   i. Decrease in preferred stock
   j. Decrease in inventory
   k. Increase in patents

3. State the effect on working capital funds of (a) borrowing $1,000 from a bank on a six-months note payable; (b) declaring and issuing a stock dividend; (c) collection of accounts receivable; (d) writing off prepaid insurance to expense.

4. A company's management undertook an agreement with a construction company whereby the construction company would build a new office building and receive capital stock in payment instead of cash. Were funds provided and applied in this case? Why or why not ?

5. Why are nonfund income statement items added or subtracted to reported profit when the statement of sources and applications of working capital funds is prepared.

6. Name several accounts whose balances should be analyzed to locate off-setting sources and applications.

7. Describe the content of the Statement of Changes in Financial Position, indicating what information is contained in it that is not readily apparent on the balance sheet and income statement.

8. Explain why the total change in nonworking capital accounts between two years will always be equal in dollar amount to the total change in working capital accounts.

9. Explain why depreciation is added back to reported profits to determine the total funds provided by operations.

10. The management of a company periodically divides the depreciation expense into the funds used for the purchase of fixed assets. What would the resulting figure indicate?

11. During times of constantly rising prices, will the funds recaptured through depreciation be adequate to replace an asset when it is fully depreciated? If not, where must additional funds for replacement be found?

Exercises

5–1   **Format of the Statement** *(30 minutes)*   Listed below are all the changes which occurred in the account balances of a company:

a. Increase in accumulated depreciation of buildings, $2,000.
b. Decrease in land due to sale at cost, $5,000.
c. Increase in mortgage payable, $10,000.
d. Increase in long-term investments, $1,000.
e. Reported net profit for the year, $7,000. (This is an increase in retained earnings.)
f. Decrease in patents, $500.
g. Increase in prepaid insurance, $200.
h. Decrease in accounts payable, $450.
i. Decrease in preferred stock, $23,000.
j. Decrease in inventory, $500.
k. Increase in cash, $350.

Instructions
Prepare a statement of changes in financial position with a supporting schedule of changes in working capital items.

5–2*   **Statement of Changes in Financial Position** *(35 minutes)*   The information given below was taken from the records of the Rightman Co.

	19X4	19X5	December 31 19X4	December 31 19X5
Cash			$20,000	$10,000
Accounts receivable			7,000	10,000
Inventory			15,000	20,000
Land			50,000	50,000
Equipment	$50,000	$70,000		
Less:				
Accumulated depreciation	10,000	14,000	40,000	56,000
Total assets			132,000	146,000
Accounts payable			4,000	6,000
Wages payable			1,000	2,000
Bonds payable (due 1980)			—0—	20,000
Capital stock			80,000	80,000
Retained earnings			47,000	38,000
Total liabilities and equity			132,000	146,000

No dividends were paid during 19X5, because the company had a $9,000 loss. Equipment which had originally cost $3,000 and on which depreciation of $2,000 had been recorded was scrapped during the year with no proceeds from salvage value.

Instructions
Prepare a statement of changes in financial position for 19X5.

5–3   **Statement of Changes in Financial Position** *(40 minutes)*   The following items were taken from the Gaspard Corporation comparative balance sheets.

	December 31:	
	19X5	19X4
Cash	$ 45,000	$ 35,000
Accounts receivable (net)	45,000	35,000
Inventory	52,000	28,000
Prepaid rent	15,000	7,000
Land	40,000	40,000
Buildings	125,000	125,000
Accumulated depreciation on buildings	25,000	20,000
Equipment	80,000	50,000
Accumulated depreciation on equipment	10,000	12,000
Accounts payable	25,000	15,000
Taxes payable	13,000	7,000
Notes payable, 1988	100,000	50,000
Common stock	100,000	100,000
Paid-in capital	100,000	100,000
Retained earnings	29,000	16,000

Net income for 19X5 was $33,000, which included $12,000 of depreciation expense and a gain from sale of equipment of $5,000. Dividends of $20,000 were paid during the year, and new equipment with a total cost of $50,000 was purchased.

Instructions
Prepare a statement of changes in financial position for the year 19X5. (Note: the equipment account and the related accumulated depreciation must be analyzed to determine the proceeds from the sale of equipment; this figure is $16,000.)

5–4   **Analysis of the Statement of Changes in Financial Position** *(15 minutes)*   The *total* working capital funds applied and provided by the following two companies are exactly the same. However, the operating policies of the two companies are entirely different.

	Company S		Company T	
Funds provided:				
By operations	$10,000		$10,000	
Issue of long-term notes	40,000			
Sale of capital stock	————		40,000	
		$50,000		$50,000
Funds applied:				
Purchase of additional				
plant	$10,000		$35,000	
Payment of dividends	30,000	40,000	5,000	40,000
Increase in working capital		$10,000		$10,000

	Increase	Decrease	Increase	Decrease
Current assets:				
Cash		$ 5,000	$10,000	
Receivables	$35,000		10,000	
Inventories	55,000		15,000	
Current liabilities:				
Accounts payable		25,000		$ 5,000
Notes payable	————	50,000	————	20,000
	$90,000	$80,000	$35,000	$25,000
Increase in working capital	————	10,000	————	10,000
	$90,000	$90,000	$35,000	$35,000

Instructions

Evaluate and compare the policies of the two companies and state which one you feel has made its financial position stronger during the year.

5–5   **Working Capital Provided by Operations** *(15 minutes)*   The income statement of the Forwardier Company appears below:

Sales		$100,000
Cost of goods sold		60,000
Gross profit		$ 40,000
Operating expenses:		
Salaries	$22,000	
Depreciation	6,000	
Advertising	4,000	
Patent amortization	1,000	
Office supplies	3,000	
Utilities	2,000	

(continued)

Bad debt write-offs	4,000	
Taxes expense	1,500	43,500
Net operating loss		($ 3,500)
Interest income (accrued)		600
Net loss for the year		($ 2,900)

Instructions

Using data from this statement, prepare a schedule showing the working capital funds provided or applied by operations.

5–6   **Computation of Cash Received from Operations** *(10 minutes)*
The following information was extracted from the balance sheets of the Collins Construction Co. for the years ended December 31, 19X4 and 19X5:

	December 31,	
	19X4	19X5
Cash	$ 2,500	$ 3,000
Accounts receivable	10,500	6,800
Inventory	23,000	25,600
Accounts payable	(12,000)	(13,000)

The company's income statement contained the following:

Sales		$109,000
Expenses and costs	$80,000	
Depreciation	20,000	
		100,000
Net income		$ 9,000

Instructions

Prepare a schedule showing the total cash received from operations and the total cash spent for operating purposes.

5–7   **Analysis of Retained Earnings** *(10 minutes)*   The retained earnings of the Bollow Company appears below:

Retained Earnings

DEDUCTIONS		ADDITIONS	
Dividends declared (unpaid on Dec. 31 of this year)	$5,500	Beginning balance, Jan. 1	$15,000
		Net income for the year	7,000
Goodwill written off	3,000	Refund of prior year's	
Loss on sale of land	1,000	taxes	1,200

Instructions

List the items contained in this account which would appear separately as either sources or applications on the statement of changes in financial position.

5–8   **Analysis of Difference Between Cash Flow and Profit** *(15 minutes)*
J. K. Lodd invested $10,500 in a concession stand at the beach. All purchases of food materials are for cash, and all sales are for cash. A total of $10,000 was invested in kitchen facilities and a wooden building, which had a life of ten years. Lodd has not withdrawn any assets from the business at the end of four years.

Instructions
Assuming that all accounting is correctly undertaken and that all cash transactions have been correctly recorded, what is the profit or loss for the first four years if his cash balance of $500 when he began business has now increased to $6,500? (Straight-line depreciation)

5–9   **Replacement of Assets During Inflation** *(20 minutes)*   The Xylier Company began business in 1955 investing $100,000 in fixed assets, with a depreciable life of twenty years. At that time the dollar was worth 100 percent. The company uses straight-line depreciation. In 1975, when the assets had to be replaced, a dollar had 60 percent of the purchasing power of a dollar in 1955. During the twenty years which the company used those assets, it had made $40,000 of profits, of which $20,000 were paid in federal income taxes, and $10,000 in dividends.

Instructions
Compute the number of dollars which the company must use to replace the worn-out machinery with identical new machinery (assuming all other conditions remain the same). Could the company replace its machinery to stay in business without issuing additional stock or borrowing money? Support your answer with computations.

Problems

5–10   **Preparation of the Statement of Changes in Financial Position** *(30 minutes)*   The trial balances of the Tramm Company as of December 31, 19X4 and 19X5 are given below, together with the income statement for the year ended December 31, 19X5:

	Trial Balance	
	Dec. 31, 19X4	Dec. 31, 19X5
Cash	$ 100	$ 600
Inventory	300	900
Land	1,000	1,400
Buildings	2,000	2,000

(continued)

Accumulated depreciation—				
buildings		$ 500		$ 800
Accounts payable		100		1,100
Capital stock		2,000		2,000
Retained earnings		800		1,000
	$3,400	$3,400	$4,900	$4,900

Income Statement
For the Year Ending
Dec. 31, 19X5

Sales		$1,500
Costs and expenses	$1,000	
Depreciation	300	
Total expenses		1,300
Net income		$ 200

Instructions

Prepare a statement of changes in financial position with an accompanying statement of changes in working capital items.

5–11   **Preparation of the Statement of Cash Flow** *(30 minutes)*   Using the same data as given in problem 5–10 above, prepare a statement of cash flow for the year. Include computations showing how the cash received from operations and disbursed for operations is computed.

5–12   **Preparation of Work Sheet and Statement** *(50 minutes)*   The Dormant Company had the following trial balances on December 31, 19X4, and 19X5:

	19X4	19X5
Cash	$ 1,500	$ 4,100
Accounts receivable	12,400	11,600
Inventory	37,500	40,400
Equipment	51,200	55,000
Accumulated depreciation on equipment	(23,800)	(27,000)
Accounts payable	(7,900)	(7,600)
Rent payable	(1,000)	(1,200)
Common stock	(40,000)	(40,000)
Retained earnings	(29,900)	(35,300)

During the year the company realized a profit of $15,400 and paid cash dividends of $10,000.

Instructions

1. Prepare a schedule of changes in working capital items to accompany the statement of changes in financial position.
2. Prepare a work sheet to determine the sources and applications of working capital.
3. Prepare a statement of changes in financial position.

5–13   **Preparation of Work Sheet and Cash Flow Statement** *(40 minutes)*
Using the data given in problem 5–12, prepare a statement of cash
flow. If problem 5–12 has been assigned, the work sheet required
for that problem may also be used in the solution to this problem. If
5–12 has not been assigned, a work sheet is to be prepared in support
of the statement of cash flow. The company's income statement contained the following:

Sales		$81,300
Costs of goods sold		
Operating expenses:		
Salaries	$53,700	
Depreciation	3,200	
Supplies	9,000	
Total operating expenses		65,900
Net income		$15,400

5–14   **Preparation of Work Sheet and Statement** *(60 minutes)*   The
balance sheets of the Karron Wholesale Company appeared as follows on December 31, 19X4, and 19X5:

	December 31:	
	19X4	19X5
Cash	$ 2,000	$ 4,300
Accounts receivable	9,200	8,100
Allowance for uncollectible accounts	(600)	(500)
Inventory	17,050	19,400
Prepaid taxes	750	900
Equipment	14,900	17,000
Accumulated depreciation—equipment	(6,200)	(8,100)
Trucks	9,250	9,250
Accumulated depreciation, trucks	(3,700)	(5,950)
Franchise costs	3,000	2,500
	$45,650	$46,900
Accounts payable	$ 4,500	$ 7,200
Accrued salaries	600	750
Taxes payable	7,000	5,000
Mortgages payable	10,000	7,000
Capital stock	10,000	12,000
Retained earnings	13,550	14,950
	$45,650	$46,900

The income statement for the year reported a profit of $9,000
computed as follows:

Sales		$114,150
Depreciation expense	$ 4,150	
Other costs and expenses	100,500	
Amortization of franchise costs	500	105,150
Net profit		$ 9,000

Dividends of $7,600 were paid during the year. In addition, capital stock of $2,000 was issued on July 17. Changes in the fixed asset accounts resulted from the purchase of fixed assets, and changes in the accumulated depreciation accounts resulted from current depreciation expenses.

Instructions

Prepare a worksheet and formal statement of the changes in financial position for the year ended December 31, 19X5.

5-15   **Preparation of Work Sheet and Statement of Cash Flow** *(50 minutes)*   Using the data given in problem 5–14 above, prepare a statement of cash flow. If problem 5–14 was completed, the worksheet for the statement of changes in financial position will be available for completion of this problem. If problem 5–14 was not completed, prepare a worksheet to accompany your statement of cash flow. Your statement should also be accompanied by computations showing how the cash receipts from operations and the cash disbursed for operations was computed. (Adjust sales by changes in both accounts receivable and the allowance for uncollectible accounts.)

5-16   **Preparation of Work Sheet and Statement** *(60 minutes)*   The Clark Company's comparative balance sheets as of December 31, 19X4, and 19X5 appear below:

	December 31:	
	19X4	19X5
Cash	$ 2,000	$ 1,700
Accounts receivable	12,000	14,000
Notes receivable from customers	6,000	3,000
Allowance for uncollectible accounts	(500)	(900)
Inventory	29,000	31,000
Prepaid rent	1,000	1,200
Land	5,600	7,900
Buildings	31,200	42,500
Accumulated depreciation—buildings	(7,400)	(9,850)
Organization costs	2,000	1,000
	$80,900	$91,550

(continued)

Accounts payable	$ 4,800	$ 5,060
Taxes payable	3,050	5,500
Salaries payable	1,800	2,100
Mortgages payable, 1978	20,000	28,000
Common stock	50,000	50,000
Retained earnings	1,250	890
	$80,900	$91,550

An analysis of the income statement for the year ending December 31, 19X5, indicated a profit of $3,000 computed as follows:

Sales		$175,450
Depreciation expense	$ 2,450	
Other costs and expenses	170,000	172,450
Net income		$ 3,000

Analysis of retained earnings indicated a profit of $3,000, amortization of organization costs of $1,000, and posting of dividends in the amount of $2,360. A new mortgage of $10,000 had been secured on the new building, and a payment of $2,000 had been made on the old mortgage.

Instructions
1. Prepare a work sheet to determine the sources and the applications of working capital funds.
2. Prepare the statement of the sources and applications of working capital funds.

5–17   **Preparation of Work Sheet and Statement of Cash Flow** *(60 minutes)*   Using the data given in problem 5–16, above, prepare a statement of cash flow. If problem 5–16 was completed, the worksheet prepared for that problem may also be used for this problem. If problem 5–16 was not completed, prepare a worksheet to accompany the statement of cash flow. Prepare computations to show the cash received from or disbursed for operations.

5–18   **Flow of Funds and Replacement of Assets** *(20 minutes)*   The Scott Carton Company purchased a building on January 1, 1962, for $100,000. The building is expected to have a twenty-five-year life and no salvage value. Between 1962 and 1974 the company had made a total of $35,000 of profits and had paid $8,000 of this in federal income taxes. A total of $1,000 had been paid in dividends during each year of this period.

At the end of 1975, the company reported a profit of $15,000, the largest profit in its history. The income taxes on this profit were estimated to be $5,000. Several stockholders were disturbed because the company's dividends were not raised, since only the usual $1,000 of dividends were to be paid in the current year.

The purchasing power of a dollar had declined from a value of 100 percent in 1962 to 80 percent of that value in 1975. The unusually high profits during the year 1975 could not be expected to continue into future years, and in fact, the profit history of the company before 1975 was more indicative of future expectations.

Instructions

Write a short report to the stockholders stating why dividends should not be raised during the current year to prevent further investment or borrowing when the building must be replaced. Include computations and amounts in your report.

5–19   **Preparation of Income Statement and Statement of Changes in Financial Position** *(40 minutes)*   The following data are given for the Malibough Company. Dividends of $1,000 were paid during the year. Common stock was issued for cash, and land was bought with cash. A worksheet is not required, unless you need one for your own purposes.

	Balance as of:	
	Dec. 31, 19X4	Dec. 31, 19X5
Cash	$ 1,000	$ 100
Accounts receivable	2,000	4,500
Land	10,000	21,500
Equipment	20,000	20,000
Accumulated depreciation—equipment	8,000 (cr.)	9,000 (cr.)
Accounts payable	3,000 (cr.)	4,000 (cr.)
Common stock	15,000 (cr.)	20,000 (cr.)
Retained earnings	7,000 (cr.)	6,000 (cr.)
Sales—cash		9,600 (cr.)
Sales—credit		15,000 (cr.)
Purchases of merchandise		11,500
Salaries		3,000
Rent		2,000
Depreciation expense		1,000

Instructions

Prepare an income statement and a statement of changes in financial position for the year ending December 31, 19X5.

5–20   **Working Capital and Cash Flow Statements** *(60 minutes)*   The balance sheet and income statement of the Taylor Boat Shop are provided on the next page.

TAYLOR BOAT SHOP
Balance Sheet

	December 31:			
	19X1		19X2	
Cash	$ 6,000		$ 5,000	
Marketable securities	1,500		2,500	
Accounts receivable	15,000		12,500	
Merchandise inventory	25,000		27,500	
Prepaid insurance	500		1,000	
Equipment	30,000		32,000	
Accumulated depreciation on equipment		$ 4,000		$ 7,000
Fixtures	20,000		22,500	
Accumulated depreciation on fixtures		6,000		7,500
Accounts payable		9,000		7,000
Taxes payable		5,000		6,000
Interest payable		3,000		4,000
Bonds payable (due 1980)		12,500		10,500
Common stock		50,000		50,000
Retained earnings		8,500		11,000
	$98,000	$98,000	$103,000	$103,000

TAYLOR BOAT SHOP
Income Statement
For the Year Ended December 31, 19X2

Sales		$100,000
Cost of sales		60,000
Gross profit		40,000
Depreciation expense	$ 4,500	
Other expenses	28,000	
Total		$ 32,500
Net profit		$ 7,500

The company paid dividends of $5,000 during the year and no assets were sold.

Instructions
1. Prepare a statement of changes in financial position with a supporting schedule of changes in working capital accounts.
2. Utilizing the same data, recast the statement so that it reflects cash flow instead of working capital flow.

5-21   **Comparison of Cash Flow and Working Capital Flow** *(60 minutes)*
The management of the Kroner Can Company was disturbed to

learn at the close of business December 31, 19X5, that their cash balance was much lower than at any time previously, although the business had been more profitable than at any time in their history. There were no beginning or ending inventories, and only $600 of dividends were paid during the year.

	Balance sheet as of:	
	Dec. 31, 19X4	Dec. 31, 19X5
Cash	$ 5,000	$ 200
Accounts receivable	4,000	10,000
Notes receivable from customers (60-day)	19,000	27,000
Land	8,000	8,000
Buildings	13,000	20,000
Accumulated depreciation—buildings	(4,000)	(6,000)
	$45,000	$59,200
Accounts payable	$ 5,400	$ 3,200
Common stock	30,000	30,000
Retained earnings	9,600	26,000
	$45,000	$59,200

Income Statement
Year Ending December 31, 19X5

Cash sales	$150,000	
Credit sales	200,000	
Total sales		$350,000
Cost of goods sold		280,000
Gross profit		$ 70,000
Expenses:		
Depreciation	$ 2,000	
Salaries	40,000	
Rent	3,000	
Taxes	2,000	
Advertising	6,000	
Total expenses		53,000
Net income		$ 17,000

Instructions

1. Using these data, analyze the funds flow and prepare a statement of changes in financial position.
2. Prepare a statement of cash flow.
3. Describe why the cash balance has decreased.

5–22 **Preparation of Work Sheet and Statement of Changes in Financial Position** *(60 minutes)* The trial balances of the Royal Metal Shop were as follows on December 31, 19X4, and 19X5:

	19X4	19X5
Cash	$ 5,000	$ 6,000
Accounts receivable	11,000	9,000
Inventory	29,000	38,500
Land	17,000	18,000
Buildings	58,000	65,000
Accumulated depreciation on buildings	(21,000)	(25,000)
Equipment	69,000	71,000
Accumulated depreciation on equipment	(36,000)	(43,000)
Accounts payable	(6,000)	(9,500)
Salaries payable	(2,000)	(1,400)
Mortgages payable, due 1985	(35,000)	(31,000)
Common stock	(55,000)	(62,000)
Retained earnings	(34,000)	(35,600)

(handwritten: (2,000))

During the year the company earned profits of $12,000 and paid dividends of $10,400. One parcel of land which cost $5,000 was sold for $7,000, and the gain was included in the computation of the $12,000 profit. Another parcel of land was acquired for $6,000.

Instructions

1. Prepare a work sheet for determining the data required for a statement of changes in financial position.
2. Prepare the statement of changes in financial position and the accompanying schedule of changes in working capital items.

5–23 **Cash Flow Statement** *(60 minutes)* Using the data given in problem 5–22, prepare a statement of cash flow. If problem 5–22 has been assigned, the work sheet required for that problem may also be used in the solution of this problem. If 5–22 has not been assigned, a work sheet is to be prepared in support of the statement of cash flow. The income statement indicated the following:

Sales		$134,200
Less:		
Cost of goods sold	$66,000	
Salaries	34,000	
Supplies	13,200	
Depreciation	11,000	
Total costs and expenses		124,200
Operating income		$ 10,000
Add gain on sale of land		2,000
		$ 12,000

5-24   **Comparison of Profit and Cash Flow Using Transactions** *(60 minutes)*   Willey Timkins bought a small neighborhood theatre called the Uptown Theatre. During the first year of operations, he completed the following transactions:

a. Invested $1,000 cash and a building valued at $50,000, issuing capital stock to himself.
b. Realized $15,000 in admissions, all in cash.
c. Paid $12,000 for salaries.
d. Purchased supplies for the concession stand for $6,000.
e. Realized $9,000 from concession stand sales.
f. Paid utility bills of $5,000.
g. Recorded the property tax of $1,000 but did not pay it, since the tax was not due until the next year.
h. Bought a new projecting machine for $500.
i. Recorded the concession supplies on hand at the year's end, $500.
j. Recorded depreciation on the building, which had a twenty-year life and no salvage value. (Use straight-line depreciation.)

At the end of the year Timkins saw that his cash balance was $1,500. Since he had only invested $1,000 in cash, he reasoned that he was making a profit.

Instructions
1. Prepare a balance sheet and income statement for the Uptown Theatre.
2. Analyze the change in the cash balance and prepare a statement of cash flow to reflect the sources and applications during the year.

5-25   **Preparation of Cash Flow and Working Capital Flow Statements** *(35 minutes)*   The Tiaband Company's trial balances for the years ended December 31, 19X4, and 19X5 appear below, with data relative to transactions affecting non-working capital accounts:

	December 31	
	19X4	19X5
Cash	$ 40,000	$ 14,000
Accounts receivable	7,000	10,000
Notes receivable	6,000	8,000
Inventory	16,000	22,000
Land	50,000	50,000
Buildings	50,000	90,000
Equipment	8,000	5,000
	$177,000	$199,000

(continued)

Accounts payable	$ 5,000	$ 6,000
Notes payable	35,000	4,000
Accrued wages and salaries	1,800	2,000
Accrued taxes	4,800	5,000
Accumulated depreciation—buildings	10,000	12,000
Accumulated depreciation—equipment	2,000	2,250
Bonds payable, due 1980	–0–	40,000
Capital stock	80,000	100,000
Retained earnings	38,400	27,750
	$177,000	$199,000

Net income for the year was $9,350. Equipment which cost $3,000, and against which accumulated depreciation of $750 had been provided, was sold for $1,600. The resulting loss of $650 appeared on the income statement. A $20,000 stock dividend was issued.

Instructions
Prepare a statement of changes in financial position with an accompanying schedule of changes in working capital accounts.

5–26   **Preparation of Cash Flow and Working Capital Flow Statements**
The balance sheets of the Pillan Grain Company for 19X4 and 19X5 appear below, along with the income statement for 19X5.

THE PILLAN GRAIN COMPANY
Balance Sheet
December 31

	19X4	19X5
ASSETS		
Current Assets		
Cash	$ 85,000	$ 65,000
Accounts receivable	71,000	82,000
Grain inventory	360,000	375,000
Total current assets	$516,000	$522,000
Fixed Assets		
Equipment	$120,000	$130,000
Less: accumulated depreciation	53,000	65,000
Net	$ 67,000	$ 65,000
Grain elevator	$290,000	$290,000
Less: accumulated depreciation	202,000	210,000
Net	$ 88,000	$ 80,000
Total fixed assets	$155,000	$145,000
Total assets	$671,000	$667,000

(continued)

LIABILITIES AND CAPITAL

Current Liabilities

Accounts payable	$ 23,000		$ 13,000	
Federal income taxes payable	21,000		20,000	
Total current liabilities		$ 44,000		$ 33,000

Long-term Liabilities

Five-year installment note payable		75,000		60,000
Total liabilities		$119,000		$ 93,000

Capital

Capital stock (10,000 shares)	$400,000		$400,000	
Retained earnings	152,000		174,000	
Total capital		$552,000		$574,000
Total liabilities and capital		$671,000		$667,000

THE PILLAN GRAIN COMPANY
Income Statement
For the Year Ending December 31, 19X5

Revenue from sales		$530,000
Cost of goods sold		260,000
Gross profit		$270,000
Expenses and costs:		
Salaries	$140,000	
Advertising	6,000	
Interest on notes	2,500	
Depreciation—equipment	12,000	
Depreciation—building	8,000	
Taxes	20,000	
Supplies	9,500	
Total expenses		198,000
Net income for the year		$ 72,000

Instructions

1. Prepare a work sheet separating working capital and non-working capital changes.
2. Prepare a statement of changes in financial position for 19X5. (The company paid $50,000 in dividends during the year.)
3. Prepare a statement of cash flow for 19X5.

PART 2

Cost Accumulation and Cost Analysis

chapter 6

Cost Behavior and Break-Even Analysis

Learning Objectives

This chapter begins Part 2, which emphasizes the problems of cost accumulation and analysis. The focus at this point shifts from overall enterprise measurement to the analysis of smaller segments of the company. The behavior pattern of individual expenses is emphasized in this chapter, as well as their summation into an expense structure for the company. You should acquire the following from your study of this chapter.

1. A knowledge of expense behavior and the nature of fixed, variable, and semivariable expenses.
2. An understanding of the methods which are utilized to determine the behavior of an expense.
3. A knowledge of how the overall expense structure of the company is determined through an accumulation of individual expense formulas.
4. An understanding of break-even analysis and its underlying assumptions.
5. An understanding of the concept of contribution margin.

Cost-Volume-Profit Relationships

The management of every business is interested in increasing the company's volume of sales, but increased sales will almost invariably result in increased expenses. Therefore, changes in expenses must be considered in evaluating the effects of an increased volume of sales.

The analysis of variations in sales volume, the resulting change in expenses, and their combined effect on net income is called a *cost-volume-profit analysis*. Such analyses are vital to management in the planning and control process. To illustrate, suppose that a company has been selling for $1.00 each a total of 1,000 units per month of a product that cost $.93 per unit to produce. The company's condensed monthly income statement appears as follows:

Sales (1,000 @ $1.00)	$1,000
Costs and expenses (1,000 @ $.93)	930
Net income	$ 70

Suppose that the company's management is considering a reduction in the sales price from $1.00 to $.95 per unit, with the expectation that sales will increase to 2,000 units per month. An evaluation of the proposed price reduction must include the effects which the increase in sales volume will have on expenses. Even though the number of units sold will be increased, profits will be reduced by lowering the sales price unless there are offsetting cost savings. The income statement after the price change is shown below. Note that the net income has decreased as a result of the price change, even though the number of units sold doubled.

Sales (2,000 @ $.95)	$1,900
Costs and expenses (2,000 @ $.93)	1,860
Net income	$ 40

However, the reduction in sales price and the corresponding increase in volume of sales may produce increased profits if per unit costs and expenses will be reduced as a result of the increased volume. If the efficiencies due to large volume cause expenses to drop to $.90 per unit, the net income will increase, as illustrated in the following condensed income statement:

Sales (2,000 @ $.95)	$1,900
Costs and expenses (2,000 @ $.90)	1,800
Net income	$ 100

In almost every case, any change in the volume of sales activity will have a direct bearing on costs and profits. This chapter is devoted to an analysis of the relationship between changes in volume, changes in cost, and the corresponding effect on net profits.

Fixed, Variable, and Semivariable Expenses

An analysis of the relationship of expenses to volume change begins with a determination of the behavior of each separate expense. In order to measure accurately the effect of volume changes, fixed expenses must be separated from those which are variable. A *fixed expense* is one which remains constant in total dollar amount at all levels of volume. A *variable expense* is one which fluctuates in total amount with changes in volume, shifting upward or downward as volume increases or decreases. Many expense items are neither completely fixed nor completely variable and are called *semivariable expenses*.

Fixed expenses   Fixed expenses are related to the passage of time and not to the number of units produced or sold; thus they are fixed in amount each accounting period and are not affected by volume. Rent expense will usually be fixed in amount, regardless of volume; depreciation expense, if computed on a straight-line basis, is equal in amount each period and is considered fixed. Property taxes, officers' salaries, and insurance are also examples of fixed expenses.

There are few fixed expenses which could not be changed by management over a sufficiently long period of time. Rent expense could be changed by buying a building instead of renting; insurance could be altered by reducing the insurance coverage or acquiring a different type of coverage; and even depreciation can be changed by using a different method of computation. No hard and fast rule exists for identifying fixed expenses, and judgment must be exercised when fixed and variable expenses are being analyzed. A useful rule to follow is to consider as fixed all those which would not change appreciably during the year, regardless of volume, *assuming management continues all present operating policies*.

A few expenses are fixed only because of management policy. Advertising and research costs, for example, can be any amount management wishes, but since they are usually programmed for a year in advance, they would be considered fixed for purposes of analysis. Other expenses, such as interest and depreciation, are the result of actions taken in the past when long-term debt was assumed or assets were acquired. These are sometimes called "committed" fixed costs, because the company has committed itself to incur them in coming periods. In any event, both programmed and committed fixed costs will remain constant during the year assuming management does not alter the nature of the company's operations or change its operating policies.

Variable expenses   Variable expenses are those which will fluctuate in close relation to the level of sales activity. A variable expense increases in total amount as volume increases and decreases in total amount as volume declines. A retail store's supplies expense for such items as wrapping paper, twine, and shopping bags will increase as the volume of sales increases and will decline to approximately zero if sales cease entirely. Sales commissions and the cost of the merchandise sold are other examples of completely variable expenses.

Semivariable expenses   A semivariable expense is one that moves with volume, but not in direct proportion to the volume change. These expenses are also known as semifixed, for they include both fixed and variable elements. The salary of a sales clerk is an example of a semivariable expense. If volume increases, additional sales clerks are hired, but the number employed will probably not vary in direct proportion to the change in volume. If the sales volume declines, the number of sales clerks will be reduced, but a minimum number must be retained unless operations cease entirely. Thus, a part of the salaries expense is fixed and part varies with volume. Heat, light, fuel, telephone and telegraph, office salaries, and delivery expense are other examples of semivariable expenses.

Analysis of Semivariable Expenses

The company's overall expense structure cannot be determined until each expense is categorized as either fixed or variable, and each semivariable expense is broken down into its fixed and variable elements. Only after the semivariable items are separated into their fixed and variable portions can the company's total fixed and total variable expenses be ascertained.

Following is an illustration of the way in which semivariable expenses such as salaries expense and telephone and telegraph expense would be stated in terms of their fixed and variable components:

Sales clerks' salaries:	Fixed	$3,000
	Variable	10% of sales
Telephone and telegraph:	Fixed	$500
	Variable	3% of sales

The sales salary expense is fixed to the extent of $3,000 and, in addition, varies at 10 percent of sales. This means that even at a sales level of zero there would still be sales salaries of $3,000, the fixed amount. This is the *stand-by* concept of fixed costs. The $3,000 is the amount which would be incurred just to maintain a readiness to do business. The variable portion of the expense then indicates the additional amount necessary to handle a particular sales volume. If sales were $100,000, for example, the company's management would expect the total sales salary expense to be $3,000 plus 10 percent of $100,000, or $13,000. Should sales increase to a level of $200,000 during the next year, the company's management would then project sales salaries expense to be $23,000, calculated as $3,000 fixed, plus 10 percent of $200,000, a total of $23,000.

The fixed and variable formula for telephone and telegraph expense in the example is $500 fixed, plus a variable portion of 3 percent of sales. This expense at a $100,000 level of sales would be calculated to be $3,500 (3 percent of $100,000 plus $500 fixed). At a sales level of $200,000, the telephone and telegraph expense would be projected to be $6,500 (3 percent of $200,000 plus $500 fixed).

The calculation of the expense formula for a particular expense can be easily accomplished with hand calculations, although very sophisticated computerized methods are sometimes used. Only three hand methods are presented in this text: (1) the scattergraph method, (2) the high-low points method, and (3) the least squares method.

The scattergraph method   The scattergraph method of breaking a semivariable expense into its fixed and variable elements is begun by plotting on a graph the monthly amount of the expense which has been incurred in the past. The vertical scale of the graph is the amount of the expense, and the horizontal scale is the volume index, which may be sales, units of production, or labor hours. Ten or twelve points are needed to establish a curve in most cases. A "freehand" line is drawn through these points on the graph so that as many points are above the line as below and so that it represents the general slope of the expense-volume relationship.

Application of the scattergraph method is illustrated in Exhibits 6–1 and 6–2. A twelve-month history of the utilities expenses incurred by a company is used in this example; the data are shown in tabular form in Exhibit 6–1, and the graph is prepared by plotting these points as shown in Exhibit 6–2. Sales is the volume index used in this example.

EXHIBIT 6–1

Twelve-Month History of Utilities Expense

Month	Monthly Utilities Expense	Monthly Volume of Sales
January	$ 970	$15,000
February	780	12,000
March	900	14,000
April	810	12,000
May	720	10,000
June	730	11,000
July	990	14,000
August	870	13,000
September	820	15,000
October	1,020	16,000
November	1,030	17,000
December	1,170	20,000

The fixed element of the utilities expense is the amount which would be incurred at zero sales volume, which in Exhibit 6–2 is $200. This is the point on the vertical axis where the free-hand trend line meets the vertical scale. The variable portion then can be determined from the free-hand line by reading the sales volume and the amount of expense from any two selected points on

EXHIBIT 6–2

Scattergraph Method

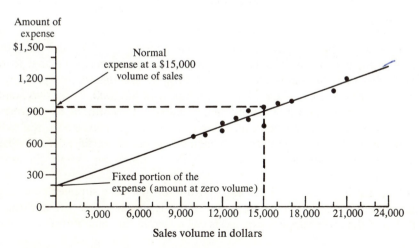

Sales volume in dollars

the line. The two points selected in this illustration are zero sales volume and a $15,000 sales volume, although other points could have been selected just as easily. Reading the graph indicates the expense would be $200 when sales are zero and $950 when sales reach $15,000. This determination is shown on Exhibit 6–2 with dashed lines. The variable element of the expense is then found by relating the change in expense and the change in the volume between the two selected points, as follows:

When sales are $15,000, the utilities expense is $950
When sales are zero,   the utilities expense is   200
Difference $15,000   Difference $750

The difference in the expense between the two selected points ($750) is divided by the difference in sales between these same points ($15,000). The resulting calculation would be: $750 ÷ $15,000 = 5%. Therefore, the variable element of the expense is 5 percent of sales. It is thus obvious that utilities is a semivariable expense in this company and that it would be stated as follows:

Fixed element $200
Variable element   5% of sales

When the utilities expense is stated with the fixed and variable elements separated, it is relatively easy to calculate the expected amount of utilities expense which the company should incur at any level of sales. For example, the expected utilities expense at $20,000 of sales would be $200 plus 5 percent of $20,000 ($200 + $1,000) or $1,200. This type of calculation is frequently used in the preparation of budgets because the amount of expense can be calculated for any level of sales.

The high-low points method   The first step in using the high-low points method of breaking down an expense into its fixed and variable components is to estimate as accurately as possible the amount of the expense at a *representative low level* of sales and the amount of the expense at a *representative high level* of sales. This method is more accurate than the use of a free-hand trend line drawn from a scattergraph, provided the two points are carefully selected.

To illustrate this method, suppose that the two points selected for analysis of the office supplies expense are sales volumes of $10,000 and $30,000. Suppose further that the normal office supplies expense was estimated to be $500 when sales were at the low point of $10,000 and this same expense was estimated to be $1,000 when sales were at a peak of $30,000. These two points are plotted on a graph and a trend line is drawn between them, as illustrated in Exhibit 6–3. From this point on, there is no difference between the high-low points method and the scattergraph method described earlier; for the fixed and variable portions of the expense would be found by exactly the same procedures.

Note that in Exhibit 6–3 the fixed portion of the office supplies expense is the amount that would be incurred at a zero sales level, or $250. The variable portion of the office supplies expense is calculated in the same way as was used

EXHIBIT 6–3

High-Low Points Method

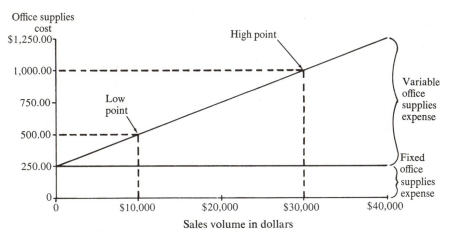

Sales volume in dollars

earlier when the scattergraph method was illustrated, except that the two points needed for the calculation are already available. The sales volume varies $20,000 (from $10,000 to $30,000), and the expense varies $500 (from $500 to $1,000). Thus, the variation in the office supplies expense is 2½ percent of the variation in sales volume ($500 ÷ $20,000). The total cost behavior of the office supplies expense is then stated as:

> Fixed $250
> Variable 2½% of sales

When the high-low points method is used, the fixed and variable elements of an expense can be computed without the use of a graph. The steps in this computation are described below. Note that the variable portion is determined first, as described previously, and then the fixed portion can be calculated.

1. Subtract the smaller expense figure from the larger. The difference is the total expense variation between the two points:

Total expense at high point	$1,000.00	
Total expense at low point	500.00	
Total expense change	$ 500.00	

2. Subtract the lower sales volume figure from the higher. The difference is the sales variation between the two points:

High sales volume	$30,000	
Low sales volume	10,000	
Sales volume change	$20,000	

3. Divide the total expense variation ($500) as figured in Step 1, by the sales variation ($20,000) as figured in Step 2, to calculate the variable portion of the expense behavior formula.

$$\$500 \div \$20,000 = 2\frac{1}{2}\% \text{ of sales}$$

4. Select either the high or the low point, and multiply the variable portion of the formula (2½ percent) by the sales volume at that level. The result of this multiplication is the portion of the expense incurred at that level which would be considered variable. Subtract this variable portion from the total expense at that volume, and the remainder will be the fixed portion.

At a sales level of $10,000:   Variable portion = 2½ % × $10,000 = $250
                                 Fixed portion = $500 total − $250 = 250
At a sales level of $30,000:   Variable portion = 2½ % × $30,000 = $750
                                 Fixed portion = $1,000 total − $750 = $250

Since volume does not affect the fixed portion of an expense, the $250 fixed portion will be the same at a sales volume of $10,000, $30,000, or any other level. Note that the expense formula of 2½ % variable plus $250 fixed is applicable at all levels once it has been calculated. Actually, the $250 fixed portion of the expense formula can be calculated using either volume and need not be calculated at both.

   The least squares method   A statistical method called the least squares method may be used to compute the fixed and variable elements of a company's expenses. This method utilizes data similar to that needed when a scattergraph is plotted, but the technique necessitates a number of calculations to compute the trend line. The technique is based upon the formula for a straight line, $Y = a + bX$, wherein Y is the amount of the expense, a is the fixed cost, b is the variable portion, and X is the volume of sales. Thus the formula $Y = a + bX$ is equal to the statement below:

   The total amount of expense (Y) is equal to the fixed portion (a)
   plus the rate of variation (b) multiplied by the volume of sales (X).

To illustrate this method of expressing the expense formula, assume that the salaries expense is $1,000 fixed and the balance variable at 5 percent of sales. The least squares formula would compute the expense at a sales volume of $50,000 as follows:

$$Y = a + bX$$
$$Y = \$1,000 + (.05)(\$50,000)$$
$$Y = \$1,000 + \$2,500$$
$$Y = \$3,500$$

Thus, a salaries expense of $3,500 would be expected at a $50,000 sales volume. The expected salaries expense can be computed easily at any sales volume if the a and b portions of the formula are known.

   The least squares calculation produces the a and b elements of the formula $Y = a + bX$ by locating a unique line which best fits a series of points similar to those illustrated for the scattergraph technique. Unlike the scattergraph method in which the line is determined by drawing a freehand trend line, the least squares calculation is mathematical and, consequently, much more accurate. The calculations, because of their complexity, are usually performed on a computer, and the adaptability of the computer for this purpose should be recognized. The past history of an expense, similar to the data used to plot a scattergraph, can be fed into the computer, and the calculations are completed in a few seconds.

The least squares calculation is based upon two formulas which contain summations of all the points included in the calculations, including the squares of the X values and the product of the X and Y values. The two formulas are:

| *Equation (1)* | $\Sigma Y = Na + b\Sigma X$ |
| *Equation (2)* | $\Sigma XY = \Sigma Xa + b\Sigma X^2$ |

When these two equations are solved simultaneously, the values of a and b are determined and the single unique line of best fit is known.

The calculations for a company's travel expenses would be undertaken as follows, utilizing only five data points to keep the example from becoming too complex:

Sales (X)	Travel Expense (Y)	X²	XY
$ 5,000	$100	$ 25,000,000	$ 500,000
7,000	120	49,000,000	840,000
6,000	110	36,000,000	660,000
10,000	150	100,000,000	1,500,000
9,000	140	81,000,000	1,260,000
$\Sigma X = \$37,000$	$\Sigma Y = \$620$	$\Sigma X^2 = \$291,000,000$	$\Sigma XY = \$4,760,000$

| *Equation (1)* | $\Sigma Y = Na + \Sigma Xb$ |
| | $620 = 5a + 37{,}000b$ |

| *Equation (2)* | $\Sigma XY = \Sigma Xa + \Sigma X^2 b$ |
| | $4{,}760{,}000 = 37{,}000a + 291{,}000{,}000b$ |

When these two equations are solved simultaneously, the values of a and b can be found. The value of b can be found by multiplying the first equation by 7,400, which equates the a values and makes subtraction and elimination of the a values possible.

Equation (1)
(multiplied by 7400) $\$4{,}588{,}000 =$ $\$37{,}000a +$ $\$273{,}800{,}000b$
Equation (2)
(subtracted) $(-)4{,}760{,}000 =$ $(-)37{,}000a +$ $(-)291{,}000{,}000b$
    $\overline{\$-172{,}000 =}$ $\overline{\quad 0 \quad} +$ $\overline{-17{,}200{,}000b}$
    $b = .01$ or 1%

Substituting the 1 percent value for b in either equation produces a value of $50 for a. The line of best fit would thus be of the form $Y = \$50 + .01X$.

Determining the Company's
Overall Expense Structure

The overall expense structure of the company is determined by accumulating the total of all fixed expenses and adding the variable expenses, so that their total is stated in terms of a single percentage of sales. Each expense appearing on the company's income statement is analyzed to determine whether it is completely fixed, completely variable, or semivariable. Each semivariable must be analyzed into its fixed and variable components, using one of the methods just described. The actual calculations are not shown in Exhibit 6–4,

EXHIBIT 6–4

Determination of a Company's Cost Structure

Income Statement			Fixed	Variable (As a % of Sales)
Sales		$100,000		
Cost of merchandise sold		60,000	—	60% of sales
		$ 40,000		
Operating expenses:				
⌐ Depreciation	$ 3,000		$ 3,000	—
√ Salesmen's commissions	1,000		—	1% of sales
⌐ Rent	5,000		5,000	—
∪ Telephone and telegraph	3,500		500	3% of sales
√ Sales salaries	13,000		3,000	10% of sales
√ Delivery expense	1,700		700	1% of sales
√ Insurance	600		600	—
√ Heat and light	4,000		2,000	2% of sales
Total operating expenses		31,800		
Net income		$ 8,200		
		Total fixed costs	$14,800	
		Variable costs		77% of sales

but the process of adding the fixed and the variable expenses to determine the overall company expense structure is illustrated. Although assumed data are used in the illustration, it is obvious that the cost of merchandise sold and salesmen's commissions are completely variable, while depreciation, rent and insurance are completely fixed. All other expenses are semivariable.

The analysis in Exhibit 6–4 indicates that the company's total fixed expenses are $14,800, and the variable expenses will total 77 percent of sales. The effects of changes in sales volume, expenses, and net income can now be determined. If, for example, sales increased by $5,000, variable expenses would increase by 77 percent of $5,000, or $3,850. Since fixed expenses will not change, the company's net profit would increase by $1,150 as a result of the increase in sales.

Increase in sales		$5,000
Less: Increase in variable expenses	$3,850	
Increase in fixed expenses	—0—	3,850
Increase in profit		$1,150

Break-Even Analysis

A company will "break even" when sales revenue exactly equals expenses. An estimate of the volume of sales necessary to break even is useful in managerial planning. A knowledge of where the break-even point lies is needed when establishing the company's pricing policy, projecting the effects of changes in operations, and ascertaining the increase in sales necessary to justify plant expansion or the incurrence of additional fixed expenses.

Break-even analysis must be based upon the company's total expense structure, since profits are realized only when sales exceed both the variable and fixed expenses and losses result when the total of both variable and fixed expenses exceeds sales. The computation of the break-even volume of sales is thus based upon the following equation:

$$\text{Sales} - \text{Variable expenses} - \text{Fixed expenses} = \text{Zero profit}$$

If a company has $10,000 of fixed expenses, and if variable expenses equal 40 percent of sales, the break-even point will be as follows:

$$\text{Sales} - 40\% \text{ of sales} - \$10,000 = 0$$
$$60\% \text{ sales} - 10,000 = 0$$
$$60\% \text{ sales} = 10,000$$
$$\text{Sales} = \frac{10,000}{.60}$$
$$\text{Sales} = \$16,667$$

The company's break-even point lies at a sales volume of $16,667, which can be proved by preparing an income statement using $16,667 of sales, variable expenses equal to 40 percent of sales, and fixed expenses of $10,000.

Sales		$16,667
Variable expenses (40% of $16,667)	$ 6,667	
Fixed expenses	10,000	
Total expenses		16,667
Profit or loss		—0—

Thus, sales in excess of $16,667 will produce a profit; but if sales fall below $16,667, the company can expect to incur losses.

The Break-Even Chart

A break-even chart is frequently prepared to illustrate in graphic form the company's break-even point and the relationship of the company's costs, volume, and profit. The break-even chart may be constructed by stating volume in terms of dollars of sales or in terms of the number of units sold. Volume in terms of units is illustrated in the following example.

If a company sells its units for $3.00 each, sales would be $3,000 at a volume of 1,000 units, $15,000 at a sales volume of 5,000 units, or $30,000 at a sales volume of 10,000 units. The sales line is thus a straight line extending from zero upward to the right, as shown in Exhibit 6–5.

The company's fixed and variable expenses are entered on the chart after the sales line is drawn. Assume, for illustrative purposes, that the company's

EXHIBIT 6–5

Sales Line on a Break-Even Chart

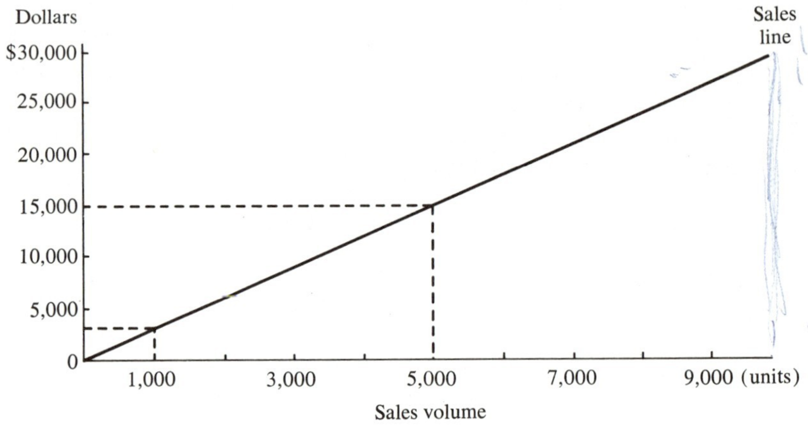

expense structure contains fixed expenses of $7,000 and variable expenses equal to 50 percent of sales. From these data, the total expenses at any sales volume can be estimated. The computation of total expenses at a level of 1,000 units and 10,000 units would go as follows:

Expenses at a volume of   1,000 units = $ 7,000 fixed + variable costs of
50% of sales
= $ 7,000 + (50% of $3,000)
= $ 7,000 + $1,500
= $ 8,500

Expenses at a volume of 10,000 units = $ 7,000 fixed + variable costs of
50% of sales
= $ 7,000 + (50% of $30,000)
= $ 7,000 + $15,000
= $22,000

Although expenses may be computed at any level of sales volume, only two points are necessary to plot the total expense line on the break-even chart. Using the two expense points computed above, and the sales line as illustrated in the Exhibit 6–5, the volume at which total expenses and total sales are exactly equal becomes evident.

EXHIBIT 6–6

Break-Even Chart

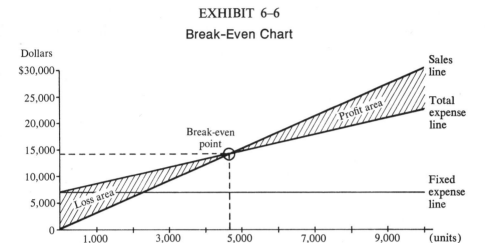

The break-even point is located on the chart where the sales line and total expense line coincide. Losses occur when sales are less than this amount, and profits when sales are greater than the break-even point. The break-even point in Exhibit 6–6 is at a sales volume of $14,000 and can be computed mathematically using the formula given previously:

$$\text{Sales volume} - \text{variable expenses} - \text{fixed expenses} = \text{zero profit}$$
$$\text{Sales} - 50\% \text{ of sales} - \$7,000 = 0$$
$$\text{Sales} - .5 \text{ sales} - \$7,000 = 0$$
$$.5 \text{ Sales} = \$\ 7,000$$
$$\text{Sales} = \frac{\$\ 7,000}{.5}$$
$$\text{Sales} = \$14,000$$

The sales volume needed to break even can be converted to units by dividing the $14,000 amount by the $3 per unit price. In this case, the break even in terms of units would be 4,667 ($14,000 ÷ 3).

The break-even chart frequently includes a separate line to indicate the company's fixed expenses. The fixed expense line is shown separately in the chart in order to emphasize the fixed expenses which will be incurred at all levels of operations, and also to indicate the relationship between fixed expenses, variable expenses, and various volume levels. Exhibit 6–6 shows a break-even chart with fixed and variable expenses indicated separately.

The angle between the total expense line and the sales line indicates the relative profit or loss potential as sales volume increases or decreases from the break-even point. If the angle is wide, there is a strong profit or loss potential. If the angle is narrow, there is a relatively small potential change in profit re-resulting from changes in sales volume. Note the difference in profit potential of the two skeletal break-even diagrams below, the first with predominantly fixed expenses and the other with predominantly variable expenses. Note that increased sales above the break-even point in the first diagram will give greater profits than the same increase would in the second diagram.

EXHIBIT 6–7

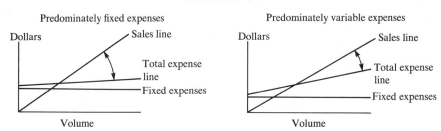

Note that where the angle is wide, the majority of the company's expenses are fixed, and variable expenses are a small proportion of the total. Where the angle is narrow, the majority of the company's expenses are variable, and increases in sales are offset in large part by increases in variable expenses.

The Margin of Safety

A company's margin of safety may be defined as the excess of its present sales volume above the break-even point. The margin of safety is computed as follows: actual sales − break-even sales = margin of safety. If a company has break-even sales of $40,000 and is presently operating at $60,000 sales volume, its margin of safety is as follows:

$$\text{Margin of safety: } \$60,000 - \$40,000 = \$20,000 \text{ of sales}$$

Sales could decrease $20,000, or 33⅓%

$$\frac{\$20,000 \text{ margin of safety}}{\$60,000 \text{ present sales}} = 33\tfrac{1}{3}\%$$

before the company will begin to incur losses.

Underlying Assumptions

Break-even analysis assumes that sales prices will remain constant. This assumption must be made if sales are shown on the break-even chart as a straight line. Very few companies sell only a single product, and price changes on one or more products are not uncommon. Thus, while the assumption of an unchanging price on every item which the company sells is not entirely valid, it does not destroy the usefulness of the break-even chart as a close approximation of the company's cost-volume-profit relationship. A new break-even analysis is usually not required unless major price changes occur.

The analysis of break-even points is also based on the assumption that the "sales-mix" will remain constant. The term *sales-mix* may be defined as that proportion of the total sales dollars produced by each of the company's several products. Many companies have several products with a high profit margin and several with a low profit margin. If the sales of high profit units increase or decrease, the break-even point will shift, even though total dollar sales remain constant. Changes in sales-mix are usually not material, but a new analysis may be needed if major shifts do occur.

A break-even analysis can be no more accurate than the analysis of the company's fixed and variable expenses. If only rough approximations are made of the fixed and variable elements of a semivariable expense, the break-even analysis should be considered in light of the accuracy of the computations that enter into the analysis. Many analysts speak of a break-even "area" instead of a point.

The primary use of the break-even analysis is to evaluate the effect of proposed changes in the company's operations. Management is constantly faced with the search for answers to such questions as, "What will happen if the price of our product is dropped by 10 percent and, as a result, volume increases by 12 percent?" "What will be our profit position if we don't satisfy the demands of the X Company, our biggest customer, and sales drop by 8 percent?" "What will be the effect of automating our plant, with a resulting increase in depreciation and taxes but a decrease in factory salaries?" Answers to such questions depend upon a knowledge of the company's expense structure, its present break-even point, and the margin of safety. Assumptions such as those concerning sales mix or the lack of absolute accuracy in the analysis of semivariable costs thus do not destroy the usefulness of this type of analysis.

Fixed and Variable Expenses in Management Reports

Statements are sometimes prepared for management's use with the fixed and variable operating expenses separated. When statements are prepared in this manner, the variable and semivariable expenses are subtracted from gross profit first. The resulting figure represents the overall contribution toward covering the company's fixed operating expenses. This type of statement is illustrated in Exhibit 6–8. Note that the contribution margin is set out clearly in the statement in order to measure the company's overall ability to cover its fixed expenses during this particular accounting period. The net income is the same as would be reported in a conventional income statement, but more insight into the company's operations can be gained from a separation of fixed and variable operating expenses.

Setting apart the fixed and variable operating expenses in the income statement has many advantages. This type of income statement reflects the company's fixed operating expenses and how much margin must be realized after

EXHIBIT 6–8

PICTAC COMPANY
Contribution Margin Income Statement
Year Ended December 31, 19X1

Sales		$361,000
Cost of goods sold		164,000
Gross margin		$197,000
Variable and semivariable operating expenses:		
Supplies	$10,000	
Clerical salaries	80,000	
Telephone and telegraph	6,000	
Salesmen's commission	13,000	
Bad debt losses	4,000	
Travel and entertainment	6,000	
Payroll taxes	2,000	
Total variable and semivariable expenses		121,000
CONTRIBUTION MARGIN TOWARD FIXED EXPENSES		$ 76,000
Fixed operating expenses		
Depreciation	$14,000	
Taxes	2,000	
Insurance	3,000	
Officers' salaries	60,000	
Total fixed expenses		79,000
Net loss		($ 3,000)

variable and semivariable operating expenses are covered in order for the company to be profitable. Showing the contribution margin in the statement provided the same information about the company's operations as that to be found in a break-even analysis. The gross margin, fixed expenses, and variable and semivariable expenses are reflected in the statement, and the company's margin of safety and the degree to which it has covered its fixed expenses can be ascertained.

Analysis of
Contribution Margin

Statements showing the contribution margin are useful in measuring the company's overall profit position. Suppose, for example, that the following condensed income statement is being analyzed:

Sales 10,000 units @ $5	$50,000
Variable and semivariable expenses	30,000
Contribution margin toward fixed expenses	$20,000
Fixed expenses	25,000
Net loss	($ 5,000)

Separating the fixed and variable expenses provides data for computing the additional contribution margin needed to cover fixed expenses and the increase in sales necessary to reach the break-even point. Since the contribution margin must be $5,000 greater to break even, sales must be increased by $12,500 to reach the break-even point. The $12,500 increase is computed as follows:

Additional contribution margin needed		$ 5,000
Contribution margin as percent of sales ($20,000 ÷ 50,000) =		40%
Sales necessary to provide the additional contribution margin	($5,000 ÷ 40%) =	$12,500

The additional $12,500 of sales represents 25 percent of the present volume, a significant increase which may be difficult to achieve. The contribution margin approach has thus provided information for a measurement of the company's current and future profit potential.

Further analysis can be undertaken to determine the amount of additional sales needed for the company to earn a fair rate of return on invested capital. If a $5,000 profit is considered a fair return, the contribution margin must be increased by $10,000 to convert the present $5,000 loss to a $5,000 profit. Sales must therefore be increased by $25,000 to realize the $10,000 additional contribution margin ($10,000 ÷ 40% = $25,000).

Summary

A knowledge of the relationships among expenses, volume, and profit is essential to sound managerial decisions which involve expense data. The reaction of a company's expenses to volume changes must be considered in such important decisions as establishing prices for the company's products, determining the effect on profitability of new capital acquisitions, or selecting the most profitable products to emphasize in an advertising campaign.

Most expenses will change when volume changes, although a few are completely fixed in nature. Those that do change with volume are either completely variable or are semivariable in nature. The semivariable expenses must be analyzed in order to separate their fixed and variable elements, and several methods are available for this purpose. Some, such as the least squares method, are relatively sophisticated, while others, such as the scattergraph method, are fairly simple. The nature of the data employed in the analysis, however, is not absolutely accurate, and thus there are limitations in the use of the expense behavior data. The results of expense behavior analyses are sufficiently accurate for long-range and strategic planning and for establishing budgetary amounts for future periods.

Summation of a company's fixed and variable expenses provides amounts which may be used for broad managerial decisions and for calculation of break-even points. It is more realistic to speak of a break-even "area" than a "point," for the assumptions which are required preclude exactness. Moreover, management is able to control expenses sufficiently to produce a shift in the total fixed and variable expenses as the break-even point is approached. Even with these limitations, however, the break-even analysis is useful for long-range planning and for estimating the effects of managerial actions. The arrangement of the income statement so that the variable expenses are segregated from fixed expenses, with the resulting contribution margin shown, is very helpful to management. This type of income statement permits the calculation of break-even points directly from the statements and also permits a direct calculation of the margin of safety and the amount of sales necessary to increase profits by a given amount.

New Terms

Break-even chart   A graphic representation of sales, fixed costs, and variable costs which shows the break-even point.

Break-even point   The point located on the revenue line of a graph where volume of sales is exactly equal to total costs.

Cost behavior   The reaction of a cost to changes in volume.

Fixed cost   A cost related to the passage of time which remains constant when volume changes.

High-low points method   A method of ascertaining the behavior of an expense utilizing one high point and one low point.

Least squares method   A method of ascertaining the behavior of an expense based upon the squares of the distance of each point from the line of best fit.

Margin of safety   The excess of actual sales over the break-even point.

Scattergraph   A graph of expense amounts incurred during several periods, prepared to ascertain the behavior of that expense in relationship to changes in volume.

Semivariable cost   A cost which varies somewhat with volume changes, but not in complete proportion.

Variable cost   A cost which increases and decreases proportionately as volume goes up or down.

Questions

1. What is meant by a cost-volume-profit analysis? Why is an analysis of one of these factors dependent upon the reaction of the other two?

2. The Kalo-Willby Company sells 4,000 units per month at a price of $2 per unit, with unit costs of $1.80. The company is contemplating an increase in the sales price to $2.50, which will reduce the number sold to 3,000 units and increase the unit cost to $2.00. Would you recommend this change?

3. Define and state the distinguishing characteristics of a variable expense, a fixed expense, and a semivariable expense.

4. How is a semivariable expense stated when the fixed and variable portions have been analyzed and segregated? Why is there a fixed element and a variable element in a semivariable expense?

5. What is a scattergraph? How is it used to determine the fixed and variable portions of a semivariable expense?

6. The accountant who is analyzing the expenses of the Bourough Company is preparing a scattergraph, using only three points. Would you have confidence in the results of such an analysis?

7. Describe the high-low method of computing the fixed and variable portion of a semivariable expense. How are the high and the low points determined?

8. The office salaries of a company are as follows: High point—sales of $100,000, salaries of $2,000; Low point—sales of $20,000, salaries of $1,000. What is the variable portion of the expense as a percent of sales? What is the fixed portion of the expense?

9. How is the overall cost structure of the company determined?

10. What is a break-even chart? Of what value is it?

11. The ABC Company has fixed expenses of $20,000 and variable expense equal to 80 percent of sales. What is its break-even point in sales volume?

12. What is the margin of safety? Of what value is this figure?

13. The break-even analysis is not absolutely accurate. What factors tend to make it a close approximation instead of an absolutely accurate analysis?

14. What is a "contribution margin income statement"? How does it differ from a conventional income statement?

15. If a company is planning to use income statements that show the contribution margin, is it necessary to record expenses differently from the way in which they would be recorded for a conventional income statement? Explain.

16. Explain how the break-even point can be roughly approximated from an income statement that shows the contribution margin.

Exercises (4)

6–1   **Definitions** *(10 minutes)*   The following terms or concepts were introduced in this chapter:

     a. Fixed expense
     b. Variable expense
     c. Scattergraph
     d. High-low points method
     e. Cost structure of a company

    f. Break-even analysis
    g. Margin of safety
    h. Contribution margin

Instructions
Define each term or concept, giving examples where possible.

6–2 **Analysis of Semivariable Expenses** *(15 minutes)*   The Yorborg Company incurred an $800 expense for telephone and telegraph at a sales volume of $100,000 and an expense of $1,200 when sales were $200,000. The company also incurred an office supplies expense of $1,500 at the $100,000 sales level and $2,000 at the $200,000 sales level.

Instructions
Compute the fixed portion and the variability of each of these two semivariable expenses.

6–3 **Break-Even Analysis** *(15 minutes)*   The Brofitt Company sells a single product for $70 per unit. The company's cost structure is $30,000 of fixed expenses and variable expenses equal to 40 percent of sales.

Instructions
1. Compute the break-even point.
2. Prepare a break-even chart.
3. If the company increases its fixed costs to $40,000 and decreases its variable expenses to 30 percent of sales, will its break-even point move up or down?

6–4 **Scattergraph Analysis of Expense Behavior** *(20 minutes)*   The sales and the sales salaries of The Robert-Snap Company were as follows during the year:

	Sales	Sales Salaries
January	$20,000	$3,750
February	21,000	4,000
March	18,000	3,450
April	16,000	3,050
May	15,000	2,800
June	17,000	3,250
July	19,000	3,550
August	20,000	3,800
September	21,000	3,950
October	22,000	4,200
November	20,000	3,850
December	18,000	3,350

Instructions
Using a scattergraph determine the fixed and the variable sales salaries for the company.

6–5*   **High-Low Method; Break-Even Analysis** *(40 minutes)*   Listed below are the expenses incurred at a representative high and also at a representative low level of sales for a company:

	Sales	Office Salaries	De-precia-tion	Sales Sup-plies	Utili-ties	Cost of Mer-chandise sold
Low point, May, 19X1	$20,000	$1,400	$4,000	$1,200	$ 800	$12,000
High point, Oct., 19X1	40,000	1,800	4,000	2,400	1,200	24,000

Instructions
1. Using the high-low points method, compute the variable and/or fixed portions of each of the expenses.
2. What is the overall cost structure of the company?
3. Compute the break-even point for the company.
4. Prove the break-even point with an income statement prepared at the break-even level of sales.
5. Prepare a break-even chart.

6–6*   **Break-Even Analysis with Changed Conditions**   *(15 minutes)* The Engert-Bearing Company sells its one product for $20 per unit. It has fixed expenses of $84,000 and variable expenses of 30% of sales. The company is contemplating spending $20,000 for additional sales fixtures, and depreciation on these fixtures will increase the fixed costs by $2,000 per year. However, these fixtures will decrease variable costs by 4 percent of sales, because fewer store supplies will be used.

Instructions
1. Compute the break-even point before the fixtures are purchased.
2. Compute the break-even point after the fixtures are purchased.
3. State briefly what has happened to the company's break-even point as a result of the purchase of the fixtures.

6–7   **Contribution Margin Statements** *(15 minutes)*   The Grattman Company sells two products, A and B. The following data have been estimated for the coming year:

	Product A	B
Unit sales price	$5.00	$7.00
Variable expenses	$1.00	$1.50
Fixed expenses ($60,000 total allocated ⅓ to A, ⅔ to B)	2.00	4.00
Net profit per unit	$2.00	$1.50

Instructions
1. How many units of each product are expected to be sold?
2. Prepare an income statement which shows the contribution margin based on the number of units computed in part 1.
3. Which product would you, as president, tell your salesmen to emphasize?

6–8   **High-Low Points Calculations** *(20 minutes)*   A company incurred the following expenses at representative high and low levels of activity:

	High	Low
Sales	$250,000	$200,000
Cost of goods sold	150,000	120,000
Depreciation	20,000	20,000
Supplies	12,500	10,000
Utilities	4,500	4,000
Delivery expense	7,700	6,200

Instructions
Compute the fixed and/or variable behavior of each expense utilizing the high-low points method.

6–9   **Expense Behavior and Break-Even Calculation** *(25 minutes)* The following expenses have been taken from income statements of the Firett Company at representative high and low levels of activity:

	Sales Volume of $20,000	Sales Volume of $50,000
Cost of goods sold	$12,000	$30,000
Administrative salaries	5,000	5,000
Office supplies	100	190
Insurance	50	50
Delivery expenses	400	520
Selling supplies	200	350

Instructions
1. Compute the behavior of each expense item in terms of its fixed and variable elements utilizing the high-low points method.
2. Compute the company's break-even point.

6–10   **Expense Behavior and Break-Even Computations** *(35 minutes)* A company incurred the following expenses at representative high and low levels of activity:

	High	Low
Sales	325,000	275,000
Cost of sales	195,000	165,000
Auto expense	15,000	13,000
Depreciation	20,000	20,000

(continued)

Office salaries	13,250	12,750
Sales salaries	29,375	25,625
Utilities	10,125	8,875

The company sells its product for $40 per unit.

Instructions
1. Compute the fixed and variable behavior of each expense.
2. Compute the break-even point in dollars.
3. Compute the break-even point in units.

6–11   **Expense Structure and Break-Even Calculation** *(20 minutes)*
Listed below are representative high and low figures for a company.

	Low	High
Sales	80,000	120,000
Cost of goods sold	50,000	75,000
Depreciation	5,000	5,000
Other costs and expenses	20,000	28,000

Instructions
1. Find the fixed and variable structure of each expense, and for the entire company.
2. Compute the break-even point.

6–12   **Expense Behavior and Contribution Margin Statement** *(40 minutes)*   The income statements of the Nelson Company, at representative high and low levels of sales are given below:

Sales		$500,000		$200,000
Cost of merchandise sold		300,000		120,000
Gross margin		$200,000		$ 80,000
Expenses				
Depreciation	$20,000		$20,000	
Supplies	5,000		2,000	
Salaries	70,000		40,000	
Utilities	10,000		7,000	
Insurance	3,000		3,000	
Taxes	1,000		1,000	
Total expenses		109,000		73,000
Net income		$ 91,000		$ 7,000

Instructions
1. Compute the fixed and variable elements of each expense, and for the company as a whole.
2. Compute the break-even point.
3. Prepare an income statement which reflects contribution margin, assuming all semivariable costs are more variable than fixed, at a sales level of $200,000.

6–13   **Contribution Margin Analysis** *(15 minutes)*   A company was requested by one of its largest customers to submit a price quotation on a shipment of 25,000 units. The company's expense structure is $1,200,000 fixed expenses and variable expenses of $12 per unit. The present sales volume is 100,000 units with a sales price of $30 each.

Instructions
1. Compute the present break-even point.
2. What is the lowest price the company can quote on the shipment and not change its present amount of profit?
3. What is the amount which should be quoted if the company wishes to earn a profit of $2 per unit on the shipment over the amount of net profit presently being earned on other business?

6–14   **Margin of Safety** *(15 minutes)*   A company has $4,500 of fixed expenses and variable expenses of $5 per unit. Its present sales are 1,000 units at $10 per unit.

Instructions
1. Compute the present break-even point.
2. Compute the present margin of safety.
3. The company is considering an increase in sales price to $11 per unit, with a drop in volume to 950 units. Compute the new break-even point and the new margin of safety.

6–15   **Change in Expense Structure** *(10 minutes)*   A company has fixed expenses of $50,000 and variable expenses of 60 percent of sales.

Instructions
1. Compute the break-even point.
2. The company is considering acquisition of a new fixed asset. If acquired, it will increase fixed expenses by $5,000 and decrease maintenance (variable) from 3 percent to 1 percent of sales. Compute the new break-even point.

6–16   **Contribution Margin Analysis** *(15 minutes)*   A company sells product A for $5 per unit and product B for $6 per unit. During the past year, it sold 10,000 units of A and 10,000 units of B with the following results:

	A	B
Sales	$50,000	$60,000
Variable expenses	10,000	15,000
Contribution margin	$40,000	$45,000
Fixed expenses (allocated)	30,000	50,000
Net profit (loss)	$10,000	$(5,000)

The company has an opportunity to sell 1,000 more units of either A or B (but not both) without changing fixed expenses. Which should it sell? Why?

Problems (3)

6–17 **High-Low Points Calculations** (25 minutes)   A company incurred the following expenses at representative high and low levels of activity:

255 060

	High	Low
Sales	$150,000	$75,000
Cost of goods sold	105,000	52,500
Advertising	10,000	10,000
Supplies	3,300	1,650
Sales salaries	25,000	17,500
Utilities	1,650	825
Insurance	4,100	4,100
Administrative salaries	20,000	12,500

46575

174075

Instructions
1. Compute the fixed and/or variable behavior of each expense.
2. Compute the break-even point.

6–18   **Scattergraph and High-Low Points Calculations** (50 minutes) Data concerning the office supplies expense of a company are presented below for a twelve-month period.

Month	Sales	Office Supplies Expense
January	$50,000	$3,200
February	55,000	3,100
March	60,000	3,150
April	75,000	3,500
May	80,000	3,650
June	75,000	3,600
July	65,000	3,150
August	70,000	3,450
September	85,000	3,750
October	60,000	3,250
November	55,000	3,000
December	70,000	3,300

Instructions
1. Prepare a scattergraph. Estimate the fixed and variable portions of the office supplies expense from the scattergraph by drawing a freehand trend line.

2. Take the highest sales volume and the lowest sales volume, and utilizing these two points prepare a high-low points analysis to determine the expense behavior of office supplies.
3. Compute the expected amount of office supplies expense at a sales level of $90,000 using
   a. The formula computed in part 1.
   b. The formula computed in part 2.

6–19   **High-Low Methods; Break-Even Analysis** *(50 minutes)*   Listed below are the expenses of a company at a representative high and a representative low level of activity.

	High	Low
Sales	$200,000	$150,000
Cost of goods sold	120,000	90,000
Gross margin	$ 80,000	$ 60,000
Operating expenses:		
Depreciation	$ 20,000	$ 20,000
Supplies	7,000	6,500
Sales salaries	30,000	25,000
Utilities	5,000	4,500
Delivery expense	8,000	8,000
Total operating expenses	$ 70,000	$ 64,000
Net income (or loss)	$ 10,000	($ 4,000)

Instructions
1. Using the high-low points method, compute the fixed and/or variable behavior of each expense.
2. Compute the overall expense structure of the company.
3. Compute the break-even point.
4. Prepare a break-even chart.

6–20   **Break-Even Analysis and Contribution Margin Statements** *(45 minutes)*   A company has the following expense structure:

	Variable	Fixed
Cost of goods sold	50% of sales	
Depreciation		$13,000
Supplies	5%	2,000
Utilities	3%	
Advertising		10,000
Administrative salaries		18,000
Sales salaries	10%	15,000
	68%	58

Instructions
1. Compute the break-even point.
2. Compute the margin of safety if present sales are $200,000.
3. Prepare a contribution margin income statement at a level of

$200,000 sales. (Place semivariable expenses with the variable expenses in the statement.)

4. The company is contemplating increasing its advertising by $10,000 with a resulting increase in sales to $225,000.
   a. Will this action be profitable? Support your answer with computations.
   b. Compute a new break-even point if advertising is increased by $10,000.

6–21   **Effect of Advertising and Price Changes** (*60 minutes*)   The Mayfield Company sells its product for $8 each, and a total of 8,000 units was sold during the current year. The company's expense structure is as follows:

Selling expenses—fixed	$10,000
Administrative expenses—fixed	8,000
Selling expenses—variable	$1.00 per unit
Administrative expenses—variable	$ .50 per unit
Cost of merchandise sold—variable	$4.00 per unit

Included in the fixed selling expenses is $2,000 of advertising. The manager wishes to increase the advertising amount to $5,000 and raise the sale price to $8.50 per unit. He feels that the same number of units can be sold under these policies.

Instructions
1. Prepare income statements and compute the break-even points under both the current and the proposed pricing arrangements.
2. Construct a break-even chart, showing with solid lines the present cost and revenue data, and with dotted lines the data as they would appear under the manager's proposal.
3. Is advertising expense a fixed or variable expense? Why?

6–22   **Computation of Expense Behavior and Break-Even Analysis** (*45 minutes*)   The following expenses were determined for the Quick-Fire Battery Company at a representative high volume and a representative low volume of activity. Each unit sells for $5.

	Sales Volume of $200,000	Sales Volume of $500,000
Cost of goods sold	120,000	300,000
Administrative salaries	20,000	20,000
Office supplies	1,000	1,900
Insurance	500	500
Delivery expenses	4,000	5,200
Selling supplies	2,000	3,500
Property taxes	1,800	1,800
Utilities	1,300	2,500
Heat and light	1,900	2,500
Sales salaries	30,000	51,000
Office salaries	12,000	18,000

Instructions
1. Compute the fixed portion of each expense and the variability of each expense as a percentage of sales.
2. Total the amounts computed in part 1 to determine the total fixed and variable expense structure of the company.
3. Compute the company's break-even point.
4. Prepare a break-even chart.

6-23   Profitability Analysis Using Contribution Margin *(35 minutes)*
The Talbart Company has the following expense structure:

Fixed expenses	$175,000
Variable expenses	$130 per unit

Their sales price is $300 per unit, and their sales have been 1,600 units per year during the past several years. The company received an offer from a large distributor not presently buying from them to purchase 1,000 units at a sales price equal to one-half the Talbart Company's normal price, or $150 per unit. This distributor had guaranteed to market the units in an area where the Talbart Company was not selling, thus having no effect on the regular sales to the Talbart Company's customers. However, the Talbart Company would incur a $10 per unit extra shipping cost to get the units to the distributor. The president of the company does not want to accept the offer, saying it cannot possibly be profitable.

Instructions
1. Ignoring any legal ramifications and assuming that the Talbart Company has the capacity to produce these additional units, should this offer be accepted? Solve this problem by preparing two contribution margin income statements, one if the Talbart Company does not accept the offer and sells only the 1,600 units to its regular customers, and the other statement if the Talbart Company accepts the offer.
2. Reconcile the difference in profit between these two courses of action.

6-24   Analysis of Expense Structure: Break-Even Analysis *(50 minutes)*
The Swenson Company is a wholesale distributor of pianos. Their sales price is $400 per unit. Analysis of operating expenses and budgets for the coming year reveals the following:

Purchase price of each piano, $220.
Advertising budget for the year is fixed at $4,000.
Salesmen are guaranteed fixed annual salaries totaling $7,000 and receive in addition $24 commission on each piano sold.
Office salaries are fixed at $6,000.

Expenses of operating the delivery trucks have been analyzed as:
  Fixed expenses including depreciation, taxes, and insurance will be $2,000;
  Variable expense of delivering each piano will be $4.
Rent will be $3,000.
Fixed office supplies costs will be $800, and variable office supplies will be $0.40 per piano sold.

Instructions
1. Compute the total fixed expenses and the total variable expenses as a percentage of sales.
2. Compute the break-even point.
3. Construct a break-even chart.
4. What would be the profit or loss if the Swenson Company sold 100 pianos? If 200 pianos are sold?

6–25   **Contribution Margin Income Statements** *(45 minutes)*   The Williamson Barker Company has the following expense structure, exclusive of the cost of goods sold, advertising, and market research:

  Operating fixed expenses $120,000
  Operating variable expenses $1 per unit

The advertising expense and market research costs of this company are determined by managerial decision, and the amounts fluctuate without any relationship to the units sold or the dollar amount of sales. The cost of goods sold fluctuates with the market price of available merchandise and has no direct relationship to sales, either in units or dollar amounts.

The company's management is trying to decide among several alternate choices of units to sell in the coming year. The company can sell only one of these units, because if two or more were sold, the advertising and market research costs would have to be increased beyond the profitability stage. The following proposals are being considered:

1. Buy a unit for $3.60, sell it for $6.00, and expend $30,000 on advertising and $10,000 on market research. Sales of 180,000 units can be expected.
2. Buy a different unit for $4.00, sell it for $6.00, and expend $15,000 on advertising and a like amount on market research. Sales of 250,000 of these units would be expected.
3. Buy still a different unit for $6.00, sell it for $10.00, and expend $50,000 on advertising and $20,000 on market research. Only 100,000 of these units could be sold.

Instructions
Prepare three contribution margin income statements to determine which alternative would produce the greatest profit. Treat advertising and market research as fixed expenses in the statement.

6–26   **Break-Even Analysis and Contribution Margin Statements** *(50 minutes)*   A company has the following expense structure:

	Variable	Fixed
Cost of goods sold	60% of sales	
Supplies	5%	$ 1,000
Sales salaries	10%	20,000
Utilities	3%	
Advertising		9,000
Administrative salaries		18,000
Delivery expenses	7%	

The company sells a single product for $10 per unit.

Instructions

1. Compute the break-even point.
2. Construct a break-even chart:
3. Compute the margin of safety if 35,000 units are currently being sold.
4. Prepare a contribution margin income statement for the sale of 35,000 units. Place semivariable expenses with variable expenses in this statement.
5. The company is contemplating increasing its price to $11 per unit, with a decrease to 33,000 in the number of units sold. Would the price change increase or decrease the company's profitability? (Restate the variability of the costs to terms of *per unit* variability to answer this part.)

6–27   **Contribution Margin Statements** *(30 minutes)*   Assume the following data:

	Product A	Product B
Number of units sold	10,000	5,000
Sales price	$ 5	$ 10
Fixed expenses	$10,000	$20,000
Variable expenses	50% of sales	30% of sales

The market is relatively stable, and increases in the unit sales of one product result in decreases of the same number in the unit sales of the other. Management is not sure just which of the two products to push in its sales effort.

Instructions

1. If the company pushed sales of A so that their unit sales increased by 20 percent, with a corresponding unit decrease in sales of B, what would be the effect on profits? Prepare a proforma income statement showing the contribution margin to support your answer.

2. Prepare a proforma income statement showing the contribution margin if sales of B were pushed so that unit sales of B increased by 2,000 units but caused an equal unit decrease in sales of A.

6–28 **Cost Behavior Applied to a Pricing Problem** *(60 minutes)* A company has the following two income statements at a representative high and a representative low level of activity.

THE QUALITY COMPANY
Representative Income Statements

	1971 (High Activity)		1970 (Low Activity)	
Sales (at $5 per unit)	$500,000		$300,000	
Cost of goods sold ($3 per unit)	300,000		180,000	
Gross profit		$200,000		$120,000
Expenses:				
Office salaries	$ 60,000		$ 50,000	
Sales salaries	80,000		72,000	
Supplies	5,000		3,000	
Advertising	18,000		18,000	
Insurance	1,000		1,000	
Depreciation	5,500		5,500	
Property taxes	3,000		3,000	
Telephone and telegraph	800		600	
Heat and light	1,600		1,000	
Total expenses		174,900		154,100
Net profit (or loss)		$ 25,100		$(34,100)

The company now sells a single unit for $5, and this unit costs $3. They are thinking of adding a lower priced unit to their line, which will cost $2.40 and which will be sold for $4. Expected sales volumes would be as follows:

	Sales Price	Units Expected to Be Sold	Cost of Each Unit
If one unit is sold	$5.00	90,000	$3.00
If two units are sold:			
Low-priced unit	$4.00	60,000	$2.40
High-priced unit	$5.00	40,000	$3.00

Instructions

The president must make a decision on pricing from these facts and estimates. Would you advise him to keep prices as they are now and sell only the one product, or to sell two products? Support your decision with computations, including at least the following:

1. The behavior of each expense, showing the fixed and variable expense on a *per unit* basis.

2. The overall expense structure of the company on a *per unit* basis.
3. The expected profit or loss which would be realized (a) if only one product is sold and (b) if both products are sold.

6–29   **Selection of Sales Price: Computation of Break-Even Point** *(60 minutes)*   The financial statements of the Hallibor Company contained the following information concerning the current year's operation:

Sales (6,000 units)		$200,000
Less: Cost of goods sold		60,000
Gross profit		$140,000
Salaries	$40,000	
Delivery expenses	30,000	
General and administrative expenses	50,000	
Other se'ling expenses	9,000	129,000
Net profit		$ 11,000

The company has no beginning or ending inventories, and the cost of merchandise sold may be considered as completely variable with sales. Assume that the salaries, delivery expenses, and other selling expenses are completely variable, and the general and administrative expenses are fixed. The expectations for the coming year have been estimated by management as follows:

a. Salaries will increase 5 percent due to raises.
b. Delivery expenses will increase 10 percent due to increases in the cost of delivery supplies.
c. The amount of other selling expenses per unit will not change.

Unit sales and selling prices will react in the following pattern:

If selling price per unit is	Number of units sold will be
$31	7,000
32	6,800
33	6,500
34	6,300
35	5,500
36	5,000
37	4,000

Instructions
1. Compute the variable expenses per unit after the expected changes, and the total fixed expenses.
2. Prepare computations to indicate which sales price should be selected for next year to realize the maximum profit?
3. Compute the break-even point, using the sales price you selected in part 2.

6–30   **Computation of Expense Behavior; Break-Even** (60 *minutes*)
Presented below are two representative income statements of the
Trillo Company:

Sales	$100,000	$60,000
Cost of goods sold	60,000	36,000
Gross margin	$ 40,000	$24,000
Less operating expenses:		
Depreciation	$ 10,000	$10,000
Salaries	15,000	12,000
Supplies	2,400	1,800
Total expenses	$ 27,400	$23,800
Net income	$ 12,600	$ 200

Instructions
1. Compute the fixed and variable portions of each of the three operating expenses.
2. Determine the overall expense structure of the company.
3. Compute the break-even point of sales.
4. Prepare a break-even chart.
5. Assume that the company can increase its sales by $12,000 with-
   out a change in sales price, provided that a $5,000 advertising
   expense is incurred. However, the company may also realize the
   same $12,000 increase in sales by lowering its sales price so that
   its gross margin on sales is 38 percent instead of the present
   40 percent. Which course of action would be most profitable?
   Show your answer in the form of two income statements, one for
   each possible course of action, using $112,000 of sales.

chapter 7

Manufacturing Cost Accumulation and Analysis

Learning Objectives

This chapter continues the section of the text which discusses cost accumulation and analysis. The primary purpose of this chapter is to describe the nature of the cost data which must be accumulated for control of manufacturing costs. Upon completion of your study of this chapter you should:

1. Understand the distinction between product and period costs and the way each type enters into the determination of net income.
2. Know the cost classifications encountered in manufacturing operations and their behavior in relation to volume changes.
3. Be able to construct a statement of the cost of goods manufactured and understand the relationship of this statement to the income statement.
4. Understand the nature of inventory costs and the need for unit cost data for inventory purposes.

Nature of Manufacturing Operations

The operations of a manufacturing company are much more complex than those of nonmanufacturing companies, since raw materials must be converted into a completed product before sales can be made to customers. An automobile manufacturer, for example, must convert thousands of raw materials into hundreds of automobile parts and then assemble these parts into a finished product. Thus, in addition to accounting for selling and administrative expenses, manufacturing companies must accumulate and report the cost of the raw materials consumed, the labor cost of workmen, and the numerous other manufacturing overhead costs incurred in the production process.

The basic difference between a merchandising company and a manufacturing company is the way in which its salable products are acquired. The merchandising company buys its products ready for sale, while the manufacturing company must acquire raw materials, train workers, design and arrange equipment which converts the raw material into finished products, and inspect its products at intervals to insure that the proper quality of workmanship is maintained.

The materials, labor, and other manufacturing costs incurred in the completion of manufactured products present a number of special accounting problems. Manufacturing costs must be accumulated separately from selling and administrative expenses to facilitate the calculation of the cost of the units sold. Since there are many more operations being performed in a manufacturing company than in a merchandising operation, accounting effort is increased substantially. Inefficient operating areas cannot be determined, and manufacturing costs cannot be held at a minimum without detailed costs on each type of raw material and each labor operation. In addition, the planning and control activities of manufacturing operations are more complex than those of merchandising companies. For example, misplanning the production of units so that they are started through the plant when all the necessary raw materials are not on hand for their completion would be a major catastrophe in many companies, since such a scheduling error could lead to costly disruptions.

Period and Product Costs

The cost to manufacture a company's products must be accumulated separately from selling and administrative expenses. Separation of manufacturing costs from nonmanufacturing expenses provides a framework for income determination that permits a more accurate computation of net profit for the period. All costs incurred in manufacturing the company's products are called *product costs*, while those incurred in selling and administrative efforts are called *period costs*. A product cost is one directly associated with getting a product into its finished state, ready for sale. These costs are assigned to specific units of product, and if a unit is not sold, its cost appears in the balance sheet as *inventory*. However, when the unit is sold, its cost is "transferred" to the income statement as cost of goods sold, and it no longer appears in the inventory. The inventory thus represents a reservoir of costs incurred in the manufacturing process, and as units are sold their cost appears in the income statement, along with such non-product expenses as advertising and salesmen's salaries. This is illustrated in Exhibit 7–1.

A period cost is not associated with the production of goods; these costs are more closely associated with the time period in which they are incurred than

EXHIBIT 7–1

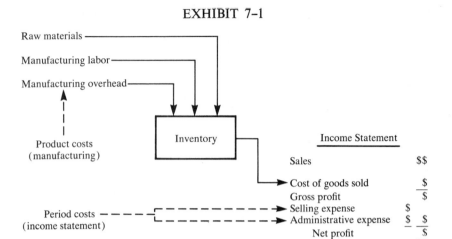

with the products which have been produced. The salary expense of employees in the general accounting department, for example, is a type of cost which is more closely associated with the time period in which the employee works than with the products which may be produced in the plant. Office supplies used in the administrative offices and the telephone and telegraph expense in the sales office, as other examples, are more aptly matched with the revenues earned during the period in which the expenses were incurred than with products which were produced. The entire process of calculating net profit for a period is one of matching with revenues earned during a given period *all* the period costs, but only those product costs associated with *sold* units. Note that in Exhibit 7–1 the period costs go directly to the income statement as incurred, and there is no deferral of period costs to another year as there would be for product costs associated with unsold units. Note also that the finished goods inventory, shown as a reservoir of costs in Exhibit 7–1, is composed of all the labor, raw materials, and manufacturing overhead associated with unsold units. The cost of goods sold represents the cost of those units which were previously in the inventory but which were sold during the period and are no longer on hand.

Determination of the Cost of Goods Sold

The computation of the cost of goods sold for a given accounting period is accomplished by adding the costs of units manufactured during the period to the cost of the inventory of unsold units at the beginning of the period. The sum of this addition gives the total available to be sold during the period. From this total, the cost of the ending inventory of unsold units is subtracted: the result is the cost of goods sold during the period.

	Cost of unsold units at the beginning of the period	$
Add:	Cost of units manufactured during the period	$
	Total cost of units available for sale	$$
Less:	Cost of unsold units at end of the period	$
	Total cost of goods sold	$

While this computation is fairly simple in concept, accumulation of the amounts may require considerable effort. A physical count of units on hand at the end of each period may be necessary, and dollar costs must be assigned to these unsold units. For this purpose, the unit cost of manufacturing each product must be computed. In addition, control of the manufacturing process necessitates separation of the labor, material, and manufacturing overhead costs. Thus, a large number of manufacturing costs and expenses must be recorded and reported separately for control purposes. They must then be brought together at some point during the accounting period in order to determine the cost of goods manufactured and to apportion this cost to sold and to unsold units.

Elements of Manufacturing Cost

The three basic elements involved in the manufacture of a product are *materials, labor,* and *overhead.* In the accounting records these three are accounted for separately, so that management can determine unit cost or locate specific costs which are higher than is considered normal. All three of these cost elements are combined at some point in the accounting process so that the total cost to manufacture the completed product may be determined.

Raw materials   Raw materials are the commodities which enter directly into the finished product. The raw materials element is sometimes called *direct materials,* since these materials enter directly into the manufacture of the company's finished products. Paper and ink were the primary raw materials for the manufacture of the book which you are now reading; wood and graphite are the raw materials used in the manufacture of a pencil; while the raw materials used in the manufacture of an automobile or a refrigerator will number into the hundreds or even thousands.

In addition to direct materials which can be easily associated with finished products, there will be some materials which either cannot be associated with specific units of product, or which are not worth the cost and effort of doing so. These are called *indirect materials.* Such materials as the glue used in the manufacture of furniture or the thread which is used to bind the back on this book are examples of indirect materials. What constitutes a direct or an indirect material depends upon management's need for cost information; but, in general, when a material cost is small in relation to other costs, it will be considered an indirect material. Direct materials always constitute the majority of the dollar costs of raw materials, while indirect materials are almost always relatively insignificant in dollar amount.

The finished product of one company may be the raw material of another company. The raw materials for a steel mill may be iron ore, coke, and coal, and its finished product is steel. This same steel becomes a raw material for a company manufacturing lawn mowers. Thus, what constitutes a "raw material" depends upon the nature of the individual manufacturing company.

Labor   The labor cost of manufacturing is made up of the wages paid to employees who work in the manufacturing process and who produce the company's products. Labor is a necessary ingredient in every manufacturing operation. Automated factories have fewer workers than those using hand labor, but the manufacturing process is impossible without the incurrence of some labor cost. Wages paid to factory employees must be accounted for separately from those paid to selling and administrative employees because the cost to manufacture must be computed apart from the cost to sell. The wages of factory employees are recorded in a manufacturing labor account, while those of selling and administrative employees are recorded as sales salaries or administrative salaries.

Some employees work directly on the manufacture of a company's products, and the wages of these persons are recorded as *direct labor*. There are other employees, however, who repair machinery, clean up the factory, transport raw materials to and from the stockroom, and—in general—do not work directly on products. Their wages are recorded as *indirect labor*. As is the case in classifying materials, management uses its discretion in classifying labor as direct or indirect; since the nature of the work of many employees could, if it were desirable, be classified either way. The informational needs of management and the relative importance of the labor cost will usually be the determining factors in how labor is classified.

Manufacturing overhead   Overhead is difficult to define, for it includes all those costs incurred in the operation of the factory other than those classified as direct materials and direct labor. In addition to indirect labor and indirect materials, overhead includes such costs as depreciation, insurance, taxes on the factory building and machinery, repairs, heat, light, power, and factory supplies. A careful distinction must be made between factory overhead costs and expenses of a similar nature that relate to the selling and administrative function. Supplies for the office of the factory supervisor would be manufacturing costs, while supplies of a similar nature for the sales manager's office would be selling expenses. The ultimate use of the supplies rather than the type of supplies will determine whether they are manufacturing or selling expenses.

One of the significant characteristics of overhead costs is that they usually cannot be associated directly with the units which are produced. While direct raw materials and direct labor can be reliably assigned to units of production, there is little direct relationship between such costs as depreciation on the factory building, factory supplies, and supervision costs and the individual units which are being produced. When a large number of different products is manufactured, the association of manufacturing overhead to specific units presents a difficult accounting problem.

The following list of overhead items illustrates the nature of those expenses which are considered overhead. It is only a partial list, for there are many costs which are unique to each industry, and a complete list is impossible. The list has been divided among variable, fixed, and semivariable costs to emphasize even further the complexity of accounting for manufacturing overhead costs.

Variable Manufacturing Overhead Costs

Factory supplies
Power
Materials spoilage
Materials handling costs
Labor overtime costs
Fuel
Small tools
Materials receiving costs

Fixed Manufacturing Overhead Costs

Salaries of factory management
Depreciation
Maintenance and repairs of buildings and grounds
Taxes
Amortization of patents
Insurance on factory assets
Rent or lease costs for factory assets
Wages of firemen and watchmen

Semivariable Manufacturing Overhead Costs

Supervision salaries
Inspection salaries
Repairs of equipment
Vacation payments
Payroll and personnel department costs
Factory office supplies
Payroll taxes
Employee welfare costs

The Statement of the
Cost of Goods Manufactured

The large number of cost accounts utilized by a manufacturing company makes the income statement quite lengthy when each cost is shown separately. Therefore, a statement of the cost of goods manufactured may be prepared for the manufacturing activity and supports the basic income statement. This financial report is designed to reflect the company's manufacturing cost data, thus reducing the income statement to a more concise presentation. The statement is arranged so that all manufacturing costs are accumulated and totaled, and the costs considered applicable to the ending inventories are subtracted from the total. The final figure on the statement is the cost of goods manufactured. This amount then appears in the income statement as part of the computation of the cost of goods which were sold during the period.

A completed statement of the cost of goods manufactured is illustrated in Exhibit 7–2. Note that the statement begins with the $16,400 balance of the work in process inventory at the beginning of the period. The three major elements of manufacturing cost—raw materials, direct labor, and manufactur-

EXHIBIT 7–2

JACKSON STAPLE MANUFACTURING COMPANY
Statement of the Cost of Goods Manufactured
Year Ended December 31, 19X1

Goods in process, January 1, 19X1			$ 16,400
Costs placed into production:			
Material			
Inventory, January 1, 19X1	$ 15,000		
Purchases	406,100		
Transportation-in	8,900		
Total raw materials available	$430,000		
Less: Inventory, December 31, 19X1	8,000		
Total material consumed		$422,000	
Labor		273,000	
Manufacturing overhead			
Factory supplies	$ 18,000		
Factory building repairs	25,200		
Superintendence	21,000		
Property taxes	8,100		
Depreciation—factory building	14,200		
Depreciation—machinery	13,750		
Patent amortization	9,250		
Factory payroll tax expense	9,740		
Machine repairs	10,070		
Heat, light, and power	8,900		
Factory insurance	6,090		
Total manufacturing overhead		144,300	
Manufacturing costs placed into production			839,300
Total beginning inventories and production costs			$855,700
Less: Goods in process, December 31, 19X1			14,200
Cost of goods manufactured (to the income statement)			$841,500

JACKSON STAPLE MANUFACTURING COMPANY
Income Statement (Partial)
For the Year Ended December 31, 19X1

Sales		$1,330,000
Cost of goods sold		
Beginning inventory of finished goods	$ 20,700	
Cost of goods manufactured	841,500	
Total available for sale	$862,200	
Less ending inventory of finished goods	42,700	
Total cost of goods sold		819,500
Gross margin		$ 510,500

ing overhead—are listed next. Their total of $839,300 represents the costs placed into production during the period. The cost of goods manufactured is then determined by subtracting the portion of these costs considered applicable to the ending goods in process inventory. This is accomplished by subtracting the $14,200 ending inventory from the $855,700 total manufacturing costs which were in process during the year.

The computation of the amount of raw materials consumed during the period appears in the first part of the statement. This section of the statement consists of adding the beginning raw materials inventory of $15,000 to the $406,100 purchases and $8,900 transportation-in costs. The $430,000 total is the raw materials available for use. The ending raw materials inventory of $8,000 is subtracted from this total to provide the $422,000 cost of the raw materials consumed during the period. The labor and overhead amounts are then added to this raw materials cost to complete the computation of the manufacturing costs placed into production during the period.

Note that the $841,500 final figure on the statement of the cost of goods manufactured is needed for completion of the income statement. The cost of goods sold as shown on the income statement is calculated in the same manner as explained in previous chapters. The beginning inventory of finished goods is added to the cost of goods manufactured to determine the total available for sale; the ending inventory of finished goods is then subtracted from this total to determine the final cost of goods sold.

Materials, labor, and manufacturing overhead, the three basic elements of manufacturing cost, are segregated and totaled separately in the statement of the cost of goods manufactured. The separation of these cost elements is based on the natural concept of the manufacturing process as consisting of people (labor) working with a physical product (raw materials) and using equipment (manufacturing overhead) to produce manufactured items. When the owner or manager of a business studies the report, his mind will, in all probability, visualize the labor, material, and manufacturing overhead expenses in this manner. In addition, different methods are used to analyze these three cost elements. The efficiency of the use of raw materials and labor, for example, cannot be judged in the same way as the employee's efficiency in repairing machinery or the accounting department's accuracy in recording depreciation. Thus, the materials, labor, repair, depreciation, and other factory costs are reported separately.

Ending Inventories

The costs to be assigned to the ending work in process and finished goods inventories are determined by computing the unit cost to manufacture the company's product. New unit costs are figured each accounting period, since the costs during one period will differ from those of the prior period. The unsold units are counted at the end of the period and multiplied by the unit cost to manufacture in order to determine the dollar cost of the ending inventory.

A portion of the raw materials cost, the labor cost, and the manufacturing overhead cost must be included in the total unit cost. To understand the cost-

ing of the finished goods inventory, assume that the total cost of goods manufactured for the period has been accumulated and consists of the following:

Raw materials consumed	$ 50,000
Manufacturing labor	150,000
Depreciation on machinery	12,000
Heat, light, and power	8,000
Factory supplies	30,000
Total cost of goods manufactured	$250,000

Suppose, further, that 1,250 units were manufactured, of which 1,000 were
sold and 250 remain on hand. The manufacturing cost during the period is
$200 per unit, determined by dividing the $250,000 total manufacturing costs
by the 1,250 units produced. This $200 unit cost is applicable to each of the
1,250 units produced during the period, whether sold or unsold. The ending
inventory would be $50,000, determined by multiplying the $200 previously
computed unit cost by the 250 unsold units. The ending inventory is thus assigned its pro rata portion of the materials, labor, and overhead incurred during
the accounting period. Note that the materials, labor, depreciation, power, and
supplies consumed in the manufacturing process thus enter into the determination of net income only when the units produced are sold; costs associated with
unsold units are held as inventory to become part of the cost of goods sold in
later periods. A full discussion of the determination of unit costs is deferred
to following chapters of this text. However, it should be clearly understood at
this point that the cost of the goods in process and the finished goods inventories
are determined by allocating the manufacturing costs of the period to all the
units produced.

Units which are only partially completed and which constitute the inventory
of work in process may be considered in terms of equivalent completed units.
Three units which are one-third complete would be the equivalent of one
finished unit. The 250 units on hand at the end of the period in the preceding
example could be either 250 units completely finished or 500 units which are
one-half finished.

To illustrate further the costing of the finished goods inventory, consider
the manufacturing costs computed in the statement of the cost of goods manufactured shown earlier in Exhibit 7–2. The $839,300 amount represents the
total materials, labor and overhead costs in the production process during the
period. If this production effort resulted in 419,650 units, the cost of each
unit of production would be $2 ($839,300 ÷ 419,650 = $2 per unit). As-
suming 21,350 units are unsold, these units would constitute the ending inventory and would be assigned a cost of $42,700, or $2 × 21,350 units. If
there were 14,200 additional units in the ending work in process inventory
which were one-half completed, these would be the equivalent of 7,100 completed units. Using the $2 per unit cost computed earlier, the goods in process
would be assigned a cost of $14,200 (7,100 units of equivalent production at
$2 per unit = $14,200.

The computation of unit manufacturing costs, as discussed and illustrated previously, is summarized in Exhibit 7–3.

EXHIBIT 7–3
Calculation of Units Produced

Units completed and sold		391,200
Units in the finished goods inventory		21,350
Units in process	14,200	
Percent completed	50%	
"Equivalent" units in process		7,100
Total production		419,650
Unit cost ($839,300 ÷ 419,650)		$2

These ending inventories of work in process and finished goods would become the beginning inventories of the next period.

Manufacturing Cost Behavior

Although the previous chapter on cost-volume-profit analysis introduced expense behavior, the discussion was directed toward nonproduct costs. The effects of manufacturing activities upon the cost structure of the firm require separate treatment. A merchandising or nonmanufacturing company has one central activity, that of selling a product or service. For this type of company, the base for measuring expense variability, for constructing break-even charts, or for computing contribution margin would clearly be the company's sales volume. Manufacturing companies, on the other hand, have two principal activities: (1) manufacturing a product and (2) selling that product. The volume activity for the manufacturing operation is closely associated with hours worked in the factory or units produced, but may have little association with sales volumes. This is true because production may exceed or be less than sales in any given accounting period. The inventory, as discussed previously, is the buffer which expands or contracts for the difference between production and sales volumes. Thus, the existence of manufacturing costs tends to complicate an analysis of the company's overall cost structure.

The cost structure of a manufacturing company is usually described with manufacturing costs and selling expenses stated separately, as follows:

Fixed manufacturing costs	$100,000
Variable manufacturing costs (based upon units produced, direct labor hours, or direct labor costs)	$5 per unit
Fixed selling and administrative expenses	$ 50,000
Variable selling and administrative expenses (based upon units sold)	$3 per unit

The raw materials cost is, in most cases, completely variable with production; one unit of a completed product requires approximately the same quantity of raw materials as any other unit of the same completed product. Thus, as production increases or decreases, the total raw materials consumed varies in almost exact proportion to the number of completed units. Similarly, the direct labor cost frequently follows the same completely variable behavior pattern, since increased or decreased production will necessitate proportionately more or less labor. However, there are notable exceptions, especially in mechanized processes, where the labor cost remains relatively fixed. In all examples and problems in this chapter, the assumption is made that the labor cost is completely variable, and the discussion of exceptions is reserved for a later chapter.

Break-Even Analysis for Manufacturing Companies

A break-even chart prepared for a manufacturing company is frequently constructed with the manufacturing costs and nonmanufacturing expenses shown separately. Exhibit 7–4 illustrates such a break-even chart. This exhibit makes

EXHIBIT 7–4

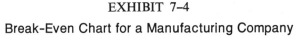

Break-Even Chart for a Manufacturing Company

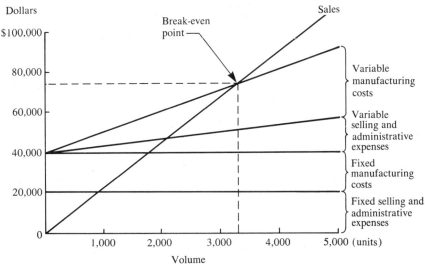

it evident that break-even analysis is based upon the long-range assumption that exactly the same number of units will be sold as will be produced. It is important to note that *the periodic accounting computation of net income does not require a balance between production and sales, for the cost of units produced but unsold is held in the ending inventory.* However, an imbalance between sales and production in any given accounting period will affect a break-even analysis, for sales at exactly the break-even point may result in either a profit or loss, depending upon whether the volume of production is greater or less than the volume of sales.

To illustrate this complex but important concept, assume that a company selling its products for $10 each has fixed manufacturing costs of $200,000, fixed selling expenses of $100,000, variable manufacturing costs of $2 per unit, and variable selling expenses of $1 per unit. The computation of its break-even point would appear as follows, where S is the number of units to be sold:

	Variable Selling Expenses	Variable Manufacturing Costs	Fixed Manufacturing Costs	Fixed Selling Expenses	
Sales −	Selling Expenses	− Manufacturing Costs	− Manufacturing Costs	− Selling Expenses	= Profit
$10S −	$1S	− $2S	− $200,000	− $100,000	= 0
				7S	= $300,000
				S	= 42,857 units

The algebraic computation may be described verbally as follows: each $10 sale results in a return of $3 of variable costs, leaving $7 to help cover fixed costs. Since there are $300,000 of fixed costs to be covered, sales must equal 42,857 units to break even ($300,000 ÷ $7). The validity of the computation may be proved as follows:

Sales (42,857 at $10 each)		$428,570
Fixed costs and expenses		
Manufacturing	$200,000	
Selling	100,000	
Variable costs and expenses		
Manufacturing (42,857 at $2)	85,713	
Selling (42,857 at $1)	42,857	
Total costs		$428,570
Net income or loss		—0—

To continue the illustration, assume now that the company manufactures 50,000 units during its first year of operation and sells exactly 42,857 of these. According to previous calculations, this volume of sales will be just sufficient to break even. In accordance with generally accepted accounting principles, the manufacturing costs would be carefully segregated from the selling costs, as required for purposes of income determination, and a unit cost to manufacture would be computed. This unit cost would then be used to compute the cost of the ending inventory and the cost of goods sold. Thus, the costs of manufacturing 50,000 units would be as follows:

Manufacturing costs	
Fixed	$200,000
Variable (50,000 at $2)	100,000
	$300,000
Per unit cost ($300,000 ÷ 50,000)	$6

The expense of selling 42,857 units would be as follows:

Selling expenses	
Fixed	$100,000
Variable (42,857 at $1)	42,857
	$142,857

The income statement which would be prepared for the period is shown below. Note that it contains sales exactly equal to the break-even amount. Note also that the cost of each unit sold is determined in accordance with the procedure described earlier, that is, by dividing the $300,000 total manufacturing cost by the 50,000 units produced, resulting in a $6 per unit cost.

Sales (42,857 units at $10)	$428,570
Cost of goods sold (42,857 at $6)	257,142
Gross margin	$171,428
Selling expenses	142,857
Net profit	$ 28,571

The net profit of $28,571 realized at the break-even point of 42,857 units is a result of the fact that *the volume of production was greater than the break-even volume of sales.* A break-even point is always computed under the assumption that both production and sales are at the same level. In this case, since production is greater, the fixed manufacturing costs are spread over a larger number of units. This produces a lower unit manufacturing cost, and therefore a profit of $28,571 is realized at the break-even sales level.

The profit of $28,571 is exactly equal to the fixed costs which are held in the inventory of unsold units. Note that in the following computation the ending inventory and the cost of goods sold each contains a portion of the fixed and the variable costs, and that the 7,143 unsold units (50,000 produced less 42,857 sold) have absorbed a portion of the fixed costs. The concept of holding a portion of fixed costs in the inventory of unsold units is difficult to grasp, but it is essential to a thorough understanding of financial reports.

	Total Cost of 50,000 Units	Assigned to 42,857 Units Sold	Assigned to 7,143 Unsold Units in Inventory
Fixed production costs	$200,000	$171,429	$28,571
Variable manufacturing costs (50,000 at $2)	100,000	85,713	14,287
	$300,000	$257,142	$42,858

To summarize, five important concepts are included in the preceding discussion:

1. When a company manufactures a single product, unit costs are determined by dividing the total manufacturing costs incurred during the period by the number of units produced.

2. The existence of fixed manufacturing costs produces high unit costs when production volume is low, and low unit costs when production volume is high.
3. Product unit costs, although dependent upon levels of production, enter into the determination of net income only when the units are sold. The ending inventory is the residual of the cost pool, or the means of holding the cost of unsold units until future periods when they will be sold.
4. Production and sales volumes may differ during any given period, with a resulting effect upon inventory, cost of goods sold, and net profit.
5. Break-even analysis assumes equal production and sales volumes.

Analysis of Manufacturing Costs

Manufacturing costs are analyzed periodically by management to ascertain the efficiency of operations and to locate those operating areas requiring attention. An accurate and effective study of manufacturing costs requires a separate analysis of each of the three major cost elements—materials, labor, and manufacturing overhead. Each cost element must be analyzed separately, because inefficiencies and weaknesses in the company's operations may affect one cost element but not another. Poor purchasing policies, for example, may increase the cost of materials but have no effect on labor costs or manufacturing overhead.

Two basic techniques used to analyze and compare manufacturing costs are *comparative analysis* and *cost-volume analysis*. *Comparative analysis* consists of comparisons of the company's costs with those of prior years, with the costs of other companies, or with the average throughout the industry. A cost-volume analysis is based upon studies of the relationship of changes in each manufacturing cost element to changes in the company's volume of manufacturing activity during the period.

Comparative Analysis

A comparative analysis of manufacturing costs may be made either internally or externally. *Internal* comparisons relate the company's current manufacturing costs with its costs of prior years. *External* comparisons are made by comparing the company's manufacturing costs with cost data of other companies.

Internal comparison   An internal comparison with the company's own prior costs will indicate whether labor costs, materials costs, or manufacturing overhead have changed significantly. This type of comparison is primarily a measurement of current operations with previous operations to locate unfavorable cost trends. Exhibit 7–5 illustrates data used in an internal comparison of the current year's manufacturing costs with those of the previous two years.

Analysis of the data contained in Exhibit 7–5 indicates that materials costs are decreasing both in amount and as a percentage of total manufacturing costs, from 56 percent of total cost in 19X1 to 50 percent of total cost in 19X3. Labor costs, on the other hand, are increasing; while manufacturing overhead has remained relatively constant as a percentage of total manufacturing costs. Assuming the level of production was approximately the same during each year, an upward trend in labor costs becomes apparent, and further investigation may be made to locate causes and determine what action, if any, should be taken. However, this type of analysis has serious limitations when the level of production changes from year to year.

EXHIBIT 7–5

Internal Comparison of Manufacturing Costs

	19X3		19X2		19X1	
Cost Element	Amount	% of Total	Amount	% of Total	Amount	% of Total
Materials consumed	$24,000	50	$27,000	53	$29,000	56
Direct labor	16,000	33	15,000	29	14,000	27
Manufacturing overhead	8,000	17	9,000	18	8,800	17
Total	$48,000	100	$51,000	100	$51,800	100

External comparison   An external comparison measures a company's manufacturing costs against similar data from other manufacturing companies and indicates those areas in the company's operations which do not compare favorably and are probable areas for improvement. Average costs are published periodically by most trade associations, usually indicating the average costs for small, medium, and large companies by geographical areas.

Industry-wide cost data published by trade associations are usually stated in terms of percentage amounts, since a comparison of absolute dollar amounts could be distorted by differences in the size, location, or personnel of the companies being compared. Exhibit 7–6 illustrates an external comparison of manufacturing cost data for the Wellington Company.

EXHIBIT 7–6

External Analysis of Manufacturing Costs

	Percent of Total Manufacturing Costs			
Cost Element	Wellington Company	Company X	Company Y	Industry Average
Materials consumed	29	43	40	41
Direct labor	32	25	27	26
Manufacturing overhead	39	32	33	33
Total	100%	100%	100%	100%

This analysis indicates that the Wellington Company has a higher labor cost, a higher manufacturing overhead cost, and a lower materials cost than other similar companies. As a consequence, the management of the Wellington Company may search for means of reducing labor costs, such as increased mechanization, improved production facilities, or more efficient utilization of workmen's time. Although remedial measures are left to management discretion, the analysis has indicated areas that should receive primary attention. As indicated above for internal comparisons, however, differences in the volume of activity by the companies being compared present a major weakness in this type of analysis.

Analysis of
Cost-Volume Relationships

One of the most effective methods of analyzing manufacturing costs is to relate the amount of change in each cost element to changes in the volume of production. For example, if production has increased by 20 percent from the previous year, the changes in each major element of manufacturing cost can be measured in relation to this 20 percent variation in volume. The reaction of each element of manufacturing cost to changes in the volume of production represents the variability of the cost.

To illustrate the cost-volume analysis of manufacturing overhead expenses, assume that a company's volume of production increased from 60 percent of capacity in the previous year to 80 percent of capacity during the current year. Production has thus increased by one-third (80% ÷ 60% = 133⅓%). An increase in materials costs of one-third would be considered reasonable, because the cost of materials will in most cases bear a direct relationship to production. An increase in labor costs of approximately one-third may also be reasonable, if changes in labor costs vary in reasonable direct proportion to production. Each manufacturing overhead expense must be studied separately, however, since some expenses in the overhead classification are fixed and some are variable.

The example in Exhibit 7–7 is presented to illustrate still further the cost-volume analysis technique. Income statements of the Boll-Mertz Company for both the current year and the prior year are presented. Note that the volume of activity increased from 75 percent of capacity in the prior year to 90 percent during the current year.

The volume of production in 19X2 is 20 percent greater than during the prior year (90% ÷ 75% = 120%). Materials costs have increased from $45,000 to $54,600, or 21.3 percent. Labor costs have increased from $32,000 to $40,000, or 25 percent. These costs are proportionately higher than the increase in the level of production, a fact which may indicate a need for management study. Labor costs, in particular, appear to be significantly out of proportion to the increase in production.

Each item of the Boll-Mertz Company's manufacturing expenses must be measured separately against the volume change. Depreciation and taxes have remained constant, as might reasonably be expected, since they are fixed costs. Heat, light, and power costs have increased from $8,000 to $9,600, a 20 percent increase, which is in direct proportion to the volume increase. If heat, light,

EXHIBIT 7-7

BOLL-MERTZ COMPANY
Manufacturing Costs
During the Year Ending December 31, 19X2

	19X2 (90% capacity)		19X1 (75% capacity)	
Materials consumed		$ 54,600		$45,000
Labor		40,000		32,000
Manufacturing expenses				
Depreciation	$5,000		$5,000	
Taxes	2,000		2,000	
Heat, light, and power	9,600		8,000	
Total manufacturing expense		16,600		15,000
Total		$111,200		$92,000

and power normally fluctuate directly in proportion to volume change, this increase would be considered normal.

Summary

Companies which manufacture their products are presented with accounting problems which nonmanufacturing companies do not have. They must segregate manufacturing costs from nonmanufacturing costs in order to compute the cost of the units produced and the cost of the finished goods and work in process inventories. A large number of additional accounts must be maintained in order to accumulate data concerning the manufacturing process, and the number of accounts is so large that, in most cases, an additional statement for the cost of goods manufactured is necessary in order to keep the income statement from becoming too cluttered.

Manufacturing costs are segregated into three main categories: raw materials, labor, and manufacturing overhead. The overhead element contains all of those costs which cannot be directly associated with specific products, while materials and labor contain those costs which are directly associated with products. There are some materials which are relatively low-cost, and there are some labor costs of a general nature which cannot be traced directly to specific units. These are called indirect materials and indirect labor and since they are not associated with specific products, they become a part of the manufacturing overhead.

The basic purpose of the statement of the cost of goods manufactured is the accumulation of the cost of raw materials, labor, and overhead in order to determine the cost of goods produced during the period. This total is necessary in order to determine the final unit cost. Manufacturing costs, similar to non-manufacturing costs, contain a mixture of fixed, variable, and semivariable items. The base for determining the variability of manufacturing costs must be related to production and is therefore different from the base used to determine the variability of selling and administrative costs. The base for measuring the variability of selling and administrative costs is usually sales, since they increase or decrease in proportion to the sales effort rather than the production effort. The existence of two bases for measuring variability (production for manufacturing costs, and sales for nonmanufacturing costs) necessitates an assumption in break-even analysis that the two volumes are equal during the period. If production differs in amount from sales, the break-even calculation will not hold true.

New Terms

Direct labor   Those labor costs which are considered sufficiently important to be associated with specific units of a product.

Direct materials   Those materials which are considered sufficiently important to be associated with specific units of product.

Equivalent production   Unfinished production stated in terms of completed units.

Indirect labor   Those labor costs which are not identified with specific units of product.

Indirect materials   Those materials which are insignificant in amount or which for some reason are not associated with specific units of product.

Manufacturing overhead   General manufacturing costs other than direct labor and direct materials.

Period cost   A cost associated with the period of time in which it was incurred.

Product cost   A cost incurred in the manufacture of products.

Raw materials   The commodities acquired for and entering into the manufacture of products.

Questions (2)

1. Why is it important to distinguish between the three major elements of manufacturing costs—materials, labor, and manufacturing overhead— when reporting on manufacturing operations?

2. What differences exist between the balance sheet of a merchandising company and that of a manufacturing company?

3. Why is a separate statement of cost of goods manufactured usually necessary for a manufacturing company?

4. What does equivalent production mean, and of what significance is it in calculating unit costs?

5. Explain what is meant by the statement that the cost of the ending finished goods and ending work in process inventories contain a portion of each manufacturing cost element?

6. Which of the following are product costs and which are period expenses?
   a. Bad debt expense
   b. Insurance on machinery
   c. Taxes on buildings, used two-thirds for factory and one-third for general office purposes
   d. Patent amortization expense
   e. Advertising
   f. Travel costs of the factory manager
   g. Light bulbs used in the factory office
   h. Christmas party for factory employees
   i. Machinery repairs
   j. Depreciation on accounting department equipment

7. What bases are used for determining variability of production costs? Why is sales not an acceptable base?

8. Explain why the break-even analysis assumes that sales and production are maintained at the same level. Include in your explanation whether a profit or a loss would be made if sales are at exactly break-even level but production is higher.

9. Distinguish between internal and external comparisons. What information can be derived from such comparisons?

10. Which of the following labor costs would vary directly with production and which would not:
    a. Janitorial work
    b. Final assembly of radios
    c. Machinery repairs
    d. Painting refrigerators
    e. Supervisory salaries
    f. Gathering scrap and waste
    g. Drilling holes in metal furniture legs

Exercises (2)

7–1   **Classifying Product Costs and Period Expenses** *(15 minutes)*
One of the basic principles of accounting for manufacturing costs is the segregation of product costs and period expenses. Presented below is a list of selected costs incurred by a company:

a. Bad debt loss from a customer who bought manufactured products
b. Insurance on plant equipment
c. Property taxes on the company's land, one-third of which is used for the sales office and the remainder for manufacturing

d. Patent amortization expense
e. Advertising
f. Travel costs of the factory management
g. Light bulbs used in the factory office
h. Christmas party for factory employees
i. Machinery repairs
j. Depreciation on general accounting equipment

Instructions
Indicate which of these costs are product costs and which are period expenses.

 Manufacturing Cost Behavior *(15 minutes)*   Listed below are a number of costs incurred in the manufacturing process of a company:

a. Janitorial work
b. Final assembly of radios
c. Machinery repairs
d. Painting refrigerators
e. Supervisory salaries
f. Gathering scrap and waste
g. Drilling holes in metal furniture legs
h. Salaries of receiving department employees
i. Overtime in the welding department
j. Social Security expenses on wages
k. Factory building depreciation

Instructions
State whether each cost would most probably be variable, semivariable, or fixed. Also select an activity base which is reasonably related to changes in the variable and semivariable costs, such as direct labor costs, direct labor hours, units produced, machine hours, etc.

7–3   **Cost Structure and Break-Even Analysis** *(30 minutes)*   A company has the following cost structure:

Fixed manufacturing costs	$170,000
Fixed administrative and selling expenses	100,000
Variable manufacturing costs (per unit of production)	$5
Variable administrative and selling expenses (per unit sold)	$3

The company has a selling price of $20 per unit.

Instructions
1. Compute the company's break-even point in number of units and also in dollars of sales.
2. Prepare a break-even chart.

3. Assume that the company produced 25,000 units and only sold 22,500 units during the year. Prepare an income statement.
4. Explain why the net income for the 22,500 units sold does not agree with the break-even computation made in part 1.

7–4* **Statement of Cost of Goods Manufactured** *(20 minutes)*   The following information was accumulated by the Malloy Manufacturing Company, Inc. during 19X1.

Finished goods, April 1	$12,000
Goods in process, April 1	2,800
Raw materials, April 1	7,000
Sales	50,000
Purchases	20,000
Labor	9,000
Repairs on machinery	1,000
Factory supplies	700
Factory depreciation	3,000
Sales salaries	4,000
Advertising	1,100
Selling supplies used	500
Finished goods, April 30	11,000
Goods in process, April 30	1,900
Raw materials, April 30	5,000

Instructions

1. Prepare a statement of the cost of goods manufactured for the month of April, using the data you feel should be included in the statement.
2. Prepare an income statement using the cost of goods manufactured from part 1.

7–5 **Analysis of Manufacturing Cost Changes** *(30 minutes)*   The manufacturing costs incurred by the Grissolm Company during 19X4 and 19X5 are shown below. Production in 19X4 was at 100 percent of capacity and in 19X5 was at 90 percent of capacity.

	Manufacturing Costs for the Year Ending December 31,	
	19X4	19X5
Materials consumed	$ 60,000	$ 50,100
Manufacturing labor	50,000	45,000
Manufacturing overhead:		
Depreciation on machinery	$8,500	$9,500
Factory supplies	1,100	1,000
Heat, light, and power	2,000	2,100
Factory building rent	9,000	9,000
Insurance	900	890

(continued)

	Manufacturing Costs for the Year Ending December 31,	
	19X4	19X5
Machinery repairs	4,800	5,100
Telephone and telegraph	600	650
Total overhead	26,900	28,240
	$136,900	$123,340

During 19X5 an additional machine was bought, which resulted in $1,000 more depreciation but a reduction of labor costs by $1,600. The machine required repairs of $500 and extra power of $300.

Instructions
Considering these changes, list the costs which you feel need further investigation because they have not changed in reasonable proportion to changes in production. State why you feel each of these costs should be investigated.

7–6* **Determination of Unit Cost** *(20 minutes)*   A company incurred the following costs during the year:

Manufacturing labor	$100,000
Raw materials used	170,000
Manufacturing overhead	60,000
Selling and administrative expenses	75,000

The company completed 8,000 units during the year, had 6,000 half-completed units in process at the end of the year, and sold 7,000 units for $50 each. There were no beginning inventories.

Instructions
Calculate the following:
1. The per unit cost of manufacturing during the year.
2. The profit made during the year.
3. The balance sheet value of the ending goods in process and finished goods inventories.

7–7 **Effect of Different Production Levels** *(35 minutes)*   A company incurred the following costs during the year:

Fixed manufacturing costs	$150,000
Variable manufacturing costs	$7 per unit manufactured
Fixed administrative expenses	$50,000
Variable administrative expenses	$3 per unit sold

During the year the company sold 26,000 units at $20 each. There were no beginning inventories.

Instructions
Calculate the following:
1. The break-even point

2. The profit which the company would realize if 21,000 units were manufactured and 20,000 were sold

3. The profit which the company would realize if 30,000 units were manufactured and 20,000 were sold

7–8   **Calculation of Unit Costs** (*35 minutes*)   The following data pertain to a company during the current year:

Beginning inventories of work in process	—0—
Raw materials purchased	$28,000
Beginning inventory of raw materials	5,000
Ending inventory of raw materials	3,000
Direct labor	50,000
Manufacturing overhead	19,000
Selling expenses	18,500
Production: 8,000 units completed; 3,000 units in process one-third completed	
Beginning inventories of finished goods	—0—
Sales: 7,000 units at $15 each	

Instructions

Calculate the following:

1. The cost of each unit manufactured (Prepare a statement of the cost of goods manufactured.)
2. The profit made during the period (Prepare an income statement.)

(Note: a calculation of unit costs to manufacture will be necessary to complete the statement of the cost of goods manufactured, since the ending work in process inventory must be assigned a value.)

Problems (3)

7–9   **Statement Preparation** (*40 minutes*)   The trial balance of the Amander Company as of December 31, 19X5, appears as follows:

Cash	$ 1,000	
Accounts receivable	6,000	
Finished goods inventory, 1/1/X5	9,000	
Goods in process inventory, 1/1/X5	3,000	
Raw materials, 1/1/X5	2,000	
Machinery	18,000	
Accounts payable		$ 3,000
Common stock		25,000
Retained earnings		7,000
Sales		51,000
Raw materials purchases	16,000	
Transportation-in on raw materials	500	
Labor	21,000	
Depreciation on machinery	3,000	

Factory taxes	1,000	
Factory supplies	800	
Advertising	1,200	
General office salaries	3,500	
	$86,000	$86,000

Finished goods inventory, 12/31/X5	$ 8,000
Goods in process inventory, 12/31/X5	2,000 ✓
Raw materials inventory, 12/31/X5	4,000

Instructions

Using these data, prepare a statement of the cost of goods manufactured for the year, and an income statement.

7–10   **Statement of Cost of Goods Manufactured** *(35 minutes)*   The management of the Troell Manufacturing Company has not received separate monthly statements showing the costs to manufacture and sell its products. You have been requested to prepare one for the month of May, 19X1, using the following information:

On the first of the month the company had on hand raw materials which cost $10,600, finished goods in the warehouse of $16,000, and partially finished products with a cost of $11,300. The purchases journal showed a total of $17,000 of raw materials had been bought. A total of $24,000 of raw material had been put into process during the month.

The payroll journal showed labor costs to be $15,000, of which $14,000 was factory payroll and $1,000 was selling payroll. Factory supplies of $1,000, depreciation on machinery of $9,000, factory taxes of $1,500, and heat, light, and power of $3,000 had been incurred. At the end of the month, the incompleted goods in process included $1,000 of material, $800 of direct labor, and $400 of manufacturing expenses. Finished goods sold during the month had a cost of $65,000.

Instructions

Prepare the statement of the cost of goods manufactured, working forward or backward from the given information to complete the statement.

7–11   **Statement Preparation** *(50 minutes)*   The Follstram Manufacturing Company's trial balance, with the related inventory data, is as follows:

Cash	$ 1,550
Accounts receivable	7,300
Finished goods inventory, 1/1/X5	9,100
Goods in process inventory, 1/1/X5	800
Raw materials inventory, 1/1/X5	1,400
Machinery	47,000

(continued)

Accumulated depreciation—machinery		$ 8,000
Patents	$ 2,500	
Accounts payable		2,800
Mortgage payable		6,000
Common stock		40,000
Retained earnings		6,000
Sales		75,000
Purchases	31,000	
Transportation-in	1,200	
Labor	18,400	
Machinery repairs	1,700	
Factory supplies	700	
Factory rent	2,000	
Depreciation expense	1,000	
Factory taxes	700	
Insurance expense	150	
Patent expense	500	
Advertising	1,400	
Office supplies	300	
Sales commissions	2,100	
Office salaries	7,000	
	$137,800	$137,800

Finished goods inventory, 12/31/X5	$ 6,200
Goods in process inventory, 12/31/X5	1,100
Raw materials inventory, 12/31/X5	900

One-half of the insurance expense for the year is on the factory building, and the balance is on the general office.

Instructions

Using the information listed above, prepare the following:
1. A statement of the cost of goods manufactured
2. An income statement for the year

7–12   **Break-Even Analysis** *(50 minutes)*   The Attwell Company has the following cost structure:

Variable selling and administrative expenses	$5 per unit sold
Fixed selling and administrative expenses	$40,000
Variable manufacturing costs	$8 per unit produced
Fixed manufacturing costs	$120,000

The company's product sells for $25 per unit. The budget profit plan established for the coming year included sales of 15,000 units and production of 16,000 units.

Instructions
1. Compute the break-even point in units and in dollars of sales, assuming production and sales are to be at the same level.
2. Prepare a break-even chart.

3. Prepare an income statement which reflects the company's profit plan for the coming year.
4. Assume that the actual sales at the end of the year were exactly 13,333 units, but that production continued throughout the year and reached the projected level of 16,000 units. Prepare an income statement to reflect the results of actual transactions.
5. Explain the difference between the break-even point in sales computed in part 1 and the profit computed in part 4.

7–13 **Break-Even Analysis** *(45 minutes)*   A company analyzed its cost structure and found the following:

Fixed manufacturing costs	$100,000
Variable manufacturing costs	$10 per unit
Fixed selling and administrative expenses	$200,000
Variable selling and administrative expenses	$5 per unit

The company's product sells for $40 per unit. The company plans to produce 13,000 units during the coming year, although it expects to sell only 12,000 units.

Instructions
1. Compute the break-even point in units and also in dollars, assuming that production and sales are at the same level.
2. Prepare an income statement showing the results of producing and selling at exactly the break-even point.
3. Prepare an income statement which reflects the company's plans for the coming year. (Assume that there are no beginning inventories.)
4. Explain the difference between the profits computed in part 2 and part 3.

7–14 **Reporting and Analysis of Manufacturing Costs** *(60 minutes)*
The manufacturing costs of the Brayville Company for 19X5 were as follows:

Factory labor	$274,000
Raw materials purchased	328,700
Factory insurance expired	8,200
Factory building depreciation	17,200
Factory equipment depreciation	9,320
Factory supplies	3,840
Heat, light, and power	7,580
Equipment repairs	63,400

The factory insurance was almost double that of the previous year because several policies had been cancelled and new policies taken. The equipment repairs expense was four times the normal amount because of extensive and unexpected repairs during the year.

The company had no beginning inventory of work in process or finished goods because changes in their products beginning in 19X5 had necessitated clearing out all old models. There were no beginning or ending raw materials inventories. During 19X5, a total of 10,000 new units was started; 8,000 units were completed; and 6,000 were sold. The incomplete units were half finished.

William Baker, the company's sales manager, had been instrumental in changing the company's products and was not disturbed when the company reported net income for the year of $87,800, which was $45,000 below the previous year. He stated, "We actually had a good year, even though profits are down, because our factory insurance and repair costs were almost $50,000 more than in previous years. If it had not been for these costs, our net income would have been $50,000 greater and would thus be higher than that of the previous year."

Instructions

1. Prepare a statement of the cost of goods manufactured.
2. Compute the per unit cost of the units manufactured during the year.
3. Comment briefly on the correctness of the statement made by Baker, wherein he claimed the $50,000 additional cost reduced profit by that same amount.

Determination and Analysis of Unit Costs (*45 minutes*)   The management of the Brenton Company was concerned in the prior year about the cost of manufacturing its product. Its per unit costs then were as follows:

Labor	$ 6.00
Materials	9.80
Manufacturing overhead	6.50
Per unit	$22.30

During 19X5, the company produced 8,000 units, and at the end of the year its trial balance and ending inventories were as shown below:

Cash	$ 2,000	
Accounts receivable	8,000	
Finished goods inventory, 1/1/X5	12,000	
Goods in process inventory, 1/1/X5	—0—	
Raw materials inventory, 1/1/X5	6,000	
Machinery	25,000	
Factory building	56,000	
Accounts payable		$ 9,000
Common stock		100,000
Retained earnings		26,000
Sales		211,000
Purchases	79,000	
Transportation-in	1,000	
Labor	53,000	

Factory taxes	3,000	
Factory supplies	2,000	
Heat, light, and power	10,000	
Machinery repairs	8,000	
Depreciation—factory building	25,000	
Depreciation—machinery	17,000	
Salesmen's salaries	12,000	
Advertising	3,000	
Selling supplies	2,000	
Administrative salaries	22,000	
	$346,000	$346,000

Ending inventories:

Finished goods, 12/31/X5	$ 14,000
Goods in process, 12/31/X5	—0—
Raw materials, 12/31/X5	8,000

Instructions

1. Prepare a statement of the cost of goods manufactured during the year. 196,000
2. Compute the unit costs of manufacturing for labor, materials, and manufacturing overhead. Indicate which of these three cost elements you would be concerned about if you were the company's general manager.   ÷ by units produced

    9.75 L
    6.625 M.
    8.125 F.O.

7–16   **Statement of Cost of Goods Manufactured** *(50 minutes)*   The trial balance of the Queens Company appears below. The ending inventories are: finished goods, $36,000; goods in process, $19,000; raw materials, $14,000.

THE QUEENS COMPANY
Trial Balance
December 31, 19X5

Cash	$ 1,000	
Accounts receivable	6,000	
Allowance for uncollectible accounts		$ 300
Raw materials inventory, 1/1/X5	2,000	
Goods in process inventory, 1/1/X5	7,000	
Finished goods inventory, 1/1/X5	10,000	
Machinery	61,000	
Accumulated depreciation—machinery		6,000
Furniture and fixtures	14,000	
Accumulated depreciation—furniture and fixtures		3,000
Accounts payable		1,850
Capital stock		50,000
Retained earnings		14,000
Sales		281,500
Sales discounts	1,400	

(continued)

THE QUEENS COMPANY
(continued)

Purchases	88,000	
Purchases returns		500
Transportation-in	1,200	
Labor	90,000	
Building rent	21,000	
Heat, light, and power	2,000	
Machinery repairs	1,800	
Taxes	700	
Depreciation—machinery	2,000	
Advertising	3,400	
Salesmen's salaries	21,700	
Selling expenses	3,650	
Office salaries	18,000	
Depreciation—furniture and fixtures	1,000	
Bad debts expense	300	
	$357,150	$357,150

The taxes are one-half applicable to the factory and one-half to the general office. The building rent is applicable two-thirds to the factory and one-third to the general office. One-fourth of the heat, light, and power is applicable to the general office.

Instructions
1. Prepare a statement of the cost of goods manufactured.
2. Prepare an income statement.
3. If 10,700 units were produced during the period, prepare a schedule showing the per unit labor, material, and manufacturing overhead cost.

7–17   **Preparation of Income Statements; Effect of Price Changes** *(40 minutes)*   In 19X5 the Pratt Products Company sold its product for $300 per unit. Manufacturing costs on this unit were $200, and the selling and administrative expenses were $80 per unit. Manufacturing costs were composed of labor 40 percent, material 25 percent, and manufacturing overhead 35 percent. A total of 2,000 units was sold during 19X5, and the company has no beginning or ending inventories.

Instructions
1. Prepare an income statement for 19X5.
2. The company's manufacturing overhead includes $50,000 of fixed costs. The labor, material, and remaining manufacturing expenses are completely variable. The selling and administrative expenses include $100,000 of fixed costs, and the remainder are variable. The sales manager wants to decrease the selling price to $280 and expects to sell 2,300 units at that price. Are the

lower price and increased volume more profitable for the company? Prepare a projected income statement for 19X6 if the price is lowered and the 2,300 expected level of sales is realized.

7–18   **Analysis of Manufacturing Costs** *(40 minutes)*   The Cortable Company has incurred operating losses for the past three years, and management is concerned about the costs to manufacture its products. They feel that their machinery is outdated and should be replaced. The following data have been collected:

			Nearest Competitor	Average of Industry
	Cortable Company			
	Amount	Percentage	Percentage	Percentage
Materials costs	$ 9,000	30	30	32
Labor	12,000	40	30	29
Depreciation on machinery	6,000	20	30	31
Repairs and maintenance	1,500	5	5	4
Factory supplies	1,500	5	5	4
Total manufacturing costs	$30,000	100%	100%	100%
Sales	$40,000		$50,000	$47,000
Gross profit (% sales)	25%		40%	39%

The company has no beginning or ending inventories, since it sells its products as they are completed. The management of the Cortable Company believes that machinery can be bought which will reduce direct labor costs by 30 percent, but will increase repairs and maintenance by 50 percent. Depreciation expense will increase by 20 percent.

Instructions
1. Would the purchase of the new machinery increase the profitability of the Cortable Company? Prepare a schedule showing the effect on manufacturing costs and on gross profit if the machinery is bought. Assume sales will stay constant.
2. Does the purchase of the machinery make the cost structure of the Cortable Company closer to the industry average? Prepare a schedule comparing the Cortable Company with the industry average, if the new machinery is bought.

7–19   **Analysis of Manufacturing Costs** *(45 minutes)*   The Aaron-Battle Company closes its books on December 31 of each year. The following information is applicable to the year 19X5:

Purchased raw materials costing $22,000.
Incurred and paid labor costs of $17,000.
Paid $1,000 of factory taxes, $500 for machinery repairs, and $3,000 for heat and power.

Recorded $4,000 depreciation on factory equipment.

Recorded $10,000 depreciation on the building. One-fourth of the building was used for the sales office and three-fourths for the factory.

Paid administrative expenses of $15,000.

Recorded the following beginning and ending inventories:

	Beginning	Ending
Finished goods	$11,000	$9,000
Goods in process	5,000	4,000
Raw materials	3,000	2,000

Instructions

1. Prepare a statement of cost of goods manufactured.
2. Production for the year consisted of 9,000 units completed and another 2,000 units one-half completed. The manufacturing costs have been previously budgeted as follows:

	Per unit of production
Materials consumed	$2.50
Labor	1.60
Manufacturing overhead	1.60
Total per unit	$5.70

Prepare a schedule comparing budgeted and actual per unit costs, indicating both total and per unit variances for each of the three major cost elements.

7–20 **Analysis of Manufacturing Costs** *(40 minutes)*   The Folsom Company was formed in 19X4 for the purpose of manufacturing a single product. At its inception it maintained only summary details of the various cost elements. At the end of 19X4, the first year of its operations, the following cost data were available from its records:

Number of units manufactured	20,000
Number of units sold	20,000
Sales price per unit	$11
Total material costs	$46,000
Total labor costs	75,000
Total manufacturing overhead	56,000

On January 1, 19X5, the company appointed a new president. He immediately made several shifts in production methods which created additional overhead costs, but eliminated the need for several employees. He also altered the type of materials used in the manufacturing process and changed the sales price of the product to $10 per unit in an attempt to increase the sales volume. The following data summarize the company's operations in 19X5:

Number of units manufactured	25,000
Number of units sold	25,000
Sales price per unit	$10
Total material costs	$60,000
Total labor costs	68,000
Total manufacturing overhead	81,000

The sales manager was very happy with the results of the new president's decisions and offered as evidence the fact that sales increased from 20,000 to 25,000 units. The production manager was not so sure, since his total manufacturing costs are higher.

Instructions
You are requested by the president to ascertain the results of his decision on profits.
1. Prepare an income statement comparing the prior year with the current year.
2. Prepare an analysis showing the per unit cost of each element of manufacturing cost in the prior year and in the current year.

7–21   **Analysis of Manufacturing Expenses Using Cost Behavior** *(60 minutes)*   The Smith Company manufactures a plastic case similar to that used for table radios. The company was formed in 19X3 by two men who knew little about accounting, and their books are kept by a bookkeeper who has no formal training in accounting.

During 19X3 the company produced 10,000 units. In 19X4 production was 20,000 units, due primarily to a large government contract. In 19X5 the company produced 13,000 units. They have no beginning or ending inventories. Their cost of goods manufactured and sold for the three years were as shown below:

THE SMITH MANUFACTURING COMPANY
Comparative Statement of the Cost of Goods Manufactured and Sold
For the Year Ending December 31

	19X3	19X4	19X5
Materials consumed	$20,000	$40,000	$26,000
Labor costs	10,000	20,000	18,000
Factory building depreciation	3,000	3,000	3,000
Supplies	2,000	3,000	2,800
Heat, light, and power	900	1,400	1,300
Insurance	500	500	500
Factory taxes	200	200	200
Machinery repairs	1,000	1,800	1,700
Depreciation on machinery	3,000	3,000	3,000
Factory telephone expense	600	900	800
Total	$41,200	$73,800	$57,300

Instructions

No production changes have been made during the three years and production costs of both 19X3 and 19X4 are representative. J. Jones, one of the two founders of the company, feels that some of the manufacturing costs in 19X5 are too high. S. Smith, the other founder of the company, points out that none of the 19X5 expenses is greater than the amount for last year and that he cannot understand why Jones considers them too high. Analyze the company's costs and describe whether you feel any of the 19X5 costs are too high. If so, indicate which ones are too high and why you feel they are too high.

chapter 8

Job Order and Process Costing Systems

, get a no. of jobs.

— continuous, can't distinguish

accumulate by cash of job

This chapter continues the discussion of manufacturing costs with an emphasis on the determination of unit costs. Upon completion of your study of this chapter you should:

1. Understand the nature of both job order and process costing systems.
2. Recognize the need for perpetual inventory records and know how a perpetual inventory system operates.
3. Know how labor and materials costs are accumulated by jobs or processes.
4. Recognize the problems of allocating manufacturing overhead to products and the methodology by which such allocations are made.

Nature of Costing Systems

The techniques for determining unit costs become very complex when a number of products are manufactured, each requiring different amounts of materials or labor, and, in many cases, passing through different manufacturing processes. The computation of unit costs is further complicated when some products are made to customer specifications, while others are standard inventory items. Management must receive information at frequent intervals on the cost to manufacture the company's various products, not only for the determination of the cost of ending inventories but also as a basis for planning and

229

control. Without unit costs, management would have difficulty in setting selling prices, determining the cost of new or altered products, planning the manufacture of specific products, or locating operations which need attention.

Two distinct types of costing systems have emerged as a result of different manufacturing methods. Some companies produce a large number of products, each requiring different amounts and types of materials and labor, while other companies use a continuous, steady process to manufacture a smaller number of unchanging products. Companies which manufacture shoes, clothing, appliances, tools, books, furniture, and radios are examples of those with a large number of different products, each costing a different amount to manufacture. This type of manufacturing process ordinarily uses a *job order* system. Companies with products such as bricks, cement, gasoline, plastics, and pulp paper are examples of those with relatively unchanging products and constant processes. This latter type of manufacturing company would utilize a *process* cost system.

The job order system is designed to accumulate costs for separate jobs, and each different product is manufactured under a separate job number. Many jobs may be in process at the same time in a job order system, and the costs being incurred on each job must be recorded separately. A company manufacturing refrigerators may make fifteen different sizes, each in eight different colors with five styles for each size. A job order would be issued each time a different size, color, and style combination is needed, and all the labor, materials, and manufacturing overhead applicable to that job would be accumulated separately in the accounting records. The resulting unit cost of that type of refrigerator would be an average of the cost of manufacturing the total number of units specified for that particular job.

In a process costing system the process as well as the products remain unchanged, and the cost accumulation system is much simpler. Costs are accumulated for the separate processes, such as mixing, baking, and packaging for a bakery. The cost of each process is then divided by the number of units produced that period in order to arrive at a unit cost.

The nature of the "unit" to be used varies, since some products are best measured by pounds, others by barrels, sets, pairs, dozens, or gross. The unit selected should be small enough to provide sufficient detail, yet large enough to permit facility in accumulating costs. A single nail would be too small to use as a basis for measuring the cost of manufacturing nails; pounds would fit that product much better. On the other hand, the use of pounds in the manufacture of pencils would be equally inadequate, for the unit is too large. Each product must be considered separately in the selection of the best unit basis for cost accumulation and analysis.

Need for
Cost Detail

For good operating control, a unit cost must be broken down into its various cost elements. While some control over costs may be maintained by comparing or analyzing *total unit costs* for each product, there is usually not sufficient information in total unit costs for management to spot inefficient areas. The following total unit cost, for instance, does not provide sufficient detail to indicate why the cost of Product A is higher than the estimated or expected cost:

deviated down 1.00

	Actual Unit Cost	Standard Unit Cost
Product A	$10.00	$9.00

While total unit cost information will inform management that costs to manufacture a product have increased, the particular element of cost that caused the increase is not known. Costs by major elements as shown in the accompanying analysis provide a better measure for cost control over the manufacture of Product A.

	Actual Unit Cost	Standard Unit Cost
Product A		
Direct labor	$ 4.00	$3.05
Direct material	4.30	4.35
Manufacturing overhead	1.70	1.60
Total	$10.00	$9.00

An analysis by cost elements, similar to that above, more nearly pinpoints the area within the manufacturing process that needs attention. Labor costs are obviously out of line for this product, since labor increased from $3.05 per unit to $4.00 per unit. Immediate steps should be taken to determine why labor costs to produce product A have increased. The difference may be the result of inefficiency, machinery breakdowns, or some similar item within the control of management. Obviously, there are cases where the reason may be beyond the control of management, such as an equipment failure necessitating a large amount of hand work. Regardless of the reason, however, unit cost data provide the basis for locating cost elements that are out of line and will provide leads as to where management's effort may be expended more profitably in controlling costs.

Perpetual Inventories

Most well-managed manufacturing companies use a *perpetual* inventory system, because it provides current data on inventory balances and the unit costs to manufacture without a physical count. The perpetual inventory system is based upon a continuous recording of receipts and withdrawals of units from the inventory so that the balance on hand is known at all times. The movement of raw materials and goods in process is recorded at frequent intervals, and as units are completed, their associated costs are removed from the goods-in-process inventory and transferred to the finished goods inventory.

The use of perpetual inventories is a prerequisite to quick and accurate determination of unit costs. While these systems require additional clerical cost to maintain, they are a ready source of information on the cost of raw materials on hand, the cost of work currently in process, and the cost of finished goods in the warehouse. Three separate perpetual inventory accounts are maintained by progressively managed manufacturing companies: one for raw materials, one for goods in process, and one for finished goods. These three accounts are increased or decreased immediately when units are bought, produced, or sold.

Raw materials   When raw materials are purchased, the raw materials perpetual inventory account in the accounting records is increased with the cost of raw materials and any related freight. The inventory is decreased by the cost of raw materials as they are consumed in the manufacturing process. The balance of the raw materials inventory account at any given time represents the amount currently on hand.

The raw materials inventory may be considered a reservoir of resources which is replenished with new materials and depleted by their use. As they are withdrawn from the store room and consumed, their cost is transferred to the cost of goods in process.

Goods in process   The goods in process perpetual inventory account is increased with the cost of all direct materials consumed, direct labor expended on that material, and the manufacturing overhead applied to production. It is decreased with the cost of the units completed. The balance in this account represents the cost of the incomplete units currently in process. Exhibit 8–1 illustrates the goods in process inventory as it relates to the raw materials and finished goods inventories.

EXHIBIT 8–1

Flow of Costs Through Perpetual Inventory Accounts

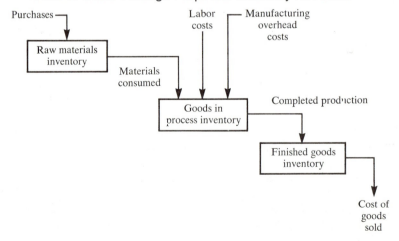

Finished goods The finished goods perpetual inventory is increased with the cost of the products completed in the manufacturing process and is decreased with the cost of those units sold. The balance represents the cost of finished goods currently on hand. The movement of costs through the perpetual inventory accounts is illustrated in Exhibit 8–1. Note that the final movement out of the finished goods inventory is to the cost of goods sold.

The use of perpetual inventories moves costs through the inventory accounts as the physical units move through the plant. The perpetual inventory records thereby provide financial information which would not otherwise be available for day-to-day control and planning.

Sp 2/24/77

Job Order
Inventory Records

Operating management must have up-to-date inventory data in considerable detail to keep the manufacturing facilities moving on schedule. There must be records of how many units of individual raw materials are on hand, how much cost has been incurred on each job, and how many units of each type of finished product are available for sale to customers. To satisfy these informational needs, a detailed inventory record is required for each different type of raw material, each job in process, and each kind of finished goods. Since an extremely large number of individual records will be required, they are maintained as subsidiary inventory records, separate from the general accounting records. This framework is shown in Exhibit 8–2. The three inventory control accounts are maintained in the general accounting office, while the three separate subsidiary inventory ledgers are maintained separately.

The *stores ledger* contains a record of each type of raw material; the *job cost record* is a ledger containing a record of each product currently in process; and the *finished goods ledger* contains a record of each finished product. Thousands of different raw materials may be used in making the company's many products, and the stores ledger contains an account for each of these. Hundreds of different jobs may be in process, and the detailed records provide data on the cost of each. The subsidiary inventory records may be separate cards in a card file or pages in a loose-leaf binder, while in contemporary computerized systems the records may be in magnetic tape, magnetic disc, or magnetic drum storage.

Exhibit 8–2 illustrates the three inventory control-subsidiary arrangements. Note the separation of the three inventory components: raw materials, with its related stores ledger; goods in process, with its related job cost ledger; and finished goods, with its related finished goods ledger. The three control accounts contain dollar totals but do not contain information on the number of units on hand, since unit data would be meaningless when many different types of units are included in the inventory. The detailed subsidiary ledgers contain information on both units and dollars. The unit information is needed at this level of detail for planning and scheduling production, while the dollar amounts are necessary for determining unit costs for inventory control.

EXHIBIT 8-2

Perpetual Inventory Control Accounts and their Subsidiary Ledgers

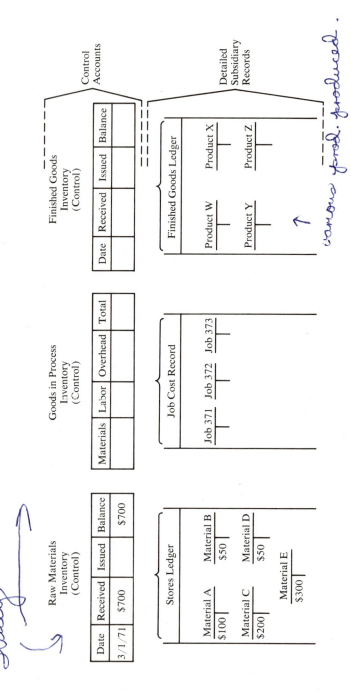

234

EXHIBIT 8-3
Raw Materials Stores Card

Material Type __Roller Bearings, 3/8", Brass__

Location __Warehouse A__

Minimum Quantity __200__

Maximum Quantity __1,000__

Stock No. __16493__

Row __15__

Bin __9__

Date	Received			Issued			Balance		
	Quantity	Unit Cost	Total	Quantity	Unit Cost	Total	Quantity	Unit Cost	Total
Jan 4	1,000	$1.00	$1,000				1,000	$1.00	$1,000
6	Freight	.10	100				1,000	1.10	$1,100
8				600	$1.10	$660	400	1.10	440
10	500	1.00	500				900	1.04	940
12	Freight	.12	60				900	1.11	1,000
13				200	1.11	222	700	1.11	778
16				400	1.11	444	300	1.11	334
19	700	1.05	735				1,000	1.07	1,069
24	Freight	.11	81				1,000	1.15	1,150
25				200	1.15	230	800	1.15	920
29				300	1.15	345	500	1.15	575
30				100	1.15	115	400	1.15	460

235

Note that the subsidiary ledger for raw materials contains an account for specific types of raw materials; the job cost record contains a separate record for each job; and the finished goods ledger contains data on each of the company's finished products. The detailed subsidiary records are more important than the control accounts for daily operating control and are updated daily. Amounts recorded in the detailed subsidiary ledgers are accumulated and summarized, and only the totals of the week's or the month's transactions need be entered in the corresponding control account. Periodically—sometimes as frequently as each month—the dollar balance in the control and the sum of the balances in the subsidiary ledger accounts are reconciled to insure that all transactions are being recorded properly. One of the major advantages of the control-subsidiary relationship is the control provided by this periodic reconciliation.

Exhibits 8–3 and 8–4 illustrate the informational content of the raw materials detailed ledger and the job cost record. While a finished goods ledger is not illustrated, the form of this ledger would be almost identical to that in Exhibit 8–3 for raw materials.

The job cost record shown in Exhibit 8–4 provides a detailed record of the costs incurred on each job currently in production. A separate job cost record is inserted in the subsidiary whenever production of a different product begins. When a job is completed, the total costs accumulated on the job cost record represent the cost of manufacturing that job. Thus, the unit cost of a manufactured product is determined directly from the job cost record.

Exhibit 8–4 illustrates the information content of the costs that are accumulated in the job cost record for Job 19349, the number assigned for the production of 200 units of electric clocks, Model 735–12. The $1,475 total cost of the

EXHIBIT 8–4

Job Cost Record

Article	Electric Clocks, #735–12		Job Number	19349
Amount	200		Date Started	7/9/X1
For	Stock		Date Finished	7/15/X1

Material		Labor			Overhead	
Date	Amount	Date	Hours	Amount	200% of direct labor	$ ~~730.00~~ 630.00
7/9	$ 20.00	7/9	20	$ 29.00		
7/10	109.00	7/10	10	16.00	Recap	
7/11	11.00	7/11	80	110.00	Materials	$ 430.00
7/14	240.00	7/14	50	90.00	Labor	315.00
7/15	50.00	7/15	35	70.00	Overhead	730.00
Totals	$430.00	Totals	195	$315.00	Total	$1,375.00
					Per unit	$ 6.875

job includes labor, materials, and manufacturing overhead, and this total provides data for the finished goods record for that model of electric clocks. Note that the $7.375 unit cost is determined by dividing the $1,475 total cost accumulated in the job by the 200 units which that job produced.

Accumulating Job Costs

Determination of the materials, labor, and manufacturing overhead associated with each job order requires a large amount of clerical effort. The necessary procedures for each cost element are described below.

Materials   The cost of all materials withdrawn from the stockroom should be assigned to specific jobs where feasible. Those materials which can be charged directly to specific jobs are called *direct materials* and are added to the goods in process control account and to the detailed job records. This procedure has been described earlier. However, there are always materials which are difficult, if not impossible, to associate with specific jobs. Glue used in the manufacture of wooden frames for furniture, and thread used in the manufacture of shirts or blouses are examples of materials costs which would require excessive effort if they were to be assigned to a specific job. All raw materials which cannot be associated directly with a specific job without undue effort are called *indirect materials*. Since they are not associated with a specific job, these materials cannot be recorded directly in the job cost records. Indirect materials must therefore be recorded as manufacturing overhead. The manufacturing overhead costs are prorated to all jobs worked on during the period, using an equitable proration base. The proration procedure is discussed later.

Raw materials costs are principally the amounts paid to suppliers for purchased materials; but transportation costs, when paid by the purchaser, should be considered a part of the cost of raw materials. The freight invoice is the basis for this entry, and allocation of freight costs to different raw materials on the basis of weight may be necessary. Exhibit 8–3, shown previously, indicates a freight cost as part of the raw materials cost. Exhibit 8–5, on page 238, illustrates the total of a supplier's invoice being recorded in the control, while the cost of the individual items is recorded in the detailed raw materials ledger accounts.

When raw materials are withdrawn for use, the workman requesting the material prepares a *materials requisition* form. This requisition lists the raw materials that are being placed into production and indicates the job on which they will be used. The cost to be transferred out of each stores account is determined by use of these materials requisitions. The total of all the requisitions is the amount by which the raw materials control is reduced.

Exhibit 8–6 illustrates the transfer of materials costs from the raw materials inventory to the goods in process records, based upon data coming into the accounting office from the stores requisitions. Note that the $240 total from the requisitions is recorded in the issued column of the raw materials control, and the individual materials withdrawn are recorded in the detailed inventory records. The same $240 is also recorded as the materials cost in the goods in

EXHIBIT 8–5

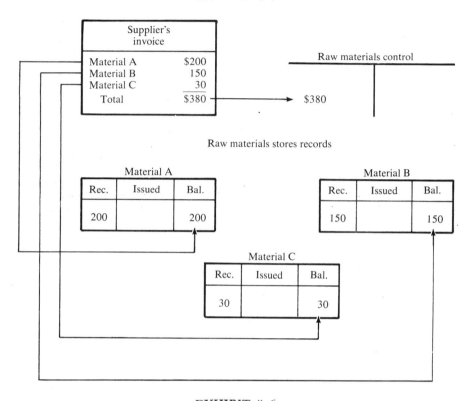

EXHIBIT 8–6

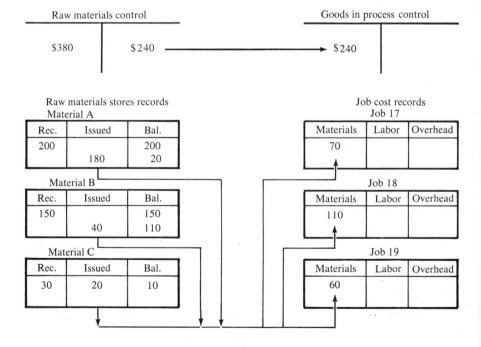

process control, and the job on which the materials were consumed is charged with the appropriate cost in the detailed job cost records.

Labor   Labor costs are assigned to different jobs by means of a work record prepared daily for each employee, indicating the number of hours spent on each job or each activity. These daily records are called *employees' time sheets*. When an employee is working directly on a job, the job number is indicated on that employee's time sheet. When he is not working on a specific job, his labor for that time is considered indirect labor, and the time sheet indicates the nature of the work he is doing, such as machinery repair, clean-up, material handling, or idle time. Analysis of the time sheets provides information for assigning direct labor costs to individual jobs; since indirect labor is not directly connected with a specific job, it is recorded as manufacturing overhead.

Note that the total payroll in Exhibit 8–7 is divided into direct labor and indirect labor. The $785 of direct labor is assigned to specific jobs and also to the goods-in-process control, while the $100 of indirect labor is recorded as a manufacturing overhead cost. Note also that the goods-in-process control and the individual job cost records now contain both direct materials (from the previous illustration) and direct labor costs; also note that the control and subsidiary records are maintained in balance.

EXHIBIT 8–7

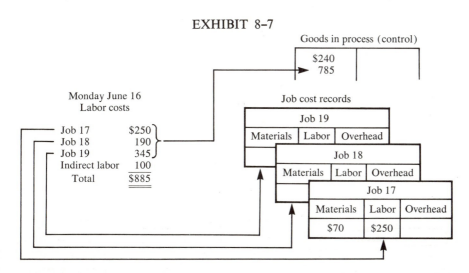

Manufacturing overhead   All factory costs which cannot be assigned directly to a job cost record are treated as manufacturing overhead. Thus, manufacturing overhead contains such costs as depreciation, insurance, taxes, indirect labor, indirect materials, supplies, heat, light, and power.

The total of the manufacturing overhead must be prorated to all jobs worked on during the period. The amounts of direct labor cost, direct materials cost, machine hours, or direct labor hours spent on each job may be used as the bases for making the prorations.

In some cases the proration is done at the end of the accounting period after the total amount of overhead costs is known. When this procedure is followed, the cost of completed jobs cannot be ascertained until the end of the accounting period. Since cost data are needed sooner than this in most instances, a predetermined *overhead rate* is used, permitting the calculation of the cost of a completed job as soon as the job is finished.

The predetermined overhead rate is frequently based on the amount of direct labor cost assigned to the job. Suppose, for example that a company has a predetermined overhead rate of 50 percent of direct labor. The cost of a job which has $70 of direct materials and $250 of direct labor would be determined as follows:

Direct materials	$ 70
Direct labor	250
Manufacturing overhead	
(50% of $250)	125
Total cost	$445

If 50 units of product A are completed on that particular job, the cost of those units would be $8.90 each ($445 ÷ 50 units).

Manufacturing Overhead Application Rates

The rate to be used in applying overhead expenses to individual jobs is usually determined annually at the beginning of each year. A predetermined rate is used, because some jobs will be completed before the actual total of the year's manufacturing expenses is known, and the cost of these completed jobs should be accumulated as soon as possible.

The predetermined application rate is computed by estimating all the overhead expenses to be incurred during the coming year and dividing this amount by an appropriate proration base. If direct labor cost is used as the proration base, the computation is as follows:

$$\frac{\text{Estimated total manufacturing overhead for 19X1}}{\text{Total estimated direct labor costs for 19X1}} = \frac{\$100,000}{\$200,000} = 50\%$$

Based upon estimates of costs for the coming year, a predetermined rate of 50 percent of direct labor cost is established. The rate of 50 percent of direct labor means that when a job is completed, the amount of manufacturing overhead to be applied to that job will be 50 percent of the direct labor cost posted to the job record.

Exhibit 8–8 illustrates the use of the manufacturing overhead rate in the overall costing system. Overhead is not applied until the job has been completed and the total direct labor assigned to it is known. However, overhead is applied to unfinished jobs at the end of each year for the amount of direct labor incurred to date. This permits a correct assignment of costs to the goods in process inventory on the balance sheet date.

At the end of the accounting period, any balance in the manufacturing overhead control represents the difference between actual manufacturing overhead

EXHIBIT 8-8

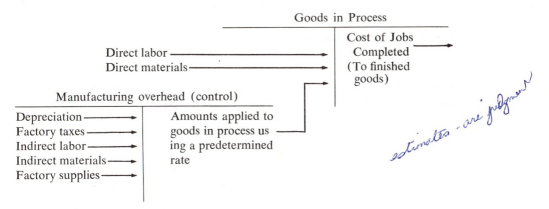

Goods in Process

Direct labor ———————————→ Cost of Jobs Completed (To finished goods)

Direct materials———————————→

Manufacturing overhead (control)

Depreciation ——→	Amounts applied to
Factory taxes ——→	goods in process us ——
Indirect labor ——→	ing a predetermined
Indirect materials ——→	rate
Factory supplies ——→	

estimates – are judgment

and the amount applied to jobs. The balance is called the *manufacturing over-head over- or under-applied*. The over- or under-applied manufacturing overhead appears on the income statement at the end of the year, since profits or losses cannot be accurately determined without considering this item. The over- or under-applied manufacturing overhead is classified in an income statement as an adjustment to the cost of goods sold. However, if the amount of the over- or under-application is abnormally large, it should be prorated between ending inventories and the cost of goods sold. The amount will usually be relatively small, however, if the predetermined rate is carefully established, and there are no major unforeseen changes in the volume of production.

The overhead rate may be based on direct labor costs as illustrated earlier, but it may also be based on direct materials cost, labor hours, or machine hours associated with each job. The selected base should be closely associated with the incurrence of overhead costs, so that there is a direct correlation between the total overhead incurred and the amount of the base. If direct labor cost is selected for the base it should provide a fair measure of the amount of overhead cost associated with each job.

if we have a debit bal. we then have credit.

Completion of Jobs

When a job is completed, that job record is removed from the detailed job ledger, and the total cost of the job is removed from the goods in process control. The finished goods completed by that job must then be entered in the finished goods inventory control and also in the finished goods detailed record. This procedure is illustrated in Exhibit 8–9.

In this exhibit, Job 18 has been completed, and the $395 total cost of that job is transferred to both the finished goods detailed record and to the related control. Note also that the goods in process control remains in balance with the two unfinished jobs. In this case overhead was applied only to the one completed job. The remaining jobs will receive their fair share of overhead, according to the application rate, either when completed or at the end of the year.

EXHIBIT 8–9

Goods in Process (control)		
Material	$240	To finished goods
Labor	785	$395
Overhead	95	

Finished Goods (control)
→ $395

Detailed Job Records

Finished Goods Detailed Records

Job 17

Materials	Labor	Overhead
$ 70	$250	

Product A

Received		Issued	Balance	
100 $395			100	$395

Job 18

Materials	Labor	Overhead
$110	$190	$95
		Total $395

Product B

Received	Issued	Balance

Job 19

Materials	Labor	Overhead
$ 60	$345	

Job Order Costs Illustrated

The following records of the Barron Company are shown to illustrate the job order costing system. The company uses three raw materials—X, Y, and Z—and manufactures two products—Model A and Model B. There were no beginning inventories, and a predetermined manufacturing expense application rate of 150 percent of direct labor has been set. Note that the final record of the cost of sales is dependent upon the accumulation of the cost of producing the units sold. The transactions are described below and should be traced through the records shown in Exhibit 8–10.

1. Purchases of raw materials were:
   - Material X   100 units @ $1   each.
   - Material Y   2,000 units @ $.10 each.
   - Material Z   500 units @ $.50 each.

2. Two jobs were placed into production:
   - Job 609 for 100 units of Model A
   - Job 610 for 50 units of Model B

3. Raw materials were issued to production as follows:
   - To Job 609— 10 units of X, 1,000 units of Y
   - To Job 610—500 units of Y,   200 units of Z
   - Indirect materials: 100 units of Y.

4. Labor costs for the period were:

On Job 609	$800
On Job 610	400
Indirect labor	100

5. Additional manufacturing overhead:

Depreciation	$1,000
Factory taxes	200
Heat, light, and power	300
Factory supplies	100

6. Manufacturing overhead was applied to jobs, using the predetermined rate of 150 percent of direct labor.

7. Job 609 was finished, completing 100 units of Model A.

8. Twenty units of Model A were sold @ $30 each.

Note that a subsidiary ledger for manufacturing overhead is shown in the illustration. A detail record of each overhead cost is necessary for analysis and interpretation of cost data. The application of overhead will destroy the balance

EXHIBIT 8–10

Raw Materials (Control)

Debit	Credit
$550	$270

Manufacturing Overhead (Control)

Debit	Credit
$ 10	$1,800
100	
1,600	

Goods in Process (Control)

Debit	Credit
$ 260	$2,110
1,200	
1,800	

Finished Goods (Control)

Debit	Credit
$2,110	$422

STORES LEDGER

Material X

100	10

Material Y

200	160

Material Z

250	100

MANUFACTURING EXPENSE SUBSIDIARY LEDGER

Indirect Materials

10	

Indirect Labor

100	

Depreciation

1,000	

Taxes

200	

Heat, Light, and Power

300	

Factory Supplies

100	

JOB COST RECORDS

Job 609

110	2,110
800	
1,200	

Job 610

150	
400	
600	

FINISHED GOODS LEDGER

Model A

2,110	422

Model B

between the control and the subsidiary, but it does not destroy the effectiveness of the subsidiary as a means of accumulating useful data.

Process Cost Systems

A job costing system is helpful to those companies that manufacture a relatively large number of different products, using different materials and methods to complete each product. However, the use of job order cost techniques is not applicable to those industries that manufacture uniform products in a constant manufacturing process. Many industries, such as cement manufacturing, flour milling, and brick making, utilize a constant process and manufacture a relatively small number of products. These companies do not need as much detail as that provided by job cost records.

In continuous process industries, unit costs are accumulated through a separation of costs by manufacturing departments or processes, instead of by jobs. The total costs incurred by a department or process for a period of time—usually a week or a month—are divided by the number of units produced during that time to determine unit costs. Suppose that a baking company manufacturing loaves of bread has set up three separate processes for cost accumulation —mixing, baking, and packaging. The company's materials, labor, and manufacturing overhead costs are accumulated by departments (or processes) as shown in Exhibit 8–11.

EXHIBIT 8–11

BAILEY BREAD COMPANY
Departmental Production Cost Report
Month of July, 19X5

	Total Costs (200,000 loaves)	Per Unit Cost
Mixing departments costs:		
Materials	$ 5,000	$ .025
Labor	7,000	.035
Manufacturing overhead	3,500	.017
	$15,500	$ .077
Baking department costs:		
Materials	$ 1,000	$ .005
Labor	9,000	.045
Manufacturing overhead	4,500	.022
	$14,500	$ .072
Packaging department costs:		
Materials	$ 3,000	$ .015
Labor	3,000	.015
Manufacturing overhead	1,500	.008
	$ 7,500	$ .038
Total cost	$37,500	$ .187

The costs for this company are accumulated by cost elements in three control accounts—one for each of the three departments—which are also called *cost centers*. No subsidiary records are used, and the information in the control accounts is sufficient. Each cost element is divided by the units produced to arrive at a unit cost. Note that there are unit costs for all three cost elements in each department. The unit cost is sometimes very small and may be carried to three or four decimal places. In this illustration, 200,000 loaves were manufactured during the period, and even $.001 per loaf would amount to several hundred dollars.

Summary

The costing system which a company uses must be constructed to fit the unique operations of that company. Job order systems are designed to accumulate costs for a large number of products, each with different materials and labor operations; process systems are designed to accumulate costs by departments or cost centers, where a small number of products are made in an unchanging process. The job order system requires considerably more clerical effort than the process system because of the necessity of assigning materials and labor costs to a large number of different jobs.

Regardless of the type of cost system utilized, perpetual inventory records must be maintained to provide current information about the status of raw materials, work in process, and finished units. Information on raw materials is necessary for planning and production scheduling, and without information concerning the availability of materials, serious scheduling problems would occur. Information on finished units should be available on a current basis so that the questions of customers or salesmen concerning the availability of units for sale may be answered. Current cost information on work in process is a prerequisite for keeping the finished goods inventory up-to-date, since completed production is the basis for replenishing the finished goods inventory.

A framework of subsidiary ledgers is the foundation of the job order system. Subsidiary ledgers are necessary for maintaining the vast amount of detail on each raw material, the cost of each job in process, and the amount of each finished product on hand. In addition, subsidiary ledgers for overhead costs provide the necessary data for planning and controlling this element of cost. A constant flow of business papers and documents provides the information to keep the subsidiary ledgers current. Vendors' invoices and receiving reports provide information on receipt of raw materials, while materials requisitions provide data on materials usage. Labor time tickets provide data concerning the jobs which employees have worked on, and completed production reports inform the cost accounting department that jobs are finished. The documents flow in such a manner that the subsidiary ledgers are posted daily and are kept up-to-date at all times, although the control accounts in the general ledger may be posted only once each week or month from summaries or totals of the documents.

Manufacturing overhead is perhaps the most difficult to control and the most difficult to assign to jobs or processes. Control of overhead costs is more complex, because its relationship to production is obscure: the direct relationship which materials and labor have to units produced does not hold true for overhead costs. Budgets and cost-volume relationships are the only means of determining if the amount spent for overhead costs is reasonable. Even the assignment of overhead to jobs or processes requires an allocation process based on a predetermined overhead rate.

Appendix

Journal Entries for Costing Systems

Job Order System Journal Entries

The journal entries which would be made for a job order costing system are shown below. These entries are numbered (1) through (8) to correspond to the illustrative problem in the chapter, which was solved in T-account form in Exhibit 8–10. The explanations to each entry contain the amounts posted to each subsidiary ledger.

(1)　Raw materials　　　　　　　　　　　　　　$ 550
　　　　　　Accounts payable　　　　　　　　　　　　　　　$ 550
　　　　To record the purchase of raw materials:

　　　　　　　　X　$100
　　　　　　　　Y　　200
　　　　　　　　Z　　250
　　　　　　　　　　$550

(2)　(No entry is required until costs are
　　　　actually incurred.)

(3)　Manufacturing overhead　　　　　　　　　$　10
　　　Goods in process　　　　　　　　　　　　260
　　　　　　Raw materials　　　　　　　　　　　　　　　$　270
　　　　To record the issuance of raw materials:

Materials		Job	
X	$ 10	#609	$110
Y	160	610	150
Z	100	Indirect	
		materials	10
	$270		$270

(4)　Manufacturing overhead　　　　　　　　　$　100
　　　Goods in process　　　　　　　　　　　1,200
　　　　　　Accrued wages payable　　　　　　　　　　$1,300

(continued)

To record payroll for the week:

Job 609	$ 800
Job 610	400
Indirect labor	100
	$1,300

(5) Manufacturing overhead $1,600
    Accumulated depreciation $1,000
    Cash   600
To record manufacturing overhead:

Depreciation	$1,000
Taxes	200
Heat, light and power	300
Factory supplies	100
	$1,600

(6) Goods in Process $1,800
    Manufacturing overhead $1,800
To record manufacturing expenses
applied to jobs using a rate of 150%
of direct labor.

Job #	Direct Labor	Manufacturing Overhead Applied
609	$800	$1,200
610	400	600
		$1,800

(7) Finished goods $2,110
    Goods in process $2,110
To record completion of Job 609:
Total job cost $2,110; completed
100 units; unit cost $21.10.

(8) Accounts receivable $ 600
    Sales $ 600
To record sales of 20 units of Model A
@ $30 per unit.

(9) Cost of goods sold $ 422
    Finished goods $ 422
To record cost of sales of 20 units of
A @ $21.10 per unit.

Process Cost System Journal Entries

The journal entries to record the costs which were illustrated in Exhibit 8–11
are shown below. Manufacturing overhead is applied, using a predetermined
rate of 50 percent of direct labor cost, and there is a small under-application at
the end of the period. Actual overhead incurrence has been added to the entries for completeness, as has the sale of the finished product.

(1)	Raw materials	$10,000	
	Accounts payable		$10,000
	To record the purchase of raw materials		

(2)	Mixing department	$ 5,000	
	Baking department	1,000	
	Packaging department	3,000	
	Manufacturing overhead	500	
	Raw materials		$ 9,500
	To record the issuance of direct and indirect raw materials to production.		

(3)	Mixing department	$ 7,000	
	Baking department	9,000	
	Packaging department	3,000	
	Manufacturing overhead	2,000	
	Accrued payroll		$21,000
	To record the incurrence of direct and indirect labor costs.		

(4)	Manufacturing overhead	$ 7,200	
	Cash		$ 5,300
	Accumulated depreciation		1,900
	To record manufacturing overhead costs, as follows:		

	Depreciation	$1,900
	Heat and power	1,200
	Supplies	2,800
	Insurance	900
	Taxes	400
		$7,200

(5)	Mixing department	$ 3,500	
	Baking department	4,500	
	Packaging department	1,500	
	Manufacturing overhead		$ 9,500
	To apply overhead, using a predetermined rate of 50% of direct labor.		

(6)	Finished goods	$37,500	
	Mixing department		$15,500
	Baking department		14,500
	Packaging department		7,500
	To record completed production.		

(7)	Accounts receivable	$50,000	
	Sales		$50,000
	To record sales for the period.		

(8)	Cost of goods sold	$37,500	
	Finished goods		$37,500
	To record the cost of goods sold.		

(9)	Cost of goods sold	$ 500	
	Manufacturing overhead		$ 500
	To close the under-applied overhead to cost of goods sold.		

Note that there is no ending balance of work in process in any of the three departments, and there is no ending inventory of finished goods. Note also that the under-applied overhead has been closed to the cost of goods sold.

New Terms

Employee time sheet Document containing data concerning jobs on which employees have worked.

Finished goods Control account for the cost of completed products.

Finished goods ledger Group of subsidiary accounts for each specific type of finished product.

Goods in process Control account for unfinished work in process.

Job cost record The subsidiary record of the costs incurred on each job.

Job order system A cost gathering system based upon individual jobs.

Manufacturing overhead over- or under-applied The difference between actual overhead costs and the amount applied to production.

Manufacturing overhead rate The rate used to apply overhead to production.

Materials requisition form A document showing what materials were used on each job.

Perpetual inventory system A method of maintaining inventory records so that the current balance on hand is known at all times.

Process system A cost gathering system based upon the accumulation of costs by activities or departments.

Stores ledger The subsidiary ledger for individual raw materials.

Questions (1)

1. What unit would you consider the best measurement device for each of the following:
   a. Cement
   b. Nails
   c. Cookies
   d. Paint
   e. Paper clips
   f. Typewriters
   g. Automobiles
   h. Wire for telephone lines

2. Name the perpetual inventory accounts used in a job order accounting system. Why are perpetual inventory accounts of value to management?

3. Name the control accounts and the subsidiary ledgers used in cost accounting in a job order system. Why are the subsidiary accounts necessary?

4. Describe the procedures by which detailed raw material costs are gathered; describe the process by which labor costs are gathered.

5. Why is a detail ledger maintained for manufacturing overhead? How detailed should the ledger be?

6. Why is a proration method used to apply manufacturing overhead to jobs or processes?

7. How is an application rate for manufacturing overhead set? Name several bases for prorating manufacturing overhead to jobs.

8. What is the source of unit costs for the finished goods inventory records in a job order system? In a process cost system?

9. Would you recommend a job lot or a continuous process costing system for the following industries:
    a. Print shop
    b. Cement manufacturing
    c. Toy manufacturing
    d. Flour milling
    e. Gasoline refining
    f. Furniture manufacturing
    g. Radio manufacturing

10. How do the computations of unit costs in job order and process cost accounting differ?

11. Why are unit costs for each separate labor operation and each raw material needed for management analysis and planning?

Exercises

8–1   **Definitions** *(15 minutes)*   The following terms or concepts were introduced in this chapter:
    1. Goods in process inventory
    2. Stores ledger
    3. Job cost ledger
    4. Materials requisition form
    5. Indirect materials
    6. Employee time sheet
    7. Manufacturing overhead

8. Overhead application rate
9. Process cost system

Instructions
Define each term or concept, giving examples where possible.

8–2 **Distribution of Raw Material Costs** *(15 minutes)* The Wilson Company lists its raw materials requisitions each week. Given below are data for the week of January 17.

Materials Requisition Number	Raw Material	Amount Withdrawn	Job on Which Materials Are Used	
			Job Number	Amount
3756	X	$300	427	$100
			431	200
3757	Y	100	427	55
			440	45
3758	Z	50	440	50
3759	X	100	431	180
	Y	200	441	120
3760	Z	120	431	120

Instructions
Prepare a form similar to Exhibit 8–6 for the raw materials control and its related stores ledger and for the goods in process control and its related job cost records. Enter the amounts to record the consumption of raw materials and incurrence of materials costs on the various jobs.

8–3 **Analysis and Distribution of Labor Costs** *(15 minutes)* The time sheets of the Kronin Company showed the following regarding Robert Kraft, employee No. 373, for the week ending July 30. Kraft's pay rate is $4 per hour, and he receives one hour for lunch from 12:00 to 1:00 pm.

Date	Began	Ended	Work Done
July 26	8 am	5 pm	Job 742
27	8 am	10 am	Job 742
	10 am	3 pm	Machinery repairs
	3 pm	5 pm	Job 780
28	8 am	12 am	Job 750
	12 am	5 pm	Clean up
29	8 am	5 pm	Job 742
30	8 am	2 pm	Job 780
	2 pm	5 pm	Idle time (no work)

Instructions
Prepare a schedule which shows the wages earned by Kraft and the costs which would be charged to specific jobs and to the manufacturing overhead detailed ledger.

Manufacturing Overhead Rates *(15 minutes)*   The Klein Company estimated at the beginning of the year that $75,000 of manufacturing expenses would be incurred during the year. In addition, the manufacturing activity was projected to be at a level of $25,000 of direct labor, 15,000 hours of direct labor, and 10,000 machine hours.

Instructions
1. Compute the manufacturing overhead rate if the company bases the rate upon (a) direct labor costs, (b) direct labor hours, and (c) machine hours.
2. Assume that during this period Job No. 456 was completed, requiring $1,000 of direct labor, 610 direct labor hours, and 405 machine hours. Compute the amount of manufacturing overhead which would be allocated to that job for each of the three possible rates computed in part 1, above.

8–5   **Process Cost Reports** *(20 minutes)*   The Johnson Company uses a continuous process costing system. Its costs for the week were as follows:

	Department 1	Department 2	Department 3
Labor	$15,450	$38,500	$4,000
Materials	10,300	19,000	1,500
Manufacturing overhead	5,150	9,600	2,000

Instructions
Prepare a Departmental Production Cost Report for the company's three departments for the week. Show total costs and unit costs in the report for each department. A total of 5,000 units was completed during the week.

8–6*   **Application of Manufacturing Overhead** *(15 minutes)*   In December the cost accountants of the Zebra Paint Company established the following base for allocating manufacturing overhead to jobs:

$$\frac{\text{Estimated manufacturing overhead} = \$100,000}{\text{Estimated direct labor} = \$133,333} = 75\%$$

During the following year actual direct labor cost was $150,000, and the actual manufacturing overhead was as shown below:

Cash expenses:	
Factory supplies	$ 7,000
Rent	36,000
Heat, light, & power	12,000
Indirect labor	9,000
Indirect materials	15,000

(continued)

Non-cash expenses:

Depreciation on machinery	25,000
Factory insurance	3,000

Instructions

1. Establish a form for the control account of manufacturing overhead similar to that in Exhibit 8–10, which accounts in the subsidiary ledger for the individual overhead items. Enter the actual manufacturing overhead costs incurred (on the left side), and the amount applied to goods in process (on the right of the control account).
2. Ascertain the amount of manufacturing overhead over- or underapplied.
3. Describe at least two factors that produced the over- or underapplication of manufacturing overhead.

8–7

Computation of Overhead Rates *(15 minutes)*   The management of the Yamast Manufacturing Company is not certain of the results which would be obtained from using different bases of applying manufacturing overhead to its jobs. The total manufacturing overhead for the next year is estimated to be $150,000. Other estimates for the coming year are as follows:

Direct labor	$300,000
Direct materials	400,000
Machine hours	600,000
Direct labor hours	200,000
Number of units to be produced	50,000

Instructions

1. Compute an application rate using five different bases of allocating manufacturing overhead.
2. Job 34–A2, which is shown below, was completed on January 17. Compute the manufacturing overhead which would be applied to this job, using each of the different rates computed in part 1.

Job 34–A2

Number of units   500

Machine Hours	Direct Labor		Direct Materials	Manufacturing Overhead
	Hours	Amount		
2,000	700	$1,200	3,000	
4,000	400	900	1,500	
1,500	800	1,400	400	
7,500	1900	3500	4,900	

4.

1,905   1,750   18,3750

8–8   **Analysis of Amounts Affecting Jobs in Process** *(15 minutes)*
The Waco Company uses a job order cost system. The goods in
process control appeared as follows:

Goods in Process

INCREASE		DECREASE	
Beginning balance	—0—	To finished goods	$19,000
Labor	$ 6,000		
Manufacturing overhead	12,000		
Materials	7,500		

Instructions
1. Describe the transaction which underlies each of the amounts in
this problem. (For example, from what document and as a result
of what activity did the $6,000 labor cost arise?)
2. From the data given, compute the rate used to apply manufacturing overhead to goods in process, if direct labor is used as the
base.
3. If the balance in the account represents the cost of one job in
process with $2,000 materials costs, what are the direct labor and
the manufacturing overhead costs in this job?

8–9   **Interpretation of Overhead Allocations** *(15 minutes)*   The Bran-
don and McFarland Company manufactures a variety of products,
including a new unit called a "Spool-Holder." This unit is made of
plastic and is sold to retail stores for $.27 each. The company has
determined that the cost of manufacturing the unit is $.23 as
follows:

Materials	$.07
Labor	.08
Overhead (applied on basis	
of 100% of labor cost)	.08
	$.23

The sales manager wants the unit discontinued, claiming that the
gross profit of only $.04 per unit is not sufficient to cover selling
costs, which are approximately $.05 per unit. He feels that competi-
tion prevents an increase in selling price of the unit.
The plant manager argues that if the unit is not manufactured, his
costs, other than material and labor, will not change. As a result, the
overhead application rate will have to be increased to 110 percent of
labor for all the company's other products. He further stated that if a
direct materials base were used to prorate overhead, the spool-holder
cost would be reduced by $.03 per unit, since the spool-holder has a
low material cost.

Instructions

Describe whether you would recommend discontinuing the product or changing the overhead application method. Include in your answer what other information you would need to make a final decision.

8–10*   **Job Cost Relationships** *(15 minutes)*   The following data are provided for the Bigman Manufacturing Company for the month of January:

Raw materials inventory, January 1: $4,000
Raw materials purchased during January: $16,000
Finished goods inventory, January 1: —0—

	Job #1	Job #2	Job #3	Total
Goods in process, January 1	$ 1,000			$ 1,000
Job costs incurred during January				
Direct labor	2,000	4,000	3,000	9,000
Overhead applied	4,000	8,000	6,000	18,000
Direct materials	4,000	8,000	6,000	18,000
	11,000	20,000	15,000	46,000

Job #1 (started in December) was finished during January and is in the finished goods warehouse not sold.

Job #2 (started in January) was finished during January and has been sold to a customer for $50,000.

Job #3 (started in January) has not yet been finished.

Instructions

Answer the following questions, using the above data.
1. What is the amount of raw materials on hand on January 31?
2. What is the amount of goods in process inventory at January 31?
3. What is the amount of finished goods inventory at January 31?
4. What is the amount of cost of goods sold during January?
5. What is the total cost of goods completed during January?
6. If overhead was applied as a percentage of direct material costs during January, what was the application rate?

Problems

8–11   **Basic Flow of Costs** *(20 minutes)*   The Jason Company uses a job order costing system with perpetual inventories. The following transactions were completed during the year:

a. Purchased raw materials costing $7,000 for cash.
b. Issued $6,000 of the raw materials to production. Of this amount, indirect materials amounted to $500.

c. Labor costs for the period were $15,000, of which $2,000 was indirect labor.

d. Paid $3,000 for power, $4,000 for factory supplies, and $200 for factory taxes.

e. Manufacturing overhead was applied to production, using a rate of 70 percent of direct labor costs.

f. Jobs with a total cost of $23,000 were completed.

g. Finished goods costing $15,500 were sold for $24,000 cash.

h. Selling expenses were $6,200.

Instructions

1. Compute the ending balance of the raw materials, goods in process, manufacturing overhead, and finished goods inventories.

2. Prepare an income statement, with the over- and under-applied overhead treated as an adjustment to the cost of goods sold.

8–12 **Basic Flow of Costs** *(25 minutes)* The Brane Company completed the following transactions during the year:

a. Purchased raw materials costing $14,090.

b. Issued $10,120 of the raw materials to production. Of this amount $720 was indirect materials which could not be traced directly to jobs.

c. Labor costs for the period were $7,625, all of which were paid in cash. Of these, $1,390 were indirect and could not be charged directly to jobs.

d. Paid $5,100 of manufacturing overhead costs in cash and recorded $1,400 of depreciation on factory equipment.

e. Manufacturing overhead was applied to work in process, using a rate of 120 percent of direct labor cost.

f. Jobs with a total cost of $21,470 were completed and transferred to finished goods inventory.

g. Finished goods costing $19,350 were sold on account for $30,000.

h. Selling and administrative expenses of $8,320 were incurred.

Instructions

1. Compute the amount of the ending inventories for raw materials, goods in process, and finished goods.

2. Compute the over- or under-applied overhead.

3. Prepare an income statement for the year, treating any over- or under-applied overhead as an adjustment to the cost of goods sold.

8–13 **Maintenance of Job Cost Records** *(30 minutes)* The Franklin Company manufactures metal lawn furniture. There were no beginning inventories except for $9,000 of raw materials. On January 6, Jobs Nos. 6431, 6432, 6433, and 6434 were started. Materials requisitions during the month were as follows:

For Job 6431	$3,000
6432	1,000
6433	1,500
6434	2,100
Indirect materials	700
Total materials	$8,300

The payroll for the month was as follows:

For Job 6431	$1,200
6432	1,400
6433	1,700
6434	1,100
Superintendence	600
Machinery repairs	200
Total payroll	$6,200

The company applies manufacturing overhead to jobs on a predetermined application rate of 150 percent of direct labor cost. Additional manufacturing overhead during the month was as follows:

Depreciation on machinery	$3,100
Factory supplies bought and consumed	3,200
Prepaid factory taxes expired	1,150

Jobs 6431 and 6433 were completed on January 31.

Instructions

1. Prepare a set of forms similar to those in Exhibit 8–10 for the raw materials, goods in process, finished goods, and manufacturing expense controls. Also establish detailed subsidiary accounts for manufacturing expenses and job cost records. Establish the appropriate titles for the subsidiary accounts and enter the transactions into the form. (Consider amounts on the left as increases to each account and amounts on the right as decreases.)
2. Prepare a job card for Job 6431 similar to Exhibit 8–4, which was for 100 units of lawn chairs (type B, white) and place the appropriate cost data given in the problem on the card.

8–14   **Job Order Cost Accumulation** *(35 minutes)*   The following transactions were completed during the year by a company using a job order system:

1. Purchases of raw materials were:

X	80 units @ $1.00 each	
Y	2,000 units @ $ .10 each	
Z	400 units @ $ .50 each	

2. Two jobs were placed into production:

Job 109 for 50 units of Model A
Job 110 for 50 units of Model B

3. Raw materials were issued to production as follows:

To Job 109: 20 units of X; 1,000 units of Y
To Job 110: 400 units of Y; 300 units of Z

Indirect materials: 80 units of Z

4. Labor costs for the period were:

Job 109	$ 900
Job 110	1,200
Indirect labor	150

5. Additional manufacturing overhead:

Depreciation	$800
Factory taxes	$300
Heat, light, and power	$400
Factory supplies	$120

6. Manufacturing overhead was applied to jobs, using the predetermined rate of 80 percent of direct labor.
7. Job 109 was finished; 50 units of Model A were completed.
8. Twenty units of Model A were sold @ $50 each.
9. Selling expenses of $250 were paid.

Instructions
Using a form similar to Exhibit 8–10, enter the transactions. Then prepare an income statement, treating any over- or under-applied overhead as an adjustment to the cost of goods sold.

8–15 **Comprehensive Job Cost System** *(40 minutes)* The Greyson Company completed the following transactions during April. The company uses a job order accounting system, and there were no beginning inventories.

a. Purchased on account 1,000 units of raw material AA at $1.10 per unit, and 500 units of BB at $2.00 per unit.
b. Issued 800 units of AA to production and 400 units of BB, as follows:
Job 61 used 200 of the units of AA and 100 of the units of BB.
Job 62 used 300 of the units of AA and no units of BB.
Job 63 used 200 of the units of AA and 300 units of BB.
100 of the units of AA were used for general factory purposes.
c. Labor for the month was as follows:

Job 61	$ 800
Job 62	200
Job 63	1,000
Superintendence	500

d. Manufacturing overhead is applied using a rate of 80 percent of direct labor.

e. Actual manufacturing overhead was as follows:

Factory building depreciation	$800
Factory supplies bought and consumed	100
Heat, light, and power expenses	200
Insurance expired	50

f. Job 61 was completed and produced 100 units of Model X.

g. Job 62 was completed and produced 50 units of Model Z.

h. 40 units of Model X were sold for cash at $25.00 each, and 20 units of Model Z were sold for cash at $18.00 each. A total of $259 was paid for selling and administrative expenses.

Instructions

1. Prepare a set of forms similar to Exhibit 8–10, including the appropriate subsidiary accounts.
2. Record the transactions in the forms. (Consider amounts on the left as increases to an item and amounts on the right as decreases.)
3. Prepare an income statement for the period. Treat any over- or under-applied overhead as an adjustment to cost of goods sold.

 Comprehensive Job Cost System (*40 minutes*)   The Borranti Company, which uses a job order costing system, completed the following transactions during February. There were no beginning inventories.

a. Purchased for cash 600 units of material Y for $2 per unit and 1,000 units of material Z for $1 per unit.

b. Issued the material as follows:

> To Job A–36: 100 units of Y and 50 units of Z
> To Job A–37: 300 units of Y and 400 units of Z
> To Job A–38: 150 units of Y and 50 units of Z
> For general factory use: 200 units of Z

c. Recorded the following labor costs:

Job A–36	$2,000
A–37	1,100
A–38	600
Indirect labor	300

d. Applied manufacturing overhead to jobs based on a rate of 60 percent of labor costs.

e. Recorded the following manufacturing overhead costs:

Depreciation	$600
Supplies bought and consumed	350
Prepaid taxes which expired	100
Prepaid insurance which expired	200
Machinery repairs not yet paid	500

f. Jobs A–36 and A–38 were completed. Job A–36 completed 100 units of product Alpha, and Job A–38 completed 200 units of product Beta.

g. Sold 60 units of Alpha for cash at $50 per unit and 120 units of Beta for cash at $10 per unit.

h. Incurred selling and administrative expenses of $460.

Instructions

1. Prepare a set of forms similar to Exhibit 8–10, including the appropriate subsidiary accounts.
2. Record the transactions in the accounts. (Consider amounts on the left as increases to an account and amounts on the right as decreases.)
3. Prepare an income statement for the period, treating any over- or under-applied overhead as an adjustment to the cost of goods sold.

8–17 **Computing Customer Billings From Job Records** *(35 minutes)* The Quick-Service Printing Shop does small printing jobs for its customers, most of which take only a few days to complete. Although it gives each customer an estimate of the cost of doing a job, the actual bill to the customer is computed after the job is completed and consists of all direct labor and direct materials charged to the job, overhead equal to 100 percent of direct labor, and 30 percent added to the total of materials, labor and estimated overhead to cover selling expenses and allow some profit on the job. On January 30 the following labor break-down for Joe Willis was given to the accounting department; he receives $2 per hour, with one hour off from 12 to 1 for lunch.

Date	Began	Ended	Work Done
Jan. 26	8 am	5 pm	Job 742
27	8 am	9 am	Job 742
	9 am	4 pm	Machinery repairs
	4 pm	5 pm	Job 780
28	8 am	3 pm	Job 750
	3 pm	5 pm	Clean up
29	8 am	5 pm	Job 780
30	8 am	11 am	Job 780
	11 am	5 pm	Idle time (no work)

That same day the raw materials requisitions for the week ending January 30 were received by the accounting department.

Materials Requisition Number	Raw Materials	Amount Withdrawn	Job on which materials are used	
			Job Number	Amount
3756	X	18	742	$10
			750	8

(continued)

Materials Requisition Number	Raw Materials	Amount Withdrawn	Job on which materials are used	
			Job Number	Amount
3757	Y	40	780	15
			742	25
3758	Z	7	750	7
3759	X	12	780	12
	Y	20	750	20
3760	Z	6	790	6
	Y	32	indirect	

Instructions

1. Prepare a schedule to reflect the wages earned by Joe Willis for the week and the jobs or overhead costs to be charged for his labor.
2. Prepare a schedule showing the materials charged to each job or to overhead costs.
3. Prepare a schedule showing how the billing amounts for Jobs 742 and 780 would be computed, if the above data include all the labor and materials costs of the two jobs.

8–18 **Comprehensive Flow of Job Order Costs** (*60 minutes*)   The Windy City Copper Plating Company, which uses a job order costing system, completed the following transactions during June. There were no beginning inventories.

a. Purchased for cash 1,500 units of material A for $5 per unit and 500 units of B for $10 per unit.
b. Issued materials to jobs as follows:

> To Job 178: 300 units of A and 100 units of B
> To Job 179: 500 units of A and 120 units of B
> To Job 180: 100 units of A and 200 units of B
> For use as indirect materials: 50 units of B

c. Incurred labor costs as follows, all of which were paid in cash:

> On Job 178: $3,200
> On Job 179: $1,400
> On Job 180: $4,000
> As indirect labor: $800

d. Incurred manufacturing overhead, all of which were paid in cash except for depreciation:

> Factory supplies: $500
> Factory taxes: $1,200
> Depreciation on factory building: $2,000
> Heat, light, and power: $1,800

e. Applied manufacturing overhead to jobs, using a rate of 80 percent of direct labor.

f. Completed Job 178 for 200 units of product M and Job 180 for 50 units of Product P.

g. Sold 150 units of M at $60 per unit and 40 units of P at $250 per unit.

h. Recorded the cost of the units sold.

i. Incurred and paid in cash $4,000 of selling expenses.

Instructions

1. Establish a form similar to Exhibit 8–10 with control accounts for raw materials, goods in process, finished goods, manufacturing expenses, and cost of goods sold. Also establish a stores subsidiary ledger for raw materials A and B, a job order subsidiary ledger for Jobs 178, 179, and 180, a finished goods subsidiary ledger for products M and P, and a manufacturing overhead subsidiary for indirect materials, indirect labor, factory supplies, factory taxes, depreciation on factory building, and heat, light, and power.

2. Enter all amounts in the form for the transactions completed by the company. (Amounts on the left are increases to an item; amounts on the right are decreases.)

3. Prepare a schedule to prove the balance between the raw materials control account and the stores ledger, the goods in process control account and the job cost ledger, and the finished goods control account and the finished goods ledger.

4. Prepare an income statement, treating any over- or underapplied overhead as an adjustment to the cost of goods sold.

8–19   **Process Cost Reports** *(35 minutes)*   The Pratt Paper Company manufactures paper from pine logs and uses a continuous process accounting system. Its operations are divided into three departments.

Department A strips the bark off the logs and chips it into small pieces.

Department B mixes the chips with chemicals in a vat.

Department C presses the chemically dissolved pulp into paper.

The process does not change, and the company's operations move at a constant speed so that beginning and ending inventories are always in the same amount and at the same stages of completion. For this reason, the inventories of goods in process are not considered in determining production for each period.

The company completed the following transactions during one week in August.

Purchased for cash three car load lots of logs for $2,700 and one tank car of chemicals for $1,000.

Placed two car loads of logs and one-half of the chemicals into process.

Labor for the week was as follows:

Department A	$1,500
B	700
C	900
Superintendence	800

Manufacturing overhead (paid in cash except for depreciation) was as follows:

Depreciation	$400
Machinery repairs	100
Power	100
Supplies	50
Taxes	100

The company applies manufacturing overhead to departments on the basis of 50 percent of direct labor costs. During the week, 200 tons of paper were produced.

Instructions

1. Prepare a departmental production cost report showing total production costs and unit costs for each element in each department for the week ending August 13.
2. Ascertain whether the overhead expenses are over-applied or under-applied.

8–20 **Process Cost Reports** *(35 minutes)* The Brane Baking Company manufactures pies in a continuous production process. Two departments are used—the mixing department and the baking department. There were no beginning or ending inventories. The records for these two departments are shown below for the month of June:

Mixing Department

Materials	$9,000
Labor	7,200
Manufacturing overhead	
(50% of direct labor)	3,600

Baking Department

Materials	$1,290
Labor	5,160
Manufacturing overhead	
(50% of direct labor)	2,580

The mixing department started 50,000 pounds of mix during the month, but spoiled 5,000 pounds of the mix, and only 45,000 good pounds were produced. The company's accountants have developed cost estimates for each pie, and these estimates have proved accurate in the past. They are as follows:

	Cost per pound
Mixing:	
Materials	$0.181
Labor	.158
Manufacturing overhead	.079
	$0.418
Baking:	
Materials	$0.030
Labor	.100
Manufacturing overhead	.050
	$0.180
Total	$0.598

During the month, the master baker was discharged, and a new baker was employed. His inefficiency due to being unfamiliar with the company's process caused labor costs to be higher than usual.

Instructions

1. Prepare a departmental production cost report showing for each cost element in each department the total costs, the expected costs, and the difference.
2. Write a short explanation at the bottom of the report explaining the more significant variances.

Unit Costs for Pricing Purposes *(40 minutes)*   The Robinson-Snell Company manufactures automobile air conditioners, as well as other appliances. Most of its parts are bought from other manufacturers. A job order accounting system is used. Its costs for each unit of the air conditioner, Model 435–2, have been as follows:

Materials:	
2-speed switch	$ 4.10
Condenser	122.00
Case	15.00
Fan	21.00
Miscellaneous other parts	12.00
Labor:	
Assembly	$ 20.00
Packing	5.00
Manufacturing overhead:	
75% of labor	

A major automobile producer requested bids from the Robinson-Snell Company for a large number of air conditioners similar to Model 435–2. The specifications which the automobile manufacturer set for the new air conditioner require a different switch that will cost $7.20 and a larger condenser, which costs 10 percent more than the one used on Model 435–2. The cost to assemble and pack the new unit will be 20 percent more than the old unit. The Robinson-Snell Company will have to construct special equipment costing $2,000, which will be of no further use after the automobile manufacturer's order is complete. Assume that the other manufacturing expenses are completely variable. The Robinson-Snell Company must earn a gross profit equal to 40 percent of cost.

Instructions

1. What price should the Robinson-Snell Company bid if the order is for:
   a. 100 units
   b. 500 units
   c. 2,000 units
2. Prepare a schedule of costs and indicate what the selling price should be for each of the possible order sizes.

8–22 **Overhead Allocations and Price Setting** *(40 minutes)* The Storey-Blatz Company manufactures and sells a line of lawn mowers. The company constructed a large plant several years ago and has never produced more than 6,000 units, which is 60 percent of capacity. At the beginning of the year, the company set the rate at which it would apply manufacturing overhead to jobs as follows:

$$\frac{\text{Estimated total manufacturing overhead at 60\% capacity}}{\text{Estimated total direct labor costs at 60\% capacity}} = \frac{\$90,000}{\$45,000} = 200\%$$

Based upon this application rate, the cost estimate for manufacturing product 123–L was as follows:

Materials	$ 20
Labor	30
Manufacturing overhead	
(200% of direct labor)	60
Total	$110

The company set its selling price on this mower at $150, since its selling expenses are $32 per unit. The company received an offer from a large chain store for 3,000 of the 123–L units at a proposed price of $90 each.

The sales manager did not want to accept the offer, maintaining the price of $90 would cause a loss on each unit sold. "Why sell a product if you lose money on every one of them?" was his contention. The production manager wanted to sell the units because it would keep his plant busy.

The president requested a study of the company's cost structure to help him decide. He found the factory fixed costs to be $30,000 and the variable portion $10 for each unit manufactured; the fixed selling expenses were $100,000 and the variable portion $15 per unit sold.

Instructions

1. Show computations to indicate whether the offer of $90 would be profitable for the Storey-Blatz Company.
2. Describe what other factors would enter into the decision.

chapter 9

Standard Costs

Learning Objectives

Upon completion of your study of this chapter you should have achieved the following:

1. An understanding of the nature of standard costs and the meaning of variances from standard.
2. A knowledge of how standards for materials, labor, and overhead costs are established.
3. An understanding of how variances are treated in the determination of net income.
4. An understanding of how overhead variances are analyzed to segregate the volume and the controllable elements.

Nature of Standard Costs

Standard costs are predetermined costs. They are usually set at the beginning of each year and are used during the year to measure and evaluate actual operating costs. A standard represents that cost which in management's opinion *should be incurred* in future operations, and a predetermined standard is thus established for each labor operation and for each raw material used in the company's manufacturing process. Careful study and analysis, utilizing past cost experience and a projection of future events, is necessary to establish realistic standard costs. This costing system is used primarily for manufacturing operations, because factory processes tend to be repetitive; however, it is occasionally utilized in nonmanufacturing operations.

Standard costs for raw materials are based upon a systematic determination of the exact size, quantity, and quality of the materials comprising the product, plus any related freight costs. Labor standards are set by detailed time and motion studies involving the workmen and their machines. Every detail of physical motion and mechanical operation is carefully timed to accumulate the labor hours necessary to produce each item that the company manufactures.

Standard labor hours are then multiplied by the predetermined wage rate applicable to each type of operation to arrive at the standard labor cost. Some operations require skilled labor, others semiskilled, and some unskilled; the different wage rates applicable to each class of labor must be used.

The standard manufacturing overhead applicable to each product is more difficult to determine and less accurate than standard labor and raw materials costs, because there is no direct relationship between many of the overhead costs and the various products which a company manufactures. The standard overhead cost for the entire manufacturing plant must first be estimated and this total prorated to all the units which the company expects to produce. The standard manufacturing overhead cost per unit of product is thus the total expected factory overhead divided by the number of units expected to be produced. The standard cost of a relatively simple product may be illustrated as follows:

Standard Cost Per Unit of Product L–134–C

Labor:	Two hours at $2.00 per hour	$ 4.00
Materials:	One gallon of material X–73,	
	at $1.50 per gallon	1.50
	Two pounds of material Y–41,	
	at $3.00 per pound	6.00
Manufacturing overhead:	$2.50 per	
	direct labor hour	5.00
	Total standard cost	$16.50

Practical vs. Ideal Standards

Standards for labor and materials may be established at either an idealistic level or at a practical level. *Ideal* labor standards would be established so that only the most efficient employees working at top speed are able to attain them; *practical* labor standards would be set at levels so that experienced employees are able to attain them with reasonable effort. Both types of standards provide management with a tool for determining the more inefficient workers or the manufacturing operations requiring attention. From a more positive perspective, standard costs are motivating devices and provide employees with a rough measurement of what is expected of them. If the standard is too tight, so that it is achieved by only the most efficient persons working under ideal conditions, the majority of the company's employees will lose confidence in either the measuring device itself or in their own performance. The standard cost in either case has failed to motivate employees to improved performance. Scientific studies have shown that practical labor standards which are "tight but attainable" are most successful.

Variations From Standard

Variations or differences between actual and standard costs are calculated and periodically reported to management. Standards must be sufficiently detailed to permit the computation of variations by areas of responsibility. If one supervisor incurs costs in excess of the standards, the resulting variation must cover only the operating area involved. Thus the responsibility for favorable or unfavorable variations can be associated with the performance of specific individuals. By watching these variations, management can quickly detect those areas which are not meeting standards and thus need attention.

Six basic types of variations are used. They are as follows:

1. *Materials price variation:* measures differences between standard prices and prices actually paid for raw materials.
2. *Materials efficiency variation:* measures differences between the standard amount of raw materials needed and the amount actually used.
3. *Labor price variation:* measures differences between the standard labor rates and the labor rates actually used in paying workers.
4. *Labor efficiency variation:* measures differences between the standard production expected of employees and their actual production.
5. *Manufacturing overhead controllable variation:* measures differences between the manufacturing overhead actually incurred and the flexible budget of overhead.
6. *Manufacturing overhead volume variance:* measures the difference between the fixed overhead costs incurred and the fixed overhead absorbed by completed production.

These six variations are the framework around which a standard cost system is constructed. They may be computed separately for each department or process, and many companies using a job order cost system compute the labor and materials variations for each job. Reports which reflect these variations are prepared at frequent intervals and in considerable detail.

Materials Standards

The standard cost of each completed product contains separate standards for each type of raw material used in that product. Raw materials standards include both a standard quantity and a standard price. Engineers assist in the establishment of the type of material and the quantity that should be used, taking into account a normal amount of material spoilage. Freight is also included in the raw materials standard costs, so that excessive freight costs will result in unfavorable variances. Purchasing department personnel, assisted by the company's engineers and cost accountants, establish the standard materials costs. The raw material standard costs of subassembly 143–A are illustrated in Exhibit 9–1. The labor and overhead standards for this same item are illustrated later.

EXHIBIT 9–1

Direct Materials Standards Subassembly 143-A

		Materials Standard Cost
1 sheet .008 gauge cold roll steel, 24″ x 32″	$1.40 each	$1.40
3 bolts, hexagon head, 3″ x ⅛″	.04 each	.12
3 nuts, hexagon, ⅛″ I.D.	.01 each	.03
4 feet copper wire, ½₂″ O.D.	.04 per foot	.16
Total standard materials for each unit of subassembly 143–A		$1.71

Materials Price Variance

When raw materials are purchased, any difference between the actual cost and the predetermined standard cost is a *materials price variance*. Computing these variances quickly and reporting them to appropriate executives is one of the primary reasons for the use of a standard cost system. If the prices paid for raw materials are above the predetermined standards, management should be appraised of this fact as quickly as possible, for the purchasing department may not be searching diligently enough for the lowest prices or buying in sufficient quantities to get the lowest prices. On the other hand, there may have been a general upward trend in raw materials prices, so that it may be necessary to change to a less expensive material or raise the sales price of the product to cover the increased cost of production.

To illustrate, assume that 1,000 sheets of .008 gauge steel, shown in Exhibit 9–1 with a standard cost of $1.40 per sheet, were purchased for $1.50 per sheet. The steel would cost a total of $1,500, but the standard cost is only $1,400. The $100 unfavorable difference is recorded separately in the accounting records as a materials price variance, while the steel would go to the raw materials inventory at its standard cost of $1,400.

Suppose that the next shipment of 1,000 sheets of steel is acquired at $1.35 per sheet. This would produce a favorable variance of $50. The favorable and the unfavorable variances for the steel would be reported as a net amount only, for variances are accumulated by groups of materials or by departments; the large number of raw materials used by most companies precludes reporting each raw materials variance separately. However, if the total variance becomes sufficiently large to warrant special study, a detailed report may be prepared which indicates which materials are causing the variance.

It is significant that the perpetual inventories contain only standard costs, and all differences between actual and standard costs are considered period costs. The reasoning underlying this procedure is that the standard reflects what the product should cost, and therefore variances should be separated and should not be permitted to exert random and unexpected influence in inventory costs. Further, unfavorable variances are considered inefficiencies, and therefore are period rather than product costs; similarly, favorable variances are considered gains and are also period costs.

Materials Efficiency Variance

When raw materials are withdrawn from the stockroom, the actual quantity used in the manufacture of a product is compared with the standard quantity, and any differences are reported as *materials efficiency variances*. A job calling for the manufacture of 980 units of subassembly 143–A, for which the raw materials standards were shown in Exhibit 9–1, should thus require only 980 sheets of .008 gauge steel. The use of 1,000 sheets would represent inefficiency or defective materials, and would produce an unfavorable variance of $28 (20 sheets at $1.40 each, standard cost). Note that the standard cost of raw material is used to calculate the materials efficiency variances. Any difference between actual price and standard price has already been recorded as a materials price variance, so that the materials efficiency variance reflects only the effects of efficient or inefficient use of raw materials. The two materials variances are calculated as follows:

Materials Price Variance
Actual cost of materials bought, 1,000 sheets at $1.50	$1,500	20,000
Standard cost of materials bought, 1,000 sheets at $1.40	1,400	
Materials price variance (unfavorable)		$100

Materials Efficiency Variance
Materials actually used, at standard price (1,000 sheets)	$1,400	
Standard materials required, at standard price (980 sheets)	1,372	
Materials efficiency variance (unfavorable)		$ 28
Total materials variances		$128

Separation of the materials price variance and the materials efficiency variance is important, since different employees are responsible for each. The workmen who use a material usually have no responsibility for its purchase price, while the person who buys the material frequently is not responsible for its use.

Labor Standards

Standard costs are established for each labor operation and include the standard time required for the operation and the standard wage rate which should be paid for that type of work. Labor standard costs for subassembly 143–A are illustrated in Exhibit 9–2.

EXHIBIT 9–2

Direct Labor Standards Subassembly 143-A

Operation	Time	Hourly Wage Rate	Standard Labor Cost
Shear one 24″ x 32″ sheet steel into strips	10 min.	$3.00	$ .50
Punch holes in strips	15 min.	2.00	.50
Bend strips	5 min.	3.00	.25
Insert bolts and tighten nuts	5 min.	3.00	.25
Attach wire	15 min.	2.00	.50
Total standard time and cost	50 min.		$2.00

Each employee's daily time sheet indicates the operation performed, the time expended on the operation, and how many units were completed. From these time sheets the labor costs can be computed, and the actual and the standard cost of each operation compared.

Labor Price Variance

Variances resulting from differences in standard wage rates are reflected in a *labor price variance*. A wage increase granted an employee or a blanket raise for the entire labor force may result in an unfavorable labor price variance. If an employee earning $3.50 per hour works for eight hours at a task which is normally performed by an employee earning $3.00 per hour, a loss of $0.50 per hour for each of the eight hours has resulted; this $4.00 loss is recorded as an unfavorable labor price variance. Any difference between actual wage rates and standard wage rates will produce a labor price variance.

Labor Efficiency Variance

A difference between the standard time and the actual time required to complete a given production task will result in a labor efficiency variance. To illustrate the computation of labor efficiency, assume that a standard production rate of forty-eight units has been set for an eight-hour day. If a workman produces only forty-five during the day, the failure to meet standard production results in an unfavorable labor efficiency variance. The three units of lost production, multiplied by the standard unit labor cost, is the amount of the labor efficiency variance. Thus, if the standard cost is $0.50 per unit, the unfavorable variance resulting from the three lost units is $1.50.

Suppose that the same workman produces fifty units the next day. Since the standard is forty-eight units, he has exceeded standard by two units. The labor efficiency variance would then include the $0.50 standard cost of the two units of extra production. As in the case of raw materials, favorable and unfavorable variances may be combined within each department or for categories of operations. There are usually too many labor operations to report each one separately; however, the accounting department gathers sufficient data to provide detailed variances should management call for that information.

Frequently, the labor price variance and the labor efficiency variance are computed simultaneously. To illustrate, assume that a workman receiving $3.10 per hour produces fifty sheets of steel in eight hours. The standard for this operation is forty-eight sheets per eight-hour day, and the standard wage is $3.00 per hour. The labor price variance is $.80 (eight hours at $.10 above standard), and the labor efficiency variance is $1.00 (standard efficiency for an eight-hour day is forty-eight pieces, but fifty were actually completed). The extra two pieces, multiplied by the $.50 standard labor cost per piece, equals a $1.00 favorable labor efficiency variance. The labor price and efficiency variance may be illustrated as follows:

Labor Price Variance

Hours actually worked × actual wage rate (8 × $3.10)	$24.80	
Hours actually worked × standard wage rate (8 × $3.00)	24.00	
Labor price variance (unfavorable)		$ .80

Labor Efficiency Variance

Actual production × standard labor rate (50 units × $.50)	$25.00	
Standard production × standard labor rate (48 units × $.50)	24.00	
Labor efficiency variance (favorable)		(1.00)
Total labor variance		$(.20)

It is important to note that the labor price variance is the difference between the actual rate multiplied by all hours worked and the standard rate multiplied by all hours worked. The efficiency variance is then computed by determining the difference between actual production multiplied by the standard rate and standard production multiplied by the standard rate. Erroneous computations are frequently made when variances are computed, but errors can be reduced by calculating the labor price variance first.

Separation of labor price and labor efficiency variances is necessary for measurement of different areas of responsibility. The workman is responsible for his own production or efficiency, but he has little control over his wage rate. The person responsible for wage rates may have no direct control over the individual workman's efficiency. Even if the same person is responsible for both areas, it is important to know whether unfavorable variances result from wage rates or from labor inefficiency.

Manufacturing Overhead Standards

Standard manufacturing overhead for each product is more difficult to establish in advance than the standard for direct materials or direct labor, because of the widely varying types of costs included in manufacturing overhead. The relationship between manufacturing overhead and specific productive operations is also less direct. However, the general process of determining the standard manufacturing overhead for each product may be described as follows:

1. Estimate the manufacturing overhead costs expected to be incurred during the coming year.

2. Estimate the standard direct labor hours expected to be worked during the year. (Assuming direct labor is the proration base.)
3. Divide the estimated manufacturing overhead costs by the estimated direct labor hours to determine a manufacturing overhead application rate. The rate will be stated as a dollar amount per hour of labor.
4. Multiply the standard direct labor hours incurred to produce a unit of each product by the overhead application rate. The result is the standard overhead cost for a unit of that product.

To illustrate the calculation, assume that the labor standard for a single unit of one of the company's products is four hours. Assume further that a total of $100,000 of manufacturing overhead is expected to be incurred during the year, with the expectation that a total of 50,000 direct labor hours will be spent on all products during the year. The manufacturing overhead rate would be:

$$\frac{\text{Estimated manufacturing overhead}}{\text{Estimated direct labor hours}} = \frac{\$100,000}{50,000} = \$2 \text{ per direct labor hour}$$

Since each unit of this product requires four hours of labor, the standard manufacturing overhead cost for that unit will be $8.00 (4 hours × $2 per hour). If the company has another product which has standard labor of only three hours, the standard manufacturing overhead for each unit of that product would be $6.00 (3 hours × $2.00 per hour). Note that the rate of $2.00 per direct labor hour is applicable to all products, and those requiring more labor will have a higher standard overhead cost. This is as it should be, since the rate assumes that there is a direct correlation between the incurrence of manufacturing overhead costs and the hours of direct labor worked. Thus, products which require a large number of labor hours should receive a larger proportion of the overhead cost.

Some companies use direct materials cost, units of raw materials, or direct labor cost as the base for prorating manufacturing overhead. When these bases are used, the process is exactly the same as that described above; that is, a rate is first calculated and then is used to compute the standard manufacturing overhead per unit.

Computing Manufacturing Overhead Variances

When manufacturing overhead is incurred, it is recorded as manufacturing overhead in a control account, exactly as described in the preceding chapter which discussed job order costing systems. When overhead is applied to completed production, it is also accounted for exactly as discussed in the preceding chapter. However, when a standard cost system is used, only the standard manufacturing overhead cost per unit is applied to each unit produced. Thus, each completed unit receives only the standard overhead, regardless of how many direct labor hours were actually incurred in its production.

The difference between the overhead costs actually incurred and the standard amount applied to production is the total over- or under-applied overhead. This process of recording and applying overhead does not differ from that discussed in Chapter 8, except that only the standard amount is applied to each unit. There are two basic factors that produce an over- or under-applied manufacturing overhead amount.

1. The rate used to determine the standard overhead per unit was based upon a misestimate of the number of direct labor hours to be worked.
2. Those responsible for incurring manufacturing overhead costs may have spent more or less than they should have.

These two factors necessitate a calculation of two separate manufacturing overhead variances. If the original overhead application rate was calculated for an expected level of activity that was not realized, a *manufacturing overhead volume variance* will be included in the over- or under-applied overhead; if those responsible for incurring overhead spend more or less than they should, a *manufacturing overhead controllable variance* will exist.

Manufacturing overhead volume variance   When the manufacturing overhead application rate is established, it is based upon some expected level of activity for the coming year. Most companies have a flexible budget which will indicate the expected overhead costs to be incurred at several levels of activity. Exhibit 9–3 illustrates such a budget, ranging from 60 percent to 100 percent of capacity. This company produces a single product, and the standard labor cost for each of those units is two hours.

EXHIBIT 9–3

PALOMAR COMPANY
Flexible Budget Schedule of Manufacturing Overhead
For the Year 1975

Expense	60% 75,000 units (150,000 DLH)	70% 87,500 units (175,000 DLH)	80% 100,000 units (200,000 DLH)	90% 112,500 units (225,000 DLH)	100% 125,000 units (250,000 DLH)
Factory supplies	$ 7,500	$ 8,500	$ 9,500	$ 10,500	$ 11,500
Supervision	30,000	40,000	45,000	45,000	45,000
Heat, light, and power	6,000	7,000	8,000	9,000	10,000
Indirect materials	17,000	20,000	23,000	26,000	29,000
Machinery repairs	8,000	8,800	9,600	10,400	11,000
Depreciation on machinery	24,000	24,000	24,000	24,000	24,000
Depreciation on factory building	15,000	15,000	15,000	15,000	15,000
Taxes on factory building	3,000	3,000	3,000	3,000	3,000
Insurance	5,000	5,000	5,000	5,000	5,000
Indirect labor	21,000	24,000	27,000	30,000	33,000
Total	$136,500	$155,300	$169,100	$177,900	$186,500
Rate per direct labor hour	$ .91	$ .887	$ .846	$ .791	$ .746

Note that the number of direct labor hours increases as capacity increases and that the total expected dollar overhead costs increase also. However, some of the overhead costs, such as depreciation, taxes, and insurance are fixed in amount and do not change, regardless of the level of activity. For these reasons, the rate of manufacturing overhead per direct labor hour decreases as the level of activity increases.

If the company budgets production of 75,000 units, it would expect to operate at a 60 percent level of activity during the coming year and would use an overhead application rate based upon that level of activity. The overhead application rate would thus be $.91 per direct labor hour, and each unit would have a standard overhead of $1.82, since there are two labor hours in each unit. However, suppose that the company actually worked at 100 percent level of activity, due to an unexpected increase in demand for its product, and actually produced 125,000 units. Each unit produced would receive the standard overhead of $1.82, regardless of how many were completed.

The 125,000 units produced would thus result in an overhead application of 250,000 direct labor hours (DLH) × $.91, or $227,500. This amount is greater than the budget schedule (Exhibit 9–3) indicates is normal at a 100 percent level of activity. The original selection of an overhead application rate at a 60 percent level of activity ($.91 per hour) when a $.746 rate would have been correct, has produced an over-application of overhead. This portion of the manufacturing overhead variance is due to volume and is calculated as follows:

Manufacturing overhead applied to completed products, using standard overhead ($1.802 × 125,000 units)	$227,500
Manufacturing overhead budget at the level of activity actually achieved (100% capacity, or 250,000 DLH)	186,500
Manufacturing overhead volume variance	$ 41,000

Manufacturing overhead controllable variance   The manufacturing overhead controllable variance is due to the expenditure of more or less than should have been spent at the level of activity actually achieved. Continuing the example above, the company's production indicates that a 100 percent level of activity was actually achieved. Had a total of $189,700 of overhead costs actually been incurred, those responsible for incurring overhead costs would have overspent $3,200 ($186,500 budget at a 100 percent volume level, as compared to $189,700 actually spent). This $3,200 is the *manufacturing overhead controllable variance,* which is unfavorable in this particular case, because more was spent than the budget indicates. The calculation would be made as follows:

Actually spent at 100% level of activity	$189,700
Budget for 100% level of activity (250,000 DLH)	186,500
Manufacturing overhead controllable variance	$ 3,200

The calculation of the two manufacturing overhead variances is shown graphically in Exhibit 9–4.

EXHIBIT 9–4

Triangle Method of Calculating Manufacturing Overhead Variances

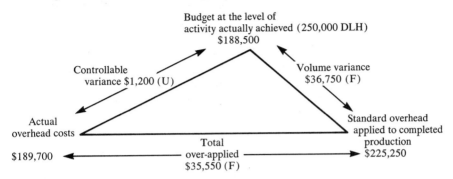

The base of the triangle is the total over- or under-applied overhead, which is the difference between the total actual overhead and the total standard overhead applied to completed production. The controllable and volume variances will total to this same amount, although one may be favorable and the other unfavorable. The unfavorable controllable variance of $1,200 in Exhibit 9–4 and the favorable volume variance of $36,750 equal the total over-applied amount of $35,550. The (u) and (f) symbols are used to indicate unfavorable and favorable variances.

Unfavorable overhead controllable variance	$ 1,200 (u)
Favorable overhead volume variance	36,750 (f)
Total over-applied overhead	$35,550 (f)

It is extremely important to remember that the apex of the triangle is the overhead which would be budgeted at the level of production achieved, *measured by the labor hours which are normal, or standard, for the units actually produced.* The actual number of hours worked should not be used to calculate the adjusted budget amount at the apex of the triangle, because there may have been a labor efficiency variance. Since this figure is used to separate the controllable variance from the volume variance, it must be based upon the standard hours in the number of units produced.

Inventories at
Standard Cost

The six variances which have been discussed in this chapter are illustrated in Exhibit 9–5. After the materials price and materials efficiency variances are removed, only the standard materials cost enters into the goods in process inventory. The same is true for labor and overhead, for the variances are

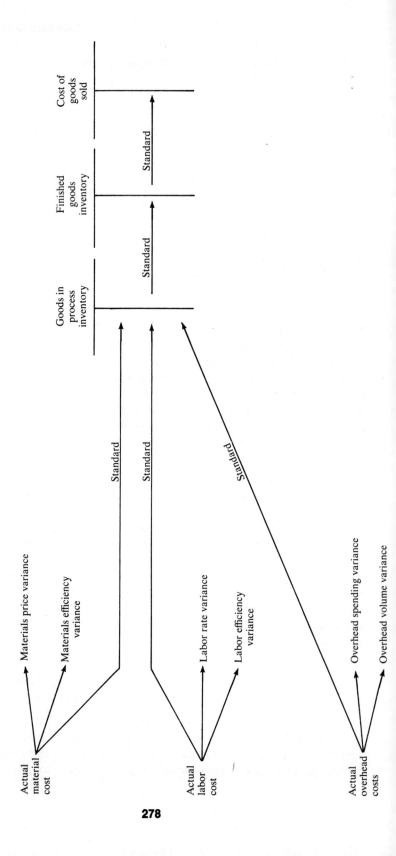

EXHIBIT 9–5
Flow of Standard Costs

recorded as the difference between the actual cost and the standard cost. Note that both the goods in process and the finished goods inventories are in the accounting records at standard cost, and that the cost of goods sold contains only the standard cost of the units sold.

Effect of Variances
on Cost of Goods Sold

Variances from standard are treated in the income statement as adjustments to the cost of goods sold. These variances are additional costs or reductions of cost and thus relate to cost of goods sold rather than to selling or administrative expenses. When the income statement is prepared for reporting to groups outside the company—such as stockholders or creditors—the variances are not shown separately, and only the final adjusted cost of goods sold appears in the statement. The variances are for management's use and are not usually of interest to others.

Some variances may be favorable, while others are unfavorable. All variances are adjustments to the cost of goods sold when their total is not unusually large in amount. When the total amount of all variances is material, it should be prorated among the goods in process inventory, the finished goods inventory, and the cost of goods sold. Assume, for purposes of illustration, that the variances total $34,222.20, and that this is considered material in amount. The allocation procedure is shown below.

	Balance as of December 31	Percent of the Total	Allocated Variance
Goods in process inventory	$ 100,000	5%	$ 1,711.10
Finished goods inventory	500,000	25%	8,555.50
Cost of goods sold	1,400,000	70%	23,955.60
Total	$2,000,000	100%	$34,222.20

Note that the $34,222.20 is allotted proportionately to the three places where overhead variances have had an effect. The work in process would be increased by $1,711.10 and the finished goods by $8,555.50. The remainder of the variance would be an adjustment to the cost of goods sold.

There is no fixed rule which indicates when the total of all variances is sufficiently material in amount to require a proration to inventories. If the variance is greater than one or two percent of the cost of goods sold, however, it begins to be material in amount. In the preceding example only $23,955.60 of the variances went to the cost of goods sold rather than the entire $34,222.20. The proration to inventories thus affects the final net profit by the amount assigned to the two inventories.

Variance Reports for
Management

Operating management needs frequent variance reports indicating favorable or unfavorable operating results for each raw material and each labor operation. Reports that show detailed variances in this manner assist management in locating those areas which differ from the predetermined standards. Any abnormal variance, whether favorable or unfavorable, should be investigated, for either could indicate weaknesses in the manufacturing operation. A large unfavorable variance for an item of raw material may indicate inferior material, inefficient usage, theft, or carelessness. On the other hand, a large favorable variance may indicate use of an insufficient amount of the material, resulting in a finished product of inferior quality.

A detailed variance report for operating management is illustrated in Exhibit 9–6. This report is prepared for production supervisors who are responsi-

EXHIBIT 9–6

Controllable Cost Report for
Direct Materials and Direct Labor

Product: Potato chips, one-ounce packages

Quantity produced: 160,000

Period covered: July 1–July 5, 1975

Materials Efficiency Variances	Standard		Actual		Total Variance from Standard
	Per Pound	Total	Per Pound	Total	
Potatoes	$.070	$ 700.00	$.074	$ 740.00	$40.00
Corn oil	.002	20.00	.002	20.00	—
Salt—plain	.001	10.00	.001	10.00	—
Salt—onion	.001	10.00	.001	10.00	—
Bags	.026	260.00	.025	250.00	(10.00)
Cardboard cartons	.040	400.00	.041	410.00	10.00
Total material	$.140	$1,400.00	$.144	$1,440.00	$40.00
Labor Efficiency Variances					
Peeling	$.061	$ 610.00	$.059	$ 590.00	$(20.00)
Slicing	.040	400.00	.042	420.00	20.00
Cooking	.052	520.00	.051	510.00	(10.00)
Packaging	.070	700.00	.076	760.00	60.00
Total labor	$.223	$2,230.00	$.228	$2,280.00	$50.00

ble for the efficiency of labor and materials, but who have no responsibility for material or labor price variances or for manufacturing overhead variances. Detailed variance reports should be submitted only to those people who have responsibility over the areas covered in the report; similar reports detailing other variances are prepared and submitted to the supervisors responsible for other areas.

Revision of
Standard Costs

Frequent changes in standard costs could result in confusion in the measurement of actual costs. For this reason, standard costs are usually adjusted annually. Standards are changed during the accounting year only as the result of a major change in expected costs, such as a steep and permanent rise in the price of raw materials. A minor shift in costs usually will not destroy the effectiveness of a standard as a cost measurement device once management is aware of the change.

Manufacturing Standard
Costs Illustrated

The following problem illustrates the operation of a standard cost system and the computation of the related variances. Note that the fixed and variable manufacturing overhead and the standard costs for the company's product are determined in advance of actual operations.

Completed prior to the current year:

Manufacturing overhead is analyzed as follows:

Total fixed manufacturing overhead	$20,000.00
Total variable manufacturing overhead per DLH	$ 1.25

32,000 direct hours are set as the expected level of production. (This is an 80% level, or 8,000 units of product.)

The standard for the company's product is:

Raw materials	10 units @ $2 per unit	$20.00
Labor	4 hours @ $3 per hour	12.00

Manufacturing overhead:

Total fixed	$20,000
Total variable 32,000 @ $1.25	40,000
Total overhead	$60,000
$60,000 ÷ 32,000 DLH =	
$1.875 × 4 hours per unit =	7.50
Total standard cost per unit	$39.50

Transactions during the current year:

Purchased and consumed 73,100 units of raw material at a cost of $153,510 ($2.10 per unit). A total of 7,300 units of finished goods was produced.

Incurred labor costs of $89,900; this cost was incurred for 29,000 labor hours at $3.10 per hour.

Incurred manufacturing overhead costs of $56,000.

There were no beginning or ending inventories of raw materials or units in process.

Since there were no beginning or ending inventories, the 7,300 units completed during the year actually cost $299,410. This total is the sum of the purchase price of materials, $153,510, the amount of wages paid, $89,900, and the manufacturing overhead incurred. However, these totals do not indicate where the company failed to meet expectations; for the total standard cost of the 7,300 completed units, at $39.50 each, is only $288,350. An analysis of the variances would indicate the following:

Total standard cost of 7,300 units		$288,350
Materials price variance	$7,310	
Materials efficiency variance	200	
Labor price variance	2,900	
Labor efficiency variance	(600)	
Overhead controllable variance	(500)	
Overhead volume variance	1,750	
Total variances		11,060
Total cost of goods sold		$299,410

These variations would be reported to management, usually with supporting schedules for the major labor operations and more important raw materials. Note that the two price variances are more significant than the efficiency variances or the overhead variances. The price paid for materials and labor accounts for $10,210 ($7,310 plus $2,900) of the total $11,060 variance. Labor efficiency is better than management's expectations, since it has a favorable variance, and the materials efficiency variance appears relatively insignificant.

The overhead variance is primarily a result of the lower volume of production than anticipated when the standard overhead was computed. Since 7,300 units were produced, while the determination of overhead application was based on an expected 8,000 unit level, a total of $1,750 of the fixed overhead was not applied to products. Thus, the overhead variance is primarily attributable to volume, rather than to spending.

Standards for
Selling and Administrative Expenses

Selling and administrative expenses are related to functions other than the production of finished goods, and therefore standards for these costs must be based on a measurement other than units produced. The processing of purchase orders, for example, has no direct relationship either to the number of units produced or the number of units sold; therefore, the number of purchase orders issued becomes the basis of measurement, and a standard cost per purchase order may be calculated for measuring the efficiency of the purchasing department. A standard cost may also be prepared for each letter typed by a stenographer, each sales order processed, each customer's statement prepared, or each check written.

Standards for selling and administrative expenses cannot be interpreted as precisely as standards for manufacturing operations, because the operation being measured is not as consistent or repetitive. For this reason, selling and administrative cost variances are rarely entered in the accounting records but are usually reported to management in special reports.

Exhibit 9–7 illustrates the accumulation of a standard labor cost for processing the payment of an account payable. Note that standard time is computed for each step in the payment process as a means of accumulating the total standard time required to process and prepare each payment; the related standard salary cost is then determined by use of the prevailing salary rate for accounts payable personnel.

The standard time necessary to complete each step in a selling or administrative process is valuable information for arranging employee work loads. The standard time required to prove extensions and totals on vendors' invoices in Exhibit 9–7 is 1.4 minutes; if approximately 500 invoices are processed daily,

EXHIBIT 9–7

Standard Salary Costs for Processing and Paying Accounts Payable

	Standard Time in Minutes	Total Minutes
Processing Purchase Orders		
Sort in numerical order	.2	
Insert general ledger account number	1.1	
File in "pending" file	.8	2.1
Processing Receiving Reports		
Sort in numerical order	.2	
File one copy with purchase order in "pending" file	2.3	
File one copy numerically	.7	3.2
Processing Vendor's Invoices		
Match with purchase orders and receiving reports from "pending" file	2.3	
Prove extensions and totals	1.4	
Write voucher	1.0	
File in "approved for payment" file	.8	5.5
Preparing Checks		
Remove from "approved for payment" file	.7	
Type check	1.3	2.0
Filing Paid Vouchers and Related Documents		
File		.6
Total standard time		13.4
Hourly salary rate		$4.00
Total standard salary cost		$0.89

the supervisor of the accounts payable section is informed that 700 minutes, or 11.7 hours, is the standard time required each day to complete the operation. As a result, one employee is assigned full-time on that operation, and one-half of another employee's time is also devoted to it. If the employees assigned to the task do not complete the work, the supervisor of the section may need to observe the employees assigned to the task to see if they are performing below standard.

Selling and administrative standards are also useful as a basis for managerial decisions. Computation of standard costs for taking orders, filling orders, and making collections assists in determining the cost of making a sale. As a result, small, unprofitable orders may be discouraged. For example, assume that a company selling wholesale builders' supplies has the following standard costs for processing each sales order:

	Standard Cost
Preparing an order	$0.53
Filling an order	.46
Preparing an invoice	.07
Posting an invoice	.04
Handling a collection	.11
Posting a collection	.04
Total	$1.25

If the gross margin on the company's merchandise is 25 percent, an order for $5.00 will realize a gross profit of $1.25, which is just sufficient to cover the cost of processing the order. As a result, the company's management may wish to consider a policy of not accepting orders of less than $5.00 or perhaps adding a $1.00 handling fee on small orders.

Standard costs for selling and administrative expenses are employed primarily in larger companies, where the volume of activity permits arrangement of the selling and administrative operations into repetitive tasks. A considerable effort is necessary to accumulate the data for selling and administrative standards, and smaller companies rarely use standards except for manufacturing costs.

Summary

Standard costs may be employed with both job order and process cost systems. When a job order system is used, the job order records accumulate actual costs. After the job is completed, the standard costs of the products completed on that job are calculated, and the variances are shown on the job record, and at that time entries are made in the accounting records to record the variances and the standard costs. In this way the controllable variances for materials price, materials efficiency, labor rate, and labor efficiency are reported for each job as it is completed.

When standards are used with a process cost system, the actual manufacturing costs are accumulated for each department or cost center on a daily, weekly, or monthly basis, depending upon the frequency of the company's cost reports. Calculation of the standard cost for the units produced is a relatively simple matter, since the products are few in number and follow a prescribed, unchanging process. Standard costs are reported with actual costs on the periodic production cost reports, and thus the controllable variances are calculated and reported to operating management at frequent intervals.

Overhead costs are controlled in both job order and process cost systems through the use of flexible budgets. The overhead controllable variance is calculated and reported each time a departmental expense report is prepared, but the volume variance is less subject to control and may not be calculated and reported until the end of each month.

Standards are frequently employed in manufacturing operations because of the repetitive nature of manufacturing activities and are utilized with less frequency for selling and administrative activities. However, every cost must be judged with some kind of standard, either explicitly or implicitly, from the viewpoint of the person making the analysis. Explicit standards for manufacturing, as well as for selling and administrative expenses, provide a way of communicating the administrator's expectations to those people being measured. For this reason, standards for any operation are useful control devices.

Appendix

Journal Entries for
Standard Costs

The following journal entries are presented for the comprehensive illustration of manufacturing standard costs appearing at the end of this chapter. The amounts are those used in the illustration and provide the basis for the variances appearing at the end of that illustration.

(a)   Purchase of raw material:

Raw materials inventory	146,200	
Raw materials price variance	7,310	
Accounts payable		153,510

Bought 73,100 units at $2.10

(b)   Consumption of raw materials:

Goods in process	146,000	
Raw materials efficiency variance	2,000	
Raw materials inventory		146,200

Used 73,100 units to produce 7,300 finished products.

(c)   Incurrence of labor costs:

Goods in process	87,600	
Labor price variance	2,900	
Labor efficiency variance		600
Accrued payroll		89,900

To pay for 29,000 hours at $3.10 per hour which produced the units.

(d)   Application of manufacturing overhead:

Goods in process	54,750	
Manufacturing overhead		54,750

To apply standard overhead to the 7,300 units produced.

(e)   Incurrence of manufacturing overhead:

Manufacturing overhead	56,000	
Cash (or other credit)		56,000

To record the incurrence of actual overhead.

(f)   Completion of finished goods:

Finished goods	288,350	
Goods in process		288,350

To record completed production.

(g)   Sale of products (7,300 sold at $50 price):

Accounts receivable	365,000	
Sales		365,000

To record sales.

(h)   Cost of goods sold:

Cost of goods sold	288,350	
Finished goods		288,350

To record the cost of goods sold.

(i)   Close manufacturing overhead:

Manufacturing overhead volume variance	1,750	
Manufacturing overhead controllable		
variance		500
Manufacturing overhead		1,250

To record overhead variance.

(j)   Close variances:

Cost of goods sold	11,060	
Labor efficiency variance	600	
Manufacturing overhead controllable		
variance	500	
Materials price variance		7,310
Materials efficiency variance		200
Labor price variance		2,900
Manufacturing overhead volume		
variance		1,750

To close variances to cost of goods sold.

New Terms

Ideal standard   A standard based upon the production of the most efficient employees under ideal conditions.

Labor efficiency variance   The difference between standard labor outputs and actual labor outputs.

Labor price variation   The difference between standard rate and actual rate.

Manufacturing overhead controllable variance   The difference between overhead actually incurred and the amount that should have been incurred in accordance with the flexible budget.

Manufacturing overhead volume variance   The difference between fixed overhead incurred and the fixed overhead applied to production.

Materials efficiency variance   The difference between the standard materials usage and actual usage.

Materials price variance   The difference between the standard price of materials and the actual price.

Practical standard   A standard based upon the production of the average employee working at rapid but attainable speed.

Questions

1. Define a standard cost and describe how it can help management control the operations of a manufacturing plant.

2. Describe how materials standards are calculated. Should the standard materials cost include freight costs? An allowance for scrap and spoilage?

3. Describe how labor standards are calculated. Should the labor standard include time for a coffee break? Should it be set at the speed of the slowest worker or the fastest worker?

4. Describe how standard overhead for a unit is calculated. Is it necessary to establish an expected or normal volume for this purpose?

5. Should materials and labor standards be established for each raw material and each labor operation, or is one total material and one total labor standard sufficient? Defend your answer.

6. How are variances from standard treated in an income statement?

7. Why should materials price variances be recorded at the time raw materials are purchased, while raw materials efficiency variances are recorded when raw materials are consumed?

8. Why are manufacturing overhead variations more difficult to determine than materials and labor variances?

9. Explain how all three inventories—raw materials, goods in process, and finished goods—are maintained at standard costs. Does this simplify or complicate the inventory record-keeping process?

10. Why should detailed variance reports by separate labor operations and materials be prepared? Who should receive these reports? Should they be sent to assembly-line workers in the plant?

11. Why are variances for selling and administrative expenses used less frequently than variances for manufacturing operations?

Exercises ⒝

9–1   Definitions *(15 minutes)*   The following terms or concepts were introduced in this chapter:
a. Standard cost
b. Materials price variation
c. Materials efficiency variation
d. Labor price variation
e. Labor efficiency variation
f. Manufacturing overhead spending variation
g. Manufacturing overhead volume variation

Instructions
Define each term or concept, giving examples where possible.

9–2   Materials Variances *(10 minutes)*   The Swenson Company set a standard of three units of raw material at $1 each for its product G19–4. The first unit completed required four units of raw material which cost $0.90 each.

Instructions
Compute the two raw materials variances and indicate whether they are favorable or unfavorable.

9–3   Labor Variances *(10 minutes)*   The Ebony Company has a labor standard on one unit of its product of six hours of labor at an hourly rate of $3.00. One unit produced in January required five hours of labor at a rate of $3.20 per hour.

Instructions
Compute the labor price and efficiency variances.

9–4*   Basic Calculation of Variances *(20 minutes)*   The Marksman Company has a standard for its product as follows:

> Labor, 8 hours at $3 per hour
> Materials, 16 units at $1 per unit
> Manufacturing overhead, $2.50 per direct labor hour

During the year, 10,000 units were completed, requiring 81,000 hours of labor at a cost of $2.90 per hour and 155,000 units of raw material at a cost of $1.02 each. A total of $198,000 of actual manufacturing overhead costs was incurred. The adjusted budget for overhead for a 10,000-unit level of activity is $198,700.

Instructions
Compute six variances from standard, indicating for each whether it is favorable or unfavorable.

9–5* **Preparation of an Operating Report** *(20 minutes)* The Barb-
son-Lott Company uses a job order system. The labor standard for
a single unit of Z–2 is as follows:

Shear into strips	10 minutes @ hourly rate of $2.40	$ .40
Weld strips	20 minutes @ hourly rate of $3.00	1.00
Paint	6 minutes @ hourly rate of $2.50	.25
Assemble	15 minutes @ hourly rate of $2.00	.50
Pack and crate	10 minutes @ hourly rate of $2.40	.40
Total labor standard cost		$2.55

The employees' time sheets contained the following information for
the week ended January 17:

Date	Operation	Hours Worked	Pieces Completed	Total Labor Cost
Jan. 14	Shear	35	200	$ 76.00
15	Weld	75	200	232.00
15	Paint	20	200	52.00
16	Assemble	52	200	95.00
17	Pack and crate	30	200	80.00
	Total			$535.00

Instructions

Prepare a detailed report setting out variances resulting from each
operation. State which operation you would investigate first if you
were the production manager.

9–6* **Overhead Variances** *(20 minutes)* The fixed and variable production costs of the Murchison Manufacturing Company are as
follows:

Total fixed costs	$120,000
Variable cost per direct labor hour	$8.00

The company estimated that production for the coming month would
be 10,000 direct labor hours and at the beginning of the month established the standard manufacturing overhead rate on that basis.
Each unit requires three hours of labor. During the month the company produced 4,100 units, and incurred $210,000 of manufactur-
ing overhead.

Instructions

1. Compute the standard manufacturing overhead to be applied to
   each unit.
2. Compute the amount of overhead applied to completed production.
3. Compute the adjusted budget of overhead at a level of activity
   equal to 4,100 units.

4. Compute the overhead controllable and overhead volume variances.

9–7   **Operating Report for Material Variances** *(15 minutes)*   The Halliburton Company computes the price variance on raw materials purchases at the time the invoice is recorded as a liability. The following materials standards have been set for the raw materials used by the company:

Wire—1⁄16" copper extruded	$1.25 lb.
Felt—1" strips	2.00 lb.
Bolts—1⁄2" x 2", hexagonal head	.02 each
Nuts—1⁄2" I.D. hexagonal head	.01 each
Paint—enamel, white	4.00 gallon

The following transactions were completed during July:

July 1   Received an invoice for 100 lbs. of copper wire, $130.00, and 70 lbs. of felt, $135.00.

2   Received an invoice for 17 gallons of white enamel paint, $72.

3   Received an invoice for $17 freight on the copper wire and felt in the transaction of July 1.

4   Returned 30 lbs. of the copper wire bought on July 1, receiving $39 credit from the supplier for the defective wire.

5   Received an invoice for 1,000 bolts, $21.00, and 1,000 nuts, $9.00.

6   Received an invoice for 10 gallons of white enamel paint, $42.

7   Received an invoice for 50 lbs. of felt, $97.

Instructions

Prepare a schedule showing for each raw material the total standard cost, total actual cost, and the materials price variance.

9–8   **Calculation of Standard Costs** *(20 minutes)*   The XYZ Corporation manufactures two products, for which the following standards have been established:

Materials

Product A: 3 pounds of M at $1.20 per pound

Product B: 2 units of K at $0.75 per unit

Labor

Product A: 2 hours at $4.00 per hour

Product B: 1 hour at $3.00 per hour

Manufacturing Overhead
(allocated on basis of direct labor hours)
Fixed costs: $15,000
Variable costs: $0.75 per direct labor hour

The corporation expects to manufacture and sell 4,000 units of A and 2,000 units of B. Overhead standards are to be calculated based upon this expected production volume.

Instructions
Calculate the standard cost of each product.

9–9   **Calculation of Variances** *(40 minutes)*   A company has the following manufacturing overhead cost structure:

Fixed costs	$100,000
Variable, per direct labor hour	$3

Only one product is manufactured and the production schedule called for the manufacture of 20,000 units during the year. Overhead is assigned to units on the basis of direct labor hours.

The standard raw material and labor cost per unit is:

Materials	3 units @ $1
Labor	2 hours @ $3

At the end of the year the company had produced 20,100 units. Actual costs were:

Overhead	$220,000
Materials	60,200 units, cost $60,100
Labor	40,300 hours, cost $120,000

Instructions
Compute the following:
1. Standard overhead per unit
2. Labor price variance
3. Labor efficiency variance
4. Materials price variance
5. Materials efficiency variance
6. Overhead controllable variance
7. Overhead volume variance

9–10   **Calculation of Variances** *(40 minutes)*   A company established the following standard cost for its product based upon an estimated volume of 120,000 direct labor hours.

Direct labor (8 hours @ $3)	$24
Direct material (10 units @ $2)	20
Overhead ($1 per direct labor hour)	8
Total	$52

The overhead cost structure of the company is $60,000 fixed plus $0.50 per direct labor hour. During the year the company actually produced 15,000 units, and the actual costs were:

Labor (124,000 hours)	$370,000
Materials (151,000 units)	$303,000
Overhead incurred	$122,400

Instructions
Compute the following, indicating for each whether it is favorable or unfavorable:
1. Labor efficiency variance
2. Labor price variance
3. Material efficiency variance
4. Materials price variance
5. Overhead under- or over-applied (state which)
6. Overhead volume variance
7. Overhead controllable variance

9–11   **Calculation of Variances** *(25 minutes)*   The Strake Company has established a standard for its product as follows:

Labor	16 hours at $6 per hour
Material	32 units at $2 per unit
Overhead per unit	$40

During the year 10,000 units were completed requiring 162,000 hours of labor costing $5.80 per hour and 310,000 units of raw material at a cost of $2.04 each. A total of $396,000 of overhead was incurred.

Instructions
Compute the following; indicating for each whether it is favorable or unfavorable:
1. The materials price variance
2. The materials efficiency variance
3. The labor price variance
4. The labor efficiency variance
5. The total over- or under-applied overhead

9–12   **Calculation of Variances** *(40 minutes)*   The Bendit Manufacturing Company established the following standard for its only product:

Labor	8 hours at $3.00 per hour
Materials	16 units at $1.00 per unit

Manufacturing overhead (allocated on a per unit basis)

Variable	$12.00 per unit
Fixed	$80,000

Estimated production is 10,000 units.

Actual results were:

> 10,000 units completed
> 81,000 hours of labor at $2.90 per hour
> 155,000 units of raw materials used
> 160,000 units of raw materials purchased at $1.02
> $198,000 actual overhead costs

Instructions

Compute the following variances:
1. Materials price variance
2. Materials efficiency variance
3. Labor price variance
4. Labor efficiency variance
5. Manufacturing overhead controllable variance
6. Manufacturing overhead volume variance

Problems ⌐³⌐

9–13   **Computation of Variances** *(20 minutes)*   Product X, manufactured by the Toolson Die Company, has the following standards for materials and labor:

Materials	3 units @ $4.00	$12	
Labor	6 hours @ $3.00	18	

During January 1,000 units were completed, requiring 3,050 units of raw materials, which were purchased for $3.90 per unit and 5,800 hours of labor, which cost a total of $18,000.

Instructions

Compute the materials price, materials efficiency, labor price, and labor efficiency variances, and state whether they are favorable or unfavorable.

9–14   **Calculation of Variances; Income Statement** *(40 minutes)*   The following basic transactions were completed by the Corrigan Co. which uses a standard cost system:

a. Materials with a standard cost of $18,000 were purchased for $18,200.
b. Materials with a standard cost of $14,000 were used to complete production which had standard materials requirements of $14,100.
c. Labor costs of $6,000 were incurred. Fifty dollars of the labor cost was due to labor rates higher than the standard rate. The labor produced units with standard labor of $6,200.
d. Manufacturing overhead of $11,000 was incurred.

e. Standard manufacturing overhead of $11,800 was applied to production.
f. All goods in process were completed.
g. All goods completed were sold for $50,000.
h. Selling and administrative costs of $12,600 were incurred.

Instructions

Prepare an income statement which sets out six variances from standard, if the overhead volume variance was $1,000 favorable.

9–15   **Calculation of Variances; Income Statement** *(40 minutes)*   The Paladium Equipment Company set the following standard on its product:

Labor	2 hours @ $3.00 per hour	$ 6
Materials	6 units @ $2.00	12
Manufacturing overhead	$2.50 per direct labor hour	5
		$23

The standard manufacturing overhead is determined on the following basis:

Normal production, 20,000 direct labor hours.
Manufacturing overhead is $20,000 fixed plus $1.50 per DLH.
Normal manufacturing overhead for 20,000 DLH = $50,000
    $50,000 ÷ 20,000 = $2.50 per DLH

The following transactions occurred during the year:

a. Purchased on account 60,000 units of raw material @ $2.10.
b. Used 53,000 units of raw material in producing 9,000 units.
c. Incurred 18,100 hours of labor @ $2.90 per hour in producing 9,000 units.
d. Incurred $46,000 of manufacturing overhead.
e. Applied manufacturing overhead to production for the 9,000 units.
f. Completed the 9,000 units and transferred them to finished goods
g. Incurred $80,000 of general and selling expenses.
h. Sold 6,000 units for $40 each.

Instructions

Prepare an income statement for the period which reflects at least six variances from standard.

9–16   **Computation and Analysis of Materials Variances** *(20 minutes)*
The Roytun Company manufactures two products, X and Y. Two supervisors are employed, one in charge of the manufacture of product X and the other in charge of the manufacture of product Y.

The company uses three types of raw materials in the manufacture of its two products, and the normal costs and requirements of these raw materials are as follows:

Raw Materials	Standard Cost per Unit	Units Required for One Completed Unit of X	Y
A	$1.00	1	2
B	.50	2	1
C	2.00	1	3

During the year the company completed 10,000 units of X and 8,000 units of Y. All raw materials are issued out of the stockroom to the supervisors at standard cost. An analysis of the raw materials usages for the period revealed that the supervisors had consumed materials as follows:

Materials	Standard Cost of Materials Used by the Supervisor in Charge of Product X	Y
A	$10,200	$15,900
B	9,800	4,500
C	20,400	54,100

Instructions
1. Prepare a schedule showing the standard cost, actual cost, and variance of each material as used by each of the two supervisors.
2. In your opinion, which supervisor was most efficient in his use of raw materials? Which material appears to have been used least efficiently, or cost more than the standard, considering both departments together?

9-17 **Reporting Material and Labor Variances** *(50 minutes)*   The Schmidt Company has two products, Beta and Theta. The unit material and labor standards for the two products are as follows:

Beta			Theta		
Material:			Material:		
A	2 units @ $2	$4.00	Y	3 units @ $1	$3.00
B	1 unit @ $1	1.00	Z	2 units @ $3	6.00
Labor:			Labor:		
Assemble	1 hour @ $2	$2.00	Paint	½ hour @ $2	$1.00
Pack	½ hour @ $1	.50	Crate	1 hour @ $1	1.00

During the month of March, the company completed the following transactions:

Purchased materials as follows:

> 2,000 units of A for $4,070
> 1,000 units of B for   980
>   700 units of Y for   750
>   500 units of Z for   1,460

Consumed materials as follows:

1,700 units of A and 780 units of B were used to complete 800 units of Beta.

610 units of Y and 380 units of Z were used to complete 200 units of Theta.

Employees' time tickets showed the following labor costs:

Assembling	800 units of Beta	—790 hours @ $2.10 per hour
Packing	800 units of Beta	—410 hours @ $1.10 per hour
Painting	200 units of Theta	— 90 hours @ $1.90 per hour
Crating	200 units of Theta	—205 hours @ $1.00 per hour

Instructions

Prepare a detailed schedule showing the materials price variance, materials efficiency variance, labor price variance, and labor efficiency variance for each material and each labor operation.

9–18   **Overhead Variances; Controllable Variance Report** *(40 minutes)*
The Wilson Abrasive Company established the following flexible budget of each manufacturing overhead expense at the beginning of the year:

	Fixed	Variable Per DLH
Depreciation on building	$ 5,000	
Depreciation on machinery	4,000	
Factory supplies		$ .04
Heat, light, and power		.02
Indirect labor	1,000	.08
Indirect materials	800	.03
Insurance	200	
Machinery repairs	2,000	.05
	$13,000	$ .22

The company's sales forecast showed that 10,000 units would be sold. No inventory is needed, since units are sold as they are manufactured. Standard manufacturing overhead per unit is based upon a normal production level of 30,000 direct labor hours. The company's only product has a labor standard of three direct labor hours per unit.

At the end of the year, the company had incurred 34,000 direct labor hours and had manufactured and sold 11,000 units. Its actual manufacturing overhead costs were as follows:

Depreciation on the building	$ 5,000
Depreciation on machinery	4,050
Factory supplies	1,400
Heat, light, and power	600
Indirect labor	3,750
Indirect materials	1,050
Insurance	200
Machinery repairs	3,600
	$19,650

Instructions

1. Compute the standard manufacturing overhead per unit.
2. Compute the overhead applied to production during the year, the total over- or under-applied overhead, the spending variance, and the volume variance.
3. Prepare a budget report for the year, showing the actual manufacturing expenses, the budgeted expenses at a volume of 11,000 units, and the controllable variance for each manufacturing expense item.

9–19 **Analysis of Operating Results** *(40 minutes)*   The Winson Manufacturing Company has a standard cost for part number 643A as follows:

Direct materials	One unit of material Y7	$1.00
Direct labor	⅓ hour, at $2.40 per hour	.80
Overhead (50% of labor cost)		.40
		$2.20

The company has two machines on which the part can be made. Both machines can be run at varying speeds, and each has a top speed of four units per hour. However, at top speeds the machines have a tendency to wrinkle the material, and thus spoilage is increased. The standard material does not include any allowance for spoilage, since the standard production is three units per hour, and the machines do not wrinkle the material at that speed. Smith operates Machine 1 and receives an hourly wage of $2.50; Barron operates Machine 2 and receives an hourly wage of $2.30.

Production statistics for the week ended August 13, when both employees operated their machines forty hours, were as follows:

	Machine 1 (Smith)	Machine 2 (Barron)
Units started	160	110
Units completed	130	108
Units spoiled	30	2

Instructions

What variances would be reported for each of the two operators? Which employee do you consider to have done the better job during the week? What factors other than those given should be considered when analyzing which did a better job?

9-20   **Calculating and Reporting Variances** *(60 minutes)*   The Smithson Company set the following standard on its product at the beginning of the year:

Materials:	
4 pounds of X @ 30¢ per pound	$ 1.20
5 units of Y @ $1.00 each	5.00
1 gallon of Z @ $4.00 per gallon	4.00
Labor:	
Molding 3 hours @ $3.00	9.00
Forming 1 hour @ $2.00	2.00
Crating 1 hour @ $1.00	1.00
Manufacturing overhead:	
$1.92 per direct labor hour	9.60
Total	$31.80

The standard manufacturing overhead rate of $1.92 per DLH was determined by dividing the normal expenses of $48,000 by the standard labor in 5,000 units. The company has fixed costs of $23,000 and variable costs of $1.00 per direct labor hour. The rate was thus computed as follows:

$$\frac{\text{Normal manufacturing overhead for 25,000 DLH} = \$48,000}{25,000 \text{ DLH}} = \frac{\$1.92 \text{ per}}{\text{DLH}}$$

At the end of the year the president received the following income statement:

Sales (6,000 units @ $50.00)		$300,000
Cost of goods sold at standard	$190,800	
Total variances from standard	3,490	194,290
Gross profit		$105,710
Selling and administrative expenses		95,000
Net profit		$ 10,710

The president was disturbed by the $3,490 variance. He asked you to investigate and prepare a report showing the variances in more detail. You analyzed the company's records and found the following costs were incurred in producing the 6,000 units which were sold:

25,000 pounds of X were purchased at a cost of $7,600 and consumed.

28,000 units of Y were purchased for $29,000 and consumed.
6,100 gallons of Z were purchased for $23,800 and consumed.
Molding operations took 19,000 hours at $3.10 per hour.
Forming operations took 5,900 hours at $1.90 per hour.
Crating operations took 6,400 hours at $1.20 per hour.
Actual manufacturing overhead incurred was $56,100.

Instructions
Reconstruct the income statement for the president showing materials price, materials efficiency, labor price, and labor efficiency variances for each product and each labor operation. Also calculate an overhead controllable and an overhead volume variance.

9–21   **Calculation of Variances; Income Statement** *(50 minutes)* . The Detecto Equipment Company established the following standard cost for its single product:

Labor	2½ hours at $4.00 per hour	$10
Materials	10 units at $3.00 per unit	30
Manufacturing overhead		?
Total cost per unit		?

The overhead standard is based upon normal production of 10,000 units, and the company's cost structure is $50,000 of fixed costs, and variable costs of $2.00 per direct labor hour.

During the year, the company purchased for cash 200,000 units of raw materials at $3.10 per unit and used 155,000 units. A total of 37,000 hours of labor were worked at a cost of $3.90 per hour; a total of $127,000 of manufacturing overhead costs was incurred. Actual production was 15,000 units of the product, of which 13,000 were sold for $60 each. The selling expenses were $100,000.

Instructions
1. Calculate the standard overhead per unit and the total standard cost per unit.
2. Calculate the materials price variance, the materials efficiency variance, the labor price variance, the labor efficiency variance, the manufacturing overhead controllable variance, and the manufacturing overhead volume variance.
3. Prepare an income statement for the period, treating the variances as an adjustment to the standard cost of goods sold.

9–22   **Calculation of Variances; Income Statement** *(50 minutes)*   The Watergate Company developed the following comprehensive budget for the month of August, 19X1:

[handwritten margin notes: R.M 3.10, 200,000, 620,000, Labor 3.90, 37,000, 144,300, M.O. $127,000]

Proforma Income Statement for August, 19X1

Sales (10,000 units at $120 per unit)	$1,200,000
Cost of goods sold at standard	
(10,000 units at $86 per unit)	860,000
Gross margin on sales	340,000
Selling and administrative expenses	300,000
Net income	$ 40,000

The company developed the following cost of goods sold at standard:

Labor standard	4 hours at $5.00 per hour	$20
Materials standard	3 units at $7.00 per unit	21
Overhead standard	($9.00 per standard machine hour,	
	5 standard machine hours per unit)	45
		$86

The overhead rate was based on the following cost structure:

Fixed overhead, $200,000
Variable overhead, $5.00 per machine hour

There is an expected level of sales of 10,000 units and therefore 50,000 machine hours (10,000 units × 5 standard machine hours per unit).

The following transactions occurred during August:

a. Purchased 45,000 units of raw materials at a cost of $319,500.
b. Used 44,000 units of the raw material in the production of 15,000 finished goods.
c. Incurred 55,000 labor hours at a cost of $283,500.
d. Used 80,000 machine hours.
e. Incurred $580,000 manufacturing overhead expense.
f. Incurred $325,000 selling and administrative expenses.
g. Completed 15,000 units and transferred them to finished goods.
h. Sold 12,000 units at a price of $120 per unit.

Instructions
1. Compute the following variances:
   a. Materials price variance
   b. Materials efficiency variance
   c. Labor price variance
   d. Labor efficiency variance
   e. Overhead controllable variance
   f. Overhead volume variance
2. Prepare an income statement, treating the variances as adjustments to the standard cost of goods sold.

9–23   **Computation of Variances; Preparing Departmental Reports** *(50 minutes)*   The Framemore Company uses a continuous process system. All materials enter into Department A, where they are liquified and pass on into Department B. In Department B, the material is molded into the desired shape and passed on to Department C, where it is finished and smoothed. The following standards were predetermined for the company's one product:

Department A:			
Materials	2 units @ $4	$8	
Labor	1 hour @ $2	2	
Manufacturing overhead	$1 per DLH	1	$11
Department B:			
Labor	2 hours @ $3	$6	
Manufacturing overhead	$1.50 per DLH	3	9
Department C:			
Labor	2 hours @ $2	$4	
Manufacturing overhead	$1 per DLH	2	6
			$26

The company has no beginning or ending inventories. During the month of February, the company completed 20,000 units, and the costs were as follows:

Materials purchased for cash and consumed: 41,000 units at $3.80 each.
    Labor: Department A   20,100 hours at $2.10 per hour
           Department B   38,000 hours at $3.05 per hour
           Department C   41,000 hours at $2.00 per hour
    Actual manufacturing overhead: Department A $19,000
                                Department B $61,000
                                Department C $40,500

Normal manufacturing overhead for 20,000 units (budget):
                Department A $20,100
                Department B   57,000
                Department C   41,000

Instructions
Prepare a report showing at least six variances for each department.

9–24   **Break-Even; Overhead Rate; Income Statement** *(60 minutes)*
The Horton Company has a flexible budgetary program and a standard cost system. The standard cost for their single product is as follows:

Labor (3 hours at $3 per hour)	$ 9.00
Materials (2 units at $2 per unit)	4.00
Manufacturing overhead $2.33	
per direct labor hour	7.00
	$20.00

The standard manufacturing overhead cost per unit is based upon expected production of 10,000 units and a cost structure as follows:

	Fixed Portion	Variable, Per DLH
Indirect labor	$ 3,000	$ .67
Indirect materials	2,000	.33
Depreciation	15,500	
Factory supplies		.33
Heat, light, and power		.17
Taxes	4,500	

During the year just ended, the company's selling and administrative costs were $15,000 fixed and $5 variable. The unit sales price is $33.50 per unit.

Instructions

1. Compute the break-even point of the company in terms of units and in terms of dollars of sales.
2. Show computations indicating how the standard overhead cost per unit was computed.
3. During the period, the company produced 11,000 units, sold 10,000, and incurred the following costs:

Labor (34,000 hours)	$100,000
Materials (21,000 units)	41,200
Indirect labor	24,800
Indirect materials	14,700
Depreciation	15,550
Factory supplies	10,800
Heat, light, and power	5,900
Taxes	4,100
Fixed selling expenses	15,100
Variable selling expenses	44,200

Prepare a budget report which reflects for each manufacturing overhead cost the budget for the 11,000-unit level of activity actually achieved, the actual expenses, and the variance.

4. Prepare an income statement for the period showing the standard cost variances in the statement. Assume that there are no beginning or ending work-in process or raw materials inventories.

chapter 10

Distribution Expenses

Learning Objectives

This chapter shifts the emphasis from the analysis of manufacturing costs to the analysis of nonmanufacturing expenses. Upon completion of your study of this chapter you should:

1. Know what distribution expenses are, what segments of a business are usually analyzed, and how a profitability analysis is applied to these segments.
2. Be able to select an acceptable proration base, make the allocation of indirect expenses to segments, and complete the segment profit analysis.
3. Understand the limitations of a segment analysis which contains prorated indirect costs and how segment contribution margins may be more meaningful than "full segment profitability."

Segment Analysis

A company's operations are frequently subdivided into separate "segments" for purposes of profit measurement. "Segments" is a broad term, used here to indicate any of the fractional parts into which the operations of an enterprise may be divided. The emphasis in this chapter is on those segments which are responsible for nonmanufacturing expenses, or the expenses incurred in the administrative and selling activities of the business. These expenses are more closely associated with the distribution of the product after it has been manufactured and the terms *distribution expenses* and sometimes *distribution costs* are frequently used. In this chapter the terms *nonmanufacturing expense* and *distribution expense* will be used synonymously.

Two frequently encountered examples of segment analysis are the profitability calculations of the different departments of a department store and the separate profit measurements of the branches of a company with physically separated outlets. Sears, Roebuck and Company, for example, has thousands of branch outlets in separate locations throughout the world, and each is measured separately to identify unprofitable stores and to provide valuable managerial information about the revenues and expenses of each outlet. Once unprofitable or undesirable segments (in this case, outlets) have been identified, appropriate action can be taken. The departments of every large department store, supermarket, sporting goods store, or clothing store constitute segments which require profitability analysis. Only through this type of profit measurement can management identify the departments which are not performing adequately.

Other types of segment analysis include the expense and revenue analysis of product lines, distribution channels, order size, and customer type. Measurement of the profitability of any branch, department, product, territory, or other fractional part of a business cannot be undertaken without assigning such revenues and expenses to each area being analyzed. Determination of the portion of the company's revenues and operating expenses which relate to each segment requires extensive analysis and this chapter discusses these methods of measuring the activities of separate profit centers.

A *profit center* is any part of the business to which both costs and revenues can be traced and a profit measurement undertaken. Revenues and costs can be traced, for example, to the separate routes of an airline—such as the nonstop Eastern flight between New York and Miami. If insufficient profits are earned on that route, the airline may undertake to discontinue it and route passengers on the company's other existing flights—through Atlanta or Washington D.C. Automobile rental agencies, to use another example, may assign revenues and costs to each location where customers come to pick up and leave rental cars. If the Hertz location at Hamilton, Ohio has insufficient revenue or excessive costs making it unprofitable, then the company will need to review the operations at that location to find ways to increase profit.

An *expense center* is an activity in the business which incurs expenses but which does not earn revenue. A company's accounting department, for example, incurs expenses but does not earn revenue. The purchasing department, heating plant, and administrative offices are other examples of expense centers. Since there are no revenues assignable to expense centers, they must be controlled by means of budgets and comparisons of expenses against the volume of activity.

Segment Responsibility

Each expense center and profit center is placed under the control of a manager. He is assigned the responsibility of operating the segment in accordance with the profit plan or the budget allowances which are approved in advance by the executives above him. One of the primary purposes of the accounting reports prepared for each department, branch, or other segment is to measure the effectiveness and efficiency of the manager. If the company as a whole is to be profitable, the executives at the top of the organization must know whether their managers are performing adequately, and accounting reports must be constructed to provide this information.

Reports concerning expense centers and profit centers are for management's purposes only and are not available to persons outside the company. Profit center information is not released because it would be valuable to competitors. It would indicate where the company's most profitable areas were and competitors would expand into those areas quickly if that type of information were available. Data on expense centers are not released because they are primarily for measurement of an individual manager's efficiency and have little value to anyone outside the company.

An analysis of the fractional parts of a business is usually undertaken by preparation of an income statement for each segment. In most cases, little difficulty is encountered in assigning revenues to segments, but the allocations and apportionments necessary to assign expenses create a number of complex problems. Selection of an adequate base for apportioning expenses is important, because the amount of the net income or loss computed for each fractional part of the business can be no more accurate than the assignment of revenues and expenses permits.

Exhibit 10–1 shows an analysis of the four product lines sold by the Mattlow Company. This analysis provides a basis for ascertaining the most profitable and the least profitable products. The statement reveals that the sale of wall-

EXHIBIT 10–1

MATTLOW COMPANY
Analysis of The Profitability of Product Lines

	Carpeting	Draperies	Floor Tiles	Wallpaper
Sales	$5,000	$8,000	$3,000	$12,000
Cost of merchandise sold	3,000	4,000	1,000	8,000
Gross profit—Amount	$2,000	$4,000	$2,000	$ 4,000
—Percent of sales	40%	50%	67%	33%
Operating expenses				
Salaries	$ 300	$1,600	$ 400	$ 2,000
Supplies	100	300	100	600
Rent	25	200	50	100
Taxes	50	200	100	300
Utilities	100	300	200	600
Total operating expenses	$ 575	$2,600	$ 850	$ 3,600
Net Income—Amount	$1,425	$1,400	$1,150	$ 400
—Percent of sales	29%	17%	38%	3%

paper produced the greatest number of dollar sales but the smallest net income. The most profitable product line per dollar of sales is floor tiles, and this fact could not have been determined without assigning revenues and expenses to each product line.

Note that "percent of sales" calculations are made for the four product lines at both the gross profit and the net income level. The gross profit percentages are indications of the effectiveness of the pricing policy of each line, while the net income percentages provide information about overall profitability. The pricing of draperies and floor tiles provides the greatest gross margin per dollar of sales, with 50 percent and 67 percent respectively, while carpeting and wallpaper produced gross margins of 40 percent and 33 percent. The expenses attributable to carpeting are low, however; so that, in the final analysis, that product line produced a net profit of 29 percent of sales, which is higher than two of the other product lines. The overall analysis thus indicates that the pricing policy of wallpaper needs attention, and the expenses of the drapery and wallpaper department are so high in relation to the gross margin realized that these two product lines are not producing a sufficient net income.

Assigning Revenues to Segments

Information about sales should be captured in sufficient detail at the point of the transaction with the customer to permit a number of different types of analysis. The amount received from the sale of a pair of shoes, for example, must be recorded so that it can be properly assigned to the correct department, to the proper product line, to the proper time period, and to the salesman who made the sale. Careful attention must be given to the types of analysis which will be needed when the accounting system is designed, because all the required information concerning a sale must be captured at the point of the original transaction with the customer. If sufficient data about sales are not recorded at that point, it becomes prohibitively expensive and sometimes impossible to try to reconstruct it later.

Many companies record sales on cash registers in such a way that a number of different subtotals are maintained. When the pair of shoes mentioned earlier was sold, the sales clerk may be instructed to utilize the keys on the cash register to indicate the amount, the department numbers, the product code, and the sales clerk's number, thus permitting a later analysis of the profitability of the department, the product line, or the sales clerks. A further breakdown of sales in this case would not be possible, however, since the necessary data were not captured at the time the sale was recorded.

Many retail stores attach a form of punched card to each item in the inventory, and the data on the card permit a larger number of sales analyses to be made. An example of a pin-punched tag is shown in Exhibit 10–2. Small pin holes in the card code data similar to that printed on the tag, each set of holes representing the code for the department, product line, color, size, price, location, and other data considered pertinent to the sale.

The tags are punched with a special machine and attached to the merchandise when it is purchased and placed in inventory. The tags are removed from

EXHIBIT 10–2

Punched Tag

the merchandise at the time of sale, and they are processed at the end of each day through machines which can interpret the holes and prepare a number of subtotals for management analysis. The tags are also utilized in the replacement of the item sold, for they help determine which sizes, colors, and styles are popular. In this way, the replacement of sold merchandise can be accomplished more quickly and efficiently, and the company's sales can be increased.

Separate subsidiary records are frequently maintained for the sales made in each department. Each day the total sales for the entire store are recorded in a general ledger control, while the sales by individual departments are entered in a subsidiary ledger. The subsidiary is reconciled with the sales control periodically, usually weekly or monthly. Such a reconciliation insures accuracy in the recording of departmental sales. Where the accounting system is highly mechanized, the subsidiary may be reconciled daily with the control. Cash sales and credit sales are sometimes separated in the accounting records also, thus providing sufficient data for analyzing the profitability of cash customers versus credit customers.

Assigning Purchases and Transportation-in to Segments

When merchandise is acquired for resale, the purchase must be assigned to the department which will stock it and sell it. A control account is maintained in the accounting records for purchases, with a separate subsidiary ledger for each department. The control and the subsidiary are reconciled at least once each month to insure that they balance and to help locate errors.

When invoices are received from suppliers, each department manager must approve those for merchandise which will be stocked and sold in his department. This method allows the accounting department to be aware of which department the merchandise is assigned to, so that the purchase can be correctly recorded. When items for several departments appear on the same invoice, the department to which each item goes must be carefully indicated.

Transportation-in must also be assigned to individual departments. As is the case with purchases, there should be a separate control account in the general ledger for all transportation-in costs, with a subsidiary ledger for the transportation-in costs incurred for each department. If the freight bill covers the transportation cost for merchandise items purchased for more than one department, an allocation of the cost must be made. Since freight costs are normally based upon weight, the weight of each item, indicated on the freight bill, can be used as a basis for the allocation of the transportation-in cost.

A separate record is sometimes kept for the data pertaining to each department. Information on sales, inventory, purchases, and freight-in for each department is kept in this record, and usually there are separate control accounts for the totals. This arrangement is illustrated in Exhibit 10–3, which shows sales information from a daily sales report being accumulated in the departmental records, with the total appearing in the control.

EXHIBIT 10–3

Department Subsidiary Records and Related Control Accounts

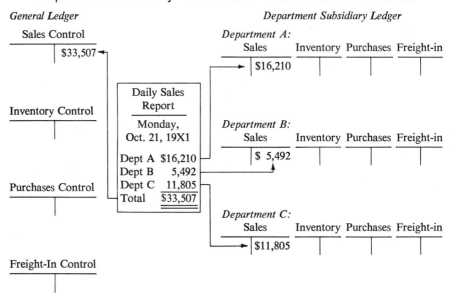

Note that all Department A accounts are grouped together in the departmental records, followed by Department B records, and so on. This arrangement permits the activities of each department to be analyzed as a unit, and also permits the subsidiary accounts for sales, inventory, purchases, and freight-in to be added and balanced with their respective control accounts.

Assigning Operating Expenses to Segments

The assignment of operating expenses to segments is more difficult than the assignment of sales, inventory, purchases, and freight-in. Operating expenses are in many cases not as closely associated with departments as are sales or purchases, and special procedures are necessary before they can be fully traced to departments. While some operating expenses may be directly traceable to the department which caused their incurrence, a large number of operating expenses may be only indirectly associated with any of the departments. Operating expenses must thus be treated as either *direct* or *indirect* expenses in a segment analysis.

Direct expenses   A direct operating expense is one which is directly traceable to a segment and which was incurred specifically for that segment. The salaries of the sales clerks are direct expenses of the departments in which they work, and the payroll records will usually indicate the salaries expense incurred for each department. For this reason, sales persons are not usually shifted from department to department during the day. Likewise, the salary of an outside salesman who sells only one product would be a direct cost traceable to that product if the segment analysis is for product lines. A direct expense is frequently one which could be eliminated entirely if that particular segment of the business were discontinued.

Indirect expenses   An indirect operating expense is one that is not directly traceable to a particular department and probably could not be fully eliminated if any one part of the enterprise were discontinued. In a profit analysis of the departments of a retail store, the depreciation expense on the store building is an indirect operating expense, because the total building depreciation would not be reduced or discontinued if any one department were eliminated. In an analysis of product lines, the sales manager's salary is also an indirect operating expense, since it is not traceable to specific products and probably would not be altered if any one product were eliminated.

A direct expense in one type of analysis may prove to be an indirect expense in another type of analysis. The special wrapping supplies used in the shoe department of a retail store would be a direct cost if departmental profitability were analyzed, but these same supplies would be indirect if men's shoes, women's shoes, and children's shoes were analyzed for profitability. The supplies are directly traceable to the department, but they are not traceable to separate lines of shoes. The nature and type of analysis being undertaken will determine whether the expense can be treated as direct or indirect.

Proration of Indirect Expenses

Since indirect expenses are not directly traceable to departments, an appropriate basis must be used in allocating or prorating these expenses. Several bases of allocation are available for each indirect expense; the base selected should be the one which measures most accurately the benefit received by each segment as a result of having incurred the operating expense. In many cases, several bases are applicable, and there is no single rule to use in locating the most accurate one. The only criteria is that there be a reasonable relationship between the proration base and the incurrence of the expense.

To illustrate the necessity of prorating indirect expenses, suppose a department store were measuring the profitability of each of its departments. How would administrative salaries be prorated to the various departments? A basis that measures the effort expended by the administrative officers for each department would be satisfactory, but measuring "effort" is difficult if not impossible.

A more objective measurement might be the proportion of administrative time spent on the problems of each department, or the number of employees in each department. Considerable judgment and care are necessary to select the proration method which produces the most reliable results.

Mechanics of allocating indirect expenses   The mechanics of allocating indirect operating expenses to segments are comparatively simple. The basic technique is as follows:

Step 1	Select an appropriate basis for allocation.
Step 2	Determine the number of units in the allocation base which are applicable to each segment, and their total.
Step 3	Divide the total operating expense which is being apportioned by the total of the "base units." The result is a cost per base unit.
Step 4	Multiply the number of base units in each segment by the cost per unit to ascertain the operating expense applicable to each segment.
Step 5	Total all the amounts as apportioned to insure that they equal the full amount of the operating expense. This step is to insure the mathematical accuracy of the proration.

To illustrate, suppose that a retail department store is analyzing each department for profitability. The telephone expense for the entire store is $950, and the five departments have the numbers of telephones shown in the accompanying table.

Department	Number of Telephones
A	6
B	5
C	3
D	1
E	4
Total	19

Step 1	The base is to be the number of telephones in each department. This appears to be an equitable basis for allocating the store's telephone expense.
Step 2	The number of telephones in each department has been given previously. There is a total of 19 telephones for the entire store.
Step 3	The telephone expense, $950, divided by 19 phones, gives a cost per phone of $50.
Step 4	The amount of the expense apportioned to each department would be:

Dept. A	6 phones @ $50 =	$300
B	5 phones @ $50 =	250
C	3 phones @ $50 =	150
D	1 phone @ $50 =	50
E	4 phones @ $50 =	200
	Total	$950

Step 5   Adding all the amounts assigned to the departments proves that the $950 total has been allocated.

Use of Expense Centers

More accurate results may be obtained by allocating indirect operating expenses through a two-step process which utilizes expense centers. As described earlier, an *expense center* is a center of activity within the organization which produces no revenue but to which many operating expenses can be traced, either directly or indirectly. After all of the expenses applicable to the center are accumulated, the total is then prorated to the revenue-producing departments.

The purchasing department in a department store is an illustration of an expense center. In a profitability analysis of the store's selling departments, all the expense of operating the purchasing department would be accumulated, including salaries, supplies, utilities, and telephone. The total of all these expenses would then be reallocated to each sales department. An appropriate proration base for the purchasing department's expenses would be the total number of purchases made for each of the sales departments.

The credit department is another example of a functional area which could be used as an expense center for allocation purposes. All the expenses of operating the credit department, including direct and indirect expenses, are accumulated, and the total is then allocated to selling departments using an equitable base, such as the dollar amount of credit sales made in each department.

The first allocation of expenses to the departments and expense centers is called a *primary* allocation. The reallocation of the total costs of the expense centers back to the revenue-producing segments is called a *secondary* allocation.

To summarize, the expense allocation process is completed by the following three steps:

Step 1   Assign all direct expenses to the revenue-producing segments and to the expense centers.
Step 2   Allocate the indirect expenses to revenue-producing segments and expense centers, using an equitable allocation base.
Step 3   Allocate the total expenses for each of the expense centers to revenue-producing segments.

This process is illustrated in Exhibit 10–4 which contains two revenue-producing departments—A and B—and one expense center—the purchasing department. Note that after the process has been completed, all the expenses have been allocated to the two revenue-producing departments. The expense center was used only as a means of gathering expenses prior to their final allocation to revenue-producing segments.

Basis for Primary Allocations

The base used to allocate the company's operating expenses to departments or to expense centers depends upon the type of analysis being made. However,

EXHIBIT 10–4

Use of Expense Centers for Allocation

		Revenue Producing Segments		Purchasing Department
		A	B	
Step 1	Assign direct expenses	⟶ $	⟶ $	⟶ $
Step 2	Allocate indirect expenses (primary allocation)	⟶ $	⟶ $	⟶ $
Step 3	Total of the expense center is allocated to revenue-producing segments (secondary allocation)	$ ⟵	$ ⟵	$
Step 4	Expenses assigned to revenue-producing segments are totaled	$$	$$	

Exhibit 10–5 is presented to illustrate the nature of allocation bases which are appropriate in most cases.

Retail Departmental Analysis Illustrated

The process of performing a segment analysis for the Sallman-Toll Department Store, a departmentalized retail store, is presented below in Exhibits 10–6 and 10–7. The company has three sales departments: shoes, notions, and men's

EXHIBIT 10–5

Frequently Used Bases for Primary Allocation of Indirect Expenses

Expense	Allocation Basis
Depreciation on equipment	Value of equipment
Taxes on equipment	Value of equipment
Insurance on store equipment	Value of equipment
Officers' salaries	Time spent
Depreciation on store building (or store rent)	Square feet occupied
Taxes and insurance on building	Square feet occupied
Taxes and insurance on inventory	Value of the inventory
Telephone expense	Number of telephones
Heat	Cubic feet occupied
Light	Number of light outlets
Supplies	Dollar sales
Miscellaneous expenses	Dollar sales

EXHIBIT 10–6

SALLMAN-TOLL DEPARTMENT STORE
Condensed Departmental Income Statement
Month Ended December 31, 19X1

Department

	Shoes		Notions		Men's Clothing		Total	
	Amount	%	Amount	%	Amount	%	Amount	%
Sales	$31,000	100	$15,000	100	$41,000	100	$87,000	100
Cost of merchandise sold	19,500	63	9,850	66	30,200	74	59,550	69
Gross margin	$11,500	37	$ 5,150	34	$10,800	26	$27,450	31
Direct expenses	4,300	14	2,680	16	7,600	18	14,580	16
Margin after direct costs	$ 7,200	23	$ 2,470	18	$ 3,200	8	$12,870	15
Indirect and allocated expenses	3,020	10	1,420	11	4,130	10	8,570	10
Net income (loss)	$ 4,180	13	$ 1,050	7	$ (930)	(2)	$ 4,300	5

clothing. Two expense centers are used: the credit department and the delivery department.

The first step is to gather data on sales and the cost of merchandise sold, and to compute the resulting gross profit for each department. This completes the first part of the departmental income statement, which is shown in Exhibit 10–6. Note that only the three revenue-producing departments appear in this statement, and that both dollar amounts and percent of sales figures are given for each department.

The second step is to assign operating expenses to the revenue-producing departments. This step is completed on a separate analysis sheet, and is illustrated in Exhibit 10–7. Note that the direct expenses are subtotalled before the indirect expenses are entered on the work sheet. The operating statistics used to prorate the indirect expenses and the expense centers are given in Exhibit 10–8.

Finally, the secondary allocation of the totals of the expense centers are made so that all expenses are ultimately assigned to the sales departments. The totals on the work sheet provide the information to complete the departmental income statement which was shown earlier in Exhibit 10–6.

In the analysis of the completed departmental income statement (Exhibit 10–6), the departmental gross profit is a significant figure, indicating the departmental manager's ability to purchase and sell merchandise at the desired rate of markup. The gross profit as a percentage of that department's sales is carefully watched by management, for if the percentage drops significantly, poor merchandising in that department may be indicated. In like manner, the margin after direct costs is a significant figure, indicating the department's earn-

EXHIBIT 10–7

SALLMAN-TOLL DEPARTMENT STORE
Analysis of Operating Expenses by Departments
Month of December, 19X1

Expense	Basis of Allocation	Sales Departments			Expense Centers		Total
		Shoes	Notions	Clothing	Credit Dept.	Delivery Dept.	
Direct							
Salaries	Direct	$3,000	$1,980	$ 5,000	$1,520	$ 710	$12,210
Advertising	Direct	1,000	500	2,000			3,500
Repairs to furniture and fixtures	Direct	300	200	600	600	400	2,100
Total direct expenses		$4,300	$2,680	$ 7,600			
Indirect							
Insurance on store fixtures	Value of assets	$ 200	$ 100	$ 300	100	100	800
General store supplies	Predetermined ratio	400	200	500	50	40	1,100
Telephone and telegraph	No. of telephones	70	50	90	30	30	300
Property taxes	Value of assets	60	30	90	30	30	240
Rent on store building	Square feet	400	200	700	300	400	2,000
Electricity	Electric outlets	250	200	350	40	60	900
Expense centers							
Delivery department	No. of deliveries	700	240	800		$1,740	
Credit department	Credit sales	940	400	1,300	$2,640		
Total indirect costs		$3,020	$1,420	$ 4,130			
Total direct and indirect expenses		$7,320	$4,100	$11,730			$23,150

EXHIBIT 10–8

SALLMAN-TOLL DEPARTMENT STORE
Operating Statistics for Allocating Indirect Expenses

	Shoes	Notions	Clothing	Credit	Delivery	Total
Value of store assets	$20,000	$10,000	$30,000	$10,000	$10,000	$ 80,000
Number of telephones	7	5	9	5	4	30
Square feet	20,000	10,000	35,000	15,000	20,000	100,000
Electric outlets	50	40	70	8	12	180
Number of deliveries	350	120	400	—	—	870
Credit sales	$ 9,400	4,000	13,000	—	—	$ 26,400

ings after direct and traceable costs are covered. If a department does not realize sufficient margin to cover its direct costs, the elimination of that department should be considered.

The net profit made by each department after the deduction of both direct and indirect expenses indicates that department's contribution to the company's net income. Care must be exercised in determining the significance of a departmental net loss after allocated indirect expenses, because any margin after direct costs helps cover the company's indirect costs which are mostly inescapable, even if the department were eliminated. Discontinuance of a department will, in most cases, result in an elimination of that department's direct costs, but the company's total indirect costs may not change appreciably. Furthermore, discontinuance of one department may result in decreases in the sales by other departments, since customers may stop buying from the company when a full line of merchandise is no longer available.

Analysis of Territories

Analysis of the profitability of sales territories helps locate unprofitable areas and provides data useful in directing the company's sales efforts. When operating expenses are analyzed by territories—such as cities, salesmen's areas, or other geographical divisions—an extensive use of expense centers is necessary. Expense centers are frequently established to include such functions as packing and shipping, billing, credit extension, collecting and accounts receivable, and general administration. Direct and indirect operating expenses are assigned or prorated to territories and expense centers, and the expense center totals are then allocated to revenue-producing territories in exactly the same manner described in the prior discussion of a departmental analysis, with the exception that a greater number of expense centers is necessary to effect an equitable distribution of indirect expenses.

Exhibit 10–9 illustrates an analysis of operating expenses by territories. The analyses of sales, cost of merchandise sold, and gross profits by territories are not included in the illustration, because these revenues and costs can be analyzed directly from sales invoices. The income statement by territories which utilizes the expense totals is shown in Exhibit 10–10.

EXHIBIT 10-9

SMYTH DISTRIBUTING COMPANY
Territorial Analysis of Operating Expenses
Month Ended December 31, 19X1

Expense	Basis of Allocation	Territories			Expense Centers				Total
		North	South	Central	Order Filling and Shipping	Credit and Collection	Warehousing	General Administrative Expense	
Direct:									
Transportation-out	Direct	$ 200	$ 100	$ 400					$ 700
Salaries	Direct	1,200	600	1,200	$700	$600	$ 500	$1,000	5,800
Advertising	Direct	100	100	300					500
Total direct expenses		$1,500	$ 800	$1,900					
Indirect:									
Insurance	Value of equipment	50	75	50	100	150	700	400	1,525
Taxes	Value of assets	10	15	10	20	30	140	80	305
Rent on building	Square footage				120	120	400	180	820
Heat	Square footage				40	40	100	60	240
Cost centers:									
Order filling and shipping	Number of orders	240	300	440	$980				
Credit and collection	Number of invoices	280	270	390		$940			
Warehousing	Cubic volume shipped	500	400	940			$1,840		
General administrative	Same ratio as direct salaries	688	344	688				$1,720	
Total indirect expense		$1,768	$1,404	$2,518					
Total operating expenses		$3,268	$2,204	$4,418					$9,890

EXHIBIT 10–10

SMYTH DISTRIBUTING COMPANY
Income Statement by Territories
Month Ended December 31, 19X1

	North		South		Central		Total	
	Amount	%	Amount	%	Amount	%	Amount	%
Sales	$22,000	100	$15,000	100	$16,000	100	$53,000	100
Cost of merchandise sold	15,500	70	10,500	70	11,000	69	37,000	70
Gross margin	$ 6,500	30	$ 4,500	30	$ 5,000	31	$16,000	30
Direct operating expenses (from expense analysis)	1,500	7	800	5	1,900	12	4,200	8
Margin after direct expenses	$ 5,000	23	$ 3,700	25	$ 3,100	19	$11,800	22
Indirect and allocated expenses (from expense analysis)	1,768	8	1,404	10	2,518	15	5,690	11
Net income	$ 3,232	15	$ 2,296	15	$ 582	4	$ 6,100	11

Note that the expense centers in Exhibit 10–9 are numerous and that the basis for distributing the totals of these centers to territories provides a reasonably equitable allocation of indirect operating expenses. The margin after direct expenses and the net income after all expenses assist management in locating territories which need attention.

Basis for Allocating Expense Centers to Territories

The basis used to allocate expense centers to territories may differ from company to company, but the bases in Exhibit 10–11 are widely used. Note that these are bases for secondary allocations and are used only after total expenses

EXHIBIT 10–11

Basis for Secondary Allocation of Expense Center Totals

Expense Center	Basis
Storage of finished goods	Cost of goods sold by territories
Accounts receivable	Number of customers
Order assembly	Number of orders
Billing customers	Invoice lines
Packing and shipping	Number of units shipped
Delivery	Truck miles (or analysis of freight bills if by common carrier)
Sales solicitation	Number of calls made

have been accumulated for each expense center. Primary allocation bases were illustrated earlier in Exhibit 10–5, and the primary allocation is completed before the secondary allocations are performed.

Other Types of Segment Analysis

An analysis of operating expenses by types of customers, channels of distribution, or other segments is undertaken in the same manner as the departmental and territorial analyses illustrated. While different bases of allocation may be used, the technique is identical. The process of selecting expense centers and completing primary and secondary allocations provides an analysis technique which assists management in measuring and comparing an almost unlimited arrangement of the fractional parts of an enterprise. The following types of analyses are undertaken periodically in most better-managed companies:

1. Commodities—such as by individual products or groups of products.
2. Channels of distribution—wholesale, retail, and jobber outlets.
3. Class of customers—such as those making small purchases and those making large purchases.
4. Method of sale—through salesmen, phone orders, or mail.
5. Terms of sale—cash, credit, or installment.

It is important to note that analysis such as these require that sales be properly coded so that they can be separated for profit analysis. Costs and expenses are then analyzed in the same manner as was previously illustrated for departments and territories, with indirect expenses assigned to expense centers where applicable and the expense center totals then allocated to the revenue-producing areas. Analyses of profitability for these segments are undertaken in most companies only once or twice each year, or when a weakness in operations is suspected.

An analysis of operating expenses is sometimes undertaken to locate means of reducing the amount of operating expenses, but more frequently the analysis is directed toward securing greater results from present expenses. Directing the company's efforts into more productive channels frequently increases net income more than a search for means of reducing expenses.

Discontinuing a Segment

The decision to discontinue an "unprofitable" segment must be based upon a comparison of the revenue that will be lost and the expenses that can be eliminated. If revenue from the sale of a product does not cover the direct costs, management is alerted to the possibility that total profits may be increased if the product is dropped. If, for example, discontinuing a product will cause a $6,000 decrease in sales and a decrease of $8,000 in expenses, profits will increase by $2,000 as a result of dropping the product.

Reduction in expense	$8,000
Loss of sales	6,000
Increase in profits	$2,000

Determination of the loss of sales or the decrease in expenses is a difficult undertaking, and estimates must be made of the expected decrease in such expenses as insurance on merchandise, office supplies, telephone and telegraph, heating, and lighting. An estimate of the loss of sales is even more difficult, for although sales of the discontinued product or department will be lost, the sales of other products or departments may increase or decrease. A grocery store with a fresh meats department may either note an increase in its sales of frozen and canned meats if the fresh meats department is dropped, or suffer a decrease in the sales of all other departments because customers stop coming to the store.

Branch Records

Many merchandising companies have outlets in different geographical locations, with each separate location considered a *branch store*. There is usually a single *home office* which houses the offices of the top executives of the company and from which control over the various branches is directed. In some cases, a company is composed of hundreds of branches under the administrative control of a single home office. Each branch is not a separate corporation or a separate company, and it has no legal existence separate from the home office. However, because each branch is physically removed from other branches and from the home office, and because it is under the immediate direction of a single person—usually called a branch manager—the home office must have some means of measuring the profitability and controlling the operations of each of its branches.

Centralized branch records In some cases all accounting records are maintained at the home office, and the branch is given only a small operating cash fund. Cash received from sales which are made at the branch are sent daily to the home office, and if credit sales are made at the branch the resulting receivables are maintained and collected at the home office. The branch does not buy its own merchandise or pay its employees their wages and salaries. These payments are made from the home office. The operating cash fund which the branch maintains is used only for small unexpected payments which can not be conveniently made by the home office, and periodically the operating cash fund at the branch is replenished.

In this type of branch control system, the branch does not have a set of accounting records. The home office maintains a set of accounts similar to the departmental records discussed previously in this chapter. Separate subsidiary ledgers for sales, purchases, transportation-in, and operating expenses are maintained at the central office for each outlet. In this way, the profitability of all branches can be calculated in much the same way as departmental profits and losses were determined in the earlier part of this chapter.

Decentralized branch records   In cases where the branch is large and can feasibly do so, it may maintain a full set of accounting records. In such cases, sales and receivables are recorded at the branch, and deposits are made in the branch's own bank account for all cash sales, and the branch collects its own receivables. It may also pay many of its own expenses and record its own liabilities. In some cases the branch will have a full set of accounting records for assets, liabilities, revenue, and expenses. The branch will submit a set of financial statements, or at least a complete trial balance, to the home office each month to reflect its financial position and the results of its operations.

However, the branch is not a separate legal entity even though its operations are accounted for separately from other branches or from the home office. Thus, the home office must establish an accounting system which facilitates combining the transactions of each branch with those of its own and its other branches in order to prepare a set of financial statements for the company as a whole. In addition, the home office must establish its accounting records in such a manner that its books reflect the investment in assets which it has made in each branch. A combined income statement which combines the revenue and expense data of a company with two branches and a home office is illustrated in Exhibit 10–12.

EXHIBIT 10–12

Combined Home Office-Branch Income Statements

	Home Office	Branch 1	Branch 2	Total
Sales	—	$372,500	$586,400	$958,900
Cost of goods sold	—	241,200	210,100	451,300
Gross margin	—	$131,300	$376,300	$507,600
Operating expenses				
Salaries	$100,000	$ 23,000	$189,500	$312,500
Supplies	3,000	1,000	13,700	17,700
Depreciation	17,000	6,000	24,100	47,100
Utilities	9,200	7,500	11,900	28,600
Rent	15,500	9,000	16,000	40,500
Taxes	2,100	1,200	5,700	9,000
Total	$146,800	$ 47,700	$260,900	$455,400
Net income (loss)	$(146,800)	$ 83,600	$115,400	$ 52,200

Note that the branch and home office statements are added to arrive at totals for the company. The format of the statements of each branch must be consistent to permit such addition; and, for this reason, a rigidly prescribed format is usually designed by a company for its branches.

Summary

The measurement and control of distribution activities is more difficult than that of manufacturing operations, because distribution expenses are only indirectly associated with individual segments of the business. While some selling and administrative expenses may be directly assigned to the segments being studied, a large portion of the company's distribution expenses cannot be so assigned. For this reason, a number of expense centers are utilized in the analysis of selling and administrative expenses. When expense centers are used, those expenses which can be assigned or prorated to the expense centers are accumulated, and the total associated with each center is then prorated back to the revenue-producing segments. In this way, all expenses are eventually assigned to those segments earning revenues, and the profitability of each revenue center can be measured.

The large number of prorations necessary in this type of analysis makes the resulting net profit figures for each segment of limited use. Both the profit after direct expenses and the profit after all indirect and allocated expenses are usually shown in segment profitability reports. The profit after direct expenses is meaningful, because it indicates each segment's contribution toward the company's general indirect costs. The profit earned by a segment after all expenses have been allocated reflects that segment's overall profitability, but this figure has only limited applicability to specific decisions relating to such actions as discontinuing the segment or pricing the company's products within that segment. For these reasons, segment analysis is undertaken only at periodic intervals—annually or semiannually in many cases.

New Terms

Branch store   An outlet of a company situated in a different geographical location from the central office.

Direct expense   An expense directly associated with and traceable to a segment of the business.

Distribution cost   A non-manufacturing cost.

Expense center   An activity within the business to which a number of expenses can be directly assigned.

Home office   The central office which administers a number of branches.

Indirect expense   An expense not directly traceable to the segments which are under analysis.

Primary allocation   The allocation of indirect expenses to expense centers.

Profit center   An activity of the business to which both revenues and expenses can be traced.

Secondary allocation   The allocation of expense totals to revenue-producing activities.

Segment of a business   Any of the parts of a business into which it may be divided.

Questions

1. Define the meaning of the term "segment" of a business. Name some of the ways a business may be "segmented" for analysis and measurement purposes.

2. Describe the basic approach to the segmenting of a business for profit measurement.

3. Define a direct expense and an indirect expense and distinguish between the two.

4. Is an expense always direct, or is it possible for the same expense to be direct in one type of analysis and indirect in another? Explain your answer.

5. How are indirect expenses assigned to segments? Is there only one basis which can be used to make this assignment in a given situation, or will there be several available bases? If so, how should the basis be selected?

6. What is an "expense center"? What role do expense centers have in expense apportionment to segments?

7. Distinguish between a "primary" allocation and a "secondary" allocation.

8. How may sales and cost of goods sold be analyzed by product, department, territory, or other segments? Is the analysis of sales and cost of goods sold as difficult as the analysis of operating expenses?

9. If a product, territory, or other segment is covering the direct costs but is not fully covering both direct and indirect costs, should it be automatically discontinued? Why or why not?

10. Why are expense centers used more extensively in an analysis of territories or products than for departments?

11. What basis would you use to allocate the following expense centers to products? To territories?
    a. Cost of warehousing finished goods
    b. Billing customers
    c. Assembling merchandise to get it ready for shipment
    d. Credit and collection
    e. Shipping dock costs

12. If a revenue-producing segment has a net loss after allocation of all expenses, including those of expense centers, should it be discontinued or abolished? Discuss the things which should be considered before a final decision is reached.

13. Name a company in your city or geographical location which has a number of branch outlets. Discuss how the general manager of that company would use financial information to measure the effectiveness and the profitability of each outlet.

14. What basis for allocating the following costs could be used if the company is a department store and the allocation is to the company's fifteen departments?
    a. The cost of outfitting and paying league fees for the company's bowling team
    b. The employee cafeteria costs
    c. The delivery department
    d. The customer complaint department
    e. The administrative office
    f. The accounting department
    g. Property taxes on the building
    h. Property taxes on the inventory
    j. Supplies, salaries, and other costs of the customers' gift suggestion booth

Exercises

10–1   **Definitions** *(15 minutes)*   The following terms or concepts were introduced in this chapter:

    a. Distribution costs
    b. Segment
    c. Direct expense
    d. Indirect expense
    e. Primary allocation
    f. Secondary allocation
    g. Expense center
    h. Allocation basis

Instructions
Define each term or concept, using examples where appropriate.

10–2   **Selection of Allocation Basis** *(15 minutes)*   The Billings Department store is analyzing its operating expenses by sales departments, and the following expenses are included in the analysis:

    a. The departmental manager's salary
    b. Property taxes on the store building
    c. Costs of advertising the departments' products in newspapers
    d. Fire insurance on the store building
    e. Salary costs of clerks who work in the department
    f. The president's salary
    g. Office supplies used in the central accounting office
    h. Depreciation on departmental fixtures and showcases
    i. Wrapping supplies bought in large lots and used by all departments

Instructions

Indicate for each expense whether it is direct or indirect and how it may be assigned, allocated, or otherwise distributed to the sales departments.

10–3   **Allocation of Store Rent Expense** *(15 minutes)*   The Attkinson Department Store is allocating its store rent to its four producing departments on the basis of the space occupied by each department. The total rent to be allocated is $5,000, and the floor space is as follows: Department A, 1,000 square feet; Department B, 4,000 square feet; Department C, 3,000 square feet; and Department D, 2,000 square feet. In addition, there is an aisle occupying 500 square feet running between departments A and B which provides passage back to departments C and D. An information booth for customers, located in the center of the store, occupies an additional 100 square feet. Department A is at the front entrance, so that all customers must pass through it to reach other points in the store.

Instructions

State how you would allocate the store rent, with computations and justifications for your answer.

10–4   **Allocation of Indirect Expenses** *(15 minutes)*   The Jones-Beckman Company is allocating its operating expenses by sales departments. The following expenses are included in the analysis:

a. Store building rent
b. Cost of electricity for lighting the store, including the large neon fixtures outside, which are on all night
c. Insurance on the inventory
d. Office supplies used in the central office, including accounting supplies
e. Telephone expense
f. Bad debts expense
g. Purchasing department salaries
h. Transportation-out to customers
i. Employee cafeteria expense
j. Air conditioning expense

Instructions

Indicate which of the expenses are direct and which are indirect in an analysis of departmental sales. Also state what basis you would use to allocate the indirect expenses.

10–5   **Allocating Expense Center Totals** *(15 minutes)*   The Centro Company is preparing an analysis of its operating expenses and has decided to use five expense centers. These are as follows:

a. Finished goods warehousing
b. Customer billing

c. Assembling orders for shipment
d. Credit and collection
e. Shipping dock

Instructions
State what basis you would use to allocate the total cost of each expense center to the sales departments if the analysis is (1) by sales territories and (2) by products.

10–6   **Allocation of Indirect Costs to Products** *(20 minutes)*   The Howard Smith Company is analyzing operating expenses by products. The sales manager's salary of $10,000 and the shipping manager's salary of $8,800 are to be allocated, using one of the bases given below:

	Product			
	A	B	C	D
Sales manager's time spent on each product	20%	30%	40%	10%
Number of units sold	800	2,000	5,000	1,000
Number of shipments made	200	600	1,000	400

Instructions
Which base or bases would you select for the allocation? State why the one you select is better and make the calculations.

 10–7   **Allocation of Occupancy Costs** *(15 minutes)*   The management of the Allread Company, a department store, feels that space on the second floor is worth only half as much as space on the ground floor. Their belief is based on the fact that more people pass through the ground floor, and that the departments on that floor therefore have more opportunity to make sales. The space occupied by the departments is as follows:

Department	Ground Floor	Second Floor
A	10,000 sq. ft.	
B	15,000	
C	5,000	
D	*30*	25,000 sq. ft.
E		5,000
		30

Instructions
If the total building rent is $21,000 for the year, how much of the rental cost should be allocated to each of the departments?

10–8*   **Expense Distribution Work Sheet** *(20 minutes)*   The Kroper Company has two sales departments, A and B, and two expense centers, C and D. Direct expenses were A, $5,000; B, $4,000; C,

$2,000; D, $1,450. Indirect expenses of $14,000 are to be allocated 30 percent to A, 30 percent to B, 20 percent to C, 20 percent to D.

Expense center C is the purchasing department, which issues twice as many purchase orders for A as for B. Expense center D is the delivery department which delivered 3,000 packages for A and 5,500 for B.

Instructions
Prepare an expense distribution work sheet for the company.

10–9*   **Expense Distribution Work Sheet** *(40 minutes)*   Prepare an expense distribution work sheet, using the data given below. You are to select the correct basis for allocation. (Distribute Building and Occupancy before Purchasing.)

	Total	Shoes	Men's Wear	Ladies' Wear	Building & Occupancy	Pur- chasing
Direct expenses	$8,110	$1,800	$2,100	$4,000	$125	$85
Indirect expenses						
Insurance on equipment	$ 900					
Electricity	700					
Telephone	400					

Data for expense allocation:

Department	Square Footage	Value of Equipment	Amount of Purchases	Number of Electric Outlets	Number of Telephones
Shoes	2,000	$10,000	$40,000	7	3
Men's wear	7,000	20,000	90,000	12	4
Ladies' wear	9,000	30,000	70,000	10	5
Building & occupancy	—	35,000		2	1
Purchasing	2,000	5,000		4	7

10–10   **Combining Branch Statements** *(25 minutes)*   The following data were gathered for the branches and home office of the Ministop Stores, Inc.

	Home Office	Branch A	Branch B
Sales	—	$100,000	$60,000
Cost of goods sold	—	60,000	38,000
Sales salaries	—	10,000	8,000
Administrative salaries	$15,000	—	—
Advertising	3,000	1,000	1,000
Supplies	800	400	300
Utilities	1,100	700	500
Rent	3,000	1,200	1,300

Instructions

Prepare an income statement with four columns: one for the home office data, one each for the two branches, and one which combines all the company amounts into a single overall income statement.

Problems

10–11   **Preparation and Analysis of Profit by Territories** *(30 minutes)*
The president of the Peterman Company requested the sales department to analyze sales and cost of goods sold for each of the company's four territories for the year. He also requested the accounting department to analyze costs by territories. As a result of these requests he received the following information:

Territory	Sales	Cost of Goods Sold	Direct Expense	Indirect and Allocated Expenses
Southwest	$20,000	$ 9,000	$ 4,000	$ 8,000
Northwest	30,000	12,000	5,000	8,000
Southeast	10,000	6,000	4,500	2,000
Northeast	25,000	13,000	4,500	3,000
Total	$85,000	$40,000	$18,000	$21,000

Instructions

1. Prepare an income statement for each of these territories showing the profit after direct expenses and the profit after all expenses.
2. Which territories would you, as president, give close attention? State why you would select those territories for closer study.

10–12   **Analysis of Costs by Size of Order** *(30 minutes)*   The sales manager and the president of the Trondike Company disagree about the large number of small orders which the company receives. The sales manager believes all orders are profitable, no matter how small, but the president is inclined to believe some of the smaller orders are unprofitable.

The Trondike Company's income statement by size of order was prepared after an expense analysis and appeared as follows:

	Less than $25 Each	Between $25 and $100 Each	Between $100 and $200 Each	Over $200 Each
Sales	$8,000	$25,000	$40,000	$8,000
Cost of goods sold	4,000	12,500	20,000	4,000
Gross margin	$4,000	$12,500	$20,000	$4,000

(continued)

	Less than $25 Each	Between $25 and $100 Each	Between $100 and $200 Each	Over $200 Each
Expenses				
Direct:				
Filling orders	$1,100	$1,200	$1,300	$200
Sending invoices	900	1,000	800	100
Recording collections	900	1,200	1,000	50
Loss on uncollectible accounts	600	300	200	—
Transportation out	800	1,100	1,800	400
Indirect:				
Other sales department expenses	500	2,000	2,800	
General and administrative expenses	400	2,100	3,050	700
Total expenses	5,200	8,900	10,950	1,450
Net profit (loss)	($1,200)	$ 3,600	$ 9,050	$2,550

Instructions

1. Why would the costs of filling orders, sending invoices, recording collections, and loss on uncollectible accounts be much higher in proportion to sales for the orders under $25 each than for orders over $25 each? Explain.
2. Describe the procedure and the probable bases used to allocate the expenses to the various classifications of order sizes.
3. What policy in regard to order size might management make as a result of this segment analysis that might increase the company's profitability?

10–13 **Expense Distribution Work Sheet** *(30 minutes)* The Blanco Forwarding Company divides its operations into a north and a west territory, with each under the direction of a district manager. The company also uses two expense centers, one for purchasing and the other for credit. Direct costs for the month of July were $6,000, $8,000, $3,000 and $2,000 for the north and west territories and the purchasing and credit departments, respectively. Indirect expenses of $17,000 for the month are to be allocated to the four on the basis of 30 percent to north, 40 percent to west, 20 percent to purchasing, and 10 percent to credit. The purchasing department issued 140 purchase orders applicable to July business in the north and 180 for the west. The credit department processed 500 credit reports during the month for the north and 425 for the west.

Instructions

Prepare an expense distribution work sheet for the company for the month of July.

10–14   **Effects of Eliminating a Department** *(30 minutes)*   The Barker Company is considering eliminating one of its two departments. Its departmental income statement is shown below.

If department B is eliminated, the sales of department A will increase 10 percent, and the cost of sales will increase 10 percent also. All the direct costs of B will be eliminated, and other costs, presently allocated to department B, will be reduced as follows: utilities, $100; insurance, $300; property taxes, $300.

	Department A	Department B
Sales	$100,000	$60,000
Cost of goods sold	60,000	40,000
Gross profit	$ 40,000	$20,000
Direct expenses:		
Salaries	$ 10,000	$ 9,000
Supplies	100	200
Advertising	1,000	500
Indirect expenses:		
Administrative salaries	9,000	9,000
Utilities	500	600
Rent on building	2,500	1,600
Property taxes on inventory	500	400
Insurance	600	700
Total expenses	$ 24,200	$22,000
Net profit (loss)	$ 15,800	($ 2,000)

Instructions

Prepare a schedule showing in detail the change in revenue, costs, and profit if department B is eliminated. Describe briefly why all expenses allocated to department B were not eliminated and whether you would discontinue department B.

10–15   **Allocation of Joint Transportation Costs** *(30 minutes)*   The Matador Bottling Company sells and delivers its bottled products to retail outlets within a 200-mile radius of its bottling plant. On the return trip from a delivery the company's trucks pick up empty containers, new containers from several bottle manufacturers in the area, and raw materials from a number of suppliers. The company's trucks do not run a scheduled route and are sent wherever needed to deliver and return with raw materials. The scheduling of truck trips is under the direction of the assistant to the president.

All the cost of operating the truck fleet are recorded as delivery expenses, and consequently there is very little transportation-in cost on raw materials and bottles. The sales manager feels that this is not an equitable method of accounting, since he is thus charged with a cost over which he has no direct control.

A typical truck run is as follows:

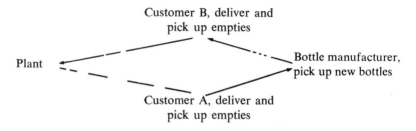

The sales manager is attempting to identify unprofitable customers and feels that the cost of delivering to some customers is greater than the profit made on sales to them.

Instructions

How could trucking costs be allocated to find unprofitable customers? How would trucking costs be divided between selling and transportation-in?

10–16   **Expense Distribution Work Sheet and Income Statements** *(60 minutes)*   The following data were accumulated by the Goode Department Store:

	Sales	Cost of Goods Sold
Dry goods department	$21,000	$11,000
Notions department	18,000	9,000
Household appliance department	35,000	21,000

Direct expenses are shown below:

	Salaries	Supplies	Advertising
Dry goods department	$3,000	$500	$1,000
Notions department	2,000	200	800
Household appliance department	4,000	600	1,600
Purchasing department	2,000	200	—
Credit department	1,000	200	—

Indirect expenses were depreciation on building, $10,000; insurance on building, $500; telephone and telegraph, $1,200; and electricity, $800.

Statistics available for allocation purposes are as follows:

	Dry Goods	Notions	Household Appliances	Purchasing	Credit	_Totals_
Square footage occupied	12,000 _(24%)_	10,000 _(20%)_	15,000 _(30%)_	7,000 _(14%)_	6,000 _(12%)_	_50,000_
Number of telephones	3	2	4	2	1	_12_
Electric outlets	4	2	5	3	2	_16_
Purchase orders	50	81	70			
Credit sales	$10,100	$5,000	$11,500			

Instructions

Prepare (1) an expense distribution work sheet and (2) income statements by departments for the Goode Department Store from the above data for the year ended December 31. (Distribute the costs of the purchasing department before distributing those of the credit department.)

10–17 **Profit by Salesman** (45 minutes) The Jackson Desk Company sells office desks in three states. The company has six salesmen, and the accounting office has accumulated the following information about each salesman for the year:

	Jones	Smith	White	Peters	Adams	Knowl
Sales made	$38,000	$27,000	$51,000	$57,000	$53,000	$45,000
Salary	7,000	7,000	7,000	7,000	7,000	7,000
Travel costs	1,000	2,000	1,200	600	1,300	500
Freight-out	900	300	800	400	200	900
Commissions	500	—	1,000	1,500	1,400	700
Cost of goods sold	20,000	15,000	25,000	30,000	28,000	22,000
Number of customers	15	8	10	12	14	11

The following costs could not be traced directly to salesmen and are to be allocated using the given basis: general sales office costs of $9,000 equally to salesmen; general office costs of $14,000 on the basis of the number of customers served; warehouse expenses of $7,000 on the basis of cost of goods sold.

Instructions

1. Prepare an income statement showing the net profit or loss generated by each salesman's efforts.
2. The company pays salesmen a commission based on the amount of sales made, above a minimum base. Do you think the commissions paid reflect the productivity of the salesmen? Why or why not?

10–18 **Profit by Product Line** (50 minutes) The Ralston Company manufactures hardware, garden tools, and utensils. The company's management is not sure which of these product lines is its most profitable, and the following data were accumulated for the year just ended:

Sales: hardware, $90,000; tools, $41,000; utensils, $62,000.
Cost of goods sold: hardware, $50,000; tools, $20,500; utensils, $31,400.

Expenses:		
	Warehouse	$ 8,000
	Order processing	12,000
	Salesmen's commissions	37,500
	Collection expense	5,000
	Advertising	10,000
	Transportation	7,500
	Packing and shipping	3,500
	Administrative	4,000
		$87,500

a. The warehouse contains 100,000 square feet, of which 62,500 are used for hardware, 20,000 for tools, and 17,500 for utensils.
b. The company processed 3,000 orders for hardware, 1,000 for tools, and 2,000 for utensils.
c. Sales commissions were paid as follows: hardware $15,000, tools $10,000, utensils $12,500.
d. Individual collections during the year were made as follows: 1,000 on sales of hardware, 800 on tools, and 700 on utensils.
e. The company spent $1,500 on general advertising, which benefits all product lines equally, and $8,500 on specific products. The specific advertising was 30 percent for hardware, 50 percent on tools, and 20 percent on utensils.
f. Transportation costs were paid as follows: hardware $3,000, tools $2,000, utensils $2,500.
g. Shipments made during the year were 600 on hardware, 800 on tools, and 350 on utensils.
h. General and administrative expenses are allocated on the basis of 40 percent to hardware, 30 percent to tools, and 30 percent to utensils. These percentages are the result of time estimates made by administrative employees.

Instructions
Prepare an income statement showing the profitability of each product. Based upon the results of your statement, discuss briefly which product line appears to be most profitable, whether or not you would eliminate a product line, and which line you would emphasize in the sales effort.

10-19   **Analysis of Allocated Costs** *(40 minutes)*   The White and Williamson Company, which is located in Buffalo, New York, has not realized a profit for the past several years. Their controller has talked several times with the sales manager and the president about the

WHITE AND WILLIAMSON COMPANY
(Problem 10–19)

	Basis	Far West	Mid-west	South	Atlantic Coast	New England	Total
Sales	Analysis of sales invoices	$35,000	$40,000	$18,000	$40,000	$54,000	$187,000
Cost of goods sold	Analysis of cost on each sales invoice	17,000	21,000	10,000	20,000	28,000	96,000
Gross profit		$18,000	$19,000	$ 8,000	$20,000	$26,000	$ 91,000
Salesmen's salaries	Analysis of payroll	$ 7,000	$ 6,000	$ 6,000	$ 7,000	$ 7,000	$ 33,000
Salesmen's travel	Analysis of expense reimbursements	5,000	2,000	3,000	1,500	2,000	13,500
Salesmen's entertainment	Analysis of expense reimbursements	700	700	200	900	800	3,300
Freight out	Analysis of freight invoices	1,600	800	900	500	600	4,400
Advertising	Analysis of radio and newspaper advertising	700	500	300	1,100	1,200	3,800
Other selling costs	Number of salesmen's calls	750	500	520	550	580	2,900
Administrative salaries	Time spent	3,000	1,000	3,000	1,000	1,000	9,000
Office supplies	Number of customers	400	500	200	1,500	1,300	3,900
Building depreciation, taxes and insurance	Total sales	1,750	4,000	900	4,500	5,500	16,650
Other administrative costs	Equally to each territory	300	300	300	300	300	1,500
Total expenses		$21,200	$16,300	$15,320	$18,850	$20,280	$ 91,950
Net profit (loss)		($ 3,200)	$ 2,700	($ 7,320)	$ 1,150	$ 5,720	($ 950)

333

company's unprofitable sales territories. The president was skeptical of the controller's opinion that a few territories are causing the losses, and the sales manager was outspoken in saying that the controller was absolutely wrong. The company sells a full line of overcoats, sweaters, and jackets.

The controller asked his staff to prepare an analysis of operating revenues and expenses by territories. The resulting analysis is illustrated on p. 333.

The controller presented this analysis to the president and the sales manager in support of his position that the far western and southern territories were causing the losses. The president studied the analysis and remarked that the bases for distributing some of the expenses were not equitable and that the profit analysis was thus incorrect. He stated that the administrative time was naturally greater for the western and southern territories, because the administration was trying to build up sales there.

The final result of the discussion was that the president, sales manager, and controller agreed that any territory would be eliminated if it did not produce more revenue than the actual direct costs of operating in the territory.

Instructions

Discuss the bases used in the controller's study and their applicability to the situation and state what territories, if any, you would recommend discontinuing.

10–20   **Analysis of the Effects of Eliminating a Department** (45 minutes)
The Williamsburg Department Store prepared the following analysis for each of its departments.

The administrative officers are considering the elimination of the ready-to-wear and the notions departments and ask you to prepare a study of the resulting effects on profit. You have estimated the following results if the two departments are eliminated:

a. Sales and cost of goods sold at the hardware department will drop 10 percent, but sales and cost of goods sold of the household goods department will increase by 5 percent.

b. All direct expenses will remain the same for the remaining departments but will disappear entirely for the two eliminated departments.

	Ready-to-wear	Hardware	Notions	Household Goods	Total
Sales	$60,000	$39,000	$15,000	$80,000	$194,000
Cost of goods sold	35,000	21,000	7,000	45,000	108,000
Gross profit	$25,000	$18,000	$ 8,000	$35,000	$ 86,000

(continued)

	Ready-to-wear	Hardware	Notions	House hold Goods	Total
Direct expenses:					
Sales salaries	$14,000	$ 8,000	$ 6,000	$13,000	$ 41,000
Advertising	500	400	100	1,000	2,000
Supplies	200	100	100	400	800
Indirect expenses:					
Depreciation on building	5,000	4,000	2,000	8,000	19,000
Telephone and telegraph	300	200	50	400	950
Electricity	400	100	100	300	900
Administrative salaries	6,000	3,000	2,500	5,000	16,500
Insurance	150	50	50	200	450
Property taxes	250	150	100	200	700
Total expenses	$26,800	$16,000	$11,000	$28,500	$ 82,300
Net profit (loss)	($ 1,800)	$ 2,000	($ 3,000)	$ 6,500	$ 3,700

c. The total telephone and telegraph expense will decrease by $200.

d. The total electricity expense will decrease by 10 percent.

e. Total insurance expense will decrease by $100.

Instructions

1. Prepare an analysis listing in detail the changes in revenue, the changes in expenses for the store as a whole, and the overall effects on the net profit of the store.

2. State whether you think the two departments should be eliminated and why you have so decided. Do you feel the above analysis, as submitted to the company's management, reflects clearly all data needed for such decisions?

10–21   Analysis of Profitability of Small Orders *(50 minutes)*   The Gale Company is considering a quantity discount system whereby customers are allowed quantity discounts for larger purchases. The

	Orders for One Unit	Orders for Two Units	Orders for Three Units	Orders for Four Units
Sales	$10,000	$100,000	$120,000	$40,000
Cost of goods sold	5,000	50,000	60,000	20,000
Gross profit	$ 5,000	$ 50,000	$ 60,000	$20,000
Direct expenses	$ 2,000	$ 10,000	$ 8,000	$ 2,000
Indirect expenses	3,000	30,000	36,000	12,000
Total expenses	$ 5,000	$ 40,000	$ 44,000	$14,000
Net profit	$ –0–	$ 10,000	$ 16,000	$ 6,000

company wants to set the discount rate by size of orders so that it will encourage customers to buy in the larger quantities, which are more profitable. A study was undertaken of the company's costs by size of order, and the accompanying condensed expense distribution worksheet for the year was prepared.

The company's product sells for $50 per unit before any discount is allowed for quantity purchases. The direct expenses were $10 for each order, regardless of the size of the order. The indirect expenses were allocated on a basis of 30 percent of sales.

Instructions

1. Compute the profit earned on each order for each of the four order sizes.
2. Suppose the company set a policy of 2 percent off of the sales price of $50 for orders of two units, 5 percent off for orders of three units, and 10 percent off for orders of four units. If the cost of goods sold remained at 50 percent of selling price, before discounts, direct expenses remained at $10 per order, and indirect expenses remained at 30 percent of sales before discounts, prepare an income statement by size of order if sales were the same in total number of units but were received as follows:

Number of orders for one unit	100
Number of orders for two units	1000
Number of orders for three units	800
Number of orders for four units	225

3. Would you recommend that the discount policy be adopted? Why or why not?

Analysis of Profitability of Products (*60 minutes*)   The advertising manager of the Nelson Company requested information about which of the company's two products to emphasize in his advertising program during the coming year. As a result of his request, the controller was asked to prepare an analysis of the profitability of the two products. The controller requested his staff to accumulate the necessary information for the analysis, which was presented as shown below:

Expense	Amount	Allocation
Salesmen's salaries	$18,000	Direct: $10,000 to A and $8,000 to B
Advertising	3,000	Direct: $2,000 to A and $1,000 to B
Insurance on inventory	700	Direct: $300 to A and $400 to B
Freight-out	2,100	Direct: $900 to A and $1,200 to B
Telephone and telegraph	800	Number of telephones: General sales department, 6; Order handling, 2; General office, 8
Building depreciation and insurance	4,500	Space occupied: General sales department, 6,000 ft.; Order handling, 4,000 ft.; General office, 8,000 ft.
Supplies	1,200	Direct: General sales department, $400; Order handling, $300; General office, $500.

Expense	Amount	Allocation
Administrative salaries	39,000	Direct: General sales department, $11,000; Order handling, $8,000; General office, $20,000
General sales department		Time spent: 60% product A; 40% product B
Order handling		Number of orders: 10,000 product A; 8,800 product B
General office		Time spent: 40% product A, 60% product B

Instructions

1. Prepare the expense distribution sheet for the company, using a worksheet for the two products, A and B, and three expense centers for the general sales office, order handling, and general office.
2. If 10,000 units of A were sold during the period and each unit produced $8 of gross margin, and 20,000 units of B were sold which produced $5 gross margin each, which product made the greatest total amount of profit?
3. Which of the two units produced the greatest *per unit* profit?
4. If the company can undertake only $15,000 additional advertising, which must be expended on either product A or product B— but not on both—and if this advertising will sell an additional 5,000 units of the product selected, which would you choose to advertise?

PART 3

Planning and Control Systems

chapter 11

Budgetary Control and Profit Planning

**Learning
Objectives**

This chapter begins a new part of the text which emphasizes planning and control systems. Upon completion of your study of the chapter you should:

1. Appreciate the role of the budgetary process in controlling and coordinating a company's activities.
2. Recognize the necessity for resolving major company policies prior to the preparation of the budget.
3. Know the sequence in which the budgetary process is undertaken.
4. Be able to prepare the budgetary schedules.

The Nature of Budgeting

Business budgeting is a process of carefully and systematically planning future activities. In some companies, plans for the future exist only in the minds of one or two top executives; but, in more progressively managed companies, formal budgets are prepared and approved by executive management well in advance of actual operations. Reports are then prepared at regular intervals which compare the results of operations with the predetermined budget.

A budget is the means by which management's plans are reduced to monetary amounts. By means of departmental breakdown, the budgetary scheduling is communicated to each operating supervisor who is affected. Since the budget provides a measure of expected future performance, the budgetary system can be a means of motivating employees to more efficient operations or to improved individual performance.

The business budget has three fundamental purposes: (1) planning future operations, (2) coordinating all the company's activities, and (3) controlling the actions of operating employees. Detailed budgetary plans for sales, expenses, production, inventories, and cash are usually necessary to satisfy these purposes.

Planning is the process of establishing future objectives and formulating means of meeting those objectives. Control, on the other hand, is the means by which management ascertains that the various parts of the business perform efficiently and progress toward the predetermined goals. A good budgetary system provides both planning and control. Planning is effected by determining in advance the expected sales volume, the expected cost of merchandise to be purchased or produced, the number of employees needed, and the expenses to be incurred. Control is then achieved by means of budget performance reports prepared for each subdivision of the company. These budgetary reports reflect the difference between actual operations and the budgetary plan and provide a means for locating those activities requiring attention.

The budget is the primary vehicle for bringing the diverse operations of a business into an overall, coordinated plan of action. The budget permits the production departments to plan their activities in coordination with sales departments, the purchasing department to plan the acquisition of raw materials to meet production requirements, and the finance officers to plan the company's cash requirements in order to pay for the materials. Without a vehicle such as the budget, the efforts of individual parts of the business might not be sufficiently coordinated to provide maximum operating efficiency.

A final benefit derived from a comprehensive budgetary program is that of calling attention, in advance, to the need for operating policies. For example, the advertising budget focuses attention upon the selection of advertising media which are expected to be effective; preparation of the production budget focuses attention upon the selection of an optimum inventory level; and preparation of the cash budget involves selection of a minimum acceptable cash balance. Establishment of these policies is an integral part of the control process, and an effective budgetary program requires that these policy decisions be made in advance, prior to the existence of a crisis situation.

The Budget Period

The budget should cover a period sufficiently short to permit the location of areas needing attention before excessive loss or waste has occurred. For this reason monthly budget reports on sales and expenses are very useful. On the other hand, annual budgets, prepared sufficiently in advance to permit long-range planning and systematic growth, have many advantages; indeed, some companies budget the purchase of fixed assets as far as five or ten years in advance. Most businesses prepare annual budgets, covering the same period as their accounting year, with a breakdown by months or quarters. The monthly breakdown is prepared to take into account all known seasonal or short-term fluctuations expected during the twelve months of the budget year. In addition to monthly budget reports, a cumulative budget report covering the year-to-date is usually prepared.

Construction
Of the Budget

The budget is prepared in the form of schedules which reflect in considerable detail the operations which are planned for the coming period. Schedules for budgeted sales, for example, should indicate the sales plan for each product in each territory for each month. Production schedules should indicate planned production for each product for each week or each month.

Budget schedules must be prepared in a logical sequence, and their preparation frequently begins months before the start of the budget period. Production schedules, for example, cannot be prepared until sales budgets have been completed and decisions have been made relative to inventory levels. Manufacturing labor, raw materials purchases, and manufacturing overhead budgets must be prepared after the production schedules have been completed, and cash budgets depend upon the expense budgets. The sequence of events in the preparation of the budget is usually as follows:

1. Project the expected sales during the budget period both in units and in dollars. The sales budget is the foundation upon which the remaining steps in the budgetary process are built.
2. Determine the desired finished goods inventory level.
3. Prepare production schedules for each product.
4. Prepare schedules of labor costs to manufacture the units included in the production plan.
5. Prepare schedules of the purchase of raw materials, considering the anticipated production and the level of raw materials inventories desired.
6. Prepare expense budgets for manufacturing overhead items.
7. Prepare selling expense and administrative expense budgets.
8. Bring together the forecasts indicated above into a "master budget," or overall plan. This step can be accomplished by preparing proforma (projected) income statements and balance sheets.
9. Based on estimated collections from cash or credit sales and the payment of expenses, prepare a cash budget. This budget indicates when additional funds must be borrowed or invested and when any borrowed funds can be repaid.

After the budget has been constructed, each subbudget and the master budget should be approved by executive management. Copies of the appropriate budgets should be given to operating supervisors, who will then know exactly what is expected of them.

The Sales Budget

The sales budget is the foundation for all other subbudgets and must be prepared first. A forecast of sales in both dollars and units of product provides the basis for budgeting selling expenses, purchases, inventory levels, personnel requirements, and cash needs. Many factors must be considered when the sales budget is established, including sales trends, limitations on the supply of merchandise or the capacity of the manufacturing plant, growth and expansion of the company's market, competing products, the expected amount of advertising, and the general level of the economy. Since most of these unknown factors must be estimated, the larger companies frequently maintain a specially trained staff to measure them. Historical data from prior periods may help in establishing the budget for the coming year, but historical amounts must always be adjusted for anticipated changes.

High-speed equipment, such as that used for punched-card or electronic data processing systems, facilitates completion of the detailed schedules required for careful sales planning. However, mechanized accounting systems are not a prerequisite for sound budgetary planning, and even the smallest companies will benefit by planning their sales activities for the coming period.

Sales should be budgeted by individual products, by sales territories, and by different marketing processes—such as wholesale, jobber, and retail—thereby permitting measurement of the performance of individuals who are responsible for different sales areas. To illustrate the preparation of a sales budget, suppose that the J. C. Treadway Company produces three products: Regular, Choice, and Supreme. All products are sold through wholesale outlets in three territories, North, South, and Central. The sales budget, illustrated in Exhibit 11–1, reflects the planned sales for the first three months of 19X1 in both units and dollars and by separate products and territories.

The Production Budget

The production budget is prepared after the sales budget has been completed. Since sales forecasts reflect the products to be sold each month, the manufacture of those products can be budgeted with little difficulty. However, fluctuations in inventory levels affect the production budget. Consequently, the number of units made in any one month may differ from the number to be sold. The production schedule must be arranged so that the inventory is sufficient at all times for the projected sales but at the same time is not excessive. Interest, insurance, and storage costs on any excess inventory reduce the company's potential profit.

Inventories should be maintained at low levels to reduce their carrying cost, but at the same time they must be sufficient to prevent stockouts. Thus the decision on inventory levels is an important part of the planning process.

When the production budget is prepared, each product must be projected separately. The inventory of each product at the beginning of the budget period and the units of that product expected to be sold are inserted in the budget schedule first. If the J. C. Treadway Company, whose sales budget is shown in

EXHIBIT 11–1

J. C. TREADWAY COMPANY
Sales Budget
First Quarter, 19X1

	January		February		March	
	Units	Dollars	Units	Dollars	Units	Dollars
Regular:						
North	150	$ 1,500	160	$ 1,400	170	$ 1,600
South	150	1,400	180	1,600	180	1,600
Central	200	2,700	210	2,900	230	3,000
	500	$ 5,600	550	$ 5,900	580	$ 6,200
Choice:						
North	1,700	$ 5,000	1,600	$ 5,500	1,600	$ 5,500
South	2,300	7,000	2,400	7,500	2,600	8,000
Central	1,600	6,800	1,800	6,700	1,700	6,000
	5,600	$18,800	5,800	$19,700	5,900	$19,500
Supreme:						
North	900	$ 3,000	1,000	$ 3,200	1,000	$ 3,200
South	1,000	3,500	1,000	3,500	1,100	3,700
Central	600	2,200	600	2,200	600	2,300
	2,500	$ 8,700	2,600	$ 8,900	2,700	$ 9,200
Total		$33,100		$34,500		$34,900

Exhibit 11–1, has a beginning inventory of 530 regular units, the following data are placed on the production budget before either new production or ending inventories are computed. These data are reflected in the following computation:

Computation of the Production Budget (in units)

(1)	+	(2)	=	(3)	−	(4)	=	(5)
Desired Inventory at End of Month		Sales for Month (From Sales Budget)		Total Needed During Month		Inventory at Beginning of Month		Required Production
Regular:								
January		500				530		
February		550						
March		580						

At this point, a policy relative to the desired number of units in the inventory at the end of each month must be formulated. Management should adopt an inventory policy in this regard to prevent overstocking and while, at the same time, maintaining adequate stocks.

Suppose, to complete the illustration, that a decision is reached by the management of the J. C. Treadway Company to maintain an inventory at the end of each month equal to next month's budgeted sales. Thus, the ending inventory on January 31 must be equal to the projected sales of February, which appear in the sales budget at 550 units. With this information, the January production can be computed as follows:

Desired inventory at the end of the month	550
Sales during the month	500
Total needed	1,050
Less units in the inventory at the beginning of the month	530
To be manufactured during the month	520

The beginning inventory for the second month would then be 550 units, and monthly production would be computed by applying the same procedure. The completed production budget, illustrated in Exhibit 11–2, follows this approach.

EXHIBIT 11–2

J. C. TREADWAY COMPANY
Production Budget (in units)
First Quarter, 19X1

Products	Desired Inventory at End of Month	Sales for Month (From Sales Budget)	Total Needed During Month	Inventory at Beginning of Month	Required Production
Regular:					
January	550	500	1,050	530	520
February	580	550	1,130	550	580
March	650	580	1,230	580	650
Choice:					
January	5,800	5,600	11,400	6,000	5,400
February	5,900	5,800	11,700	5,800	5,900
March	6,100	5,900	12,000	5,900	6,100
Supreme:					
January	2,600	2,500	5,100	2,000	3,100
February	2,700	2,600	5,300	2,600	2,700
March	3,000	2,700	5,700	2,700	3,000

The beginning inventories of the Choice and Supreme products are assumed to be 6,000 units and 2,000 units respectively, and the plan of the company is to have an ending inventory equal to the expected sales of the following month.

After the production budget is completed in terms of units, the labor, materials, and overhead costs to be incurred must be scheduled. The projection of manufacturing costs must take into consideration anticipated price changes and general price trends in raw materials and labor costs.

Labor Budgets

The schedules of manufacturing labor requirements cannot be prepared until the production schedules are completed. Labor requirements are computed by multiplying the hours of labor in each product by the units of that product to be manufactured. If there is one-half hour of labor required for each unit of Regular, three-fifths of an hour for Choice, and three-fourths of an hour for Supreme, the labor required for the first quarter of 19X1, as indicated by the production schedules of the J. C. Treadway Company, would be that shown in Exhibit 11-3.

EXHIBIT 11-3

J. C. TREADWAY COMPANY
Manufacturing Labor Budget
First Quarter, 19X1

	Scheduled Production	Required Labor Hours Per Unit	Total Hours Required	Expected Hourly Rate	Manufacturing Labor Cost
January:					
Regular	520	1/2	260		
Choice	5,400	3/5	3,240		
Supreme	3,100	3/4	2,325		
			5,825	$2	$11,650
February:					
Regular	580	1/2	290		
Choice	5,900	3/5	3,540		
Supreme	2,700	3/4	2,025		
			5,855	$2	$11,710
March:					
Regular	650	1/2	325		
Choice	6,100	3/5	3,660		
Supreme	3,000	3/4	2,250		
			6,235	$2.10	$13,004

From these schedules, the required number of factory employees can be projected. Exhibit 11-3 indicates that 5,825 hours of labor will be required in January, 5,855 hours in February, and 6,235 hours in March. To illustrate how these schedules provide plans for future operations, note that the difference between the expected labor requirements for January and March is 410 hours (6,235 − 5,825) and represents the labor of approximately two employees. Thus, the company's executives know in advance either two additional workers must be hired and trained, or a considerable number of overtime hours will have to be worked by present employees.

Conversion of the hours into dollar costs also necessitates a plan for employee wage changes. This is especially important where wage costs constitute a major element in the total cost of the company's products. Note that an average wage increase from $2 per hour to $2.10 per hours is expected in March.

Raw Materials Budget

The raw materials requirements are directly dependent upon scheduled production. However, purchases must be made in the most economical quantities. Many companies give discounts for large quantity purchases, and these "quantity discounts" must be considered when inventory levels and purchases of raw materials are being planned. Costs of carrying an increased inventory during periods of low production must be matched with the savings realized by purchasing in large quantities. Assume, for simplicity, that there is one unit of raw material in each unit of the J. C. Treadway Company's products. Further, assume that the raw material presently costs $.50 per unit but is expected to increase to $.60 in March, and that the units purchased each month must equal the production for that month. The raw materials purchases budget of the J. C. Treadway Company would appear as shown in Exhibit 11–4.

EXHIBIT 11–4

J. C. TREADWAY COMPANY
Schedule of Monthly Purchases (in dollars)
For the First Quarter, 19X1

	Raw Material Units to Be Purchased	Raw Materials Purchase Price	Purchases Total
January:			
Regular	520	$0.50	$ 260
Choice	5,400	.50	2,700
Supreme	3,100	.50	1,550
			$4,510
February:			
Regular	580	$0.50	$ 290
Choice	5,900	.50	2,950
Supreme	2,700	.50	1,350
			$4,590
March:			
Regular	650	$0.60	$ 390
Choice	6,100	.60	3,660
Supreme	3,000	.60	1,800
			$5,850

Manufacturing Overhead Budget

The projection of manufacturing expenses other than labor and raw materials entails a thorough study of each expense and its reaction to volume changes. The amount of fixed expenses will remain constant at all levels of production, but variable and semivariable manufacturing expenses will change. The techniques of analyzing expenses described in the earlier chapter on cost-volume-profit analysis must be applied, using the level of activity in the production schedule. The schedule of manufacturing expenses for the J. C. Treadway Company appears in Exhibit 11–5.

EXHIBIT 11–5

J. C. TREADWAY COMPANY
Manufacturing Overhead
First Quarter, 19X1

Expense	January (5825 DLH)	February (5855 DLH)	March (6235 DLH)	Total
Depreciation on machinery (fixed)	$ 800	$ 800	$ 800	$2,400
Heat, light and power (semi-variable; $100 fixed, plus $.04 per labor hour)	333	334	349	1,016
Supervisory salaries (fixed)	1,200	1,200	1,200	3,600
Factory supplies (variable; $.05 per direct labor hour)	291	293	312	896
Factory taxes (fixed)	100	100	100	300
Repairs and maintenance (semi-variable; $50 fixed plus $.02 per direct labor hour)	167	167	175	509
Factory payroll taxes (semi-variable; $.02 per labor hour)	117	117	125	359
Total	$3,008	$3,011	$3,061	$9,080

Note that the number of direct labor hours shown in the schedule of manufacturing labor (Exhibit 11–3) is the activity base used to project the manufacturing expenses. While the number of units produced could have been used, there is probably a closer relationship between expenses incurred and the number of hours worked. This is especially true when a number of different products are being manufactured.

Cost of Goods Sold Schedule

The cost of goods sold can be budgeted after the manufacturing labor, raw materials, and manufacturing overhead schedules are completed. These three schedules are brought together and the unit costs to manufacture can be computed. Based upon these unit costs, the cost of goods sold and the cost of unsold units held in inventory can be calculated. Exhibit 11–6 illustrates the cost of goods sold schedule, using assumed amounts for the beginning and ending inventories.

Selling and Administrative Expense Budget

The projection of selling expenses and administrative expenses also entails a study of each expense and its reaction to volume changes. The behavior of each expense of the J. C. Treadway Company is indicated in Exhibit 11–7 to emphasize the manner by which the amounts are computed. However, note

EXHIBIT 11–6

J. C. TREADWAY COMPANY
Cost of Goods Sold Budget
First Quarter, 19X1

	January	February	March
Beginning finished goods inventory	$16,300	$17,258	$18,119
Manufacturing labor (Exhibit 11–3)	11,650	11,710	13,004
Raw materials (Exhibit 11–4)	4,510	4,590	5,850
Manufacturing overhead (Exhibit 11–5)	3,008	3,011	3,061
Total	$35,468	$36,569	$40,034
Ending finished goods inventory	17,258	18,119	19,414
Cost of goods sold	$18,210	$18,450	$20,620

that the selling and administrative expenses budget is based on the sales volumes computed in the sales budget and has no necessary relationship to factory productivity.

Profit Planning

All the schedules shown previously must be brought together to reflect the company's profit plan for the budget period. A proforma statement, which contains the data in the budget schedules, is used for this purpose. *Proforma* means

EXHIBIT 11–7

J. C. TREADWAY COMPANY
Expense Budget
For the First Quarter, 19X1

	January	February	March	Total
Selling:				
Depreciation on store equipment (fixed)	$1,000	$ 1,000	$ 1,000	$ 3,000
Store supplies (variable; 2% of sales)	662	690	698	2,050
Insurance on store equipment (fixed)	300	300	300	900
Sales salaries (semivariable; $1,000 fixed, balance 5% of sales)	2,655	2,725	2,745	8,125
Total selling expenses	$4,617	$ 4,715	$ 4,743	$14,075
Administrative:				
Officers' salaries (fixed)	$1,000	$ 1,000	$ 1,000	$ 3,000
Telephone and telegraph (semivariable; $100 fixed, balance 1% of sales)	431	445	449	1,325
Clerical salaries (variable; 10% of sales)	3,310	3,450	3,490	10,250
Office supplies (semivariable; $100 fixed, balance 1% of sales)	431	445	449	1,325
Taxes (fixed)	200	200	200	600
Total	$5,372	$ 5,540	$ 5,588	$16,500
Total expenses	$9,989	$10,255	$10,331	$30,575

that the statement contains anticipated amounts instead of historical amounts. The preparation of proforma statements, undertaken after all subbudgets are completed, is the final step in the budget plan. These statements are prepared to reflect the effects of all the budgeted transactions on the company's profitability and financial position.

The proforma income statement which would be prepared from the subbudgets illustrated in this chapter is shown in Exhibit 11–8. The source of each amount in the proforma statement is indicated in the body of the statement so that these amounts can be traced to the schedules shown previously. The projected income statement provides a means of determining the overall effects of the budget plan: if the budgeted net income is too low, these budgets are reviewed, and means of reducing expenses or increasing revenues are sought.

A proforma balance sheet is frequently prepared to project the company's financial position at the end of the budget period. However, a projected balance sheet is less significant than a projected income statement, since the cash budget provides sufficient data for planning the receipts and disbursements of cash. A projected balance sheet for the J. C. Treadway Company is not shown.

EXHIBIT 11–8

J. C. TREADWAY COMPANY
Proforma Income Statements
For the First Quarter, 19X1

	January	February	March
Sales (from Exhibit 11–1)	$33,100	$34,500	$34,900
Cost of goods sold (from Exhibit 11–6)	18,210	18,450	20,620
Gross profit	$14,890	$16,050	$14,280
Selling and administrative expenses (from Exhibit 11–7)	9,989	10,255	10,331
Budgeted net income	$ 4,901	$ 5,795	$ 3,949

Exhibit 11–8 shows, for example, that the profit for March is considerably lower than for the prior two months. This reduction is principally due to the anticipated increases in wage rates and raw material costs. After seeing the profit plan, management may decide that increases in selling prices are necessary in March to maintain an acceptable profit level. Even if prices cannot be raised, management is forewarned that profit reductions are imminent.

The sequence in which the schedules are prepared is shown in Exhibit 11–9. Note that the sales budget is prepared first and that the proforma income statement cannot be prepared until all other schedules are complete.

The Cash Budget

The cash budget is prepared after all other schedules have been completed, because cash is affected by more transactions than any other asset. The cash budget is one of the most important budgets, for it indicates the cash requirements

EXHIBIT 11–9

Sequence Followed in Preparing Budget Schedules

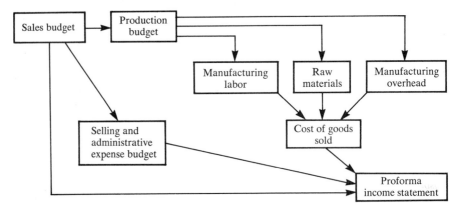

necessary to complete the budgeted activities. The cash budget indicates the extent and timing of any need for additional monies, as well as the anticipated repayment date.

The cash budget is constructed by scheduling receipts and disbursements from all budgeted activities. A cash budget may be subdivided into monthly, weekly, or even daily periods, depending upon the company's cash position. Projected disbursements are subtracted from budgeted receipts to determine the anticipated cash balance at the end of each period.

The cash budget of the J. C. Treadway Company is illustrated in Exhibit 11–10. Note the indication that borrowed funds will be needed in January and February and that the company should be able to repay both the loans in March. Preparation of the cash budget begins with the cash balance on January 1. Receipts and disbursements for January are entered, and the projected cash excess or deficiency at the end of the month can be determined. Anticipated borrowings or repayments of borrowed funds are then considered, and the final projected cash balance at the end of the month is computed. The ending balance of one month is the beginning balance of the next month, and the process is repeated for each succeeding month until the cash budget is completed.

The budgeted sales, expenses, and purchases must not be incorporated into the cash budget without prior adjustment for noncash items. For example, the total sales budgeted for January will not be realized in cash if some of the sales are made on credit terms. However, receivables arising from sales in prior months will be collected and must be included in the cash budget. The terms of raw materials purchases determine the time of payment and must be considered when the cash budget is constructed. If the creditors' terms allow payment to be made on or before the tenth day of the following month (commonly stated as 10EOM), the payment for a month's purchases need not be made until the following month.

Adjustment of an expense budget to a schedule of cash disbursements requires the subtraction of such noncash expenses as depreciation and the amor-

EXHIBIT 11–10

J. C. TREADWAY COMPANY
Cash Budget
First Quarter, 19X1

	January	February	March
Projected cash balance, first of month	$ 1,200	$ 1,211	$ 696
Receipts:			
Cash sales	14,000	15,000	18,000
Collection of receivables	12,000	13,000	16,000
Collection of notes receivable			4,000
Total available cash	$27,200	$29,211	$38,696
Disbursements:			
Payment of labor, materials, and manufacturing overhead	$19,000	$20,360	$20,620
Selling and administrative expenses	8,989	11,155	8,831
Purchase of new machine			1,200
Total disbursements	$27,989	$31,515	$30,651
Excess of available funds over disbursements	$ (789)	$ (2,304)	$ 8,045
Borrowed funds needed	2,000	3,000	
Repayment of borrowed funds			(5,000)
Projected cash balance, end of month	$ 1,211	$ 696	$ 3,045

tization of prepaid taxes or insurance. The budgeted selling and administrative expenses of the Callaway Company which were shown in Exhibit 11–7 may be assumed to require adjustment as follows:

	January	February	March
Total budgeted expenses	$9,989	$10,255	$10,331
Less: Depreciation expense	(1,000)	(1,000)	(1,000)
Taxes expense	(200)	(200)	(200)
Insurance expense	(300)	(300)	(300)
Add: Payment of year's taxes		2,400	
Payment of a one-year insurance premium	500		
Total cash expenditures for expenses (to cash budget)	$8,989	$11,155	$ 8,831

The total cash expenditures for expenses for each month, as shown in Exhibit 11–7, must not be inserted into the cash budget until adjustments have been made for noncash expenditures. Note that the expenditures of $8,989, $11,155, and $8,831 for January, February, and March, respectively, are the amounts which appear in the cash budget shown in Exhibit 11–10.

Summary

A budgetary system is one of the strongest planning and control tools available to management. Such a system provides a mechanism for coordinating the activities of the company throughout the year, as well as a means of establishing and estimating the effects of major policies prior to their actual implementation. The budget plan necessitates a careful consideration of such policies as pricing the company's products, establishing inventory levels, scheduling production, and estimating selling and administrative efforts well before the beginning of the period. In addition, the combined effects of these decisions can be tested by completing the budget schedules. This is an important aspect of the budget system, because two or more of the company's policies may be in conflict and produce undesirable results. The budgetary plan provides a mechanism for resolving such imbalances, so that plans can be better coordinated before being placed into operation.

The sales budget is prepared first, usually several months prior to the beginning of the period. Based upon sales forecasts and inventory level policies, the production budget can then be set. Once production has been planned and scheduled, the materials, labor, and overhead budgets are completed. These projections permit a cost of goods sold calculation, and the adequacy of the pricing decisions which were used in establishing the sales budget can then be tested. If the cost of a unit is too high in relationship to the sales price originally set, management is alerted that it must either increase the sales price, decrease the costs, or be content with a reduced profit figure. In this way, a viable coordinated plan for the coming year is established.

Business budgeting is a process of carefully & systematically planning future activities

New Terms

Budgetary coordination   The integration and synchronization of the activities of a company through a comprehensive budget.

Cash budget   A schedule of expected cash receipts and disbursements.

Inventory policy   Operating directives for the planned amount and levels of inventory.

Labor budget   Schedule of expected labor costs.

Manufacturing expense budget   Schedule of expected overhead costs.

Proforma means that the statement contains anticipated amounts

Production budget   Schedule of production, in either units or dollars.

Raw materials budget   Schedule of required raw materials, in either units or dollars.

Sales budget   Schedule of expected sales.

Selling and administrative expense budget   Schedule of expected selling and administrative expenses.

Questions

1. Define "budgeting." Why would a company install a budgetary system?

2. What is meant by the statement that "a budget is a means of communication and motivation"?

3. Describe the functions and responsibilities of a budget officer. Should he enforce adherence to budgetary policy?

4. A foreman of the Pratt Company exceeded his budget of expenses for seven consecutive months. As a result, the budget officer terminated the foreman's employment. Do you feel the budget officer should be given the authority to take action such as this? Why or why not?

5. What steps should be completed in establishing a budgetary system preliminary to the actual setting of budgetary amounts?

6. Why is the sales budget or forecast the first step in the accumulation of budgetary amounts? Can you think of any circumstances where production amounts instead of sales amounts would be the beginning point?

7. What is a proforma financial statement? Of what use is a proforma income statement?

8. What is meant by the statement that "the value of a budget report is exactly equal to the confidence which executives have in the accuracy of the budgeted amounts"? Do you agree with this?

9. How long should the budget period be? Could the length of time used for budgeting expenses, cash, and fixed assets be different?

10. The vice-president in charge of sales would very likely want to see the sales budget broken down by types of products. Describe other detailed breakdowns of the sales budget which he might find useful.

11. Describe the procedure used in establishing inventory and purchases budget amounts.

12. Describe the nature of a cash budget and name some of its uses.

13. Why are the amounts in the sales budget and in the expense budget not always applicable to the cash budget?

14. Describe and name some of the purposes of a report on capital asset expenditures.

Exercises

11–1   **Budgetary Schedules** *(20 minutes)*   The following budgetary schedules were described and illustrated in this chapter:

a. Sales budget
b. Production budget

    c. Raw materials purchases budget
    d. Direct labor budget
    e. Expense budget
    f. Cash budget
    g. Proforma income statement

Instructions
1. Describe the content and purpose of each schedule.
2. Describe the order in which the schedules would be prepared.
3. Describe which official would be most interested in receiving each schedule to guide him in his operations.

11–2   **Sales Budgets** *(20 minutes)*   The Garrison Company sells its Regular product at a price of $2 per unit and its Choice product at $5 per unit in each of its three territories, North, West, and Central. During the current year, the company's sales of Regular have been 12,000 units per month in each of the North and West territories, but only one-half that amount in the Central area. Its sales of Choice have been 5,000 units per month in the Central and North territories but twice that amount in the West. A 10 percent increase over the current year in units sold has been budgeted for each of the first three months of the coming year, January, February, and March.

Instructions
Prepare a sales budget for the first three months of the coming year showing sales by product for each territory, with both unit and dollar amounts.

11–3   **Raw Materials Budgets** *(20 minutes)*   The Metallic Products Company has estimated the production of its three products as follows:

	Product X	Product Y	Product Z
January	1,000	8,000	10,000
February	1,200	7,000	12,000
March	1,500	6,000	8,000

Each unit of Product X consumes one unit of raw material, while Y consumes two and Z consumes three. Raw materials now cost $5 per unit, but an increase to $6 is expected in February. The beginning inventory of raw materials on January 1 is 23,000 units, and an inventory policy has been adopted to maintain ending inventories of raw materials equal to the next month's production requirements.

Instructions
1. Prepare a raw materials purchases budget in units for January and February.

2. Compute the dollar cost of the purchases for January and February.

11–4*   **Purchases Budget** *(30 minutes)*   The Quicksand Company buys and sells three products: Quality, Regular, and Supreme. The inventories on June 30 were:

	Units	Unit Cost
Quality	2,000	$ .50
Regular	3,000	1.00
Supreme	5,000	2.00

The company's president has ordered a 10 percent reduction in inventories by July 31, another 10 percent by August 31, and another 20 percent by September 30. (All percentages based on June 30 amounts.) Forecasted sales in units for the quarter are:

	July	August	Sept.
Quality	3,000	3,300	3,500
Regular	4,000	5,000	5,100
Supreme	6,000	6,100	6,000

Instructions
Prepare a purchases budget for the three-month period in both dollar and unit amounts.

11–5   **Cost of Goods Sold Projections** *(30 minutes)*   The Webfoot Corporation has forecast sales of 42,000 duck decoys in January. It takes one-half hour of labor at an expected cost of $3.00 per hour to produce one decoy. It also takes one pound of plain plastic at $.12 per pound and one-half pint of colored plastic at $.40 per pint for each decoy. Beginning inventories are:

3,000 completed ducks
500 pints of colored plastic
2,000 pounds of clear plastic

The company would like to keep materials inventories constant but double the inventory of finished ducks. Overhead is allocated to each unit equally, and a total of $4,500 of overhead costs is expected to be incurred.

Instructions
Calculate the projected cost of goods manufactured, indicating both total costs for the month of January and unit costs for materials, labor, and overhead.

11-6*   **Expense Budget** *(20 minutes)*   Listed below are amounts of expenses expected at the high point of activity and at the low point:

	Expense at Sales Volume of $100,000	Expense at Sales Volume of $300,000
Telephone expense	$ 300	$ 500
Depreciation expense	2,000	2,000
Sales commissions	5,000	15,000
Supplies	100	200

During November, actual expenses were: telephone, $410; depreciation, $2,000; commissions, $12,500; and supplies, $160.

Instructions
1. Compute the fixed and variable elements of each expense.
2. Using the expense behavior computed in part 1, above, determine the amount of each expense which the company would expect to incur if actual sales are budgeted at $250,000.
3. Compute the amount by which actual expenses vary from the budgeted expense as computed in part 2.

11-7*   **Cash Budgets** *(30 minutes)*   The Cambay Company has projected its cash transactions as follows:

	January	February	March
Cash sales and collections of accounts receivable	$15,000	$20,000	$18,000
Merchandise purchases	14,000	13,000	12,000
Salaries expenses	3,800	2,200	2,100
Annual rent payment		2,400	
Purchase of equipment			3,000

The January 1 cash balance is $1,200. When the cash balance is expected to be below $1,000, cash is borrowed in even thousands to maintain a minimum $1,000 balance; when cash exceeds the minimum balance, payments in even thousands are made on a large note payable which the company owes. (The cash balance is not to be less than $1,000 at any time.)

Instructions
Prepare a cash budget for the first three months of 19X1.

11-8   **Comprehensive Budget Plan** *(90 minutes)*   A company sells two products, A and B, for $10 and $20, respectively, in two territories, East and West. The budget plan calls for unit sales as follows for the first three months of the coming year:

	January		February		March	
	A	B	A	B	A	B
East	3,000	1,000	3,500	1,000	4,000	1,000
West	2,000	1,000	1,800	1,300	1,500	1,500

Two units of raw material are required for each unit of finished product, and one-half hour of labor is required for each unit of A and one hour for B. A unit of raw material costs $2, and an hour of labor costs $4. Inventories on January 1 are 10,000 units of raw material, 6,000 units of A, and 1,600 units of B. The cost behavior of the company's factory overhead and selling costs is as follows:

> Factory overhead
> > Depreciation (fixed) $10,000 monthly
> > Supplies (completely variable) $1 per unit manufactured
> Selling expense
> > Sales salaries (fixed) $8,000 monthly
> > Travel and entertainment
> > > (completely variable) $0.50 per unit sold

The cost of each month's production is to be computed by dividing the anticipated factory overhead equally among all units of A and B produced.

Instructions

Prepare the following schedules:

1. Sales budget showing sales for each product in each territory for each month of the three-month budget period.
2. Production budget for each product for each month, if monthly ending inventories of A and B are to be equal to that month's budgeted sales.
3. Direct labor budget for each month.
4. Raw materials purchases budget for each month, if raw materials inventory at the end of each month is to be equal to that month's production requirements.
5. Budget of factory overhead costs showing amounts for each month.
6. Budget of selling expenses showing amounts for each month.
7. Schedule of the unit cost to manufacture A and B each month, if overhead is applied equally to all units produced each month.
8. Proforma income statements using a FIFO inventory for finished goods. Assume that the beginning inventory of A costs $9 per unit and that of B costs $11 per unit.

Problems

11-9 **Sales Budgets** (*30 minutes*)   The Saltree Company sells a product called Amora at a price of $5 and a second-line product called Gusta at $3 per unit. It has separated its sales areas into three territories, Chicago, Cleveland, and Columbus. During the current year, the company's sales of Amora have been 9,000 units per month, divided equally among the three areas. Gusta has been selling at a rate of 15,000 per month, with 8,000 of these in the Chi cago area, 4,000 in the Cleveland area, and 3,000 in the Columbus area. The company's budget plan for the coming year calls for an increase of 10 percent in the unit sales of Amora for all three months in all areas, a 5 percent increase in Gusta in all territories in January, and a 15 percent increase in Gusta in all territories in February and March. (All increases are based on the present volume and are not cumulative.)

Instructions
Prepare a sales budget for the first three months of the coming year reflecting sales for each territory for each product, and including both unit and dollar amounts.

11-10 **Sales Budgets** *(30 minutes)*   The Noble Novelty Company carries three major lines of products: gifts, games, and party supplies. Their sales territory is divided into eastern, central, and western territories. Total sales are estimated to be $100,000 in October, $120,000 in November, and $150,000 in December. The eastern territory is expected to produce 30 percent of the sales each month, the central territory 40 percent, and the western 30 percent. The major lines are expected to produce the following portion of the monthly sales in each territory:
Eastern and central: gifts, 20 percent; games, 30 percent; party supplies, 50 percent. Western: gifts, 30 percent; games, 20 percent; party supplies, 50 percent.

Instructions
Prepare a sales forecast showing the expected dollar sales by product lines and territories for each month of the three-month period.

11-11 **Purchases Budget** *(20 minutes)*   A company has established a sales budget for its only product as follows:

January	10,000 units
February	15,000 units
March	8,000 units

Each unit purchased will cost $3, and the December 31 inventory is 5,000 units. The company's management wishes to have an inventory of 8,000 units on January 31, 12,000 units on February 28, and 7,000 units on March 31.

Instructions
Prepare a purchases budget showing both unit and dollar purchases for each of the three months, January through March.

11-12 **Production Budget** *(30 minutes)*   The Queensberry Company sells three products, Quality, Regular, and Supreme. The inventories on June 30 were as follows:

	Units
Quality	2,000
Regular	3,000
Supreme	5,000

The president was disturbed because the number of units on hand was excessive and ordered his operating executives to reduce the inventories by 10 percent in July, another 10 percent in August, and 20 percent in September (all percentages based on June 30 amounts). Sales in units are budgeted as follows for the three months:

	July	August	September
Quality	3,000	3,300	3,500
Regular	4,000	5,000	5,100
Supreme	6,000	6,100	6,000

Instructions
Prepare a purchase budget for each month of the three-month period.

11–13 **Expense Analysis and Budgeting** (50 minutes) The Nordic-Freeman Company is having difficulty controlling the expenses of its sales department. The general manager contends that sales expenses should be carefully budgeted, and all contemplated expenditures in excess of budgeted amounts should be approved by him before the expense is incurred. The sales manager contends that this procedure will not work, because frequently the salesmen must incur expenses on the spur of the moment when travel or customer entertainment is necessary to close a sale.

		Sales Expenses Incurred					
Month	Amount of Sales	Office & Clerical Salaries	Enter-tain-ment	Depre-ciation	Travel	Sales-men's Salaries	Sales-men's Com-missions
Jan.	$300,000	$22,700	$7,620	$4,000	$10,450	$9,000	$6,000
Feb.	280,000	22,200	7,200	4,000	10,000	9,000	5,600
Mar.	300,000	22,800	7,600	4,000	10,350	9,000	6,000
April	290,000	22,400	7,410	4,000	10,200	9,000	5,800
May	310,000	23,100	7,840	4,000	10,500	9,000	6,200
June	330,000	24,000	8,200	4,000	11,000	9,000	6,600
July	340,000	24,500	8,400	4,000	11,150	9,000	6,800
Aug.	360,000	25,400	8,800	4,000	11,600	9,000	7,200
Sept.	350,000	24,850	8,580	4,000	11,400	9,000	7,000
Oct.	320,000	23,550	8,000	4,000	10,800	9,000	6,400
Nov.	300,000	22,900	7,650	4,000	10,400	9,000	6,000
Dec.	320,000	23,650	8,070	4,000	10,750	9,000	6,400

The general manager's budget for the sales department has been prepared in the past without careful analysis of the relationship between fixed and variable portions of sales expenses. As a result, the budget was sometimes based on an expected sales volume which differed from the actual sales volume.

The general manager has called you in to help him budget the sales department expenses so that comparisons of actual amounts with budget amounts will be meaningful. The company's records contain the data shown on p. 361.

Budgeted sales are $320,000 in January, $340,000 in February, and $360,000 in March.

Instructions

1. Compute the monthly fixed and variable portions of each selling expense (use high-low sales volume).
2. Prepare the expense budget for January, February, and March.
3. Actual sales in January were $345,000, and actual expenses were as follows:

Office and clerical salaries	$25,400
Supplies	7,800
Depreciation	4,000
Travel	11,800
Salesmen's salaries	9,000
Salesmen's commissions	6,900

Construct a budget report for the sales department setting out the budgeted amounts, the actual expenses incurred, and the over- or under-budget amounts.

11–14   **Sales, Purchases, and Expense Budgets; Proforma Statements**
(70 minutes)   The Forrest Products Company is a merchandising company which buys its products, A and B, ready for resale to customers. A and B sell for $20 and $40, respectively. Product A cost $12, and product B costs $22 per unit. The company's monthly selling expenses have been analyzed as follows:

	Fixed	Variable, Per Unit Sold
Advertising	$ 5,000	—
Salaries	10,000	$2.00 per unit sold
Delivery expenses	4,000	$ .05
Telephone and telegraph	1,400	.30
Supplies	2,000	.20
Taxes	2,200	—
Depreciation	10,800	—

The company's beginning inventories were 4,000 units of A and 1,000 units of B, and it wishes to decrease its inventories by 100 units of A and 50 units of B during each month of the next three months.

The company expects its sales to be as follows:

	Product A	Product B
January	6,000 units	2,000 units
February	6,150 units	1,800 units
March	7,000 units	1,500 units

Instructions

Prepare the following schedules:
1. A sales budget.
2. A purchases budget (Since the units are acquired ready for sale, the purchases budget will be the same as a production budget.)
3. An expense budget with amounts for each of the three months.
4. A proforma income statement with three columns, one for each month.

11–15   **Comprehensive Budget Plan** (60 minutes)   The sales department of the Craftsman Company prepared a sales budget for its single product for the next quarter as follows:

	April	May	June
Budgeted unit sales	4,500	5,000	5,500

The product has a sales price of $10 and requires the following costs:

> One hour of labor at $3.00 per hour
> Two units of raw material at $1.00 per unit

The company's cost structure is:

Manufacturing overhead	
Depreciation (fixed)	$1,500
Supplies (variable)	$ 1.00 per unit manufactured
Administrative expenses	
Salaries (fixed)	$6,000
Supplies (variable)	$ .50 per unit sold

An ending inventory policy is to be implemented for finished goods such that the ending inventory will be equal to that month's sales. Raw materials are bought as required and no change in the raw materials inventory is anticipated. Inventory status at April 1 is:

Finished goods	5,000 units (cost $6 per unit)
Raw materials	7,500 units (cost $1 per unit)

Instructions

Prepare the following:
1. Production budget of finished goods
2. Purchases budget of raw materials
3. Labor budget
4. Manufacturing overhead budget

5. Administrative expense budget
6. A cost of goods manufactured schedule showing both total and per unit costs for each month.
7. Proforma income statements for each month of the budget period using a FIFO inventory method.

11–16 **Comprehensive Budget Plan** *(60 minutes)* The Winston Company sells two products, X and Y, for $10 and $15 per unit, respectively. The company's monthly selling expenses are projected to be $18,700 for January. Beginning inventories are 2,000 units of Product X at a cost of $6.00 each and 500 units of Y at $12 each, and inventory levels are to be maintained at the same level throughout the period. Raw materials are to be purchased each month for that month's production at a cost of $1.00 each. One unit of raw material is required for one unit of X and three for a unit of Y. One hour of labor is required for a unit of X and two hours for a unit of Y at a cost of $3.00 per hour. Factory overhead is $1.00 for each unit manufactured, plus $4,000 fixed per month. Fixed overhead is to be allocated equally to all units manufactured. The company expects to sell units as follows in January:

3,000 units of X
1,000 units of Y

Instructions
Prepare for the month of January:
1. Sales budget
2. Raw materials purchases budget
3. Manufacturing labor budget
4. Cost of goods manufactured schedule
5. Proforma income statement using FIFO inventory showing profit contribution (gross profit) for each product

11–17 **Comprehensive Budget Plan** *(70 minutes)* The Barnstrom Company sells two products, X and Y, for $10 and $20 per unit, respectively. The company's monthly selling expenses have been analyzed as follows:

	Fixed	Variable (Per unit)
Depreciation	$5,000	
Taxes	1,000	
Supplies	1,000	$0.20
Telephone and telegraph	500	0.30
Delivery expenses	2,000	0.05
Salaries	5,000	1.00
Advertising	2,000	

Beginning inventories were 2,000 units of Product X at a cost of $5 each and 500 units of Y at $10 each. The company wishes to maintain inventories at these same levels throughout the year; raw materials are purchased each month for that month's production and cost $1 each. One unit is required for X and three for Y. One hour of labor is required for a unit of X and two hours for Y; each hour costs $3. Factory overhead is $1 for each unit of X and Y.

The company expects to sell units as follows:

January	3,000 units of X, 1,000 units of Y
February	3,500 units of X, 1,200 units of Y
March	4,000 units of X, 1,500 units of Y

Instructions
Prepare
1. Sales budget
2. Production budget
3. Raw materials purchases budget
4. Manufacturing labor budget
5. Overhead budget
6. Calculation of the per unit cost of goods manufactured
7. Proforma income statement

11–18 **Comprehensive Budget Plan** *(90 minutes)* A company sells two products, X and Y, for $20 and $30, respectively, in two territories, east and west. The budget plan for the coming year calls for unit sales as follows for the first three months of the coming year:

	East		West	
	X	Y	X	Y
January	300	1,000	100	500
February	350	900	200	600
March	400	800	300	400

Two units of raw materials are required for each completed unit of X, and three are required for a unit of Y. One hour of labor is required to produce each unit of X, while two hours are required to produce a unit of Y. Raw materials current costs $3 per unit, but an increase to $3.50 is expected in March. Labor costs $3 per hour, and no change is anticipated. Inventories on January 1 are 5,000 units of raw material, 500 units of X, and 1,300 units of Y. Factory overhead and selling expenses have the following characteristics:

Factory overhead (monthly amounts)
Depreciation (fixed)	$10,000
Utilities (semi-variable)	$2,000 fixed, plus $0.30 per unit manufactured
Supplies (variable)	$0.20 per unit manufactured

Selling expenses (monthly amounts)
Sales salaries (fixed)	$9,000
Selling supplies (variable)	$0.10 per unit sold
Utilities (semi-variable)	$3,000 fixed, plus $0.20 per unit sold

The cost of each month's production is to be computed by dividing the factory overhead equally among all units, both X and Y, manufactured during the month.

Instructions

Prepare the following schedules:

1. Sales budget showing sales for each product in each territory for each month of the three-month budget period.
2. Production budget for each product for each month if ending inventories of X and Y are to be equal to that month's budgeted sales.
3. Direct labor budget for each month.
4. Raw materials purchases budget for each month if the raw materials inventory at the end of each month is to be equal to that month's consumption of materials.
5. Budget of factory overhead costs showing amounts for each month.
6. Budget of selling expenses showing amounts for each month.
7. Schedule of the unit cost to manufacture X and Y during each of the three months. Use a FIFO inventory method for raw materials (beginning inventory has a $3 per unit cost).
8. Proforma income statements using a FIFO inventory for finished goods. Beginning inventories of X cost $15 per unit and Y cost $20 per unit.

11–19   **Cash Budget** *(50 minutes)*   The Howard Company has a cash balance of $3,000 on December 31, 19X1. It has projected sales as follows for the first three months of 19X2:

	Jan.	Feb.	March
Cash sales	$ 2,000	$ 6,000	$ 4,000
Credit sales	60,000	72,000	48,000

Credit sales are collected 50 percent in the month of sale, 40 percent in the following month, and 10 percent in the second month. Credit sales for the previous November were $40,000, and for December, $50,000.

Purchases will be 50 percent of total sales for each month and will be paid in full in the month following the purchase. Purchases in December were $30,000.

Cash expenses are expected to be as follows:

January	$18,000
February	$21,000
March	$16,000

The mortgage payment in January will be $20,000. Dividends in March will be $6,000, and there will be a purchase in February of equipment for cash in the amount of $16,000. In March, the company expects to sell for cash equipment costing $20,000, which has accumulated depreciation of $12,000, at a loss of $1,000.

The company will borrow when necessary to maintain a cash balance of $2,000 and will make as large a repayment as possible in those months in which it has an excess of cash over the $2,000 minimum balance.

Instructions
Prepare a cash budget for the three-month period.

11–20 **Cash Budget** *(50 minutes)*   On December 31, 19X1, the Stillwater Company had a cash balance of $7,000, accounts receivable of $32,000, and accounts payable arising from raw materials purchases of $48,000. The company's subbudgets indicate the following expectations for 19X2:

	January	February	March
Cash sales	$15,000	$13,000	$12,000
Credit sales	60,000	62,000	68,000
Purchases of raw material	50,000	40,000	60,000
Labor	16,000	17,000	17,000
Taxes	—	—	2,000
Dividends	—	—	10,000
Payment on mortgage	5,000	5,000	5,000

It is expected that $24,000 of the December 31 receivables will be collected in January and the balance in February. It is anticipated that the collection of credit sales will be 30 percent in the month of sale, 60 percent in the next month, and 10 percent in the third month. Purchases of raw material are paid for in the month following the purchase. The company does not want its cash balance to fall below a $2,000 minimum balance and borrows from the bank in even thousand dollar amounts each month that funds are needed. The company repays these loans in even thousand dollar amounts whenever it has available cash, but the cash balance is not to be less than $2,000 at any time.

Instructions
Prepare a cash budget by months for the first three months of 19X2.

11–21 **Cash Budget** *(45 minutes)*   The following items have been budgeted for the Lemmon Hardware Company for January:

Sales (30% cash, balance collected 60% in month of sale, 30% in the following month, and 10% in the third month.	$120,000
Accounts receivable expected to be collected in January	50,400
Purchases (40% paid in month of acquisition, 60% paid in the following month)	135,000

(continued)

Dividends	20,000
General expenses (includes monthly depreciation of $1,200 and tax expense of $300. The annual tax bill of $3,600 is paid in February.)	19,000
Selling expenses (includes monthly insurance expense of $200. The annual insurance premium of $2,400 is paid in March.)	24,000

The desired cash balance at the end of each month is $2,000. Cash is to be borrowed when the balance is below this amount and a large note payable is to be repaid in even thousands when the balance exceeds $2,000. The beginning cash balance is $2,400.

Instructions
Prepare a cash budget for the month.

11–22   **Proforma Statements; Cash Budgets** *(50 minutes)*   The trial balance of the Dante Company appeared as follows at the beginning of the budget year:

Cash	$ 2,000	
Inventory	6,000	
Equipment	60,000	
Allowance for depreciation—equipment		$10,000
Accounts payable (to be paid in January)		5,000
Mortgages payable		25,000
Accrued property taxes		2,200
Capital stock		20,000
Retained earnings		5,800
	$68,000	$68,000

The company is a merchandising company and buys its products ready for resale. Its sales are all on cash terms, and sales for the next two months are budgeted as: January, $30,000, February, $40,000. Gross profit on sales is expected to be 40 percent, and the merchandise inventory is to be reduced 50 percent during the month of January and is to remain at that amount; all merchandise purchases are for cash. The mortgage is payable each February 1 in annual installments of $5,000; interest is paid monthly at 6 percent on the unpaid balance. Fixed cash administrative and selling expenses, exclusive of property taxes, are $4,000 per month, and variable cash administrative and selling expenses are 10 percent of sales. The property tax is accrued at $200 each month, and the annual tax of $2,400 is paid on January 28. Depreciation is $1,000 per month. Extensive advertising costs of $2,600 are to be incurred in January but will not be paid until February.

Instructions
Prepare the following:
1. A proforma income statement for January and for February.
2. A cash budget for January and February.

3. A proforma balance sheet as of February 28.
4. Write a brief statement concerning whether the company can expect to be in a weaker or sounder financial position at the end of the two-month period. (Hint—work backward from gross profit to ascertain purchases.)

11–23   **Proforma Statements; Cash Budget** *(60 minutes)*   The condensed balance sheet and income statement of the Hatiflax Distribution Company for the year ended December 31, 19X1, were as follows:

HATIFLAX DISTRIBUTION COMPANY
Balance Sheet
December 31, 19X1

ASSETS		EQUITIES	
Cash	$ 13,000	Accounts payable	
Accounts receivable	6,050	(for merchandise)	$ 8,000
Inventory (5,000 units)	14,500	6% notes payable	20,000
Buildings and equipment		Capital stock	60,000
(net)	71,500	Retained earnings	33,450
Land	16,400		
Total assets	$121,450	Total equities	$121,450

HATIFLAX DISTRIBUTION COMPANY
Income Statement
For the Year Ended December 31, 19X1

Sales (30,000 units)		$150,000
Costs of units sold		87,000
Gross profit		$ 63,000
Selling expenses	$21,000	
Administrative expenses	30,000	
Interest expense	1,200	
Total expenses		52,200
Net income		$ 10,800

The company is a wholesale distributor which buys its products ready for resale to customers. The budget committee has approved a budget of sales as follows for the first three months of 19X2: January, 2,500 units; February, 2,600 units; March, 3,000 units. The sales price is not expected to change, but the unit cost is expected to increase to $3 on January 1. A FIFO inventory method is used, and the number of units in the inventory is to remain unchanged.

Sales are 50 percent for cash, and the other 50 percent is collected in the month following. All units bought for sale are paid for in the month following purchase.

Selling and administrative expenses are primarily fixed in nature, but the total is expected to increase by 6 percent. They are incurred and paid evenly throughout the year, except for annual depreciation of $2,400. Depreciation is included in administrative expenses, requires no cash outlay, and will not change during the coming year. Interest on the notes payable is paid monthly, and dividends of $10,000 are to be paid in January.

Instructions

1. Prepare proforma income statements for each of the three months.
2. Prepare a cash budget for January, February, and March.

11–24   **Analysis of Budget Variances** *(30 minutes)*   Charles Gessman was appointed budget officer of the Maclin Oil Company in 19X1. He had no previous background in budgeting, and the president of the company told him to "set up a budgetary program and see that it works. After I approve the budget for next year, it is your responsibility to see that actual expenses stay within those amounts."

Gessman ordered the accounting department to supply him with budget reports each week showing the budgeted amount of each expense for the week (computed by dividing the annual budgeted amount by fifty-two), actual expenses incurred during the week, and the variance for each expense. He also told all supervisors that any continued excess of actual expenses over budgeted amounts would be cause for dismissal.

The first week's budget report on the sales department showed the following:

	Actual	Budget (1/52 of Annual Total)	Variance Over (Under)
Sales	$217,000	$188,000	$29,000
Depreciation	$ 2,000	$ 2,010	$ (10)
Salesmen's travel	3,170	2,700	470
Telephone and telegraph	861	740	121
Office supplies	419	390	29

Gessman was highly disturbed over the unfavorable expense variances and told the sales manager that continued unfavorable variances would be sufficient cause for terminating his employment. The sales manager then went straight to the president and said that "either the new budget officer leaves, or I'm quitting."

Instructions

Would you consider the expenses "unfavorable"? If you were president, which of the two men, Gessman or the sales manager would you support, and why? Suggest a means of improving the budgetary program.

chapter 12

Analysis of Budgetary Variances

Learning Objectives

This chapter continues the treatment of budgetary systems with an emphasis on variances. Upon completion of your study of this chapter you should:

1. Know the meaning of and know how to calculate the price and quantity elements in budget variances.
2. Appreciate the importance of separating controllable and non-controllable costs on budgetary reports.
3. Understand the concept of responsibility accounting and how proper organization and assignment of responsibility provides control.
4. Recognize the limitations and dangers of overly strict interpretations of budgetary variances.

Variance Analysis

Budgetary control is exercised by establishing a detailed plan for future operations, recording transactions so that they may be compared with predetermined plans, reporting to management differences between actual and planned operations and taking corrective action wherever indicated. The construction of the budget plan was discussed in the preceding chapter, while the comparison of actual transactions with those plans and the analysis of the resulting variances is discussed in this chapter.

The significance of a variance depends not only upon its size, but also upon the accuracy with which the budget was formulated. Thus, the analysis of budgetary variances requires a knowledge of how budget plans were constructed. Variances indicate deviations from the plan but do not indicate the cause, and ascertaining the underlying reason for a variance is one of management's most difficult tasks. Intelligent analysis and interpretation of a variance necessitate judgment, analytical ability, perception of human motivations, and a thorough understanding of the accounting process.

 There are two basic factors which produce variances between planned and actual operations. These are (1) the effect of changes in volume and (2) the effect of changes in price. The volume and price effects were first introduced in Chapter 9, where the analysis of over- and under-applied overhead was discussed. At that point they were called "volume variance" and "controllable variance." That same type of analysis may be applied to variances in sales, cost of goods sold, direct labor, raw materials, and selling and administrative expenses. For sales, the two variances would be called "price variance" and "quantity variance"; for direct labor they may be called "wage rate variance" and "efficiency variance"; for raw materials they may be called "cost variance" and "quantity variance." In all cases, however, these variances represent the effect of volume and the effect of price. The primary emphasis in this chapter is the analysis of these two different causal factors.

Variances in Sales

The difference between planned sales and actual sales is one of the most important budget variances. The profit which a company is able to realize depends upon its ability to compete in the market, and if sales are not up to expectations, the profit plan is in jeopardy. One of the first analysis problems which management encounters is the location of that part of the company's operations causing the variance. It is for this reason that the individual products and territories of the sales budget are shown in considerable detail. Matching this detail with actual sales helps locate the segment which may be causing a problem.

The preparation of the detailed sales budget of the J. C. Treadway Company was illustrated in the previous chapter in Exhibit 11–1. That budget is incorporated in the sales report shown in Exhibit 12–1, which matches actual sales with the budget. The total sales variance for the month is unfavorable by $1,800, although it should be noted that there are several favorable and several unfavorable variances.

Analysis of the larger variances shown in the report discloses the following facts:

Regular product in North territory	$ 500 under budget
Choice product in North territory	1,000 under budget
Supreme product in North territory	400 under budget
Total	$1,900

Thus, an unfavorable variation of $1,900 may be attributed to the company's North territory, and management must investigate to ascertain the

EXHIBIT 12–1

J. C. TREADWAY COMPANY
Sales Report
Month of January, 1975

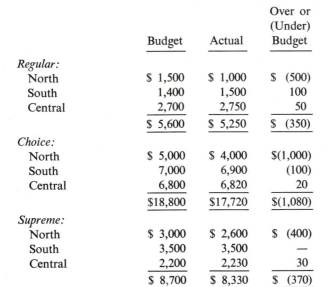

	Budget	Actual	Over or (Under) Budget
Regular:			
North	$ 1,500	$ 1,000	$ (500)
South	1,400	1,500	100
Central	2,700	2,750	50
	$ 5,600	$ 5,250	$ (350)
Choice:			
North	$ 5,000	$ 4,000	$(1,000)
South	7,000	6,900	(100)
Central	6,800	6,820	20
	$18,800	$17,720	$(1,080)
Supreme:			
North	$ 3,000	$ 2,600	$ (400)
South	3,500	3,500	—
Central	2,200	2,230	30
	$ 8,700	$ 8,330	$ (370)
Total	$33,100	$31,300	$(1,800)

cause. The other sales areas produced no significant variances, and none of the company's products had unfavorable variances in all territories. As shown here, an analysis of the detailed variances assists in locating the area needing managerial attention.

Sales Price and Quantity Variances

Having isolated the unfavorable variance in the North territory, management must now ascertain what caused it. The variance may be caused by either not selling the expected quantity of units or not realizing the expected sales price. The unfavorable variance should be analyzed to separate the effects of quantity changes from the effects of price changes.

To illustrate the computations with a simplified example, suppose that the Binton Company established a budget plan which indicated sales of 10,000 units each month at a price of $1 each. Assume further that on February 1 management reduced the sales price to $.90 per unit, and as a result, 11,000 units were sold during the month. Actual sales for February were thus $9,900 (11,000 units @ $.90 = $9,900), and the budget report reflected these events as follows:

Budgeted sales	$10,000
Actual sales	9,900
Unfavorable variance	$ (100)

The $100 total unfavorable variance is the result of an increased number of units sold at a decreased price. The separate effects of the price and quantity factors are computed as follows:

Sales price variation

Actual quantity sold at the budgeted price (11,000 @ $1.00)	$11,000
Actual quantity sold at actual sales price (11,000 @ $.90)	9,900
Variance due to price reduction (unfavorable)	$(1,100)

Sales quantity variation

Budgeted quantity at budgeted price (10,000 @ $1.00)	$10,000
Actual quantity at budgeted price (11,000 @ 1.00)	11,000
Variance due to quantity increase (favorable)	$ 1,000

The total $100 unfavorable variance thus resulted from a $1,100 unfavorable price change offset by a $1,000 favorable quantity change. It is important to note that the quantity is held constant when the price variance is calculated. The actual quantity sold, 11,000 units, is multiplied by the budgeted price of $1.00 and also by the actual price of $.90. The result is the effect of reducing the price by $.10. Note also that the price is held constant when the quantity variance is calculated, and that the *budget* price is used in the calculation. The budget price of $1.00 in this case is multiplied by the budgeted quantity of 10,000 units, as well as by the actual quantity of 11,000 units. The result is the effect of selling 1,000 more units. Finally, note that the sum of the price variance and the quantity variance will equal the total $100 variance.

Cost of Goods Sold Variance

Variances in the cost of goods sold should also be analyzed to separate the effect of quantity and cost. Suppose, for example, that the company whose sales budget was analyzed in the preceding discussion had budgeted its cost of goods sold at 10,000 units at $.60 each, but sold 11,000 units which had an actual cost of $.50 each. The total budget variance would be as follows:

Budgeted cost of goods sold (10,000 units @ $.60)	$6,000
Actual cost of goods sold (11,000 units @ $.50)	5,500
Actual under budget (favorable)	$ 500

The total $500 favorable variance contains the effect of both cost and volume changes, which may be separated as follows:

Cost variance

Actual quantity sold at budgeted cost (11,000 @ $.60)	$6,600
Actual quantity sold at actual cost (11,000 @ $.50)	5,500
Variance due to cost decrease (favorable)	$(1,100)

Quantity variance

Budgeted quantity sold at budgeted cost (10,000 @ $.60)	$6,000
Actual quantity sold at budgeted cost (11,000 @ $.60)	6,600
Variance due to quantity increase (unfavorable)	$ 600

Note again that the cost is held constant when the quantity change is computed, and the quantity is held constant when the cost change is computed.

The computation of the price and quantity factors may also be shown in graphic form. When this is done, the total variance which is being analyzed is shown as follows:

Actual cost of ←—————————→ Budgeted cost
goods sold $500 difference   of goods sold
$5,500   ($6,000)

When the actual quantity sold at budgeted cost is inserted between the actual and budgeted amounts, the price and quantity factors included in the total variance become apparent. This computation is illustrated in Exhibit 12–2.

EXHIBIT 12–2

Computation of Cost and Quantity Variances

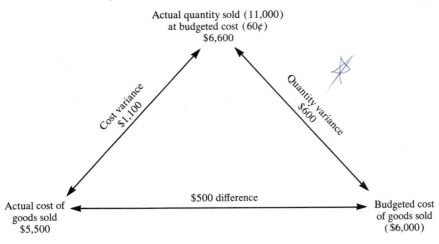

Gross Profit Variances

The variance between planned and actual gross profit can be explained by combining the analysis of sales and cost of goods sold as described in the preceding sections. The amounts previously illustrated, for example, might appear in the budget report as follows:

EXHIBIT 12–3

THE BINTON COMPANY
Partial Budget Report
February, 19X1

	Budget	Actual	Over or (Under) Budget
Sales	$10,000	$9,900	$(100)
Cost of goods sold	6,000	5,500	(500)
Gross profit	$ 4,000	$4,400	$ 400

The $400 favorable variance in gross profit is the result of combined sales and cost of goods sold factors. A separate statement reconciling the changes in gross profit may be prepared and reported to management as a schedule supporting the budget reports.

Analysis of Variance in Gross Profit

Sales variances are caused by the following:

Variances due to sales price	$(1,100)	
Variances due to quantity sold	1,000	
Total sales variances		$(100)
Cost of goods sold variances are caused by the following:		
Variances due to changes in cost	$(1,100)	
Variances due to changes in quantity	600	
Total cost of goods sold variances		(500)
Total variances in gross profit		$400

Operating Expense Variances

Budget variances for selling and administrative expenses will also have volume and spending elements. The volume variance in operating expenses is due to the fixed and variable nature of this type of expense, and is the result of preparing a budget for one level of activity and then not operating at that level. The volume variance should be calculated and separated from the spending variance, since the spending portion of the variance is controllable while the volume variance is the result of random economic events.

The separation of the volume and the spending variances for selling and administrative expenses begins with the calculation of the fixed and variable cost behavior of each expense. In fact, the original budget estimate should have been based upon this type of analysis, as described in Chapter 11. At the end of the budget period, after the actual level of activity is known, a revised budget is calculated for the actual level of operations achieved. The spending variance is the difference between the actual expense and the revised budget calculations. Separation of the two variances could thus be illustrated as shown in Exhibit 12–4.

EXHIBIT 12–4

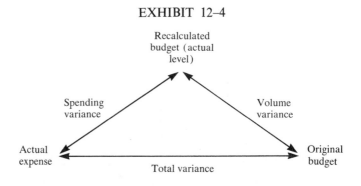

Note that the spending variance is the difference between what was actually spent and what should have been spent at that same level of activity. On the other hand, note that the volume variance is the difference between two budget calculations made at two different levels of activity. The spending variance is the result of the responsible individual's efforts to keep his spending in line with the amount he is expected to spend at that level of activity. Budget reports which reflect the spending variance but exclude the volume variance are prepared for each individual responsible for incurring expenses. Such a report is illustrated later in Exhibit 12–6.

As an illustration of the calculation, suppose that the salaries expense of the delivery department is semivariable, with a $1,000 fixed amount and the variable portion 2 percent of sales. If sales are budgeted at $50,000, delivery salaries will be budgeted at $2,000 ($1,000 fixed plus 2 percent of $50,000 sales). If delivery salaries for the period are actually $2,250 and sales are actually $65,000, computation of the adjusted budget of salaries expense should be based on the expected salaries expense at the $65,000 level of sales. It is possible, for example, that a higher than expected volume of sales may have necessitated payment of considerable overtime and the adjusted budget for the higher sales level should be used to calculate the spending variance. These facts may be shown as follows:

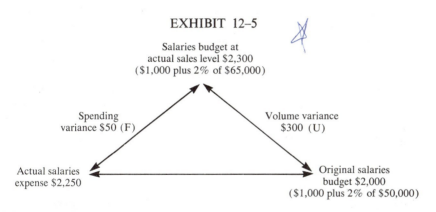

EXHIBIT 12–5

Note that the $250 difference between the original salaries budget of $2,000 and the actual salaries expense of $2,250 is composed of a $50 favorable spending variance offset by a $300 unfavorable volume variance. The spending variance is controllable, while the volume variance is the result of whatever factors produced the increase in sales.

Expense Reports

To illustrate the control reports based upon spending variances, assume that the J. C. Treadway Company had planned a sales volume of $35,000 but realized actual sales of $30,000. The budget, adjusted for the change in volume, is compared with actual expenses in Exhibit 12–6, using assumed amounts for the actual expenses.

Each expense in the report has been adjusted to the actual level of sales, which was $30,000. The fixed and variable nature of each expense is shown in parentheses, but normally will not appear in a formal report. It is important to recognize at this point that the original profit plan was constructed on a projection of $35,000 of sales, and expense projections would have originally been based on this same level. However, the expense report prepared at the end of the period reflects only the spending variance, and thus must contain adjusted budget amounts.

EXHIBIT 12–6

J. C. TREADWAY COMPANY
Expense Report
For the Month of January, 19X1

	Budget Based on Actual Sales Volume of $30,000	Actual	Over or (Under) the Original Budget
Selling:			
Depreciation on store equipment (fixed)	$1,000	$1,000	$ —
Store supplies (variable, 2% of sales)	600	670	70
Insurance of store equipment (fixed)	300	300	—
Sales salaries ($1,000 fixed, balance			
variable at 5% of sales)	2,500	2,700	200
Total selling	$4,400	$4,670	$270
Administrative:			
Officers' salaries (fixed)	$1,000	$1,000	$ —
Telephone and telegraph ($100 fixed,			
balance variable at 1% of sales)	400	420	20
Clerical salaries (variable, 10% of sales)	3,000	3,300	300
Office supplies ($100 fixed, balance			
variable at 1% of sales)	400	435	35
Taxes (fixed)	200	200	—
Total administrative	$5,000	$ 5,355	$355
Total expenses	$9,400	$10,025	$625

The discussion thus far concerning flexible budgets and spending variances is summarized in the following three basic points:

1. A budgetary plan is necessary to coordinate all the activities of the company and is completed prior to the beginning of the period for which the budget is prepared.
2. A system of budgetary reports is necessary to inform management of the company's success or failure in meeting its predetermined budgetary objectives. For this purpose, the budgetary reports should compare the

original budget with amounts actually realized. This type of report is especially necessary for sales and the cost of merchandise sold.

3. The measurement of how well supervisory employees have held to budgetary requirements in the incurrence of expenses necessitates a careful matching of actual expenses with adjusted budgeted amounts which are restated to the level of activity achieved. Thus, reports using flexible budget techniques are especially applicable to operating expenses such as those incurred in the selling and administrative activities.

Comprehensive
Analysis of Variances

The two primary tools for understanding and analyzing the results of operations, as presented in earlier chapters, are:

1. A knowledge of the company's cost structure, with each expense having been analyzed into its fixed and variable elements.
2. A comprehensive profit plan for the period, determined in advance, with each expense computed for the anticipated level of activity.

With these two tools it is possible to account for all variances between the original profit plan and the actual results of operation. To illustrate, assume that a company establishes the following profit plan at the beginning of the period:

XYZ COMPANY
Profit Plan Budget
For the Period Ending December 31, 19X1

Sales (10,000 units at $10 each)		$100,000
Cost of goods sold (10,000 units at $6 each)		60,000
Gross profit		$ 40,000
Operating expenses		
Depreciation (fixed)	$ 5,000	
Salaries ($10,000 fixed, balance variable at $1 per unit sold)	20,000	
Supplies (variable at $0.50 per unit sold)	5,000	
Total operating expenses		30,000
Net income		$ 10,000

Assume also that at the end of the period the following actual revenues and expenses were reported by the accounting department:

XYZ COMPANY
Income Statement
For the Year Ending December 31, 19X1

Sales (11,000 units at $9 each)	$99,000
Cost of goods sold (11,000 units at $5.50 each)	60,500
Gross profit	$38,500

(continued)

Income Statement
(continued)

Operating expenses		
Depreciation	$ 5,000	
Salaries	19,800	
Supplies	5,100	
Total operating expenses		29,900
Net income		$ 8,600

The $1,400 unfavorable difference between the original profit plan of $10,000 and the realized profit of $8,600 may be analyzed into the component variances shown in Exhibit 12–7.

EXHIBIT 12–7

XYZ COMPANY
Analysis of Budget Variances
Period Ending December 31, 19X1

			Favorable or (Unfavorable) Variance	
Variance in sales				
Due to price differences ($1 for 11,000 units)			$(11,000)	
Due to quantity differences (1,000 units at $10)			10,000	
Total sales variance				$(1,000)
Variance in cost of merchandise sold				
Due to cost differences ($.50 for 11,000 units)			$ 5,500	
Due to quantity differences (1,000 units at $6)			(6,000)	
Total cost of merchandise sold variance				(500)
Variance in gross profit				$(1,500)
Variance in operating expenses				
Due to spending differences				
Actual expenses		$29,900		
Budget adjusted to the level of realized sales, (11,000 units)				
Depreciation	$ 5,000			
Salaries	21,000			
Supplies	5,500	31,500		
Total spending difference			$ 1,600	
Due to volume				
Original profit plan		$30,000		
Budget adjusted to the level of realized sales (computed above)		31,500		
Total volume variance			$ (1,500)	
Total operating expense variance				100
Total profit variance				$(1,400)

Responsibility
Accounting

Responsibilty accounting may be defined as a process of accumulating and reporting expenses by areas of responsibility. Costs should also be budgeted by the same areas of responsibility, with a separate budget for each supervisor who has authority to incur costs.

To illustrate, consider the organization chart in Exhibit 12–8. While not all company divisions or departments are indicated, a complete line of authority is shown from the president down to the supervisor of Department 3.

Costs assigned to person with significant influence.

EXHIBIT 12–8
Partial Organization Chart

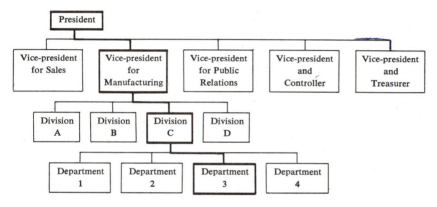

The responsibility reports prepared for the department heads, division managers, vice-presidents, and president are illustrated in Exhibit 12–9. Note that the data in the reports become somewhat less detailed at the higher levels of authority, but sufficient information is available for each executive to locate the areas within his responsibility which demand immediate attention.

The departmental reports contain a complete breakdown of expenses, subdivided into those within the control of the departmental supervisor and those beyond his control. The manager of Department 3 has exceeded his budget by $90, primarily because salaries were above the expected amount.

The reports to the division managers summarize the performance of each departmental supervisor. Note that the $90 unfavorable budget variance of Department 3 assumes less significance to the division manager, since both Departments 1 and 2 have larger unfavorable variances.

The division managers' reports to the vice-president and president include summaries of each of their respective areas of responsibility. The president will probably hold a conference with the vice-presidents of sales and manufacturing to ascertain the causes of their large unfavorable variances. Each of these executives will have conferred with his subordinates in anticipation of the president's questions. Through this process a business is coordinated and its

Cont. Costs may be strongly influenced by manager

EXHIBIT 12–9

ABC COMPANY
Expense Budget Report
Department 3

	Budget	Actual	Actual Over (Under) Budget
Controllable:			
Salaries	$5,000	$5,100	$100
Supplies	1,000	930	(70)
Heat and power	700	750	50
Noncontrollable:			
Depreciation	2,000	2,000	—
Taxes	500	510	10
Insurance	100	100	—
Total	$9,300	$9,390	$ 90

ABC COMPANY
Expense Budget Report
Division C

	Budget	Actual	Actual Over (Under) Budget
Department 1	$10,500	$10,600	$ 100
Department 2	11,000	13,000	2,000
Department 3	9,300	9,390	90
Department 4	8,100	8,030	(70)
Total	$38,900	$41,020	$2,120

ABC COMPANY
Expense Budget Report
Manufacturing

	Budget	Actual	Actual Over (Under) Budget
Division A	$ 51,600	$ 51,400	$ (200)
Division B	41,200	41,350	150
Division C	38,900	41,020	2,120
Division D	36,700	36,680	(20)
Total	$168,400	$170,450	$2,050

ABC COMPANY
Expense Budget Report

	Budget	Actual	Actual Over (Under) Budget
Sales	$132,700	$134,100	$ 1,400
Manufacturing	168,400	170,450	2,050
Public Relations	23,200	22,900	(300)
Controller	59,750	57,600	(2,150)
Treasurer	18,740	18,800	60
Total	$402,790	$403,850	$ 1,060

various segments welded into a unified operation. It should be reemphasized that the budget amounts are adjusted to the actual levels of activity, so that the reports contain only the spending variance.

Controllable Costs

A *controllable cost* is one which may be strongly influenced by a manager within a reasonable time period. It may be either a fixed cost or a variable cost, for both are controllable at some level in the organization. Rent may not be controllable by the department supervisor, but it would be at the presidential level where the decision is made to rent, lease, or own the building. All costs are controllable by someone in the organization, given a sufficient time frame, but the degree of control which is possible within a period of one or two months is not always evident. Thus there is no clearly definable point at which an expense would be considered controllable or non-controllable, and the separation of these two types of expenses on a company's budget reports becomes a matter of judgment.

Note that the expense report of Department 3 shown in Exhibit 12–9 indicates that the salaries, supplies, and heat and power expenses are controllable, while depreciation, taxes, and insurance are not. The departmental supervisor is able to increase or decrease the salaries expense within a short time by hiring or terminating exployees or by increasing the efficiency of his people. He may, however, have no authority to grant pay raises or even to set the pay scale of his workers; this authority is usually reserved for the plant manager. Thus the departmental supervisor has considerable control over salaries expense, but the plant manager also has partial control. It is not unusual for several individuals to be able to exercise some control over the same expense, and therefore controllability need not be absolute before an item is classified as controllable in a budget report. The most important criterion in a decision to list an expense as controllable or non-controllable is whether such a classification instills a cost consciousness in the person who receives the report. In the final analysis, budgetary reports should be designed to motivate employees to improved performance, and the distinction between controllable and non-controllable expenses in budgetary reports is meaningful only for that purpose.

Limitations of the Budget Program

Many executives expect the budget program to solve automatically all the company's planning and control problems, but it can be no more effective than the operating supervisor's understanding of its purposes and its limitations. The budget cannot plan or control, but it is a useful tool. Control is exercised by people, who communicate plans and evaluate the efficiency and performance of others, taking action when efficiency and performance are substandard. The executive must rely on his own judgment in determining substandard performance; in his analysis of budgetary variances, he must consider such questions as the following:

1. Is the variance significant enough to warrant investigation?
2. If the variance is from a controllable expense, can steps be taken to eliminate future unfavorable variances?
3. How accurate is the budgeted amount? If the amount was approximated, can the amount of the variance be the result of an error in the budgeted figure? If it is an approximate figure, the size of the variance may reflect an error in budgeting.
4. How accurately have actual amounts been accumulated to match with budgeted amounts? Is the process of matching actual costs with budget figures sufficiently accurate to produce a reliable variance?

These questions relate to both the accuracy and the amount of the variance. It is possible to waste valuable time following up insignificant variances and to produce unrest by holding supervisors responsible for variances resulting from accounting or budgetary errors.

Motivation is the key to a successful budgetary program. A business budget cannot achieve the desired purposes unless the persons who operate under it are motivated by the budgeted amounts to greater achievement. However carefully established, the budget plan cannot be effective if those who use it are not motivated to operate within its limits. One form of motivation is to discharge those supervisors who do not "meet the budget," but this procedure discourages company loyalty and has proved highly unsuccessful. Some companies reward adherence to the budget with bonuses or pay increases. This procedure has serious limitations, for the supervisor may attempt to "beat the system" by falsifying his performance.

The key to successful budgeting is to set attainable budget figures so that persons affected by it can meet the budget with reasonable effort. Psychologists have found many different motivating factors active in individuals, and a good budgetary plan should implement these human desires. The motivating factor may be a monetary reward or recognition, but the soundest motivating factor, although perhaps the hardest to instill, is the feeling of a job well done.

Planning Fixed
Asset Acquisitions

The fixed assets budget reflects the company's plan for acquiring, improving, or retiring its income-producing assets. This part of the budget plan should be extended further into the future than the operating budget and is frequently projected for periods up to five, ten, or twenty years. Long-term planning is necessary to insure that funds are available as needed for the acquisition of fixed assets, either through retained profits, borrowing, or investment.

The acquisition of any asset that is to be capitalized and depreciated or amortized over a period of years should be included in the fixed assets budget. The fixed assets budget does not include ordinary repairs and maintenance, which are part of the current operating expense budget. However, such extensive repairs as the rebuilidng of a blast furnace or a major reconstruction of a refinery would be included in the fixed assets budget.

Assume, for example, that the Butterfield Company, a relatively new operation, has a plant with a production capacity of 100,000 units annually. Current and anticipated sales are as follows:

Actual units sold:	1971	40,000
	1972	50,000
	1973	62,000
	1974	76,000
	1975	90,000
Projected units to be sold:	1976	100,000
	1978	125,000
	1980	155,000
	1982	180,000
	1984	210,000
	1986	250,000

The projected sales indicate that the company will need an enlarged plant soon, since its capacity will be reached during the next year, 1976. Even if capacity is doubled by new construction in 1976, additional capacity will be needed again in 1984. Thus, planning for the acquisition of additional fixed assets must be begun years in advance. The length of the construction period necessary to build the enlarged plant must also be considered when acquisitions of fixed assets are planned.

The fixed assets budget must be flexible enough to allow for fluctuating economic conditions which may alter the projected need for fixed assets. Suppose the board of directors of the Butterfield Company, whose sales projections are shown above, decide that construction of a new building and purchase of additional equipment are to begin immediately. A compromise between over-expansion and underexpansion must be reached; overexpansion increases fixed costs and multiplies the risks of financial failure, while underexpansion will create loss of sales due to the inability to match production with demand. One possible compromise in the case of the Butterfield Company appears to be a doubling of capacity, thus accommodating the next seven years' growth. If expansion continues as projected, construction of additional fixed assets will then be necessary in 1984 or 1986; if the projected increase in sales does not materialize, the overcapacity will be minimized.

The Capital Assets Expenditures Report

When fixed assets are constructed, periodic reports must be prepared to match actual cost with the previously approved budget cost. Although the board of directors will have budgeted a given amount for plant expansion, final requirements may be more or less than this figure. A *capital asset expenditures report* is thus prepared, as illustrated in Exhibit 12–10.

EXHIBIT 12-10

BUTTERFIELD COMPANY

Report on Capital Asset Expenditures

As of June 30, 19X1

Description	Amount Approved	Expected Completion Date	Original Cost Estimate	Actual Costs to Date	Total Expected Costs
Extend left wing of plant	$ 80,000	1/ 4/X6	$ 78,000	$23,000	$ 79,500
Enlarge power plant	30,000	11/15/X6	30,000	19,000	29,600
New machinery	63,000	1/10/X7	60,000	5,000	62,000
Totals	$173,000		$168,000	$47,000	$171,100

This report informs management of the expected completion date, the amounts originally approved for the projects, amounts already spent, and the current estimate of the final cost. These reports are especially useful to upper management personnel, who are responsible for many widely dispersed acquisitions covering a span of several years.

Summary

A profit plan is essential for managerial control and is of assistance in insuring that the company's efforts are coordinated. Such a plan provides a base for measuring individual performance and motivating employees toward improved efficiency, and periodic reports which show budgetary variances are of importance to management in the location of areas requiring attention. The total difference between planned profit and realized profit may be reduced to a series of variances, thus providing for management a valuable summary of causal factors.

The difference between the original budget projection and the revenues which were actually realized may be divided into a price and a quantity variance. These two variances separate the effects which changes in price have had from the effects which volume shifts have produced. In similar fashion, the cost of goods sold can be segregated into a cost and a volume variance, and operating expenses can be divided into spending and volume variances. These calculations permit the controllable variances to be reported separately, without being obscured by the less controllable volume variance.

Insistence upon strict adherence to budgeted amounts often destroys the effectiveness of the budgetary program, since there may be valid reasons for deviating from the original plan. Therefore, variances serve only as indicators, triggering a search for underlying reasons. Locating and remedying unfavorable factors require managerial skill and talent, and the budget plan, with its related variance reports, permits management to concentrate on the company's more significant problems.

New Terms

Capital asset   A fixed asset.

Capital asset expenditure report   A report on planned fixed asset acquisitions.

Comprehensive variance analysis   A variance analysis which explains the entire difference between realized profit and the original profit plan.

Controllable cost   A cost which is under the control of a particular individual.

Flexible budget   A budget which is expressed in such a way that budget amounts can be calculated for any level of activity.

Gross profit variance   The difference between budgeted and realized gross profit.

Operating expense spending variance   The difference between actual operating expenses and budgeted operating expenses calculated with a flexible budget formula.

Operating expense volume variance   The difference between budgeted operating expenses calculated with a flexible budget formula and the original budget of expenses.

Sales price variance   The difference between budgeted and actual sales which is due to price.

Sales quantity variance   The difference between budgeted and actual sales which is due to volume.

Responsibility accounting is a process of accumulating and reporting expenses by areas of responsibility.

Questions

1. Describe the process of budgetary control. How does a budgetary variance assist in the control process?

2. Budgetary planning usually begins with a sales budget. How can information drawn from monthly comparisons of planned sales and actual sales, by-products and territories, assist management in locating sales areas needing attention?

3. A difference between budgeted sales and actual sales may be due to either price changes or quantity differences. Describe how these two elements may be separated into a price and a quantity variance.

4. A company budgeted sales of 1,000 units at $5 each. During the period the price was increased to $5.50, and 900 were sold. What would the total variance be? The price variance? The quantity variance?

5. Does the cost of merchandise sold variance contain a price and a quantity variance? Are they computed the same way as for sales?

6. Describe how the total of the sales and cost of merchandise sold variances explains the total variance in gross profit.

7. What is a flexible budget? Why should budgetary amounts be adjusted to the level of operations actually achieved when the variance of an operating expense is computed?

8. What is meant by the term "accounting by areas of responsibility"?

9. What are controllable and non-controllable expenses? Why should expense reports segregate controllable and non-controllable expenses?

10. Why are budgetary and expense reports more detailed for operating executives—such as foremen and supervisors—than for top-level executives such as the president?

11. What is meant by the statement "motivation is the key to a successful budgetary program"?

12. Describe how an employee who is given a bonus each month for meeting his budget could, if not carefully watched, manipulate expenses to make it appear that he has met the budget.

Exercises

12–1   **Definitions** *(15 minutes)*   The following terms and concepts were introduced in this chapter:

    a. Price variance
    b. Quantity variance
    c. Flexible budget
    d. Budgetary motivation
    e. Capital expenditures report
    f. Responsibility accounting

Instructions
Define each term or concept, giving examples where possible.

12–2   **Sales Variances** *(10 minutes)*   A company budgeted sales for the month of October as follows:

        15,000 units @ $5.00 each

Actual sales were as follows:

        14,000 units @ $5.50 each

Instructions

Compute the following variances, indicating whether the variance is favorable or unfavorable.
1. Sales price variance
2. Sales quantity variance
3. Total sales variance

12–3 **Sales Variance Computation** *(15 minutes)* The Frost-Dip Ice Cream Company forecast its sales and costs for February as follows:

100,000 gallons to be sold at $1.00 per gallon; cost $.75 per gallon

Actual results were:

> Sales of 103,000 gallons
> Revenue of $106,150
> Cost of goods sold, $79,310

Instructions

Compute the following:
1. The sales price variance
2. The sales quantity variance
3. The cost of goods sold price variance
4. The cost of goods sold quantity variance

12–4* **Expense Variations** *(15 minutes)* Shown below are the budget and the actual expenses for a company for the month of January.

	Budget (Expected Sales Volume of 15,000 Units)	Actual Results (Sales Volume of 12,000 Units)
Selling		
Advertising (fixed)	$ 5,000	$ 5,000
Supplies (variable, $.50 per unit)	7,500	6,000
Salaries ($5,000 fixed + $1.00 per unit)	20,000	20,000
Total sales expense	$32,500	$31,000
Administrative		
Officer's salary (fixed)	$ 1,000	$ 1,000
Sales clerks' salaries and commissions ($2,000 fixed + $2.00 per unit)	32,000	20,000
Communication (variable, $.10 per unit)	1,500	1,150
Supplies ($100 + $.01 per unit)	250	225
Taxes (fixed)	150	150
Total administrative expense	$34,900	$22,525
Total expenses	$66,400	$54,525

Instructions
Compute the following:
1. The expense volume variance
2. The expense spending variance

12–5 **Expense Variance Computation** *(15 minutes)*   A company's
selling and administrative expense behavior is as follows:

Fixed	$10,000
Variable	5% of sales

Sales were budgeted at $100,000. Actual sales and selling and
administrative expenses were as follows:

Sales	$90,000
Selling and administrative expense	$14,250

Instructions
Compute the following selling and administrative expense variances,
indicating whether favorable or unfavorable:
1. Spending variance
2. Volume variance
3. Total variance

12–6 **Computation of Price and Quantity Variances** *(10 minutes)*
The Marx Company prepared a budget profit plan as follows:

Sales	10,000 units at $7.30 each
Cost of sales	10,000 units at $4.10 each

Actual sales were 10,200 units at $7.40 each, and the actual cost
was $4.25 per unit.

Instructions
Compute the price and quantity variances for both sales and cost
of merchandise sold, and prepare a schedule reconciling the entire
gross profit variance.

12–7 **Computing Flexible Budgetary Amounts** *(10 minutes)*   Supplies expense has been analyzed and determined to be $100 fixed
per month and variable at $.02 per dollar of sales. In April, sales
were $7,000 and supplies expense was $280.

Instructions
Compute the expected supplies expense which should have been
incurred at the $7,000 level and the difference between expected
and actual supplies expense.

12–8 **Computing Flexible Budgetary Amounts** *(10 minutes)*   The
salesmen's travel and entertainment expense is $3,000 when sales
are $300,000 and $4,000 when sales are $500,000.

Instructions
Compute the fixed and the variable elements of the expense. If actual travel and entertainment expenses were $3,300 in a month when sales are $400,000, compute the difference between actual expense and the expected expense at that sales volume.

12–9 **Form of the Budget Control Report** *(15 minutes)* Analysis of the monthly expenses of the Marylin Mattress Company indicated the following:

	Fixed Portion	Variable Portion (Per Unit Sold)
Salaries	$11,000	$0.20
Travel and entertainment	600	.12
Supplies	200	.06
Depreciation	4,000	
Delivery expense	1,200	.30
Taxes	1,000	
Building rental	5,000	
Insurance	400	
Repairs	200	.15
Telephone and telegraph	100	.08

January sales were 6,000 mattresses, and actual costs incurred are shown below.

Salaries	$12,900
Travel and entertainment	1,240
Supplies	500
Depreciation	4,000
Delivery expense	3,200
Taxes	1,000
Building rental	5,000
Insurance	400
Repairs	1,020
Telephone and telegraph	700

Instructions
Prepare a budget report which reflects actual expenses, budgeted expenses, and the budget variances.

12–10* **Comprehensive Analysis of Budget Variances** *(30 minutes)*
The budget profit plan of the Atwell Company was as follows:

Sales	7,000 units at $12.50 each
Cost of merchandise sold	$8.30 per unit

Operating expenses:
Salaries—$5,000 fixed and the balance variable at 8 percent of sales.

Depreciation—$9,000 fixed.

Supplies—variable at 1 percent of sales.

Utilities—$200 fixed and the balance variable at one-half of one percent of sales.

At the end of the period the income statement reflecting actual operations was as follows:

Sales (6,800 units)		$88,400
Cost of merchandise sold		57,800
Gross margin		$30,600
Operating expenses:		
Salaries	$13,000	
Depreciation	9,000	
Supplies	850	
Utilities	700	
Total expenses		23,550
Net income		$ 7,050

Instructions

Prepare a schedule showing variances which will explain the entire difference between the net income in the original profit plan and the net income actually realized.

Problems

12–11 **Flexible Budget Reports** *(20 minutes)*   The expenses of department 15 of the Maybelle Company were analyzed into fixed and variable components as follows:

Salaries	Fixed $4,000; variable 5% of sales
Telephone and telegraph	Fixed $ 200; variable ½% of sales
Supplies and postage	variable ½% of sales
Travel and entertainment	Fixed $ 700; variable 1% of sales
Depreciation	Fixed $1,000
Equipment repairs	Fixed $ 400; variable 1% of sales
Insurance	Fixed $ 500

The actual expenses at the end of March, when sales totaled $100,000, were as follows:

Salaries	$8,500
Telephone and telegraph	680
Supplies and postage	470
Travel and entertainment	1,900
Depreciation	1,000
Equipment repairs	1,380
Insurance	500

Instructions
Prepare a report showing actual expenses, budgeted expenses for $100,000 of sales, and the resulting variances. Comment on any variances which you feel warrant an investigation.

12–12   **Flexible Budget Reports** *(20 minutes)*   The cost structure of the trucking department of the Pulpwood Paper Company is as follows:

Salaries ($1,300 fixed; variable 1% of sales)
Depreciation on delivery trucks ($400 fixed)
Gas and oil ($500 fixed; variable $\frac{1}{10}$% of sales)
Truck repairs ($250 fixed, variable $\frac{1}{10}$% of sales)
Insurance ($100 fixed)
Taxes and licenses ($120 fixed)
Utilities ($50 fixed, variable $\frac{1}{10}$% of sales)
Supplies (variable $\frac{1}{10}$% of sales)

In November, the company's sales totaled $400,000 and actual expenses were: salaries, $5,500; depreciation on delivery trucks, $400; gas and oil, $910; truck repairs, $600; insurance, $100; taxes and licenses, $120; utilities, $480; supplies, $460.

Instructions
Prepare a budget report for the trucking department, using budgeted amounts adjusted to the actual level of operations, and showing variances for each expense.

12–13   **Computations of Variances** *(15 minutes)*   A company budgeted sales of 15,000 units at a sales price of $10 and a unit cost of $7. Actual sales were 12,000 units which produced a total of $156,000 revenue and a cost of goods sold of $96,000.

Instructions
Calculate the following:
1. Sales price variance
2. Sales quantity variance
3. Cost of sales cost variance
4. Cost of sales quantity variance
5. Total variance in gross profit

12–14   **Price and Quantity Variances** *(15 minutes)*   The Holsum Company budgeted sales of 11,000 units at a sales price of $12 each and a cost of $7 each. At the end of the period, a total of 12,000 units had been sold for $141,600, and the cost of merchandise sold was $83,400.

Instructions
1. Prepare a budget report showing budgeted, actual, and variance figures for sales, cost of merchandise sold, and gross margin.

2. Separate the total variance between budgeted gross margin and actual gross margin into four separate factors: (a) sales price variance, (b) sales quantity variance, (c) cost of merchandise sold cost variance, and (d) cost of merchandise sold quantity variance.

12–15   **Price and Quantity Variances** *(15 minutes)*   A company budgeted sales of 4,500 units at $50 each, with a cost of $35 each. Actual sales were 4,300 units at a price of $52 each, and the actual cost was $36 each.

Instructions
Compute the following:
1. Total variance in sales
2. Sales quantity variance
3. Sales price variance
4. Total variance in the cost of merchandise sold
5. Cost of merchandise sold cost variance
6. Cost of merchandise sold quantity variance

12–16   **Price and Quantity Variances by Product** *(25 minutes)*   The annual budget of the Hydren Company contained expected sales of its three products as follows for March:

Product 11–A	1,000 units at $3
Product 19–C	2,000 units at $5
Product 20–B	3,000 units at $10

On March 1, the prices of the products were changed to $3.10, $5.50, and $11.00, respectively. The number of units sold were 1,100, 1,800, and 3,100, respectively.

Instructions
1. Compute the total variance between budgeted sales and actual sales for each product.
2. Compute the portion of each variance due to price variations and to quantity variations.

12–17   **Price and Quantity Variances by Product** *(30 minutes)*   The Mayhall Company has three products. Its sales and cost of sales were budgeted as follows for July:

	July Sales Budget		July Cost of Sales Budget	
Product A	(10,000 @ $1)	$10,000	(10,000 @ $.50)	$ 5,000
Product B	(5,000 @ $3)	15,000	(5,000 @ $2)	10,000
Product C	(3,000 @ $5)	15,000	(3,000 @ $3)	9,000
		$40,000		$24,000

At the end of July, the budget report to the president contained the following figures:

	Budget	Actual	Variance Over or (Under)
Sales	$40,000	$39,300	$ (700)
Cost of sales	24,000	24,740	740
Gross profit	$16,000	$14,560	$(1,440)

The president was disturbed because the actual sales were lower than budgeted sales and requested a report showing price and quantity variances for sales and cost of sales for each product (all factors affecting the gross profit variance).

Instructions

Using the following actual data for July, prepare the report for the president:

Actual Sales		Actual Cost of Sales	
A (11,000 @ $ .95)	$10,450	A (11,000 @ $ .52)	$ 5,720
B (5,200 @ $2.90)	15,080	B (5,200 @ $2.10)	10,920
C (2,700 @ $5.10)	13,770	C (2,700 @ $3.00)	8,100
	$39,300		$24,740

12-18   **Comprehensive Variance Report** *(40 minutes)*   A company reported the following to its executive manager for the month of July:

	Budget	Actual	Variance
Sales (12,500 units budgeted, 10,000 actual)	$100,000	$120,000	$20,000
Cost of goods sold (variable)	50,000	62,000	12,000
Gross Profit	50,000	58,000	8,000
Expenses			
Depreciation (fixed)	7,000	7,000	—0—
Supplies (variable)	2,000	2,100	100
Salaries ($4,000 fixed, balance variable)	12,000	13,700	1,700
Utilities ($600 fixed, balance variable)	1,600	2,100	500
Total expenses	$ 22,600	$ 24,900	$ 2,300
Net Income	$ 27,400	$ 33,100	$ 5,700

All variable and semivariable expenses are computed as a percentage of sales.

Instructions

Compute all variances required to explain the difference between budgeted net income and actual net income.

12-19   **Comprehensive Variance Analysis** *(30 minutes)*   The original budget plan of a company and the results of actual operations are given on the following page:

	Original Budget Plan	Actual Operations
Sales: 10,000 @ $10	$100,000	
11,000 @ 9		99,000
Cost of sales: ($6)	60,000	
($5)		55,000
Gross profit	$ 40,000	$44,000
Supplies (2% of sales)	$ 2,000	$ 1,880
Depreciation (fixed)	10,000	10,000
Salaries (15,000 fixed plus 3% of sales)	18,000	17,870
Total expenses	$ 30,000	$29,750
Net income	$ 10,000	$14,250

Instructions
Compute the following and indicate for each whether it is favorable or unfavorable.
1. Sales price variance
2. Sales quantity variance
3. Cost of sales cost variance
4. Cost of sales quantity variance
5. Expense volume variance
6. Expense spending variance

12–20 **Comprehensive Variance Analysis** *(50 minutes)*   The budget of the RST Company for the month of May included sales estimates of 100,000 units at a unit sales price of $10 and a cost of $5 per unit. The company's monthly flexible expense budget included the following:

Administrative salaries
  Fixed $50,000, variable $.06 per unit sold
Depreciation
  Fixed $60,000
Supplies
  Fixed $10,000, variable $.20 per unit sold
Taxes
  Fixed $10,000
Travel and entertainment
  Variable $1.05 per unit sold
Utilities
  Variable $.10 per unit sold
Sales salaries
  Fixed $20,000, variable $.05 per unit sold

At the end of May the records indicated the RST Company had sold 110,000 units for a total of $1,210,000 and that the cost of goods sold was $550,000.

Actual operating expenses were:

Administrative salaries	$ 56,600
Depreciation	60,000
Supplies	35,000
Taxes	10,000
Travel and entertainment	110,000
Utilities	12,300
Sales salaries	25,000
	$308,900

Instructions

1. Prepare a proforma income statement for the month based on budget expectations.
2. Prepare a budget report as of the end of the month in the form of a three-column income statement, one column for actual amounts, one for the original budget plan, and one for variances.
3. Prepare a schedule which fully analyzes the variances between the original budget and actual operations. The schedule should include a price and quantity variance for sales, a cost and quantity variance for the cost of goods sold, and a volume and a spending variance for operating expenses.

12–21 **Comprehensive Analysis of Variances** *(60 minutes)* The budget of the Neff Casting Company for the month of August included sales of 50,000 units at a unit sales price of $15 and a unit cost of $6.50. The company's monthly flexible expense budget included the following:

Depreciation (fixed, $45,000)
Supplies (variable, $0.50 per unit sold)
Sales salaries ($100,000 fixed, plus $1.00 per unit sold)
Utilities ($0.25 per unit sold)
Taxes ($20,000 fixed)
Administrative salaries ($85.000 fixed, plus $0.05 per unit sold)
Delivery expenses ($0.40 per unit sold)
Travel and entertainment ($15,000 fixed, plus $0.10 per unit sold)

At the end of the month, the accounting records indicated that the company had sold 53,000 units for a total of $768,500 and that the cost of merchandise sold was $333,900. Actual operating expenses were: depreciation, $45,000; supplies, $27,000; sales salaries, $151,000; utilities, $14,000; taxes, $20,000; administrative salaries, $90,000; delivery expenses, $20,100; and travel and entertainment, $21,000.

Instructions

1. Prepare a proforma income statement for the month based upon budget expectations.
2. Prepare a budget report as of the end of the month in the form

of a three-column income statement, one column for actual amounts, one for the original budget plan, and one for variances.

3. Prepare a schedule which fully analyzes the variances between the original budget and actual operations. The schedule should include a price and a quantity variance for sales, a cost and a quantity variance for the cost of merchandise sold, and a volume and a spending variance for operating expenses.

12–22   **Comprehensive Analysis of Variances** *(60 minutes)*   The budget of the Upton Company for the month of February of the current year included sales estimates of 70,000 units at a unit sales price of $9 per unit and a cost of $5.50 per unit. The company's monthly flexible expense budget included the following:

Administrative salaries (fixed $45,000, plus variable $0.05 per unit sold)

Sales salaries (fixed $30,000, plus variable $0.20 per unit sold)

Delivery expenses (variable $0.60 per unit sold)

Taxes (fixed $15,000)

Depreciation (fixed $49,000)

Supplies (fixed $11,000, variable $0.15 per unit sold)

Travel and entertainment (variable $0.40 per unit sold)

At the end of the month, the accounting records indicated that the company had sold 60,000 units for a total of $546,000 and that the cost of merchandise sold was $324,000. Actual operating expenses were: administrative salaries, $48,000; sales salaries, $40,400; delivery expenses, $40,500; taxes, $15,000; depreciation, $49,200; supplies, $19,100; travel and entertainment, $24,750.

Instructions

1. Prepare a proforma income statement for the month based upon budget expectations.
2. Prepare a budget report as of the end of the month in the form of a three-column income statement, one column for actual amounts, one for the original budget plan, and one for variances.
3. Prepare a schedule which fully analyzes the variances between the original budget and actual operations. The schedule should include a price and a quantity variance for sales, a cost and a quantity variance for the cost of merchandise sold, and a volume and a spending variance for operating expenses.

12–23   **Comprehensive Analysis of Variances** *(40 minutes)*   The Maxwell Company's budget was established as shown on p. 399, for the month of May.

At the end of May, the accounting records indicated the following actual sales and expenses: sales, 3,100 units at $6.10 each, with a

Sales (3,000 units at $6 each)		$18,000
Cost of merchandise sold ($4 each)		12,000
Gross margin		$ 6,000
Operating expenses:		
Depreciation (fixed)	$1,000	
Supplies ($0.40 per unit)	1,200	
Salaries ($800 fixed, plus $0.30		
per unit)	1,700	
Utilities ($500 fixed, plus $0.10		
per unit)	800	
Total operating expenses		4,700
Net income		$ 1,300

cost of $4.06; depreciation, $1,000; supplies, $1,250; salaries, $1,650; utilities, $810.

Instructions

1. Prepare an income statement reflecting the original budgeted amounts, actual amounts, and total variances for each item on the income statement.
2. Prepare a schedule analyzing in full the variance between the budgeted profit and the actual profit.

12–24   **Preparation of Budget Plan and Budget Reports** *(50 minutes)*
The Adkins Chemical Company projected its income statement for the first quarter of 19X1 as follows:

ADKINS CHEMICAL COMPANY
Proforma Income Statement
January through March, 19X1

Sales		$400,000
Cost of merchandise sold (60% of sales)		240,000
Gross profit		$160,000
Operating expenses:		
Selling expenses:		
Sales salaries	$42,000	
Store supplies	1,600	
Sales commissions	4,800	
Advertising	15,900	
Depreciation—store equipment	2,700	
Total selling expenses		$67,000
General and administrative expenses:		
Office salaries	$57,000	
Rent expense	3,000	
Bad debt expense	3,600	
Depreciation—office equipment	6,600	

(continued)

ADKINS CHEMICAL COMPANY
(continued)

Supplies	4,800	
Total general and administrative expenses	75,000	
Total expenses		142,000
Net income before income taxes		$ 18,000
Income taxes (30%)		5,400
Net income after income taxes		$ 12,600

[handwritten margin notes: Inc. Taxes back 3 yrs. forward 5 yrs.]

Revenues in the quarterly budget are expected to be realized as follows: $100,000 in January, $140,000 in February, and $160,000 in March.

The company's cost structure is as follows:

Fixed costs—advertising (equal amounts monthly), depreciation, sales salaries, office salaries, and rent expense. Income taxes are 30 percent of net profit before taxes.

Variable costs—all operating expenses not listed above as fixed are considered completely variable with sales.

Data for actual operations, taken from the company's accounts on January 31, were as follows:

[handwritten margin notes: End up with Jan. 36100 loss, Feb. 7724 inc, March 10977 inc.]

Sales	$130,000 (cr)
Cost of merchandise sold	76,100
Sales salaries	16,000
Store supplies	530
Sales commissions	1,500
Advertising	5,400
Depreciation—store equipment	900
Office salaries	18,800
Rent expense	1,000
Bad debt expense	1,300
Depreciation—office equipment	2,200
Supplies	1,300

Instructions

1. Using the data in the proforma income statement for the quarter and the data provided relative to the company's cost structure, prepare a profit plan in the form of income statements for January, February, and March.

2. Prepare a budget report in the form of an income statement, with columns for actual, budget, and variance, comparing the original January budget with the actual results of January transactions. (The tax expense is not entered in the books until the end of the year and must be computed from net income for monthly statement purposes, and a loss of one month carries forward to reduce the taxable income of the next month.)

12–25   **Cost Structure; Break-Even; Budget Plan Preparation and Analysis**
(80 minutes)   The executive vice-president of the Pratt Company requested his accountant to supply him with two income statements, one at a representative high and the other at a representative low level of operations. The accountant gave the following two statements to him in answer to his request:

	For the Period June 1 to May 31			
	19X1		19X2	
Sales		$70,000		$120,000
Cost of merchandise sold		39,970		68,520
Gross margin		$30,030		$ 51,480
Salaries	$14,000		$20,000	
Supplies	700		1,200	
Depreciation	8,000		8,000	
Travel and entertainment	3,000		4,000	
Taxes	1,000		1,000	
Total expenses		26,700		34,200
Net income		$ 3,330		$ 17,280

The vice-president feels that, with concentrated effort, the firm will be able to sell 10,000 units during the next fiscal year ending May 31, 19X3. He expects the sales price to hold steady at $11 per unit and that the units can be bought for $5.70 each.

Instructions
1. Using a high-low points method, determine the cost behavior of each operating expense. From these compute the cost structure of the company. For this purpose the cost of merchandise is variable at 57 percent of sales.
2. Compute the break-even point for the company.
3. Prepare a break-even chart.
4. Prepare a profit plan for the company for 19X3 in the form of a proforma income statement, using the vice-president's expectations.
5. At the end of the period, the actual sales were 9,400 units at $11.10 each and the total cost of merchandise sold was $50,760. The operating expenses were as follows:

Salaries	$19,000
Supplies	1,100
Depreciation	8,000
Advertising	4,000
Taxes	1,000

Prepare a schedule which reconciles the actual net profit realized with that in the original profit plan of the vice-president, showing as many significant variances as you feel are appropriate.

12–26	**Responsibility Accounting Reports** *(40 minutes)*	The Bracken-ridge Company has instituted a system of responsibility accounting wherein costs and expenses are broken down by the areas of responsibility in the organization chart. Each officer of the company who is responsible for incurring costs has an approved expense budget, which is divided between those over which the individual can exercise control and those over which he has no control.

Approved Budget

Expense	Sales Manager	Office Manager	Public Relations Manager	Personnel Manager
Controllable:				
Salaries	$20,000	$ 9,000	$6,000	$4,000
Supplies	1,000	2,500	500	200
Telephone	200	100	400	100
Advertising	3,000	—	50	—
Furniture and fixture repairs	300	400	100	150
Miscellaneous expenses	100	50	50	50
	$24,600	$12,050	$7,100	$4,500
Non-controllable:				
Depreciation	$ 2,000	$ 1,000	$ 400	$ 300
Insurance	500	200	100	50
	$ 2,500	$ 1,200	$ 500	$ 350
Total	$27,100	$13,250	$7,600	$4,850

The accounting process was designed to accumulate actual cost by individual areas of responsibility, and during the period the following actual expenses were incurred:

	Sales Manager	Office Manager	Public Relations Manager	Personnel Manager
Salaries	$20,100	$9,050	$6,500	$4,100
Supplies	1,050	2,400	600	160
Telephone	190	100	700	80
Advertising	3,400	—	100	—
Furniture and fixture repairs	280	395	80	130
Miscellaneous expenses	90	45	250	40
Depreciation	2,100	1,050	400	400
Insurance	480	210	100	50

Instructions
1. Prepare four budget schedules, one for the operations of each of the four managers, showing the budget, actual, and variance from budget figures for each expense.

2. Prepare a report for the general manager which shows budgeted, actual, and variance information in summary form (totals for each department) for each of the four departments.

12–27 **Responsibility Reports** *(45 minutes)* Cameron and Browne, Inc., has three productive departments in the casting division. Each of these three departments is assigned to a supervisor, who receives budget reports monthly on the expenses he has incurred.

Data for the month of January for the casting division were as follows:

	Department A		Department B		Department C	
Casting Division	Budget	Actual	Budget	Actual	Budget	Actual
Controllable:						
Labor	$10,000	$10,200	$20,000	$19,700	$ 8,000	$ 8,100
Materials used	15,000	16,100	31,000	31,200	12,000	11,900
Supplies	2,000	1,700	3,000	2,800	1,000	980
Machinery repairs	1,500	1,400	4,500	4,600	700	690
Non-controllable:						
Depreciation	4,000	4,000	8,000	8,000	2,000	2,000
Insurance	800	780	1,000	1,000	400	400
Taxes	1,100	1,100	1,400	1,450	600	620
Total	$34,400	$35,280	$68,900	$68,750	$24,700	$24,690

The casting division is one of four divisions making up the entire company. A plant manager is in charge of each division, and the vice-president in charge of manufacturing heads all divisions. Budget reports are prepared monthly for each departmental supervisor, the plant manager, and the vice-president in charge of manufacturing.

Data for the month for the other three divisions (in totals only) were as follows:

	Budget	Actual
Milling division	$180,000	$181,000
Electrical division	105,000	104,000
Assembly plant	200,000	207,000

Instructions
1. Prepare individual budget reports for the supervisors of Departments A, B, and C which show actual, budget, and variations.
2. Prepare a report for the casting division plant manager.
3. Prepare a report for the vice-president in charge of manufacturing.
4. If you were the casting division plant manager, which department would you feel warrants study first? Why? If you were the vice-president in charge of manufacturing, which division or plant would you investigate first? Why?

12–28   **Capital Expenditures Report** *(30 minutes)*   The board of directors of the Ohio-Western Company approved the following projects at its November 17, 19X0, meeting:

	Approved Budget	Expected Completion Date
New building at the St. Louis factory	$340,000	April 1, 19X1
New equipment for the Wisconsin branch	69,000	May 1, 19X1
New electronic data processing equipment for home office	650,000	Nov. 1, 19X1
New equipment for the Alabama branch	102,000	June 1, 19X2

Watch labor costs because budgeted ones are fouled up.

The board of directors then authorized the managers of each branch and the president of the home office to request bids on these capital expenditures and proceed with the installation or construction. By March 31, 19X1, the following had been accomplished:

1. A bid for the construction of the St. Louis factory building had been accepted for $332,000, but completion was not expected until May 1, 19X1. A total of $280,000 had been expended, and additions of $6,000 had been made to the original construction contract.
2. The new equipment for the Wisconsin branch had been ordered at a total cost of $69,500 and is to be delivered on May 1, 19X1. No expenditures had been made as yet for the equipment.
3. The electronic data processing equipment had been ordered at a total cost of $639,000, and $300,000 had been paid. The equipment is to be delivered and installed, ready for operation, on October 15, 19X1.
4. The equipment for the Alabama branch could not be acquired for less than $115,000. Equipment costing $37,500 had been acquired and paid for, and the remainder was to be delivered on July 16, 19X2.

Instructions
Prepare a report on capital expenditures for the board of directors for its next meeting.

12–29   **Budget Control Reports for Production Workers** *(40 minutes)*
The Beachwater Manufacturing Company assigns employees to designated crews, each composed of three men. Each crew is assigned to a particular machine, and transfers of men between crews, or of crews between machines, is relatively rare. The budgeted hourly labor cost of a crew is $6 ($2 per hour per man). The machines operate at different speeds, and budgeted production of each machine is as follows:

Crew Chief	Machine	Expected Budgeted Production Per Hour
Warren	1	100 units
Killeen	2	80
Roberts	3	90
Landrum	4	120
Waters	5	80
Neff	6	100

If a machine breaks down or needs adjusting, the crew does the repair work and makes up for lost production in overtime hours, receiving time and one-half pay for any hours worked over eight in any one day. Management watches the production and costs of each crew very carefully to prevent abuse of the overtime payment.

At the end of the week the accounting department reported the following:

Crew	Total Hours Worked	Units Produced	Total Week's Labor Cost
1	44	4,000	$290
2	40	3,400	240
3	42	3,600	270
4	48	5,800	320
5	40	3,500	240
6	42	4,200	260

Instructions

Prepare a report showing for each crew (a) actual production (in units), (b) expected production (in units) for the hours worked, (c) production variance (in units), (d) actual labor costs for the week, (e) budgeted labor cost for the week (hours worked at $6 per hour), and (f) labor cost variance (due to overtime).

How would you rank the crews in order of their efficiency, with the most efficient crew first?

12–30 **Budgetary Variances and Motivation** *(30 minutes)* As budget officer of the Pulpwood Paper Company, Cary Denbow had carefully studied the cost behavior of labor costs of the yard gang. The primary function of this group of men was to move materials, unload flatcars of pine logs, and clean the outside premises of the plant. Their monthly labor cost was $2,000 fixed and $1.00 variable for each ton of raw materials consumed.

In July, the plant was at half capacity and several men who were normally employed in the stripping and chipping departments were assigned to the yard gang rather than being laid off temporarily. These were specially trained men who might find another job if laid off. Their hourly wage was considerably higher than the usual hourly wage paid to members of the yard gang. They were paid their usual wage while working in the yard, and, being inexperienced in the work, they were somewhat inefficient. As a result, a large unfavorable variance in the labor cost of the yard gang for the month appeared. The budget report showed the following:

Yard gang:	Budget		Actual		Variance	
	Hours	Cost	Hours	Cost	Hours	Cost
Labor	2,500	$5,000	2,900	$8,100	400	$3,100

Instructions

The supervisor of the yard gang was unhappy with the budget program and insisted that the variance should not be charged against his operations. Describe in detail how the accounting and budgeting system should have been constructed in order to provide control data and yet not weaken the confidence of the company's employees in the budgetary program.

12-31   **Accounting and Budgetary Control; Motivation** (*30 minutes*)
The supervisor of the Welding Department of the Jones-Hartner Company received the following budget report for the month of May:

	Budget	Actual	Variance Over or (Under)
Labor—spot welding	$13,200	$13,280	$ 80
Labor—arc welding	22,900	22,700	(200)
Labor—material handling	1,400	4,800	3,400
Welding supplies	3,500	3,520	20
Machinery repairs	7,900	9,850	1,950
Power costs	4,300	5,400	1,100
Heat, light	900	870	(30)
Depreciation on equipment	2,700	2,700	—
Insurance	600	585	(15)
Taxes	500	490	(10)
	$57,900	$64,195	$6,295

The welding supervisor was a conscientious employee and had never had a total unfavorable variance before. He was very concerned about the $6,295 variance, which is an unusually large variance for any of the company's departments. He went to the accounting department to find what had caused the variance and was told the following:

(a) Total costs of operating the company's power plant are accumulated, then prorated to each department based on total labor costs. Since the labor costs in the welding department were high in May, and labor in other departments was low, a large portion of the power costs were prorated to the welding department.

(b) The mechanics from the repair department, who repair machines, keep time records on each repair job they perform. The total costs of the repair department are prorated to each department receiving their services, based on the time spent repairing equipment in each department. The mechanics had very little work to do all month, and thus each job they did received a large prorated "cost."

The accounting department could not explain the large variance in material handling labor. They had received time tickets from the timekeepers with that amount of labor on them. The supervisor went to the timekeeper for an explanation, and the timekeeper reminded him of Job 174L, where 1,000 heavy, unwieldy units had to be brought back from the assembly department, reworked, and returned one at a time. The material-handling costs had been charged to the welding department. The supervisor remembered that the units had to be reworked because the blueprints he used for the original welding had been incorrect.

The supervisor then returned to his welding department completely disgusted with the budgetary program. He felt that any effort to keep expenses in line with the budget was useless in view of the way expenses were charged to him.

Instructions
Describe in detail how the accounting and budgeting system should be constructed to handle the power costs, the machinery repairs, and the material handling costs.

chapter 13

Internal
Check Systems – *Known as internal control*

Learning
Objectives

This chapter continues the discussion of planning and control systems with an emphasis upon methods by which assets are safeguarded, the accuracy of data is assured, and the efficiency of clerical duties is controlled. Upon completion of your study of this chapter you should:

1. Understand the nature of the internal check system.
2. Recognize the importance of the arrangement of duties and the flow of work in the construction of a system of internal check.
3. Appreciate the role in the control process of such devices as subsidiary ledgers, document registers, bank reconciliations, and prenumbered multicopy documents.
4. Be able to trace the flow of documents and understand the arrangement of duties in cash receipts, cash disbursements, vouchers payable, and fixed asset control systems.

The Nature of
Internal Check

The first chapter of this text described control as the process of establishing objectives, setting plans, and measuring actual operations in such a way that management can know whether the objectives and plans are being met. This type of control is usually characterized as *management control* and was so labeled in that earlier chapter. One of the elements which make up a part of the total management control process is the system of *internal check,* and that element is emphasized in this chapter.

The system of *internal check* may be defined as *all the measures taken to protect the company's assets against irregularities, to insure the accuracy of recorded transactions, and to assure management that the information on which it must base decisions is authentic and reliable.* Internal check is narrower in scope and more concerned with internal operations than management control, since it is primarily concerned with the safeguarding of assets against theft and embezzlement and with the arrangement of duties so that individual clerical tasks are performed efficiently, with a minimum of error.

Internal check is one of the major tools used by management in controlling a company's operations. Individual performance of management personnel who have been assigned supervisory duties is measured with financial reports containing data related to their activities, and this process has been described in the topics discussed in earlier chapters. Nonsupervisory personnel performing clerical duties are controlled through formal work systems, arrangement of duties, and a prescribed flow of business papers. That control system is emphasized in this chapter. The financial control process includes not only the financial reports concerning responsibility centers headed by management personnel, but also includes the business papers and work arrangements through which the data contained in the reports are gathered. For this reason, internal check is one of the more important control subsystems employed within the company.

The distinction between management control and internal check is not precise, and these two aspects of control tend to blend together. Their distinction is also obscured because the term *internal control* is sometimes used synonymously with management control and sometimes synonymously with internal check. The basic distinction lies in the different level and different scope of the two control methods. Their differences are contrasted in the following table.

Attribute	Management Control	Internal Check
Scope	Covers all aspects of the company's operations	Concerned with clerical duties, work flow, and assignment of duties
Level	Upper levels, where strategic planning and management decisions are made	Operational or clerical level
Purpose	To guide the company in the face of competition and keep it healthy and strong	Asset protection and clerical accuracy of data
Persons involved	Managerial personnel	Nonsupervisory clerical personnel

Systems of internal check must be carefully constructed and constantly monitored to insure that assets are not subjected to theft and embezzlement and that errors are not permitted in the data gathering process. For this reason, the system of internal check is based upon two very fundamental principles:

1. Responsibilities of all clerical personnel must be fixed and clearly communicated.
2. A system of checks and balances must be maintained whereby one clerical activity within the company is automatically checked by another clerical activity with a minimal duplication of effort.

Seperate Duties

The principle of fixed responsibilities requires little elaboration, since it is obviously necessary for employees to be held accountable for their actions. However, the system of checks and balances is more complex and warrants clarification and discussion. Most of the discussion in this chapter is concerned with that topic.

Subsidiary Ledgers and Control Accounts

Subsidiary or detailed ledgers are used as a means of controlling both assets and liabilities. A subsidiary ledger is a part of the accounting records, separate from the general ledger, wherein a detailed record is kept of those individual items constituting the balance of the control account. Subsidiary ledgers for inventories were described in the chapter on job order costing systems, although the discussion at that point was concerned with the accumulation of job costs. However, the use of a control account for jobs in process, with subsidiary records for each job, also provides a check on the accuracy with which materials, labor, and overhead costs are assigned to jobs. A total of the balances in the jobs in process subsidiary records is accumulated periodically and matched with the balance in the control account, thus insuring that all costs have been assigned to a job. Other examples of control accounts with related subsidiary ledgers include the records of the receivables from each customer (an accounts receivable ledger), the record of the payables owed each supplier (an accounts payable ledger), and the plant and equipment in use (a fixed asset ledger).

This process is illustrated in Exhibit 13–1. That example shows the materials requisitions for withdrawal of materials being routed to the cost accounting department, where they are entered in the correct job subsidiary ledger account. A total of the materials withdrawn is accumulated on an adding machine tape, and this total is sent separately to the person maintaining the control account. If the materials are not correctly entered in the job subsidiary ledger, the total of the subsidiary records will not balance with the control. Note that there is minimal duplication of effort in this arrangement. The total of the materials requisitions had to be accumulated at some point, and the arrangement of duties was such that the total was accumulated prior to the forwarding of the requisitions to the cost accounting department for entry in the job subsidiary ledger accounts. Having this *batch total* prepared in advance insures that none of the materials requisition forms becomes misplaced and fails to be entered as a cost of some job.

EXHIBIT 13–1

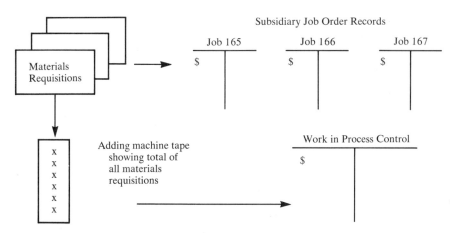

In order to provide maximum control, the detail or subsidiary ledger should be maintained by someone other than those persons having physical control of properties or those who prepare or post entries to control accounts. Separation of the control account from the subsidiary ledger is a form of automatic check to ascertain that the detailed ledger is being maintained accurately. The detailed ledger, in turn, is used to control and account for specific assets or properties.

The accounts receivable ledger may be used as another illustration of how control can be provided by the use of subsidiary ledgers. This process is shown in Exhibit 13–2. When a credit sale is made, at least three copies of the credit sales slip are prepared. One copy is sent to the person maintaining the customers' detailed ledger for use in posting to customers' accounts. Another copy is forwarded to the person who maintains the control account in the general ledger. At the end of each month, the total of all the customers' accounts is compared with the total in the control account. Any difference must be reconciled. If the subsidiary total and the control balance agree, there is assurance that all credit sales were posted to *some* customer's account. There is no assurance that the proper customer's account was posted, however. The customers are relied upon to inform the company if a credit sale was posted to the wrong account. All customer complaints are directed to someone other than the person who maintains the subsidiary ledgers, thus affording an independent check on the accuracy of posting credit sales.

Control and subsidiary ledger accounts are valuable control measures when duties of employees are separated properly. However, if the same person is permitted to maintain the customers' ledger, prepare and post entries to the general ledger control accounts, and receive monies from customers in payment of their accounts, control over receivables is nonexistent. Cash can be extracted without authorization and both the control and subsidiary accounts adjusted so that the disappearance is never discovered.

EXHIBIT 13–2
Accounts Receivable Controls

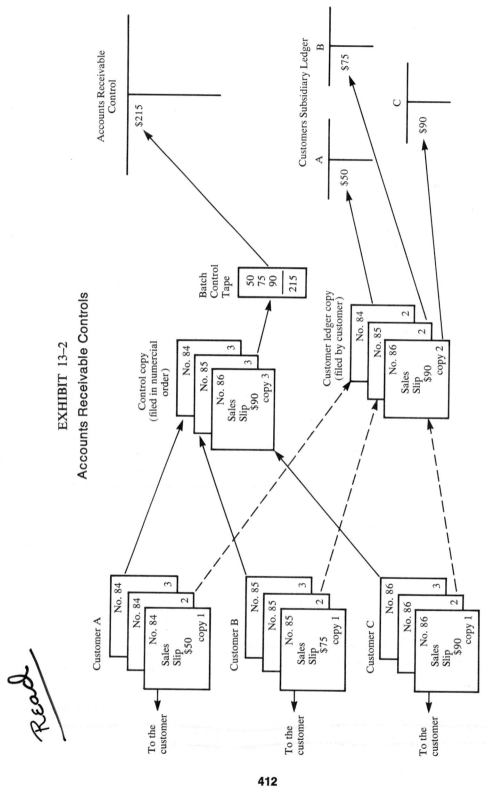

A sound system of internal check cannot be achieved without separation of three basic functions: (1) record keeping, (2) physical custody of assets, and (3) authority to move assets or incur liabilities. If authority for more than one of these three functions is placed in the hands of any one individual, the duties of that individual are not properly assigned.

To illustrate the need for separation of these three functions, consider the arrangement of duties shown in Exhibit 13–2. The sales slip is prepared in triplicate by the sales clerk, and the original (copy one) is given to the customer. The sales slips are prenumbered so that none will be lost or misplaced without detection. The customer copy is a "check" on the work of the sales clerk, for any errors will be detected quickly by the customer. Copy three of the sales slip goes to the person maintaining the control, which represents the accounting, or control, function. The receivable from the customer represents an asset, and the person maintaining the customers' subsidiary ledger performs the custody function. Copy two of the sales slip goes to the person maintaining the subsidiary ledger.

Function	Responsible Person	Explanation
Authority to move assets	Sales clerk	Prepares the sales slip and allows the customer to take the merchandise
Control of the assets	Person maintaining the subsidiary ledger	Maintains each customer's account and sends monthly statements
Record keeping	Person maintaining the control account	Periodically balances the total of the control against the total of the subsidiary ledger

Note that this system involves a minimum of duplicated effort. Each function is undertaken at a point and in a sequence that permits segregation of the three functions and reduces the possibility of embezzlement or error in the handling of accounts receivable.

The fact that a good system of internal control will not *prevent* fraud must be recognized. However, the early detection of fraud is one of the key advantages of a sound system. Should the sales clerk deliberately lose one of the sales slips, that fact would be noticed when the slips are arranged in numerical order by the person maintaining the control. If a sale is not posted to a customer's account, that omission will be discovered when the subsidiary and control accounts are reconciled. Thus, the system provides the mechanism by which errors or fraud are quickly detected. However, when two or more persons work together on an embezzlement scheme, the system may not detect the fraud, since the "separation of duties" aspect of the system no longer exists.

— Cash Receipts Controls —

Cash is the most liquid asset of a business and therefore must be controlled carefully to prevent theft and embezzlement. Exhibit 13–3 illustrates the segregation of duties and flow of work necessary to achieve control over cash

EXHIBIT 13–3
Cash Receipts Controls

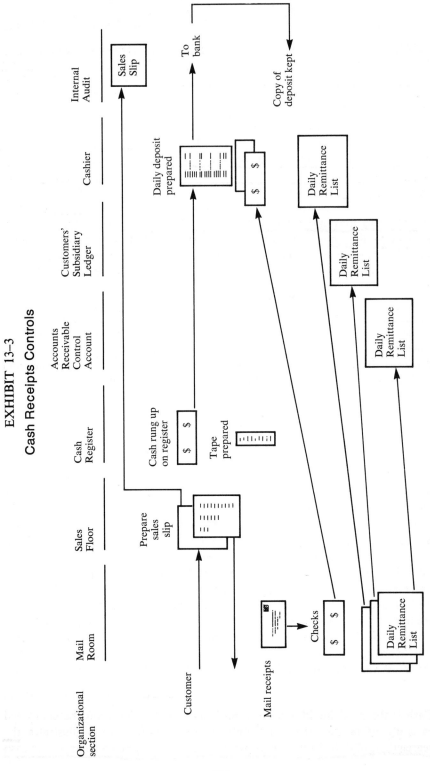

414

receipts. Note that recordkeeping, physical custody, and authority for movement are carefully separated.

Cash sales   When cash is received for cash sales, a sales slip is prepared, and the cash is immediately rung up on a cash register. The cash register has a locked-in tape, which records each transaction with indelible ink and accumulates a total of the day's sales. Separation of recordkeeping and physical custody of cash begins at this point; for the salesperson, who has access to cash, is not given access to the tape. At the end of each day, the cash in the register is transferred to an employee who deposits it in the bank. This employee likewise does not have access to the tape. The locked-in tape is removed by still another employee and becomes the basis of the daily cash sales entry. Each day management receives a report of the cash over and short, which is computed as the difference between the cash deposit and the total of the locked-in tape. Small cash overages and shortages are to be expected, but large shortages or continued small shortages indicate possible manipulation of cash. To prevent loss of control over cash, it is most important that the person who has access to cash not have access to the records. If these functions were performed by the same individual, cash could be extracted, the records altered, and the disappearance of cash would never be discovered.

Collection of receivables   Cash payments by customers toward their accounts receivable balances are normally received by mail in the mail room. Lists of checks are prepared at that point. One copy of this daily remittance list, as shown in Exhibit 13–3, is sent to the accounts receivable control, and a second copy is forwarded to the customers' subsidiary ledger. The checks are sent directly to the cashier where the deposit is prepared. Note that a copy of the deposit slip from the bank is forwarded to the auditor, who will use it in the reconciliation of the bank balance, as described in this chapter.

Cash Disbursement Controls

An authorized signature converts a blank check to the equivalent of cash. Therefore, the persons authorized to sign checks should not be given access to the accounting records. The payment which is to be made with the check should be authorized by one person (authority for movement of an asset), the check should be recorded by another person (recordkeeping), and it should be signed by another (physical custody). In this way, control over cash payments is achieved, so that no one individual can extract cash without detection.

A stronger control over cash is achieved when all cash receipts are deposited daily and all payments are made by check. This procedure precludes the comingling of receipts and disbursements and reduces the possibility of mishandling either one. It also permits a comparison of daily cash receipts with the deposits appearing on the bank records. Furthermore, all checks written can also be compared with the figures which are subtracted by the bank from the company's account. This procedure is illustrated in Exhibit 13–4. Note that each check is authorized with a voucher and supporting documents.

EXHIBIT 13–4

Control Over Cash Disbursements

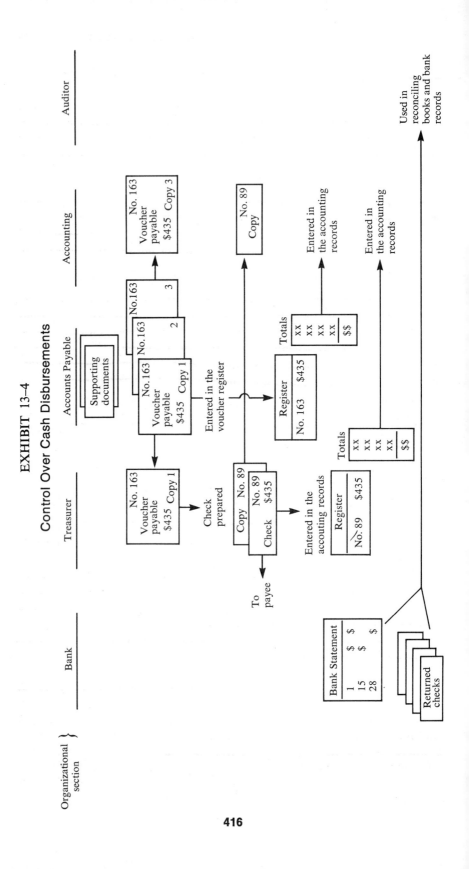

The checks are recorded in a check register, with totals forwarded to the general ledger. A copy of the voucher is the basis for recording purchases and expenses, and each voucher is recorded in a voucher register. When the checks have cleared the bank, they are returned by the bank to the company, and the internal auditor receives them for later use in the bank reconciliation process. Both checks and vouchers are prenumbered to insure that none is lost or fails to be recorded.

Exhibit 13–5 is part of a check register which is used to account for all checks written. Note that checks are recorded in numerical sequence in the check register and that voided checks are recorded, although no dollar amount appears in the money columns. A voided check must be clearly marked *void* to prevent its later use. Tearing off the signature portion of a check is one method of insuring that a voided check is not used later.

Small cash payments   The necessity of making many small cash payments quickly and without prior notice is frequent in business affairs. Immediate cash payment is necessary, for example, when office supplies are purchased, when a collect telegram is received, or when freight charges must be paid upon receipt of merchandise. Since preparation of a check is often a lengthy process, a means of making small payments quickly is necessary.

A *petty cash fund* is established for the purpose of making small cash disbursements, and its existence permits a tighter control over the issuance of checks. A limit such as $25 or $50 may be placed on the size of the payment which can be made from the petty cash fund, and anything over this amount must be paid by check. When a petty cash fund is established, a specific amount of cash is placed in the fund, and one designated person makes all payments from the fund. The amount of the fund may range from $100 to $1,000, depending upon the company's needs.

As cash is expended from the fund, the person in charge of the fund prepares a *petty cash voucher*, which contains information relative to the amount spent, what it was spent for, and any other pertinent information about the payment. Exhibit 13–6 illustrates a petty cash voucher, which is prenumbered and requires the signature of the person who receives the payment. The remaining cash, plus the completed petty cash vouchers representing payments from the fund, must always equal the original amount of the fund. When additional cash is needed in the fund, the completed petty cash vouchers are submitted for reimbursement, and a single check is written on the general bank account to replenish the fund by the amount of the paid petty cash vouchers. The expenses that were incurred when the petty cash was expended are then recorded.

This type of fund is called an *imprest* fund, which means that cash has been "advanced" to the petty fund cashier, who will be reimbursed when the money in the fund is expended. Control exists because the person responsible for the fund must account at all times for the full amount of the fund, either with unspent cash or with properly completed documents indicating how the balance was used.

EXHIBIT 13-5
Check Register

Date	Payee	Check Number	Voucher Number	Accounts Payable Dr.	Purchase Discount Cr.	Cash in Bank Cr.
April 19	Indiana Abrasives Co.	3241	7430	1,000.00		1,000.00
20	Travis Publications	3242	7520	900.00	18.00	882.00
20	Wilson-Toole, Inc.	3243	7540	200.00	4.00	196.00
20	Office Supply House, Inc.	3244	7541	97.00		97.00
21	J. A. Biggers	3245	7556	850.00	17.00	833.00
21	Evans Company	3246	7560	36.00		36.00
24	Southern Supply Company	3247	Void	—		—
24	Abbott and Fitch	3248	7542	500.00	15.00	485.00
24	Wm. J. Hoffman	3249	7497	150.00	3.00	147.00
30	Totals			18,200.00	263.00	17,937.00

Petty cash vouchers should be marked PAID when they have been reimbursed, to prevent their reuse. Otherwise, control over the fund ceases to be effective.

EXHIBIT 13–6

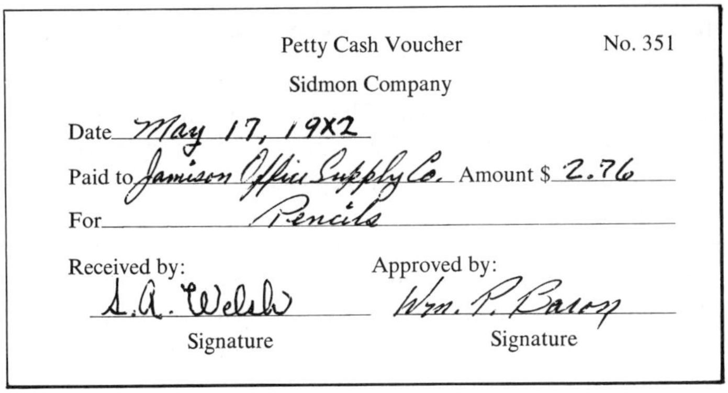

Petty Cash Voucher   No. 351

Sidmon Company

Date_ *May 17, 19X2*_

Paid to_ *Jamison Office Supply Co.*_ Amount $_ *2.76*_

For_ *Pencils*_

Received by: Approved by:

L.A. Welsh   *Wm. P. Basey*

Signature   Signature

Bank Reconciliations

All banks maintain detailed records for each of their depositors. These records show each deposit made to the customer's account and all checks written against the company's account which have reached the bank. Each month the bank sends a *bank statement* to each depositor. The bank statement, illustrated later in Exhibit 13–8, is a detailed record of all deposits and checks which have cleared the depositor's account at the bank.

If a company deposits its cash receipts daily and disburses only by check (except for petty cash disbursements), the bank statement should contain the same figures as the company's books. Daily cash receipts in the company's records will appear as deposits on the bank statement; checks recorded in the company's check register will appear as withdrawals on the bank statement. The bank statement is thus a second record of a company's cash transactions, providing another means of locating unauthorized transactions.

However, the cash balance on the bank statement and that on the company's books will seldom agree exactly even when there are no unauthorized transactions. This discrepancy is due to the lag between (1) the date a check is issued and the date it clears the company's bank account, or (2) the date cash is received and recorded and the date the deposit reaches the bank. The time lag on deposits is normally not more than one or two days, but it may be several weeks for checks. Differences between a company's cash records and the bank's records may also result from clerical errors on the part of either the company or the bank.

The cash balance on the bank statement and that recorded on the company's books should be reconciled each month. The reconciliation is made to insure that each cash transaction appearing on the bank statement is recorded currently on the books. If unauthorized checks are drawn, or if cash is extracted before deposit, the bank reconciliation should reveal the discrepancy. The monthly reconciliation of the bank account should not be performed by an employee who has access to cash, signs checks, or records cash transactions. The reconciliation is a proof of cash transactions as recorded on the company's books, and it should be assigned to an employee who has no other duties connected with cash transactions.

The following steps are necessary in reconciling the cash balance on the bank statement with that appearing on the company's records:

1. Trace daily cash receipts on the company's records to the deposits appearing on the bank statement. The deposits on the company's books which have not yet reached the bank are "deposits in transit" and should be added on the reconciliation work sheet to the balance of cash which the bank statement shows.

2. Compare the cleared checks returned by the bank and deducted on the bank statement with the record of checks in the cash disbursements journal. Any checks that have been issued by the company but have not yet cleared the bank represent "outstanding checks" and must be subtracted from the bank balance on the reconciliation work sheet.

3. The above two steps should account for all deposits and checks. Any other items appearing on either the company's records or the bank's records must be investigated to determine whether the bank or book balance should be adjusted. For example, the bank may have recorded a service charge against the company's cash balance. Since this charge does not appear on the company's records, it must be subtracted from the cash balance on the books. As a further illustration, the bank may have collected a note receivable owed the company by one of its customers and deposited the proceeds directly to the company's account. If the company has not yet recorded the collection of the note, the cash must be added on the reconciliation work sheet to the cash balance on the company's books. The form of a bank reconciliation work sheet is shown in Exhibit 13–7.

EXHIBIT 13–7

Bank Reconciliation Work Sheet
July 31, 19X5

Balance per books, July 31, 19X5	$	Balance per bank, July 31, 19X5		$
Add: Note collections by the bank which have not been recorded on the books	(+)	Add: Deposits in transit which have not yet reached the bank		(+)
Less: Expenses and costs charged by the bank and deducted from the bank balance but not entered on the books	(−)	Less: Checks written which have not yet cleared the bank		(−)
		Bank errors	{	(+)
Book errors	{ (+)		{	(−)
	{ (−)			
Corrected cash balance	$	Corrected cash balance		$

Exhibit 13–8 illustrates the reconciliation process, showing the relationship of the company records and the related bank statement used in the reconciliation process. The two ending cash balances—$2,498 as shown on the bank statement, and $2,288 as shown in the company's books—are adjusted by adding to or subtracting from each until the corrected cash amount is determined. The accompanying bank reconciliation for the Wilson Company was prepared from these documents. Each of the checks outstanding, deposits in transit, book errors, and unrecorded service charges can be determined by tracing the amounts in Exhibit 13–8 between the book figures and the amounts on the bank statement.

WILSON COMPANY
Bank Reconciliation

Balance per books, Jan. 31, 19X5	$2,288	Balance per bank, Jan. 31, 19X5		$2,498
Add: Error in recording deposit of Jan. 2. Actual deposit was $200; recorded in books as $190	10	Add: Deposits in transit: Deposit of Jan. 31		120
	$2,298			$2,618
Less: Unrecorded service charge	5	Less: Checks outstanding:		
		Number	Amount	
		746	$100	
		749	65	
		750	90	
		755	70	325
Corrected balance	$2,293	Corrected balance		$2,293

Disbursement Approvals

The authority to approve a disbursement is a major responsibility and is usually vested in only a few responsible officers of the company, who receive and review all documents, invoices, and papers relating to a disbursement.

The documents surrounding the purchase of merchandise may be used to illustrate the accumulation of paperwork prerequisite to issuing a check. A *purchase requisition* is prepared by designated persons to inform the purchasing department that merchandise is needed. When the purchasing department receives the requisition, a *purchase order* is prepared and forwarded to the supplier. When the goods arrive, the receiving department inspects and counts the merchandise and prepares a *receiving report*. Finally, the supplier submits his invoice, which shows the amount owed him for the merchandise. Signed copies of all four documents, which have been prepared independently, are accumulated in the vouchers payable department and are sent to the officer who will authorize payment. He reviews the papers to ascertain that the merchandise was needed (purchase requisition), that it was actually ordered (purchase order), that it was received in good condition (receiving report), and that the amount owed is correct (invoice). If all documents are in order, payment is approved—but the official who approves the disbursement should not also sign the check.

EXHIBIT 13–8
Illustration of Bank Reconciliation Procedures

COMPANY RECORDS

CHECK REGISTER

Date	Payee	Check Number	Accounts Payable	Purchase Discounts	Cash
Jan. 1	M. L. Peters	744	$ 40		$ 40
4	N. A. Owens	745	10		10
4	F. Y. Jones	746	100		100
5	A. B. Cox	747	15		15
12	James Stone	748	133	$3	130
13	Lillian Miller	749	65		65
19	X-Tons Company	750	90		90
20	A-B-C Company	751	100	2	98
22	Tri State Corp.	752	25		25
22	L. T. Mann	753	50	1	49
28	Peter G. Hayes	754	20		20
30	Abbott Corporation	755	70		70
	Totals		$718	$6	$712

CASH RECEIPTS JOURNAL

Date	Account	General	Sales	Accounts Receivable	Cash
Jan. 1	Cash sales		$190		$190
3	A. R. Burna	$50		$100	100
9	Interest income				50
17	Cash sales		300		300
21	Doris Kroett			80	80
28	Wm. A. Beckett			60	60
31	Kay Farnesworth			120	120
	Totals	$50	$490	$360	$900

Cash in Bank

Balance, Jan. 1	$2,100	Cash Payments	$712
Cash Receipts	900		
Balance, Jan. 31	$2,288		

Checks compared to locate checks outstanding

Receipts and deposits compared to locate deposits in transit.

BANK RECORDS   STATEMENT

Wilson Company
6100 30th Street
Boston, Mass.

Checks	Deposits	Date	Balance
Balance brought forward		Jan. 1 'X5	$2100
$ 40	$200	Jan. 2 'X5	2060
10	100	Jan. 3 'X5	2260
15	50	Jan. 4 'X5	2350
5 (service charge)		Jan. 10 'X5	2385
130	300	Jan. 12 'X5	2380
98 25	80	Jan. 18 'X5	2550
20 49	60	Jan. 22 'X5	2507
		Jan. 28 'X5	2498

1ST FEDERAL BANK   This is your balance
BOSTON

Please reconcile with your records and report any errors on this statement to us immediately.

Voucher System

The voucher system is a term applied to an orderly flow of documents similar to that just described but containing an additional control arising from the preparation of a formal document called a *voucher*. The system operates in the following manner:

1. When all copies of purchase requisitions, purchase orders, receiving reports, invoices, and other papers supporting a disbursement have been accumulated in the vouchers payable department, the *voucher* authorizing the payment is prepared, with full information concerning the disbursement. A copy of a voucher is illustrated in Exhibit 13–9.
2. The voucher and all related documents are sent to the person who will approve payment. His signature on the voucher is authority for payment. All documents supporting the payment are stamped or perforated at this point to prevent their reuse with another voucher.
3. The authorized voucher is recorded in a voucher register. Vouchers are prenumbered and must be listed in numerical order in the register. Exhibit 13–10 illustrates a voucher register.
4. The approved voucher is then filed according to due date in an unpaid voucher file containing all authorized but unpaid vouchers.
5. Vouchers are removed from the unpaid voucher file on their payment date. Checks are prenumbered; and as they are prepared, they are recorded in a check register, together with the number of the supporting voucher. Thus, every check is supported by a voucher, and a complete cross reference between checks and vouchers is maintained in the check register.
6. The checks and vouchers are forwarded to the officer whose signature is authorized to appear on the checks, where they are signed and mailed. Each voucher is stamped *paid* and returned to the accounting department, where the check number is recorded in the voucher register to indicate that payment has been made. In the illustration of the voucher register in Exhibit 13–10, note that some of the vouchers have been paid and some have not. The unpaid vouchers, which have no check numbers beside the voucher numbers, are still retained in the unpaid voucher file. The entire voucher system is illustrated in the flow chart in Exhibit 13–11. Note particularly the separation of the three functions necessary for sound internal control.

Fixed Asset Control

Many companies have more dollars invested in fixed assets than in any other type of property. Fixed asset control is achieved by (1) establishing a control account and subsidiary ledger for each class of asset, (2) establishing fixed responsibility for use of the assets, (3) segregating the granting of authority to move the asset from the physical custody of the asset, and (4) periodically examining the fixed assets and accounting for their existence.

A subsidiary ledger for fixed assets is shown in Exhibit 13–12. The fixed asset ledger card should be prepared at the time the asset is purchased. All

EXHIBIT 13–9

Voucher

Acme Pulp Company
Ft. Wayne, Indiana

No. 7563

Payee: Pure Chemical Company
6302 Whitis Avenue
Chicago, Illinois

Date	Details	Amount
April 29, 19X5	600 lbs. chemical 34X–2	
	Invoice 4921, dated April 18	$723.00

Accounting distribution:
Debit   Purchases $723.00

Total credit to accounts payable $723.00

Date prepared	April 30, 19X5
Date of payment	May 10, 19X5
Documents assembled by	B.C.A.
Documents received by	B.R.G.
Approved for payment	m. whitley
Recorded by	J.R.S.

Note that this voucher has been approved for payment but will not be paid until May 10, 19X5. The voucher has been entered in the voucher register and would remain in the unpaid voucher file until the payment date.

EXHIBIT 13–10

Voucher Register

Date	Payee	Voucher number	Check number	Accounts payable cr.	Purchases dr.	Store supplies dr.	Delivery expense dr.	Sundry debits Account	Post ref.	Amount
April 17	Tracey Supply Co.	7538	3240	175.00			175.00			
18	Hauling Steel Co.	7539		100.00				Bldg. repairs	4132	100.00
19	Wilson-Toole, Inc.	7540	3243	200.00	200.00					
19	Office Supply House, Inc.	7541	3244	97.00		97.00				
20	Abbott and Fitch	7542	3248	500.00	500.00					
20	Drakes-Landow Company	7543		50.00	50.00					
21	McFarland Supply	7544		82.00				Adv. expense	5160	82.00
22	Hovart Chain Products	7545	3230	1,400.00	1,400.00					
22	Outland Company	7546	3260	600.00				Office equip.	2310	600.00
23	Patts Metal Company	7547	3219	510.00	510.00					
23	Armco Products	7548		192.00		192.00				
24	Midstates Oil Company	7549		41.00			41.00			
24	Lerno Company	7550	3238	750.00	750.00					
25	Trainer Insurance Company	7551		120.00				Prepaid ins.	1728	120.00
25	Ralph Newman	7552	3251	422.00	422.00					
30	Pure Chemical Company	7563		723.00	723.00					
				723.00	723.00					
30	Totals			19,520.00	13,140.00	650.00	329.00			5,401.00

EXHIBIT 13–11

The Voucher System Illustrated

Record keeping function	Authority to move assets	Physical custody of asset
Accounting department	Officer who approves voucher for payment	Check signer

1. Purchase requisitions, purchase orders, receiving reports, and invoices accumulated.

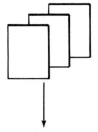

2. Voucher prepared, and documents attached.

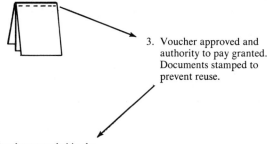

3. Voucher approved and authority to pay granted. Documents stamped to prevent reuse.

4. Voucher recorded in the voucher register, then placed in unpaid voucher file.

5. Voucher removed from unpaid voucher file. Check prepared and data entered in check register. Voucher and check sent to check signer.

6. Check signed and mailed. Voucher stamped "Paid" and returned.

7. Voucher placed in paid voucher file. Check number entered in voucher register to indicate payment.

pertinent data are entered on the card, including information about how depreciation is to be computed and the department responsible for the asset. If responsibility for the physical custody of the asset is later transferred to another department, that information should be noted on the card. Responsibility for assets must be fixed, and the assets must not be transferred without proper authority. If the detailed asset records are maintained by the person who has physical custody of the assets or access to the general ledger control account, adequate control is difficult to maintain. Periodically, the detailed fixed asset cards should be used to "inventory" the fixed assets and ascertain that each asset still exists and is in the possession of the person responsible for it.

EXHIBIT 13–12

Fixed Asset Subsidiary Ledger Card

Delta Manufacturing Company
Fixed Asset Ledger

Description	Drill press	Asset number	375
Location	Machine department	General ledger classification	Machinery
Manufacturer's serial number	8427–A–325	Cost	$8,100
Purchased from	Waco Machinery Co.		
Date purchased	July 1, 19X0		

Person responsible for the asset   Foreman, machine department

Depreciation information:

Estimated life	10 years
Estimated salvage value	$100
Depreciation method	Straight-line
Monthly depreciation	$66.67
Annual depreciation	$800

Final disposition _____

Depreciation Record

Date	Depreciation expense	Balance of accumulated depreciation	Undepreciated balance
19X0	$400	$ 400	$7,700
19X1	800	1,200	6,900
19X2	800	2,000	6,100
19X3	800	2,800	5,300
19X4	800	3,600	4,500
19X5	800	4,400	3,700

━ The Internal Audit Function ━

A company's control system is a complex framework, including the formulation of detailed plans and budgets, preparation of reports by responsibility areas, independent preparation of bank reconciliations, flow-of-work arrangement, the use of voucher and other subsidiary ledger systems, and such mechanical devices as cash registers with locked-in tapes. In many companies, management maintains a staff of internal auditors whose function is to review the control system to see that it is adequate and effective.

The internal audit staff is most frequently under the responsibility of the controller, who is the company's top accounting executive. Internal auditors periodically review the arrangement of duties, flow of work, adequacy and content of the company's documents, and the accuracy of financial data, making recommendations as to how any weaknesses and inefficiencies can be eliminated. Although the internal auditor does look for more efficient ways of performing a job, he is not considered only an "efficiency expert." He is an expert in controls, and it is his duty to establish and maintain a strong system of control throughout the business.

Summary

Management control over supervisory personnel is exercised through an organizational framework with specifically assigned responsibilities and an accounting system designed to report separately on the activities of each responsibility area. Control over nonsupervisory personnel, however, is more effectively accomplished through a system of internal check. The principal components of internal check are work arrangements and division of duties. Thus, without undue duplication of effort, one person automatically checks the accuracy of another person's work. The system of control consists of such accounting methods as bank reconciliations, voucher systems, locked-in cash register tapes, prenumbered documents, subsidiary ledgers which must balance with control accounts, and internal audits for periodic review of the entire system.

Separation of the record-keeping and physical custody functions from the authority to transfer is a prerequisite to a sound internal check system. No two of these functions may be vested in the same individual without a resultant weakening of the control system. When two or more persons conspire together, the detection of fraud or error becomes more difficult, for such action in effect places at least two of the three separate functions in the same hands. However, if the system is properly constructed, even collusive action will be automatically detected in the long run.

New Terms

Bank reconciliation   The process of matching the book balance of cash with the bank's record, and reconciling any differences.

Bank statement   A statement received monthly from the bank showing all deposits and all checks cleared.

Batch total   The total of a group of documents.

Check   A negotiable instrument authorizing the bank to pay someone from the balance of an account.

Check register   A list of checks written.

Fixed asset register   A subsidiary record containing data on each asset.

Imprest fund   A fund which is reimbursed periodically for the amount of expenditures from it.

Internal audit   Review of the company's activities undertaken by employees whose specialty is locating and strengthening weaknesses in internal controls.

(control)

Internal check   All the measures taken to protect assets, insure accuracy, and assure management that the information on which it bases decisions is correct.

Petty cash fund   A fund of cash used to pay for small items immediately.

Petty cash voucher   The document evidencing payment from a petty cash fund.

Purchase requisition   A document requesting that a purchase be made.

Purchase order   A document authorizing a vendor to supply or send an item.

Receiving report   A document indicating receipt of supplies, materials, or assets.

Voucher   A document authorizing a check to be prepared.

Voucher register   A list of vouchers which have been prepared.

Subsidiary ledger - a part of the accounting records, separate from the general ledger; wherein a detailed record is kept of those individual items constituting the balance of the control account.

Questions

1. Distinguish between management control and internal check.

2. Discuss in general terms the role of accounting in the process of business control and give several examples of how accounting may be used as a control mechanism.

3. What part does the organization of a business have in the control process? Is a formal organization more likely in a large or a small business?

4. What is responsibility accounting? How does it work? Is "responsibility accounting" a different form of accounting from that which you have studied in previous chapters, or is the performance of control functions an application of the accounting process?

5. Define a "system of internal control." What are the three basic functions which must be separated to provide good internal control?

6. Describe how an imprest petty cash fund works and why it is established.

7. Describe the process of reconciling a bank account. Explain (a) why a bank account should be reconciled, (b) what is meant by an outstanding check, and (c) a deposit in transit.

8. Why is control over the payment of liabilities necessary? Describe some of the documents used in the control over liabilities.

9. Describe in detail how the voucher system works.

10. What purpose is served by entering check numbers in the voucher register and voucher numbers in the check register when a voucher is paid?

11. How can a subsidiary ledger and control account be used as a control device?

12. Describe the process of maintaining control over fixed assets.

13. Discuss the function of the internal auditor. Is he an "efficiency expert"?

14. On December 31, 19X6, the bank statement showed a balance of cash of $800. If there were $600 of checks outstanding and a deposit of $300 in transit, what is the correct cash balance?

15. An invoice dated July 16 with terms of 2/10, n/30 was received and approved on July 17, and a voucher was prepared on July 18. If it could not be paid on the due date because of a lack of cash, who should approve the deferral of payment? If a return was made so that less than the amount of the voucher is actually owed, who should approve a reduction in the amount of the voucher?

Exercises

13-1   **Definitions** (*15 minutes*)   The following terms or concepts were introduced in this chapter:

a. Responsibility accounting
b. System of internal control   *p. 429*
c. Internal check
d. Imprest petty cash fund *- used to keep from writing checks for small amounts*
e. Bank reconciliation *- 428*
f. Voucher system *★ gains control over cash disbursements*
g. Internal audit function *- locating weaknesses*

Instructions
Define each term or concept, giving examples wherever possible.

13-2   **Locating Weaknesses in Internal Control** (*15 minutes*)   Several independent internal control situations are described below:

a. The accountant of the Zorill Company is in charge of all accounting records and documents. He also signs checks and reconciles the bank account monthly. *has physical custody + record keeping*
b. The foremen are in charge of the assets and materials used in a company's manufacturing operations. They are authorized to

buy new assets and report what they bought to the accounting department, where payment for the asset is made. They are also authorized to sell or scrap assets, which they also report to the accounting office. *no limit on what bought, no check on sales,*

c. The officer in charge of purchasing is authorized to place orders for any items which come to him on signed purchase requisitions. He sends a copy of the purchase order which he processes to the accounting department but does not have authority to sign a purchase requisition himself. He can, however, cancel any purchase order that he sends at any time he chooses. He insists that he be allowed to cancel orders so that he can take advantage of better prices if there is a price change. *None,*

Instructions
Describe any weaknesses in the systems.

13–3 **Design of a System of Internal Control** *(30 minutes)* John Grimmit owns a neighborhood movie theatre. His principal sources of revenue are the sale of admission tickets; the sale of candy, popcorn, and cold drinks; and receipts from leasing the theatre to special groups. He has lower admission prices before six o'clock in the afternoon and has different prices for children, teenagers, and adults. In addition, a special movie is often shown at "popular prices," which means that the prices are higher than the regular prices.

Instructions
Describe in detail how a system of internal control could be constructed for the operations of the theatre. The system should be designed so that it safeguards the assets and also provides adequate financial detail for administrative control. Care must be exercised to insure that the system is not overly elaborate.

13–4* **Control Over Cash Receipts** *(30 minutes)* Outline the steps necessary for a system of control over the cash receipts for: (a) a vending machine company; (b) a restaurant.

13–5 **Bank Reconciliation** *(20 minutes)* From the following information for the Fahren Company, prepare a bank reconciliation statement and determine the correct available cash balance.

Balance per bank statement, July 31, 19X1	$8,150
Book balance, same date	7,325
Credit for note collected by bank	500
Bank charges	5
Deposits in transit	462
Customer's check deposited July 3, but returned by bank and marked N. S. F. ("not sufficient funds")	42

Check drawn on another company's account and deducted in
  error by bank   25
Outstanding checks: No. 22   212
                      No. 27   450
                      No. 28   197

13–6*   Bank Reconciliation *(20 minutes)*   The Wisconsin Company
reconciles its bank account monthly. On January 31 the bank
statement showed a balance of $7,996, and the books showed a
balance of $7,591. A comparison of the detail of the bank state-
ment and the books revealed that a deposit of $800 had not yet
reached the bank, and checks numbered 6013 for $720, 6142 for
$105, and 6151 for $490 had not yet cleared the bank. In addition,
the bank had made a $10 service charge which had not been
recorded by the Wisconsin Company, and check number 6011
which cleared the bank was recorded as $400 on the books but was
actually for $500. This check was a salary check.

Instructions
Prepare a bank reconciliation.

13–7   Voucher and Check Register *(40 minutes)*   The Brigham Development Company uses a voucher system which includes a
voucher register and a check register with the headings as shown in
Exhibits 13–5 and 13–10.

Aug.   3   Purchased merchandise from the Lackey-Bone Com-
           pany, with an invoice price of $1,000, terms 2/10, n/30.
       4   Purchased store supplies from the Johnston Company,
           $400, terms n/30.
       5   Bought gas and oil for the delivery truck from the Snead
           Company for $60, which was paid immediately.
      10   Paid the Lackey-Bone Company invoice of August 3, less
           discount.
      12   Purchased merchandise from the Lackey-Bone Com-
           pany $3,000, terms 3/10, n/60.
      14   Received an invoice from the KLRN radio station for
           advertising, $140, due September 1.
      15   Purchased a typewriter from the Acme Supply Company
           for $250, terms n/30.
      28   Paid KLRN radio station invoice of August 14.

Instructions
1. Enter the transactions into the registers, beginning voucher numbers with 5016 and check numbers with 4219.
2. Total the accounts payable columns from both journals and determine the amount of unpaid vouchers.
3. Prepare a list of unpaid vouchers to reconcile with the control
   balance as determined in part 2.

13–8   **Use of Fixed Asset Subsidiary** *(40 minutes)*   The Woolsey Company maintains a subsidiary ledger card for each fixed asset similar to the form shown in Exhibit 13–12.

July   9   Purchased an electric typewriter for the sales department, manufacturer's serial number 740–31A–2, from the Office Supply Company for $430. The asset will have a ten-year life and a salvage value of $30.

      17   Purchased an executive desk for the accounting department, serial number 321463, from the Wales Desk Company, for $620. The desk will have a ten-year life and a salvage value of $20.

      29   Purchased an electric calculator for the billing department, serial number AY346–13, from the Monroe Company, for $500. It will have a twelve-year life and a salvage value of $20.

Instructions
Insert the data for the three assets into subsidiary ledger cards. Begin the assets numbers with 376. The company uses a straight-line depreciation method.

Problems

13–9   **Design of a System** *(30 minutes)*   Troy Rayford owns a restaurant near a large university campus. He serves meals in the main dining area, has a cocktail lounge in an adjacent area, and has two private dining rooms for large groups and special meetings. An advance reservation is necessary for use of one of the private dining rooms, and all business is for cash except for recognized groups, meeting in the special rooms. These groups, such as the Lions Club, fraternity and sorority groups, or private parties sponsored by an individual well known to Mr. Rayford, are allowed thirty-day terms. Approximately four cooks, seven kitchen helpers, twelve waitresses, two bartenders, and three receptionist-cashiers are presently employed.

Instructions
Describe in detail how a system of internal control over cash receipts and disbursements could be constructed for the restaurant. The system should be designed so that it safeguards the company's assets and also provides adequate financial detail for administrative control. Care must be exercised to insure that the system is not overly elaborate.

13–10   **Control Over Merchandise** *(30 minutes)*   The manager of a summer resort hotel noticed after a few month's operations that the receipts of the cigar counter had been less than those in the corresponding periods of the previous seasons. The receipts from other hotel activities had not decreased, and upon investigation the following was found:

1. Four office employees were allowed to serve customers at the counter.
2. All sales were at the established unit selling prices.
3. All cash in excess of a $10 change fund, representing the day's receipts, was deposited with the main hotel cashier at the close of the day.
4. No stocks had been carried over at the counter from the previous season.
5. Cigars and cigarettes and candy were added to the counter from the general storeroom in full boxes and cartons as needed.
6. No inventory records were kept at the counter.

Instructions
1. Determine how you would find the amount of a shortage, if any.
2. Describe an adequate system of internal control. Set up weekly inventory.

13–11   **Bank Reconciliation** *(20 minutes)*   The Paprill Company reconciles its bank amount monthly. On August 31, the bank statement showed a balance of $7,832, and the company's books showed a balance of $7,096. A comparison of the detail of the bank statement and the general ledger revealed that a deposit of $489 had not yet reached the bank, and checks numbered 339 for $793, 362 for $195, and 387 for $702 had not yet reached the bank. In addition, the bank had made a $6 service charge and a $9 charge for printed checks which had not been entered in the general ledger, and check number 321 which cleared the bank was recorded as $387 in the general ledger, but was actually for $837. This check was a payroll tax check.

Instructions
Prepare a bank reconciliation.

13–12   **Bank Reconciliation** *(30 minutes)*   The bank statement of the Baker Company is shown on page 435, together with the cash receipts book, check register, and cash account. By tracing all checks written and recorded in the check register to those clearing the bank, the outstanding checks can be located. Deposits in transit can be found by tracing cash receipts in the books to the deposits on the bank statement. Other reconciling items such as errors in the books or bank service charges can also be located by the above procedures.

Cash

July 1	5,140	July 31	2,105
31	2,490		
Balance	5,525		

FIRST NATIONAL BANK		Baker Company 6108 South Street	
CHECKS CLEARED	DEPOSITS	DATE	BALANCE
		July 1 'X1	$5,140
$ 50		July 4 'X1	5,090
100	$800	July 6 'X1	5,790
20	420	July 9 'X1	6,190
940		July 11 'X1	5,250
10 (service charge)	510	July 17 'X1	5,750
60 120	190	July 20 'X1	5,760
	220	July 28 'X1	5,980
200		July 31 'X1	5,780

Check Register

Date	Payee	Check No.	Ac- counts Payable	Pur- chase Dis- counts	Cash
July 1	Smith and Company	7015	$ 20		$ 20
2	Able Stationers	7016	50		50
3	Triple X Company	7017	40		40
4	Wilson Company	7018	310		310
5	ABC Company	7019	100		100
10	Sam P. Wortham	7020	1,000	$60	940
14	Gardner Jones	7021	75		75
17	Lindley Company	7022	125	5	120
18	Contrable Company	7023	60		60
21	Lester Abbot	7024	300		300
30	Trable Company	7025	90		90
	Totals		$2,170	$65	$2,105

Cash Receipts Journal

Date	Payee	Sales	Accounts Receivable	Cash
July 5	Cash sales	$ 800		$ 800
8	Robert P. Marple		$ 420	420
17	Wilson Company		510	510
19	Cash sales	190		190
27	Cash sales	220		220
31	Samuel Barker		350	350
	Totals	$1,210	$1,280	$2,490

Instructions

Prepare a bank reconciliation from these data. Check #7024 was actually for $200 and was the last check which cleared the bank during the month. The check was for equipment repairs.

13–13 **Bank Reconciliation** *(30 minutes)* The bank reconciliation of the Trimble Company prepared by the company's accountant at the end of the prior month, March 31, is shown below. The company's check register, cash receipts journal, and the bank statement for April also appear below:

TRIMBLE COMPANY
Bank Reconciliation
March 31

Balance per bank statement		$425.80
Add: Deposits in transit		263.00
		$688.80
Less: Outstanding checks		
#31	$84.17	
#32	15.00	99.17
		$589.63

Bank Statement
April

April	Checks		Deposits	Balance
1		Balance forward		$ 425.80
5	$91.42		$263.00	
6	23.98		136.72	
10	84.17			
12	45.65		192.45	
13			198.00 CM	
15	61.06			
18	30.45		286.13	
20	56.67			
22	1.83 DM		112.11	
25	16.12			
26	84.54		172.80	
27	76.67			
28	41.50 NSF			
30	67.76			1,105.19

CM A note receivable was collected by the bank, $200.00, less a $2.00 collection fee ($198 CM on the bank statement).

DM Bank service charge.

NSF   Bob Brogan's check returned because of lack of funds. (Brogan is a customer.)

Check Register			
April	Ck. No.	Payee	Cash
1	33	Adel Co.	$ 45.65
4	34	Bake Co.	91.42
6	35	Cris Co.	23.98
8	36	Dead Co.	61.06
10	37	Excel Co.	30.45
16	38	Foil Co.	56.67
20	39	Gore Co.	16.12
24	40	Hare Co.	84.54
26	41	Iris Co.	76.67
27	42	Jack Co.	67.76
28	43	Kohn Co.	15.00
30	44	Lyon Co.	37.92
			$607.24

Cash Receipts	
April	Cash
5	$ 136.72
10	192.45
15	286.13
20	112.11
25	172.80
30	147.55
	$1,047.76

Add to books:
Collection of note
Less:
Fees
L C.
NSF

Deposit in Transit
3 outer checks

$1,

Cash in Bank

589.63	607.24
1,047.76	
1,637.39	

1637.39
607.24
1030.15

Instructions

From these documents prepare a bank reconciliation for April.

13–14   **Determine Cash Shortage With a Bank Reconciliation** (*30 minutes*)
The W. W. Demont Company has just discovered that one of its most trusted employees has been embezzling money from the company. The system of internal control was very weak, and the employee had been given authority to sign checks and also to reconcile the bank statement with the books. He had been writing unauthorized checks payable to himself and reporting incorrectly that the bank statement reconciled. You have been called in to determine

the amount of the employee's embezzlement. You find that the cash per bank figure is $7,692 and the cash per books figure is $10,432. Outstanding checks are the following:

No.	1152	$700
	1153	612
	1154	50
	1160	119
	1172	73
	1180	210

One deposit for $2,792 is in transit. The bank had charged the company with a $20 service charge for printing checks and this had not been entered on the books. The bank had also collected a $500 note for the company and deposited this to the company's account, but the company had not yet recorded the collection. In addition, check #1156 payable to the Young Company for office supplies had been erroneously recorded on the books as a $60 check when it was actually a $6 check and had cleared the bank as such.

Instructions

1. Determine the extent of the cash shortage by using a bank reconciliation work sheet. The reconciliation will not balance, and the difference will be the shortage.
2. What recommendation would you make that would prevent such shortages in the future?

Techniques of Voucher and Check Control *(60 minutes)*   The Yale Company uses a voucher register and check register with headings similar to those in the illustrations in this chapter. They also have a $200 petty cash fund maintained by the office manager. On January 1, the following vouchers are unpaid, all having been incurred for the purchase of merchandise:

Voucher Number	Payee	Amount
6005	ABC Company	$1,200
6016	Tanner Company	300
6017	Jack Trimble	705
Total unpaid vouchers		$2,205

Enter the unpaid vouchers in a form similar to Exhibit 13–10. The following transactions were completed during January:

Jan. 2 Purchased merchandise from the Noble Company for $600, terms 2/10, n/30.
    3 Purchased office supplies from the Jackson Company for $220. Payment is to be made immediately.
    5 Paid voucher number 6005 less a 2 percent discount.
    7 Wrote a check to a special payroll bank account to pay semimonthly salaries of $6,000.

8 Purchased store supplies from the Yarbrough Company for $190, terms n/30.

9 Paid voucher number 6016.

12 Reimbursed the petty cash fund. Paid petty cash vouchers were for:

Delivery expenses	$30
Store supplies	10
Purchases	20
Office supplies	12

(Use a single voucher for the reimbursement.)

12 Paid the Noble Company for voucher 6018.

18 Purchased merchandise from the Noble Company for $1,600, terms 2/10, n/30.

24 Repaired the delivery truck. The invoice (from the Taylor Company) for $60 was paid immediately.

30 Purchased merchandise from the McFarland Company for $290, terms 3/20, n/60.

31 Wrote a check to the special payroll bank account to pay semimonthly salaries of $5,800.

Instructions

1. Record the transactions for the month of January using forms similar to those in Exhibits 13–5 and 13–10. The first voucher number in January is 6018, and the first check number is 4813.
2. Total the vouchers payable columns of the voucher register and check register, and determine the amount of unpaid vouchers at the end of the month.
3. Prepare a schedule of unpaid vouchers, proving the total to the amount calculated in part 2.

13–16 **Control System for Fixed Assets** *(30 minutes)*   The Manor Electric Company has a large number of fixed assets which are used in its manufacturing operations and which are classified as electrical equipment. Many of these are small electronic testing equipment items that are relatively expensive. Several of these have disappeared recently, and no one knows who used them last or what they were last used for. Several employees have informed the president that the missing assets could have been scrapped, since they remembered seeing assets scrapped without any paper work being prepared. The president of the company has instructed that a complete physical inventory of all fixed assets be taken and complete data on each asset accumulated. The inventory is now finished.

By searching through old invoices, the cost of every asset was determined, and depreciation has been calculated to the present date on each item. The books show a balance in the equipment ledger account of $73,492, and the book figure of accumulated depreciation is $14,722. The physical inventory shows fixed assets on hand of $71,465, and the correctly computed depreciation is $13,528.

Instructions

(handwritten margin note: 73492 / 71,465 / 2,027 / 1,194 Depn)

How would you recommend that the facts disclosed by the physical inventory be treated from an accounting standpoint? What procedure should be instituted so that the company will know (1) what assets should be on hand, (2) who is responsible for a missing asset, and (3) whether scrapped assets are properly recorded?

(handwritten margin note: $833 loss)

13–17   **Control System for Purchase of Materials** *(45 minutes)*   The Dalton Manufacturing Company was formed by James Dalton in 1958, and the cash and vouchers payable system was installed at that time. Very few changes in the company's procedures have been instituted since 1958, and as a result the system is not designed for the company's present scope of operations. Approximately a million dollars is received and disbursed each year, and the company's average bank balance is $40,000. There are six persons in the accounting department, two in the purchasing department, and four in the administrative department.

(handwritten margin notes: (1) Record loss / Outsiders / OP / Fr. Acct. record / Should have name of person in custody & asset transfer form. / Must have authority to scrap it.)

When a foreman or department head needs an item, he tells the purchasing department manager in person or over the telephone. The purchasing department manager places an order for the needed item, sending one of the two copies of the purchase order to the supplier and keeping the other copy in his files. When the merchandise is received, the receiving dock personnel count and inspect it and send a single copy report of its acceptance to the manager of the purchasing department. The purchasing department manager also receives the invoice from the supplier. When the invoice and receiving report have both been received, the retained copy of the purchase order is attached by the purchasing department manager, and these three documents are sent to the accounting department for payment.

When the accounting department receives the three documents, a voucher is prepared. The voucher is then entered in the voucher register to record the materials bought and the liability to the supplier.

When the date of payment arrives, a check is prepared by the accounting department, and the check, with the voucher and the three related documents, is sent to the administrative vice-president for approval of the voucher and signing of the check. All the documents are returned exactly as received to the accounting department. The check is then entered in the check register and mailed to the supplier. Monthly bank reconcilations are also prepared in the accounting department.

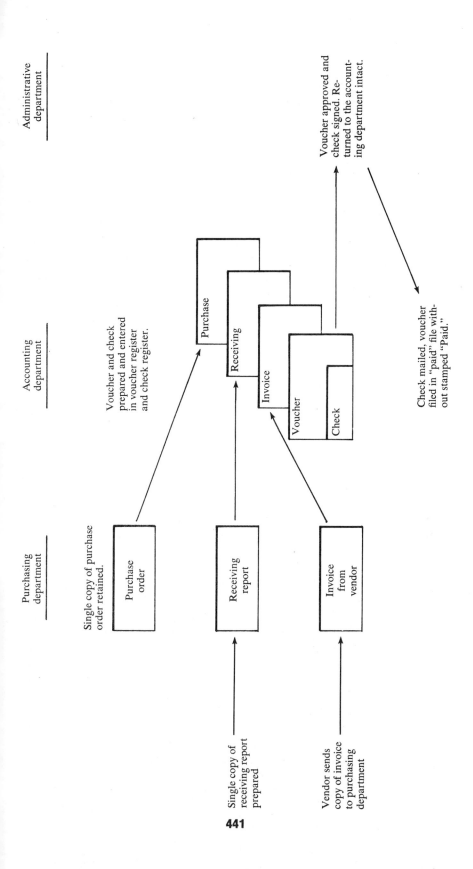

Purchasing department

Accounting department

Administrative department

Single copy of purchase order retained.

Purchase order

Voucher and check prepared and entered in voucher register and check register.

Purchase

Receiving

Invoice

Voucher

Check

Voucher approved and check signed. Returned to the accounting department intact.

Single copy of receiving report prepared

Receiving report

Check mailed, voucher filed in "paid" file without stamped "Paid."

Vendor sends copy of invoice to purchasing department

Invoice from vendor

Mr. Dalton has been very disturbed by the increasing amounts paid by the company for raw materials. Costs of raw material have increased as a percentage of the cost of goods sold as follows:

Year	Material Costs as a % of Cost of Goods Sold
19X1	32%
19X2	33
19X3	32
19X4	36
19X5	45

Mr. Dalton has reviewed the manufacturing process and concluded that the proportions of raw material used have not changed in the past five years. He has also reviewed the changes in market prices of the materials which the company uses and concluded that the increase in the company's costs from 32 percent to 45 percent in three years is higher than the price changes. He has become increasingly aware of the weaknesses in internal control in his organization and wants to strengthen them, especially since there may be some possibility of fictitious purchases of material.

Instructions
1. Diagnose the system of internal control and determine if it is possible for someone in the company to institute a fictitious materials purchase.
2. State how the system of internal control over purchases can be strengthened without the necessity of hiring new employees and by a rearrangement of the work flow.
3. Is the control over cash payments satisfactory? Is it possible that cash could be illegally extracted and the materials account increased in the accounting department? What recommendations would you make for better cash control?

13–18   **Control Over Scrap** *(30 minutes)*   In the course of its normal operations, the Midwest Products Company accumulates diversified scrap metals. The scrap consists of the usual odds and ends of pipe, wire and similar miscellaneous materials. All of this is dumped into a junk pile. In the past, when a quantity had been accumulated, several local scrap dealers were approached. When they saw what was available in the pile, they were not interested, saying that it would not be worth the trouble of picking it up.

One of the plant guards proposed that he rent a truck on his day off, pick up the scrap and take it to a small scrap dealer who would buy it, so long as it is delivered to him. Payment was to be at a flat price for each lot, set when delivery is made, not by weight or type of scrap. The guard proposed that the net proceeds then be divided equally between him and the company. As the company would benefit and had nothing to lose from the proposal, an arrangement was concluded on these terms. It was provided that the company's share be turned over by the guard to his supervisor, who in turn gave it to the plant cashier.

You have found that receipts from sale of scrap have been received at fairly regular intervals, in what would appear to be reasonable amounts. However, there has been a lapse of receipts during the past few months. You questioned the guard, who said that he has made several sales during the period and has turned the company's share over to his supervisor. You then saw the supervisor, who admitted receipt of the payments but stated that he has used the funds for purposes such as payment of temporary labor and minor supplies required in his work. The supervisor showed you evidence of some of these payments, but he has no record of amounts, nor has either the guard or the scrap dealer.

Instructions

Describe in detail a system of control over the sale of scrap, assuming the plant guard is to continue making scrap delivery, since it is the only way the company can sell the scrap.

PART 4

Applications of Cost Data

chapter 14

Analysis of
Costs and Revenues

**Learning
Objectives**

This chapter begins a new section of the text dealing with applications of cost and revenue data to specialized managerial decision-making areas. Upon completion of your study of this chapter you should:

1. Understand the cost and revenue concepts as applied to the decisions which management makes.
2. Be able to analyze cost and revenue data for make-or-buy, plant shut-downs, product discontinuance, and asset replacement decisions.
3. Recognize how irrelevant costs may be included in the analysis and will result in incorrect decisions.

**Role of
Cost Data**

The process of decision making was discussed early in Chapter 1 in order to provide a framework for the analysis techniques and processes to be discussed in subsequent chapters. At this point, specific areas of decision are discussed in more detail, and considerable emphasis will be given to the possibility of including irrelevant costs in the analysis. As described in Chapter 1, decision making is one of the basic functions of management. It is a continuous process, concerning such problems as what products to sell, the most efficient and in-expensive method of production, what duties to assign to employees, what quantities to produce or buy, where, how, and when to sell the company's products and at what prices. There are usually several possible courses of action in solving any given business problem. All pertinent cost and revenue data must be considered and comparisons must be made of the relative effects of each on the company's profits. The best course of action is usually the one that produces the greatest profit, considering the long-range objectives of the company.

Historical cost and expense information from a company's records serves only as a beginning point in analyzing any problem. Considerable care must be exercised in using historical cost and expense data, because succeeding events may make past data inapplicable. The solution to most business problems requires an estimate of the effect of future events on the company's costs and revenues, and historical data must be adjusted accordingly.

One of the most useful techniques in selecting a course of action is a comparison of the effects of each possible solution to a problem. Since maximum profit is one of the basic objectives of business, the course of action producing the greatest long-range increase in revenues, or decrease in costs, will probably be the best choice. The first step in selecting a course of action is to compute the *differential revenue* or the *differential cost*. These terms are used to designate the difference in revenue, or cost, among alternative choices. Suppose, for example, that a company has a limited amount of a new product and is able to supply only one market location. If data indicate the probability of $3,000 more in sales in the city of Flagstone than in the city of Genoa, this figure is the differential revenue between the two location choices. If selling expenses are expected to be $2,500 greater in Flagstone than in Genoa, this figure is the cost differential. The sum of the revenue and cost differential is the *profit differential,* which in this case indicates $500 more profit to the company if the product is marketed in the Flagstone territory.

There is no universal procedure in making an analysis of cost and revenue differences, but the following steps are generally applicable:

1. Clearly define the alternate courses of action.
2. Ascertain the costs or revenues pertinent to each.
3. Determine the extent to which each alternate course of action will affect revenues and costs.
4. Compare the revenue and cost changes to determine the differential cost, the differential revenue, and the sum of these two—the differential profit.
5. Assess the importance of these factors which cannot be assigned dollar values.
6. Select the course of action producing the greatest profit differential, taking into account the objectives of the company, the cost and revenue amounts, and the nonquantitative factors.

One of the most difficult of these steps is the determination of which costs or revenues will be affected by the change and to what extent they will be affected. The inclusion of irrelevant costs in the computations may very easily result in the selection of an unprofitable, or less profitable, course of action. Unfortunately, selection of the less desirable course of action may not become apparent for some time, if at all.

In a decision concerning whether to add a new product to the company's line, for example, the expected revenue in the form of dollar sales can be estimated, as well as the costs to make and sell the unit. Estimates can be made for the expected volume of units to be sold and for such related costs as an altered production schedule and an increase in the investment in inventory. However, there would be some effects of introducing the new product which cannot be subjected to dollar calculations, such as the effect upon the morale of the salesmen if they have to handle an additional product, the change which may occur in the company image in the eye of the customer, or the public's reaction to its introduction. These nonquantitative aspects may be minimal, as would be the case when a paint manufacturer introduces a new type of paint brush made of a foam material instead of bristles. The effects may be major, however, in the case of a manufacturer of food stuffs who begins to market a poisonous insecticide.

Cost and revenue data will always be an important part of most management decisions, but they are only the starting point. Quantitative data concerning costs and revenues are prerequisites to the assessment and evaluation of the nonquantitative aspects of a management problem. While this chapter discusses the more important quantitative factors, the importance of the other more qualitative elements must not be minimized.

Cost Concepts for Decision Making

The discussion in preceding chapters of this book has placed primary emphasis on the accumulation and analysis of *historical* costs. These costs are the result of events which occurred in a unique set of circumstances which may never occur again in exactly the same way. Thus, when historical data are applied in making a decision among alternate courses of action, such data must be adjusted to reflect anticipated future events which will occur in a different set of circumstances. A number of important cost concepts are employed in the blending of historical and projected data. Since many of these are anticipated future amounts, they are not found in the traditional balance sheet or income statement and must be calculated outside of the formal recordkeeping system.

Marginal Costs and Revenues

Marginal revenue is the revenue which will be realized from the sale of additional units; *marginal cost* is the added cost incurred in the production of additional units. The terms *marginal cost* and *differential cost* are sometimes used synonymously. The unit used to measure marginal cost or revenue may be one, one thousand, one carload, one half-dozen, or any other appropriate measure. If the company is able to sell 980 units for $1,000 and 990 units for $1,015, the marginal revenue of the ten additional units is $15.

Cost and revenue differences are constantly being computed and analyzed by management. The decision process is basically one of comparing alternate courses of action, and the marginal costs and revenues of each alternative must be projected. The cost of one type of new equipment may be $10,000, while another type will cost $12,000. The marginal, or differential cost, is $2,000. In this case, the $2,000 additional cost of the second type is also an *incremental cost,* because it is greater. Had it been lower, it could have been called a *decremental cost,* since this term is used for a difference which is negative, occurring when one alternative action costs less than another.

In specialized cases, the marginal cost to produce additional units will be the variable costs of production, but care must be exercised when the terms "variable cost" and "marginal cost" are equated, since they are not always synonomous. Marginal cost is measured between two explicit courses of action, while variable cost relates to a wide range of possible levels of production and includes those costs which normally move in relative proportion to volume changes. It is entirely possible that the marginal cost of producing additional units will necessitate some additional variable costs for material and labor and, in addition, will necessitate the acquisition of new equipment. The new equipment may result in additional fixed costs for depreciation, insurance, and taxes; consequently, the marginal cost of additional production may include more than those costs normally considered variable.

Relevant Costs and Revenue

Not all costs and revenues are relevant to every decision among alternate courses of action. The terms *relevant* and *irrelevant* cost are used to distinguish between those amounts which should and those which should not be applied to the solution of a particular problem.

To illustrate, assume that a company operates a fleet of trucks to transport its products and that management is analyzing the marginal costs to be incurred in operating the trucks for two additional hours each day. The drivers' salaries, gasoline, and truck repairs would be relevant costs in this case, since two hours of additional driving time will increase the amount of these costs. On the other hand, the cost of truck licenses and insurance would be irrelevant, for these costs will not change, regardless of the number of hours the trucks are used. However, the licenses and insurance would be relevant in the calculation of the cost differential between discontinuing use of the company's own trucks and employing a commercial transport company, for the license and truck insurance costs would not be incurred if commercial transport facilities were used. What constitutes a relevant cost in one situation may be irrelevant in another, and care must always be exercised to insure that the irrelevant costs are excluded. A knowledge of the particular situation, coupled with careful study of each cost element, will insure that only relevant costs are included in an analysis.

Opportunity Costs

An *opportunity cost* may be defined as a possible revenue which is sacrificed in order to achieve some other objective. In choosing one alternative, management must sometimes consider what could have been derived from the rejected alternative. The cost of a parking lot for employees, for example, will include the labor and materials to construct the facility and will also preclude the use of the land for another purpose. If the land could be leased to another company, the rental income which is given up would be an opportunity cost of constructing the parking lot. Funds invested in additional land to be held for expansion purposes, as another example, could have been invested in income-producing securities, had management so desired. The revenue which would have been received from the investments in income-producing properties represents the opportunity cost of acquiring and holding the property for expansion.

Although opportunity costs are not actually incurred, they are helpful in the selection of a course of action or in making a choice among alternatives. This type of cost never appears in the accounting records, but it is necessary for decision-making purposes and is frequently included in special cost analyses.

Sunk Costs

A *sunk cost* is a cost previously incurred which, within the context of the decision currently being considered, cannot be recaptured or decreased. Thus, by definition, a sunk cost will almost always be an irrelevant cost in a given decision. It may be either a variable or a fixed cost, the important point being that it has already been incurred and will neither affect nor be affected by the possible actions being considered. To illustrate, assume that a company has acquired a special machine at a cost of $10,000 and that it has no salvage value. If the machine is continued in use, its cost will be written off as depreciation; if it is scrapped, the cost will also be written off—in this case, as a loss on the disposition of fixed assets. Thus, the $10,000 is a future cost in any event and is considered irrelevant to the choice between continuing or discontinuing the manufacture of the product for which the machine was acquired. If the machine has a salvage value, however, this amount would be of interest in the analysis. Sunk costs include only nonrecapturable or nonalterable costs, and if some portion of the cost of the machine may be recovered as salvage value, that portion of the cost is not sunk.

Out-of-Pocket Costs

An *out-of-pocket cost* is one which requires a current outlay of resources. It may be a fixed cost or a variable cost, and it may be marginal or incremental, but so long as it will require a current utilization of working capital, it is an out-of-pocket cost.

This type of cost is important in choosing among alternate courses of action, especially when a company has a limited amount of available working capital. The cash flow required for various alternative solutions to a problem, including both outflows for equipment and expenses and inflows from revenues, should be carefully calculated so that the out-of-pocket requirements may be accurately judged.

Make or Buy Decisions

Frequently management must decide whether to make parts, materials, and equipment, or have them supplied from an outside source. Such decisions require special cost studies which are as important as any the managerial accountant must make. Even after the final decision has been reached, the cost to make as compared with the cost to buy from outside sources must be constantly reviewed in the light of changing production levels and methods, available working capital, and shifting competitive pressures. A make-or-buy decision is based upon a comparison of (1) the incremental costs to buy and (2) the incremental costs to make. If the parts or assets are bought from outside suppliers, the full purchase price will be their cost. If the parts are manufactured, the incremental cost to make them will include only the marginal costs which will be incurred in their manufacture. Thus, the full cost from an outside supplier must be matched with the marginal cost to manufacture.

To illustrate, assume that the Bolton Company is studying the feasibility of buying or making part No. 164–B1, used in the manufacture of their main product. Approximately 1,000 of these parts will be needed. This part could be bought from outside suppliers for $5.70 each. The company's cost accounting records show that the full unit cost to manufacture the part, computed with a job order costing system, has been as follows:

Direct cost		
Material	$2.42	
Labor (one hour)	1.87	
Depreciation on special equipment which was bought to make this part and which has no salvage value	.40	
Total direct costs		$4.69
Indirect cost		
Fixed manufacturing expenses, apportioned to all the company's products (supervision, insurance, and taxes on the factory buildings, etc.)	$ .94	
Variable manufacturing expenses, computed to be $.60 per direct labor hour	.60	
Total indirect costs		1.54
Total cost		$6.23

The decision should not be made by comparing the $5.70 outside purchase price with the total $6.23 unit cost to manufacture. Only the incremental costs, or those which would be incurred as a direct consequence of manufacturing the part, should be included for comparative purposes. The $6.23 total historical cost must be adjusted as follows:

Total historical cost to manufacture		$6.23
Less: Depreciation on special equipment, which has no salvage value and is therefore a sunk cost and irrelevant	$ .40	
Fixed manufacturing expenses which will not change, whether the part is made or bought, therefore irrelevant	.94	
Total deductions		1.34
Total incremental cost to manufacture		$4.89

The $.40 per unit depreciation cost for special equipment with no salvage value represents a sunk cost which will be incurred whether or not the part is manufactured. The general fixed manufacturing cost of $.94 would also be incurred whether or not the parts were manufactured. Consequently, only the $4.89 cost incurred as a consequence of manufacturing the part should be compared to the $5.70 cost of buying the unit from outside sources.

Cost if purchased	$5.70
Incremental or additional cost if manufactured	4.89
Savings if manufactured	$ .81 per unit

If the Bolton Company has the capacity available, it should manufacture the part, since the net savings or profit differential between the two choices is $.81 per unit. This $.81 is a contribution toward covering the company's fixed costs, which would be lost if the parts were purchased.

Additional Processing Decisions

Another problem necessitating an analysis of cost and revenue differences is whether to add further steps to the company's manufacturing process in order to make a more valuable product. The decision must be based on a comparison of the additional processing cost and the additional revenue which would be realized by having a better quality product or a different type of finished product.

Further processing will obviously require additional labor and overhead costs. In addition, the decision to process further necessitates the use of costs which are assumed, or *imputed*. An imputed cost is one that is not actually incurred and is more closely akin to an opportunity cost or an income given up. For example, if additional investment in equipment is needed for further processing, the funds required for the new equipment, if invested in other properties, would earn income. The income which these funds would earn if they were not sunk in additional equipment for further processing is an imputed cost which must be considered in the analysis.

To illustrate the analysis involved in additional processing decisions, assume that the Farley Manufacturing Company sells its product for $50 per unit as presently manufactured. If the unit is processed further—resulting in a better quality product—the sales price could be increased to $55 per unit. The revenue differential is thus $5 per unit. Assume further that the present sales volume of 10,000 units per year would not be affected by the proposed additional processing and the increase in price. Consequently, the total revenue differential is $50,000 (10,000 units at $5 each). Assume further that the following estimated annual costs would be incurred in the additional processing effort:

Additional labor, per year	$28,000
Additional variable manufacturing expense per year	8,000
Additional annual fixed manufacturing expense (depreciation on one new special-purpose fixed asset, cost $100,000, life ten years)	10,000
Total annual cost of further processing	$46,000

If the decision to process further involved only a comparison of the expected costs of $46,000 with the additional revenue of $50,000, it would appear that a profit of $4,000 would be realized by further processing. However, as indicated above, an investment in fixed assets of $100,000 is necessary to complete the additional processing. If this $100,000 could be invested in other income-producing properties that would yield a 6 percent return (or $6,000), the return from such investment would be more profitable, other things being equal, than investing it in equipment for further processing.

In the final analysis, the $50,000 additional revenue from further processing should be compared with the $52,000 actual and imputed costs to process further.

Actual costs to be incurred	$46,000
Imputed interest on the additional investment ($100,000 @ 6%)	6,000
Total additional costs to process further	$52,000
Incremental revenue	$50,000
Loss in profit (if further processing is undertaken instead of investing @ 6%)	$ (2,000)

With this analysis it becomes evident that further processing is not the best course of action and that, other factors being equal, the company's funds should be invested in other ventures.

Plant Shutdown

Sometimes a decision must be made between continuing operations at one of the company's plants, even though losses are being incurred, or ceasing operations and keeping the plant on a "stand-by" basis. There is always hope that the plant's profit picture will improve. However, an immediate decision is necessary concerning whether a smaller loss would be incurred by continuing operations or by temporarily closing the plant.

The losses on a shutdown basis will approximate the fixed costs. Since no operations are being performed, there will be no revenue and no variable costs; consequently, the fixed costs measure the extent of the loss incurred when the plant is shut down. Thus, as long as revenues exceed *variable* costs, the plant is realizing a contribution margin and is covering a portion of its fixed costs. If any contribution is made toward fixed costs by continuing operations, the plant should not be shut down.

The following case illustrates the differential analysis necessary in deciding between shutdown and continued operations at a loss. Assume that the Smith Company is presently selling 1,000 units per year, at $100 each, with annual fixed costs of $50,000, and variable costs of $80 per unit. Its present profit position would thus be:

Sales (1,000 units @ $100)	$100,000
Less: Variable costs (1,000 units @ $80)	(80,000)
Fixed costs	(50,000)
Net loss	$(30,000)

Temporary shutdown If the Smith Company were to shut down temporarily, but remain on a "standby" basis, it would cease to have revenue and would be able to discontinue its variable costs. The fixed costs would continue, however, and a net loss equal to their total of $50,000 would be incurred. On a temporary basis, then, the company should continue operations so long as revenues exceed variable costs, since the resulting contribution margin helps to cover the fixed costs.

Permanent shut down On a long-run basis, sale of the plant may be indicated if the sale price produces an inflow of cash in excess of the contribution margin which will be realized over the life of the assets. The above figures indicated a contribution margin of $20,000 per year, as the rearranged statement indicates:

Sales, 1,000 units at $100	$100,000
Less variable costs, 1,000 units @ $80	80,000
Contribution to fixed costs	$ 20,000
Less fixed costs	50,000
Net loss	$(30,000)

Suppose, for example, that the $50,000 of fixed costs are made up of $35,000 in depreciation and $15,000 in salaries. Suppose further that the prospect for improved performance in future years is poor and that the fixed assets can be sold for $120,000. The contribution margin of $20,000 per year will continue for the life of the asset, which is twenty years. The decision to discontinue operations permanently and to sell the assets should focus on whether the contribution toward depreciation is greater than the sale price of the assets.

Contribution to fixed costs per year	$ 20,000	
Fixed salaries	15,000	
Contribution toward depreciation per year	$ 5,000	
Total for twenty years	$100,000	

In this case, the $120,000 present market value of the assets is greater than the total $100,000 contribution toward depreciation over the twenty years of their life and other things being equal—the assets should be sold.

Note that the short-run decision to shut down or to continue operations was based on a comparison of the costs at shutdown with the contribution made toward total fixed costs. This was, of course, a short-run course of action. The decision to cease operations and sell the assets, however, was a long-run decision based on the difference between two ways of recapturing the cost of the assets: (1) through sale or (2) through contributions toward depreciation. Both are ways by which the investment in assets may be recovered, and—in this case—the sale price was the most advantageous course of action.

Discontinuing a Product

Dropping a particular product from a company's line is a difficult decision because it is impossible to foresee all the possible consequences. However, the basic approach to this problem begins with an analysis of the direct and indirect costs applicable to each product. Direct costs are those incurred specifically to sell that particular product, while indirect costs are not traceable to products. Direct and indirect costs should not be confused with variable and fixed costs, for a fixed cost may be either direct or indirect, and a direct cost may be either fixed or variable. The salary of a shoe clerk working for a department store may be considered fixed so long as shoes are sold, but is direct and would probably be terminated if shoes were no longer sold. Therefore, it is direct as well as fixed. Supplies, on the other hand, may be directly associated with departments but would be variable with sales.

Chapter 10, on distribution expenses, contains a discussion of which costs are direct and which are indirect. To illustrate the effects of indirect costs when making an analysis of whether to discontinue a product, however, consider the following case of a company which sells three products. The company's accountants have prepared a conventional income statement, with indirect costs prorated to products as follows:

	Product A	Product B	Product C	Total
Sales	$100,000	$60,000	$40,000	$200,000
Cost of goods sold	55,000	35,000	25,000	115,000
Gross profit	$ 45,000	$25,000	$15,000	$ 85,000
Selling and general expenses	40,000	24,000	18,000	82,000
Profit (loss)	$ 5,000	$ 1,000	$(3,000)	$ 3,000

This statement indicates that net losses are being incurred by Product C, while the other two products are profitable. Suppose, however, that both the cost of goods sold and the selling and general expenses were more fully analyzed, and the following breakdown of direct and indirect costs were determined:

	Product A	Product B	Product C	Total
Direct costs in cost of goods sold	$30,000	$25,000	$14,000	$ 69,000
Indirect costs in cost of goods sold				46,000
Total cost of goods sold				$115,000
Direct costs in selling and general expenses	25,000	15,000	8,000	$ 48,000
Indirect costs in selling and general expenses				34,000
Total selling and general expenses				$ 82,000

The indirect expenses are prorated in the conventional income statement and thereby tend to give an erroneous impression of the results of selling Product C. An income statement rearranged to reflect the contribution margin after direct costs expresses more clearly whether or not Product C is contributing to general indirect costs. Such a statement would appear as follows:

	Product A	Product B	Product C	Total
Sales	$100,000	$60,000	$40,000	$200,000
Total direct expenses	55,000	40,000	22,000	117,000
Contribution toward indirect costs	$ 45,000	$20,000	$18,000	$ 83,000
Total indirect costs				80,000
Net profit				$ 3,000

The contribution of Product C toward direct costs is almost as great as that made by Product B. Profits would decrease by $18,000 if Product C were dropped. The following income statement reflects the effect on profits if Product C were to be eliminated. Note that while indirect costs remain at $80,000, there is less contribution to cover them.

	Product A	Product B	Total
Sales	$100,000	$60,000	$160,000
Direct expenses	55,000	40,000	95,000
Contribution margin	$ 45,000	$20,000	$ 65,000
Total indirect costs			80,000
Total net loss			$ (15,000)

The company would incur a loss of $15,000 with Product C eliminated, instead of the $3,000 profit currently realized. The $18,000 difference between the $3,000 profit and the $15,000 loss is the contribution made by Product C toward indirect costs. In the absence of unusual market conditions, when a product covers its direct costs and contributes toward indirect costs, the company's profits will decrease if the product is discontinued.

An important assumption was made in the preceding analysis that indirect costs will not be reduced when Product C is eliminated. Some reduction in indirect costs will probably be realized, but the exact amount may be difficult to ascertain. Further, an assumption was made that no change would occur in the total sales of the other two products. A more complete analysis might include an estimate of these two changes if their amounts are subject to projection.

Asset Replacement Decisions

A differential analysis is frequently necessary in determining whether to replace an existing asset. Assuming that such an asset is essential to the operation of the business, the alternate choices are clearly (1) to retain the old asset, or (2) to buy a new one. However, determining the effects of each choice on costs and revenues is more difficult, and both historical data and future estimates must be included in the computations.

To illustrate the nature of such a decision, assume that a company's management is considering the replacement of one of its factory machines with a more efficient machine with the same remaining life as the old. If the machine currently in use is retained, management does not anticipate any appreciable change in its operating costs, which in past years have been as follows:

Two operators' wages, total	$14,000 per year
Related payroll taxes on operators' wages	840
Machinery maintenance	1,000
Power	500
Material spoilage	1,200
Total annual cost	$17,540

If the new machine is bought, management estimates that operating costs will decrease as follows:

One operator's wages, total	$ 8,000 per year
Related payroll taxes on operator's wages	480
Machinery maintenance	1,500
Power	1,000
Material spoilage	800
Total annual cost	$11,780

The *annual* cost differential, favoring the purchase of the new machine, is $5,760, computed by subtracting the $11,780 annual operating cost of the new machine from the $17,540 annual operating cost of the old machine. For purposes of simplification, if the life of both the assets is five years, the differential cost over the entire life of the machines would result in a total cost savings of $28,800 ($5,760 × five years) with the purchase of this new machine.

Following the determination of the differential in operating costs between the two machines, a second computation is necessary to ascertain whether this cost saving is sufficient to cover the purchase price of new equipment. Suppose, for example, that the new machine will cost $21,000. In this case, the company's profit would be increased by $7,800 and, other things being equal, the old asset should be replaced. This is illustrated in the following computation:

Five-year cost saving by using the new machine	$28,800
Cost of the new machine, with a five-year life	21,000
Increase in profits over five years	$ 7,800

In general, purchase of a new asset is indicated when the savings resulting from its acquisition exceed its purchase cost. Obviously, if the purchase price of the new asset exceeds potential savings, replacement would not be wise. Note, however, that the sunk cost of the old machine is irrelevant to the decision.

Use of net cost   In the above example the new asset was assumed to cost $21,000. This cost is the *net cost* of acquiring the new machine and would be computed as the list price of the new asset, less any trade-in value received for the old asset or any proceeds from its sale.

To illustrate, assume that the old asset has an undepreciated cost of $15,000, with a current trade-in value of $4,000 and that the new asset has a list price of $25,000. The net cost of $21,000 is computed by subtracting the trade-in value of $4,000 from the list price of $25,000. The net cost of the new machine must be used in the cost analysis, since the savings and the net cost of realizing these savings must be compared if a correct analysis is to be made.

Depreciation expense on both the old machine and the new is excluded in computing the cost savings; nor is a gain or loss on the trade or sale of the old asset considered in the computation (excluding income tax considerations). The depreciation expense and any loss on the trade, as such, should be considered irrelevant costs in this analysis.[1] The only relevant data are (1) the cost in dollars to buy the new machine, as compared with (2) the dollars in operating costs saved by the new machine. Note that neither depreciation nor loss on disposition of the old machine required an outflow of dollars; these two costs are therefore irrelevant to the analysis.

Exclusion of book losses   A book loss which requires no outlay of funds should not be included in the analysis. Inclusion of such a loss may lead to an incorrect decision. To continue the preceding example, assume that the old asset with a book value of $15,000, plus $21,000 cash, is traded for the

---

1. If discounted cash flow were applied to this example, the depreciation and gain or loss on disposition would, for income tax reasons, enter into the computations. This aspect is treated in another chapter.

new asset with a list price of $25,000. Thus, a book loss of $11,000 would be realized as follows:

Book value of old asset (undepreciated cost)	$15,000
Trade-in received	4,000
Book loss	$11,000

The $11,000 loss recorded when the trade is made must not be included in the analysis; if it is included, an incorrect decision to retain the old equipment may be reached. Such an *incorrect* analysis follows:

Incorrect Analysis

Five-year operating savings (from previous example)	$28,800
Less book loss on trade	11,000
Net savings	$17,800
Cost of new machine	21,000
Decrease in profits if the new machine is bought	$(3,200)

This computation is incorrect because of the inclusion of a non-fund loss in an analysis which is based on cash savings versus out-of-pocket costs. Depreciation expense on both the new and the old equipment was also excluded from the analysis, because it is a non-fund expense.

Income statement analysis   The increase in profits over the five-year period can also be calculated, using an income statement format over the life of the assets. Assuming that equal revenue totaling $120,000 over the five-year period would be produced by either machine, Exhibit 14–1 illustrates two income statements, one resulting from retention of the old asset and the other from purchase of the new asset. Note that depreciation expense and loss on the trade have been included in the income statements, even though they did not enter into the computations leading to the replacement decision.

EXHIBIT 14–1

Five-Year Income Statement If Old Asset Is Kept			Five-Year Income Statement If New Machine Is Acquired		
Sales		$120,000	Sales		$120,000
Expenses			Expenses		
$17,540 × 5 years	$87,700		$11,780 × 5 years	$58,900	
Depreciation on old machine	15,000	102,700	Depreciation on new machine	25,000	
			Loss on trade	11,000	94,900
Net income		$ 17,300	Net income		$ 25,100

The net income is $7,800 greater if the new machine is acquired ($25,100 less $17,300). Note that this is the same amount computed in the earlier example when depreciation and losses were *excluded* from the differential analysis. Had the loss on the trade been used in making the analysis, an entirely incorrect decision would have been reached.

Summary

The managerial decision-making process is complex and covers an almost infinite range of topics. Both historical cost and future cost estimates are involved in most analyses, and care must be exercised to insure that only relevant costs are included in an analysis. A number of concepts are applicable to the decision area, including differential costs, incremental costs, decremental costs, opportunity costs, sunk costs, out-of-pocket costs, and imputed costs. These costs are not identified as such in the accounting records and are cost concepts only as they relate to specific decisions.

A large number of the computations and special cost studies underlying managerial decisions require segregation of fixed and variable costs. Make-or-buy, plant shutdown, product discontinuance, and further processing problems are representative of those whose solution is based upon a variable cost analysis and calculation of the contribution toward covering fixed costs. The asset replacement decision is one of the most important which management must make. The cost of the old asset is a sunk cost, and its depreciation and any loss on its disposition are irrelevant to the analysis. Their inclusion may result in an incorrect decision.

New Terms

Book loss   Any loss which is recorded on the books.

Decremental cost   Any cost which is lower than the preceding cost.

Differential cost   A difference between two costs.

Historical cost   An actual cost incurred in the past.

Imputed cost   An assumed cost which will not actually be incurred, but which may be attributed to a given course of action.

Incremental cost   The additional cost of one alternative over another.

Marginal cost   The added cost for the next unit or units. Synonymous with differential cost and incremental cost.

Opportunity cost   A possible revenue which is given up for another course of action.

Out-of-pocket cost   A cost which must be paid for with an outlay of resources.

Sunk cost   A cost previously incurred which cannot be recaptured.

Questions

1. Define differential costs, differential revenue, and differential profit. Why are these terms of primary importance in problems concerning managerial decisions?

2. One factor which is considered in reaching most business decisions is the cost to be incurred. Why are costs from previous income statements not always applicable in reaching decisions affecting the future?

3. Is it possible that a decision which maximizes profit in the immediate future may be detrimental to the company's long-range future?

4. When a decision must be reached concerning the purchase of a new machine, is it generally true that the machine should be replaced if the cost of the new machine is less than the savings realized by its use?

5. If the answer to question four above is "yes," why is depreciation on the new machine not considered when the savings and cost are being compared?

6. What is an irrelevant cost? Can a cost be relevant to one decision but irrelevant to another?

7. What is a "make-or-buy" decision? Describe how incremental costs enter into such a decision.

8. What is an "additional processing" decisions? How do incremental costs and revenues enter into such decisions?

9. What is an imputed cost? Are these costs included in the traditional income statement?

10. Is the statement true that losses incurred on a "shutdown" basis are equal to the company's fixed costs? Explain.

11. When a decision is being considered relative to the discontinuance of one of a company's products, why must the variable (or incremental) costs incurred in the manufacture of that product be computed?

12. When reaching a decision relative to pricing "additional sales," how do incremental revenues and incremental costs enter into the decision?

Exercises

14–1   **Definitions** *(15 minutes)*   The following terms or concepts were introduced in this chapter:
a. Differential cost
b. Marginal cost
c. Relevant cost

d. Sunk cost
e. Opportunity cost
f. Historical cost
g. Imputed cost
h. Out-of-pocket costs

Instructions
Define each term or concept, giving examples where possible.

14–2   Make-or-Buy Decision *(10 minutes)*   ABC Corporation is currently purchasing an assembly part for $7.00. Estimated costs to manufacture the product, if the ABC Corporation decides to undertake the production of the part, are:

Estimated costs to manufacture:

Direct material	$2.00
Direct labor	3.20

Variable manufacturing costs are 100 percent of direct material. Fixed manufacturing costs are allocated at 25 percent of direct material.

Instructions
Prepare computations to indicate whether the part should be bought from the outside supplier or should be manufactured.

14–3   Make-or-Buy Decision *(15 minutes)*   A company uses a small one-sixth horsepower motor in one of its products. The motor can be acquired from an outside source at a cost of $5.75 each. The company's accountants have computed the following total costs to manufacture the motor:

Direct materials	$1.70
Direct labor	2.50
Variable manufacturing expenses (50% of labor)	1.25
Fixed manufacturing expenses (20% of labor)	.50
Total	$5.95

Instructions
1. Assuming that the company has sufficient manufacturing capacity, should the motor be bought or manufactured? Support your answer with computations.
2. Assuming that the company uses 10,000 motors per year, how much will be saved each year by manufacturing (or buying)?

14–4*   Additional Processing Decision *(15 minutes)*   A company presently sells its units for $12.00 each, and its average volume of sales is 100,000 units per year. The company's cost structure is $400,000 of fixed costs and variable costs of $4 per unit.

The company's market analysts have estimated that if the company adds a high-speed, three-way switch to the unit, it could be sold for $12.50. The number of units sold would not change. New equipment costing $100,000 with a five-year life and no salvage value must be acquired to manufacture the switch, and additional material and labor costs of $.25 per unit would be incurred in making and installing the switch.

The $100,000 for the necessary equipment must be borrowed from the bank at 6 percent interest.

Instructions

Would you recommend that the switch be added (excluding any market considerations)? Support your answer with computations. Would your answer differ if the company had sufficient funds and did not have to pay 6 percent interest for the $100,000?

14–5*   **Pricing Additional Business** *(20 minutes)*   The Fong Company produces a single product in large quantities. The company's fixed costs are $20,000 per year, and the variable costs are $2.00 per unit. In 19X1, production was 20,000 units, and the sales price was $3.50 per unit. The company's annual capacity is 40,000 units. There are no selling costs.

Instructions

1. Compute the average unit cost for 19X1.
2. Should the company accept a government contract in 19X2 for 10,000 units at a price of $2.40 each if nongovernment business is expected to remain the same as in 19X1? Support your answer with computations.
3. Prepare two income statements—one assuming the government contract is accepted and another assuming it is not.

14–6   **Discontinuing a Product** *(20 minutes)*   The Evertrue Manufacturing Company has three product lines: A, B, and C. The company's management requested an income statement by product lines and received the following:

| | Product | | | |
	A	B	C	Total
Sales	$400,000	$100,000	$300,000	$800,000
Cost of goods sold	250,000	60,000	200,000	510,000
Gross profit	$150,000	$ 40,000	$100,000	$290,000
Operating expenses	130,000	70,000	80,000	280,000
Net income (loss)	$ 20,000	($ 30,000)	$ 20,000	$ 10,000

The company's president and principal stockholder argued that such an analysis is misleading, and he requested further information about the company's operating expenses. He was given the following:

| | Product | | | |
	A	B	C	Total
Variable operating expenses	$110,000	$ 30,000	$ 50,000	$190,000
Total fixed operating expenses				90,000
Total				$280,000

Instructions

1. Prepare an income statement showing the contribution made by each product toward covering the company's fixed costs. Would you recommend discontinuance of Product B?
2. Prepare an income statement if Product B is discontinued, assuming no change in sales or cost of goods sold of the other products.

14–7   **Equipment Replacement** *(15 minutes)*   The ABC Company is considering buying a new machine for $15,000, which would replace a machine with a book value of $6,000, a remaining life of six years with no salvage value at that time. The replacement machine would have a life of six years and no salvage value. The old machine could be sold now for $2,000. Annual operating costs would be $16,000 with the old machine and $14,000 with the new machine.

Instructions
Prepare computations to indicate whether the new machine should be acquired.

14–8   **Equipment Replacement** *(25 minutes)*   The Henderson Manufacturing Company is considering buying a new machine for $14,000. The cost of operating the old machine is $15,000 per year, and the new machine can be operated for $12,000 per year. Both the old and new machines have remaining useful lives of five years. The old machine has an undepreciated cost of $10,000 and can be sold now for $1,000, and neither the old nor the new machine will have any salvage value at the end of five years.

Instructions

1. Assuming either machine will produce revenues of $100,000 over the next five years, would you buy the new machine? Show your computations to support your answer.
2. Prepare two income statements to reflect the results of operations for a five-year period if (a) the old machine is kept and (b) the new machine is bought.

Problems

14–9 **Make-or-Buy Decision** *(20 minutes)* The Cascade Company is presently making all parts for its product and at 100 percent capacity would use 7,000 units of Part 79C. The standard cost for the part is:

Raw Materials (6 units at $1)	$ 6.00
Labor (2 hours at $3.50)	7.00
Variable overhead ($1 per DLH)	2.00
Fixed overhead ($.50 per DLH, based on 100% capacity)	1.00
Total per unit cost of Part 79C	$16.00

The company is presently operating at 75 percent of capacity but continues to allocate fixed overhead at 100 percent, and as a result there is a large unfavorable volume variance at the end of each year.

An outside vendor approached the company and offered to manufacture the part for a price of $14 each. If the offer is accepted, the Cascade Company could dispose of equipment with an undepreciated cost of $30,000, receiving $20,000 in cash for the equipment. The equipment has five years of life remaining and no salvage value at the end of that time. In addition, the Cascade Company receives a quarterly discount on the purchase of raw material, and if part 79C is not manufactured, the cost of raw materials on all other parts will increase by one cent per unit. A total of 800,000 units of raw material is used each year in the manufacture of other parts.

Instructions
Prepare an analysis to indicate whether Part 79C should be manufactured by the Cascade Company or acquired from an outside manufacturer.

14–10 **Make-or-Buy Decision With Sunk Costs** *(25 minutes)* The Graff Corporation manufactures each year 1,000,000 units of a particular type of carton, which it uses as a container for one of its products. A special machine which two years ago cost $100,000 and has eight years of remaining life is used exclusively in the manufacture of the container. The machine can be sold now for $56,000 but will have no value at the end of eight years. The annual cost to manufacture these cartons is as follows:

Depreciation on the machine	$10,000
Labor and other variable costs	27,500
	$37,500

The company received a letter from another manufacturing company which contained an offer to manufacture the cartons for the Graff Company for $.032 each. The Graff Company reasoned that this would be a wise course of action, since they were presently costing $.0375 each.

Instructions
1. Present arguments and computations to indicate whether the company's analysis is correct. (Assume an eight-year period of time.)
2. Would your answer differ if the company did not own the machine, but leased it for an annual payment of $8,000?
3. What would your answer be if the machine were owned by the Graff Company but had a present resale value of $56,000?

14–11   **Make-or-Buy Decision** *(25 minutes)*   The Grand Company is presently making all parts for its product. It uses 10,000 units of part A which has a standard unit cost of:

Raw materials (2 units at $5)	$10.00
Labor (2 hours at $3.50/hour)	7.00
Variable overhead ($1 per direct labor hour)	2.00
Fixed overhead ($1.50 per direct labor hour)	3.00
Total per unit cost of part A	$22.00

An outside vendor approached the company and offered to manufacture part A for a price of $20 each. If the offer is accepted, Grand Company could dispose of equipment used to manufacture part A for $50,000 in cash.

In addition, Grand Company receives a volume discount on the purchase of raw materials; and, if part A is not manufactured, the cost of raw materials on all other parts will increase by $2.00 per unit. A total of 10,000 units of the raw materials is used each year in the manufacture of other parts. The equipment used to manufacture part A has a remaining useful life of ten years.

Instructions
Prepare an analysis to indicate whether part A should be manufactured by Grand Company or acquired from the outside vendor. Use a ten-year period of time.

14–12   **Additional Processing Decision** *(20 minutes)*   A company with an annual volume of 10,000 units per year sells its product for $20. The company's cost structure is $80,000 of fixed costs and variable costs of $3 per unit.

The company's management has decided that an additional part can be added to the unit, resulting in the sale of the same number of units at a price of $22. Special equipment would be needed, costing $120,000, with a ten-year life and no salvage value since its only use would be to manufacture the new part. Labor and materials for the new part would cost $.50 per unit.

Instructions
1. Prepare computations to indicate whether the new part should be added, assuming that the special machine would have to be financed with borrowed money costing 8 percent per annum.
2. Would your answer differ if the machine could be bought for cash without borrowing?

14–13   Additional Processing Costs at Different Volumes *(40 minutes)*
The Mayfield Company incurred the following costs when 10,000 units were produced and sold:

Direct labor	$25,000
Direct material	30,000
Variable manufacturing costs	40,000
Fixed manufacturing costs	20,000
Variable selling and administrative expenses	10,000
Fixed selling and administrative expenses	30,000

The company's units sell for $17.50 per unit. A notice was received that the state government was receiving bids on 3,000 units similar to those manufactured by the Mayfield Company. The state specifications required an extra part not usually installed on the company's unit. Making and installing this part would necessitate the purchase of a special machine at a cost of $5,000, and additional materials and labor costing $1 per unit. The machine would have no further use after the 3,000 special units were made, and it could then be sold for $2,000. Variable selling and administrative costs would apply to the 3,000 units if the company is awarded the contract.

Instructions
1. What is the lowest bid price per unit which could be quoted without a resulting reduction in present profits?
2. What is the price which should be bid to produce a profit of 10 percent of the sales price?
3. Prepare an income statement, assuming that the company manufactured and sold 10,000 units at their regular price of $17.50 and also received and completed the contract at a price of $13.50 per unit.

14–14   Effects on Profit When a Product Is Discontinued *(40 minutes)*
The Arrow Company manufactures and sells three products, with the per unit data shown on the following page applicable to each. The company's fixed costs are $100,000, and 4,000 economy units, 5,000 regular units, and 3,000 deluxe units are sold each year. A proposal is being considered by the company's management that would eliminate the economy unit from the company's line. Market research indicates that if the economy unit is discontinued, the sales of regular units will increase to 7,000 units, and the sale of deluxe

	Economy Unit	Regular Unit	De Luxe Unit
Sales price	$25.00	$40.00	$50.00
Direct material	$ 8.00	$13.00	$16.00
Direct labor	4.00	5.00	7.00
Variable manufacturing expenses	5.00	7.00	9.00
Variable selling and administrative expenses	3.00	4.00	5.00
Total	$20.00	$29.00	$37.00
Contribution to fixed costs	$ 5.00	$11.00	$13.00

units will increase to 4,000 units. Further, special equipment used only for the manufacture of the economy unit would be sold, so that total fixed costs (depreciation, insurance, and taxes on the equipment) would decrease by $5,000.

Instructions

1. Prepare an income statement assuming that all units are continued.
2. Prepare an income statement assuming that the economy unit is discontinued.
3. State whether you would recommend discontinuing the economy unit and describe the factors causing the profit differential between the income statements in parts 1 and 2.

14–15 **Maximizing Contribution With Constraints** *(40 minutes)* A company has three products, A, B, C, which have sales prices of $17, $16, and $10, and variable manufacturing overhead costs of $12, $12, and $6 per unit, respectively. The raw material costs $6 per unit, and the company's manufacturing process is such that either A or B is manufactured from the same raw material, each requiring one unit of the raw material. For each unit of either A or B manufactured, one unit of C emerges automatically and must be either sold or scrapped. The variable manufacturing costs of $6 per unit apply only to sold units of C, and there is no variable cost for those units scrapped. In addition, the demand for C is fixed, so that no more than 400 units can be sold each period. There are sufficient raw materials each period for the manufacture of 500 units of either A or B, or some combination of both and demand for the products is sufficient to sell all that can be produced.

Instructions

1. Compute the contribution toward the company's fixed costs if only A and C are manufactured.
2. Compute the contribution toward the company's fixed costs if only B and C are manufactured.

3. Assume that the production of C occurs only when B is manufactured. How should the units of raw materials be utilized in this case?

14–16   **Comprehensive Problem With Alternate Courses of Action** *(60 minutes)*   The Pringle Candy Company operates a chain of candy stores throughout several states. Each store manufactures and sells a special chocolate packaged in one-pound boxes. Mr. Pringle is president of the company and the only shareholder. He is particularly concerned about Store #8. This store, located in Dallas, was at one time one of the most profitable in the chain, but in recent years it has incurred losses. The volume of business has leveled, and the losses have been about the same for the past three years. Store #8 has its own candy-making equipment, which has an expected remaining life of fifteen years and undepreciated cost of $45,000. The store building is under lease for fifteen years and it has the capacity to accept additional business.

The operating results for the year ended December 31, 19X1, are shown below. (Inventories are negligible and may be ignored.) The year 19X1 is representative of the operations of Store #8 over the past several years. There appears to be little likelihood of increasing profits except by changing prices or expanding the market.

Sales (50,000 one-lb. boxes @ $1.50)		$75,000
Less: Direct candy-making wages		
(50,000 lbs. @ 30¢)	$15,000	
Manager's salary	7,500	
Two sales clerks' salaries (These two can		
handle any volume of sales.)	7,000	
Direct materials (50,000 lbs. @ 65¢)	32,500	
Candy boxes (50,000 @ 3¢)	1,500	
Rent	5,000	
Depreciation	3,100	
Insurance	1,000	
Maintenance	500	
Advertising	400	
Telephone	150	
Gas and electricity (primarily for		
candy-making)	600	
Allocated head office overhead	4,500	78,750
Net loss		$ 3,750

The telephone, manager's salary, sales salaries, advertising, maintenance, insurance, depreciation, and rent of Store #8 are fixed expenses. The company's head office is in Little Rock, and each year the total head office expenses are allocated equally to each store.

Mr. Pringle is currently attempting to reach a decision relative to Store #8. Any one or all of the following possibilities are available to him:

a. He has been offered $30,000 by a local businessman for the equipment and lease, which will be used so as not to compete with the Pringle Candy Company.
b. He can reduce the selling price of candy at Store #8 from $1.50 per lb. to $1.30 per lb. and thereby increase the number of boxes sold by 10,000 per year.
c. A candy distributor in Shreveport, Louisiana, has offered to buy 30,000 one-pound boxes of the candy each year for $1.10 per box, FOB Shreveport. Freight costs to Shreveport are $.04 per lb., and there is little likelihood that sales in Shreveport would affect the Pringle Candy Company's market.
d. An additional advertising expenditure of $6,000 will increase the sale of candy by 10,000 boxes.

Instructions
Would you recommend that the business be sold? If not, would you recommend that the regular sales price be reduced to $1.30, or that the candy be sold to the distributor at $1.10?

14–17   **Equipment Replacement** *(25 minutes)*   A company has an old machine which cost $100,000, has accumulated depreciation of $60,000, has a remaining life of four years, has a present salvage value of $20,000, and will have no salvage value at the end of four years. Its annual operating costs are $15,000.

A new special-purpose machine to replace the old one is being considered. It will cost $50,000, will have a four-year life with a $5,000 salvage value at the end of four years, and will cost $4,000 annually for operating costs.

Instructions
1. How much will the company's profits be changed over the four-year period if the new machine is acquired? Substantiate your answer with computations.
2. Assume either machine will produce exactly $100,000 of revenue over the four-year period. Prepare two income statements for the entire four-year period—(a) one assuming the old machine is kept, and (b) one assuming the new machine is acquired.

14–18   **Alternate Equipment Replacement Possibilities** *(20 minutes)*   The Lester Bakery has an oven which should be replaced because it is inadequate to meet the necessary volume of production. The old oven can be sold for $1,000 at the present time, and its operating costs are $19,000 per year. The company has narrowed prospective replacement ovens down to two choices:

Choice A: This oven has a ten-year life, will cost $20,000, and operating costs will be $16,000 per year.

Choice B: This oven has an eight-year life, will cost $29,000, and operating costs will be $14,000 per year.

Instructions

If both ovens have the same capacity and no salvage value at the end of their useful lives, which one would you recommend that the company buy?

14–19 **Equipment Replacement With Several Options** *(30 minutes)* The Omaha Sheet Metal Company is considering the replacement of an old machine. The old machine is adequate and is to be replaced only if the new machine is a good investment. Data relative to the old machine and two possible replacements are as follows:

	Old Machine	New Machine A	New Machine B
Cost	$80,000	$100,000	$110,000
Accumulated depreciation	$50,000		
Present market value	$ 1,000		
Remaining useful life	10 years	10 years	10 years
Salvage value at end of remaining useful life	$ 1,000	$ 1,000	$ 25,000
Annual operating costs	$21,000	$ 10,000	$ 12,000

Instructions

1. Would you replace the machine with a new one? If so, state which one and present computations in support of your decision.
2. If the company does not invest any funds unless the expected return is at least 10 percent, would you recommend that the machine be replaced? Compute the expected return by dividing the annual savings by the net cost of the machine.

14–20 **Equipment Replacement With Supporting Income Statements** *(30 minutes)*   A company is considering acquiring a new machine which has a list price of $106,000 and a life of ten years. The present machine has a remaining life of ten years and does an acceptable job but is slower and must be operated for two shifts to produce sufficient units. The annual cost of operating the old machine is $29,000 per year and the cost of operating the new machine would be $20,000. The old machine has an undepreciated cost on the books of $63,000 and could be sold at the present time for only $15,000. Neither of the machines would have any salvage value at the end of ten years.

Instructions
1. Prepare calculations to indicate whether you would acquire the new machine.
2. Assuming either machine would produce revenues of $400,000 over the next ten years, prepare two income statements to reflect the results of (a) keeping the old machine and (b) acquiring the new machine.

14–21   **Equipment Replacement With Supporting Income Statement** *(30 minutes)*   The management of Washing Machines, Incorporated, is searching for a new machine to speed up its production. One of the machines presently in use cost $30,000 and has a remaining life of five years. It has accumulated depreciation of $15,000 and can be sold or traded at this time for $4,000. At the end of its five years of remaining life, it will have no salvage value. A new machine which is being considered as a replacement for the present machine costs $40,000 and has an estimated life of ten years and no salvage value. The annual operating costs of the present machine and the proposed new machine are as follows:

	New Machine	Old Machine
Labor	$7,300	$11,240
Maintenance	2,000	4,000
Power	200	800
Taxes and insurance	200	400
	$9,700	$16,440

Instructions
1. Showing all computations clearly, prepare an analysis which indicates whether or not the new machine should be acquired.
2. Prepare two income statements, one to reflect the results of acquiring the new machine and the other to reflect the results of keeping the old machine. For these statements assume sales of $20,000 each year and no other costs, expenses, or losses except those related to the machines. Both the statements should cover a full five-year period beginning at the point of trade (or rejection of the trade). Assume that straight-line depreciation is used.
3. Reconcile any differences which may appear between your answer in parts 1 and 2 of this problem.

14–22   **Equipment Replacement With Incorrect Analysis** *(25 minutes)* The Nesford Company has a hydraulic press which cost $70,000 seven years ago. The machine had a twenty-year life, and the accumulated depreciation is now $24,500. The machine has a present market value of $20,000, and annual operating costs applicable to the machine are as follows:

Labor	$4,000
Materials spoilage	500
Power	1,000
Fixed and variable overhead,	
apportioned at 100% of labor	4,000
	$9,500

A machinery salesman approached the Nesford Company officials and explained that his company had developed a new semiautomatic machine which could reduce the company's operating labor by one-half. (The Nesford Company engineers agreed that labor costs would probably be reduced by 50 percent.) The new machine costs $90,000 and has a twenty-year life. The salesmen presented the following proof that his machine should be bought:

	Annual Operating Costs of New Machine		
Labor	$2,000		
Materials spoilage	400		
Power	800		
Fixed and variable overhead,			
apportioned at 100% of labor	2,000		
	$5,200		
Operating cost of old machine		$ 9,500	
Operating cost of new machine		5,200	
Annual savings			$ 4,300
Savings over 20 years (4,300×20)			$86,000
Price of new machine		$90,000	
Proceeds from sale of old machine		20,000	
Net cost			70,000
Savings by using new machine			$16,000

Instructions

Prepare a corrected analysis to support a decision to accept or reject the salesman's offer.

chapter 15

Cost Analysis
For Pricing

Pricing a company's products is a difficult and complex task which requires judgment, skill, and insight. Upon completion of your study of this chapter you should:

1. Appreciate the role which cost data have in the pricing decision.
2. Understand the marginal analysis approach to pricing.
3. Understand the nature and meaning of price-cost-profit graphs.
4. Be able to distinguish between and appreciate the nature of the full cost pricing technique and variable cost pricing.
5. Understand the problems and the suggested solutions involved in pricing joint products.

The Pricing
Decision

Establishment of sales prices for the company's products represents one of the most strategic decisions which management must make. Both the financial position and profitability of the company are directly dependent upon decisions in this area; for such decisions, once made and put into effect, are frequently difficult and costly to alter. A sales price set too high will reduce revenues below the optimum range, while a price set too low may increase the number of units sold but decrease the company's net income. Even after management realizes its error, there may be significant losses in attempting to change the pricing policy. Thus, the use of financial data in formulation of this decision is an important segment in the study of managerial accounting.

Selection of the price for a specific product should not be undertaken without consideration for the pricing of the company's other products. The company should have a pricing policy, applicable to the full line of products, which has been carefully considered and approved by management. In some companies, the pricing policy is established by the board of directors, and the operating executives determine individual prices within this board policy. However, in some companies prices are informally set—frequently without a clear policy to provide consistency and balance in the company's pricing structure. A company's pricing policy includes the basic philosophy as well as the methodology used in the establishment of its prices.

Maximizing the company's profits is not the only objective to be considered in establishing a pricing policy, although it is an important one. There are almost always a number of other considerations, and the exact weight given each would be included in the pricing policy. Some of the more important objectives, other than profits, are (1) rate of company growth, (2) national welfare, (3) share of the market, (4) steady employment for employees, and (5) compliance with governmental regulations. The pricing policy is a carefully considered combination of all these objectives, such that the achievement of each is maximized.

Were maximization of profits the sole consideration in the company's pricing policy, the needs of employees or community might be sacrificed for quick profits, or the requirements for national security and welfare might be ignored for personal gain. Businessmen, in general, recognize that objectives other than profit maximization must be considered, and our history contains many examples of the heavy weights given these objectives. During times of national emergency—such as World Wars I and II—and during recent years when inflationary pressures were strong, the federal government imposed price restrictions on almost every type of consumer product, thus insuring that all businesses would give adequate consideration to the national welfare. During these periods, price changes had to be approved by a federal agency established specifically for that purpose.

As has been repeatedly emphasized in earlier parts of this text, there are "figure" and "non-figure" aspects to every business problem. Those aspects which can be quantified may be reduced to specific amounts, but there will always be a number of considerations which cannot be quantified. This is particularly true of the pricing decision, for considerations such as the national interest or employee welfare usually cannot be quantified. For this reason, the emphasis in this chapter will be upon the profit maximization element of the pricing decision. It is important to keep in mind that after the price which will produce the maximum profit has been determined, it is then adjusted in subjective fashion to consider the nonquantitative aspects. Thus, pricing for profit maximization provides a starting point or foundation, without which management would not be able to consider adequately the other objectives included in the pricing policy.

Role of Cost in Pricing

There is an intuitively appealing connection between cost and sales price such that one may incorrectly be led to believe that the sales price of a product is a direct consequence of its cost. According to this concept, products with a higher production cost will always sell for more than those with lower costs, and vice versa. This, either fortunately or unfortunately, is not necessarily true. After ascertaining the cost to manufacture and sell a unit, a company does not always establish a selling price sufficiently high to cover those costs and realize a profit. There is some reason to believe that cost is as much a function of sales price as sales price is a function of cost. This is true because (1) price affects volume, which can cause lower or higher unit costs, and (2) a company can alter the cost of a product after ascertaining the sales price. Costs can be changed by the use of more- or less-expensive materials, elimination of expensive features, or reengineering of the product. In this way cost is brought into line with the selling price.

The sales price-cost relationship is so uncertain that it becomes almost circular, each element in turn affecting the other. These relationships may be summarized as follows:

1. Unit price affects the volume of units sold: high prices reduce volume, and low prices increase volume.
2. Unit price affects the total sales revenue, but not in relationship to volume changes: higher volume at lower prices does not necessarily produce more total revenue than a lower volume at a higher price.
3. Volume affects units costs directly: the allocation of fixed costs over a larger number of units will produce a lower unit cost, but the necessity of arbitrarily allocating such costs to all products manufactured gives rise to questions of accuracy and equity in unit cost data.

These relationships and cross-effects make pricing much more than a matter of computing "cost" and adding an amount for profit. The pricing decision is affected by cost data to a large extent, but judgment and nonquantitative elements exert a significant influence.

The Economics of Pricing

The theory of pricing has received considerable attention by economists for centuries, and a major portion of our present microeconomic theory deals with pricing. While this body of theory is rarely applied directly by executives in reaching a pricing decision, it is of value in understanding the general problem of price determination. The traditional economic model consists of calculating marginal cost and marginal revenue and determining from these the price which will produce the maximum profit. The steps in this type of analysis are as follows:

1. Calculate the total revenues expected from the feasible range of prices.
2. Calculate the total costs to be incurred for this same feasible range.
3. Calculate the unit marginal revenue and unit marginal costs for each step in the feasible range.
4. Plot the marginal revenues and costs; the point at which they are equal will be the optimum price for that product.

Revenue functions   The revenue function of a product represents the relationship between price and volume. If the total revenue expected to be realized at various possible unit prices is plotted on a graph—with total dollars on the Y axis and the individual prices on the X axis—the resulting line would represent the *revenue function* of that product. To illustrate, assume that a new product is projected to sell as follows in the price range from $0 to $8 per unit:

EXHIBIT 15–1

Revenue Function

If the price is	Expected unit sales will be	Total revenue will be
$8	800	$ 6,400
7	2,000	14,000
6	3,400	20,400
5	4,900	24,500
4	7,000	28,000
3	9,000	27,000
2	12,500	25,000
1	17,000	17,000
0	Infinite	0

Note that the total revenue is a result of both quantity sold and sales price. The lowest price does not always produce the greatest total revenue, nor does the highest price. Exhibits 15–1 and 15–2 reflect the revenue function in table and in graphic form. Exhibit 15–1 shows the total revenue in table form and Exhibit 15–2 shows the unit marginal revenue function. Both illustrations emphasize the fact that in this case total revenue increases with each price decrease to a peak of approximately $4 per unit and then declines as prices continue to drop.

Cost functions   The cost function of a product represents the relationship between total cost and the volume of units sold. Continuing the example used in the preceding discussion on revenue functions, assume that the company has $10,000 of fixed costs and that variable costs are $1.00 per unit. The total costs incurred at the various volume levels would then be as follows:

Price	Units Sold	Fixed Costs	Variable Costs	Total Costs
$8	800	$10,000	$ 800	$10,800
7	2,000	10,000	2,000	12,000
6	3,400	10,000	3,400	13,400
5	4,900	10,000	4,900	14,900
4	7,000	10,000	7,000	17,000
3	9,000	10,000	9,000	19,000
2	12,500	10,000	12,500	22,500
1	17,000	10,000	17,000	27,000
0	Infinite	10,000	Infinite	Infinite

Note that the total cost increases as the unit price decreases, since more units will be sold at the lower price levels. Also note that the total cost is very close to the fixed cost when prices are at the high extremes, since very few units are sold.

Marginal revenues and costs   Marginal revenues are computed by calculating the differences between the revenue realized at one price level and those which would be realized at the next price level. Marginal costs are computed the same way. The table on page 480 illustrates the calculation of marginal revenues and costs, using amounts from the cost and revenue table shown previously.

Note that the marginal revenues in column (5) decrease steadily in this case, reaching negative amounts after a price of approximately $4.00 is exceeded. The total marginal costs in column (7) continue to increase as prices decrease, because variable costs go up as volume increases. However, the *unit marginal cost* is equal to the variable cost of $1 per unit.

Equating marginal revenues and costs   Note that marginal costs and revenues are calculated on a unit basis in the two columns at the right of the marginal cost table. As the price is decreased, additional units are sold and the unit marginal revenue can be computed by dividing the change in the number of units sold by the change in the total revenue realized. The unit marginal cost is computed by dividing the change in the number of units sold by the change in the total cost which will be incurred. The unit marginal revenue and unit marginal cost amounts in the preceding example are plotted in Exhibit 15–2. Note that unit marginal revenues decrease until they become negative, while unit marginal costs are always equal to the per unit variable costs, which in this illustration are $1 per unit. Economists maintain that the unit marginal cost line is bowl-shaped, increasing at high volumes and at low volumes due to diseconomies of scale. In this example, however, the variable costs are assumed to be consistent at all ranges.

The cost and revenue lines cross at a price of approximately $4.00. This point indicates the price at which the next unit will result in a lower marginal revenue than its marginal cost. Thus, the company's profits will be maximized

Calculation of Marginal Revenue and Marginal Cost

(1) Price	(2) Units Sold	(3) Marginal Units Sold	(4) Total Revenue	(5) Marginal Revenue	(6) Total Cost	(7) Marginal Cost	(5) ÷ (3) Unit Marginal Revenue	(7) ÷ (3) Unit Marginal Cost
$8	800	—	$ 6,400	—	$10,800	—	—	—
7	2,000	1,200	14,000	$ 7,600	12,000	$1,200	$6.33	$1.00
6	3,400	1,400	20,400	6,400	13,400	1,400	4.57	1.00
5	4,900	1,500	24,500	4,100	14,900	1,500	2.73	1.00
4	7,000	2,100	28,000	3,500	17,000	2,100	1.67	1.00
3	9,000	2,000	27,000	(1,000)	19,000	2,000	(.50)	1.00
2	12,500	3,500	25,000	(2,000)	22,500	3,500	(.57)	1.00
1	17,000	4,500	17,000	(8,000)	27,000	4,500	(1.78)	1.00
0	Infinite	—	—	—	Infinite	—	—	—

EXHIBIT 15–2

Unit Marginal Revenue and Costs

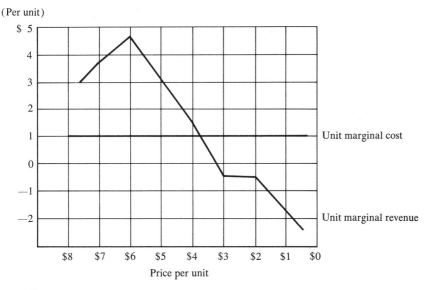

(Per unit)

at the $4.00 price, since all units sold up to this point have more marginal revenue than marginal cost.

Conceptually, such a marginal analysis is based on the assumption that as long as a particular price produces a volume of sales that creates less additional (marginal) cost than additional (marginal) revenue, the price should be increased to that point. At the point where the price increase produces less marginal revenue than marginal cost, no further price increase should be considered. Since the two unit marginal lines cross at the point where marginal revenue and marginal cost equate, that point indicates the optimal price. The $3.00 price, for example, produces $1,000 less marginal revenue and $2,000 more marginal cost than the $4.00 price. Thus, a decrease in price to $3.00 would decrease the company's profits by $3,000 and—other things being equal —would not be the optimum price.

Total Price—Total Cost Graphs

The traditional marginal analysis as presented indicates only the optimal price; it does not indicate the relative profitability of the several feasible prices, nor does it indicate the range of prices which would produce a profit. Use of total revenue and total cost instead of unit marginal amounts overcomes these limitations and is thus more useful to executives in the pricing decisions which they must make. The data used in the previous discussion on marginal analysis, which is the traditional economic approach, have been recast in the accompanying table and in Exhibit 15–3. These data are presented to illustrate the additional information provided by relating total cost and revenue instead of marginal amounts.

Price	Total Revenue	Total Cost	Profit (or Loss)
$8	$ 6,400	$10,800	$ (4,400)
7	14,000	12,000	(2,000)
6	20,400	13,400	7,000
5	24,500	14,900	9,600
4	28,000	17,000	11,000
3	27,000	19,000	8,000
2	25,000	22,500	2,500
1	17,000	27,000	(10,000)
0	—	Infinite	—

The profitable price range extends from a price of $6.00 to a price of $20.00, with the maximum profit falling at approximately $4. Further, the decrease in profits as the price is increased beyond $4.00 to $5.00 and $6.00 is slight, with profits falling not too far below those received at the optimum $4.00 price. Thus, with this type of analysis, management is provided information about the relative profitability of the several feasible prices. Such considerations as share of market, consumer satisfaction, corporate image, and community service may then be used to establish the final selling price.

EXHIBIT 15–3
Total Price—Cost Graph

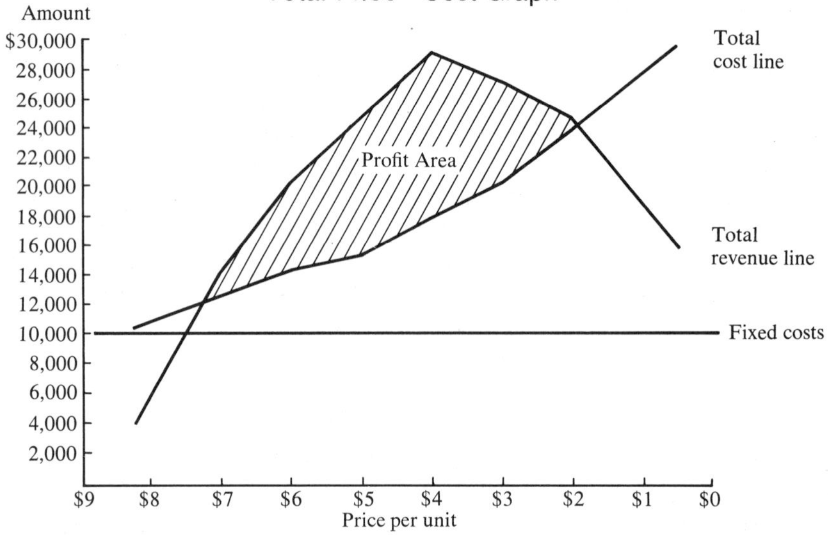

Full-Cost Pricing

The preceding discussion has been based upon two very important assumptions. The first is that the number of units which will be sold at each price level is ascertainable with an acceptable degree of accuracy. The second is that the "cost" of each product can be known with a reasonable degree of accuracy. The first assumption depends upon the ability of management to "read the market" and is beyond the scope of this text. The second assumption, which is concerned with the determination of a unit's "cost," is one of the most significant topics discussed in this text. Most of the chapters to this point have stressed the difficulty of assigning indirect and overhead costs to products when more than one product is manufactured or sold. Indeed, it can be said that there is no such thing as the "true cost" of a unit. There are many ways of assigning indirect costs to units, with widely varying results, and what constitutes a given product's fair share of these indirect costs is subject to considerable debate.

For long-range profitability, each product must have a price sufficiently high to cover its variable costs plus a "fair share" of the company's fixed costs. When more than one product is sold, the central problem thus focuses on the question of what constitutes a "fair share." One pricing method is called *full-cost pricing* because the price is determined by first computing a "full cost" for that unit. "Full-cost" in this context is synonymous with "full absorption" costing, wherein all indirect costs are allocated or assigned to units through application and allocation processes. The sales price is calculated by adding together the variable costs of the product, a prorated portion of the company's fixed costs, and a final percentage of the total for profit. The profit percentage may range from 3 percent or 4 percent of the direct and allocated costs in some high-volume industries to more than 20 percent or 30 percent in others. The full-cost method is illustrated in Exhibit 15–4. Note that allocations are an important part of this method and that a "20 percent of cost" pricing formula is used.

The full-cost pricing technique is relatively simple in concept but is difficult to apply in actual practice, primarily because of the difficulties of allocating the fixed overhead. In Exhibit 15–4, for example, the allocated manufacturing overhead was arbitrarily set at $5, $4, and $8, for the company's three products, respectively. There is no direct association, in most cases, between the company's several products and the incurrence of fixed manufacturing overhead costs. Even though the total fixed and variable costs of the company can be

EXHIBIT 15–4

Full-Cost Pricing Method Illustrated

	Product A	Product B	Product C
Direct materials, per unit	$ 6.00	$ 1.00	$ 4.00
Direct labor, per unit	7.00	3.00	1.00
Total variable costs	$13.00	$ 4.00	$ 5.00
Allocated manufacturing overhead	5.00	4.00	8.00
Allocated general expenses	7.00	2.00	7.00
Total costs	$25.00	$10.00	$20.00
Profit margin (20% of cost)	5.00	2.00	4.00
Proposed selling price	$30.00	$12.00	$24.00

computed precisely, there is no exact method for allocating the indirect costs to products, and the method is in most cases arbitrarily selected.

To illustrate the assumptions underlying the allocation of fixed costs to arrive at a full-cost figure for pricing purposes, assume that a company has $100,000 of fixed overhead costs. Assume further that there are three products, A, B, and C, over which the fixed costs must be spread. The first step in the allocation process would be to estimate the number of units which will be sold, so that the $100,000 can be allocated to these units. However, the number of units which can be sold is dependent upon the price at which they will be placed on the market. Thus, cost and price are both cause and effect: if the price is low, the number sold will be high, resulting in a low cost per unit; if the price is high, the number of units sold will be low, and the unit cost will be high. Thus, when many products are sold, the allocation of fixed overhead can be no more than an approximation, subject to considerable error.

One possible approach to the allocation problem is illustrated in Exhibit 15–5. An estimate of the value of the product to the company is used as the basis for proration; this estimate may be based upon the importance of the products in holding customers, in utilizing raw materials, or in any number of similar factors. Its arbitrary nature, however, is readily apparent.

EXHIBIT 15–5

Computation of Overhead Allocation To Products

	Product A	Product B	Product C
Estimated value of the product to the company (arbitrarily set)	3/5	1/5	1/5
Allocation of the total $100,000 based upon overall value	$60,000	$20,000	$20,000
Units expected to be sold	20,000	10,000	5,000
Per unit fixed costs	$3	$2	$4

Note that an estimate of the number of units expected to be sold was necessary before the allocation could be completed. It is important to recognize that realization of the total profit expected for the company is directly dependent upon achieving the sales volume used in making the computations. For example, if the sales volumes of 20,000, 10,000, and 5,000 units shown in Exhibit 15–5 are not achieved, the fixed cost per unit will be greater than the $3, $2, and $4 used in the pricing formula. If only 15,000 units of A are sold instead of the projected 20,000, for example, the fixed cost will be $4 instead of $3. This reduces the profit realized on each unit by $1, and the intended 20 percent profit margin will not be achieved.

In summary, full-cost pricing is based upon a computation of the product's full cost, which has inherent limitations. Selection of a volume for overhead allocation purposes is necessary, and yet this volume is eventually dependent upon the final selected sales price. Thus, the price-volume-cost relationships react upon each other, making full-cost computations in most cases a matter of arriving at a projected price-cost relationship which appears reasonable but which is recognized as being less than 100 percent accurate.

Pricing Joint Products

In many industries the processing of raw materials is such that two or more products emerge automatically from the same materials. In the meat-packing industry, for example, production of T-bone steaks is hardly possible without production of other meats, hides, and by-products. Petroleum refining companies, as another example, find that in addition to gasoline, it is economically feasible to produce kerosene, fuel oils, petrolatum, and lubricating oils at the same time.

Where joint- and by-products emerge, the computation of the "cost" of each product becomes more complex, for fewer costs can be directly associated with specific products. In such cases cost is computed by first segregating the raw materials and other processing costs incurred prior to the point at which a product emerges and becomes separated from the other products. These joint costs are then allocated to all the products which are produced from the common raw material. Such an allocation may be calculated using as a base (1) a ratio of the number of units produced by the common raw material, (2) a ratio of the market value of the products, or (3) a ratio of the relative effort necessary to produce a completed marketable product.

Units of production method   To illustrate the costing of joint products, assume that a company has three products, A, B, and C, which emerge from a single raw material. Exhibit 15–6 illustrates the production flow, wherein A and B require further processing but C does not. Three separate departments are utilized in the manufacturing process: Department 1 for the common raw material from which the three products are made; Department 2 for Product A after it emerges; and Department 3 for Product B. The third product, C, is completed as soon as it emerges from Department 1.

EXHIBIT 15–6

Joint-Product Processing

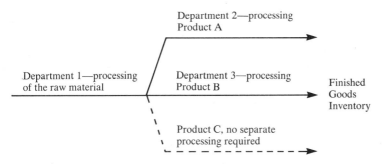

Assume that during the month of March the costs shown below were incurred in the manufacturing process.

	Department 1	Department 2	Department 3
Raw materials	$30,000	$ 5,000	$12,000
Labor	10,000	2,000	9,000
Overhead	15,000	11,500	2,100
Total	$55,000	$18,500	$23,100

Production during the period was:

Product A	55,000 units
Product B	30,000 units
Product C	15,000 units
Total	100,000 units

Assume further that the costs prior to the point of split-off are to be allocated to production on a per unit basis. This allocation method assumes that each unit of a product is equal to a unit of all the other products, and the $55,000 costs of Department 1, which were incurred prior to the separation of the three products, would be allocated as follows:

$$\frac{\text{Costs prior to split-off}}{\text{(Department 1)}} \div \frac{\text{Total units}}{\text{produced}} = \frac{\text{Unit cost prior to}}{\text{split-off}}$$

$$\frac{\$55,000}{} \div \frac{100,000}{} = \frac{\$0.55}{}$$

Allocated to:	A	55,000 units × $0.55 =	$30,250
	B	30,000 units × $0.55 =	16,500
	C	15,000 units × $0.55 =	8,250
		Total	$55,000

The final costing of the three products would then be completed by adding the additional costs incurred in Department 2 and Department 3 to the products which those departments produced. The following schedule shows this computation which, with a 20 percent profit factor, provides a basis for calculating a selling price based on "full cost."

	Product A	Product B	Product C
Common costs prior to split-off	$30,250	$16,500	$ 8,250
Further processing costs:			
Department 2	18,500		
Department 3		23,100	
Total cost	$48,750	$39,600	$ 8,250
Units produced	55,000	30,000	15,000
Unit cost	$ 0.886	$ 1.320	$ 0.550
Profit at 20% of cost	.177	.264	.110
Selling price (rounded to the nearest $0.05)	$ 1.95	$ 1.60	$ 0.65

That the sales prices as computed by this method are somewhat arbitrary is readily apparent. One unit of C receives as much cost prior to split-off as a unit of B, although B has a much higher sales price. Further, a much higher portion of the company's efforts go into Product B, assuming the incurrence of costs after split-off are any indication of effort expended.

Relative market value method   Another method of allocating joint costs is based upon the relative market value of the products. When this procedure is used, the value of the three products in terms of their total sales value would be used to determine the allocation ratio. Suppose, for example, that the products will probably have a selling price approximately as follows:

Product	Sales Price
A	$1.00
B	2.00
C	0.60

The relative sales value of the three products is the result of multiplying the units produced by their selling price, and these amounts become the basis for allocating the joint costs. The complete calculation is shown below.

Product	Units of Production	Price	Relative Sales Value	Percent of Total Sales Value	Joint Cost Allocation
A	55,000	$1.00	$ 55,000	44.4%	$24,420
B	30,000	$2.00	60,000	48.4%	$26,620
C	15,000	$0.60	9,000	7.2%	$ 3,960
			$124,000	100.00%	$55,000

This calculation assigns a portion of the joint cost to the three products based upon their value in the market place. The full cost of each unit would be the allocated cost plus the additional processing costs, as follows:

	A	B	C
Costs prior to split-off	$24,420	$26,620	$3,960
Additional processing costs	18,500	23,100	—
Total costs	$42,920	$49,720	$3,960
Unit cost	$ 0.780	$ 1.657	$0.264

Note that when the relative sales value method is used, the cost of the product is determined by its market value, and the traditional economic approach using marginal revenue and cost cannot be applied. In some cases, this method produces widely varying profit percentages, because some products require additional processing after the split-off point. Note that the variance in profit expressed as a percentage of sales for the three products in the preceding example ranges from 17 percent for Product B to 57 percent for Product C.

Product	Unit Sales Price	Unit Cost	Unit Profit	Profit as a Percentage of Sales
A	$1.00	$0.780	$0.220	22%
B	$2.00	$1.657	$0.343	17%
C	$0.60	$0.264	$0.336	57%

Variable-Cost Pricing

The full-cost pricing method described previously necessitates an allocation of fixed costs. In order to eliminate this troublesome problem, a calculation using only direct costs may be used. This type of pricing is called variable-cost or marginal-cost pricing, since only variable costs are included in the computation. When this method is used, the profit percentage, or mark-up, must be higher than that which would be used for a full-cost pricing method. The higher percentage of mark-up is required to cover the fixed costs which are not included in the computation.

To illustrate this method, assume that a company has $100,000 of fixed costs and manufactures several products. One of its products has variable costs of $8 per unit, and its sales are expected to total 10,000 units. If a full-cost method is used, a profit percentage is applied to the total costs assigned to the product, including overhead; the variable cost method applies a higher profit percentage, but includes only the variable costs. The full-cost method is contrasted with the variable costing method below.

	Full-Cost Pricing Method	Variable-Cost Pricing Method
Variable costs, per unit	$20	$20
Fixed costs, (75% of variable costs	15	—
Pricing base	35	20
Mark-up	15	30
Sales price	$50	$50

Note that the $20 variable cost is the base for pricing when the variable-cost method is used, and that the mark-up is 150 percent of variable cost. The 150 percent price policy must be sufficient to cover the fixed costs, which were not included in the base, plus some remainder for profit.

The mark-up percentage used for the full-cost method is 30 percent of total cost. However, the pricing base is higher because fixed costs have been allocated to each product; so that, for this illustration, the same sales price is established. The central point is that variable costing methods do not attempt to allocate fixed costs, eliminating the necessity to do so by using a higher percentage of mark-up. However, even this simplification does not eliminate the uncertainties of pricing a particular product.

Pricing Additional Business

Sometimes a company will receive a request to fill an unusually large order at a discount price or will submit a bid on a large order. If the company has idle productive capacity, a decision must be reached concerning whether or not the order would be profitable. There are sometimes marketing and regulatory problems involved, such as the effect on existing customers if they learn that the company is selling to others at lower prices. These marketing problems are beyond the scope of this text. However, there are certain cost analysis problems inherent in such decisions.

Generally, increased sales volume will be profitable whenever the incremental revenue received exceeds the incremental costs. To illustrate, assume that the Carlson Container Corporation's accountants have developed the following full cost for container No. 167:

Direct materials	$.07
Direct labor	.05
Variable manufacturing expenses	.04
Allocated fixed manufacturing expenses	.08
Total	$.24

The container is normally sold for $.35. A distributor in Mexico, where the Carlson Container Corporation does not normally market its products, has offered to buy 10,000 containers exactly like No. 167 for $.20 each. Assuming sales to this customer would have no effect on the company's existing market and no governmental regulations concerning fair trade were violated, should the offer of $.20 per container be accepted?

Fixed costs should not be included in the per unit amount when the differential costs are analyzed for this purpose. The fixed costs of $.08 per unit should be subtracted from the full-cost of $.24, leaving an incremental cost of $.16 to produce the additional containers. The company would thus realize a contribution margin of $.04 per unit on the proposed sale (sales price $.20 less incremental cost of $.16).

Caution should be exercised, however, in pricing additional sales below full cost. A tendency to be overly volume conscious while cutting sales prices below full cost can be dangerous; for each customer, product, or territory should contribute equitably toward the fixed costs if the company is to be profitable in the long run. Any product sold below full cost is not carrying its fair share of fixed costs, and only sales prices at or above full cost represent the most stable long-run pricing policy. Sales prices which do not cover variable costs and a fair share of fixed costs should be used only in special cases and as temporary measures.

Direct Costing

The problems encountered in the allocation of fixed costs to products has been one of the major factors responsible for the development of a costing method entitled *direct costing*. When this method of costing is employed, the only costs assigned to specific units of product are the direct costs; thus only the direct materials, direct labor, and those overhead costs directly variable with production would be considered product costs. If a job order system is used, only the variable costs would be assigned to individual jobs, and fixed costs would not be prorated. Direct costing permits prorations to be reduced to a minimum, since fixed costs are not included in the computation of product unit costs.

To illustrate the direct cost method and to contrast it with the conventional job order and process costing methods illustrated in previous chapters, assume that a company has incurred costs of $50,000 for direct labor, $30,000 for direct materials, $25,000 for fixed manufacturing costs, and $20,000 for variable costs The production for the period was 20,000 units.

	Full Cost Method	Direct Cost Method
Direct labor	$ 50,000	$ 50,000
Direct materials	30,000	30,000
Variable manufacturing costs	20,000	20,000
Fixed manufacturing costs	25,000	none
Total costs associated with production	$125,000	$100,000
Per unit manufacturing costs	$5	$4

The full-cost method includes all manufacturing costs as product costs, so that the total costs assigned to products is $125,000. Since 25,000 units were manufactured, the unit cost is $5.00, and each unit has assigned to it a portion of the fixed costs. On the other hand, the direct cost method does not assign fixed costs to units. Under this method, only $100,000 is considered product costs; and the unit cost is $4.00. The fixed manufacturing costs would appear on the income statement as a period cost, along with fixed selling and fixed administrative expenses.

Under the full-cost method, each unit sold would result in a cost of goods sold of $5.00, and the inventory of unsold units would be carried at $5.00 each. Under direct costing, however, each unit sold or left in inventory would carry a $4.00 cost. The full $25,000 of fixed costs appears in the operating expense part of the current year's income statement, and there would be no attempt to allocate the $25,000 of fixed costs to sold and unsold units.

The direct costing method does not in any way solve the complex problems inherent in establishing a sales price for a product. However, it is compatible with the marginal-cost pricing method. Whether a $5.00 full cost or a $4.00 direct cost is used in the inventory records, the problem of pricing the product to maximize profits remains to be solved.

Summary

Pricing represents one of the most strategic decision areas facing management. Both the short-range and the long-range future of the company are directly affected by such decisions, which by their very nature must be based on incomplete evidence. A sound pricing policy should be formulated as a guide to the determination of individual product prices, and relationships between cost, price, and volume should be carefully considered prior to establishing the pricing policy. Projecting total costs and total revenues for several of the more probable prices at which the product may be offered is perhaps the most effective way of approaching the pricing of a product. Total price-cost graphs are useful in determining the range of prices which will produce a profit, for this method provides some insight into the differences in expected profit among the several feasible prices. The tentative nature of the revenue and cost data which are used in pricing analyses makes the total price-cost approach more useful than the traditional economic marginal analysis.

Either full cost or marginal cost may be used in the determination of prices, and there is no single "best" way to establish a pricing policy. Prices affect volume, and volume affects cost, so that the cause-effect relationship between cost and price is not always clear. There is reason to believe that cost is as much a function of price as price is a function of cost.

Pricing joint products is especially difficult, for there is no effective method of determining the cost of an individual product when several products arise from a common material and a common process. In such cases, arbitrary allocation of the joint costs to the several products is necessary, and pricing is undertaken so that the entire group of products will be profitable. In such cases, there is little to be gained by making price analyses for each product individually, because the joint products are interdependent.

New Terms

By-product   A product with a relatively small value which arises automatically in the production of a main product.

Cost function   The behavior of cost in relation to changes in volume.

Direct costing   A costing method which does not allocate fixed costs to products.

Full absorption costing   Costing products by allocating all overhead to them.

Full-cost pricing   A pricing policy based upon cost calculations which include allocation of all overhead to products.

Joint-product   One of several products which arise from a single common raw material.

Price policy   The basic philosophy and methodology used to determine prices.

Revenue function   The behavior of total revenue in relation to price and volume changes.

Variable-cost pricing   A pricing policy based upon cost calculations which include only variable costs and no fixed costs.

Questions

1. What is meant by a *pricing policy?* Give some of the considerations which should be taken into account when establishing such a policy.

2. Explain how cost determines price and, at the same time, how price has a bearing on cost.

3. Explain what marginal revenue and marginal cost mean in the traditional economic marginal analysis of pricing. Explain how the optimal price is located in such an analysis.

4. What is a total price-total cost graph? What advantages does such an analysis have over the economic marginal analysis?

5. What is meant by full-cost pricing? Include in your answer the mechanisms of calculating a full-cost price.

6. What is mean by variable-cost pricing? Include in your answer the mechanics of calculating a variable cost price.

7. What is a joint-product? A by-product?

8. What are some of the methods by which common costs are allocated to joint-products?

9. What is "direct costing"? Would the inventory cost of finished goods differ between two companies identical in all respects except that one uses full absorption costing and the other uses direct costing?

10. Is it true that the variable costs of a unit constitute the floor below which a company cannot sell additional units without lowering its profits? Explain.

Exercises

15–1 **Definitions** *(15 minutes)*   The following terms or concepts were introduced in this chapter:
 a. Pricing policy
 b. Revenue function
 c. Cost-price-profit graph
 d. Full-cost pricing
 e. Variable-cost pricing
 f. Joint product
 g. Direct costing

Instructions
Define each term, using examples where possible.

15–2 **Preparation of a Price-Cost-Profit Graph** *(25 minutes)*   The price at which a new product is to be offered on the market is under consideration. The company has fixed costs related to the product of $10,000 and variable costs of $4 per unit. Estimates of sales volumes which could be realized at various sales prices are as follows:

Price	Estimated Unit Sales
$ 10	1,500
20	1,000
30	750
40	600
50	500
60	400
70	250
80	150
90	100
100	50

Instructions
Compute the revenue and costs which would be realized or incurred at each price. Then plot the revenue, fixed cost, and total cost lines on a price-cost-profit graph, indicating on the graph what price would produce the maximum profit.

15–3* **Preparation of a Price-Cost-Profit Graph** *(25 minutes)* Assume the same projected sales prices and quantities as in Exercise 15–2 above, except that the company has $15,000 of fixed costs and the variable costs are $3.00 per unit.

Instructions
Compute the revenue and costs which would be realized or incurred at each price. Then plot the revenue, fixed cost, and total cost lines on a price-cost-profit graph, indicating on the graph what price would produce the maximum profit.

15–4 **Marginal Revenue-Cost Graph** *(30 minutes)* Utilizing the data in Exercise 15–2 above, prepare a unit marginal revenue-marginal cost graph similar to Exhibit 15–2 with a table of supporting data similar to that supporting Exhibit 15–2. (Reverse the order of prices, listing the highest price first as is done in Exhibit 15–2.)

15–5 **Computation of Full and Variable Cost Price** *(20 minutes)* The Camden Company allocates fixed overhead to its products using a rate of 200 percent of the direct labor cost in each product. The price at which a new product is to be placed on the market is presently being considered. The direct labor cost in the product is estimated to be $5.00, and all other variable costs are estimated to be $11.50. The company's price objective is to earn a profit equal to 20 percent of total cost.

Instructions
1. Compute the sales price of the product using a full-cost method.
2. Assume that the company includes only variable costs in its price computation, with a profit margin of 100 percent of the total variable cost. Compute the sales price using this method.
3. Describe the process of computing the allocation rate of 200 percent of direct labor if it is based upon an expected volume of 5,000 units. Then describe the effect upon profits if only 4,000 units are sold; that is, using the pricing method in part 1, will the expected 20 percent profit be realized?

15-6*   **Joint Costs Prior to Split-Off** *(20 minutes)*   The Adden Company has two products and two producing departments, and a process cost system is used in the manufacturing process. All raw material enters the first department, and upon completion of that process Product A is completed and is transferred to the finished goods warehouse. The remaining incomplete material enters the second department, where Product B is completed. During the period, 10,000 units of raw material were consumed in the manufacture of 4,000 units of A and 2,000 units of B. There were no beginning or ending inventories. The costs incurred during the period were as follows:

	Department 1	Department 2
Material	$20,000	$ –
Labor	7,000	19,000
Overhead	6,000	10,000

Instructions
1. Compute the unit cost of each of the two products if all costs prior to split-off are allocated on the basis of the number of units produced.
2. What would be the sales price of each product if the pricing policy is to add 30 percent of cost for profit.

15-7   **Offer to Buy Excess Production** *(15 minutes)*   The Bake Mite Company has analyzed its costs as follows for its Product 175–LY:

Direct labor	$3.00
Direct materials	2.00
Variable manufacturing expenses	1.00
Fixed manufacturing expenses (apportioned at 33⅓ % of labor)	1.00
Total	$7.00

The product normally sells for $10.00 per unit. A foreign wholesaler approached the company with an offer to buy 10,000 units at $7.00 each. Sales to the foreign customer would not affect the company's domestic market, but an additional cost of $.50 per unit for overseas transportation would be incurred.

Instructions

Ignoring other factors not stated in the problem, would you accept the offer? Support your answer with computations.

15–8   **Calculating the Effect of a Price Change** *(15 minutes)*   The XYZ Corporation has determined its cost structure to be as follows:

Variable	$ 2.00 per unit produced
Fixed	$200.00

a. If the price is $2.50 per unit, sales next year will be 450 units.
b. If the price is $3.00 per unit and the variable expense is increased 10 percent (due to an increase in the quality of the unit) sales will also be 450 units.

Instructions

1. As a manager, which alternative would you choose. (Show figures substantiating your decision.)
2. Compute the breakeven point for each alternative.

Problems

15–9   **Selection of Price; Price-Cost-Profit Graph** *(40 minutes)*   The Overwood Company is introducing a new plastic toy called a horti-cycle; and, since it is new, the company's management is not sure what the market acceptance will be. The toy is a three-wheeled, off-balance tricycle with slightly oval-shaped wheels and when a child rides on it, up-and-down, side-to-side motion is produced as it rolls.

The market research staff of the company has estimated the following expected volumes at several possible prices:

Price	Expected Volume in Units
$ 6	4,000
8	3,800
10	3,500
12	3,000
14	2,600
16	2,400
18	2,000
20	1,600
22	1,000
24	600
26	400

The company will have to invest in machinery, equipment and special tools costing $100,000, which will have a ten-year life and no salvage value. Materials, labor, and other variable costs will be $7 per unit.

Instructions
1. Prepare a table showing for each possible price the total revenue, the total cost, the unit cost, and the total profit or loss.
2. Prepare a price-cost-profit graph.
3. Select the price which will maximize profits.

15–10   **Marginal Revenue-Cost Graph** *(40 minutes)*   Using the data given in problem 15–9 above, prepare a unit marginal revenue-marginal cost graph similar to that in Exhibit 15–2, with a table of supporting computations similar to that supporting Exhibit 15–2. (Reverse the price order, listing the highest price first as in Exhibit 15–2.)

15–11   **Pricing Without Fixed Costs: Price-Cost-Profit Graph** *(40 minutes)* Assume the same facts as in problem 15–9 above, except that the company will buy the heavy parts of the horticycle from an outside contractor. Under this arrangement, the investment of $100,000 for machinery and equipment will not be necessary, but an additional cost of $3 per unit will be incurred for the outside machine work. Thus, no fixed costs will be incurred, but the variable costs will be $10 per unit.

Instructions
Prepare a table showing, for each possible price, the total revenue, the total cost, the unit cost, and the total expected profit or loss. Also prepare a price-cost-profit graph.

15–12   **Pricing for Profit and Safety Maximization; Price-Cost-Profit Graphs** *(60 minutes)*   The board of directors of the Decanto Company is considering the price at which one of its new products will be offered to the public. They wish to maximize profits and at the same time provide maximum assurance that the product will be profitable. They have estimated the sales volumes to be as follows for each of the possible prices:

	Estimated Range of Units Which Might Be Sold	
Price	Low Estimate	High Estimate
$ 1	100,000	120,000
2	90,000	110,000
3	85,000	90,000
4	70,000	70,000
5	55,000	55,000

Estimated Range of Units Which
Might Be Sold

Price	Low Estimate	High Estimate
6	40,000	45,000
7	30,000	36,000
8	22,000	30,000
9	18,000	25,000
10	10,000	20,000

The product is to be produced by a mechanized process resulting in fixed costs of $160,000 and variable costs of $1 per unit.

Instructions

1. Prepare a table showing the total revenue, total cost, and profit or loss for the low estimates.
2. Perform the same calculations for the high estimates as was done in part 1.
3. Plot the two sets of data in parts (1) and (2) on a single price-cost-profit graph and state what price you would select to satisfy management's requirements for both profit and safety maximization.

15–13   Marginal Revenue-Cost Graphs *(40 minutes)*   Using the low estimate data in Problem 15–12 above, prepare a unit marginal revenue and marginal cost graph similar to Exhibit 15–2 with a supporting table of data similar to that supporting Exhibit 15–2. (Reverse the order of prices, listing the highest price first as is done in Exhibit 15–2.)

15–14   Full and Variable Costing in a Multiproduct Setting *(60 minutes)*
The Truetone Company has $216,000 of fixed costs and is attempting to compute costs for pricing purposes. In order to compute a sales price, the company follows a policy of adding 20 percent to each product's total cost and rounding to the nearest even dollar (prices are not to be in odd dollars). The variable costs of the company's three products are as follows:

Product A	$ 6 per unit
B	9 per unit
C	12 per unit

The company expects to produce 5,000 units of A, 10,000 units of B, and 50,000 units of C.

Instructions

1. Compute the selling price for the three products if fixed costs are allocated on the basis of the total variable costs expected to be incurred in the manufacture of each of the three products.

2. Assume that the market research staff estimates the market demand at several different price levels as follows:

Product	Unit sales if the price is:										
	$6	$8	$10	$12	$14	$16	$18	$20	$22	$24	$26
A	15,000	12,000	10,000	8,000	6,000	4,000	2,000	1,000	500	–0–	–0–
B	28,000	24,000	20,000	18,000	14,000	10,000	6,000	3,000	2,000	–0–	–0–
C	120,000	100,000	80,000	74,000	60,000	50,000	40,000	20,000	8,000	3,000	–0–

Determine which price would produce the greatest profit for the company for each product. Different prices may be used for the three products, and since fixed costs are arbitrarily allocated, a contribution margin must be calculated for each product for each price level.

3. Explain why the prices as computed in part 1 do not produce the maximum profit as computed in part 2.

15–15 Contrast Between Full and Variable Costing *(60 minutes)* The Ebony Company has $149,000 of fixed costs and prices its product by adding 20 percent to the total cost of each unit. The amounts thus computed are rounded to the nearest odd dollar for the final price. The variable costs of their three products are as follows:

Product X	$3 per unit
Y	5 per unit
Z	6 per unit

The company expects to produce 6,000 units of X, 8,000 units of Y, and 40,000 units of Z.

Instructions

1. Compute the sales prices for the three products, using a full-cost computation which allocates fixed costs on the basis of the total variable costs expected to be incurred in the manufacture of each product.

2. Compute the sales prices using a contribution approach—i.e., by computing the contribution each product makes toward fixed costs at the various price levels. Assume for this purpose that the market research staff estimates the market demand at several different price levels as follows:

	$3	$5	$7	$9	$11	$13
X	10,000	8,000	6,000	4,000	2,000	1,000
Y	20,000	18,000	14,000	10,000	6,000	3,000
Z	80,000	75,000	60,000	50,000	40,000	20,000

If a different price may be used for each of the products, what prices would maximize the company's profits?

3. Will the prices computed in part 1 approximate those computed in part 2 in this particular set of circumstances? If not, explain the differences.

15–16   **Contrast Between Variable-Cost and Full-Cost Prices** *(50 minutes)*
The Pribble Company is newly formed, and its management is attempting to establish a price for each of its four products—Good, Better, Best, and Super. The president and founder has arbitrarily estimated the products' importance in a ratio of 40 percent, 30 percent, 20 percent, and 10 percent, respectively; and production has been budgeted at 10,000, 6,000, 3,000, and 1,000 units. The company has $200,000 of fixed costs, and the four products have unit variable costs of $2, $3, $4, and $5, respectively. The company's management wants its prices to be sufficiently high to provide a 10 percent profit on each product after all costs have been covered.

The sales manager favors a full-cost pricing computation which allocates the fixed costs on the basis of the number of units of each item produced, but the president thinks the allocation basis should be either the arbitrary ratio listed above, a ratio of the variable cost per unit, or a ratio of the total variable costs to be incurred in the manufacture of each product line. Both the president and the sales manager are willing to compromise and select a price "reasonably close" to the average price produced by these allocation techniques, provided the differences in the results of the several methods do not vary significantly.

Instructions
1. Compute a full-cost price for each product if allocations of fixed costs are based on the number of units. Allow a profit of 10 percent of total cost.
2. Compute a full-cost price if allocations of fixed costs are based on the ratio of importance to the company. Allow a 10 percent profit.
3. Compute a variable-cost price based on a factor of 400 percent of variable cost to cover both fixed costs and profit.
4. Compute for each pricing method the profit which would be realized for the company, based upon the scheduled production for the coming year.

15–17   **Joint Product Costs and Prices** *(20 minutes)*   ABC Corporation has two products, A and B, and two manufacturing departments, 1 and 2. Both products emerge from a common raw material, which is processed in Department 1. Product A is completed at that point, but Product B is further processed in Department 2. The costs incurred by the two departments during the past year were:

	Department 1	Department 2
Materials	$42,000	$ 3,000
Labor	21,000	40,000
Overhead	28,000	14,000

Costs of operating Department 1 are allocated to the two products on the basis of units processed. There were no beginning or ending inventories. There were 4,000 units of Product A and 3,000 units of Product B processed during the month.

Instructions

1. Compute the cost to manufacture a unit of A and B.
2. Using a 20 percent profit percentage based on full cost, compute the sales price of A and B.

15–18   **Pricing Joint Products Using Full-Cost Method** *(30 minutes)*
The Taylor Company uses a single raw material and produces three joint-products from it, called Primera, Segunda, and Tercera. There are five producing departments, as illustrated below. Department A receives and processes the raw material, and at the end of that department's work Tercera is separated from the raw material. Tercera goes on to Department D, where it is completed, while the remaining uncompleted raw material proceeds into Department B. At the end of the processing in Department B, Segunda emerges and is sent to Department E where it is completed. The final remaining materials go on from Department B into Department C, where Primera is completed. The entire process may be illustrated as follows:

Department A—raw material processed	Department B—material continues processing	Department C—material completely processed, Primera completed

Department E—Segunda completed

Department D—Tercera completed

The raw materials cost entering Department A was $110,000. The labor and overhead costs of the departments, as well as their production, is given below:

	Costs Incurred	Units Produced
Department A	$10,000	—
B	7,000	—
C	7,000	4,000
D	8,000	8,000
E	12,000	12,000

Instructions

1. Compute a unit cost for each of the three products if allocation of all costs prior to the point of split-off is made on the basis of the number of units produced.
2. If the company's pricing policy is to add 20 percent to the cost, what would the price of each product be?

15–19 **Analysis of an Offer to Buy at a Reduced Price** *(20 minutes)*
The Prodan Company has three products with production costs as
follows:

	Product A	Product B	Product C
Direct labor	$10	$ 5	$ 8
Direct materials	20	3	4
Variable overhead	5	3	8
Fixed overhead	10	5	8
	$45	$16	$28

The fixed overhead is allocated on the basis of 100 percent of direct
labor, and the company's over- or under-applied overhead has been
very small in prior years. Thus, the company's controller feels that
the costs are accurate. The present regular catalogue prices for the
products are $75, $25, and $40, respectively, and approximately
1,000, 8,000, and 20,000 units of A, B and, C, respectively, have
been sold each year.

Harold Stafford, the purchasing agent for a large mail-order
house, contacted Mr. Prodan, president of the company, and extended an offer to buy 20,000 units of product B at a price of $11
per unit. He told Mr. Prodan, "If you will sell these to me at your
variable cost, I will sell them in areas where you do not market, so
that your sales will not be affected. Where you will increase your
profits in this deal is in the allocation of overhead. You will have a
great deal more direct labor, and your allocation rate will not be as
high as 100 percent of direct labor, as it now is. Thus, the unit cost
of all products will drop, which is common when the volume of
production goes up, and your company will realize increased profits.
Further, you will get lower prices on your raw material as a result of
quantity purchases, and more efficient labor will result from the
increased production. Why, you can't lose on a deal like this."

Instructions
Prepare a reply to the offer, giving calculations to support your
decision.

15–20 **Dumping Excess Production at Reduced Prices** *(30 minutes)*
The Rondwell Company has the following cost structure:

Fixed manufacturing expenses	$100,000
Fixed selling and administrative expenses	80,000
Variable manufacturing expenses (per unit):	
Direct labor	2
Direct material	4
Variable overhead	1
Variable selling and administrative expenses	
(per unit)	2

Instructions
1. Compute the total cost per unit to manufacture the company's product if
   a. 100,000 units are produced
   b. 50,000 units are produced
   c. 200,000 units are produced
2. Assume that the company sells its product for $13 per unit. A request was received from a wholesaler for 50,000 units at a special price of $10 each. (Assume this order will not affect the company's present market.) Prepare computations which indicate whether the offer would be profitable.
3. Assume further that the company sells 100,000 units at regular prices. Prepare two income statements, one to reflect the results of operations if the special order is accepted and the other to reflect the results of operations if the special order is rejected. (The *difference* between the two should be the same as the result of computations in the preceding part.)

15–21   **Pricing to Maximize Profits with Changing Demand** *(30 minutes)*
The Syndicate Company sells 4,000 units per month at a price of $2 per unit, with unit costs of $1.80. The company's president is contemplating an increase in the sales price to $2.50, which will reduce the number sold to 3,000 units and will increase the unit cost to $2.00.

Instructions
1. From the data given, compute the total costs to be incurred if the $2 and the $2.50 sales price is used, and from these amounts compute the company's total fixed and variable costs at the resulting volume.
2. The company's sales manager feels that the president's price increase is too small and wishes instead to increase the price to $2.70 per unit. This price would reduce the number of units sold to 2,700. Compute the company's break-even point at the $2, the $2.50, and at the $2.70 unit price. Explain why the three break-even points differ.
3. Which course of action would you choose—i.e., which price would you recommend, ignoring other factors not included in the problem?

15–22   **Computation of the Effects of Price Reductions** *(30 minutes)*
Harold Watts was appointed controller of the Tinsdale Sales and Promotion Company on July 1. His first task was to review the company's cost structure, and as a result he developed the following from the company's past financial records:

	Monthly Average in 19X4	Monthly Average in 19X3
Units sold	1,000	800
Sales price	$ 20	$ 25
Fixed costs	$10,000	$10,000
Variable costs ($8 per unit)	$ 8,000	$ 6,400

The sales price of the company's product was decreased at the beginning of 19X4 from the old price of $25 to the current price of $20 in an attempt to increase profits. An estimate of 1,150 units per month was forecast when the price was reduced. The company's officers had been disappointed when the price decrease had reduced profits instead of increasing them. A return to the old price of $25 had not been effected, because the officers felt a price increase might cause a loss of customer goodwill.

Mr. Watts discussed the company's pricing policy with the sales manager and was told that if the price is lowered still further, to $18 per unit, a total of 1,200 units could be sold; if the sales price is lowered still further to $16, a total of 1,800 units could be sold. These estimates were deemed accurate, since the company now had some experience in the effect of price reductions on the number of units to be sold. In view of the results of the recent price reduction, the sales manager had been discouraged in his attempt to persuade the company's officers to lower prices still further.

Instructions

Prepare calculations to reflect the effects of a reduction in price (1) to $18, and (2) to $16. What considerations other than financial data would you assess before making a final recommendation?

15–23   **Contribution Margin Approach to Advertising, with Flexible Demand Schedule** *(50 minutes)*   The board of directors of the Hornsby Company is in the process of setting the total advertising budget for the coming year. The company's cost structure, exclusive of advertising, is as follows:

Fixed manufacturing costs	$60,000
Variable manufacturing costs (per unit)	$ 10
Fixed selling and general costs	$40,000
Variable selling and general costs (per unit)	$ 5

The present advertising expenditure is $20,000.

The company is currently producing and selling 10,000 units per year at a sales price of $28.00 and has an annual capacity of 20,000 units.

K. C. Taylor, a new member of the board of directors and an experienced market analyst, developed the following data:

If the annual advertising expenditure is	The total number of units sold will be
$ 5,000	5,000
10,000	7,000
15,000	8,500
20,000	9,500
25,000	10,500
30,000	11,000
35,000	11,400
40,000	11,700
45,000	11,900

Instructions
1. At what amount would you recommend the advertising budget be set? Prepare data to support your decision. (Set up a table showing (1) *increased* revenue and (2) *increased* advertising and variable costs at each advertising level. The difference is increased profit.)
2. Prepare three income statements, one at the level of advertising you selected in part (1), one at the next lowest level, and one at the next highest level. (The statements should support your selection of the best level, since the level you select should produce the highest profit.)

15–24 **Planning an Advertising Policy, with Product Mix Changes** (*40 minutes*)   The Midtown Specialty Company sells two appliances, regular and deluxe. The market for the two products is relatively stable, and increases in the unit sales of one product decrease proportionately the unit sales of the other. Management is not sure which of several courses of action to take:
a. Push sales of regular
b. Push sales of deluxe
c. Leave the sales "mix" in its present proportions with no additional advertising effort

Unit statistics on sales, prices, and costs are presently as follows:

	Regular	Deluxe
Units sold	6,000	3,000
Sales price	$20.00	$28.00
Unit costs of materials and labor	$10.00	$11.00
Transportation-in	$ 1.00	$ 2.00
Fixed overhead expenses ($61,200 total)	$ 6.00	$ 8.40
Variable selling expenses	$ 2.00	$ 4.00

An additional expenditure of $4,000 for advertising will not produce additional unit sales, but will shift sales of 2,000 units from regular to deluxe, or vice versa, depending upon which product is to be emphasized. All remaining costs are not expected to change.

Instructions

Would you leave sales as is, with no additional advertising? If you decide to increase the advertising expenditure would you emphasize regular or deluxe? Must the decision be made before budgets for the coming period are established? If a decision to change the advertising program is made during the period, how should previously budgeted amounts be altered?

chapter 16

Capital Budgeting Decisions

Learning Objectives

This chapter discusses the important area of selecting from among alternative investment choices, which is one of management's most strategic decision areas. Upon completion of your study of this chapter, you should:

1. Understand how alternative investment choices may be compared.
2. Know how to compute payback period, discounted cash flow, excess present values, and discounted rates of return.
3. Recognize the advantages and disadvantages of each method of comparing dissimilar investment choices.

The Investment Decision

There is always a limit to the amount of funds which a company has available for investment in income-producing activities, and selecting the most profitable projects for investment of these funds is one of management's most critical decision areas. The process of selecting from among alternative investment proposals is called the *capital investment decision*. A capital investment is one which yields income over a number of accounting periods, and there is usually the acquisition of income-producing assets involved in the decision. Such actions as building a new plant, acquiring new equipment, undertaking an extensive advertising campaign, or acquiring the ownership of an existing business are examples of capital investment decisions.

Since each investment possibility is unique, a consistent method of comparing them should be utilized. Even though estimates of cost and future revenues are less than 100 percent accurate, they must nevertheless be made if the alternative choices are to be compared. The methods discussed in this chapter include:

1. Return on investment
2. Payback period
3. Excess present value
4. Discounted rate of return

Return on Investment

The return that an investment is able to generate is usually expressed in annual percentage amounts. Unless specific information is given to the contrary, for example, a 20 percent rate is assumed in all cases to be the rate per year. An investment of $100,000 which produces a profit of $20,000 per year is said to give a 20 percent rate of return.

The rate of return is calculated by dividing the annual profit from the investment by the amount of the investment itself. However, major problems arise in the use of this method, because the profit is not always the same from one year to the next, and the amount of the investment itself frequently will change from one period to another. Consider, for example, the investment of $10,000 for an asset which will produce revenues of $2,000 per year for ten years, at which time it will have no salvage value. Each year the profit will be $1,000, computed by subtracting $1,000 depreciation (straight-line on a ten-year basis) from the $2,000 revenue. The investment will decrease, however, because each year the depreciation expense provides a "recapture" of a part of the investment. The resulting return on investment for each year of the investment is shown in Exhibit 16–1.

The annual rate of return calculated in Exhibit 16–1 ranges from 10 percent in the first year to 100 percent in the tenth, because the investment base is decreasing. For this reason it is necessary to calculate the return on investment using *average investment* and *average net profit*.

$$\text{Rate of return} = \frac{\text{Average net profit}}{\text{Average investment}}$$

The average net profit on an annual basis is clearly $1,000. The average investment in this case is $5,000, since each year a portion of the original $10,000 investment is being "recaptured through depreciation." Average investment can generally be calculated as one-half the original investment, if it is depreciable and a straight-line method is used.

EXHIBIT 16–1

Annual Rates of Return

Year	Investment Balance	Net Profit	Rate of Return
1	$10,000	$1,000	10%
2	9,000	1,000	11%
3	8,000	1,000	12%
4	7,000	1,000	14%
5	6,000	1,000	17%
6	5,000	1,000	20%
7	4,000	1,000	25%
8	3,000	1,000	33%
9	2,000	1,000	50%
10	1,000	1,000	100%

The rate of return which an investment produces is not one of the most reliable measures for comparing investment alternatives. This is true because the rate does not take into account the size of the required investment or the timing of the revenue inflows. Consider the following example:

	Investment A	Investment B
Cost	$10,000	$40,000
Life	2 years	3 years
Revenues:		
Year 1	$ 6,000	—
Year 2	6,000	$22,000
Year 3		$30,000

Return on Investment A:

Total profit	$12,000 − $10,000 = $2,000
Average profit	$ 2,000 ÷ 2 = $1,000
Average investment	$10,000 ÷ 2 = $5,000
Rate of return	$\dfrac{\$ 1,000}{\$ 5,000} = 20\%$

Return on Investment B:

Total profit	$52,000 − $40,000 = $12,000
Average profit	$12,000 ÷ 3 = $ 4,000
Average investment	$40,000 ÷ 2 = $20,000
Rate of return	$\dfrac{\$ 4,000}{20,000} = 20\%$

Both investments produce a 20 percent rate of return, although investment B requires a much greater investment and does not produce revenues until the second year. Thus, comparison of the 20 percent rates of return could be misleading unless the size of the required investment and the timing of net cash flows are also considered.

Acceptable Rate of Return

The scarcity of funds available for capital acquisitions necessitates that some investment possibilities be rejected. Obviously those with the highest rates of return will be accepted, and those with the lowest rates will be rejected. However, the capital acquisitions with the highest rates of return are not always known in advance when other, less profitable investments are being considered. For this reason, most companies establish a minimum rate of return and will automatically reject any investment that does not provide at least this minimum rate.

The rate used by the company must be high enough to cover (1) the interest expense which is incurred in making the funds available, (2) the risk involved in making capital acquisitions, and (3) income taxes which must be paid on the return from the investment. The rate of return may have to be as high as 20 percent to 30 percent to cover these elements; and, in very risky ventures—such as oil and gas exploration and plant construction in another country—the rate is sometimes more than 50 percent.

Measuring Cash Flow

As indicated in the earlier discussion on the calculation of rates of return, the timing differences in the flow of cash from several investment possibilities is of primary importance. Most capital budgeting techniques are based on the flow of cash rather than the accrual principles of accounting which underly the balance sheet and the income statement. Use of cash flow is possible because each investment alternative is analyzed separately and can be considered from its inception all the way to its termination. Generally accepted accounting principles are based on the necessity of dividing a company's life into years and accruing or deferring revenues or expenses to assign them properly to these periods. Analysis of a capital budgeting possibility, however, does not necessitate such careful matching of expenses and revenues, since only the timing of the cash inflows or outflows needs to be considered.

Capital budgeting techniques are based on cash flows throughout the life of the investment and may be compared to a bank account where deposits (inflows) and checks (outflows) are recorded. When the investment reaches the end of its life and no longer exists, there will be more cash in the account than at the beginning, if the investment has been profitable. Consider the case of an investment in a fixed asset which will require a $10,000 outlay now and will have a life of three years. It will produce revenues of $6,000 per year during each of the three years, and $1,500 of other expenses will be incurred each year to maintain the investment. At the end of the three-year period, the asset will have a salvage value of $700. The cash flows during each year would be measured as follows:

	Cash In	Cash Out	Cumulative Balance
Year 1 Purchase		$10,000	
Revenues	$ 6,000		
Expenses		$ 1,500	$(5,500)
Year 2 Revenues	6,000		
Expenses		1,500	(1,000)
Year 3 Revenues	6,000		
Expenses		1,500	
Salvage value	700		4,200
Totals	$18,700	$14,500	

Note that depreciation on the asset is not considered, since it is a noncash expense and since only cash inflows or outflows are taken into account. Since the analysis covered the entire life of the investment and includes the original $10,000 cost and the final $700 salvage value, the cost of acquiring and using the asset is already included.

If a rate of return were calculated for this investment in accordance with the method discussed earlier in this chapter, it would be as follows:

Average investment: ½ ($10,000 − $700) = $4,650

Annual profit:	Revenue	$ 6,000
	Expenses	(1,500)
	Depreciation (⅓ of $9,300)	(3,100)
	Profit	$ 1,400

Rate of return: $\dfrac{\$1,400}{\$4,650} = 30\%$

Note that the $1,400 annual profit calculated using depreciation in accordance with generally accepted accounting principles would, for the three-year period, equal the $4,200 calculated in the cash inflow-outflow schedule. Thus, the average annual profit could have been determined in this case by dividing the $4,200 net cash inflow by 3, the number of years of the investment's life.

Payback Period

The payback period is the length of time required for the proceeds from an investment to return the original cost, and it is usually stated in years or fractions of years. If an investment of $10,000 produces revenues of $2,000 per year, its payback period is five years. Another $10,000 investment possibility, producing $4,000 revenue per year, would have a payback period of two and one-half years. The shorter payback period is obviously more desirable, other things being equal.

The payback period should not be used as the only indicator of the relative merits of alternate investment possibilities, since it reduces only one part of unlike investments to common terms—i.e., the period required to recapture the *principal* of the investment. It does not reflect in any way the relative profitability of investments, because it ignores the length of time revenue will continue to be earned after the payback period. One investment possibility may have a payback period of two and one-half years and cease to produce revenue after that year; another investment may have a payback period of five years and continue to produce revenue for twenty additional years. For this reason, the payback computation must be combined with other techniques in comparing investment possibilities.

The payback period, which considers the recapture of the principal, and the rate of return, which considers income from the investment, are frequently used together as dual measurement devices to compare the investment alternatives from which a company may choose.

To illustrate these dual measurements, assume that a company is studying two alternatives: (1) whether to invest $100,000 in a coal mine in order to have a ready source of raw material and (2) whether to use the $100,000 to modernize the manufacturing plant. Assume further that the first alternative would result in savings of $5,000 in raw material costs the first three years, and $20,000 per year for seven years thereafter. Modernization of the plant would save the company $12,000 in production costs annually for twelve years. Using payback period and rate-of-return calculations, the management of the company would compare these two investment possibilities as follows:

First Investment Possibility
(Purchase of a raw material supply)

	Annual Savings	Total Savings
Years 1–3	$ 5,000	$ 15,000
Years 4–10	20,000	140,000
Total savings		$155,000
Cost of the investment		100,000
Total profit		$ 55,000
Annual profit ($55,000 ÷ 10 years)		$ 5,500
Rate of return ($5,550 ÷ ½ of $100,000)		11.1%

Payback period:

Year	Annual Revenue	Cumulative Revenue
1	$ 5,000	$ 5,000
2	5,000	10,000
3	5,000	15,000
4	20,000	35,000
5	20,000	55,000
6	20,000	75,000
7	20,000	95,000
		→7¼ years payback
8	20,000	
9	20,000	
10	20,000	

Second Investment Possibility
(Modernization of the plant)

Total savings, 12 years @ $12,000	$144,000
Cost of the investment	100,000
Total profit	$ 44,000
Annual profit ($44,000 ÷ 10 years)	$ 4,400
Rate of return ($4,400 ÷ ½ of $100,000)	8.8%

Payback period:

Year	Annual Revenue	Cumulative Revenue
1	$12,000	$12,000
2	12,000	24,000
3	12,000	36,000
4	12,000	48,000
5	12,000	60,000
6	12,000	72,000
7	12,000	84,000
8	12,000	96,000
		→ 8⅓ years payback
9	12,000	
10	12,000	
11	12,000	
12	12,000	

The first investment proposal would yield a return of 11.1 percent per year, with a payback of 7¼ years, while the second investment proposal would yield an 8.8 percent return with a payback in 8⅓ years. The two investments are thus placed on a comparative basis as far as yield and return of investment are concerned. Of course, a final decision would involve other factors, such as raw materials shortages or whether present plant equipment can meet expected demands for the next twelve years. The subjective factors must be weighed individually, but having the return of principal and the income of the two alternate investments reduced to comparable terms assists in the evaluation.

Note that the average investment, which is one-half of the total investment, is used to calculate the rate of return percentage. Note also that the uneven flow of revenue from the first proposal necessitated calculating a total profit for the entire ten-year period and taking one-tenth of this total as the annual profit. The cost of the investment is subtracted in computing the profit from the investment, and thus the calculation of rate of return presumes the principal of the investment will be recaptured in full.

Present Value Concepts

Money presently owned is more valuable than money to be received at some point in the future. This concept is based on the fact that money may be invested and will earn income, so that one dollar held today will accumulate to more than one dollar a year from now. In like manner, a dollar to be received a year from now is worth less than one dollar at the present moment. Suppose, for example, that a friend owes you $10, due in one year, and he offers to pay $9.00 right now to discharge the entire debt. If you could earn 11 percent on your investments, you could invest the $9.00, and by the end of the year it would have grown, with the income added, to equal the original $10 of the debt. Thus, it could be said that $10 due one year from now has a present value of approximately $9.00, using 11 percent as the rate.

Note that the $10 has a present value of approximately $9.00 only if a rate of 11 percent is used. If you could earn only 6 percent on your investments, you must receive $9.43 if it is to accumulate to $10.00 by the end of the year. Thus, the present value of a sum of money to be received in the future cannot be calculated until a *discount rate* has been established.

Discount is the amount which must be subtracted from a future sum in order to determine the present value. *Interest* is the amount which must be added to a present amount to determine its value in the future. The difference between interest and discount are illustrated as follows:

Present amount	Interest added	Future amount
Present amount	Discount subtracted	Future amount

When the present amount is known, a future value is calculated using an interest rate. When only future amounts are known—as in the case of money inflows from an investment—their present value is calculated using a discount rate. We thus speak of discounting a future receipt to find its present value.

Exhibit 16–2 provides a table of present values. The first part of the table is for a single amount to be received in the future, and the second part is for a constant stream of money which will be received over a period of years. The tables are constructed for fifteen years, at selected rates ranging from 1 percent to 50 percent. More complete tables are available in financial publications, but have not been reproduced in this text.

Lump-Sum Receipts

To illustrate the first section of Exhibit 16–2 (*The Present Value of* $1), assume that $5,000 is to be received eight years from now and that a discount rate of 10 percent is to be used. Where the 10 percent column and the row for eight years in the future intersect, the figure .467 is located. This amount (for a single dollar, as the title of the table indicates) must be multiplied by the $5,000 to ascertain the present value. Since $5,000 × .467 = $2,335, we know that $5,000 to be received at the end of eight years at 10 percent discount has a present value of $2,335. Most people are surprised at how much difference there is between present and future amounts.

The calculation of present values assumes constant reinvestment each year. This means that the income from an investment made today must be rein-

EXHIBIT 16-2
Present Value of $1

Years Hence	1%	2%	4%	6%	8%	10%	12%	14%	15%	16%	18%	20%	22%	24%	25%	26%	28%	30%	35%	40%	45%	50%
1	0.990	0.980	0.962	0.943	0.926	0.909	0.893	0.877	0.870	0.862	0.847	0.833	0.820	0.806	0.800	0.794	0.781	0.769	0.741	0.714	0.690	0.667
2	0.980	0.961	0.925	0.890	0.857	0.826	0.797	0.769	0.756	0.743	0.718	0.694	0.672	0.650	0.640	0.630	0.610	0.592	0.549	0.510	0.476	0.444
3	0.971	0.942	0.889	0.840	0.794	0.751	0.712	0.675	0.658	0.641	0.609	0.579	0.551	0.524	0.512	0.500	0.477	0.455	0.406	0.364	0.328	0.296
4	0.961	0.924	0.855	0.792	0.735	0.683	0.636	0.592	0.572	0.552	0.516	0.482	0.451	0.423	0.410	0.397	0.373	0.350	0.301	0.260	0.226	0.198
5	0.951	0.906	0.822	0.747	0.681	0.621	0.567	0.519	0.497	0.476	0.437	0.402	0.370	0.341	0.328	0.315	0.291	0.269	0.223	0.186	0.156	0.132
6	0.942	0.888	0.790	0.705	0.630	0.564	0.507	0.456	0.432	0.410	0.370	0.335	0.303	0.275	0.262	0.250	0.227	0.207	0.165	0.133	0.108	0.088
7	0.933	0.871	0.760	0.665	0.583	0.513	0.452	0.400	0.376	0.354	0.314	0.279	0.249	0.222	0.210	0.198	0.178	0.159	0.122	0.095	0.074	0.059
8	0.923	0.853	0.731	0.627	0.540	0.467	0.404	0.351	0.327	0.305	0.266	0.233	0.204	0.179	0.168	0.157	0.139	0.123	0.091	0.068	0.051	0.039
9	0.914	0.837	0.703	0.592	0.500	0.424	0.361	0.308	0.284	0.263	0.225	0.194	0.167	0.144	0.134	0.125	0.108	0.094	0.067	0.048	0.035	0.026
10	0.905	0.820	0.676	0.558	0.463	0.386	0.322	0.270	0.247	0.227	0.191	0.162	0.137	0.116	0.107	0.099	0.085	0.073	0.050	0.035	0.024	0.017
11	0.896	0.804	0.650	0.527	0.429	0.350	0.287	0.237	0.215	0.195	0.162	0.135	0.112	0.094	0.086	0.079	0.066	0.056	0.037	0.025	0.017	0.012
12	0.887	0.788	0.625	0.497	0.397	0.319	0.257	0.208	0.187	0.168	0.137	0.112	0.092	0.076	0.069	0.062	0.052	0.043	0.027	0.018	0.012	0.008
13	0.879	0.773	0.601	0.469	0.368	0.290	0.229	0.182	0.163	0.145	0.116	0.093	0.075	0.061	0.055	0.050	0.040	0.033	0.020	0.013	0.008	0.005
14	0.870	0.758	0.577	0.442	0.340	0.263	0.205	0.160	0.141	0.125	0.099	0.078	0.062	0.049	0.044	0.039	0.032	0.025	0.015	0.009	0.006	0.003
15	0.861	0.743	0.555	0.417	0.315	0.239	0.183	0.140	0.123	0.108	0.084	0.065	0.051	0.040	0.035	0.031	0.025	0.020	0.011	0.006	0.004	0.002

Present Value of $1 Received Annually for N Years

Years (N)	1%	2%	4%	6%	8%	10%	12%	14%	15%	16%	18%	20%	22%	24%	25%	26%	28%	30%	35%	40%	45%	50%
1	0.990	0.980	0.962	0.943	0.926	0.909	0.893	0.877	0.870	0.862	0.847	0.833	0.820	0.806	0.800	0.794	0.781	0.769	0.741	0.714	0.690	0.667
2	1.970	1.942	1.886	1.833	1.783	1.736	1.690	1.647	1.626	1.605	1.566	1.528	1.492	1.457	1.440	1.424	1.392	1.361	1.289	1.224	1.165	1.111
3	2.941	2.884	2.775	2.673	2.577	2.487	2.402	2.322	2.283	2.246	2.174	2.106	2.042	1.981	1.952	1.923	1.868	1.816	1.696	1.589	1.493	1.407
4	3.902	3.808	3.630	3.465	3.312	3.170	3.037	2.914	2.855	2.798	2.690	2.589	2.494	2.404	2.362	2.320	2.241	2.166	1.997	1.849	1.720	1.605
5	4.853	4.713	4.452	4.212	3.993	3.791	3.605	3.433	3.352	3.274	3.127	2.991	2.864	2.745	2.689	2.635	2.532	2.436	2.220	2.035	1.876	1.737
6	5.795	5.601	5.242	4.917	4.623	4.355	4.111	3.889	3.784	3.685	3.498	3.326	3.167	3.020	2.951	2.885	2.759	2.643	2.385	2.168	1.983	1.824
7	6.728	6.472	6.002	5.582	5.206	4.868	4.564	4.288	4.160	4.039	3.812	3.605	3.416	3.242	3.161	3.083	2.937	2.802	2.508	2.263	2.057	1.883
8	7.652	7.325	6.733	6.210	5.747	5.335	4.968	4.639	4.487	4.344	4.078	3.837	3.619	3.421	3.329	3.241	3.076	2.925	2.598	2.331	2.108	1.922
9	8.566	8.162	7.435	6.802	6.247	5.759	5.328	4.946	4.772	4.607	4.303	4.031	3.786	3.566	3.463	3.366	3.184	3.019	2.665	2.379	2.144	1.948
10	9.471	8.983	8.111	7.360	6.710	6.145	5.650	5.216	5.019	4.833	4.494	4.192	3.923	3.682	3.571	3.465	3.269	3.092	2.715	2.414	2.168	1.965
11	10.368	9.787	8.760	7.887	7.139	6.495	5.988	5.453	5.234	5.029	4.656	4.327	4.035	3.776	3.656	3.544	3.335	3.147	2.752	2.438	2.185	1.977
12	11.255	10.575	9.385	8.384	7.536	6.814	6.194	5.660	5.421	5.197	4.793	4.439	4.127	3.851	3.725	3.606	3.387	3.190	2.779	2.456	2.196	1.985
13	12.134	11.343	9.986	8.853	7.904	7.103	6.424	5.842	5.583	5.342	4.910	4.533	4.203	3.912	3.780	3.656	3.427	3.223	2.799	2.468	2.204	1.990
14	13.004	12.106	10.563	9.295	8.244	7.367	6.628	6.002	5.724	5.468	5.008	4.611	4.265	3.962	3.824	3.695	3.459	3.249	2.814	2.477	2.210	1.993
15	13.865	12.849	11.118	9.712	8.559	7.606	6.811	6.142	5.847	5.575	5.092	4.675	4.315	4.001	3.859	3.726	3.483	3.268	2.825	2.484	2.214	1.995

vested and accumulated over the number of years used in the calculation if the present value is to be compatible with the future amount. Consider the example just given, where $5,000 has a present value of $2,335 for eight years at 10 percent. The following calculation shows how the 10 percent assumed earnings are added each year and behave cumulatively over the life of the investment.

Year	Principal at Beginning of the Year	Income at 10% of the Balance	Principal at End of the Year
1	$2,335	$233	$2,568
2	2,568	256	2,824
3	2,824	282	3,106
4	3,106	311	3,417
5	3,417	341	3,758
6	3,758	375	4,133
7	4,133	413	4,546
8	4,546	454	5,000

Annuities

The second part of Exhibit 16–2 contains the data to calculate the present value of a future stream of money. If $5,000 is to be received each year for four years, the present value of each dollar of the annual inflow, using a 10 percent rate, would be $3.170. This $3.170 is multiplied by $5,000 to give the present value of the annuity, which would be $15,850. An *annuity* is a payment which is received in equal amounts over a period of time, and the above example would be described as a $5,000, four-year annuity. Although a total of $20,000 would be received during the four years, its present value is only $15,850.

The rates in the annuity portion of the table in Exhibit 16–2 are nothing more than accumulations of the amounts in the first part of the table. To illustrate this point, consider the example of a stream of money to be received in the amount of $2,000 during each of the next five years, at 10 percent discount.

One way to calculate the present value would be to multiply each $2,000 receipt by the present value amount for that year. This is done in Exhibit 16–3, indicating a present value of $7,580. When the individual present values are

EXHIBIT 16–3

Year	Cash to Be Received	Present Value of a Dollar at 10%	Present Value of Cash Proceeds
1	$ 2,000	.909	$1,818
2	2,000	.826	1,652
3	2,000	.751	1,502
4	2,000	.683	1,366
5	2,000	.621	1,242
Total	$10,000		$7,580

Present value of the annuity 3.790

added, the sum is 3.790, which equals the 3.791 in the annuity section of the table. (Rounding causes the .001 difference.) Thus, the $7,580 present value could also have been calculated by multiplying $2,000 by 3.791, which equals $7,582.

Present Value Method

Present value concepts are used to reach capital investment decisions by comparing the present value of the cash inflow from an investment with its cost, measured as the required cash outflow. The minimum rate of return which the company will accept for its investments must be used in this calculation. The basic underlying premise is that if the cash inflows from an investment have a present value greater than the required outflows (at the minimum acceptable rate of return), the investment should be accepted.

Returning to Exhibit 16–3, the stream of money from that investment produced, at 10 percent, a present value of $7,580. If the cost of the investment was $7,000, and if the company accepts investments which return 10 percent or more, that investment would be accepted. The present value calculations have indicated that the discounted cash inflows are greater than the required cash outflows and the investment thus meets the criteria for acceptance. Note that this same investment would not be accepted if 20 percent were used as the minimum acceptable rate:

$$\$2,000 \times 2.991 \; (20\% \text{ annuity for five years}) = \$5,982.$$

The present value at 20 percent is only $5,982, which is not equal to the $7,000 cost. The present value of the investment proceeds is thus not sufficient, and the investment would be rejected. Note again the importance of including in the minimum acceptable rate a factor for risk, cost of capital, and profit.

When several cash outlays must be made at different times and cash inflows also differ in amount each year, the net cash inflow or outflow can be calculated and discounted. Consider the case of an investment which has the following cash flows:

Year	Original Investment	Revenues	Expenses	Additional Investment	Net Cash Inflow (or outflow)
1	$4,000	$2,000	$1,000		$(3,000)
2		5,000	1,000		4,000
3		4,000	3,000	4,000	(3,000)
4		5,000	2,000		3,000
5		3,000	—		3,000

The annual cash flows in this example are sometimes negative and sometimes positive. The present value method permits both inflows and outflows to be discounted to the present, thus providing a way of determining whether the minimum rate of return will be earned. Using a 10 percent rate, that investment would have the following net present value:

Year	Net Cash Flow	Present Value at 10%	Net Present Value
1	$(3,000)	.909	$(2,227)
2	4,000	.826	3,304
3	(3,000)	.751	(2,253)
4	3,000	.683	2,049
5	3,000	.621	1,863
Total			$2,736

The fact that there is a net positive total indicates that the investment will produce the required 10 percent return; a negative value would have indicated that it would not produce the required 10 percent. The amount of the net present value, $2,736, is not of primary concern at this point, the important fact being that it is a positive amount.

Present Value Index

The amount by which the present values of the revenue inflows exceed the present value of the expenses—excluding depreciation or amortization—provides a measure of the net return from the investment. When this amount is related to the cost of an investment, it produces a *present value index*. This is illustrated in Exhibit 16–4.

EXHIBIT 16–4

	Cost	Net Return Discounted at 10%	Present Value Index
Investment A	$100,000	$101,700	101.7
Investment B	20,000	26,200	131.0
Investment C	80,000	83,500	104.7
Investment C	150,000	145,700	98.9

If the index is less than 100, the present values are less than the cost, and the investment will not produce the desired rate of return. The highest index will indicate the investment which is most profitable, although the actual discounted rate of return is not known. The index does provide a convenient method of comparing investments, but it may be difficult to apply when the cost of the investment requires several separate cash outflows at different times. When this occurs, it may be necessary to calculate the present value of the investment's cost separately from the present values of the net return. The present value of the investment's cost is then used as the amount of the investment to calculate the present value index.

Discounted
Rate of Return

The above discussion has been directed toward ascertaining whether an investment possibility is acceptable or not, given a minimum rate of return. A method for finding the actual discounted rate of return which would be realized has not been calculated. If the actual rate is to be found, it is necessary to apply several discount rates until one that is too high and one that is too low are located. Then, working between these two, an approximation of the actual rate can be determined.

To illustrate this procedure, assume you are considering an investment costing $100,000 which produces $40,000 in each of three years. The several iterations necessary to determine the actual rate would be performed as follows:

	Annual Receipts	Value from the Table of Annuities (Exhibit 16–2)	Present Value	Result
1st estimate	$40,000	(8%) 2.577	$103,080	Too low; use higher rate.
2nd estimate	40,000	(12%) 2.402	96,080	Too high; try a rate between 8% and 12%.
3rd estimate	40,000	(10%) 2.487	99,480	Close; the rate is approximately 9.9%.

Comparing the actual discounted rate of return is sometimes done in the selection of investment alternatives. The difficulty of making the calculations can be great, however, especially when uneven flows of cash are produced. For this reason, the actual discounted rate is used less frequently than the other methods discussed in this text.

Tax Effects of
Asset Write-Offs

When a capital investment involves disposition of an existing asset, any tax deduction resulting from the write-off of the assets being replaced should be considered a reduction of the investment for the new asset. If the loss resulting from the write-off is deductible for tax purposes, the tax reduction in effect should be considered a reduction of the cost of the asset. To illustrate, assume that a company paying taxes of 50 percent is considering the replacement of an asset which has no scrap value but has an undepreciated book value of $5,000. The new asset will cost $40,000 and will reduce operating costs by $7,000 each year of its ten-year life. The computations are shown below using a 12 percent discount rate. The book loss of $5,000 has a value of $2,500 because it saves that amount in taxes. This savings is treated as a reduction in the cost of the new asset.

Cash outlay for the investment	$40,000	
Less: Reduction in taxes due to book loss in writing off the old asset (50% of $5,000)	(2,500)	
Net cost of the investment		$37,500
Present value of $7,000 per year for ten years at 12% discount rate		39,550

Thus, the investment meets the company's criterion of a 12 percent return, although it does not do so before consideration of the tax aspects of the loss on disposition of assets. The discussion in a previous chapter on the replacement of assets indicated that a book loss on the disposition of an old asset is irrelevant to replacement computations. The loss itself is irrelevant, because there is no cash flow involved in the writeoff; however, any reduction in future income taxes as a result of the write-off affects the cash flow and must be considered in the computations. Thus, it is not the loss but the tax reduction that is significant to the capital budgeting computations.

Tax Effects of Depreciation Methods

The more important methods used to compute depreciation were described early in the text, and all of those methods are acceptable for the computation of taxable net income. Of these, the three principal methods used in corporate tax returns are the straight-line, constant percentage of a declining balance, and sum-of-the-years' digits methods. Other methods—such as those based upon units of production—are permitted, but may be used only if they can be shown to be reasonable. The straight-line method is utilized more frequently than any other, but the proportion of corporate assets depreciated by the declining balance and sum-of-the-years' digits methods has steadily increased since these methods were first permitted in 1954.

If the company elects to use a constant percentage of a declining balance method, the percentage used cannot exceed twice the rate which would be used if a straight-line method were employed. Thus, an asset with a ten-year life would be depreciated one-tenth, or 10 percent, each year on a straight-line basis. The percentage to be used for that same asset employing a constant percentage of a declining balance method would be limited to 20 percent, or twice the 10 percent straight-line rate. The illustrations in this chapter and the assignment problems utilize a declining balance rate exactly equal to twice the straight-line percentage.

Since depreciation cannot exceed the cost of the asset, reduced by a reasonable salvage value, the amount of depreciation taken during the total life of the asset will be the same regardless of the depreciation method used. However, the *timing* of the depreciation charges will differ greatly, and the present value of large depreciation charges in the early years of the life of the asset makes the declining balance and sum-of-the-years' digits methods more advantageous in many cases. To illustrate, consider the timing of the depreciation charges for the two most frequently used depreciation methods applied to an asset which cost $100,000, has a life of ten years and a scrap value of $10,000 at the end of its useful life. A 50 percent tax rate is assumed in the illustration.

The total depreciation in both cases is $90,000. However, noticeable differences are evident in the amount of depreciation during the early and the later years of the life of the asset. The larger depreciation deductions in the earlier years make the declining balance method much more attractive for tax purposes and will, in most cases, produce significant differences in present value calculations. The net difference in present value between the two methods for a ten-year period, as shown in Exhibit 16–5, is $4,442 and would be even greater if the time period were longer.

EXHIBIT 16–5

Comparison of the Present Value of Straight-Line and Declining Balance Depreciation

Year	Straight-Line Depreciation	Declining Balance Depreciation	Before-Tax Difference	After-Tax Difference (50% Tax Rate)	Present Value of $1	Present Value of the After-Tax Difference
1	$ 9,000	$20,000	$11,000	$5,500	.909	$5,000
2	9,000	16,000	7,000	3,500	.826	2,891
3	9,000	12,800	3,800	1,900	.751	1,425
4	9,000	10,240	1,240	620	.683	423
5	9,000	8,190	(810)	(405)	.621	(252)
6	9,000	6,550	(2,450)	(1,225)	.564	(692)
7	9,000	5,240	(3,760)	(1,880)	.513	(964)
8	9,000	4,200	(4,800)	(2,400)	.467	(1,121)
9	9,000	3,360	(5,640)	(2,820)	.424	(1,196)
10	9,000	3,420	(5,580)	(2,790)	.386	(1,072)
Total	$90,000	$90,000	–0–	–0–	6.145	$4,442

An investment which does not meet the company's minimum return using a straight-line depreciation method may be sufficiently attractive if present value computations are made using a declining balance method. To illustrate, assume that a company's management is considering the possibility of acquiring an investment at a cost of $102,300. The machine is expected to produce savings of $40,000 during each of the next four years and will have no salvage value at the end of that time. The company is subject to income taxes of 40 percent. An old machine will be scrapped, with no cash proceeds but with a tax deductible loss of $4,000. Assume further that the company will not accept investments which do not produce at least a 15 percent return after taxes. The computations comparing the present value of the investment and the resulting cash returns are given below.

Cost of the Investment

Cash outlay	$102,300	
Less reduction in taxes on the write-off of the old asset ($4,000 @ 40%)	1,600	
Net cost of the investment		$100,700

Present Value of the Savings, Using Straight-line Depreciation

	Year 1	Year 2	Year 3	Year 4	
Net proceeds, before taxes	$40,000	$40,000	$40,000	$40,000	
Depreciation	27,500	27,500	27,500	27,500	
Taxable difference	$12,500	$12,500	$12,500	$12,500	
Taxes, at 40%	$ 5,000	$ 5,000	$ 5,000	$ 5,000	
Cash inflow (net proceeds less taxes)	$35,000	$35,000	$35,000	$35,000	
Present value @ 15%	.870	.765	.658	.572	
Present value of cash proceeds	$30,450	$26,775	$23,030	$20,020	$100,275

Present Value of the Savings, Using Declining Balance Depreciation

	Year 1	Year 2	Year 3	Year 4	
Net proceeds, before taxes	$40,000	$40,000	$40,000	$40,000	
Depreciation	55,000	27,500	13,750	13,750*	
	($15,000)	$12,500	$26,250	$26,250	
Less excess depreciation in prior years		(15,000)†	(2,500)†		
Taxable difference	–0–	–0–	$23,750	$26,250	
Taxes, at 40%	–0–	–0–	$ 9,500	$10,500	
Cash inflow (net proceeds less taxes)	$40,000	$40,000	$30,500	$29,500	
Present value at 15%	.870	.765	.658	.572	
Present value of cash proceeds	$34,800	$30,600	$20,069	$16,874	$102,343

The investment will produce a return of 15 percent after taxes only if the declining balance or sum-of-the-years' digits method is used. When the straight-line method is employed, the net investment of $100,700 is greater than the $100,275 value of the cash proceeds.

The tax regulations permit separate choice of depreciation methods for each asset. One asset may be depreciated on a straight-line basis, while the next asset acquired may be subjected to another of the several acceptable methods. In certain cases, the tax regulations even permit a change in the method used to depreciate a particular asset, but care must be exercised in such instances to prevent violation of the regulations.

Summary

All companies have limited funds available for investment and must select investment opportunities carefully. A minimum rate of return is employed to screen out unacceptable investments. The minimum rate must be sufficient to cover the cost of capital which will be used, as well as the risks which are inherent in the investment, and to provide a satisfactory profit.

The payback period coupled with the basic rate of return provides a means of equating unlike investments. Payback provides a measure of the recapture of principal, and the rate of return provides a measure of profitability. Together these two techniques can be used as an effective measure of an investment's potential.

The discounted cash flow concept is another useful measure of an investment's acceptability. This technique is based on the fact that a present dollar is more valuable than a future dollar. The method necessitates the selection of a rate of discount for the calculation of the present value of future receipts. When applied to an investment possibility, the future returns from the investment are estimated and their present value is calculated, using the predetermined minimum acceptable rate of return. The present value of future receipts is then compared with the presently required outlay for the investment.

Present value calculations assume constant reinvestment of cash inflows, and these reinvestments are assumed to produce earnings equal to the discount rate which was used in computing the present value amounts. Without such reinvestment, the equating of future streams of money with a present outlay for the investment would not be valid.

New Terms

Annuity   A payment of equal amounts over several periods.

Capital investment   An investment in an asset which has a life extending over several periods.

Discount rate   The percentage used to calculate the subtraction from a future sum in order to determine a present value.

Interest rate   The percentage used to calculate the addition to be made to a present value to determine its future value.

Payback period   The length of time required to recapture the principal of an investment.

Present value   The value of a sum to be received in the future which has been discounted back to the present.

Present value index   The ratio of the present value of inflows to the present value of outflows of an investment.

Questions

1. Describe what is meant by "a capital investment decision." Give several examples.

2. Describe how the return on investment calculation is made. Include in your answer how the amounts used in the calculation are derived when the investment is a depreciable asset giving a cash inflow that differs from one year to the next.

3. An investment was bought for $10,000 and is a depreciable asset with a two-year life; straight-line depreciation will be used. It will produce total cash inflows of $6,000 the first year and $8,000 the second year. What is the rate of return for the investment?

4. Why would a company need to have a minimum acceptable rate of return? Why can't a decision be made on each investment as it arises without the need for an established minimum rate of return?

5. Why is the payback period used to compare investment possibilities? If it is used as the only comparison technique, what would its major weakness be?

6. Describe the concept of present value of a future receipt.

7. Suppose that a friend owes you $100, due in one year, and that his credit is absolutely good. Would you take $90 now instead of the $100 due in one year? Would you take $80? Would you take $70? Select a minimum amount that you would take now to discharge the debt and calculate from that amount what your personal present value discount rate might be.

8. Distinguish between interest and discount.

9. What is an annuity? Describe, using the amounts in Exhibit 16–2, the relationship between the present value amounts in the first part and the second part of the table.

10. Why is depreciation used in computing after-tax cash flow, even though depreciation is a "noncash" expense?

11. Why is a book loss on the sale of an asset being replaced a part of the after-tax cash flow calculation, even though the loss is a noncash item on the income statement?

Exercises

16–1   **Computation of Present Values** *(20 minutes)*   Given below are a number of independent exercises. You are to compute the present value in each case, using the values given in the table in Exhibit 16–2.

1. Present value of $1 received in five years, at 10 percent discount rate.
2. Present value of $6,500 to be received in four years using a 20 percent discount rate.
3. The total present value of $2,000 to be received at the end of the fourth year, $3,000 at the end of the sixth year, and $5,000 at the end of the tenth year, using a 20 percent discount rate.
4. Present value of an annuity of $1 received for six years using a 10 percent discount rate.
5. Present value of a $2,000 annuity to be received for the next seven years using a 30 percent discount rate.

16–2   **Computation of Present Values** *(15 minutes)*   Compute the present value of the following, using a 20 percent discount rate:
1. $2,000 to be received four years from now.
2. $2,000 to be received each year for the next four years.
3. $2,000 to be received in each of the sixth through the tenth years from now.

16–3*   **Comparing Investment Alternatives** *(25 minutes)*   The Pepper Company is comparing three investment possibilities. The cost, annual cash inflow, and life of each is given below:

	Cost	Annual Cash Inflow	Life of the Investment
Investment A	$100,000	$20,000	7 years
Investment B	40,000	10,000	6 years
Investment C	80,000	15,000	10 years

Instructions
For each investment compute (1) the payback period, (2) the rate of return, (3) the present value, using a 10 percent rate, and (4) the present value index.

16–4   **Computation of Payback, Rate of Return, and Present Value** *(20 minutes)*   The White Investment Company is considering the possibility of investing $100,000 in a special project. This venture will return $25,000 per year for five years.

Instructions
Compute (1) the payback period, (2) the annual rate of return, and (3) the present value of the investment using a 10 percent rate. (Use the table in Exhibit 16–2.)

16–5   **Comparison of Two Investment Proposals** *(20 minutes)*   The Paper-Mill Company is considering two investment possibilities; the first requires an investment of $100,000 and the second an investment of $80,000. The first investment will return $20,000 each year for ten years, while the second will return $10,000 for seven years and $20,000 for the next three years. Neither investment has any salvage or residual value at the end of the ten-year period.

Instructions
1. For each investment proposal, compute (a) the total dollar return, (b) the payback period, (c) the annual rate of return, and (d) the present value of the investment at 20 percent, using the tables in Exhibit 16–2.
2. State which investment you feel is most profitable.

16–6 **Comparison of Investment Proposals** *(30 minutes)*   The Salt Company is comparing three investment possibilities. The cost, annual cash inflow, and the life of each is given below:

	Cost	Annual Cash Inflow	Life of the Investment
A	$100,000	$40,000	5 years
B	200,000	50,000	6 years
C	300,000	60,000	7 years

Instructions
For each investment compute:
1. The payback period
2. The rate of return
3. The present value of cash inflows, using a 20 percent discount rate
4. A present value index

16–7* **Analysis of an Investment Possibility** *(15 minutes)*   A company is considering an investment possibility which will return $10,000 each year for three years. The cost of the investment is $20,000 with no salvage value at the end of the three years.

Instructions
1. What is the payback period?
2. What is the rate of return?
3. What is the present value of the investment at 10 percent?
4. What is the present value index?

16–8* **Present Value With Straight-Line Depreciation** *(25 minutes)* The Merim Company is considering the acquisition of an asset for $10,000. The asset will have a five-year life with no salvage value and will produce income of $4,000 annually before depreciation. It will replace an asset with no scrap value but with a $2,000 present book value. Assume that the company is subject to a 40 percent tax rate and requires a 16 percent return after taxes.

Instructions

Assuming a straight-line depreciation method, present computations indicating the present value of the after-tax cash flow for each of the five years of the asset's life.

16-9   **Present Value Using Sum-of-the-Years' Digit Depreciation** *(30 minutes)*   Assume all the data in Exercise 8, except that a sum-of-the-years' digits depreciation method is used. Compute the present book value of the after-tax cash flows if the asset is bought.

Problems

16-10   **Selection of an Investment** *(20 minutes)*   A company can borrow at 6 percent to make investments. Investment A will provide $5,000 at the end of each year for ten years. Investment B will provide $10,000 at the end of each year for five years. The costs of the investments are:

A	$30,000
B	$40,000

Instructions

1. If you are absolutely certain of the cash flows, which investment is better? Show computations of the payback period, rate of return, present value at 10 percent, and present value index to support your selection.
2. If you are not absolutely certain of the cash flows, would you change your selection? Justify your answer.

16-11   **Comparison of Investment Alternatives** *(30 minutes)*   The Anderson Company is comparing four investment possibilities. The cost, annual cash inflow, and life of each is as follows:

	Cost	Annual Cash Inflow	Life of the Investment
Investment A	$ 50,000	$10,000	9 years
Investment B	90,000	15,000	8 years
Investment C	100,000	25,000	7 years
Investment D	70,000	20,000	7 years

Instructions

For each investment compute:
1. The payback period
2. The rate of return
3. Present value, using a 12 percent rate
4. A present value index

16–12   **Comparison of Two Investment Proposals** *(30 minutes)*   The Glasson Company is considering two investments, each requiring a present expenditure of $36,000. Proposal A will return $6,000 each year for ten years, while proposal B will return $10,000 each year for five years.

Instructions
For each investment proposal compute (1) the total dollar return, (2) the payback period, (3) the annual rate of return, (4) the present value of the investment, using an 8 percent rate (from the table in Exhibit 16–2), and (5) the present value index.

16–13   **Ranking of Investment Alternatives** *(40 minutes)*   Presented below are the cash proceeds which are expected to be received from alternate investments. Each investment requires an outlay of $80,000 and produces cash inflows totaling $110,000, but the company has funds to accept only one of them.

	Cash Expected to Be Received						
	Year 1	Year 2	Year 3	Year 4	Year 5	Year 6	Total
Investment A	$10,000	$10,000	$20,000	$20,000	$25,000	$25,000	$110,000
Investment B	30,000	30,000	20,000	10,000	10,000	10,000	110,000
Investment C	40,000	40,000	10,000	10,000	5,000	5,000	110,000
Investment D	5,000	5,000	20,000	20,000	30,000	30,000	110,000
Investment E	60,000	30,000	5,000	5,000	5,000	5,000	110,000
Investment F					50,000	60,000	110,000

Instructions
1. Compute the total present value at a 10 percent rate (using the present values in Exhibit 16–2), the payback period, and the rate of return for each of the investments.
2. Rank the investments in the order in which you would accept them, placing the most desirable first.

16–14   **Computation of Present Values of Investment Alternatives** *(30 minutes)*   Bill Mecker is considering several investment properties. Two of the most promising of these are an apartment house and a small printing company. The rental property will cost $40,000 and has a remaining life of ten years with a salvage value of $10,000 at the end of the tenth year. Rentals will be $10,000 annually, and repairs and taxes will be $1,000. The printing company will require an investment of $30,000 and may be assumed to have a reasonable life expectancy of eight years. The equipment will have a salvage value of $5,000 at the end of the eighth year, and annual profits after all expenses and depreciation are expected to be $5,000.

Instructions
Prepare a table for each investment, showing the cash inflow each year and the present value of these inflows, using a 10 percent dis-

count rate. State which you would accept if only one could be acquired.

16-15   **Comparing Investment Possibilities** *(35 minutes)*   The Slick Company is comparing four investment possibilities. The cost, annual cash inflow, and life of each is given below:

	Cost	Annual Cash Inflow	Life of the Investment
Investment A	$ 60,000	$15,000	6 years
Investment B	90,000	20,000	7 years
Investment C	80,000	10,000	12 years
Investment D	100,000	20,000	8 years

Instructions
For each investment compute:
1. The payback period
2. The rate of return
3. Present value, using a 12 percent rate
4. A present value index

16-16   **Effect of Tax Loss on Asset Replacement Decisions** *(30 minutes)*
The Robertson Company is presently using a hand-operated machine which cost $100,000 four years ago and has a remaining life of ten years. It has a $60,000 undepreciated cost and a present market value of $20,000. A new machine has just been introduced, costing $150,000 with a ten-year life and no salvage value. It would produce annual savings of $25,000 in labor costs over the present machine. The company does not accept investments which return less than 10 percent after taxes. Assume the company's tax rate is 40 percent and that straight-line depreciation will be used. Should the Robertson Company acquire the new machine?

Instructions
Compute the present value of the cash flow using a 10 percent rate to ascertain whether the investment should be made. Consider in your answer the tax loss on the sale of the old asset, deduction of depreciation for tax purposes, and the tax on the annual savings. The old machine would be sold and would not be traded on the new asset. .

16-17   **Present Value Using Straight-Line Depreciation** *(40 minutes)*
Assume that a company paying taxes of 50 percent is considering the replacement of an asset which has $2,000 scrap value and remaining book value of $20,000. The new asset will cost $90,000, will produce additional revenues of $18,000 a year for ten years, and will be sold at the end of the tenth year for $6,000. The company uses a discount rate of 10 percent when evaluating investment possibilities and straight-line depreciation.

Instructions
Compute the following:
1. Net cost of the investment (subtract the value of the tax loss on the sale of the old asset)
2. Annual after-tax cash inflow
3. Present value of total after-tax cash inflow for the ten-year period at 10 percent
4. Excess (if any) of the present value of after-tax savings over the cost of the investment
5. The present value index

16–18   **Present Value With Straight-Line Depreciation**   *(30 minutes)*   The Martin Company has been experiencing a decline in sales volume and profits on their product recently. The vice-president in charge of consumer research reports that recent technical innovations in their field point to an expected further decline in market potential. It has been suggested that the company turn its effort toward the production of certain plastic toys, since the present facilities could easily be adapted to these products. If the company does make toys, a new machine costing $12,000 with a five-year life and no salvage value would have to be purchased. It is estimated that income after all expenses (except depreciation) will be $5,000 annually from the manufacture of toys. Assume that the company is subject to a 50 percent tax rate and requires a 15 percent return after taxes.

Instructions
Assuming a straight-line depreciation method, present computations indicating whether the asset should be acquired and the toys manufactured.

16–19   **Present Value Using Straight-Line Depreciation** *(30 minutes)*
The company is considering buying equipment for $100,000. The asset will have a ten-year life, no salvage value, and will be depreciated by the straight-line method. It will produce revenue of $30,000 annually before the deduction of depreciation expense. The asset to be replaced has a book value of $6,000 and can be sold now for $2,000.

Instructions
Compute the following:
1. The payback period of the new asset
2. The present value of cash inflows using a 50 percent tax rate and a 12 percent return after taxes
3. The present value index of the investment

16–20   **Tax Effects on Decisions to Acquire Depreciable Assets** *(30 minutes)*   The Plachard Corporation has the alternative of investing $300,000 during the current year for new equipment or spending a like amount for advertising. Assume that either expenditure would produce savings or profits of $80,000 per year for the next five years, before depreciation or taxes. The equipment has no salvage value at the end of the five years, and the company uses a straight-line depreciation method for tax purposes.

The advertising may be expensed in full during the first year, and the company has sufficient profits from other sources to absorb it. Assume that the company is subject to a 40 percent corporate tax.

Instructions

Compute the net after-tax cash flow from each of the two investment possibilities—that is, cash inflows less cash outflows—for each year of the five-year period. Comment on the difference in both amount and timing of the net after-tax cash flows.

16–21   Present Value Using Straight-Line Depreciation *(60 minutes)*
The Hokum Company is considering the acquisition of an asset for $25,000. The asset will have a five-year life with no salvage value and will produce income of $8,000 annually after deducting all expenses except depreciation. It will replace an asset with a present market value of $3,000 and a present book value of $5,000. Assume that the company is subject to a 50 percent tax rate and requires a 16 percent return after taxes.

Instructions

Assuming a straight-line depreciation method, present computations indicating whether the asset meets the company's investment criteria.

16–22   Comparative Tax Effects on Asset Replacement Decisions *(80 minutes)*   The Fox-Batrix Company is considering the acquisition of an asset for $110,000. It will have a five-year life, will produce labor savings of $35,000 each year, and will have a salvage value of $10,000. The company is subject to 40 percent taxes on its income.

Instructions

1. Compute the after-tax cash flow during each of the five years, using (a) straight-line depreciation, (b) sum-of-the-years' digits depreciation, and (c) declining balance depreciation with a rate equal to double the straight-line rate.
2. If the company does not accept investments returning less than 10 percent after taxes, should the investment be acquired?

16–23   Tax Effects on Lease vs. Purchase Agreements *(40 minutes)*
The Damas Company is considering an investment possibility which requires cash outlays of $100,000. One alternative is to acquire new equipment which will have a ten-year life and a $15,000 salvage

value at the end of the ten years and which will be subject to a constant percentage of a declining balance depreciation method at a rate double that of straight-line depreciation. It will produce labor savings of $20,000 per year before depreciation or taxes.

The second alternative is to acquire the same equipment through a lease arrangement instead of a purchase. The $100,000 could then be invested in bonds yielding a 6 percent interest income and maturing in ten years. The lease payments for the machine would be $15,000 per year for each of the ten years. Assume that the company is subject to income taxes of 50 percent.

Instructions

1. Compute the after-tax cash inflow and outflow for each of the two possibilities for the ten-year period. (Round calculations to the nearest even dollar.)
2. Assuming that an after-tax return of 10 percent is the minimum acceptable rate, will these investments meet the company's investment requirements?

chapter 17

Enterprise Valuation Decisions

Learning Objectives

Valuation of a going concern is a difficult and complex task and one which depends upon a synthesis of the techniques utilized in the analysis of financial statements and capital budgeting. Upon completion of your study of this chapter you should:

1. Recognize the complexities encountered in valuing an enterprise.
2. Know how to analyze a financial statement, obtaining the necessary data to value an enterprise.
3. Recognize the capital budgeting processes which are applicable to the valuation process.
4. Appreciate the processes of measuring the performance of segments of an enterprise.

Valuation Complexities

The purchase and sale of businesses or major portions thereof, which occur with some frequency, necessitate the placing of a value on the business as a continuing entity. However, determination of the market value of an entire business enterprise or a significant portion of it is a complex and difficult task, and the methodology used in such a determination depends upon the intended purpose of the valuation. A bank or insurance company considering a loan application may value the assets and earning power of its client company in terms of the current resale value. A governmental agency valuing a public utility for purposes of approving its rate structure would use a different method. Finally, a prospective buyer of a company may employ still other valuation techniques to determine a purchase price. In all cases, however, a thorough understanding of the meaning and limitations of financial statements is a prerequisite to assigning a value, and the purpose of this chapter is to introduce the problems inherent in such analysis and to illustrate how accounting data are employed in their solution.

The current market value of the ownership rights in a business enterprise depends in large measure upon the value of its assets and its profit potential. The balance sheet, income statement, and statement of retained earnings, which report current financial position and the result of past operations, are the foundation for appraising the company's value. The data in these financial statements must be analyzed thoroughly for a realistic and reliable valuation of the firm.

To illustrate the problem of valuing an enterprise, assume that Logan Brail owns 90 percent of the capital stock of a company and that the remaining 10 percent is owned by several other individuals. Mr. Brail, having reached retirement age, is interested in withdrawing from active management and selling his stock. The value of Brail's stock ownership is directly dependent upon the value of the business enterprise. Even though shares owned by one of the other stockholders have recently been traded, the price received by such minority shares does not provide a basis for evaluating Brail's holdings, since his 90 percent ownership controls the company. Only by placing a valuation on the enterprise as a going concern can an intelligent appraisal of the value of the controlling interest in the company be made.

Accounting data are of value in solving this type of business problem, but factors outside the scope of financial data enter into the solution of almost all business problems. When a value is placed on a business enterprise, the seller will usually assess a higher value than will a prospective purchaser. The final price is a product of bargaining between the two parties. The methods discussed in this chapter provide a means of quantifying or reducing to dollar amounts some of the factors which the buyer and seller must consider. Several alternative procedures are discussed in this chapter, any one of which could be applied to a given situation. Data from more than one method establish a reasonable range of values within which the buyer and seller will negotiate.

Valuation of Assets
and Earnings

In measuring the value of a business, the company's assets and earning power must be evaluated separately. Properties presently owned must be included in assessing the value of an enterprise, but the value of present assets standing alone will not in most cases reflect the value of a going concern as a future source of net income. For example, one business whose assets have a present market value of $100,000 may have annual profits of $15,000, while a similar business with the same dollar value of assets may realize annual profits of only $5,000. The first company, which has a greater profit potential, is obviously more valuable as a continuing enterprise, even though its tangible assets are worth no more than those of the second company.

The need for a separate evaluation of the assets and the profit potential of a company may be illustrated by a simple example. Consider the case of a cold drink vending machine located in a choice spot. Both the machine and the monopoly it enjoys because of its location will be included in the sales price, and a value must be assigned to each. The current value of the machine is $300, without consideration of the location; this amount measures the value of the asset itself, whether in its present location or at another site.

The value of the location is determined by appraising the "excess profits" which it produces. If the average net income from the use of similar machines in other locations is $70 annually while this particular site returns a profit of $100, the excess profit is $30 per year. *Capitalization* of this excess profit is one method by which the extra earning power may be valued. The term "to capitalize" means to compute the amount of investment which, at a selected rate of interest, will produce, in this case, $30 annual income. If 20 percent is a mutually agreeable rate of interest, the capitalized value is found by dividing $30 by 20% (or .20).

$$\$30 \div .20 = \$150$$

An investment of $150, earning 20 percent annually, will produce $30 of income; consequently, the excess profits are worth $150. Using this method of evaluation, the vending machine, in its present location, is worth $450, determined by adding the $300 value of the asset to the $150 valuation of the location. An investor would therefore pay $450 for the machine in expectation of a $100 return each year, $70 of which is the normal return and $30 of which is a 20 percent return of the price he paid for the location.

Steps in the Valuation Process

The valuation process involves four basic steps, which were followed in appraising the value of the vending machine in the previous example. These are:

1. Determine the value of the assets.
2. Project into the future the annual net income of the business and determine the amount which may be considered excess earnings.
3. Place a value on the excess earnings.
4. Add the total asset values in step 1 to the total value of the excess future earnings in step 3 to arrive at the computed value of the business as a continuing enterprise.

There are several ways in which each of these steps may be accomplished, with varying results. These alternate procedures and the application of financial data to the valuation process are discussed in the remainder of this chapter.

Role of Accounting Data

The historical data in financial statements do not always reflect future expectations, and the value of a business enterprise must obviously be based on its potential. For this reason, financial statements serve only as a beginning point in the valuation of a business and must be adjusted in the light of future expectations.

With the exception of cash and receivables, which should appear on the financial statements at realizable value, all the assets on the balance sheet reflect only the unexpired cost. This amount at any given time is dependent upon the selected depreciation or amortization policy and usually has no relationship to current value. For example, the method of recording depreciation, computing the cost of the ending inventory, and amortizing intangible assets will directly affect the book value of an asset at any given moment in its useful life.

The net income which a business reports each accounting period is also directly affected by the company's accounting policies. The choice of a depreciation method (such as straight-line vs. declining balance) and the selection of an inventory valuation method (such as FIFO vs. LIFO) play major roles in the determination of reported profits. In addition, fluctuations in the value of the dollar may prevent accurate comparisons of one year's net income with that of another. A net profit of $10,000 in 1950 should not be equated with a profit of $10,000 in 19X1 without adjustment, because the dollar in 19X1 does not have as much purchasing power as the dollar enjoyed in 1950. If the financial statements of past years are used as a basis for estimating future income, the data must be so adjusted that the net incomes of all periods included in the analysis are comparable.

Valuation of Assets

There are three different concepts which may be applied in the valuation of the assets of a business. The assets may be assigned (1) their value if sold individually on the open market, (2) the cost of procuring similar assets, or (3) their value as a collective group of income-producing assets. The latter is generally considered the most appropriate valuation basis.

The concept of assigning to assets a value equal to their proceeds if sold individually on the open market is based on a liquidation assumption, rather than on a going concern basis. Assets sold in this manner almost invariably realize less than their value as a group of productive assets. The liquidation value of individual assets is relevant only in certain instances when the company has incurred consistent losses or when its profits have been considerably less than those of similar companies within the industry. In such cases, the assets should be sold and the proceeds invested in properties that will produce a normal return.

Replacement value, or the estimated cost of procuring similar assets in like condition, is not always a good measure of the value of the collective assets of a going concern, because the costs incurred and the time consumed in gathering and arranging the assets into productive properties are not usually considered. Furthermore, assignment of replacement value assumes that similar assets in like condition are available.

The best measure of the value of a company's total assets is their present worth as a group of related, income-producing properties. There is no absolute method by which this value can be assessed, but it is generally replacement cost plus the cost of the time, effort, and expense of bringing the assets together.

To illustrate the valuation of a company's assets, assume that the Crandall Company has been earning average annual profits of $10,000, which is above the average in the industry. Their trial balance appears as follows:

Cash	$ 2,000	
Inventory	10,000	
Machinery and equipment	60,000	
Accumulated depreciation—		
machinery and equipment		$10,000
Common stock		40,000
Retained earnings		22,000
	$72,000	$72,000

Assume further that the machinery and equipment could be sold for a total of $50,000 and the inventory would bring $5,000 on an immediate liquidation sale basis. Machinery and equipment similar to the existing assets would cost $67,000 if acquired individually, however, and the inventory has a replacement value of $11,000. In addition, an estimated $4,000 would be spent in acquiring similar machines and equipment, transporting them to the company's location, installing and testing them.

The liquidation value of the company's total assets would be $57,000. This amount consists of the following:

Cash	$ 2,000
Inventory	5,000
Machinery and equipment	50,000
	$57,000

The value of the assets on a going concern basis, however, would be $84,000, determined by using the following amounts:

Cash		$ 2,000
Inventory		11,000
Machinery and equipment	$67,000	
Plus cost of assembly	4,000	
		71,000
		$84,000

The going concern valuation should be used only when the company has a value as a profit-making organization. Similarly, a liquidation value is applicable only when the return on investment is less than normal and liquidation is a distinct possibility. In the above example, the company's profits of $10,000 provide a reasonably sound return on investment, and use of the going concern valuation is justifiable.

Estimation of Future Earnings

After the valuation of the assets, the next step in the process is to estimate future earnings. Past earnings are the beginning point in determining future profits, but such expenses as depreciation and amortization must be adjusted to reflect the new valuation that has been placed upon the assets. In prior years, the company's profits were computed using depreciation and amortization expenses based on the original cost of the assets; when future earnings are estimated, depreciation and amortization expenses should be based on the adjusted value of the assets. If the business is sold, the new owner must compute future earnings using depreciation and amortization costs based on the price he will have paid for the assets.

In the previous illustration, the inventory was reflected on the books of the Crandall Company at $10,000, and the machinery and equipment at an undepreciated cost of $60,000. Their adjusted market values were estimated in that illustration to be $11,000 and $71,000, respectively. Assume that the machinery and equipment have a remaining useful life of five years and that a FIFO inventory method is to be used. A buyer, paying the adjusted market value for the assets, could expect his future profits to be lower than those reported in previous years by the amounts shown in Exhibit 17–1, other factors being equal.

EXHIBIT 17–1

Profit Reduction Resulting From Changed Asset Costs

	Cost on Seller's Books	New Cost to Purchaser	Reduction in Future Years' Profits				
			1	2	3	4	5
Inventory	$10,000	$11,000	$1,000				
Machinery and equipment	60,000	71,000	2,200	$2,200	$2,200	$2,200	$2,200
Decrease in expected profits			$3,200	$2,200	$2,200	$2,200	$2,200

Assuming that the company has been earning $10,000 annually, and that present operations will continue unchanged in the future, the new owner paying current market value for the assets can expect a profit of only $6,800 in the first year after acquisition and $7,800 for the next four years.

Obviously, many factors in addition to the adjusted market value of the assets will affect future profits. Upward cost trends, population shifts, and improved production or marketing methods, for example, should be considered when future profits are estimated. Both purchaser and seller must reach an agreement on the probable effects of such factors before they can be quantified and included in the estimation of future earnings.

Valuing Excess Earnings

Future earnings will command a purchase price only if it is anticipated that they will be in excess of a normal return on invested capital. A purchaser paying the adjusted market value for a company's assets expects a normal return on his investment. If he cannot anticipate such a return, in the absence of other considerations, he will not buy the assets and continue them in their former use.

To illustrate, assuming that 6 percent is considered a normal return on invested capital, a purchaser paying $100,000 for the assets of a business would expect earnings of at least $6,000 per year. If future profits are estimated at only $4,000 annually, or less than the normal return, the assets are not worth $100,000 as a group of related income-producing properties. The assets may in this case produce more income if they are sold individually and the proceeds invested elsewhere at 6 percent.

If expected profits are $6,000, assets worth $100,000 and earning only 6 percent will produce only a normal return and there will be no excess profits. Expected earnings of $8,000 per year, however, will yield excess earnings of $2,000. In addition, an estimate must be made of the period of time over which excess earnings will continue. Obviously, the longer these profits can be expected to continue, the greater will be their value. Since there is no reliable way by which this time period can be ascertained, it is necessary for both seller and purchaser to arrive at a mutually acceptable estimate.

The value of a company's excess earnings may be considered (1) the total excess earnings for a specified number of years, (2) the capitalized value of annual excess earnings or (3) the present value of future excess earnings.

Specified number of years   When excess earnings for a specific number of years are used to value the company's profits, a relatively short period of time is normally selected. With some notable exceptions, a period longer than five or six years has not been allowed in the valuation cases settled in court. If excess profits are $2,000 per year, use of a five-year period would place a $10,000 valuation on the company's profits, which would be added to the adjusted market value of the assets to determine the total valuation of the enterprise. If the assets are valued at $100,000, the business would be considered worth a total of $110,000.

Capitalization   Assuming that a 20 percent after-tax rate of interest is mutually acceptable, the capitalized value of excess profits of $2,000 per year is determined by dividing the annual excess earnings by the selected percentage, as follows:

$$\$2,000 \div .20 = \$10,000$$

The $10,000 capitalized valuation indicates that an investment of $10,000 earning a 20 percent return will produce a $2,000 income each year.

The selected interest rate must be sufficient to provide a satisfactory return on the investment and, at the same time, cover the risk involved in projecting excess profits into the future. Consequently, the selected rate may be as high as 20 to 30 percent.

Present value   Use of present value computations is based on the premise that the inflow of future dollars from excess earnings will not be as valuable as an equal number of current dollars. Therefore, future excess profits for a specified period may be valued by discounting them back to the present at a selected discount rate. The discount rate should be sufficient to provide a normal return and also cover the risk inherent in buying future excess profits.

To illustrate, assume that excess profits are estimated to be $2,000 per year, that a 10 percent rate is to be used, and that the excess earnings are not reasonably assured for more than ten years. The total present value of the estimated excess profits is computed by using amounts from a present value table similar to that exhibited in an earlier chapter. Each dollar of excess profits over the ten-year period is discounted back to the present to determine its current value. The computation would be made as shown in Exhibit 17–2.

EXHIBIT 17–2

Year	Expected Excess Profits	Present Value of a Dollar at 10%	Present Value of Excess Profits
1	$2,000	.909	$ 1,818
2	2,000	.826	1,652
3	2,000	.751	1,502
4	2,000	.683	1,366
5	2,000	.621	1,242
6	2,000	.564	1,132
7	2,000	.513	1,026
8	2,000	.467	934
9	2,000	.424	848
10	2,000	.386	772
Total			$12,292

The stream of expected excess profits is thus estimated to have a present value of $12,292, dependent upon selection of a 10 percent rate and a ten-year period. Use of other percentage figures or a different number of years could produce significantly different valuations.

An Illustration

The case shown below is given to illustrate the entire valuation procedure. The current financial position of the Graybell Company and its profit position are reflected in the following financial statements.

All the capital stock of the company, which is owned by T. R. Graybell, is to be sold. The Wycoll Company is interested in acquiring the business and wishes to purchase all of the stock from Graybell. Representatives of the Wycoll Company and Mr. Graybell arrive at the following decisions after considerable negotiation.

EXHIBIT 17–3

GRAYBELL COMPANY
Condensed Balance Sheet
December 31, 19X1

ASSETS			EQUITIES		
Cash		$ 2,000	Accounts payable	$2,000	
Accounts receivable	$ 8,000		Accrued taxes		
Less: Allowance			payable	1,000	$ 3,000
for uncollectible			Two-year note		
accounts	500	7,500	payable		2,500
Inventory		10,000	Capital stock		20,000
Equipment	$19,000		Retained earnings		4 000
Less: Accumulated					
depreciation	9,000	10,000			
Total assets		$29,500	Total equities		$29,500

GRAYBELL COMPANY
Income Statement
For the Year Ended December 31, 19X1

Sales		$100,000
Cost of goods sold		63,000
Gross profit		$ 37,000
Expenses:		
Depreciation on equipment	$ 2,000	
Salaries	21,500	
Supplies	1,500	
Rent	5,000	30,000
Net income		$ 7,000

1. The Wycoll Company agrees to accept the valuation of all assets and liabilities as presented on the balance sheet, with the exception of the equipment, which has a current market value $10,000 greater than its book value and five years of useful life remaining.
2. The $7,000 net income for 19X1 is representative of the company's operations, and no foreseeable events are expected to change its profit position materially.
3. A 10 percent return on invested capital is a normal return in this industry.
4. Excess profits, if any, are to be discounted at 16 percent for a five-year period to determine their present value.
5. The price to be paid for the company's stock is the current market value of the net assets plus the present value of any excess profits.

Valuation of assets   The net assets (assets less liabilities) total $24,000 on the books. Their market value is $10,000 greater than their book value; therefore, the agreed current market value of the net assets is $34,000.

Computation of excess profits   The depreciation expense has been $2,000 per year, as reflected by the company's income statements, but will be $4,000 when based on the equipment's current market value of $20,000 and its remaining five-year life. Thus, the increased depreciation expense will reduce anticipated future profits to only $5,000 per year.

A normal return on the $34,000 valuation of the company's assets at the agreed 10 percent rate would be $3,400 per year. Thus, only $1,600 of the expected $5,000 net income is excess profits ($5,000 expected profits less $3,400 normal profits = $1,600 excess profits).

Present value of excess profits   The two parties agreed that future excess profits are to be discounted to their present value using a five-year period and a 16 percent rate.

The present value of the excess profits is computed as follows:

Year	Excess Profits	Present Value of a Dollar	Present Value of Excess Profits
1	$1,600	.862	$1,379.20
2	1,600	.743	1,188.80
3	1,600	.641	1,025.60
4	1,600	.552	883.20
5	1,600	.478	764.80
Total			$5,241.60

The present value of future excess profits is thus $5,241.60, and a total valuation of $39,241.60 is placed on the business, computed by adding the $34,000 current market value of the net assets to the $5,241.60 present value of the excess profits.

Comparing Partnership and Corporation Financial Data

Two factors of major importance should be considered when the financial statements of a partnership or proprietorship are compared with those of a corporation. First, the income taxes paid by a corporation are an expense of the business, while profits of partnerships and proprietorships are taxable as personal income to the owners. Second, the services of partners or proprietors are not reflected in the salaries expense accounts, since any assets they withdraw are recorded as personal withdrawals and not as a salary expense.

Consider, for example, the following two income statements for the Atlas Corporation and the Hale-Bartt partnership. For the purpose of illustration, assume that these companies are identical in every respect, except in the form of ownership.

ATLAS CORPORATION Income Statement *For the Year Ending Dec. 31, 19X1*			HALE-BARTT PARTNERSHIP Income Statement *For the Year Ending Dec. 31, 19X1*		
Sales		$300,000	Sales		$300,000
Cost of goods sold		160,000	Cost of goods sold		160,000
Gross profit		$140,000	Gross profit		$140,000
Expenses:			Expenses:		
Depreciation	$10,000		Depreciation	$10,000	
Salaries	90,000		Salaries	50,000	
Supplies	5,000		Supplies	5,000	
Insurance	3,000	108,000	Insurance	3,000	68,000
Net income			Net income		$ 72,000
before taxes		$ 32,000			
Federal income					
tax expense		10,600			
Net income					
after taxes		$ 21,400			

The partnership net income of $72,000 appears on the surface to be much better than the $21,400 corporate net income after taxes. However, note that the sales, cost of goods sold, gross profit and depreciation, supplies, and insurance expense are identical. Only the salaries expense differs in amount, and only the statement of the corporation reflects a federal income tax expense. The salaries of all administrative officers are considered expenses to the corporation, but the services of the partners are not reflected in the salaries expense account of the partnership. If the salaries expense of the partnership contains an additional $40,000, an amount assumed to be comparable to the salaries received by the two top executives, the statements of the companies would reflect identical operating results. Therefore, when the value of a partnership is computed by a prospective corporate purchaser, partnership profits should be adjusted to the corporate form, or vice versa.

Value of a Decentralized Segment

As a company grows, the problems facing management in controlling and coordinating that company's activities become increasingly complex. Many large companies have attempted to solve the problem of organizational complexity by decentralizing. A decentralized company is one which is divided into separate segments, each with its own "top" management. Although legally there is only one company, for organizational purposes the equivalent of several different companies will exist.

One of the major automobile companies in the United States provides an excellent example of a completely decentralized organization. In addition to a "corporate management" group in the "head office" there are sixteen separate divisions, each with a manager in charge. Each manager operates his division like a smaller, separate company. Materials are sold from one division to another only if the sales price is less than that offered by an outside vendor, and shipments are billed and paid for in regular fashion between the divisions.

The value of each decentralized operation must be measured by the "profit" it is able to generate. A profit goal is frequently set for each segment by corporate management, and the performance of the manager of that segment is measured by his ability to meet this profit target. Corporation management must give relatively broad executive authority to each manager and normally will intervene in the operations of a segment only when a manager's actions are detrimental to some other segment of the corporation. The establishment of interdivisional transfer prices to be charged by one segment to another segment is one area wherein top corporate management sometimes intervenes. The "profit" earned by a segment is thus directly affected by the "controlled" prices between divisions.

Return on Investment as a Valuing Method

Periodic computations of the rate of return realized by a decentralized segment of the company constitute one way in which the value of a decentralized segment is frequently measured. The rate of return in such cases is determined by use of the simple formula which follows:

$$\frac{\text{Annual net income of the segment}}{\text{Assets invested in the segment's operations}} = \text{Annual rate of return}$$

If a company has invested $600,000 in the assets of a small plant to produce parts for the main assembly plant, and the decentralized parts operation reports annual profits of $65,000 annually, the return is $65,000 divided by $600,000, or 10.8 percent. In many cases the division manager must prepare and administer his own budgetary program, and his effectiveness in the independent operation of his division is measured by his ability to earn profits. Since high profits are assumed to be a fair measure of the manager's effort, the manager who is able to realize a high return on the company's investment in the assets used by his division is considered to be doing an efficient and effective job.

To illustrate the need for a calculation of the return on investment, consider the case of a company with four divisions, operated by four division managers, who report profits as follows:

	Net Profit
Division A	$10,000
Division B	50,000
Division C	30,000
Division D	20,000

Although the manager of Division B has the highest net profit, the amount of net profit does not indicate the full extent of each manager's effectiveness until it is related to the amount of invested assets. The following table indicates the assets employed, profits realized, and the resulting return on investment:

	Net Profit	Net Assets Invested	Return on Investment
Division A	$10,000	$ 70,000	14.2%
Division B	50,000	500,000	10.0
Division C	30,000	400,000	7.5
Division D	20,000	100,000	20.0

The return on investments indicates that the manager of Division D is utilizing his assets much more effectively than any of the other managers. Division C shows a rate of return much lower than the other divisions, and, other things being equal, management may want to give further attention to the operations of that division.

Care must be taken, however, to insure that the balance sheet and income statements of the various divisions are prepared in a comparable fashion. Their incomes are not comparable, for example, if one division uses a LIFO inventory method while another uses a FIFO method, or if one uses straight-line depreciation and another uses the sum-of-the-years' digits. In such cases, adjustments to the net income figures are necessary to make the return on investment amounts comparable.

Determining profit of a decentralized segment   A particularly difficult problem exists in the determination of "profit" realized by a decentralized segment. This problem exists because frequently a large portion of the revenues of a decentralized unit are received from other segments of the same company under a price structure not fully subject to open competitive pressures. A transfer of materials or services between divisions at cost would be entirely possible from a strict accounting standpoint, but transfer at cost would not permit the computation of a divisional profit or a divisional rate of return. Some of the most frequently used bases for determining intercompany transfer prices are as follows:

1. *List price.* The list price is sometimes used when merchandise is also sold to outside customers. Thus, other segments of the company must pay the same price as any other customer. This method is equitable for computing divisional "profit," but such a price is not always available, especially when the entire output of the plant goes to other segments of the same company.
2. *Cost plus a profit.* Cost plus a fixed amount of profit is frequently used for intercompany billing purposes. Cost in such cases may be (a) full cost, including some portion of home office overhead which is allocated to each segment, (b) manufacturing cost, not including allocated general overhead, or (c) variable cost, which excludes all allocated and fixed overhead items. The profit may be (a) a fixed percentage of cost or (b) a fixed amount per unit. Thus, there are several variations of the "cost plus a profit" computation.

3. *Negotiated price.* A negotiated transfer price set by top corporate management is frequently used. Such a price results in an arbitrary "profit" in many cases and necessitates careful interpretation of the results of the transactions of the division. Thus, although rate of return on a decentralized operation is a useful measure of the contribution of a segment of the company, the absence of a fully competitive environment in which the price structure can operate interjects into the divisional profit an element of management's particular biases.

Summary

In a free, competitive society, the ownership of business enterprises changes hands with some frequency, and a method of determining the value of the entire ownership or a substantial portion of the ownership equity must be available. While the exact method used in any given situation is subject to bargaining, both the value of the assets and the present value of the stream of future profits should be considered. The assets may be assigned a liquidating value, a replacement value, or a going-concern value. Profits may be valued by taking the sum of the expected excess earnings for a specified number of years, by capitalizing the value of annual excess earnings, or by computing their present value. The value of a single operating segment of the company is even more difficult to compute than the value of the entire enterprise, especially if an intercompany transfer price is involved. Management frequently employs a return on investment (ROI) calculation to measure the effectiveness of separate operating segments. The base of the calculation is the amount of assets employed by the segment being measured; care must be taken in interpreting the results, because the asset base is stated at cost. The cost of assets to one branch or division may be entirely different from the cost of the same type of asset within another division, and the resulting rates of return may therefore not be comparable.

New Terms

Capitalization   The value of an investment computed by dividing the income from an investment by a selected rate of interest.

Decentralized segment   A division or part of a company which is physically separated and usually separately managed.

Earning power   The excess of actual earnings of a company over earnings normal in that industry.

Going concern value   A value based upon replacement cost plus a factor for the cost of organization and startup.

Liquidation value   A value based upon what could be received in an immediate, forced sale.

Replacement value   A value based upon the full cost which would be incurred in replacing something.

Valuation   The calculation of a present market value.

Questions

1. Why is the determination of the current value of a business entity necessary? Name several events which necessitate placing a value on the business enterprise.

2. Presently owned assets and the earning power of a business must be evaluated separately when placing a value on the enterprise. Explain why this is necessary.

3. Describe briefly the four steps in the valuation process.

4. Why are past financial data valuable, but nevertheless only a beginning point in the valuation of a business?

5. Accounting policies adopted by a company directly affect the balance sheet amounts of assets and also the periodic net income. Contrast the balance sheets and reported income of two companies, where one uses a LIFO inventory and sum-of-the-years digits depreciation while the other uses straight-line depreciation and a FIFO inventory method.

6. Do you feel that a company that has made a consistent profit of $10,000, without fluctuation, since 1933, has "remained steady" or has its profitability decreased in terms of purchasing power? Explain.

7. Distinguish between the valuation of assets based on (a) a liquidation assumption, (b) a replacement basis, and (c) a collective group of productive assets. Which is more appropriate to a profitable going concern?

8. When an attempt is being made to set a value on a business enterprise and future profits are being estimated, explain why past profits must be adjusted to take into consideration current asset values.

9. Why is a relatively short period of time, such as five or six years, normally used when the value of excess future profits is considered the total excess for a specified period of time?

10. Describe the process of "capitalizing" excess profits.

11. Describe the process of discounting excess profits back to the present. Is a specified period of time necessary for this computation?

12. How can a deficit of one company be of value to another company if the two are jointly owned and file a joint return?

13. Why do salaries and federal income taxes make the income of proprietorships and partnerships not comparable with corporations? Would you consider a corporate net income of $50,000 equal to a partnership net income of $50,000?

Exercises

17–1   **Definitions** *(15 minutes)*   The following terms or concepts were introduced in this chapter:
a. Capitalization of excess earnings
b. Liquidation value of assets
c. Replacement value of assets
d. Excess profits
e. Decentralized company
f. Negotiated intercompany transfer price

Instructions
Define each term or concept, giving examples where possible.

17–2   **Value of a Concession Right** *(15 minutes)*   John Crain owns the cold drink concession at a ball park and pays several university students to operate it for him. Crain paid $5,000 for the concession rights two years ago, and it has three remaining years of life. His other assets used in the operations of the concession are of negligible amount. Profits have averaged $3,000 each season.

Instructions
If a 10 percent return is considered normal on investments of this nature, and if the present level of profits can reasonably be expected to continue for three years, discount the earnings back to present value and place a valuation on the concession rights. (Use the table in Exhibit 16–2.)

17–3   **Valuation Based on Excess Earnings** *(15 minutes)*   William Hott is considering the purchase of all the stock in a company which has net assets of $100,000. Profits have been $18,000 each year, after deduction of depreciation expenses of $8,000. Profits are expected to continue unchanged if Hott buys the business, with the exception of the increased depreciation expense. A profit of 10 percent is considered normal in this industry.

Instructions
If the net assets have a current value of $120,000 and a remaining life of ten years, and if excess profits are to be assigned a value equal

to their amount over the next five years, compute a total valuation of the enterprise.

17–4*   Value of Excess Earnings *(35 minutes)*   Compute from the data given in the following three independent cases the value which would be assigned to excess profits:

a. Normal earnings in the industry are 10 percent on net assets, and excess profits are to be given a value equal to the total excess profits to be earned during the next five years. The company has net assets worth $200,000, and total profits are expected to be $27,000 annually.

b. Normal earnings in the industry are 8 percent of net assets, and excess profits are to be capitalized at 10 percent. The company has net assets of $100,000, and total profits are expected to be $11,000 annually.

c. Normal earnings in the industry are 15 percent on net assets, and excess profits for the next five years are to be discounted to present value at 20 percent. The company has $200,000 of net assets, and profits are expected to be $40,000 annually. (Use the table in Exhibit 16–2.)

17–5   Rate of Return with Differences in Accounting Policy *(20 minutes)*
Mercle Department Stores, Inc., has retail outlets in several major cities. The effectiveness of the manager of each outlet is measured by the return on the investment of his particular store. The following data were included in the financial reports received from seven of the company's stores:

Store	Net Income for the Year (on the Income Statement)	Total Investment
A	$10,000	$100,000
B	20,000	250,000
C	5,000	80,000
D	1,000	70,000
E	30,000	200,000
F	10,000	100,000
G	8,000	80,000

All accounting policies relative to inventories and depreciation are similar, except that Store C uses a LIFO inventory method and Store D uses a sum-of-the-years' digits depreciation method. If these stores had followed the same policies as other stores, their net incomes would have been $8,000 and $12,000 respectively.

Instructions
Compute the return on investment for each store, and rank them in order, highest return listed first.

Problems

17–6 **Valuation Using Alternate Methods For Earnings** *(40 minutes)*
The amounts appearing on the Redline Company's books and the estimated present value of the assets on December 31, 19X1, appear below.

Negotiations are in process for the Donahue Corporation to purchase the entire common stock of the Redline Company. Both parties agree that the equipment has a seven-year remaining life and the buildings a twenty-year remaining life. Depreciation used in past profit determinations has been $6,000 annually for equipment and $7,000 annually for buildings. Both parties agree that the company's sales will continue to average $300,000 annually over the foreseeable future, and that expenses, exclusive of depreciation and income taxes of 50 percent, will average $260,000.

	Book Value		Estimated Present Value
Cash	$ 7,200		$ 7,200
Accounts receivable (net)	11,400		10,800
Inventory	24,200		24,200
Equipment (net)	36,400		35,000
Buildings (net)	87,000		100,000
Land	18,700		25,000
Accounts payable		$ 24,600	
Mortgages payable		50,000	
Capital stock		80,000	
Retained earnings		30,300	
	$184,900	$184,900	

Instructions
Compute valuations of the business for each of the following three independent assumptions if normal return on investment in the industry is 10 percent and if excess profits are valued (1) as being equal to the total excess profits earned during the next five years; (2) by capitalizing at 10 percent; (3) by discounting excess earnings for the next ten years at 16 percent to determine present discounted value. (Use the table in Exhibit 16–2.)

17–7 **Valuation Using Various Techniques For Excess Profits** *(30 minutes)* The fair market value of the assets of the Comprador Company is $400,000, and they have ten years of life left. The company is currently earning an annual profit of $60,000 with a depreciation expense of $30,000. A 10 percent return is considered normal in the industry.

Instructions
Compute a value of the enterprise if excess profits are to be assigned a value equal to: (a) the total amount for the next three years, (b) their capitalized value at 20 percent, (c) their present value for ten years discounted at 20 percent. (Use the table in Exhibit 16–2.)

17–8   **Assessing a Value; Comparing Actual Return to the Value** *(40 minutes)*   Harvey Wayton agreed to purchase the entire common stock of the Midway Corporation for $159,000. The trial balance of the Midway Corporation was as follows at the time the stock was acquired by Wayton:

Cash	$ 3,000	
Accounts receivable (net)	17,000	
Equipment (net)	36,000	
Buildings (net)	80,000	
Land	10,000	
Accounts payable		$ 11,000
Mortgages payable		25,000
Common stock		70,000
Retained earnings		40,000
	$146,000	$146,000

The building has a fair market value of $100,000 and a twenty-five-year remaining life; the land has a present value of $15,000; receivables a value of $16,000; and equipment a value of $40,000 with a ten-year remaining life. All other assets have a value equal to the amounts in the trial balance.

The company's past profits have averaged $20,000, based on annual depreciation of $3,000 on the building and $3,000 on equipment. Other than for depreciation changes, these profits should remain constant. Normal profits in the industry are 10 percent on investment, and Wayton agreed to compute a value for excess profits by capitalizing them at 20 percent.

In order to acquire the Midway Corporation, Wayton formed a new company, the Wayton Corporation, and invested $159,000 for its common stock. He then paid the $159,000 to the Midway Corporation for its assets and liabilities.

In the first year after acquiring the corporation's assets and liabilities, the Wayton Corporation rendered services to customers for cash, $300,000, and paid selling and administrative expenses of $270,000 in cash. Depreciation was recorded at the new cost and expected life of the assets. Goodwill, recorded when the Wayton Corporation acquired its properties, was the amount paid for the excess profits and is to be amortized using a five-year life.

Instructions
1. Reconstruct the computations which were used to arrive at the $159,000 value of the business when Wayton purchased it.
2. Prepare an income statement from the transactions completed during the first year of the life of the new company.
3. Compute the percentage return which Wayton realized on his investment (net profit from part 2 divided by his investments for the business.)

17–9   **Projection of Profits and Computation of Enterprise Value** *(40 minutes)*   The Parsons Corporation offered Joe Killan $120,000 for his business, the Midgett Company, which was owned entirely by Killan. The Midgett Company was formed five years ago, and it has realized profits as follows:

First year	$ 1,000 loss
Second year	2,000 net income
Third year	5,000 net income
Fourth year	8,000 net income
Current year	11,000 net income

The Midgett Company has net assets on its books of $80,000. A conservative estimate of their market value is $90,000, although they cost Killan $120,000 five years ago. They have a ten-year remaining life. Most companies in the same industry consider 10 percent on investment a normal return.

Instructions
1. Estimate the profits which will be earned in the next five years, assuming the present trend continues.
2. Compute the value of the business using
    a. market value of the assets plus present value of ten years of excess earnings discounted at 20 percent
    b. market value of the assets plus present value of five years of excess earnings discounted at 10 percent
    c. market value of the assets plus the full amount of excess earnings for the next four years.
3. Comment on whether you think the $120,000 price suggested by the Parsons Company is a reasonable offer.

17–10   **Computation of a Valuation and a Rate of Return** *(45 minutes)*   Mr. Robert Holt, president and sole owner of the Hillside Hotel, a corporation, is considering selling his stock in the company and retiring.

Mr. Holt had an independent appraiser examine the assets of the company, and the appraiser's report indicated that the balance sheet amounts represented current value except for land and buildings. The report stated that the land has a current value of $50,000 and the buildings a value of $120,000 with a thirty-year remaining life.

Mr. Holt has been receiving a salary of $5,000 annually from the business. He set his salary low, since he preferred to take the profits of the company in the form of dividends. Presidents of similar hotel corporations receive a salary of $15,000. Average return on invested assets in the industry may be assumed at 10 percent.

Instructions

1. Do you think Mr. Holt has received a fair rate of return on the $150,000 he paid for the hotel three years ago? Compute the rate of return he has received each year on his investment.
   a. Using the profit, corrected by the items shown in the statement of retained earnings.
   b. Using only the cash flow to Mr. Holt (salary plus dividends).
2. Using a 10 percent discount rate for ten years of excess profits, plus the net market value of assets, compute a value for the business.

HILLSIDE HOTEL
Comparative Balance Sheet

	December 31		
ASSETS	19X1	19X2	19X3
Cash	$ 7,500	$ 16,100	$ 3,300
Accounts receivable	12,000	12,700	13,000
Less: Allowance for uncollectible accounts	(700)	(700)	(800)
Supplies	10,100	10,300	10,900
Buildings	190,000	190,000	190,000
Less: Accumulated depreciation	(72,000)	(77,000)	(82,000)
Furniture, fixtures, and equipment	63,500	73,500	79,100
Less: Accumulated depreciation	(23,900)	(28,000)	(40,100)
Land	30,000	30,000	30,000
Total assets	$216,500	$226,900	$203,400
EQUITIES			
Accounts payable	$ 20,700	$ 34,900	$ 21,800
Mortgage payable (annual principal payments of $5,000)	75,000	70,000	65,000
Capital stock	100,000	100,000	100,000
Retained earnings	20,800	22,000	16,600
	$216,500	$226,900	$203,400

HILLSIDE HOTEL
Income Statement

For the Year Ending
December 31

	19X1	19X2	19X3
Revenues:			
From room rental	$100,000	$105,000	$104,000
From food and beverage sales	37,000	39,000	40,000
Total revenues	$137,000	$144,000	$144,000
Operating expenses:			
Salaries	$ 69,000	$ 71,000	$ 74,000
Utilities	14,500	14,700	15,100
Depreciation	9,100	9,100	9,100
Supplies	6,800	7,000	7,200
Total operating expenses	$ 99,400	$101,800	$105,400
Net income before taxes	$ 37,600	$ 42,200	$ 38,600
Federal income taxes	$ 13,000	$ 17,000	$ 16,000
Net income after taxes (to retained earnings)	$ 24,600	$ 25,200	$ 22,600

HILLSIDE HOTEL
Statement of Retained Earnings

For the Year Ending
December 31

	19Xi	19X2	19X3
Retained earnings, beginning balance	$ 11,200	$ 20,800	22,000
Understatement of prior year's taxes		(4,000)	
Correction of depreciation expense of prior year			(8,000)
Corrected beginning balance of retained earnings	$ 11,200	$ 16,800	$ 14,000
Current year's income	24,600	25,200	22,600
Dividends paid	(15,000)	(20,000)	(20,000)
Retained earnings, ending balance	$ 20,800	$ 22,000	$ 16,600

17-11   **Comparison of Corporate and Partnership Valuation** *(40 minutes)*
The entire ownership equity of Collins, Inc., a corporation, and
that of the Jones-Bertram Company, a single proprietorship, are
for sale. Both companies are in the same industry. The Collins

Corporation pays its president and only stockholder, Mr. J. C. Collins, a salary of $20,000 each year. Mr. L. K. Jones, sole owner of the Jones-Bertram Company performs the same function as does the president of a corporation, but receives no salary. The corporation pays 30 percent of its profits in taxes, while the proprietorship pays no taxes as a business entity, but would pay the same percentage as the Collins Corporation if incorporated.

The assets of both companies cost $150,000 twenty years ago and have been depreciated using a total life of thirty years. The assets of both companies have a present going concern value of $110,000 with a ten-year remaining life. The reported profits of the corporation were $20,000 in 19X1, while the profits of the proprietorship that same year were $50,000. No changes are expected in the future profitability of the two companies.

Instructions
1. Compute the value of each business to a corporate purchaser if normal profits in the industry are 10 percent of investment, and excess profits are capitalized at 20 percent.
2. Describe briefly any other factors which you would want to investigate before acquiring either business for the amount computed in part 1.

17–12   **Computation of Division Profitability** *(35 minutes)*   The Wilson Plastics Company has two divisions. The Twinston division makes raw plastics materials which it ships to the Extrusion division, where plastic household utensils are molded from the raw materials. The Twinston division is allowed to sell its entire production of raw plastics to outside customers if it desires, and the Extrusion division is permitted to buy raw materials from outside sources if the price is lower. The company's combined income statement is as follows:

Total sales		$400,000
Cost of goods sold:		
Beginning inventories—both divisions	–0–	
Raw materials consumed—Twinston	$ 90,000	
Labor—Twinston	110,000	
Overhead—Twinston	60,000	
Additional materials—Extrusion	28,000	
Labor—Extrusion	52,000	
Overhead—Extrusion	45,000	
	$385,000	
Less ending inventory—Twinston	$10,000	
—Extrusion	25,000	
Total ending inventories	35,000	
Total of cost of goods sold		$350,000
Gross profit		$ 50,000

(continued)

Operating expenses:

Selling and administrative—Twinston	$ 4,500	
Selling and administrative—Extrusion	11,200	
Central office overhead	20,000	
Total operating expenses		35,700
Net profit		$ 14,300

The ending inventory of the Extrusion division is based upon the cost of production in the Twinston division. It is unprocessed and has a market value of $30,000. The $400,000 sales in the income statement were all made by the Extrusion division except for $55,000 made by the Twinston division to outside customers. The market value of the raw plastics transferred to the Extrusion division was $220,000. Central office overhead is estimated to be 30 percent attributable to the Twinston division and 70 percent to the Extrusion division.

Instructions

The company's management is attempting to measure the "profitability" of the two divisions. Prepare separate income statements for the two divisions if market price is used as the intracompany transfer price. Treat each division as a separate company to the fullest extent possible in preparing the income statements.

17–13 **Return on Investment** *(35 minutes)* A company has five divisions, each under the direction of a vice-president. The company's Board of Directors measures these executives by the return they are able to generate from the assets under their control. The financial statements of the five divisions for the current year show the following:

Division	Net Income	Net Assets (assets less liabilities)	Total Assets	Depreciation Expense
A	$10,000	$ 80,000	100,000	6,000
B	20,000	200,000	210,000	18,000
C	30,000	250,000	310,000	25,000
D	20,000	180,000	190,000	10,000
E	10,000	110,000	115,000	12,000

Division 3 acquired its plant twenty-five years ago when the dollar was worth 150 percent of its present value, and Division D when the dollar was worth 120 percent. All others are assumed to have acquired their assets with current dollars.

Instructions

1. Compute a return on investment for the five divisions as follows:
   a. Using net assets as the base
   b. Using total assets as the base

c. Using total assets and profits adjusted for the heavier depreciation which B and D should use. (Their depreciation should be increased by $5,000 and $6,000, respectively, which will decrease their profit by a like amount.)
2. Rank the five divisions, placing the one which you feel has earned the highest return first.

17-14   **Return on Investment Adjusted for Changing Value of the Dollar** *(40 minutes)*   The Monahan Company has five plants in principal cities throughout the United States. The investment in the plants appearing in the company's records is given below, along with the year in which the investment was made and the net income of each plant for 19X1:

Plant	Year of Investment	Investment Original	19X1 Reported Income
A	1940	$100,000	$20,000
B	1950	130,000	20,000
C	1960	100,000	10,000
D	1970	180,000	20,000
E	19X1	200,000	30,000

The purchasing power of a dollar has declined steadily and may be assumed (for purposes of this problem) to have changed as follows, using 19X1 as the base year (100 percent): 1940, 160 percent; 1950, 140 percent; 1960, 120 percent; 1970, 110 percent; 19X1, 100 percent.

Instructions
1. Compute the return on investment, using 19X1 net income and the investment appearing on the company's records.
2. Convert the investments into terms of 19X1 dollars, so that all investments will be stated in terms of a dollar with uniform purchasing power. (For example, multiply the $100,000 investment in Plant A, made in 1940, by 160 percent.) Compute the return on investment using the adjusted investment amounts.
3. Comment on any differences between the two procedures. How would you rank the plants in terms of their return on investment?

17-15   **Effect of Full Cost in Intercompany Prices** *(40 minutes)*   The Hammond Company has two divisions, A and B. A is a subassembly plant producing parts for B, the main assembly plant. A full costing procedure is used to compute the intercompany transfer prices, as illustrated in the following computations:

Part Number	Variable Cost Per Unit	Fixed Cost Per Unit	Total Cost	Intra-company 10% Profit Margin	Sales and Transfer Price
X-12	$ 3.00	$1.00	$ 4.00	$ .40	$ 4.40
Y-4	5.00	1.00	6.00	.60	6.60
Z-29	10.00	1.00	11.00	1.10	12.10

The budget prepared at the beginning of the year indicated production expectations for the year as follows: X–12, 10,000 units; Y–4, 20,000 units; Z–29, 30,000 units. Since a total of 60,000 units is to be produced, the company's management decided to prorate $1 per unit of fixed cost to each unit.

The manager of division B is given full authority to purchase from outside sources if the parts are available at a lower price. These outside prices fluctuate and currently are X–12, $3.60; Y–4, $6.60; and Z–29, $11.80. The assembly plant at B uses 8,000 units annually.

Instructions
Discuss fully the implications to the Hammond Company if the manager of division B buys his year's supply of unit Z–29 from outside sources. What would you recommend as an intercompany pricing policy? Provide computations where possible to support your answer.

chapter 18

Quantitative Decision Techniques

**Learning
Objectives**

This chapter continues the discussion of costs and revenues as they are utilized in the management decision process. Upon completion of your study of this chapter you should:

1. Appreciate the role of quantitative methodology in the process of reaching workable solutions to business problems.
2. Know how to calculate optimal order quantities, probability estimates, probability rates of return, and prepare control charts based upon normal probability distributions.
3. Recognize the limitations of quantitative decision tools and how they provide important information if interpreted in light of the underlying assumptions.

**Nature of
Quantitative Techniques**

Management control of a business is not a simple, uncomplicated process. Most of the decisions required of management are complex, and there is usually no assurance that the final decision is the best of all possible alternatives. The number of variables which may affect the outcome of a particular course of action is almost infinite, and consideration of the effects of each variable becomes extremely difficult. However, quantitative concepts and techniques have been developed in recent years to aid those who must evaluate the more significant variables.

A quantitative technique is, broadly defined, any methodology which attempts to evaluate in quantitative terms a number of different factors, thereby arriving at a tentative solution to the given problem. These techniques frequently make use of *models*. A model, in this context, is a mathematical formula or other expression of relationships. The mathematical expression given in the earlier chapter on cost-profit-volume relationships for the fixed and variable portions of an expense is a form of model. The statement that a "particular cost is $1,000 fixed, and the balance is variable with sales, at the rate of 2 percent of sales" provides a model of the behavior of that cost.

Several quantitative techniques will be introduced in this chapter, but those discussed will not in any way exhaust the possibilities of this type of analysis. The examples selected for treatment in this chapter were chosen because they illustrate the interrelationships of cost and revenue data with quantitative methodology. Throughout this chapter, special attention should be given to the types of costs and revenues which are utilized in the models, and the need to quantify events, in terms of their probability of occurrence, and to estimate quantities, costs, and revenues.

An Illustration: EOQ

To illustrate and contrast an essentially subjective approach with a quantitative technique, consider the problem of selecting the quantity of merchandise to be ordered. Assume that John Grimmitt, formerly assistant manager of the hardware department, has recently been promoted to manager. The previous manager had always ordered $100 of product A each time that the inventory of that product was depleted, and Grimmitt can find no definite reason for ordering that particular quantity. He is therefore interested in determining what quantity should be ordered each time the stock runs low.

Subjective method One possible solution would be to continue the custom of issuing a $100 order. While this procedure utilizes the experience and judgment of the former manager, there is no assurance that this is the best quantity. Grimmitt has therefore decided to list all the advantages and disadvantages of increasing and of decreasing the order quantity.

Effects of Increasing the Order Quantity

Desirable Features	Undesirable Features
1. Fewer orders will be placed, thus saving clerical ordering costs.	1. There will be a larger inventory with the resulting increased costs of carrying the inventory.
2. Should the purchase price rise, the larger inventory will produce a "savings."	2. There is increased danger of obsolescence losses
3. Quantity discounts may be secured.	
4. The danger of loss from stockouts is reduced.	

After having listed the more significant factors requiring consideration, Grimmitt may reach a decision without further analysis, but in so doing he will be interjecting his personal biases. He may, for example, be overly concerned with the danger of obsolescence losses and therefore permit that factor to color his judgment.

At this point, however, Grimmitt may begin to apply quantitative techniques by placing weights on each of the factors and examining the numeric result of these weights. The possibility of obsolescence loss may be weighted as "3," while the likelihood of stockouts may be weighted "2." In this manner, a quantitative amount is produced, but since the weights also are the result of personal bias, the value of the numerical amount is almost as subject to question as if a purely intuitive decision had been made.

Quantitative methodology   A close examination of the desirable and undesirable features listed by Grimmitt will indicate that reasonably accurate dollar costs may be ascertained for most of them. Costs of carrying inventory can be computed, as can the cost of issuing purchase orders. Only obsolescence and stockout losses cannot be computed with reasonable accuracy, although a probability of occurrence may be estimated. It is the estimation of costs and probabilities and their use in a model that constitutes a quantitative solution to the problem.

Fortunately, Grimmitt does not have to construct his own model, for there is an existing formula for determining order quantities. This model is based upon the concept of equating the costs of ordering merchandise with the cost of carrying inventory. If the order quantity is too large, the inventory will be too high and its carrying cost will be excessive; similarly, if the order quantity is too low, a large number of orders must be placed with a resulting high ordering cost. The objective, therefore, is to find that point where the total cost is

EXHIBIT 18–1

Inventory Order and Carrying Cost

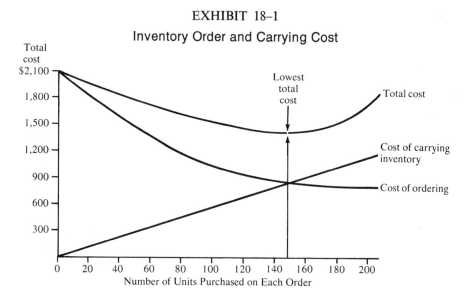

Number of Units Purchased on Each Order

the lowest. The model used in this case is based upon the fact that the point of lowest total cost will always be the point where order cost is exactly equal to the cost of carrying inventory.

Exhibit 18–1 illustrates in graphic form the behavior of the cost of ordering, the cost of carrying inventory, and the total of the two costs. Note that the cost of ordering is high when order quantities are low, since a large number of orders must be placed. On the other hand, the total cost of carrying inventory decreases as the order quantity decreases, since the average number of units on hand is lower. The total cost is the sum of these two costs and is found at the point where the two cost curves cross. The proof that this point will always produce the lowest total cost is possible with elementary calculus, but such proof is not considered necessary at this point.

The calculations necessary to determine the optimum order quantity may be reduced to a simple formula requiring only three amounts. These are the incremental cost of placing one purchase order, the cost of carrying inventory stated as a percentage of inventory value, and the expected demand for the product during the coming year. Using mathematical notations,

Let X = The unknown (order size)
      K = The incremental cost of placing an order
      R = The cost of carrying \$1.00 of inventory for one year, expressed as a percentage
      D = The expected sales of the product for the year

From these factors, some additional quantities may be derived. The number of orders placed during the year can be expressed as D/X, or the total sales during the period divided by the size of the orders to be placed. If sales are expected to total \$80,000 each year, and if the order size is \$8,000, then \$80,000 ÷ \$8,000, or 10, will be the number of orders placed during the year. Further, the average inventory during the period can be expressed as $X/2$, or one-half the amount ordered each time. The inventory is assumed to go from a high equal to the number of units ordered, to a low of zero, at which time another order will be placed and received. Thus, the average inventory will be equal to one-half the quantity ordered.

With these amounts expressed in mathematical form, the cost of carrying inventory and the cost of placing orders may be expressed as follows:

1. The total cost of carrying inventory = $X/2 \times R = XR/2$ (Since $X/2$ is the average inventory, and R is the rate of carrying inventory, then $XR/2$ is the total cost of carrying inventory.)
2. The total cost of ordering = $D/X \times K = DK/X$ (Since D/X is the number of orders placed and K is the cost of an order, then DK/X is the total cost of ordering during the year.)

Now, since it is seen that the optimum order quantity will be found where the cost of carrying inventory equals the cost of ordering, these two factors may be equated and a model for determining order quantities formulated, as follows:

$$\frac{XR}{2} = \frac{DK}{X}$$

$$X^2R = 2DK \qquad (\text{multiplying by } X)$$

$$X^2 = \frac{2DK}{R} \qquad (\text{transposing } R)$$

$$X = \sqrt{\frac{2DK}{R}} \qquad (\text{solving for } X)$$

Thus, the problem of determining order quantities may be reduced to a single calculation, which expressed non-technically is as follows:

$$\frac{\text{The optimum}}{\text{order size}} = \sqrt{\frac{2 \times \text{The cost of placing an order} \times \text{The expected sales}}{\text{The cost of carrying inventory}}}$$

With this model available, the only problem remaining for Grimmitt is to determine the costs of carrying inventory and the cost of placing purchase orders. Cost studies will be necessary, but they should not prove excessively difficult. Suppose, for example, that Grimmitt finds the following costs applicable to carrying inventory and placing purchase orders:

Cost of Carrying $1.00 of Inventory for One Year		Incremental Cost of Placing One Purchase Order	
Insurance	$0.05	Supplies	$0.12
Taxes	0.03	Postage	0.10
Storage costs	0.01	Clerical costs	1.18
Imputed interest	0.06	Office space costs	0.40
	$0.15		$1.80

Note that the cost of carrying inventory includes storage costs and imputed interest. The storage costs would be included only if they are direct costs which may be discontinued as the inventory is reduced. Sunk storage costs, such as depreciation and taxes on a building, which are inescapable, would be irrelevant to this problem. The imputed interest is included since the funds tied up in increased inventory could be invested in other revenue-producing ventures. Further, the clerical and office space costs included in the cost of ordering must include only the variable, or incremental costs.

With these quantitative tools, Grimmitt is now able to compute the optimum order quantity for Product A. The only additional figure required is the expected demand for the product during the year. Assuming that total sales are expected to be $1,000, the amounts can now be inserted into the model and solved for the unknown order quantity.

$$X = \sqrt{\frac{2DK}{R}}$$

$$X = \sqrt{\frac{2 \times \$1.80 \times \$1,000}{.15}}$$

$$X = \sqrt{\frac{\$3,600}{.15}}$$

$$X = \sqrt{\$24,000}$$

$$X = \$155$$

If the D factor used in the formula (demand) is the retail value of sales, the answer will also be in terms of sales value; if K is the cost of sales, the answer will be in terms of cost. In the illustration, assume cost is used, and the results indicate that the prior practice of ordering $100 may have been unnecessarily costly, for too many purchase orders were placed. If Grimmitt increases the order quantity to $155, the total cost of ordering and of carrying inventory will be reduced.

The model constructed for determining the order quantity of Product A is applicable to most of the company's other products as well. The order cost and the cost of carrying inventory, once computed, will be applicable to a large number of products, the only variable being the demand or expected sales. Application of the model, using the same cost of ordering and carrying inventory as used in the previous computation, but assuming expected sales of $5,000 annually, will produce an optimum order quantity of $346. A product with expected sales of only $100, on the other hand, would have an optimum order quantity of $49.

The use of quantitative models is increasing rapidly. Many of the more important business activities have been subjected to study, and useful models have been constructed. The results thus obtained are in most cases far superior to those produced by pure intuition or guess. Grimmitt, in the illustrative case, might have continued indefinitely with a costly order quantity had he not undertaken the quantitative analysis just described.

Probability estimates   The degree of probability of the occurrence of a particular event is either subconsciously or consciously considered in the solution to most business problems. Such statements as "I wonder if taxes will be increased next year," and "There is some chance that our labor costs will increase next year," are verbal expressions of the concern about events which have varying degrees of probability. The quantification of these probabilities and their incorporation into the decision-making process has gained momentum recently, and the use of this type of data has paralleled the use of quantitative models and the application of computers to business problems.

The application of probability theory is based upon two important considerations.

1. An absolute impossibility is assigned a chance of zero, and an absolute certainty a chance of one. However, in all areas where probability is of concern, neither extreme can be assumed, and the total of the various probable outcomes must total to one. Thus, if there are three possible outcomes, they may be expressed as follows:

Outcome A has a probability of 1/8
Outcome B has a probability of 4/8
Outcome C has a probability of 3/8
Total   8/8 = 1

2. Probability analysis of business problems is useful only when meaningful categorizations of probabilities are possible. The possible outcomes for which probabilities are computed must be mutually exclusive, which means that one and only one of the possible outcomes can occur. The occurrence of two of them in combination is not considered in the assessment of probabilities.

Use of Weighted
Probabilities

One of the most easily understood uses of probabilities is in forecasting the amount of future costs or revenues. Since the most significant amounts used in business planning are estimates of the results of future events, the use of probabilities in management planning has considerable potential.

To illustrate the use of weighted probabilities, assume that the sales manager of the Wattsbury Company is preparing a sales forecast for the coming year. The entire budget of the company will be constructed around this estimate. He examines prior years' sales, studies the condition of the market for his company's products, reads news bulletins which forecast the state of the national economy, and arrives at the data shown in Exhibit 18–2. Note that several levels of sales have been estimated, with the probability of achieving each. The combined result of multiplying each probability by its related level of sales provides a sales forecast much more accurate than a single guess. Even though the probabilities are subjectively determined, they provide a useful mechanism for projecting the result of future events.

EXHIBIT 18–2
Estimation of Sales Using Probability Estimates

Possible Sales Levels (1)	Probability Estimates (2)	Weighted Results (1 × 2)
$15,000	.2	$ 3,000
20,000	.2	4,000
25,000	.4	10,000
30,000	.1	3,000
35,000	.1	3,500
Total	1.0	$23,500

Multiplying the probability and the related level of sales provides a consistent, uniform method of considering the various probabilities in one final answer. Although the likelihood of realizing sales of $25,000 is given a heavy probability, the chances of realizing less than this amount exceed the chances of realizing more. Consequently, the most likely sales projection would be $23,500.

Simple Min-Max
Analysis

Probabilities are useful in minimizing losses and maximizing profits, in determining optimum production quantities, establishing sales prices, and solving similar problems. Such analyses may be extremely complex, although some such as a simple minimum-maximum analysis—may be undertaken by slight elaboration of the weighted probability analysis discussed in the preceding section. To illustrate, consider the decision facing a vendor of corsages, specially made with school colors, who sells his product outside the football stadium immediately preceding football games. Assume that the cost of each corsage to the vendor is $3.00 and that he has a sales price of $5.00 each. Those left at the end of the game are of no value, since they will not keep until the next game and may be considered a total loss for purposes of this illustration. Thus, each unit produces a $2.00 profit if sold but a $3.00 loss if unsold. Note carefully that the decision facing the vendor is entirely different from that in the economic order quantity example discussed earlier in this chapter. Reorder without loss was possible in the earlier case where the problem was one of balancing order costs with carrying costs. In the case of the vendor of corsages, there is but one order, regardless of amount, and there are no carrying costs. The vendor's problem is to buy that amount of corsages which will maximize his profits at the same time that it minimizes his losses.

The first requirement in such a problem is to formulate probabilities concerning the number of units that can be sold. Suppose that the vendor has records which indicate the following sales history:

Event	Number of Times Achieved	Calculated Probability
Sales of exactly 0 units	—	0/30
1	4	4/30
2	6	6/30
3	10	10/30
4	7	7/30
5	2	2/30
6	1	1/30
7 or more	—	0/30
Total	30	30/30

Conversion of the past history of sales into probabilities is readily accomplished by converting the individual amounts into a fraction of the total. Since there are thirty times for which historical data are available, and four of these thirty produced a sale of only one unit, the probability of selling no more than one unit is 4/30. The probability of selling no more than two units is 6/30, since six times out of 30 only that number of units was sold. When this method is used, the total probabilities will always equal unity. Note that in Exhibit 18–3 the total is 30/30, which equals one, or unity.

Determination of the optimum quantity to buy is then undertaken by comparing the probability of a $2.00 profit from one additional sale with the probability of a $3.00 loss if the unit is not sold. The fractions used in these calculations must be cumulative probabilities, however. A cumulative fraction measures the probability of achieving at least that level of sales. This is illustrated in Exhibit 18–3.

EXHIBIT 18–3

Cumulative Probabilities of Achieving Various Levels of Sales

Event	Probability (From Previous Calculation)	Cumulative Probability of:	
		Loss	Profit
Sale of no unit	—	—	—
Sale of 1st unit	4/30	0/30	30/30
Sale of 2nd unit	6/30	4/30	26/30
Sale of 3rd unit	10/30	10/30	20/30
Sale of 4th unit	7/30	20/30	10/30
Sale of 5th unit	2/30	27/30	3/30
Sale of 6th unit	1/30	29/30	1/30
Sale of 7th unit	—	30/30	0/30
Total	30/30		

The data shown in Exhibit 18–3 indicate that the probability of selling at least one unit is 1, or 30/30, since the vendor has never sold less than that amount. The probability of selling two is only 26/30, however, because in four out of the thirty cases less than two were sold. Similarly, the probability of selling three units is 20/30, since in ten cases out of thirty less than three were sold. Note also that the probability of a loss is the difference between unity (one) and the computed probability of realizing a profit. This is true because each unit must produce either a profit or a loss, one or the other, and the sum of these two possibilities must also equal one.

The final step in computing the optimum number of units to buy is completed by multiplying the cumulative probabilities for each sale by the $2.00 profit and subtracting from this amount the product of multiplying the probability of a loss by the $3.00 potential loss on each unit. This computation is illustrated in Exhibit 18–4.

The data in Exhibit 18–4 indicate that the net expected profit or loss on the first unit is $2.00, resulting from a "certainty" or 30/30 probability of selling that number of units and a "certainty" of 0/30 probability of loss. The second unit has a 26/30 probability of sale and a 4/30 probability of loss, with a resulting net profit probability of $1.33. The third unit has a profit probability

EXHIBIT 18–4

Event	Per Unit Potential Profit	Probability	Probable Profit	Per Unit Loss Potential	Probability	Probable Loss	Net Profit or Loss Probability
Sale of 1 unit	$2.00	30/30	$2.00	$3.00	0/30	$0.00	$2.00
Sale of 2 units	2.00	26/30	1.73	3.00	4/30	.40	1.33
Sale of 3 units	2.00	20/30	1.33	3.00	10/30	1.00	.33
Sale of 4 units	2.00	10/30	.67	3.00	20/30	2.00	(1.33)
Sale of 5 units	2.00	3/30	.20	3.00	27/30	2.70	(2.50)
Sale of 6 units	2.00	1/30	.07	3.00	29/30	2.90	(2.83)
Sale of 7 units	2.00	0/30	.00	3.00	30/30	3.00	(3.00)

also and should be bought. However, the fourth unit has a loss probability and should not be acquired since its profit probability is 67¢ and its loss probability is $2.00. Thus, the vendor is able to maximize the probability of profits at the same time that he minimizes his chances of losses by buying only those units which have a net profit probability.

Caution must be exercised to use only incremental costs and revenues in such an analysis. The results may be distorted if fixed or sunk costs are used. In the illustrative example, both revenues and costs were completely variable, and a distinction between fixed and variable costs was not necessary. In most business problems, however, a careful cost analysis is necessary to segregate the relevant and the irrelevant costs prior to applying probability analysis.

Probabilities and
Capital Investments

The techniques of evaluating capital investments using such comparative data as the payback period, rate of return, and present value have been discussed in previous chapters. These techniques provide a means by which alternative investments are compared, but the comparison is enhanced when a factor for measuring probability is included in the computations. The probability of realizing the projected cash inflows differs from one investment to another, and by incorporating probabilities into the computations, the risk factor can be taken into account.

One very effective means of using probabilities in capital investment computations is to assign probability estimates to the life of the investment. Thus, an investment with a three-year maximum expected life may have a probability of 10 percent of terminating at the end of the first year, a 20 percent probability of terminating at the end of the second year, and a 70 percent chance of terminating at the end of the third. These probabilities are then used to weigh the returns which would be realized upon termination of the investment at each of the three possible points. To illustrate, consider the comparison of two different investments using a 10 percent discount rate. Investment A is a machine costing $100,000, which has a possible five-year life and is expected to contribute savings of $40,000 per year. The probabilities of the sudden obsolescence of this machine at the end of each of the five periods are 5 percent, 10 percent, 20 percent, and 45 percent, respectively. Investment B, on the other hand, is a stable piece of equipment with a four-year life, a cost of $50,000, and expected savings of $25,000 during each of the four years. The probability of obsolescence is 5 percent during each of the first three years and 85 percent in the last year of the machine's expected life.

The computations in Exhibit 18–5 illustrate the manner in which probability estimates are used to weight the returns realized during each year of the investment's life. The result is a probability-rate-of-return. These overall rates may then be used to compare the alternative investments. The procedure is as follows:

1. Compute for each year of the investment's life the present value of the cash inflow it produces.
2. Compute the cumulative sum of the present values, determined in step 1.
3. Compute the cumulative profit or loss realized by the investment. This would be accomplished by subtracting the cumulative discounted cash inflow from the investment's original cost. This step provides an indication of when the investment has returned its cost and begins to produce profits.
4. Divide the cumulative profit or loss for each year by the investment's original cost. This provides a rate of return should the investment terminate during the year.
5. Multiply the probability of termination during each year by the rates of return computed in step 4. The total of these amounts is the probability-rate-of-return.

The inclusion of probabilities in the investment comparison indicates that investment B will produce a higher probability-rate-of-return. The relative risks of the two investments are such that the higher return and greater safety of investment B is clearly indicated.

The Normal Curve

The normal curve is a powerful quantitative tool which is being applied with increasing frequency to business problems. A normal curve is the term applied to a smooth, symmetrical, bell-shaped curve with the maximum height at the center and one-half of its area on each side of the center line. One of the principal features of the normal curve is that it provides a means of measuring the grouping or dispersion of items around the average of the group. It is frequently used to measure the significance of the difference between a given amount and the average of all the amounts in the group. Exhibit 18–6 shows the shape of the normal curve.

EXHIBIT 18–5

Computation of Probability-Rate-of-Return

(1) Year	(2) Cash Inflow	(3) Present Value of $1 at 10%	(4) Total Present Value	(5) Cumulative Return	(6) Cumulative Profit or Loss (Cost Less Column 5)	(7) Rate of Return if Terminated	(8) Probability of Termination	(9) Probability-Rate-of-Return (7) × (8)
INVESTMENT A ($100,000 cost)								
1	$40,000	.909	$36,360	$ 36,360	$(63,640)	(63.6)	.05	(3.18)%
2	40,000	.826	33,040	69,440	(30,600)	(30.6)	.10	(3.06)
3	40,000	.751	30,040	99,440	(560)	(.5)	.20	(.10)
4	40,000	.683	27,320	126,760	26,760	26.8	.20	13.40
5	40,000	.621	24,840	151,600	51,600	51.6	.45	23.22
TOTAL FOR INVESTMENT A								30.28 %
INVESTMENT B ($50,000 cost)								
1	$25,000	.909	$22,725	$ 22,725	$(32,275)	(58.7)	.05	(2.94)%
2	25,000	.826	20,650	43,375	(11,625)	(21.1)	.05	(1.10)
3	25,000	.751	18,775	62,150	7,150	13.0	.05	.07
4	25,000	.683	17,075	79,225	24,225	44.1	.85	27.49
TOTAL FOR INVESTMENT B								33.52 %

To illustrate the use of such a curve, assume that the labor time for product X as shown on all job orders for that product during the year has been grouped as follows:

Required Labor to Complete One Unit of Product X	Number of Job Orders
60 to 65 minutes	2
65 to 70	8
70 to 75	14
75 to 80	28
80 to 85	26
85 to 90	15
90 to 95	9
95 to 100	1
Total	103

If plotted on a bar graph, the manufacturing time per unit of product X would appear as shown in Exhibit 18–6. A curved line is drawn to indicate the type of curve which these data produce. This particular curve is illustrative of a normal curve, where the items in the group are dispersed around the average. A non-normal curve would have more items on one side of the average than on the other or would drop more sharply on one side than on the other.

One of the most significant features of the normal curve is that the average of the group is exactly at the center. Thus, the probability that any one item in the

EXHIBIT 18–6

Manufacturing Time For One Unit of Product X, as Shown on Job Orders

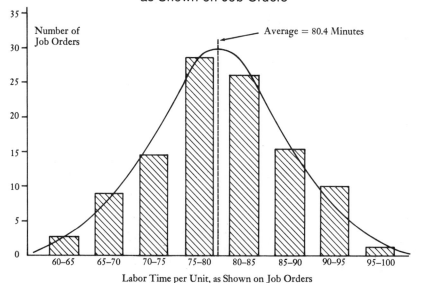

Labor Time per Unit, as Shown on Job Orders

group will fall on one side or the other is exactly 50 percent. In addition, the curve is such that 68 percent of all probabilities will fall not more than plus or minus one *standard deviation* on either side of the average; 96 percent will fall not more than ± 2 standard deviations; and 99 percent will fall not more than ± 3 standard deviations from the average. The term *standard deviation* is given to the measure of dispersion around the average. Although the calculation of this measure is shown in a later footnote, its mastery is considered beyond the scope of this text. The significant point to remember is that the chances of any item being a given amount greater or less than the average can be measured by means of the standard deviation.

To illustrate the use of the standard deviation, consider the labor time as reflected by job orders shown in Exhibit 18–6. The standard deviation for those data is 7.4 minutes, as computed in the footnote below.[1] This means that 68 percent of the job orders can be expected to show a labor time that deviates no more nor less than 7.4 minutes from the average of 80.4 minutes. Thus, 68 percent of the labor costs can be expected to fall between 73 and 87.8 minutes. Similarly, labor times for 96 percent of the job orders will fall within ± 2 standard deviations, or between 65.6 and 95.2 minutes. Examination of the original data indicates that the range of two standard deviations contains 100 of the 103 cases, which further validates the calculation.

Exhibit 18–7 illustrates three normal curves, with the area under one, two, and three standard deviations shaded.

---

1. A standard deviation is found by computing the difference between each item in the group and the average of all items in the group, squaring the individual differences, summing the squares, dividing the sum by the number of items in the group to get an *average squared deviation*, and taking the square root of this average. In mathematical form the computation would be

$$\sqrt{\frac{\Sigma(X - \overline{X})^2}{N}}$$

with N = the number of items, and $\overline{X}$ = the average of all items. The computation below is for the items shown in the illustration of job order times for product X. An average cost for each group was used (the items in the 60- to 65-minute group were averaged at 62.5 minutes, etc.).

Group Average	Deviation from the 80.4 Average	Deviation Squared	Number of Items in Each Group	Squared Deviation Times the Number of Items in Each Group
62.5	18	324	2	648
67.5	13	169	8	1,352
72.5	8	64	14	896
77.5	3	9	28	252
82.5	2	4	26	104
87.5	7	49	15	735
92.5	12	144	9	1,296
97.5	17	289	1	289
Total			103	5,572

Average of the squared deviations (5,572 ÷ 103)   54.1

Square root of the average squared deviation ($\sqrt{54.1}$)   7.4

EXHIBIT 18–7

Normal Curves With Areas Under the Standard Deviations Shown
(σ = Standard deviation)

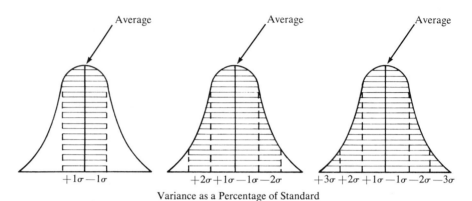

Variance as a Percentage of Standard

Statistical Analysis for
Cost Control

Standard deviations provide management with a tool for locating those significant variations from standard, budgeted, or anticipated costs which should be given attention. The budgeted or standard cost may be considered the average, and an excessive deviation on either side of this amount should be investigated. Determining what is an excessive deviation has always been a particularly vexing management problem, but the use of standard deviations can help establish control limits in many instances.

To illustrate the way in which a standard deviation may help in interpreting a variance, consider the following data:

Operation	Actual Cost	Standard Cost	Variance	Variance as a % of Standard	Variance in Terms of Standard Deviations away from the Average
Painting—Department A	$10,089	$9,500	$589	6.2%	.8
Welding—Department B	2,900	2,752	148	5.1	2.3
Crating—Department C	4,601	4,300	301	7.0	1.3

Since an executive rarely has time to study causal factors for all variances, he must select those which are most significant. The central question, then, is which of the three variances reported above indicates an out-of-control situation. The largest dollar variance occurred in Department A, which, if amounts alone were considered, would be the most significant variance. As a percentage of standard cost, however, the 7 percent variance for crating in Department C indicates a relatively greater margin of error. Finally, the variance in Department B is smaller in dollar amount and as a percentage of standard, but in terms of deviation from the average variance it is the most significant. The 2.3 standard deviations indicate that there are less than two chances out of one hundred that a variance as large as that in Department B could occur without a significant causal factor. The probability that the variances in Departments A and C would occur is much greater, for their standard deviations indicate less spread from the average.

It must be remembered, however, that the purpose of cost control is to confine or to reduce costs, consistent with quality, safety, and other similar considerations. Thus, large dollar variances cannot be ignored, regardless of how small the standard deviation may be. Probabilities in terms of standard deviations are valuable aids in interpreting the meaning of a variance, however, and provide a consistent device for measuring its significance.

The Control Chart

One means by which costs may be observed from one period to another is through the use of a control chart. Such a chart is based upon the normal curve, standard deviations, and a graphic portrayal of the cost behavior of that particular cost. A separate chart must be constructed for each cost. The chart for indirect labor in Department B is shown in Exhibit 18–8. Visual presentations such as these aid management in interpreting the significance of a variance.

The chart in Exhibit 18–8 is drawn for an expense item whose past history indicates that 68 percent of the time the variation will not exceed standard by more than ± 4.3 percent. Thus, plus or minus one standard deviation encom-

EXHIBIT 18–8

Control Chart For Indirect Labor Costs in Department B
(Standard deviation $\sigma = 4.3\%$)

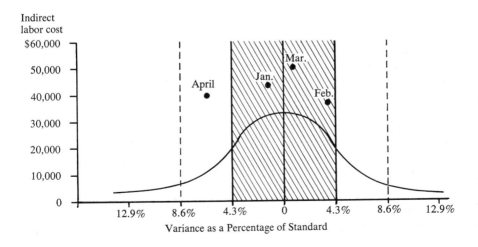

Variance as a Percentage of Standard

passes all variations which are less than 4.3 percent of the budget. The significance of this chart is that it permits visual surveillance of the expense. If a variation does not exceed ± 4.3 percent of standard, it is considered to be within control; if it is greater than 4.3 percent, it is considered to be "out of control."

The normal curve itself is placed in the chart for illustrative purposes only. The significant features are the shaded areas for plus and minus one standard deviation, which is considered the control area. As long as the variances remain within this area, as they did in January, February, and March, the indirect labor cost is considered to be within the limits of the control established for it. When a variance exceeds this tolerance, as occurred in April, management is warned that the cost is being influenced by a factor other than those considered normal, and investigation of the causal factor may be in order.

Note that the amount of the indirect labor cost for the month is indicated on the scale at the left and the percentage variance on the scale at the bottom. The significance of the size of the variance is indicated by the fact that the variance is outside the shaded control area.

Summary

Model building is a relatively new technique, but it can be valuable in testing the results of various courses of action. A quantitative model usually takes the form of an equation or a formula, thereby necessitating the quantification of large portions of the input data. Models for inventory control, investment decisions, and cost analysis are descriptive of those currently being applied to business problems. Additional areas of application are frequently discovered, and the use of models will undoubtedly continue to grow.

Many individuals, including experienced businessmen, are not receptive to the concept of using a formula or of applying subjective probabilities to business and economic data. However, decisions must be made, and it is usually more helpful to work with fractions of a problem, bringing the individual parts together into a final quantified result, than to attempt a subjective analysis of many factors at the same time.

Most business decisions depend first of all upon a clear definition of the problem, followed by the gathering and sorting of data, recognition of possible courses of action, and the determination of the probable outcomes of each alternative. Scientific management also calls for a logical and consistent recording of the facts which lead to the decision. When this is done, the data are then available for use in solving similar problems which may arise at a later time. If careful thought is given, even subjective probabilities may be supported by objective data.

New Terms

Control chart　A graph which shows allowed deviations from standard and actual deviations, thus highlighting those deviations considered unacceptable from a control standpoint.

E. O. Q.   Economic order quantity.

Min-max   A methodology which balances the results of minimization and the results of maximization.

Model   A formula or expression of relationships.

Normal curve   A bell-shaped curve with the average, or mean, at the center.

Probability estimate   An estimate of the probability that an event will occur.

Quantitative technique   Any methodology which attempts to evaluate something in terms of a given quantity, such as dollars, pounds, or minutes.

Standard deviation   A term used to express the dispersion of items around the mean, or average.

Weighted probability   A method of estimating the most probable amount, utilizing the average of amounts multiplied by probabilities.

Questions

1. What is a model? Is the accounting equation ASSETS = LIABILITIES + PROPRIETORSHIP a type of model? If so, what does it represent a "model" of?

2. Distinguish between the "subjective" and the "objective" approach to a problem. Explain whether the system by which grades are determined in this class would be considered an objective or a subjective approach.

3. What are the elements which enter into the determination of an economic order quantity? Would the EOQ amount increase or decrease as the result of higher costs to place an order?

4. Why should only variable costs enter into the calculation of EOQ ordering costs and inventory carrying costs? Name some fixed costs of ordering and carrying inventory.

5. Why is it better to have the sum of all probable outcomes of an event equal one (unity) instead of ten, or eight, or some other number?

6. What is a weighted probability? Give an example.

7. What is meant by a "min-max" calculation? Give an example.

8. What is a normal curve? Is it possible for the average amount in a group of different amounts to be located somewhere other than in the exact center of the group? If so, would the group exactly fit a normal curve?

9. Explain what is meant by a standard deviation when related to a normal curve.

10. Explain what a control chart is when constructed around the concept of a normal curve.

Exercises

18–1 **Definitions** *(15 minutes)*   The following terms or concepts were introduced in this chapter:
a. Quantitative technique
b. Economic order quantity
c. Economic model
d. Probability estimate
e. Probability-rate-of-return
f. Normal curve
g. Standard deviation
h. Control chart

Instructions
Define each term or concept, giving examples where possible.

18–2 **Computing and Graphing Inventory Cost Data** *(40 minutes)*   A company has a product with an annual volume of sales of 1,600 units. The ordering cost is $8 per order placed, and the cost of carrying inventory is 15 percent of the value of the inventory. The units cost $40 each. Prepare a table with columns for the following data:

> Units per purchase order
> Number of orders necessary
> Total variable ordering costs
> Units in the average inventory
> Cost of the average inventory
> Cost of carrying inventory
> Total cost of ordering and carrying inventory

Instructions
1. Compute the data for the table for each order size which is a multiple of ten—that is, for ten units per purchase order, twenty units per purchase order, thirty units per purchase order, etc.— up to a total order size of 140 units per order.
2. Prepare a graph similar to Exhibit 18–1 to reflect the data in the table.

18–3 **Computation of Economic Order Quantity** *(15 minutes)* The cost structure of a company includes fixed costs of $10,000 per year to operate the purchasing department and $8 variable costs for each order placed. The company's cost accountants have estimated that money invested in inventory costs 10 percent per annum, that taxes are 2 percent of inventory value, and that inventory insurance is 3 percent of the inventory's value.

Instructions
Compute the economic order quantity of a product with an annual sales volume of $40,000. (You may round your answer to the nearest $100, thus permitting an estimation of the square root portion of the computation.) If the product sells for $50, how many units would be ordered?

18–4 **Use of Probability Estimates to Forecast Sales** *(15 minutes)* The vice-president of sales is preparing his budget for the coming year. He knows that sales will be dependent upon the extent of advertising which will be undertaken but is not sure what amount the advertising budget should be. He therefore is estimating the sales which will be realized at several different advertising levels, using probability estimates as follows:

If advertising is	Then sales may be	With a probability of
$10,000	$200,000	.3
	300,000	.5
	400,000	.2
		1.0
$15,000	$200,000	.1
	300,000	.3
	400,000	.5
	500,000	.1
		1.0
$20,000	$300,000	.1
	400,000	.3
	500,000	.4
	600,000	.2
		1.0

Instructions
Compute the probability expectation for the amount of sales most likely to be realized at the three different advertising levels.

18–5* **Profit Minimum-Maximum Computation** *(20 minutes)* A vendor sells for $10 a product which costs $6 per unit to make. The unit will spoil overnight, and the number bought each day from his supplier should not exceed anticipated sales. Past history of sales on Saturday indicates the following expectations for that day of the week:

	Number of Occurrences
Sales of 9 or fewer units	never
Sales of 10 units	2
Sales of 11 units	10
Sales of 12 units	15
Sales of 13 units	10
Sales of 14 units	8
Sales of 15 units	5
Sales of 16 units or more	never

Instructions

Prepare a schedule similar to Exhibit 18–4 to indicate how many units should be bought to maximize the probabilities of profits and yet minimize the possibilities of losses.

18–6*   **Computation of Probability-Rate-of-Return** *(30 minutes)*   The Ajax Company is analyzing two investment possibilities and will select the one which has the highest probability-rate-of-return. Investment A will cost $200,000 and has an expected return of $70,000 annually for five years. It is a reasonably safe investment, and the probability of its continuing only until the end of each of the five years is .05, .15, .20, .25, and .35, respectively.

There is more risk involved in investment B, and the possibilities of its continuing for the full five-year period are considerably less. It will also require an investment of $200,000, but the expected returns are $80,000 each year for five years. The probability of its continuing only until the end of each of the five years is .10, .30, .30, .20, and .10, respectively.

Instructions

Compute the probability-rate-of-return using a 10 percent rate for each of the two investments using a table similar to Exhibit 18–5.

18–7   **Preparation of a Control Chart** *(20 minutes)*   A control chart similar to that illustrated in Exhibit 18–8 is being prepared for the overtime expense of the Dragnet Furnace Company. One standard deviation is plus or minus 6 percent of the budget, and any deviation in excess of plus or minus 9 percent of budget (one and one-half standard deviations) is considered out of control.

The expense for the past four months has been as follows:

	Budget	Actual
January	$71,400	$70,320
February	60,200	66,700
March	51,000	54,000
April	62,000	60,390

Instructions
Construct a control chart for the overtime expense. Plot the variations, expressed in percentages of budget, for the four months. Superimpose on the chart a normal curve, as in the illustration in Exhibit 18–8.

Problems

18–8   **Computing and Graphing Economic Order Quantity** *(35 minutes)*
A company has a $3 variable cost of placing purchase orders, and the cost of carrying inventory is 15 percent of the value of the inventory. The units cost $10 each.

Instructions
1. Compute the economic order quantity of a product with an annual volume of $1,000. After computing the economic order quantity, rounded to the nearest $100, divide by the $10 per unit cost to arrive at an approximate number of units on each purchase order.
2. Prepare a table with the following headings:

> Units per purchase order
> Number of orders necessary
> Total variable ordering costs
> Units in the average inventory
> Cost of the average inventory
> Cost of carrying inventory
> Total cost of carrying and ordering

Complete this table using units per purchase order in multiples of five—i.e., five, ten, fifteen, etc.—up to thirty units per order.

18–9   **Computation of Economic Order Quantities** *(20 minutes)*   The purchasing department of a company has $100,000 of fixed costs and variable costs of $2.10 per purchase order. The company has $30,000 fixed costs of carrying inventory (depreciation, taxes, and insurance on the warehouse) plus variable costs of 20 percent of the inventory's value.

Instructions
Compute the economic order quantity for a product (1) with $10,000 annual sales, and (2) with $100,000 annual sales.

18–10 **Computation of Economic Order Quantities** *(20 minutes)* The Maxfield Company has gathered the costs of carrying inventory and placing purchase orders as follows:

Costs of Carrying $1 of Inventory for One Year		Costs of Placing One Purchase Order	
Insurance	$ .03	Supplies	$ .30
Taxes	.04	Postage	.10
Imputed interest	.10	Typing, filing	2.40
Fixed costs, prorated	.13	Fixed costs, prorated	1.20
	$ .30		$4.00

The fixed inventory carrying costs are computed by prorating warehouse depreciation and other fixed storage costs on the basis of average inventory carried during the year. The fixed purchasing costs are allocated equally to each order placed during the year.

Instructions
Compute the economic order quantity for an item of merchandise whose annual volume is (1) $10,000, (2) $30,000, and (3) $100,000.

18–11 **Testing Sensitivity of Economic Order Quantity** *(25 minutes)* The Kellon Company is attempting to establish economic order quantities for several of their inventory items. They have computed ranges of costs which their controller feels are representative of their normal operations. The president and the sales manager are skeptical of the results of such computations and request that the range include both pessimistic and optimistic figures.

The cost of placing a purchase order is computed to be $4, and considering all possible errors in this computation, the controller feels that the most pessimistic figure would be $5 and the most optimistic would be $3. The average cost of carrying inventory is 20 percent, with a possible high of 25 percent and a low of 15 percent.

Instructions
1. Compute the economic order quantity for an item with an annual sales volume of $50,000, using (a) the lowest carrying and lowest ordering cost, (b) the expected carrying and expected ordering cost, (c) the highest carrying and highest ordering cost, (d) the highest ordering and the lowest carrying cost, and (e) the lowest ordering and the highest carrying cost.
2. Considering the results of part 1, what economic order quantity would you select?

18–12 **Use of Simple Probability Estimates** *(20 minutes)* William Toone, as Vice-President of Sales for the Massachusetts Novelty Company, established the following probabilities for next month's sales:

Sales	Probability of Occurrence
$100,000	1/20
120,000	2/20
140,000	6/20
160,000	7/20
180,000	2/20
190,000	1/20
200,000	1/20

In addition to the above probabilities, there is a one-third chance that a labor strike will occur at a large local manufacturing company. Should this happen, sales of the Massachusetts Novelty Company will be 20 percent lower than if the strike had not occurred.

Instructions
Compute the most probable amount of sales which the Massachusetts Novelty Company will have.

18–13   **Production to Minimize Losses and Maximize Profits** *(40 minutes)* The Bronston Company produces a perishable product with no salvage value. The selling price is $6.75 each, and the variable costs to produce and sell each unit are $5.25. The units spoil if not sold immediately, and the company's history of sales during the month of August indicates the following:

Daily Sales	Number of Occurrences
Less than 100,000 units	never
100,000 units	20
200,000 units	60
300,000 units	110
400,000 units	90
500,000 units	20
More than 500,000 units	never

Instructions
Prepare a schedule similar to Exhibit 18–4 to determine the amount of production which would maximize the probability of profits and minimize the probability of losses. (Use total profit and total loss amounts for each level of sales instead of unit amounts.)

18–14   **Min-Max Determination of Production** *(45 minutes)*   The Tripoli Dairy sells eggnog during the Christmas season, using a special formula which is popular in the area. The eggnog will not last longer than one week, when it must be picked up from the retail stores. At that time it has no commercial value. The Tripoli Dairy refunds the retail stores when the eggnog is not sold, so that the dairy must absorb the full loss. The management of the dairy is attempting to ascertain how much eggnog should be produced during the month of December, using the statistics for the past five years given as follows:

Daily Sales	Number of Occurrences
Less than 20,000 quarts	never
20,000 quarts	7
30,000 quarts	13
40,000 quarts	34
50,000 quarts	26
60,000 quarts	10
70,000 quarts	7
80,000 quarts	3
More than 80,000 quarts	never

Each quart of eggnog costs $.25 to produce and sells for $.34. The $.25 cost is composed of $.15 variable costs and $.10 allocated fixed costs.

Instructions
Determine the amount of eggnog which should be produced in order to maximize the probability of profits and at the same time minimize the probability of losses. Prepare a schedule similar to Exhibit 18–4 to support your answer, using total profit and total loss amounts instead of unit amounts.

18–15   **Min-Max Computations With and Without Loss** *(60 minutes)* The operator of a newsstand has agreed to carry Tiempo magazine. Each copy will cost him $.35, and he will sell it for $.55. Demand by his customers for each issue appears to follow the following probability pattern:

Demand	Probability
100 copies	.10
150	.20
200	.30
250	.30
300	.10

Instructions
Compute the optimum number of copies which he should buy to maximize profits and minimize losses if (1) he cannot return unsold copies to the publisher, (2) he can return unsold copies for full refund, and (3) he can return unsold copies for refund of half his cost.

18–16   **Computation of Probability-Rate-of-Return** *(40 minutes)*   Wilton Smith is considering two investments, each requiring an expenditure of $100,000 and having a maximum life of four years, with no remaining value at the end of that time. The first will have a return of $40,000 each year with a probability of terminating at the end of the first, second, third, and fourth year of .10, .30, .30, and

.30, respectively. The second has an annual return of $40,000 with a probability of termination of .05, .10, .40, and .45 during each consecutive year of its life.

Instructions
Compute a probability-rate-of-return for the two investments with the table shown in Exhibit 18–5. Use a 10 percent discount rate.

18–17　　**Computation of Probability-Rate-of-Return** *(60 minutes)*　　A company has two investment possibilities, both requiring an investment of $200,000. The first will produce a return of $75,000 for each of the next five years, and the probability of its continuing only until the end of the first year is .05 ,to the end of the second is .15, and to the end of the third, fourth, and fifth year is .20, .25, and .35, respectively.

There is more risk to the second investment, and although it will return $90,000 for each of five years, the probabilities of its terminating at the end of each of its five years of life are .10, .30, .30, .20, and .10, respectively. Neither of the two investments will have a residual value at the end of five years.

Instructions
Compute a probability-rate-of-return for the two investments, using a table similar to Exhibit 18–5 and a 10 percent discount rate.

18–18　　**Preparation of a Control Chart** *(30 minutes)*　　The Cost Control Department of the Borrough Company has analyzed the factory supplies expense and found that one standard deviation is 5 percent of the average cost of supplies. A control chart is being constructed for this expense, with the normal curve superimposed on it for graphic emphasis of the fact that any variations in excess of one standard deviation are considered out of control.

During the first four months of the year the supplies expense per budget and the actual expense were as follows:

	Budget	Actual
January	$3,420	$3,280
February	3,900	3,820
March	3,100	3,500
April	3,700	3,710

Instructions
Construct a control chart similar to the illustration in the text. Plot the variations, expressed in percentages of budget, for the four months.

18–19　　**Control Chart, Including Standard Deviation** *(60 minutes)*　　The Abelard Company has listed its supplies expenses for the past few years, rounded to the nearest $50, with the results as shown below. The expense has in the past been considered relatively fixed.

Expense	Occurrences
$ 800	2
850	20
900	60
950	55
1,000	16
1,050	1
Assumed Average $925	

Instructions
1. Following the illustration in the text, compute the amount of one standard deviation.
2. Assume that in the following month the expense was $1,080. Using the standard deviations computed in part 1, what is the approximate chance that the expense would be this high as a result of pure random chance?

Appendix

Solutions to
Selected Exercises

Chapter 1

1-4   a. The line of command goes as follows: Board of Directors to President to Vice-President of Marketing to Manager of Product Y to the Advertising Department head.

b. The payroll department calculates pay amounts and prepares pay checks for advertising personnel.

c. The excess of the actual payroll of the advertising department over its budget would be reported by the controller to one or all of the following: Vice-President of Marketing, Manager of Product Y, and the advertising department head. These executives, and not the controller, would take any required corrective action. The controller supplies information but should not be permitted to exercise authority in correcting whatever caused the variance.

Chapter 2

2-6

JADE-WAIT COMPANY
Balance Sheet
December 31, 19X1

ASSETS

Current assets		
Cash	$ 3,750	
Accounts receivable	7,500	
Merchandise inventory	14,100	
Office supplies	100	
Store supplies	175	
Prepaid insurance	650	
Total current assets		$26,275

Fixed assets

Store equipment	$ 3,250	
Office equipment	1,900	
Buildings	6,000	
Land	2,250	
Total fixed assets		$13,400
Total assets		$39,675

EQUITIES

Current liabilities

Accounts payable	$ 7,825	
Notes payable	$ 2,500	
Taxes payable	375	
Salaries payable	250	
Total current liabilities		$10,950

Fixed liabilities

Mortgage payable in 1980		2,500
Total liabilities		$13,450

Owners' equity

Capital stock	$20,000	
Retained earnings	6,225	
Total owners' equity		26,225
Total equities		$39,675

2-8
a. The cost concept is violated, because the inventory is stated at sales price instead of cost.
b. Revenue has not been realized, because the customer may never actually buy the merchandise. The periodicity concept has been violated, because revenue should not be recorded until there is an enforceable receivable from the customer.
c. The matching concept is violated, because there is no systematic periodic apportionment of the cost of the asset to accounting periods.
d. The matching concept has been violated. The loss from the fire should be recorded and reported during the period in which the loss occurred.
e. Matching is incorrect, for there should be no depreciation recorded if the asset has been completely depreciated.

Chapter 3

3-1   MATSON COMMISSION AGENCY

1. *Generally accepted accounting principles*

Sales		$ 27,000
Less:		
Salaries	$24,000	
Advertising	6,000	
Total expenses		30,000
Net loss		$ (3,000)

2. *Cash basis income*

Receipts	$ 23,000
Less disbursements:	
Salaries	23,000
Net income or (loss)	—0—

3. *Economic income*

Market value of net assets at the beginning of the period	$ 15,650
Market value of net assets at the end of the period	16,650
Economic income	$ 1,000

3-4

THE STRANE COMPANY
Income Statement
For the Year Ended July 31, 19X1

Revenues from the sale of products		$56,500
Cost of products sold		28,000
Gross profit		$28,500
Salaries expense	$7,000	
Fuel	2,400	
Insurance	1,000	
Supplies used	700	
Advertising	3,200	
Utilities	2,000	
Rent	4,100	
Total expenses		20,400
Net operating income before extraordinary gains		8,100
Extraordinary gains on sale of assets		2,000
Net income before taxes		$10,100
Federal income taxes		2,100
Net income after federal income taxes		$ 8,000

3-9

OPAL COMPANY

	Depreciation expense		
	19X4	19X5	19X6
1. Straight-line	$1,000	$1,000	$1,000
2. Sum-of-the-years' digits	1,667	1,333	1,000
3. Units of output	500	1,250	750
4. Constant percentage of declining balance	2,200	1,320	792

Chapter 4

4-2 ROMMEL COMPANY

a. Current ratio: $\dfrac{\$6,000}{\$3,000} = 2$ to 1

b. Acid-test ratio: $\dfrac{\$3,000}{3,000} = 1$ to 1

c. Number of days' sales in receivables: $\dfrac{\$\,2,000}{\$27,000} \times 365$ days $= 27$ days

d. Inventory turnover: $\dfrac{\$18,000}{\$\,3,000} = 6$ times

e. Earnings per share: $\$3,000$ profit $\div\ 200$ shares $= \$15$ per share

f. Price earnings ratio: $\$150 \div \$15 = 10$ to 1

4-3 DONOVAN COMPANY

a. Current ratio: $\dfrac{\text{Current assets}}{\text{Current liabilities}} = \dfrac{\$140,000}{60,000} = 2.3$ to 1

This ratio indicates the company's short-term liquidity or its ability to pay its debts.

b. Acid-test ratio: $\dfrac{\text{Cash} + \text{receivables}}{\text{Accounts payable}} = \dfrac{\$60,000}{60,000} = 1$ to 1

This ratio indicates the company's *immediate* ability to pay its debts.

c. Earnings per share: $\dfrac{\text{Earnings}}{\text{Number of shares}} = \dfrac{\$14,000}{1,200 \text{ shares}} = \dfrac{\$11.67}{\text{per share}}$

This ratio indicates the earnings accruing to each share of stock outstanding.

d. Ratio of owner's equity to debt: $\dfrac{\text{Owner's equity}}{\text{Total debt}} = \dfrac{\$160,000}{160,000} = 1$ to 1

This ratio indicates the proportion of the assets supplied by investors and by owners and the relative protection of the creditors.

e. Net income as a return on invested capital:

$$\frac{\text{Net income}}{\text{Invested capital}} = \frac{\$\,14,000}{160,000} = 8.8\%$$

This ratio indicates the return received by the capital invested in the business.

f. Price-earnings ratio: $\dfrac{\text{Price}}{\text{Earnings per share}} = \dfrac{\$175}{\$11.67} = 15$ to 1

This ratio indicates the rate of return on an investment made by buying a share of stock.

Chapter 5

5-2

RIGHTMAN COMPANY
Statement of Changes in Financial Position
For the Year Ended December 31, 19X5

Sources	
Operations:	
Net loss	$ (9,000)
Add: Loss on scrapped equipment	1,000
Depreciation	6,000
Total from operations	$ (2,000)
Issuance of bonds payable	20,000
Total sources	$ 18,000
Applications	
Purchase of equipment	$ 23,000
Decrease in working capital	$ 5,000

5-6

COLLINS CONSTRUCTION COMPANY

Sales from the income statement	$109,000	
Add: Decrease in receivables (representing		
additional collections)	3,700	
Total cash from operations		$112,700
Total costs and expenses, exclusive of depreciation		
which is a non-cash item	$ 80,000	
Add: Increase in inventory, representing purchases		
not on the income statement as cost of goods		
sold	$ 2,600	
Less: Increase in accounts payable, representing		
purchases of material or other items not paid		
for this period	(1,000)	
Total cash disbursed for operations		81,600
Net cash inflow from operations		$ 31,100

5-9   The 1975 dollar equals 60/100 of the 1955 dollar, or stated in reverse, the 1955 dollar equals 100/60 of the 1975 dollar.
The 1955 cost of the asset of $100,000 × 100/60 = $166,667 to replace the asset.

XYLIER COMPANY

Profits		$ 40,000
Less: Taxes	$20,000	
Dividends	10,000	30,000
Earnings retained		$ 10,000
Original cost "recaptured through depreciation"		100,000
Total possible available for replacement		$110,000
Needed to replace		166,667
Additional borrowings or investment needed to		
replace		$ 55,667

The company thus must borrow or issue stock to retain its current position. Even if no taxes or dividends had been paid, the company would still have to have additional funds to stay in business with the same assets.

Chapter 6

6-5   1.

	Fixed	Variable
Office salaries	$1,000	2%
Depreciation	$4,000	—
Sales supplies	—	6%
Utilities	400	2%
Cost of goods sold	—	60%
	$5,400	70%

2. The expense structure is $5,400 fixed plus variable at 70 percent of sales.

3. S − 70%S = $5,400
   .30S = $5,400
      S = $18,000

4.

Sales		$18,000
Office salaries	1,360	
Depreciation	4,000	
Sales supplies	1,080	
Utilities	760	
Cost of goods sold	10,800	18,000
Net profit		—0—

5.

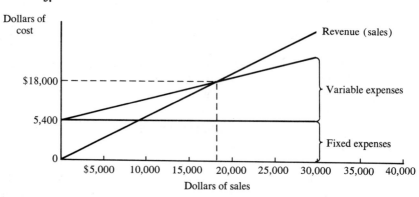

6-6   1. S − 30%S − $84,000 = 0
      S −   .30S = $84,000
          .70S = $84,000
             S = $\dfrac{\$84,000}{.70}$
             S = $120,000

2. $S - 26\% - \$86,000 = 0$
$$S - \quad .26S = \$86,000$$
$$.74S = \$86,000$$
$$S = \frac{\$86,000}{.74}$$
$$S = \$116,216$$

3. The break-even point is lower because each unit contributes more to fixed expenses, and the additional contribution is greater than the additional fixed expenses.

Chapter 7

7-4   1.   MALLOY MANUFACTURING COMPANY, INC.
Statement of the Cost of Goods Manufactured
For the Month Ended April 30, 19X1

Goods in process, April 1			$ 2,800
Cost placed into production			
Material			
Inventory, April 1	$ 7,000		
Purchases	20,000		
Total materials available	$27,000		
Less inventory, April 30	5,000		
Total materials consumed		$22,000	
Labor		9,000	
Manufacturing overhead			
Repairs on machinery	$ 1,000		
Factory supplies	700		
Factory depreciation	3,000		
Total manufacturing overhead		4,700	
Manufacturing costs placed into production			35,700
			$38,500
Less: Goods in process, April 30			1,900
Cost of goods manufactured			$36,600

2.   MALLOY MANUFACTURING COMPANY, INC.
Income Statement
For the Year Ended April 30, 19X1

Sales		$50,000
Cost of goods sold		
Beginning inventory of finished goods	$12,000	
Cost of goods manufactured	36,600	
Goods available for sale	$48,600	
Ending inventory of finished goods	11,000	
Total cost of goods sold		37,600

Income Statement
(continued)

Gross margin		$12,400
Sales salaries	$ 4,000	
Advertising	1,100	
Selling supplies used	500	
Total expenses		5,600
Net profit		$ 6,800

7-6   1.

Manufacturing labor	$100,000
Raw materials used	170,000
Manufacturing overhead	60,000
Total manufacturing costs	$330,000
Units completed	8,000
Equivalent units in process	
(6,000 × ½)	3,000
Total production	11,000
Unit cost to produce	

$330,000 ÷ 11,000 units = $30 per unit

2.

Sales (7,000 × $50)	$350,000
Cost of goods sold (7,000 × $30)	210,000
Gross margin	$140,000
Selling and administrative expenses	75,000
Net profit	$ 65,000

3. The balance sheet value of the finished goods ending inventory would be 1,000 units @ $30, or $30,000 (8,000 completed units less 7,000 sold). The balance sheet value of the goods in process inventory would be 3,000 equivalent units (6,000 actual units one-half completed) × $30, or $90,000.

Chapter 8

8-6   1.

Factory supplies		Rent	
$ 7,000		$36,000	

Manufacturing Overhead Control		Heat, light, power		Indirect labor	
$107,000	$112,500	$12,000		$ 9,000	

Indirect Materials		Depreciation	
$15,000		$25,000	

Insurance	
$ 3,000	

2. The overhead is overapplied by $5,500.

3. The overapplication was caused (a) by a manufacturing activity greater

than expected, and (b) because the company's management incurred more or less overhead costs than had been expected.

8-10

1.
Raw materials on hand January 1	$ 4,000
Raw materials purchased	16,000
Total available	20,000
Raw materials used during January	18,000
Raw materials on hand January 31	2,000

2. Job 3 is unfinished and constitutes the work in process as of January 31. $15,000

3.
Finished goods inventory January 1	—0—
Completed production	
Job #1	$11,000
Job #2	20,000
Total available	$31,000
Sold (Job #2)	20,000
Ending balance of finished goods (Job #1)	$11,000

4. Cost of sales (Job #2) $20,000

5. Cost of goods completed (Jobs #1 and #2) $31,000

6.
Materials costs during January	$18,000
Overhead applied in January	18,000
Overhead rate	100% of materials cost

Chapter 9

9-4

Labor price variance (81,000 units at $0.10 each)	$(8,100)	favorable
Labor efficiency variance (1,000 units at $3 each)	3,000	unfavorable
Material price variance ($0.02 for 155,000 units)	3,100	unfavorable
Material efficiency variance (5,000 units at $1 each)	(5,000)	favorable
Overhead controllable variance	(700)	favorable
Overhead volume variance	(1,300)	favorable
Total	$ 9,000	favorable

9-5

BARBSON-LOTT COMPANY
Variance Report
Week Ended January 17, 19X1

No. of units 200	Standard	Actual	Variance (favorable) and unfavorable Total	Efficiency	Rate
Shear	$ 80.00	$ 76,00	$(4.00)	$ 4.00	$(8.00)
Weld	200.00	232.00	32.00	25.00	7.00
Paint	50.00	52.00	2.00	—	2.00
Assemble	100.00	95.00	(5.00)	4.00	(9.00)
Pack and crate	80.00	80.00	—	(8.00)	8.00
	$510.00	$535.00	$ 25.00	$ 25.00	$ 0

The welding operation has the largest unfavorable variances and should be investigated first.

9-6

1. Variable ($8 × 10,000) = $ 80,000
   Fixed   120,000
   Total $200,000

   Per DLH $20
   Per unit (3 hours) $60

2. Applied: 4,100 × $60 = $246,000

3. Adjusted budget: 4,100 units × 3 hours each = 12,300 hours
                Variable costs   12,300 × $8 = $ 98,400
                Fixed costs   = 120,000
                      Total   = $218,400

4. Overhead controllable variance:
          ($210,000 − $218,400) = $8,400 favorable
   Overhead volume variance:
          ($218,400 − $246,000) = $27,600 favorable

Chapter 10

10-8

KROPER COMPANY
Expense Distribution Worksheet

	Department A	Department B	Department C	Department D	Total
Direct costs	$ 5,000	$ 4,000	$2,000	$1,450	$12,450
Indirect costs	4,200	4,200	2,800	2,800	14,000
Expense center C Allocation	3,200	1,600	4,800		
Expense center D Allocation	1,500	2,750		4,250	
Total	$13,900	$12,550			$26,450

10-9

Expense Distribution Work Sheet

	Total	Shoes	Men's Wear	Ladies' Wear	Building Occupancy	Pur-chasing
Direct expenses	$ 8,110	$1,800	$2,100	$4,000	$125	$ 85
Insurance (value of equip.)	900	90	180	270	315	45
Electricity (outlets)	700	140	240	200	40	80
Telephone (number of telephones)	400	60	80	100	20	140
Building and occupancy (sq. ft.)		50	175	225	$500	50
Purchasing (purchases)		80	180	140		$400
Total	$10,110	$2,220	$2,955	$4,935		

Chapter 11

11-4

	Desired Inventory (end of the month)	Sales for the Month	Total Needed During the Month	Inventory at the Beginning of the Month	Required Units	Dollars
Quality						
July	1,800	3,000	4,800	2,000	2,800	$ 1,400
August	1,600	3,300	4,900	1,800	3,100	1,550
September	1,200	3,500	4,700	1,600	3,100	1,550
Regular						
July	2,700	4,000	6,700	3,000	3,700	$ 3,700
August	2,400	5,000	7,400	2,700	4,700	4,700
September	1,800	5,100	6,900	2,400	4,500	4,500
Supreme						
July	4,500	6,000	10,500	5,000	5,500	$11,000
August	4,000	6,100	10,100	4,500	5,600	11,200
September	3,000	6,000	9,000	4,000	5,000	10,000

11-6   1.

	Fixed	Variable
Telephone expense	$ 200	1/10 of 1%
Depreciation	2,000	—
Sales commissions	—	5%
Supplies	50	1/20 of 1%

2. and 3.

	Budget	Actual	Actual Over Budget
Telephone expense	$ 450	$ 410	$(40)
Depreciation	2,000	2,000	—
Sales commissions	12,500	12,500	—
Supplies	175	160	(15)
Total	$15,125	$15,070	$(55)

11-7

CAMBAY COMPANY
Cash Budget
1/1/X1 to 3/31/X1

	January	February	March
Cash balance first of month	$ 1,200	$ 1,400	$ 1,800
Receipts:			
Cash sales and collection of receivables	15,000	20,000	18,000
Cash available	$ 16,200	$21,400	$19,800

Cash Budget
(continued)

	January	February	March
Disbursements			
Merchandise purchases	$ 14,000	$13,000	$12,000
Salaries expenses	3,800	2,200	2,100
Annual rent payment		2,400	
Purchase of equipment			3,000
Total disbursements	$ 17,800	$17,600	$17,100
Excess of cash available over disbursements	$ (1,600)	$ 3,800	$ 2,700
Borrowed funds	3,000		
Payment of borrowed funds		2,000	1,000
Cash balance end of month	$ 1,400	$ 1,800	$ 1,700

Chapter 12

12-4

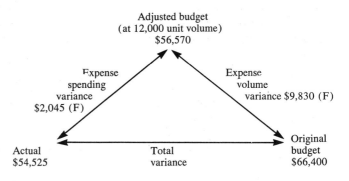

Calculation of adjusted budget (12,000 units)

Advertising	$ 5,000
Supplies	6,000
Salaries	17,000
Officer's salary	1,000
Clerk's salary	26,000
Communications	1,200
Supplies	220
Taxes	150
	$56,570

12-10 ATWELL COMPANY

	Original Budget Plan	Actual Operations	Variance	
Sales	$87,500.00	$ 88,400.00	$ 900.00	(F)
Cost of merchandise sold	58,100.00	57,800.00	300.00	(F)
Gross margin	$29,400.00	$ 30,600.00	$1,200.00	(F)
Salaries	$12,000.00	$ 13,000.00		
Depreciation	9,000.00	9,000.00		
Supplies	875.00	850.00		
Utilities	637.50	700.00		
Total expenses	$22,512.50	$ 23,550.00	1,037.50	(U)
Net income	$ 6,887.50	$ 7,050.00	$ 162.50	(F)

Sales ($88,400 ÷ 6,800 = $13 unit price)

Price: $.50 for 6,800 units		$ 3,400.00	
Quantity: 200 units at $12.50		(2,500.00)	$ 900.00

Cost of merchandise sold (57,800 ÷ 6,800 units = $8.50 unit cost)

Price: $.20 for 6,800 units		$ (1,360.00)	
Quantity: 200 units at $8.30		1,660.00	300.00
Gross margin			$1,200.00

Expenses	Original Plan	Budget Adjusted to Actual Sales	Variance	
Volume variances:				
Salaries	$12,000.00	$12,072.00	$72.00	
Depreciation	9,000.00	9,000.00	—	
Supplies	875.00	884.00	9.00	
Utilities	637.50	642.00	4.50	
Total volume variance				$85.50

Spending variances:	Budget Adjusted to Actual Sales	Actual Amount	Variance	
Salaries	$12,072.00	$13,000.00	$928.00	
Depreciation	9,000.00	9,000.00	—	
Supplies	884.00	850.00	(34.00)	
Utilities	642.00	700.00	58.00	
Total spending variance			952.00	
Total expense variances				$1,037.50
Total variance in net income				$ 162.50

Chapter 13

13-4

1. Control over the cash receipts of a vending machine company is achieved primarily by controlling the merchandise that is put into the machine. Such items as candy, cigarettes, and packages of potato chips are counted and recorded as they are issued to those employees who refill the machines. For each item placed into the machine for refill purposes, there should be a cash receipt for the sale of the item being replaced. When the employee returns from his day's work, he either returns the items not placed into machines or the money for the sold items which were replaced. Rotating employees on their routes also helps to insure that an employee is not manipulating the receipts, since records are kept for each machine.

2. Restaurant receipts are controlled through the tickets or "bill" given to each customer. A copy may be kept by the waitress or in the kitchen, and they may be prenumbered to insure that all are accounted for. The cashier inserts the ticket into the cash register when the amount is rung up, so that the amount received is imprinted on the ticket. At the end of the day, the total imprinted on the tickets (which are placed in numerical sequence and all accounted for) must equal the cash in the cash register.

13-6

WISCONSIN COMPANY

Balance per books		$7,591	Balance per bank		$7,996
Error in check #6011	$100		Deposit in transit		800
Service charge	10	110			$8,796
			Checks outstanding		
			Number		
			6013	$720	
			6142	105	
			6151	490	1,315
Corrected balance		$7,481	Corrected balance		$7,481

Chapter 14

14-4

Increase in revenue if switch is added		
(100,000 units @ $.50)		$50,000
Increase in costs if switch is added		
Additional materials and labor (100,000 @ $.25)	$25,000	
Depreciation on new equipment		
($100,000 ÷ 5 years)	20,000	
Interest on borrowed funds (6% of $100,000)	6,000	
Total costs		51,000
Net loss if the switch is added		$ 1,000

The answer should not differ if the company has funds to buy the equipment, since imputed interest of $6,000 would then enter into the computation.

14-5   a.

	Fixed costs	$20,000
	Variable costs	40,000
	Total	$60,000
	Per unit	$3.00

b.

Government contract price	$2.40
Variable costs	2.00
Contribution per unit	$ .40

Additional profit if the contract is accepted: $10,000 \times \$0.40 = \$4,000$

c.

	With Government Contract	Without Government Contract
Sales		
(20,000 @ $3.50)	$70,000	$70,000
(10,000 @ $2.40)	24,000	
Total	$94,000	$70,000
Cost of goods sold		
Variable		
20,000 @ $2.00		$40,000
30,000 @ $2.00	$60,000	
Fixed	20,000	20,000
Net income	$14,000	$10,000

Chapter 15

15-3

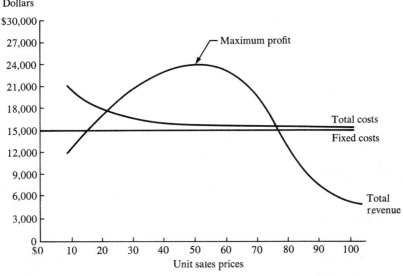

Price	Units Sold	Total Revenue	Total Cost
$10	1,500	$15,000	$19,500
20	1,000	20,000	18,000

Price	Units Sold	Total Revenue	Total Cost
30	750	22,500	17,250
40	600	24,000	16,800
50	500	25,000	16,500
60	400	24,000	16,200
70	250	17,500	15,750
80	150	12,000	15,450
90	100	9,000	15,300
100	50	5,000	15,150

15-6   1.

ADDEN COMPANY

	Product A	Product B
Costs prior to split-off (from Dept. 1)		
Labor	$ 7,000	
Materials	20,000	
Overhead	6,000	
	$33,000	
Allocation on the basis of units		
4,000 units of A equals 2/3	$22,000	
2,000 units of B equals 1/3		$11,000
Costs after split-off (Dept. 2)		
Labor		19,000
Overhead		10,000
Total costs	$22,000	$40,000
Units completed	4,000	2,000
Unit cost	$5.50	$20.00

2.

	Product A	Product B
Cost	$5.50	$20.00
Profit (30% of cost)	1.65	6.00
Selling price	$7.15	$26.00

Chapter 16

16-3

PEPPER COMPANY

	Investment A		Investment B		Investment C	
1. Payback period		5 years		4 years		5.3 years
2. Rate of return						
Total receipts	$140,000		$60,000		$150,000	
Cost	100,000		40,000		80,000	
Total return	$ 40,000		$20,000		$ 70,000	
Annual return	$ 5,714		$ 3,333		$ 7,000	
Rate of return		11.4%		16.6%		17.5%
3. Present value						
$20,000 × 4.868	$97,360					
$10,000 × 4.355			$43,550			
$15,000 × 6.145					$92,175	
4. Present value index		97.4		108.9		115.2

16-7   a. Payback period = 2 years
   b. Rate of return:

Inflow		$30,000
Cost		20,000
	Total profit	$10,000
	Annual profit	$ 3,333
	Average investment	$10,000

   Return ($3,333 ÷ $10,000) = 33⅓%
   c. Present value (2.487 × $10,000) = $24,870
   c. Present value index   124.4

16-8

	Year 1	Year 2	Year 3	Year 4	Year 5	Total
Cash inflow	$4,000	$4,000	$4,000	$4,000	$4,000	$ 4,000
Depreciation	2,000	2,000	2,000	2,000	2,000	2,000
Taxable income	$2,000	$2,000	$2,000	$2,000	$2,000	$ 2,000
Taxes (40%)	800	800	800	800	800	800
After tax income	$1,200	$1,200	$1,200	$1,200	$1,200	$ 1,200
Add: Depreciation	2,000	2,000	2,000	2,000	2,000	2,000
Add: Value of book loss on old equipment ($2,000 × 40%)	800					
Cash inflow after taxes	$4,000	$3,200	$3,200	$3,200	$3,200	$ 3,200
Present value at 16%	$3,448	$2,378	$2,051	$1,766	$1,523	$11,166

Chapter 17

17-4   a.

Net assets	$200,000	
Normal return	10%	
Normal profits	$ 20,000	
Expected profits	27,000	
Excess profits per year	$ 7,000	
Excess profits for the next five years		$ 35,000
Value of the assets		200,000
Value of the business		$235,000

   b.

Net assets	$100,000
Normal return	8%
Normal profits	$ 8,000
Expected profits	11,000
Annual excess profits	$ 3,000

(*continued*)

Excess profits of $3,000 capitalized at 10%	$ 30,000
Value of net assets	100,000
Value of the business	$130,000

c.

Net assets	$200,000
Normal return	15%
Normal profits	$ 30,000
Expected profits	40,000
Excess profits	$ 10,000

Year	Excess Profits	Value of a Dollar at 20%	Value of Excess Profits
1	$10,000	.833	$ 8,330
2	10,000	.694	6,940
3	10,000	.579	5,790
4	10,000	.482	4,820
5	10,000	.402	4,020
	Present value of excess profits		$ 29,900
	Present value of net assets		200,000
	Total value of the business		$229,900

Chapter 18

18-5

Event	Profit Potential	Profit Probability	Profit Potential	Loss Potential	Loss Probability	Loss Potential	Net Profit or Loss Potential
Sale of 9th unit	—	Certainty	—	—	—	—	—
10th	$4	50/50	$4.00	$6	—0—	—0—	$ 4.00
11th	4	48/50	3.84	6	2/50	$ .24	3.60
12th	4	38/50	3.04	6	12/50	1.44	1.60
13th	4	23/50	1.84	6	27/50	3.24	(1.40)
14th	4	13/50	1.04	6	37/50	4.44	(3.40)
15th	4	5/50	.40	6	45/50	5.40	(5.00)
16th	4	—0—	—0—	6	50/50	6.00	(6.00)

18-6

AJAX COMPANY

Investment A

Year	Cash Inflow	Present Value	Cumulative Return	Cumulative Profit or Loss	Cumulative Rate of Return	Probability	Probability Rate of Return
1	$70,000	$63,630	$ 63,630	$(136,370)	(68.2)%	.05	(3.4)%
2	70,000	57,820	121,450	(78,550)	(39.3)	.15	(5.9)
3	70,000	52,570	174,020	(25,980)	(13.0)	.20	(2.6)
4	70,000	47,810	221,830	21,830	10.9	.25	2.7
5	70,000	43,470	265,300	65,300	32.7	.35	11.4
Total							2.2 %

AJAX COMPANY
(continued)

Investment B

Year	Cash Inflow	Present Value	Cumulative Return	Cumulative Profit or Loss	Cumulative Rate of Return	Probability	Probability Rate of Return
1	$80,000	$72,720	$ 72,720	$(127,280)	(63.6)%	.10	(6.4)%
2	80,000	66,080	138,800	(61,200)	(30.6)	.30	(9.2)
3	80,000	60,080	198,880	(1,120)	(.6)	.30	(.2)
4	80,000	54,640	253,520	53,520	26.9	.20	5.4
5	80,000	49,680	303,200	103,200	51.6	.10	5.2
							(5.2)%

Index